HOMESCHOOL OPEN HOUSE

"I've just read the last entry and I loved it! Being pulled into the lives and ways of so many individual families was thought-provoking, entertaining, and emotion-stirring all at the same time. I found myself with water-filled eyes as I read the last entry. Was it that particular entry that aroused my emotions or the culmination of the whole reading experience over the last several weeks? I'm not sure."—L.T., Illinois

"I wanted to thank you from the bottom of my heart for your book. And thanks, but no thanks, for all the sleep I've lost sitting up reading it the last few nights after my daughter was in bed! This is by far the most exciting and inspiring book I have read on the subject—and any doubts I had about homeschooling were taken away. It confirmed what I knew in my heart—that homeschooling is for us! It helped me realize that there are many ways to homeschool and the *joy* is in finding what works for your family and your children, and in growing and learning together as you go along. Now, if I could just get some sleep!" —J.J., Georgia

"I really enjoyed the emphasis on the thoughts and reflections about the past five years of homeschooling by the original contributors from HOMESCHOOLING: A PATCHWORK OF DAYS, and the pleasure of meeting almost thirty new families. I've read about large and small families living in the city, the suburbs, or in the country; Christian based and non-religious homeschooling; liberal arts approach; very strong structuring and no structure; and combinations of learning and teaching styles. More than any other book, this book gave me in-depth support for homeschooling."—J.R., Maine

"My children are grown but I was intrigued by the cover of your book and found myself skimming through it. It didn't take me long to realize that skimming was no way to read this book! Within minutes I had it tucked under my arm at the check-out counter. I was so riveted that spent the week reading through the entire book. This book is essential for anyone who has a family of any age. There is so much insight and helpful information that even grandparents would truly profit from reading this special book. Thank you for an unexpected treat!"—R.M., Colorado

Also by Nancy Lande

HOMESCHOOLING: A PATCHWORK OF DAYS
Share a Day with 30 Homeschooling Families

HOMESCHOOL OPEN HOUSE

Nancy Lande

Interviews with 55 Homeschooling Families

WindyCreek Press
Bozeman, Montana

WindyCreek Press
 For information contact WindyCreek Press: WindyCreek@aol.com
First WindyCreek Printing: 2000
Most recent printing indicated by the last digit below:
10 9 8 7 6 5 4 3 2
Library of Congress Card Number: 00-106629
Lande, Nancy 1947-
Homeschool Open House
Paperback ISBN 0-9651303-1-2
CIP
SAN 298-9425
Printed in the United States of America

TO MY FAMILY

Gary
To my husband whose presence is more ingrained
in me with each passing moment.
Thank you for making decisions, implementing
changes, working through difficulties, and sharing
all that is meaningful in our lives.

Brian
The first to turn our family experiment into a stunning
reality. You grew into a young man I
admire as much as your father.

Kate
My only daughter—you hold the place right
in the center of my heart and stand bright and beautiful
among the very finest of people.

Neil
Born with a smile on your face, and it's still there.
I cherish your gusto and goodness in experiencing life.

Kevin
You create a world of joy, humor, intelligence,
wisdom, and song for all of us.

Thank you all for being the constellation
of my world.

FOREWORD

By Susan Richman

This new book of Nancy's is lavish—it's a feast of homeschooling worldwide and all around the United States. Like HOMESCHOOLING: A PATCHWORK OF DAYS, the interviews in this book help us all get a glimpse inside another family and see how they make decisions, move through their days, deal with ranges of ages of kids, experience vastly different situations, set in varied locales. Through it all we see caring families, putting in the time needed to raise good kids. And rather unique kids—kids who know quite a bit more of life than the standard fare of the world of television and the school yard. You'll be inspired, and you'll find yourself calling in your kids so you can read them aloud a chapter or two, letting them find new friends in the children in these families.

And the book continues to confound any stereotypes the media may at times seem to promote about homeschooling—the range of families and lifestyles is truly astonishing. There are families who homeschool very happily with organized texts and correspondence programs, families who espouse a looser unschooling approach, and everything in between and beyond. There are homeschooling families raising dairy goats out in the country and families who live in neat suburban neighborhoods. You'll meet families where homeschooling moms juggle working part-time, often in a family business; blended families fully enjoying homeschooling stepchildren; single parents struggling with meeting needs to support themselves and their children while homeschooling; families in

Alaskan wilderness settings hopping into airplanes to do shopping; families in the midst of Africa homeschooling in remote village areas. Several older children helped to write their family descriptions, and their writing ability in itself shows what a fine success their homeschooling has been. There are families with lots of children and more on the way, and single-child families. The depth of sharing and the uniqueness shown is awesome. It's truly the sort of book you can curl up with for hours and hours and not notice the outside world for the duration, like when you find an engrossing novel where you forget all about your own current concerns. But when you do emerge and see your own home and family again, I guarantee you'll be doing so with new perspective.

And besides the many new and fascinating family interviews, there are the five-year follow-ups from the original families who shared their lives and wonders and hopes in HOMESCHOOLING: A PATCHWORK OF DAYS. Reading through these, I've especially been touched, moved, and amazed. I think these updates of our "old friends" from the first book really offer a new view of homeschooling, a sort of first-time longitudinal study of homeschooling and it's impact on families, learning, aspirations, and future goals. I think the book is in many ways a real contribution to the whole field of homeschooling research, and not in the usual research sense of collecting statistics and test scores and norms and bell-shaped curves of this or that. But in the really human sense of recording firsthand how homeschooling has changed these families's lives over many years.

And just like you'll find all types of families in the section of new homeschoolers, here you'll find that homeschooling families don't all take the same route as their kids grow older and circumstances change. Many families moved, or mothers needed to work full-time, or illnesses intervened that caused real disruption and stress. Many are still homeschooling or continued until their kids completed high school, but some have found other paths that are better for them at this time—and they all have things to teach us about perspective and self-evaluation and really searching for what is best for our own families. They will give you the courage to be your own family, and not feel that you need to be one certain type of homeschooler, or that you have to keep homeschooling indefinitely if it's no longer the best plan for your family.

What is so heartwarming, maybe even especially in those stories where families have made different schooling decisions as their children have grown older, is the close sense of family that they still maintain—along with a continuing sense of personal responsibility to show enthusiasm and interest in their children's education and new endeavors. They've often become the type of parents that all teachers in schools hope for—those who are involved, helpful, encouraging, appreciative. And these parents know better than to just say "now education is someone else's responsibility—we're done." Truly, no matter where kids are educated, the base of family life and parental interest and encouragement is always key.

It's also so encouraging to hear how so many of these children we all got to know from PATCHWORK have now become such responsible, good people, leading purposeful lives, doing positive work to make this world a better place. This maybe crazy homeschooling idea some of us had way back so many years ago really has panned out. Some of these homeschoolers are now married (including my first son—and to a homeschool grad!), many are in college and doing extremely well. Others are sought after for work opportunities because they've continually shown themselves to be trustworthy, capable, and caring. Homeschooling for so many of us was a real leap of faith—we had no idea how these kids might possibly turn out, as we had no road map to follow, and few stories from others who had gone the whole route and ended up with fine young adults on the other end. Now you can start hearing those stories—they are realities, not just dreams.

Susan Richman
Author of:
Writing From Home
The 3 R's at Home
Math By Kids!
Pennsylvania Homeschoolers Newsletter

ACKNOWLEDGEMENTS

Grateful acknowledgement is made
for permission to quote and reproduce
the following material: excerpts from
The Home School Source Book
by Donn Reed. Copyright © 1991, 1994
by Donn Reed. Reprinted by permission of
Jean Reed, executor of the author's estate.
Reprinted by permission of Brook Farm Books (publisher).

Very special thanks to Jean Reed for premission to include
"Enduring Family Bonds" as excerpts from
The Home School Source Book, third edition,
by Jean Reed. Copyright © 2000 by Jean Reed.
Reprinted by permission of
Brook Farm Books (publisher).

My sincere appreciation to Patric Larum
for his sketches of the homes
on the title page of each chapter in Part 1.

COVER DESIGN: Nancy Lande
COVER ART: Original oil pastel, "Open House," by Nancy Lande
HOUSE DRAWINGS for Part 1 chapter headings: Patrick Larum
PATCHWORK QUILT: The patches of the quilt that is shown on the heading of Part 2 were designed by the families who were interviewed in Nancy Lande's HOMESCHOOLING: A PATCHWORK OF DAYS. When pieced together, the whole quilt presents a vision of homeschooling that is varied, colorful, energetic, and is sewn together with the common threads of family, love, and learning.
QUILTING: Pieced and hand quilted by Barbara Zook
QUILT PHOTO: by Eric Mitchell
QUILT PATCH SKETCHES for title page and Part 2 chapter titles: by Nancy Lande

CONTENTS

INTRODUCTION

Tour Notes

While driving down a street in town, I love to look at houses, especially at night when caramel-colored lights glow in windows. I look at the purple and pink gingerbread trim on a carefully restored Victorian house and wonder about the people who live there. What kind of work do they do? How many children fill the rooms? What enticed them to buy this historic home? Do they live a gingerbread life?

Or, I see a cozy cottage on the edge of town, with children's bicycles tipped over on the freshly cut lawn and a small but colorful garden with vines stretching up and holding on to high windows. I wonder who taught the children to ride the bikes and how long it took to go from wobble to balance. Where is the family originally from? Do they laugh a lot? Do the children play piano or soccer? What dreams do they have?

Then, on my way home as I wind up the mountain, I pass by a trailer park with lots of families in close proximity. Toddlers play among each other, and small storage sheds are scattered at the ends of the box-like homes, holding (I imagine) lawn mowers, bicycles, skis, sleds, ladders . . . and what else? Is this a close-knit little community bound by their years together—or a transient one where people make friends quickly? Do families share the mountain views but value their privacy? Are most of them from "here"? Are their lives freer than those with large homes to support?

As I head further up the mountain toward home, I see grayed and tilted outbuildings. Was *this* one an original homestead? And *that* one over there, was it a school or church from a thriving community of the 1890s? What is the story behind the large barn up the hill where rusted tractors are sunk in the tall grass? Who used to live there? Were they happy? What stories could they tell?

My lifelong curiosity about people and life has led me to be an asker of questions and a collector of stories. What is that are you doing? How did you think of the idea to build that? What brought you *here* from so far away? Are you reconciled to being in a wheelchair? How did you manage to cope when your husband died? Why does your fireplace have so many different varieties of stone? How does it feel to have a daughter who looks just like you did at her age? What sparked your interest in collecting antique buttons?

I have repeatedly been surprised and delighted that things are *not* what they seem. For me, every day is an unknown journey. I search for the patterns in people's lives that tell a story. I seek clues to answer my endless questions about how people live and about the "culture" of their families.

The Tour

I invite you to tour the homes of families from downtown to rural mountains. Beyond the porticos and porches of these homes are living, interconnected stories. Come along and visit fifty-five families during this HOMESCHOOL OPEN HOUSE. See how people interact, what activities they enjoy, how they organize their lives, and how they deal with both the mundane and the tragic events in their lives. Although the families were selected because they have all participated in homeschooling, you will see not only how homeschooling works but how *families* truly live. Allow me to guide you and introduce you to families who will articulate the broad concerns of homeschooling. Get ready, put on your walking shoes, pack lightly, take a camera, bring your passport, and don't forget tissues for the end of the trip. We will travel across 11,000 miles, from Alaska to Zimbabwe. This is not a trip for the timid traveler, so I suggest you also pack courage, curiosity, and respect. Please, though, do leave your old, worn-out ideas, assumptions, and quick judgments at home.

Many of you may be first-time travelers on the homeschool path, wondering whether it's a journey you'll want to continue and whether you'll find anything worthwhile to bring back for your family. Others, however, may have been touring the homeschool roads for a long while, ever looking to find just the right souvenirs to take back home. There is something for all of you in these visits with other families.

You will glean elements of successful homeschooling and roadblocks that interfere. You will not find answers on this trip; rather, you will find that critical questions are raised to aid you in making your own decisions. It is my hope that through these intelligent reflections, you will become an informed tourist.

The first part of your journey brings you to meet volunteers who offered to be interviewed for HOMESCHOOL OPEN HOUSE by letter or by responding to my Internet request to participate in this project. The interviews were conducted by e-mail, with several pages of detailed "guidelines" I provided to outline the interviewing process and the categories I wanted covered. A few examples of the many detailed questions include the following: What are relationships like among spouses, siblings, relatives, neighbors, and community? What do you think about your "day" and what you accomplish? How do you address varying emotions, insights, reflections, and ideologies? What are your goals and frustrations? Each topic included questions to help stimulate thinking and fullness of expression. At each stage I responded and asked even more questions to clarify and flush out ideas. Although a few chapters made the rounds only two or three times, most took up to a dozen back-and-forth drafts, always with the aim of focusing deeply and clearly, flushing out the world of ideology, belief, and reality.

Several interesting dynamics emerged from the interviewing process. Many parents found the process eye-opening because it gave them a chance to step back and look closely not only at their homeschooling day, but at their entire homeschooling experience. Some who initially felt their day (or their homeschooling in general) was rather disappointing, found it upon closer reflection fuller and more productive than originally experienced. The result of the dialogues for some was a growth process and an opportunity to make major changes within the security of sharing thoughts back and forth. Parents were willing to continually refine their thoughts, assess their ideas, reevaluate themselves, and make changes, They also shared their resources (in *italics* so you can easily spot them). By the end, I felt the stories revealed the larger picture of the "culture" of each family and how and why they made the decisions they did.

To this day I am truly awed that hundreds of PATCHWORK readers took the time to write and share the depth of their reactions. As the pile of letters grew and as my children grew, I felt compelled to plan another homeschool tour. The second part of your journey is an interesting trek back to the family homes of HOMESCHOOLING: A PATCHWORK OF DAYS five years after they were originally interviewed. Previous PATCHWORK travelers wrote that they were saddened to leave families who deeply affected their thinking and touched their hearts. We revisit these original families to find out how they are faring five years later. If you want to test your own powers of prediction, read PATCHWORK first, and see if you can guess what the families are doing now. You will learn what *really* happened, not what you *imagined,* or what the families themselves *hoped* would happen. Many things have occurred that you wouldn't expect if you are someone who thinks life just keeps on going in a straight path that you can control. There were complicated twists and turns in the road that required thoughtful and difficult decisions to keep on course.

Idealization

Ahead, you will find tour notes that are meant to help you focus on critical issues and make informed decisions. Before visiting these families, it might help to see "the family" in its broader setting. The complexity of family life is often obscured by the hidden forces of idealized images of the way things "used to be" or "should be." There is no one standard definition of "family," which is revealed over and over through the unique visits in this book. Most parents *imagine* the success of others and measure themselves against those images. Homeschooling parents who have removed themselves from the American-apple-pie world of schooling feel the added necessity to do *better* than the schools and to prove themselves capable. They undertake a task they've never done before and expect to produce better religious training, academic skills, character-building tools, and self-actualization abilities for their children. For homeschooling parents, this is a particularly treacherous process, as they take the entire responsibility for educating their children upon their own shoulders, without being able to blame what they define as failures on the school, the teacher, classmates, or society. The price paid for exercising the option of taking control is personal responsibility when things do not go well. When children do well personally or socially, parents take refuge in the success of family ideals, often forgetting the ambivalence and conflict that underlie the successes. But when things are going poorly, they painfully blame all the problems on their own inadequacies, inexperience, lack of innovation or creativity, or on their own family members. It is a burden.

These visits reveal the importance of rejecting idealized fantasies of being "perfect" parents, children, or families. Instead, a realistic model based on *actual* families needs to be formed. Stories and family cultures need to be shared so that parents can make more informed decisions. Fantasies and myths that create unrealistic expectations about what can or should be done only erode family solidarity and diminish confidence in the problem-solving abilities of all families. While feelings of failure and inadequacy may be a common burden for modern families, it is a particular burden to homeschooling families since child-rearing is so central to their lives.

The discordance between fantasy and reality causes families to react with guilt and anger. They feel a sense of failure when they cannot live up to the exacting standards they set for themselves, based on the way they imagine is the "right way," the "best way," or the "perfect way" to conduct family life. Families struggle with serious dilemmas, make choices they regret, and fail their highest ideals. Generally, though, *all* families try to be "good enough" in the face of feeling that they alone are responsible for their children's successes or failures. As you will see, their standard of "good enough," though far from perfect, is remarkable.

Social Environment

While visiting, notice how easy it is for parents to forget that the process of raising children is also influenced by social, cultural, and economic factors that are beyond their control and that social and economic disruptions have enormous impact on the smaller "culture" of family. Families must interface with schoolchildren, neighborhood activities, television, and political trends. All families are impacted by external opportunities and threats. Homeschooling families need to recognize and take refuge in the shared experiences they have as a community, rather than suffer in isolation. It is apparent that the families in HOMESCHOOL OPEN HOUSE don't exist purely within the context their own self-made environments but are shaped by outside society and bond together in homeschool or church communities.

Family Culture and Environment

Homeschooling is a decision that directly involves and impacts each family member. There are also internal forces that directly shape daily life such as similarities and differences in temperament, learning style, attitude, behavior, and performance. Observe how each family has its own values, models, traditions, beliefs, judgments, rituals, stories, and child-rearing practices. Patterns make up the "culture" of the family, and the families along this route give keys to help you define those microcultures, whether children go to school, homeschool, or have stopped homeschooling. Pay attention to the degree that parents encourage or discourage their children from innovation and risk taking, to the attention they pay to detail, and to their orientation toward outcome or process. All families operate within the constraints of these continuums. Evaluate which external and internal forces affect *your* family and try to get a feel for where your own comfort zone lies between stability and growth. It may take you a while to even begin to determine your own family culture, but searching for it can be very constructive.

Learning Environment

As you travel, you can't help but be aware of the large chasm between traditional teaching and actual learning. All too often in our society, "teaching" becomes a rote, dull, and uninvolved process of imparting information to someone who has little interest to begin with. Many homeschooling families have chosen to emphasize the learning *process* for their children. You will find that parents utilize their childrens' natural abilities, curiosity, and creativity as the major avenues of obtaining mastery of knowledge and skills. They guide their children to develop interpersonal skills; to think, speak, and write effectively; and to understand and appreciate the wide variety of peoples and cultures. Generally, they train their children from a very young age to make complicated moral and ethical choices and to solve problems. Parents often take on the role of facilitators, mentors, and research assistants for their children's interests and passions. There is a wide spectrum between fully structured curriculum and child-directed learning. Each family settles into a balance along this spectrum that suits their family. The more child-directed learning is, the more parents must exercise patience, trust, observation, and being right there when the moment is ripe. This is not to say that no demands are placed on children who direct their own learning or that highly structured families offer no choices to their children.

A Good Fit

On your tour, you will also notice that homeschooling choices are most successful when there is a good fit between family culture and style of homeschooling. To bend family culture to suit an inappropriate learning/teaching method or curriculum is bound to end in disaster, as one or the other snaps. Parents and children become frustrated, feel they have nowhere to turn, and are distressed if there is not a good fit between family and learning. Many of these families have more than once thrown out a homeschool approach to begin anew. You'll meet families who are most comfortable with a casual structure, fondly live with the clutter around them, pack up the car at the drop of a hat, learn at any moment and at any place, and use or create a similar style of learning. Other families thrive with family structure based on strong organization, neatness, and routines and, therefore, enjoy preplanned curricula. Some families thrive on a new journey that has no map or promised outcomes, whereas others are more comfortable with steady structure and known destinations. Within any family, different members have different learning styles, weaknesses, and gifts. Sometimes the parent and child have similar styles or ones that may clash, resulting in misunderstanding, frustration, and anger. Understanding style and structure leads to more harmonious households. Do you know what *your* style of learning is? What learning styles do your children have?

Parenting

You may be wondering, "What exactly *are* the ingredients for a successful homeschooling environment?" Since there are no scientifically verified "homeschool truths," parents must construct a creative "new" reality for what they've not yet experienced. Think of the experience of planning a family vacation. Does everyone agree where to go, what to do, whether to camp out or enjoy the luxury of a hotel, whether to plan every detail ahead of time or just wing it? More so than planning a vacation, there are many differing opinions to take into consideration when making the decision to homeschool. It appears that parents who feel most successful at the task of raising their families are able to set goals, anticipate change, correct poor performance, exploit opportunities, and keep on heading toward family objectives. Most of the families have always been in transition and are occasionally in crisis. Parents who feel successful have dared to take a chance, make a commitment, and define their goals—often from scratch. Outside events often force families into situations where the self-evident "shoulds" are challenged, and a new path must be found in order to deal with a crisis, most often leading to opportunity. Are you prepared to lead your family in a new direction to a planned destination? Do you feel enthused about looking at your family in a fresh, new way? Are you willing to enter the world of uncertainty and the unknown?

Family Management

It is useful to think about how these parents have taken on the responsibility of being effective managers of their family, home, schooling, and business. What does this entail? How do parents know if they are effective or ineffective? Will they know whether their children are "on track" or not? You can't help but notice how parents find it crucial to plan and define goals for their children and themselves in order to answer these questions. They often work backward and imagine what results they would like to see in their children as they reach their mid-twenties. What important aspects do they want to nourish as their children grow? Ask yourself how you define what is important in life. Can you constantly direct your plans and decisions toward your goals? Can you organize what needs to be done in order to meet your goals? Will you be able to lead, direct, and motivate your children, while resolving conflicts that arise between current actions and long-term goals? Can you continually review your goals and make finely tuned adjustments? As managers of families, parents in this book have revealed many insights. They encourage experience (from art to zoology), reward both success and failure (keep on trying!), celebrate mistakes (the extra time is worth it), accept ambiguity (do *you* know it all??), tolerate the impractical (unless it's a really, *really* big mess!), lower external controls of rules and regulations (with lots of hands-on training), tolerate risk and conflict (a nap, a soak in the tub, an hour out of the house, or a cry on a spouse's shoulder here and there), and focus on the end results and not the means (most of us take refuge in the big picture when the immediate moment seems lost). Also, observe how parents continually build in their children the capacity to make decisions. Parents can instill in their children ownership, empowerment, the ability to work well as a team, and the opportunity to work intensely and without interruption. Which of these qualities do you and your children have? Which would you like to build upon?

Decision Making

Many questions and problems are presented daily that need solutions —beyond what most families face. The combined responsibilities of childrearing and education, multiplied by the number of children, call for an extraordinary amount of decision making. Parents are constantly facing problems and defining discrepancies between what is occurring and their long-term goals. They monitor tasks to see if they are moving in the planned direction and develop alternatives. Setting goals gives parents the foundation for evaluating decisions. Families you'll visit have tried to work through what is trivial or important in making good decisions. They've had to judge themselves and look at what those judgments are based on. These stories also show that certainty is tenuous and difficult in the face of judgment. How will this OPEN HOUSE influence your decision making?

Change

Travel on and contemplate the most common thread that runs through *all* these families—change. Parents and children constantly react and make changes in order to preserve the balance of day-to-day living and growth as a family. You will read about change in every story, yet you will notice that change is not always welcome, nor does it always come easily. Change is like playing games never played before, where the rules fluctuate as the game develops. Parents find themselves uncertain and resistant at times but must deal with change nevertheless.

You will see families cope with change by determining which forms of authority work best, what role independence plays, and what type of leadership is most successful. Most people are happiest and most productive when they understand the large scope of their own or their family's objectives. Parents feel good when they successfully allocate authority in a manner that encourages responsibility in their children, when they allow family members varying amounts of control. When parents and children have a sense of choice and participation in *how* goals are met, they feel empowered and enthusiastic. The most satisfied parents continuously and incrementally evaluate what they do right and what could be improved, rather than resorting to anger and guilt. It is necessary to address the problems that arise, to assess them, to find creative solutions, and always, *always* to expect the constant of *more* change. The families demonstrate how innovative change leads to success and what is required to accomplish it.

Powerful motivators of change for these families are often external factors (jobs, health, etc.), poor results, unacceptable behavior, fear of failure in the eyes of others, and inefficient processes. Conflict is often the flashing red light that warns us when change is needed in order to proceed in a new and creative direction. If a child isn't responding to a curriculum, is resistant to helping out in the house, or has an undesirable attitude—you will see these families reevaluate goals and change curriculum, reorganize chores, or allocate more responsibility. Additionally, *positive* sources of change are new information, insight, creativity, requests, brainstorming, and serendipity. Homeschooling is an ideal arena for flexibility and change, since there is no administration, regulation, red tape, or formal structure to follow. Change can occur instantly if problems are seen as opportunities to seek solutions. This means asking difficult questions about yourself, what you are doing, and what you could be doing differently. How do you deal with change?

Relax

Notice that empowered children work in teams toward accomplishment and satisfaction and how they take on more and more responsibility for setting their own direction. Many of these parents have developed competency in their children by spending a great deal of time training for results, acting as facilitators for their children's ideas and projects, providing motivation to keep on exploring, and helping their children to become leaders. Almost all of the families relaxed when they gave up the idea that children "don't want to learn." Because they have gained experience based on actual results, experimentation, success, and real data, they realize they can gradually relax their minute-to-minute set of expectations and micromanagement without giving up their standards. They no longer need to worry so much about how they look or whether their children will fail, and can begin to trust their intuition and enjoy spending time with their children. As families relax in their homeschooling, they grow ever stronger in their desire to instill integrity, character, and honesty in their children. You will see that relaxing is a process that families come to over time, as they find their own way and feel more confidence as a result of their children's successes.

Tour Evaluation

As your tour ends, there are important questions to ask yourself, as the thoughtful parents in these stories have done. It is imperative to understand your family culture, to stay open, to make connections, and to take the time to question, rather than jump to quick judgments. These questions might include the following:

•Would I be comfortable running a house full-time with children around most of the day—with all the planning, management, and work entailed?

•Would I be able to educate or facilitate the learning of a number of children across many, many areas, while at the same time looking after the emotional, social, and physical needs of myself and my family?

•If necessary or desirable, could I work full-time or part-time while homeschooling?

•Would I be able to keep developing myself in a way that pleases me?

•Do I have the managing skills to handle children, noise, and activity all day long? What is my management style?

•Who am I? Who are they? What do we want for and from them?

•Can we determine what our mission, goals, and values are?

•Can I repeatedly guide my children without being overcome by too much frustration, anxiety, doubt, or anger? Do I understand what "training" is about?

•Do I understand that we can only behave in ways consistent with our family culture and that our homeschooling must fit our family culture rather than the other way around?

•Will I be able to seek out appropriate new curricula, activities, interests, and resources, as the needs of my children change?

•If I sense failure, will I have the incentive to seek new solutions?

•How would I feel if, after years of managing the emotional, intellectual, and physical needs of family and their learning, I weren't judged as qualified for satisfying work when my children were grown and no longer at home?

•Can I handle outside pressures or commitments from church, family, and society, along with the pressure that I "should" homeschool?

•Would I rather let my children suffer at home than be seen as a homeschool parent who might fail, even if the best decision is to put our children in school?

•How would I feel about *not* being part of the neighborhood chat circle or PTA? Will I get enough adult interaction through outside homeschool activities?

•Will my children *lose* anything (or too much?) by not being part of school sports, music, friends, or advanced classes? Do I need to feel responsible for or make up for their losses ?

•How will I fare without outside reinforcement, encouragement, direction, and others who will reassure me of the status of my child?

Bon Voyage

Growing and learning are about making choices. The decision to homeschool should be an informed and knowledgeable decision, based on the specifics of family culture and on the rewards and losses such a decision entails. The more questions are asked, the easier it will be to identify personal and family needs and values. Homeschooling is not an easy commitment to make without first considering the risks, costs, benefits, and alternatives—many of which can be explored on your tour of HOMESCHOOL OPEN HOUSE. I hope it will be a memorable journey.

HOMESCHOOL OPEN HOUSE

Part I

Jim, age 31
Mary, age 30
Ethan, age 10
Jase, age 5
Simon, age 3
Quinn, age 18 months
Mamie, age 5 months

Interview with Mary after a hot, dry summer in the midlands of South Carolina

CHOOSING GOOD OR BEST

7:00 a.m., October 18—I am awakened by a little voice at my head.
Simon: "Hi, MOMMY!!" (yelling)
Mommy: "Oh, hi, Simon. Did you sleep well?"
Simon: "YES, I DID!!!"
Mommy: (placing pillow over head) "Please tell Ethan to start the coffee, Simon."

SLAM! Sound of little feet running in the other direction. Simon is almost three and is the most enthusiastic person I have ever met. I am blessed that he has begun, in his "old age," to sleep in; he used to be up every morning, ready to go, at 5:30 a.m. Seven o'clock feels like a scandalously late hour in comparison.

Even the goats are letting us sleep in these days. We homeschool in a little log house on twelve acres of pastureland in the midlands of South Carolina, where we raise dairy goats. We have a herd of twenty registered Saanen and LaMancha goats and raising them has been an education in itself. In the spring, the newborn goat kids live in a playpen in our living room and demand our attention in much the way a newborn child might—sometimes around the clock. The children take turns bottle-feeding them. In addition to providing us with milk (and occasionally meat), the dairy goats have afforded our children and us a great education in all facets of biology—having seen first-hand birth, death, and everything in between. We do our own veterinary care, and the children are comfortable seeing us drawing blood, giving injections, trimming hooves, dis-budding goat kids, etc. They know that animals sicken and sometimes die, and that's just part of life for them.

Right now, following a very hot summer during which our dairy goats were unable to drink enough water to keep making milk, all of our herd is "dry," so we're not milking at all. That's a treat for us, since when they are in milk, we have to be home twice a day for milkings, twelve hours apart—part of the year, this means milking before sunup and after dark. None of our females is due to kid until February. When they kid, we'll be back to twice-daily milkings—the upside of which is a huge savings at the supermarket, with all the milk the child-ren can guzzle, and the fun of making lots of bread puddings, custards, and goat-milk fudge in order to "use up" the milk. We plan to milk only four of our twelve does in the spring, letting the rest raise their own kids (and, if we're lucky, an "adoptee" or two), but that still means at least three gallons of milk a day.

7:05 a.m.—I'm out of bed after a quick moment of prayer for patience and sufficient strength during the day and for help in remembering my priorities. My first priority is taking care of the emotional and spiritual needs of the household, and next is taking care of the physical home—in other words, focusing on home-life, not the house. It's so difficult to do those things that are "invisible" (like reading to the children, praying with them, making time to cook with them and including them in my little jobs around the house) when the "visible" things have a way of piling up and causing me to dread unexpected guests! Additionally, it's important for me to remember that I need to concern myself more with my child-ren's character than with their handwriting. It's so easy to get wrapped up in the tangible, measurable things and lose sight of what's really important. I have a hard time choosing the "best" because the "good" is so very tempting and there is so much of it.

I have taken over moderating an e-mail digest for mothers with many child-ren eight years and under. This list has about four hundred subscribers and is a lot of fun for Jim and me. Jim is an invaluable part of the operation. He handles the technical end and makes sure the mail goes out every day over our mail server. In addition, he handles some of the administrative tasks that can pile up, and he is always available for me to get feedback on how to handle difficulties. I was a subscriber for a few years before taking over moderating, and it is a great blessing to me, living in the "sticks" as I do, to have such a large fellowship. There is always something to work on as I strive to compile all the helpful recipes, tips, encouragements, and advice mentioned on the digest.

7:10 a.m.—While the computer downloads the new e-mail messages from the digest list, I brush my teeth and throw on my clothes. I might as well confess now that I am no fashion plate. I have about four favorite outfits—jumpers with t-shirts or turtlenecks under them, or skirts and sweaters—and those are what I nearly always wear. Simplicity has made me a happier mother. I know that's almost a homeschooling-mom cliché, but it's true—in a denim jumper, I feel ready to face the day. I lift the blinds and peek out the window—ahhh, sunshine and blue skies. I love autumn, and it is approaching fast.

We live five miles outside a small town with perhaps a population of 1,000. About thirty minutes away is the closest large town of Columbia, the state capital of South Carolina. We are blessed in that our little town is conservative and fairly old-fashioned for these modern times. Many still farm their land (cotton, mostly) or raise cattle.

7:20 a.m.—Having read the incoming e-mail, I head out to face the morning. Jase, age five, is clamoring for "horse mash" (skillet granola)—whole oats fried in butter and honey. I don't often make this because of the terrible potential for disasters involving my carpeting (yes, I have a carpeted dining room; don't ask why), but today he is so sweet and cute, I can't refuse him. I make the horse mash extra special today with coconut and a handful of chocolate chips, then sit the little boys down at the dining table to eat, with just a splash of milk in each bowl. "Now be careful, little boys!" Off I go to feed five-month-old Mamie in the privacy of our bedroom and to drink my morning cup of coffee with Jim.

7:30 a.m.—I am now reminded *why* I don't usually make horse mash. Jase comes to get the little vacuum. I sigh deeply and count to ten before saying anything; while counting, I pray for patience. By the time I hit "ten," I don't feel like doing anything except smiling patiently (hopefully not patronizingly) at Jase and thanking God, a little ruefully, that I have these mess-making little ones in the first place.

I get really bent out of shape about mess and noise, although this doesn't mean that my house is always neat and quiet. As a matter of fact, it is almost never neat and quiet; but that's a goal I work toward. I try hard to at least keep the living room and dining room clean and picked-up all the time. I find that I am calmer if things "look" calm, by which I mean uncluttered. Short (two-minute) pick-ups several times a day, plus vacuuming at least daily, have helped with this. When we married, I was a terrible housekeeper. Needless to say, I have learned a lot as our house has filled up with children—especially children who are home all the time, going behind me to undo the housework!

I try hard to clean enthusiastically and cheerfully and to make lots of comments about how nice everything looks when we are done. Jase and Simon have caught the spirit, and although they do not pick up on their own yet, they do work cheerfully under my direction. I did not do this with Ethan, preferring to "do it all myself" since it was easier than teaching him, and that was a mistake for which Ethan and I are still paying. I hope I can instill in the children the ability to work diligently and to "see" what needs to be done.

We don't have a formal chore chart; I usually just enlist the help of whichever child is handy when I notice that something needs to be done. The rule in our household is that the job should go to the "youngest competent child." This motivates Ethan to make sure he and I are instructing his younger brothers to do his current chores! Simon and Jase are good at picking up and both like to load and unload the dishwasher, washing machine, and dryer. They love to run the vacuum. They aren't very skilled as far as actual cleaning, but that will come in time. Right now, my major concern is for them to feel fulfilled by a job done earnestly.

7:45 a.m.—Mamie's done with breakfast and so are Ethan and the little ones. Leaving Jim still in bed (he's not a morning person), I traipse back out to the living room to examine the damage. Mamie goes in her doorway jumper (hung not in a doorway, but from a hook in the ceiling placed there just for the jumper) and spends the next thirty minutes or so bouncing around and commenting on everything in baby talk. I remind Ethan to unload the dishwasher, and I march into the boys' bathroom to do a quick cleanup, pick up clothing, and load the washing machine.

Two things have revolutionized my "chore life." One is doing a load of laundry every day, and the other is wiping down the toilet and sink every time I go into the bathroom. I try to get the laundry going every morning right away; that way I don't get depressed about the messy bathroom (which doubles as a laundry room) each time I walk in there during the day.

Some time ago, it was pointed out to me that if I could just get on top of all the chores *once*, I could then start "maintaining" the house instead of always doing emergency housecleaning. In other words, I could do house-"keeping." I've tried to make that my goal—the house always in more or less good shape all the time and maintained like that by my frequent attention to things before they get noticeably out of control. I am not always successful, but at least I have something to aim for.

After finishing in the bathroom, I stick my head into the boys' bedrooms—Ethan's room (also known as the playroom) that he shares with eighteen-month-old Quinn, and the "bunk room," that Simon and Jase share. Ethan's room is neat as a pin (thanks, Ethan), but the little boys' room looks like a train wreck. I sigh and call them to help me pick it up.

I try to ensure that both of the bedrooms are picked up completely at least once a day. They are always immediately a mess again, but at least I know, facing the room each morning, that it can't be *that* bad—after all, fewer than twenty-four hours earlier, it was spotless!

8:00 a.m.—The room is clean. I get the little boys (Jase, Simon, and Quinn) involved in building a *Brio* train track in the playroom (Ethan's bedroom) and then give Ethan some instructions for his schoolwork. Writing his assignments out on a sheet of paper, I remind him to work diligently without getting distracted.

I try to do those school-related things that require my direct involvement—like explaining math, discussing things Ethan is reading, finding and marking places from his reading on the *Mark-It* map in our dining room, calling out his spelling words to him, or reading poetry aloud—while the little ones are occupied elsewhere. Some days, depending on how exciting the morning is, that doesn't happen until nap time. *Some* days it doesn't happen at all!

Today, we work on fractions. Ethan sits next to me on the sofa while I correct work done on a previous day and he listens as I explain what went wrong with his missed problems. We do a few example problems, then he goes off to the dining table to work on the next page. Currently, he is working through the workbooks *Key To Fractions* from *Key Curriculum Press* to make sure he has fraction concepts down solidly before he begins the next *Saxon Math* book.

We have never been text-bookish homeschoolers. As students, both Jim and I disliked textbooks, finding them predigested and boring, so we have always preferred that the children's learning come from real books. As such, I suppose you could label us Charlotte Mason homeschoolers, although we don't follow all of her principles. Sometimes I get overwhelmed with daily details (housework and other interests) and am tempted to just hand my child a sheet of schoolwork and say, "Here, let me know when you're done," I do know that when I do this, it is a distant second best. Although we value independence in learning, our involvement is terribly important and might be the most challenging task in providing a quality home education.

We have used *Sonlight Curriculum*, which has a strong emphasis on history and geography and emphasizes a Christian worldview. I think *Sonlight's* language arts materials are excellent, but I haven't used them much though they coordinate with the history readers and read-alouds. Ethan is able to read and comprehend at a much higher level than he is able to express himself in writing. Therefore, for his basic studies (reading, history, science, Bible) we use materials that are several grades higher than his written-language abilities. We have had to "go it alone" as far as Ethan's language arts materials. We've used *Winston Grammar, Daily Grams*, and various spelling programs. Mostly, I think he has needed time to mature into writing. This year he is at grade level on spelling and written grammar, although his handwriting is still behind. Jim assures me that in the Information Age it will not matter; but I, priding myself on my perfect *Palmer Method* curlicues, am still working on Ethan's penmanship.

As far as science goes, I am slightly embarrassed to admit that we have done very little in the way of formal science education. *Sonlight* offers a great science

---

program that we've ordered a couple of years; but we never seem to have time to do the experiments, so he ends up merely reading through the books and answering the discussion questions. I suppose that's fine, since Ethan already reads widely and subscribes to several science-related magazines. Jim is very technologically savvy, and Ethan has worked with him on many projects. One year, we read through *The Way Things Work* and now Ethan can explain the innards of nearly every machine. We felt that this book would give him a great footing for applied physics. He consistently scores off the charts on standardized tests, so I suppose our inattention to formal science hasn't hurt him.

Our present plan for Jase is fairly unstructured, using no formal history or science for him until he is perhaps eight years old and has facility in writing. We expect that, like Ethan, Jase will read widely as his interests lead. As far as math curriculum, we are using *Miquon Math* and flash cards this year, but do not plan to use a formal textbook curriculum with him until he able to do the four basic operations solidly from flash cards. From having already taught one child in the primary grades, I know that we can just relax and enjoy these early years. We do try to take advantage of our young children's impressionable minds and fabulous memory by using lots of educational cassette tapes, especially the ones put out by *Audio-Memory*. They are just amazing in their ability to teach loads of information to little ones painlessly. At six, Ethan could recite all the countries in the world according to their continents.

8:20 a.m.—With Ethan involved in his work, I have Jase come read with me. Jase is reading from the Pathway Readers' *More Days Go By*. This series is especially nice for us since the books are Amish, and the lives of the children in those books are similar to our family's life—chickens, goats, making hay, and getting along with *lots* of little siblings. We snuggle on the sofa and I listen to him read, offering gentle correction as needed.

Meanwhile, Simon and Quinn come to me with various crises involving the need for ice water, the bathroom, and mediation of their joint efforts to manage the newly-built *Brio* railway. Jase patiently reads aloud to himself while I take care of the little boys' grievances. Finally, I have had enough of the interruptions, and I instruct Ethan to please make some microwave popcorn. The little boys take it back their bedroom to spill it all over the floor, and I urge Jase to finish his story before everything falls apart.

8:40 a.m.—At my direction, all the little boys put on their shoes and go play on the porch with a big inflatable ball and some salt dough. I check in on Ethan, who is finishing up his third page of fraction work. I grade his work, congratulate him on a job well done, and instruct him to read a couple chapters in his history text (Joy Hakim's *A History of US*, part of *Sonlight's* seventh year program). I take this rare quiet moment to go back to the bedroom to check on Jim. He's up and dressed, working on a shopping-cart program he's been writing on the com-

---

puter. He says it's like solving a big puzzle. Since my sons are so very like him, I try to be polite and actually listen when he explains a complex programming detail. I figure that, even if it wasn't necessary to do so in order to be a supportive wife, I surely should do so to get experience in how to listen when my *children* start sharing these tidbits with me.

It's kind of funny that I'm not more attracted to unit studies, because "unit study" seems to be the best description for how Jim and I tend to live our lives. We get passionately interested in something, find out everything there is to know about it, suck all the marrow out, and move on to something else, having satisfied our need to know. The first year we were in this house, we had four dairy goats, two Jersey bull calves (for meat), a Jersey cow (for milk), almost a hundred chickens (some for eggs, some for meat), and various ducks and geese. We learned almost everything there was to know about small-animal husbandry, and it seems during that year Carla Emery's *Encyclopedia of Country Living* was always in someone's lap.

The year before, we were immersed in all the details of building our own house—fantastically complicated and absorbing. Magazines everywhere, graph paper coming out our ears, nightly trips to the home supply store. The house took us six months to build from the time we started the foundation and it was built with minimal help from subcontractors. We subcontracted out the footer and foundation, the drywall, the shingling of the roof, and the plumbing and electrical. Everything else was done by Jim, with help from the rest of us—grading the site and the driveway; building the girders, joists, and subfloor; unloading the logs from the truck using a forklift; stacking, caulking, and staining the logs; setting the trusses and sheathing the roof; installing the doors and windows; all the interior framing, including a 1" x 6" tongue-and-groove wood ceiling throughout the house; building and installing the kitchen cabinets; priming and painting throughout; building the front porch that runs the length of the house; and building the eight-foot fence around the backyard—not to mention building the dairy shed and chickenhouses. Whew, we were tired by the time we finally moved in! No wonder we left most of the finish carpentry (trim work) undone until this year!

The log home we built is a four-bedroom, two-bath, ranch-style house—one level, since we knew we were building it by ourselves and figured we'd never manage to build a two-storey without a crane. The living room, kitchen, entry hall, and dining room are "open" to one another, leaving the children lots of room to run around. A master bedroom and bath are at one end and the children's rooms (a bunk room and playroom) are at the other end, along with a combination bath/laundry room. There is a study also, which will one day be a children's bedroom, but which now stores all that "necessary" stuff that is too important to throw away, but not quite important enough to actually use every day.

We designed the house ourselves with a large family in mind. We made some hideous mistakes during the building, but we learned a lot and we have a wonderful feeling of ownership that we wouldn't have had if we'd merely bought a tract house. The older two children will always remember helping to build the house—fetching tools, wheeling the compressor around—and even Simon, who was a baby when it was being built, knows that "Daddy built our house." In this age, so many things have been contracted out to professionals (education comes to mind). Jim and I want our children to know that they can do things for themselves. Some nights when we get into bed, Jim looks up at the ceiling and says wonderingly, "I built this house." The feeling I get when he says that is priceless.

This year, we are in the swing of web design and site management, and we're thoroughly enjoying that. Jim designed the web site for our state's homeschoolers' organization and has done several other sites for various Christian businesses. Like everyone else designing web pages, I suppose, we hope that one day the business will grow to the point where it can support our family. Right now it pays for new computer goodies, and we're happy with that. We have two computers networked together to share a hard drive and an Internet connection. We sit across from one another so we can talk face to face as we work.

While I listen to the details of Jim's latest programming victory, trying not to visibly glaze over, I check e-mail on my computer and find twenty messages for the digest! Wow, I guess the last digest that went out must have been pretty interesting. I process them as quickly as possible, adding comments where necessary.

9:00 a.m.—Hilarious screams erupt from the living room. "Get her out! Get her out!" I hear little Quinn screeching with delight while some sort of mayhem goes on just on the other side of my bedroom door. I shoot a look at Jim and get up from the computer to check it out. Just as I feared—a goat kid in my house. "I wonder *who* let her in?" I say cynically to Ethan, who is still on the sofa with his book in his lap, watching the fracas and laughing. While the children whoop and holler behind me, I use a piece of bread to lure Constant Comment (one of our nicest doe kids from this season) to the front door, then stuff her out before she can realize she's been evicted.

An occasional goat in the house is not uncommon. Thankfully, we've never had a buck, only the rare bold doe, and the goat kids. Having spent their first days in a playpen in our living room, they are convinced they have the right to come in whenever they please! The chickens, too, hang around by the front door, hoping for snacks.

The children are a mess from playing in the yard, and Mamie is falling apart from all the excitement. I instruct Jase to start a bath and Ethan to help undress his brothers, while I put Mamie to bed in her nice, safe playpen—in the corner of

---

Ethan (10), Jase, (5), Simon (3), Quinn (18 mo.), Mamie (5 mo.)

our master bath, where neither goat kids nor brothers are permitted to enter. I am sure I hear her sigh with relief as she snuggles in to sleep with her blanket doll. Then I go out to make sure all three little ones make it into the bathtub and to "redirect" Ethan to continue with his reading. Ethan is dying to tell me an interesting point from his book, so I listen as I do a quick pick-up of the boys' clothes (which have been left on the floor, wherever they shucked them).

Ethan is a quick learner and is very verbal. Sometimes he does not stay focused and follow through on tasks. I try to be patient. I am, by nature, a quiet, visual type, as are my husband and two of our other sons. Ethan and Simon are the garrulous auditory learners; I often lament that they were born so far apart. As twins they would have been wonderful—they could have simply talked one another's ears off.

Knowing that Ethan is auditory, I have tried to provide auditory input as much as possible. During our first few years homeschooling, he listened to dozens of books on tape. They were able to hold his attention through many very long and involved stories like the unabridged *Robinson Crusoe,* when he was just seven and eight years old. Hearing excellent writing read by good readers has no doubt influenced his ability to "hear" in his head the proper inflections as he reads silently now. We no longer do the books on tape, since he doesn't seem to need them; at ten, he reads at an adult level.

9:15 a.m.—My listening to Ethan has delayed my checking the still-running bath. The whole bottle of bubble bath has been poured into the bathtub. Bubble bath solution, in our house, lasts for about 1.8 baths, unfortunately. I try to maintain my perspective about this, remembering that it's only a dollar a bottle, but I am still annoyed. After a minute or two of standing there in front of the bathtub, watching my delighted children in a mountain of bubbles, I run to take refuge in my husband, who is still ticking happily away at the computer.

"They're trying to get me!!!" I wail. "Don't worry, honey, it's almost naptime," he reminds me. "And where there are no oxen, the stall is clean." Grumbling something about how it certainly *ought* to be clean, with all those soap bubbles in there, I go out to make sure I head off any further developments.

Occupying the little ones is, without a doubt, my biggest challenge in homeschooling this houseful. We have a couple of locking cabinets filled with toys and gadgets to busy their hands and minds. We place a high value on basic educational toys for teaching spatial relationships and basic engineering concepts, not to mention cooperation. Our favorites are *Brio* train sets, *Lego* and *Duplos,* wooden blocks, and our new favorite, *Gears, Gears, Gears!* The children also enjoy making blanket forts and then playing with flashlights in their temporary "clubhouse." We are amazed at the incredible imaginations that even our little children have. I would like to use more art supplies, but find that I do not have the patience for the cleanup. I am always a little sad when I hear about some-

---

body's great art project, and I realize that my children will probably never have that sort of free art experience in early childhood. I suppose they can always explore that when they are older—or while visiting Grandma! They also have their own computer and lots of software, most of which is from Humongous (*Freddi Fish, Spy Fox, Putt-Putt,* etc.) or part of the *Jump-Start* series. Although I think the computer certainly has its value, only rarely do we use it for "school."

9:30 a.m.—Ethan starts talking the instant my bedroom door opens. "Ethan, is this about school?" "Well . . . not exactly, but . . . ." "Please finish your reading, and then you can tell me all about it, okay?" Ethan has heard this one before. He returns to his reading; he's finished with the assignment in the Hakim book and has moved on to *Peace Child*, a missionary story.

I look in on the bathing beauties. All is well, but I can tell that Quinn is not going to go for this much longer. Looking at the clock, I decide to slap together some peanut butter and jelly sandwiches as a snack before nap time.

My interest in cooking seems to be cyclical; when I am pregnant, I am passionately interested in food. Right now I am not, so my poor children have to eat the same thing pretty often. Most of the time we have quesadillas, peanut butter and jelly sandwiches, buttered noodles, tuna casserole, macaroni and cheese, leftovers, or ravioli (the frozen kind, not the can) for lunch. I admit to not being very imaginative in the kitchen.

9:40 a.m.—By the time I finish, Quinn is out of the bath and dripping water through the living room. Simon is hot on his trail. "Get back *in*, Quinn!" I assure Simon that Quinn is just fine and that I will get him dressed and feed him; I send Simon back to the bath. In a stroke of genius, I decide to feed Quinn *before* I dress him, though I do put his diaper on him. Quinn has long ago eschewed the high chair, preferring to sit at the table like a big boy, on a bar-stool. He sits and happily eats his sandwich half, and I can almost hear the wheels turning inside his head as he contemplates climbing up on the table to fiddle with the chandelier.

9:50 a.m.—Now Simon is out of the bath for good and requesting not only a sandwich, but also a cup of milk. He is very adamant that he does not want his milk in a sippy-cup. As I explain the way it will be, he rolls around on the floor for a moment, cursing his fate, but then, threatened with an early nap, he gets up and calmly takes his sandwich and sippy cup to the table. Ethan rolls his eyes at me. Simon is a great actor and his antics are well-known in our family; this morning's scene is not one of his finer ones. Perhaps Simon just feels obligated to protest? Ethan claims his two sandwiches (a growing boy!) and joins the little ones at the table to mediate their meal.

10:05 a.m.—Jase is still not out of the bathtub, but the little boys are finished with their sandwiches, and Ethan and I decide that now is a very good time to put Quinn and Simon down for their naps. As Ethan puts Quinn into his outfit and

---

puts him to bed in his crib, I break the news to Simon.

10:15 a.m.—Three stories and a prayer later, Simon agrees to go to sleep. Quinn is already asleep—the bath has apparently done him in. On my way to the living room to see what Ethan is doing with his time, I look in on Jase, still happily playing in the bathtub. He can spend literally hours in there, pouring water from container to container and telling himself stories about tugboats and barges and sailors. He has a fantastic imagination and is rarely bored when he is alone. I remind Jase to play very quietly so that his brothers can have good naps.

Obedience—the instant, cheerful kind—is critical to successful home-schooling. I'm very grateful that our children have been trained to obey and that I can count on them to be truthful. Whatever other character flaws they may have, at least I can trust them to do as I ask, even when my attention is turned.

Ethan is in the living room on the sofa, reading his Bible study book. He stops me on my way through to the kitchen to ask me a fairly complex doctrinal question. I sit down and try to explain our stance on it, but run into a problem and go get Jim. While Jim sits across from Ethan and explains, I listen from the kitchen and put a few dishes from breakfast and lunch into the dishwasher.

Hmmmm . . . what to have for dinner? I peek into the freezer; ah, hamburger meat. Tacos! I have tomatoes, lettuce, sour cream; and although I don't have shells, I know we have corn tortillas in the fridge, and we can deep-fry them. I take out the hamburger to thaw, and while I'm at it, I take out a package of chicken too, for tomorrow's dinner.

10:30 a.m.—Ethan's question answered to his satisfaction, I sit down on the sofa across from him with our poetry book. Although he is now old enough to read the poetry himself with the proper inflections, meters, etc. inside his own head, I still read it aloud to him. It is important to me that when my children are grown, they will always remember their mother reading these timeless poems to them. I want them to love poetry as I do. I have read poetry to him since he was about seven and my only regret is that I didn't start even sooner.

After nearly every poem, he talks about how that particular poem reminds him of something, about how the meter was similar to another poem, or "isn't that the same poet who wrote Thus-and-Such Poem?" Often, he will ask me to re-read a poem that struck his fancy. Some of our favorites have been read so many times that we both know them by heart—like Frost's *Stopping by Woods on a Snowy Evening*, or Jonathan Bing and his poor manners in the court of the king, or the one about Father William losing his patience with his inquisitive son.

I can relate to Father William. I work on patience, so this time of poetry reading is a wonderful "recharge" for my emotions. I do not do it every day, but I wish I did; it seems to knit me closer to Ethan whenever I manage to find the time to do it.

11:00 a.m.—Ethan has done a fair amount of reading and had a really good

---

attitude so far today, so I send him out of the house (to his delight) to go ride his horse, a twenty-year-old Appaloosa mare named Crow. Last year, Ethan took horseback riding lessons once or twice a week. The lessons were a pain to fit into our lives, and once Ethan was good enough at riding to be able to control a horse without falling off, we stopped the lessons and decided to simply buy him a horse. Living thirty minutes from civilization, however, and having five (so far) children, I do know that we cannot afford (financially or time-wise) to start indulging each child with his own special activity every week. I do not intend to wind up being a chauffeur for age-segregated activities—not when I kept my children home in the first place under the assumption that the family home is the best environment in which to learn. Therefore, we do not intend to join "formal" extra-curricular organizations or activities for things we are already learning and doing at home. Some folks feel that experience one gains on one's own isn't valid—that it must pass through the hands of some sort of accredited organization in order to "count."

While Ethan exercises Crow, I go take care of some digest business. This gives me a chance to spend some time with Jim, too, whom I fear may be growing moldy sitting in front of his computer all day. I convince Jim that it would be in his best interest to get out of the bedroom for a few minutes and make a new pot of coffee; remarkably, he falls for my ploy. When he comes back from the kitchen, we lie down on the bed together to talk about a few things that have been on our minds. Jim and I are very, very close, and by having heart-to-heart talks two or three times a day, we stay in fellowship.

While we're talking, Mamie starts to stir, waking up from her nap. Time to eat! Mamie and I enjoy a snuggle as she feeds and Jim and I tell her all about how sweet and pretty she looks today and what a great little girl she is. Mamie is so flattered that she can hardly stand it, and she has to stop feeding several times so that she can "goo" at us, to tell us that the feeling is definitely mutual.

12:00 noon—Ethan comes in with the mail; he rode Crow up to the mailbox (about a quarter mile) and is wiped out. "May I have an apple?" He goes back outside to share his apple with Crow, taking a *Sonlight* book with him to read on the front porch. It is a nice day and I hate for him to be cooped up in the house. I know that later today he will be minding his brothers in the playroom so he'd better get his outdoor time while he can.

Meanwhile, I have some organizing to do. Our bedroom is one of the two rooms in the house that I do not insist be kept neat and, boy, is it ever a mess. I do a total cleanup of our bedroom about every two weeks and every time I do, I am struck by how much better it looks clean. But, I can't help it, the mess has to go somewhere and I am a piler, not a filer, so it usually starts accumulating next to my side of the bed the very day I clean up. By three days post-cleanup, it looks like no one has cleaned the room in months.

Jase has finished with his bath, finally, and has eaten his sandwich; now he is playing with his gears set in the living room, while Mamie rolls around on the floor next to him, gumming a teether toy.

12:30 p.m.—Simon greets me at the door, complaining that I left him all alone in his bedroom and how did I expect him to sleep without someone there with him, anyway? As usual, I cuddle with him on my bed for ten minutes or so, rubbing his back and telling him his favorite stories, until he is more awake and happy. Today he is a hard sell, wanting to hold a grudge; he agrees to let me pray for him briefly, interjecting his customary supplication to the Lord to protect him from "momsters and fire." Then I ask him if he'd like to call Grandma on the phone and, of course, he immediately brightens.

Jase hears Simon talking to Grandma and has to get in on the act, too. The two can be quite entertaining to their grandparents and, after about five minutes of news from each of them (most of which sounds suspiciously similar to yesterday's news), she asks to speak with Jim. They chat for a few minutes while Simon and Jase wander into the living room to forage for lunch. I give them each permission to eat an apple and send them both outside, after giving them firm instructions to eat the apples themselves and *not* to feed them to the horse. Meanwhile, I put on a pot of water to boil. I'm going to make buttered egg noodles for all interested parties. Then I duck back into the bedroom to see how Jim is doing and run the digest again.

1:00 p.m.—Time to put on the noodles; I hear Quinn complaining in his crib. Guess he's awake! I put in the noodles and go to check on him.

1:10 p.m.—Simon, Jase, and Ethan have discovered the noodles and are standing around panting, waiting for me to dole them out. Everyone gets noodles, butter, salt, and sippy cups of water, while I flop down on the sofa, tired, with my teacher's manual. Time for a cup of herb tea, and time to check off the things we have accomplished today and to make notes on Ethan's progress.

1:30—Oh, no! Jim's pager is going off! Don't tell me he's going to have to work at his Real Job today?! Jim's employed full-time by a company that manufactures hospital lab equipment. His job is to be available to fix the instruments when they go down or have problems. He's salaried, but only has to go somewhere if something is broken or needs to have preventive maintenance. Sometimes he is very busy for weeks on end, leaving the house before daylight and spending the night in another state. Other times, like now, he can go all week without having to go somewhere. It's a perfect job for a homeschooling dad.

Sure enough, he has a call in Columbia, about thirty minutes away. An instrument is down and they have to have service today. Jim tells me that the instrument is a quick fix. He just has to put in a new part and he can come home; the call itself probably won't take over ten minutes. Do I want to come with him? I debate for a minute, then decide to go; after all, the children have all had their naps and I do need to go to the grocery store for a thing or two.

2:00 p.m.—In near-record time, everyone is respectably dressed and in the car. We are not a small family and there are a lot of things to remember: a bottle of warm water for the baby, sippy cups for the three little boys, one of Ethan's school books (so he can make use of the idle time), Simon's "blankie," everyone's shoes and socks, the part for Jim's instrument, his computer and tool case, the mail that really should go out today, and since we're going right by the cleaner's, we might as well drop off Jim's shirts.

When we had fewer children, we took more "formal" field trips with other homeschool groups. A combination of increasing family size and increasing confidence in our family's ability to instruct our own children has greatly diminished the number of those trips. We now rely more on our everyday trips out of the house to teach the children the things that formal field trips might. We keep a zoo membership and a membership to our state museum. We have, at other times, held memberships to museums as far as an hour and a half away and actually made time to go see those museums regularly, but these days we are too busy with "real life" to do so. To the alert and caring parent, a trip anywhere out of the house is an educational experience—an opportunity to learn about occupations, manufacturing, other cultures, etc.

I often scratch my head over the saying that "homeschooling is fine, but eventually those children need to enter the Real World." Whatever do those folks mean? If anyone lives in the Real World, it is my family. All our experiences are "real," never mocked-up or simulated. I laugh, thinking of the preschools with little toy ovens and sinks and refrigerators or, for that matter, toy dolls and cradles. Obviously *that* isn't the Real World. In the Real World that my children live in, the appliances are real and so are the babies; and they don't have to do a unit in primary school about The Mailman, because they already know all about him.

It seems to me that if anyone is in for a shock about how the Real World operates, it is schoolchildren who grow up without the advantage of daily contact with people of all ages and from different walks of life; who didn't accompany Mom to shop for sales at the supermarket; who were at soccer practice when Dad changed the oil in the car; who haven't heard their parents, day in and day out, modeling the way to deal graciously with all sorts of people, in person and on the phone. All of our children are friendly and easily adaptable to any social situation. As you might expect from children coming from a large family, they play well with children of all ages and they are at ease conversing with adults. *That* is the Real World. We like to say that they have been "vertically socialized," as opposed to "horizontally"; in other words, they get along well in social groups comprised of varying ages, as opposed to being "socialized" to get

---

Ethan (10), Jase, (5), Simon (3), Quinn (18 mo.), Mamie (5 mo.)

along best in that unique and highly artificial group the schools would put them in. It's so funny how "education" is never the issue with homeschooling; everyone seems to take it for granted that we couldn't possibly do any worse at educating the children than the schools are doing!

2:45 p.m.—After stopping at the post office, the cleaners, and the dump, Jim arrives at his account, hands me the car keys, and takes Simon and Jase in to show them off. This customer is one of his favorites—it's the hospital where our last two children were born. Simon and Jase are terribly excited and, although Quinn is unhappy to see his brothers go, he is mollified by the promise of French fries from the nearby drive thru.

3:00 p.m.—Back to the hospital to find Jim and the boys waiting under the portico. The boys have to tell me all about their experience, sitting in the waiting room of the small lab and making chitchat with the elderly patients. They are both very friendly and love to make conversation and, apparently, they were a hit. Jim eats a few French fries and tells me about the call. It was uneventful but he does need to come back tomorrow and bring them some sort of gadget. The boys make a play to accompany him on tomorrow's call as well, but he looks doubtful. "I think your mommy needs you at home tomorrow, boys."

The children are fascinated by Jim's work and often put on his lab coats and walk around pretending to "go fix an instrument." Like many children, I suppose, they want to grow up to do exactly what their father does. Will they? I doubt it, but it's likely, having grown up in a "technophilic" home, that some of them will indeed want to do something technical, whether it be engineering, software design, or programming. Ethan is such a great talker that we have always joked that he should become a lawyer; perhaps he will. And Mamie? We are hoping that ultimately she will marry and be a mother to her children so we are equipping her to excel at that. When she finishes high school, she will be encouraged to further her education with something that will be of use to her future family, such as going to nursing school. We want our sons and daughters to be fulfilled adults, and to the best of our understanding, this means that they are to fulfill Biblical roles for men and women.

We have questions about the value of a college education. Clearly, anyone can see that college education is not what it used to be; instead, standards and expectations in education have fallen so much that at most colleges, the first two years of general education coursework are designed to bring the student up to the standard that used to be expected of every high school graduate. We intend to insure that our children, at the end of their high school education, are competent to read, write, and cipher at college level, in addition to possessing fluency in a second language and a broad knowledge of history and science. We want them to have the ability to effectively analyze and synthesize information and to meaningfully apply that information to their lives. In other words, to be able to use their "head knowledge" for some useful purpose. We don't see college education as necessary to that end, although we know that many people do. If our children do go to college, we want to be certain that they are firmly rooted and grounded in their faith and their Christian worldview. They need to be able to intelligently defend their beliefs and to be able to recognize anti-God bias. In our experience, many a Christian child whose parents have left his religious education largely up to the Sunday School and youth pastor, has had his faith destroyed during his first semester in college. We want our children to be well-prepared to be intelligent, educated, and winsome spokesmen for Christianity, able to graciously, yet thoroughly, counter any argument against their faith.

If our children are called to a profession that requires college education, like medicine, law, or engineering, we will certainly send them to get the education they require. However, they are not going to college "because everyone else is." In the event that they are obviously not called or suited to a specific "white collar" profession, we will encourage them to fulfill the Bible's admonition to work with their hands, to obtain a technical degree in something like machining, welding, auto mechanics, plumbing, or electricity. Possibly, they will be called to ministry or the mission field; that's fine, too, and we want them to have the education necessary to equip them to be effective there.

It is important that our sons be able to support their wives and families, but of course money should not be the only reason for choosing a particular employment. They need to be able to work to the glory of God, holding a job that they can perform well and produce a product or service of use to society.

3:10 p.m.—While we're in Columbia, this is the perfect time to duck into the grocery store; Jim treats everyone to twenty-five-cent sodas while I'm in the store. Making ends meet was a big challenge when we first gave up my high-paying job as a critical care Registered Nurse, but over time I've gotten better and better at budgeting. Part of this, I am sure, is our family's willingness to sacrifice temporal things like dinners out and "new" (as opposed to thrift-store or hand-me-down) clothes in order to be able to provide them with full-time parenting and a superior education.

I loved being a nurse, and I admit I do miss the authority that my job gave me. In the Intensive Care Unit, I knew what I was doing; it was all textbook. Motherhood is uncharted territory, comparatively speaking, full of subjective advice and observations. Whereas I knew exactly how much lidocaine to give a patient in v-tach, I do not know for sure how much or what kind of correction to give a disobedient child. My actions as a nurse provided immediate feedback. When I gave an injection, the patient either got better fast, or didn't. As a mother, I get to wait, sometimes for years, to find out whether I am doing it right.

I don't miss the money anymore, but I do miss the respect and the way, at the

---

end of a shift, I could punch my time card and know that, no matter what was happening in the ICU that day, it was not my problem once I was off the clock. Someone else would handle all the emergencies for the next twelve hours, while I went home and recharged. Now, of course, I am always on, and there will be no "off time" to recharge; I am "on call" for every emergency for the next eighteen years. The upside of this is that I have gotten very good at recharging while still on my feet!

The job I am doing at home is of huge consequence to the children God gave me to raise. Years ago, I heard a quote which has stuck with me—I cannot recall it verbatim, but it was an old woman looking back through time at a snapshot of herself with her then-small children. She said (and I am paraphrasing), "A woman walked down a furrow in a New England cornfield. She walked down that furrow with the Governor of Massachusetts in her arms, and the Governor of New Hampshire clinging to her skirts."

I don't know who my children will grow up to be; I don't know whether they will be rulers or peasants. I do know, though, that they are the children I was given to bring up. Having put my hand to the plow, I cannot turn back to look at the life of relative ease (wealth and respect, not to mention having someone else responsible for the children's education) that I would have if I went back to work.

4:00 p.m.—Home again. Jim and I are wiped out; we banish the children to play in the back bedroom and go to our room to hide. Mamie stays with us —time to feed her again. Jim checks e-mail for both of us.

5:00 p.m.—We make dinner as a joint effort. I fry the hamburger meat and season it; Jim chops the produce and grates the cheese. While I was in the grocery store, I remembered to buy taco shells, so nobody has to deep-fry the tortillas tonight!

I try to involve the children in cooking whenever possible, knowing that education for life is not limited to book learning. As I mentioned earlier, I was woefully unequipped as a new bride, and I want my own children to be competent in every area of life: housekeeping, cooking, marketing, budgeting, personal relationships, work ethics, etc. I'm glad that homeschooling affords us the opportunity to see our children's weaknesses close up so that we know exactly which life skills they still need. Also, they can see how those skills are necessary to the smooth function of a household and, indeed, even of an individual life.

5:30 p.m.—Everyone lines up to get plates. The night is mild and pleasant so the boys make a pitch to eat on the front porch, which I gladly grant; my carpeted dining room has seen enough action for one day. Quinn stays inside with us to bumble around and mooch off of us. For messy meals, he does not get his own plate. The boys run in and out of the house several times for various urgent needs, including more food, more water, more ice in their water, hand washing, face wiping, and a shoulder to cry on. Surely, this is true quality time—the opportunity to be there when your child needs a hand. A child's need for his parents cannot be scheduled into little blocks of time and then parceled out at the convenience of those parents.

6:00 p.m.—The boys are a mess again—taco sauce and sour cream. Back in the bath they go, and this time *I* pour the bubble bath myself, then then take it *out* of the room. While I wait for the tub to fill, I finally remember to move the morning's laundry into the dryer. Quinn, though clean, urges us to let him play in the tub also. We comply. While the boys riot in the tub, Ethan starts on the evening's dishes; first he has to go back outside to get the dishes left on the porch.

6:20 p.m.—The boys are out of the tub and dressed. It's time for Jase to read us a Bible story out of his easy-reader Bible. He has not been reading for long, so he struggles with the words he doesn't know. Tonight it is a story with which he is familiar—Noah and the Great Flood. He misses some key words (like "dove") but gets others that I am surprised about, like "beautiful" and "rainbow." After he finishes, Ethan rereads the story aloud so that everyone can hear it again and we talk about it briefly. Next, we read out of the *Westminster Shorter Catechism*; Jim and Ethan and I have just begun memorizing it. The younger boys are bored stiff, but I make them sit still; who knows how much they will absorb just from hearing us repeat it over and over? Finally, when they cannot stand it any longer, we sing a few of Steve Green's Scripture songs. These are much-beloved by our family, and even Quinn knows to clap and hum when his brothers sing them.

7:00 p.m.—*Bedtime* for the little boys! Ethan is finished with the kitchen and goes outside to give the goats a bucket of grain before dark. He comes back in and decides to play *Flight Sim* on his computer until bedtime in an hour. Naturally, he comes into our room at least twice to tell us of his virtual adventures piloting a 747.

Every winter, we read aloud as a family in the evenings, with Jim and I taking turns. I suppose this year Ethan will be taking his turn at reading too, since at the age of ten, he is finally fluent enough at reading aloud to do so expressively and unselfconsciously, with few mistakes. For some reason, we fall away from this during the summer, perhaps because the days are so long or because there is so much to do on our little farmlet. Right now, it is October and I'm looking forward to our yearly reading. One year, the first year we read aloud, it was the *Little House* series. Last year, we read Kenneth Roberts' *Northwest Passage*—a long and involved historical novel. The years in-between we read various books from the *Sonlight* read-alouds. We feel that this knits us together as a family and is good for the children to hear books, written far above their reading level, read aloud.

Ethan (10), Jase, (5), Simon (3), Quinn (18 mo.), Mamie (5 mo.)

8:00 p.m.—Bedtime for Ethan is a little early tonight, but I know Jim will be gone tomorrow and I want to be sure Ethan is as fresh and rested as possible so that we don't have any problems the next day. He grumbles, but goes off to bed more or less cheerfully. I know he will lie awake for the next hour or so, before falling asleep, but rest is rest.

The little boys' bedtimes are etched in stone, but Ethan's is really very flexible and, depending on what's going on, he often stays up until ten or later.

Jim wants to watch a movie tonight, so that's what we do—*Groundhog Day*, which is our family's favorite and which we have seen probably a hundred times. We pop popcorn in the microwave and watch it yet again. When it's over, we'll check e-mail once again, then retire. We always seem to need to spend at least thirty minutes talking before we go to sleep and, of course, Mamie needs to get fed and changed one last time, so we'll probably finally fall asleep by about eleven.

Our lives are highly satisfying and, although there is a lot of work involved in keeping it all together, we have never doubted that homeschooling is the right decision for our family. There was never a time when I didn't want to homeschool my children; long before Ethan was born, I knew it was the right thing to do. I am blessed that Jim agreed from the beginning and that the two of us are so like-minded about the goals of education. Both of us were good and eager students who were not stimulated in school, so homeschooling seemed like a natural alternative. By homeschooling, we can give our children a highly tailored education, delivered using the methods and materials that best suit each child. We feel that homeschooling equips a child for real life, which is, after all, the whole point. We see wonderful fruit in the lives of our children and, indeed, even in our own characters. Homeschooling is work, and mothering is work, and both require patience. I have had lots of opportunities to improve my character as I try to remember the Bible's admonition that "pleasant words promote instruction." We're closely knitted to the children and they to us and to one another. Our days are full and that is good. We are usually exhausted when we finally get to bed, but rarely so tired that we don't remember to thank God for leading our family into this land of milk and honey. We have been blessed beyond imagination by following this lifestyle of learning.

Ethan (10), Jase, (5), Simon (3), Quinn (18 mo.), Mamie (5 mo.)

Dave, age 50
Trish, age 40
AJ, age 5

Interview with Trish, while trucking across the country

ON THE ROAD

The Beginning

I couldn't wait to be sixteen. As a child, I would sit in the backseat behind my dad and pretend to drive, sitting on his fireman's turnout coat and steering with his "brush-pot" helmet. I dreamed of getting my license and worried that some future event would prevent me from driving. My dad taught me and one of my two younger sisters to change oil, change or replace sparkplugs and wires, and other car care basics. My youngest sister declined to learn, as she was planning on marrying a rich man who would buy her new cars.

Every other summer we would take a trip "back East" to make a whirlwind visit to relatives in the Midwest and on the East Coast. It was the greatest gift my parents ever gave me—wanderlust. After high school and some classes at the local junior college, driving a truck seemed like a logical step.

Although my mom it was unusual my parents were very supportive. She helped me track down a course at the county trade school so I could begin the classroom portion of getting a commercial license. When I first got my "Class A," I started out driving locally. After I gained a little experience, I got a job running coast-to-coast, also known as over-the-road (OTR). I was based out of Utah and went by myself to places that terrify me now. When I first began driving, there weren't many women drivers and most of them ran "team" with their husbands.

Amenities for women drivers were scarce. Most showers were located in the men's restrooms, and some older truck stops didn't even have women's restrooms. Once, while at the only truck stop in Los Banos, California (ironically, "bathroom" in Spanish), I had to take a shower in a janitor's closet because they didn't have a shower for women. In South Dakota, a truck stop provided a shower for women by putting a redwood fence across the communal men's shower! I encountered lots of hostile truck stop waitresses. I was barred so many times from sitting in the drivers' section that I would carry my logbook (the Department of Transportation's means of regulating hours spent driving) into the café to defend my right to be there.

Then about twenty years ago, I met a widower with two young children. I helped Dave as much I could, given my erratic lifestyle. We married six years later, and I got a local job running a concrete mixer. There was a long period of adjustment as we all tried to get used to our new situation.

My husband got injured at work eight years ago, requiring surgery and ending his career as a journeyman carpenter. Dave's daughter had a baby about the same time, so we also became grandparents. I went back on the road, because with only one paycheck at this point, the money was better. Another year later, I taught Dave to drive a truck and we ran over the road together for a summer.

And this is how we arrived to be walking across the parking lot of a truck stop in Winslow, Arizona. We had just gotten the results of a pregnancy test. Although it was late at night, we were too excited to sleep. We got back out on I-40 heading east toward Hunt's Point, New York. I experienced all the stereotypical symptoms of pregnancy, and just the smell of truck stop food made me sick. Despite my doctor's insistence that pioneer women stopped along the trail to have their babies and then went right back on walking, when we finally got back to California, I got off the truck because I had lost so much weight. And because I was already past thirty, there were some complications, but nothing life-threatening. Five years ago in April, we had a little boy we named AJ, short for Austin James.

When AJ was about six months old, the company I had been driving for offered me a job as terminal manager. This included dispatching trucks and scheduling their maintenance, hiring mechanics, stocking parts for the shop, doing paperwork for payroll, and keeping in compliance with DOT regulations. But the most difficult aspect of this job was babysitting the fifteen or twenty truck drivers who were left in my care. When I agreed to take the job, it was with the understanding that AJ would be coming to work with me. I fixed up my office with a playpen, baby food, and all the other trappings of "mommyhood" and posted NO SMOKING and NO WHINING signs.

AJ met all kinds of people from all over the United States and beyond. Two drivers who were Russian immigrants tried to teach AJ the Russian equivalent to (I hope) "Give me five!" The downside, of course, was the colorful language. When irate, most truck drivers can spew obscenities that rival sailors on shore leave. How's that for socialization? It was a little unconventional, but it worked for us—for a while anyway.

When AJ was about two years old, and the stress of my six-day work week began to take its toll, my husband was offered a dedicated run (the closest thing to a regular job) if we would relocate to Dallas, Texas. We made the move, and a little while after we got settled, the company called and asked whether I could fill in for a driver who was out sick. I had to get written permission for AJ to be on the truck, as some states have rules regarding unauthorized passengers. It took me a little time to think of all the things I would need to take on an overnight trip. It turned out to be "stuff"—lots and *lots* of stuff.

Before I knew it, I was back on the road, and this time I had someone to talk to. My husband Dave was (and still is) driving for the same company. While I was headed east, he was headed west on a semi-regular run to California. We began to coordinate our runs to get us all back in Texas together on the weekends. We used voice mail to keep in touch and checked it each time we stopped. We often met at a nice little truck stop just inside the Georgia state line.

AJ and I started finding ways to pass the time. We filled the hours with stories and songs, and I talked to him constantly. I was surprised by how much he could remember at three years old. That's when I realized I should take advantage of our many hours together and not wait until he was school-age. I began to teach him geography, and though he couldn't read very much, he always recognized the state by its outline and location on the map. I tried to explain the concept of state capitals by characterizing them as the "boss" of each state. That's when we developed the "refrigerator-magnet-state-capital program." For each new state name and capital he learned, we bought a new magnet. I put schoolroom-style American Sign Language strips above the switch console (at the edge of the cab ceiling) where he would see them all day long. It wasn't long until that paid off. If he were asked his name (a daily occurrence) but was feeling shy, he would "sign" his name instead.

I bought a copy of Siegfried Englemann's *Teach Your Child to Read in 100 Easy Lessons* and kept it in the truck to use while we were stopped somewhere, picking up or delivering a load. We played our Spanish language tape a few times a week.

Once while we were having dinner at a truck stop café, AJ began talking to a driver in the next booth. The man spoke in the melodic dialect of the southern Louisiana Cajun. He taught AJ how to say the names of our flatware in the modified French language that the Cajuns brought with them as refugees from Nova Scotia, which led us to add a conversational French tape to our play list. He learned the days of the week by using a dated medication dispenser to store his vitamins. We also subscribed to Brighter Vision's *Learning Adventures and Scholastic's At-Home Phonics and Reading Program*, which, by the way, work just as well *away* from home. They both included catchy songs and colorful workbooks and games.

In addition, most of the larger truck stops across the country have a program that allows you to rent a book-on-tape at one location, and after a few days, to return it to another. When AJ was almost four years old, we listened to Ken Burn's books on the *Civil War*, the *Lewis and Clark Expedition*, and baseball. We learned about Eleanor Roosevelt, the Panama Canal, Hoover Dam, and countless other topics, plus fiction that I wouldn't ordinarily have time to track down, much less read. We kept colored pencils and markers (but *never* crayons, due to the meltdown factor), paper, books, and child-sized maps. For us, trucking was not just driving!

Now come back in time with us for a couple of journeys "over the road." Our home was a 1996 black conventional truck. That means it had a long shiny hood and lots of chrome. A cool ride by any standard and much revered in the trucking world. It was owned by my employer, but for all intents "belonged" to the driver. We had a small bedroom with bunk beds, closets, a refrigerator, TV/VCR, a portable potty, shelves for our books and toys, a zoo of stuffed animals, and the basics required to travel with a child. We could always tell what day it was by where we were.

Tuesdays

I wake to a series of small tremors on the pillow near my head. AJ is dropping *Thomas the Tank Engine and Friends* wooden trains one at a time from the top bunk to mine. I get up, open the curtains, and look out the window.

If it's Tuesday, this must be Ozark. Ozark, Arkansas, is located in the northwest corner of the state. That means we left Dallas yesterday afternoon. We traveled northeast on State Highways 69 and 75, and we crossed the Red River into Oklahoma. We continued on to Atoka, Oklahoma, and stopped at a small chain truck stop. We took on about 100 gallons of fuel and grabbed a couple of turkey sandwiches at the sandwich shop inside. We took a minute to call into dispatch, just to make sure there were no last-minute changes or load cancellations. There weren't many places we could stop after this—my dispatch office in New York is an hour ahead and would be going home soon.

There weren't any changes, so we got back out to the truck and headed north again, and just outside Atoka where the highways fork, we stayed right on Highway 69. We crossed a series of lakes near Eufala, Oklahoma, in the Arrowhead State Park.

There is a set of scales just south of McAlester, Oklahoma, but fortunately they were closed. They exist in every state to make sure all commercial vehicles comply with weight, logbook, and permit regulations. We were "deadheading," which means our trailer was empty, and so we weren't worried about the "Coops"—as in "chicken coops" and "weighing your chickens." (Don't ask, I didn't make it up!) In the northeast corner of Oklahoma, we got on 412, which is a short toll road that took us east into Arkansas. We got into Arizona, which some referred to as "Chickendale" because of the many chicken processing plants. We were early for our loading appointment, but they had a loading dock door empty, so I backed most of the way in, opened the trailer doors, backed the rest of the way in, and "bumped the dock."

We felt the trailer moving slightly, which meant they had begun loading our twenty-four pallets of baby wipes. We straightened up in the back and did a reading lesson. Afterward, AJ practiced writing the letters from his lesson, and I did my paperwork, which usually includes updating my logbook and recording all the load information. We practiced counting and number recognition, and before long the truck stopped moving, which usually meant they've finished loading. We went inside to sign our bills and then went back out to the truck. I pulled forward and stopped again to close the trailer doors. It was dark by then, and we slowly made our way out of town south on Arkansas Highway 71. I hoped for continued dry weather as we climbed almost 2,800 feet on the narrow, winding two-lane road through the Ozark National Forest. It can be considerably foggy or icy at night, so we lose the spectacular view at the top and the realization of just how far down it really is.

It took more than an hour, but we safely reached the bottom and merged onto I-40 eastbound. It is usually a stressful ride over the hill, so after about thirty miles or so; we stopped at another small truck stop. There wouldn't be another safe place to stop 'till Little Rock, so we backed into a spot, brushed our teeth, and went to bed. And that is how we woke up in Ozark on Tuesday morning.

Wednesdays

If I wake up and look out the window at the flat terrain of Louisiana, it means it must be Wednesday, and this must be Shreveport. Yesterday we would have been home, doing all our errands and lessons before leaving at night, and then would have made it the 200 or so miles to the Texas-Louisiana state line. After rolling across the Louisiana truck scales without incident and a few miles farther, we would have gone to bed at a truck stop west of Shreveport/Bossier City and awakened here today.

Many trucks come equipped with satellite communication for direct contact with the company, but we don't have one, so we have to make contact the old-fashioned way. We get dressed, then go inside and call dispatch to check in. Sometimes we have breakfast first. Then we head to downtown Shreveport, back the truck in, and load twenty-four pallets of specimen cups. Not very glamorous, but necessary. We take a few minutes to check under the hood, which involves unlatching it, and while standing on the bumper, using my body weight to tilt the all-steel hood forward. We check everything, and AJ helps by washing and wiping everything at his level. I reverse the process and latch the hood back down. We get to work on the next reading lesson—letter writing and numbers. I ask him where we are on the atlas, and although he isn't reading yet, he points to the state we're in and knows where we are bound by state shape and by repetition. We go for a walk over to a nearby creek and watch the ducks. Then we go back to the truck, and AJ gets his trains out. I get caught up on my paperwork and update my logbook, where I must record my last change of duty—such as driving, on-duty not driving, sleeper-birth, or off-duty. Truck drivers are subjected to logbook inspections at any time by any local, county (or parish, in Louisiana), state, or Department of Transportation officer. They may even wake you from sleep at a rest area or private truck stop and demand to see your logbook, search your truck, and subject you to a roadside drug test. Obviously it is much easier to keep in compliance. Although I have been stopped for at least my share of logbook and truck inspections, no officer has ever demanded to see proof of authority to have AJ on board—he is my good-luck charm.

The guy in the warehouse bangs on the walls of the trailer signaling that we are loaded. We go in, sign the bills, and then pull away from the dock and close the trailer doors. We drive through Shreveport's historic district and wind our way back to I-20 and cross the Red River, eastbound. About an hour and a half later, we stop in Calhoun, Louisiana, to get a bite to eat or just call in. Whenever we load (or unload) freight, our company requires its drivers to call in the piece-count and weight. We are then issued a load number, which I record on a weekly report that I send into payroll. While I "call in our numbers" and have brunch, we check our voice mail and find out where Daddy is. Then we walk across the road to the shop where they sell and repair citizen band radios. It is the goal of many drivers to have a "big radio"—the point being to have a radio signal strong enough to cancel out or "walk all over" any other radio within range. The only alternative to being walked on is to have a bigger radio or a faster truck. But AJ and I are there to visit the resident mascots, two dachshunds: Oscar-Meyer-Wiener-Dog and his sister, whose name escapes me. They have the run of the place, as does AJ. They chase each other for a while, and then we head back to the truck. AJ is a "self-napper" and can lie down in the back whenever the mood strikes, so he goes to lie down and rest.

Whether we continue across Louisiana, Mississippi, and Alabama to Birmingham, or leave Arkansas, drop south through West Memphis, and "cut through the woods" of Mississippi and hit Birmingham from the north, our destination is Suwanee, Georgia. We deliver to a large hospital supply company that has a distribution center in this suburb north of Atlanta.

Usually, we cover the same ground each week. I say usually, because in trucking there is no sure thing. With variations only in our approach to "B'ham," we began to learn the best places to stop, whether to make call, stretch our legs, or get a bite to eat. We find the cleanest showers, the most convenient laundry facilities, and the places least likely to be clogged with tour buses or RVs.

Contrary to popular belief, big trucks don't always stop at the places with the best food. They stop because there is ample parking, access to phones, or if it is the closest truck stop to where they unloaded or will be reloading. The food is sometimes edible at big truck stop chains, but is always expensive. We have a refrigerator in the truck, so we can wait to eat at the better ones. We are well-known at a few of the smaller truck stops because AJ seems to bring out the grandma or grandpa in the truck drivers and waitresses we meet.

We also know the location and hours of operation of every fast-food restaurant with a playground and every interstate rest area along the way. Before AJ was reading, he memorized the characteristics of each of the different places we stop. One station in Lake Mississippi he calls the "duck place" because of the wicker ducks used to hold sugar. He calls another one, right near the Mississippi-Alabama state line, the "ice cream place" because they have a soft-serve ice cream machine that is included in the all-you-can-eat buffet.

Our favorite place to stop is a truck stop in Tallapoosa, Georgia, just east of the Alabama state line. It is about an hour-and-a-half or two-hour ride from Tallapoosa to Suwanee. We are regulars there, stopping to gather our strength for the final leg of the trip and to reward ourselves for having made it safely back out of Atlanta. The waitresses are friendly; the food is great, and even the man who owns the truck-wash knows us. A clean truck is less likely to draw the attention of the Georgia State Troopers at the truck-scales that lie between Tallapoosa and Atlanta.

For the record, I would like to say that this truck stop has the best tomatoes in the United States, and possibly North America. But for AJ and me, the best part of stopping at Tallapoosa is that we regularly meet my husband there for dinner. If we are headed back west, then he is usually headed east (with the whole night to get to Suwanee) so he can afford to spend the evening with us. Sometimes we are both headed in the same direction and run together into Atlanta or west toward home.

On January 28, we left Suwanee and were headed to meet Dave for dinner in Tallapoosa. He was bound for Suwanee and then on to Chicago. I was relieved to have survived the "watermelon 500," as the I-285 loop around Atlanta has been nicknamed. Headed west on I-20, we were still surrounded by heavy evening traffic all racing to the suburbs. AJ was strapped in his car seat, sleeping. Coming up a grade, another big truck changed lanes and moved in front of me. I noticed a wobble that was developing on his left rear set of wheels and tires. It grew worse, and as I was reaching for my "mike" to warn him, the whole tandem broke off his trailer and came at me like a missile. It was all I could do to keep from hitting anyone else. My truck was totaled, traffic was held up for hours, and it took a while to get in touch with Dave. Although AJ was fine, I was hurt to the extent that I wouldn't ever be driving again. Without running the road, the rest of our homeschooling adventure would take place at home in Texas—more or less.

The Present

Once back home, we discovered that our "truckschooling" might have actually been the same as "homeschooling." I realized that we couldn't be the only parents in Texas to ponder the idea of school at home, but I was unable to get any information about it. Meanwhile, we continued a very unstructured type of learning, between doctors visits and physical therapy. We now had the time to visit museums, parks, and even join an early childhood PTA group. We visited the local library and found a little information about a homeschooling group, but the information was outdated, and the trail was cold.

I decided to check the Internet, but there were so many web sites with links to other web sites that it became information overload. Without knowing a name for groups, or their initials, I couldn't look them up. And few advertise in the *Yellow Pages*. I eventually found a local group that meets at a nearby church. We joined and met other families, even a few with "only" children. Like any good support group, it offered glimpses into the way other families learn, and it gives a yardstick with which to measure our own progress. We came away with the things that work for us and discarded the rest.

Our homeschooling has taken on a more traditional look, inasmuch as we have a regular curriculum and set hours. We school at night though, because Dave works nights and sleeps days. We have found this to be most productive. AJ is really thriving and making great progress in math (which he pretends not to like) and handwriting (which seems to come naturally). As a result of my difficulty in obtaining homeschooling information, I began writing a column in two local papers about resources available to area families. I've helped several families get the information and support they are seeking. It has been like a pencil sharpener for my mind and offers distraction from pain and physical limitations. The one thing it can't quiet though is the call of the road. It is the stuff of countless cowboy songs, corny and sincere. But it is as real as the knot in my stomach every time I get near an interstate highway, with its promise of east to Shreveport or north to Oklahoma. Amazingly, AJ feels the pull of the road too. During these first few months after the accident, he keeps asking when we are going back to Atlanta. I hope I can figure it out and take full advantage of homeschooling's flexibility to travel and see all the history this country offers.

When I was in school, neither American history nor geography made much of an impression on me, so when I began traveling on my own, I felt as if I were learning it all for the first time. History comes to life when you can feel the cold, rough stone of a church visited by George Washington during the Revolutionary War, or read the headstones of long-gone soldiers buried at *The National Cemetery* in Vicksburg. History becomes more personal when you know the names of the dead. To stand at Gettysburg and look across the peaceful pasture where so many lost their lives surely makes an impression. Whether we dip our toes in the Mississippi, stand on the rocky coast of Maine, or walk the broad, flat beaches along the Gulf of Mexico, I hope I can inspire my son to explore this great country and appreciate the history that is everywhere, just off the highway.

Trish, Dave
AJ, John

Derek, age 39
Elise, age 38
Tasha, age 7
Taralyn, age 5
Calvin, almost 3

Interview with Elise on a spring day in the little town of Mutare, Zimbabwe

FANNING THE SPARKS

The sky is a permanent azure that contrasts with the greens, purples, and blues of the mountains that surround us. Our hundred-year-old, quiet little town occupies the valley between the mountains, and the views from almost anywhere can be breathtaking. Our roads and suburbs are dotted and lined with jacaranda and flamboyant trees that explode with color in their seasons, leaving purple and red carpets strewn beneath them. The spring weather couldn't be more perfect. The sun rises and sets at six o'clock, and the indoor temperature barely varies from comfortably cool all day. This is the impression that visitors to our town take home with them. Our house is about a five-minute drive from the town center (and from everyone else's house too!). It is a very social town, and everyone seems in some way connected to everyone else, whether as friends, relatives, clients, or business associates.

Here in Zimbabwe, I write from the small town of Mutare, where my husband grew up. Mutare has about 131,000 people, mostly made up of black folk. There are a large Indian community and a coloured community (between white and black). The whites make up something like 1% of the population. Generally, racial harmony is fairly good. We once had a very vibrant economy, but we now sit in extremely harsh economic conditions with persistent inflation. The national language of Zimbabwe is English, though there are two main African dialects that divide down ethnic lines, with a long-standing rivalry between these two groups. Derek and I are not fluent in either of these languages. Looking at the whole picture of how things are in Zimbabwe, we have long-term visions of hope and energy.

I first fell in love with Mutare when I traveled here with my high school tennis team. I decided right then that I would one day come to live here. I grew up on a farm forty miles north of the capital city of Harare. My brother, two sisters, and I went to board through high school in Harare. I went on to teacher's training college to prepare for teaching primary school. As soon as I could, I applied to teach in Mutare, where I met and became friends with Derek and his beautiful family. We married and later moved to Cape Town where Derek did his theological training. During our stay in Cape Town, we were very blessed to be able to participate in the infertility program there, and through in-vitro fertilization, God gave us our three wonderful children. We returned to Zimbabwe when our girls where four and two, and I was four months pregnant with Calvin. We started a church, and Derek began his work writing Bible commentaries for use in Third World countries. They are not simplistic, but use simple English with the layperson and speakers of English as their second language in mind. As commentaries are usually written by and for theologians, we saw a need for this work. Many local rural pastors cannot afford to get any Bible training, and they are using Derek's commentaries to help them study further. He distributes them without charge. Many others use them for their own personal Bible study. He also writes a monthly paper on current issues like taxation, just war, education, etc., challenging people to think Biblically on these issues. His work is currently being translated into Shona, the major national African dialect in Zimbabwe. We are very happy here and know that this is the calling we have for our lives.

Our day begins with the 6.00 a.m. news on the radio alarm clock that petrol has gone up 20% and will increase by this amount every three months. Of course, we are only mildly shocked, as chronic inflation has become a way of life for us. Every day our money devalues and evaporates. We lie in bed listening to the rest of the local news. Derek dresses and heads off to his office at the church—he will have breakfast there. I take longer to wake up, so I lie in bed for a while, enjoying the peace and quiet of the morning—the calm before the storm! I get up, dress, and open the bed to air. I brush my teeth and wash my face, then go to the kitchen to make a tray of tea and coffee for us. I sit down to read my Bible until the children come padding through one by one. They cuddle up and drink tea while I read to them from their Bibles. This time together is not compulsory. They are not always there, but usually don't like to miss it. I find that if we don't do this at the beginning of the day, it doesn't seem to fit in later as the day picks up momentum, and the children get involved in their projects and games. It is a very relaxed, cozy time (under blankets in winter) of "connecting" before the day begins, while everyone else on our street rushes their children off to school. We believe that "the fear of God is the beginning of wisdom"

Tasha (7), Taralyn (5), Calvin (3)

(*Proverbs 1:7*), and a key part of our day is knowing what God wants us to do. We have many other spontaneous times of spiritual discussion during the day, but they often flow out of what we read in these morning times together.

When this time ends, the children reluctantly go off to "get ready" for their first "time-box" of the day—brush teeth, dress, make beds, hang up pajamas, and tidy their room. That is so easily said, all in one little sentence! I prefer to stick to this routine as it is a productive use of time and does control chaos. However, this morning routine has been the most difficult accomplishment for me and is the time of day when the greatest amount of character training takes place. For too long I took the children's responsibility upon myself and found that while they had a fun time playing and taking as long as they possibly could to get ready, I was an uptight and frustrated person before the day had even begun. I didn't feel at all like doing anything fun or productive with them by the time they were ready. After a few "support group" meetings with Derek, we came up with a game plan. We now tell the girls what we expect them to do or not do during this "get ready" time, and when it is all done, I *check*. The key to the plan is that I put away the breakfast at 8.00 a.m. and whoever has not eaten by then goes directly onto their next responsibility, which is chores (this is not easy for a mother to enforce!). They soon discovered that it was no fun doing chores on an empty stomach. It took quite a few hunger pangs for them to learn that I was serious. It leaves me free to get breakfast and myself ready and to be a cheerleader when I see effort being made to assume responsibility. It is a learning process, yet now and then, hunger pangs are felt. They are fully aware that my aim is for them to do all the necessary preparations for the day by themselves, in any order they wish (just as I do) without being "watched." I make a distinction between getting ready for the day (personal chores) and cleaning and tidying the house (community chores).

When we are all finished getting ready, we have toasted homemade bread that I bake twice a week or whole wheat rusks (dried biscuits) that I load with all sorts of healthy stuff. These were eaten by the Dutch on their trek north from the Cape in South Africa. They are very tasty when dipped into coffee or hot tea to soften. Sometimes I also make whole-wheat pancakes or muffins, and on Sundays we have bought cereal with milk, which is a treat as it is too expensive to have every day. Because of the high cost of living, we found that we were eating mostly store-bought bread all day, so we invested in a little mill. That way we can mill our own flour from wheat bought from local farmers and use it whole and fresh. Today we have toast and tea, and no one goes hungry. When we are together over breakfast, we look at a few *Proverbs* and how they apply to our lives. For example, *Proverbs 13:11* reads "Dishonest money dwindles away, but he who gathers money little by little makes it grow." I explain that, generally, getting much money quickly usually has some kind of dishonesty connected to it.

Thus, we must be prepared to work hard and save patiently to advance ourselves. It is usually those who know how hard it is to make a dollar who will not squander what they have. We also discuss what we are hoping to achieve during the day, and I make suggestions. Sometimes I write down what the children need or want to achieve, but usually we just discuss it. I want them to know that they need to have a planned approach to the day, as time is precious. Most things they do are creative and constructive.

We have quite a number of government schools in our town, however, most of the children I know attend the same private school. People's general response to what we do is admiration. They feel that they could not commit themselves to such a challenge. When pressed for reasons why, they usually claim to be unqualified, or don't feel that their children would respect them as the teacher. They say they could not put in the effort and commitment required, that they like the competitive sport the school offers, or they want their children to progress through the British accreditation system.

The next routine "time-box" (usually about 8.30 a.m.) is chores—another training opportunity! I have yet to meet anyone who loves doing chores. We usually discuss what needs to be done so we can begin the day with order and a resemblance of tidiness. I am aiming at the children being willing to do as much or as little as necessary to help. I divide the chores fairly, aware of each individual's most and least favorite chores, though I also feel that in preparation for real life they must be willing to do whatever is necessary. Today Tasha (seven) is vacuuming and Taralyn (five) is doing the kitchen. Calvin (almost three) puts away the dried dishes. I put a load of washing in the machine and get Taralyn started with sweeping. I have really had to learn to relax my perfectionist approach to housekeeping, to live with a bit of untidiness and mess, and to accept the children's best effort as good enough. Chore time, from breakfast onwards, takes us altogether about an hour. There is not a lot to do, but the time involved depends upon how motivated everyone feels and how much training will be necessary to improve their motivation. Any responsibility the children are given or have taken upon themselves, we expect to be done willingly, cheerfully, quickly, and thoroughly (so easy to say!). This is where I believe they will learn the vital characteristics of hard word, task completion, responsibility, accountability, helpfulness, teamwork, etc. I don't like to use learning opportunities (education) to train these characteristics. For example, I never say, "If you don't finish this story you won't be allowed to ride your bike." We believe learning to be a privilege and not a right. Chore time has been a tough and challenging time. (I grew up having domestic workers doing everything.) It has been character building for me, as I also must be patient, helpful, self-controlled, and motivated. I help with their chores if I have time and if I see good effort being made, as I also want to set an example of seeing a need and offering help. When their assigned chores are complete, they come to me to offer any further help that I might need. The chores that involve cleaning, tidying, and washing our own mess, the children understand to be their rightful privilege to perform as part of belonging to our family. Other maintenance jobs they do can earn them money, such as working in the garden. My aim is to produce in the children a mature and willing attitude toward responsibility and work. As the girls are almost eight and six now, they are beginning to understand that it is more beneficial to work cheerfully, quickly, and properly the first time without the training being necessary! They are working well and come to offer further help. I don't need help today, so the children are now free to do whatever they want to do. We made up this little song together that we sing sometimes while we are working. It goes:

First you do what you have to do,
Then you do what you want to do,
This is pleasing to God above,
This is how you truly love.

If you do what you want to do,
Before you do what you have to do,
You'll never get anything done at all,
You'll always live in a mess!

Once chores are complete, we all feel free to get into "projects." This "timebox" from mid-morning onwards, is the largest, and lasts from after chores until pack-up time at 4.00 p.m. It is interrupted only by lunch, visitors, outings, and short breaks from working here and there. We don't follow a schedule or term timetables. We aim for a relaxed, consistent pace, six days a week (taken from the Biblical work ethic of working for six days and resting for one), roughly fifty weeks a year, aiming at our long-term educational goals. As much as we are physically and financially capable, we are committed to encourage and facilitate any interest shown by our children toward any subject, topic, or skill. This is a big commitment on my part as it requires me to be available to answer questions, discuss and research topics, help with projects, and just be there. It also requires me to know my children and their talents, weaknesses and strengths, learning styles, individual characters, and eventually, their callings. It is 9.30 a.m. and today's "project time" sees Calvin on his toy motorbike in full gear—a helmet, sunglasses, toy watch, and talking on his toy cell phone. He is off to say "hello" to Granny who lives about twenty yards from our back door. Our home faces west and captures the spectacular blazes of color from African sunsets—something all the children have come to appreciate. Calvin talks all day with his volume on high, so we all find it a relief when he has his midday nap. He is definitely the family comedian and performs all the more when he has an amused audience. The children often go down to visit my parents, and my mom loves to read and tell stories to them. They are also a great help with baby-sitting and sleep-overs! My parents built their cottage behind our house when the Government, as part of the "resettlement program," reclaimed their farm where I grew up. They were paid a token for it, and after running a small business in Harare for a while, we suggested that they move here and live with us.

We have an open-plan kitchen that my dad altered for us. It is open to the dining room and the main living area. We wanted this feature so that I could be involved with the children's projects while I work in the kitchen. A large counter divides the kitchen from the dining room. Taralyn brings her paints and organizes herself to get started there. I am not one who is keen on mess, and I usually groan when anyone wants to paint, but I have taught the girls how to work carefully and how to clean up afterward. The deal is that before they embark on a messy project, they understand first that they must clean up the whole mess at the end. This works well. Taralyn loves to experiment with different mediums—chalk, pastels, painting with feathers, toothbrushes, sponges, etc. She is adventurous with her creativity.

Our open-plan kitchen leads into the dining room and most projects take place at the dining room table. Where one would normally have a sideboard, we have a big desk with our computer on it. In the drawers are writing materials and paper, crayons and activity books for easy access, and a pile of curriculum books that are not touched very often. Off the dining room is a "den" where the main hive of activity is. This open area contains most of the books, toys, games, and puzzles. There are maps, a large blackboard on the walls, an artwork display area, and a bug-box for specimens collected on walks. Field guides are on a nearby shelf with binoculars and a bird book that we take with us on walks. We have a fair amount of trees and bush around our suburb, though we can't venture too far, as it is not safe these days. (Due to the harsh economic conditions and soaring unemployment, assaults and robbery are common if one ventures into isolated areas.) On one of the walls in this room we also have the girls' "bookworm." As Tasha and Taralyn complete a book, they add a circle with the title of the book to their bookworm's body. When the worm reaches the end of the wall (about fifty books), the girls will have a reading light put on their bunk beds for nighttime reading, as all the children share one room and can't have the main light on after Calvin is in bed.

Off the dining room is the lounge where Tasha is setting up a toy farmyard made out of *Lego* and toys. She is our outdoor girl who dreams of horses, farms, and animals. Ever since she was little, she has been catching lizards, chameleons, butterflies, or anything else that creeps and crawls. She and Taralyn have a rabbit and a guinea pig, and that seems to take care of her needs for now. I am not an animal person, even though I grew up on a farm. It took me a while to come to terms with her need for pets, and I have since grown fond of them. We are in the middle of a debate about keeping or selling two baby guinea pigs who are almost big enough to proliferate, and I have nightmares about being overrun by baby guinea pigs. We will enter diplomatic relations tonight when Dad comes home and, hopefully, gain a peaceful solution.

The lounge has bookcases for older children, including many *National Geographics*. There is also a music corner where there is a simple keyboard, my guitar, music books, and a tape recorder. So far, I see only Calvin taking an interest in music and singing. Being keen myself, I would like for all my children to learn music, but will not force them, since it is difficult to learn and needs motivation from within. I will continue to encourage them to join me when I play my guitar and sing. I play for our little church, and it has forced me to feel the need to improve! Time to practice is the main challenge. I manage about two to three hours a week. The children sit down at the keyboard from time to time to "tinkle." I have made simple charts about the ABC's of reading music and placed them on the wall above the keyboard. We also have a sewing corner. This is my other passion. I have been sewing for more that twenty-five years and would sew all day if I could. We have bought two old second-hand sewing machines in addition to my electric sewing machine and overlocker, which are safe for the children to use. The girls have made "clothes" for their soft toys (they never did get into dolls). They have also made hair "scrunchies" and even sold a few. They have made beanbags, a little bit of patchwork for their toys, and are now keen to make something that they can wear. (That will be a challenge!) Under the machine table is a basket of all my fabric scraps that they play around with and sew whenever the urge takes them.

Calvin comes back from Granny's house with a big story about the time Granny fell and hurt her leg. He settles down in the den with *Lego* and toys. He loves to make cars and guns. Sometime during the morning I make it a priority to read with each of the children. First the girls read to me as much or as little as they like from a book that we both agree they can manage, then I read to them from any book they choose. We have had some great times of reading wonderful stories. Then I call Calvin to choose a book and we cuddle in the den and look at a picture book on racing cars. (I sincerely hope this is not a passion in his life—I don't know whether I will encourage this one!)

After Calvin's story, I put another load of washing in the machine and head outside to hang out the first load. I do two loads every two days. That way I have every second day without laundry and bake bread instead. Today is such a beautiful, mild spring day. My baby peach trees are bearing this season. The peaches are the size of golf balls. If you have ever planted a fruit tree yourself, you will know what a thrill it is to see the fruit begin to grow. I love standing out in the morning sun to hang out the washing. It is relaxation therapy for me, and I take the time to enjoy the sunshine. Often, one of the children follows me to "help" and chat. Today they are inside with their painting and toy animals.

I had a wisdom tooth taken out two days ago. It became infected and is very sore, so I take two painkillers and lie down on my bed. It is now 10.30 a.m. and I call Tasha to come and read with me. She tries very hard at reading and plods on through to the end of the book. She needs the reward of progress on her "bookworm" and works towards the ultimate goal of the reading light on her bed. Her reading level does not stimulate her imagination enough, but I am sure the former will catch up to the latter in time. I read to her from *The Railway Children*, which we are enjoying very much. Taralyn joins in and reads to me from her book. She is self-taught, fluent, and is motivated by the stories that she reads. She doesn't care too much about the bookworm. When she has had enough, I read to her from *Bunny Tales*.

We began looking at books with our children before they could talk. As their attention span increased, we told the stories briefly with lots of expression and animation (hard work at the end of a long day when there is a great temptation to "blob" in front of the television). One of the reasons we decided to sell our television was because we felt we would rather our children relax with a book instead. We had to set the example! It was actually one of the best decisions we ever made. Derek and I began talking more, and I rediscovered the pleasure of curling up with a good book at the end of the day.

The focus on books has paid off because our children all love them. My own interest in reading had to be rekindled, as I had been very de-motivated by compulsory reading and book-related projects at school. After school and college, I wouldn't touch anything resembling academic discipline. My husband is the "bookworm." He has built up an excellent theological library over the years and especially loves secondhand bookshops. I would groan when he went into a bookshop of any description and would stand at the door twiddling my thumbs. His passion and patient example have rubbed off on me, and we are both like kids in a sweet shop (candy store) when we go book hunting. In Zimbabwe, with our economy crashing and all our books being imported, a good dictionary can cost a third of an average person's wage. We have been very fortunate over the last few years to find a number of second-hand books to add to our little collection. We dream and pray of one day having a resource center as part of our church to provide resources for homeschoolers and anyone else wanting to advance in education. This will be for people of any social or cultural backgrounds who appreciate the enormous value of books. We have the beginnings of it and will do all we can to move toward that goal.

Both Derek and I began formal education before we were ready. The system here dictates that children enter the first grade the year they turn six. I only

turned six at the end of the year, and Derek started when he had just tu
Being a "late bloomer," I was fortunate that my mother taught me for
two years, as I was too young to go to boarding school. That gave me
with reading and writing that kept me from failing. I did not excel in anything and was not inspired by very much. I believe my talent lay in the area of music and there was not much offered by our school to inspire this. Being a boarder didn't help, as my parents were not in touch with this desire and interest of mine. Derek was exceptionally good at sport, which overshadowed the rest of his education, and he did not even begin to put his writing talent into practice until he went to Bible College. One of the reasons we have always wanted to homeschool our children (even before we had them) was to be in touch with their talents, learning styles, and (eventually) their callings, and to do all we could to prepare them for this. In preparing to homeschool, I read a fair amount of books (that we sort of stumbled upon) on the philosophy and methods of homeschooling. They were: HOMESCHOOLING: A PATCHWORK OF DAYS, by Nancy Lande; *For the Children's Sake*, by Susan Schaffer Macaulay; *Schoolproof,* by Mary Pride; *Home Educating with Confidence*, by Rick and Marilyn Boyer; *The Relaxed Home School*, by Mary Hood; *The Christian Home School*, by Gregg Harris; *Educating the Whole Hearted Child*, by Clay and Sally Clarkson; and, of course, Charlotte Mason's six volume set. I was so very grateful to the authors of these books for putting their advice and experience on paper and making it available to others. I devoured them. I read and reread them and have to say that I could not have had the confidence to step out and do what I am doing if it weren't for them. I would have liked to have had books recommended to me before I started homeschooling. I give advice along these lines to others that have expressed an interest.

I get up to go and get the first load of wash off the line and hang up the second. The girls wander around a little aimlessly, so I remind them that if they are bored I have plenty of work (housework) to keep them occupied. Suddenly, they are not bored any more. Taralyn goes back to her painting, and I inspect what she has been doing on my way outside. She was painting in her coloring book. She decides that she has had enough so begins cleaning up. She wants to put one of the pages on the art wall, but I convince her that it would ruin the coloring book, so we leave it in. Tasha feels like drawing. She doesn't experiment very much but is talented at drawing and likes to get proportion right. She fetches paper from the desk drawer and sets up a picture of an elephant to copy. She always draws animals.

We believe that each person is made by God with a totally unique calling in this life and is, therefore, gifted specifically and uniquely for that calling—having different talents, gifts, character and learning style. I believe Derek's and my responsibility is to fan the sparks of interest by knowing each of the children and loving, training, encouraging, inspiring, and preparing them for their calling. (*Proverbs 22:6*) This philosophy has motivated us to take the lion's share of time at this early stage to train the children in godly character— obedience to parents, love and respect for sibling's (what a challenge!), and loving service and honor to all. We also focus on facing and dealing with personal responsibility and self-government—doing what is right whether we feel like it or not. The rest of the time is spent in seeking to inspire them through the love of "living books" written by the masters of their subjects—to learn, think about, and research the wonders of this world that God has made for us. We have very recently come across the *Robinson Self-Teaching Curriculum.* This curriculum, which is twelve years of education on twenty-two CD-ROMs, will be an invaluable resource in helping us achieve our educational goals.

The pain pills are working now, and I don't feel too sore. (The pain hasn't stopped me from eating though!) I fetch in the washing and put it in the tumble-dryer to fluff out so that most of the clothes will only need folding and not ironing. Laundry is done very differently in this country. Everyone I know has domestic workers, so it is no problem to hang everything out in the sun to dry and then iron it all. The reason for ironing everything is that flies can lay their eggs on the damp laundry while it is hanging outside, and then the larvae burrow beneath the skin of the wearer. These larvae develop into maggots. Ironing everything kills the eggs that might be there. We take our chances with the flies, as ironing everything would be almost impossible for me.

When I come back, Tasha has finished her picture and has left it on the desk. It is a pencil drawing and the proportion is fairly accurate. She and Calvin are both playing with the bucket of *Lego*. They have tipped it out, cleared roads through little piles of *Lego*, and are driving toy taxis around, offering each other lifts. Taralyn is drawing monsters on the blackboard.

Since it was payday yesterday, I now give the children some money for their savings. This is part of the real-life math that we do. I have my "shop" that contains whatever the children are saving for in a glass cabinet in the dining room. I buy it, price it, and put it in my shop. This is to counter inflation for them or in case it can no longer be found when they have saved enough. On another wall in the dining room, the girls have a chart to map the progress of their savings. Tasha is patiently saving for, you guessed it, a toy horse. Taralyn likes to buy activity and puzzle books, and Calvin buys only sweets! I must say that he is very generous though, always buying sweets (candy) for everyone. He reminded me today that my sweet supply needs replenishing! They fetch their wallets and count their money (except Calvin, of course). Tasha spreads hers out all over the carpet to admire it and plays with it a bit. We discuss how much she has and how much she still needs to save, adding on the ten-percent tithe to the church as well. She and Taralyn color in their charts and compare their totals. Calvin

---

Tasha (7), Taralyn (5), Calvin (3)

doesn't map the progress of his savings because he doesn't make any! The girls sometimes make extra money by doing extra yard work or selling something. They have sold guinea pigs, clothes, and hair scrunchies.

Math has been a concern to me, as I know no other approach but formal curriculum. I have decided to avoid this for now and focus on practical real life opportunities. I collected a bucket of a thousand counters and strung half of them together in tens. I use these to illustrate any number stories or problems that come up. Sometimes the children like me to make up hypothetical stories for them to solve. This can be quite a mental and creative strain when instantly called for. I keep a little box of cards on the desk for this. I write new ones when I have inspiration so that I am prepared when the opportunity arises (mostly at the kitchen counter when we eat breakfast or lunch). I try to make numbers as integral a part of our day as reading and writing, but it does take seizing the opportunities as they arise and making an effort to create them. I am aiming for the children to have a very solid understanding of the value of numbers and to be able to manipulate them to solve problems, before they have to spend much time learning how to write them and set them out. This is hard for me because I am a trained primary schoolteacher and often feel the temptation to make them sit down and do math from the book. I do not ooze confidence about our approach, but I do know that it would be pointless to force them to do something that they see no need to know. When they see the need to know, I believe it will take them a very short time to learn the technical side of setting out. I believe it to be much the same as the way they learned to walk or use the potty. When they have the inward motivation based on need, it doesn't take long to learn. These things happened when they were ready, irrespective of how frequently I tried to force them. I think we don't realize how powerful our example is to our children. They will do what we do, and value what we value, if it is shown with enthusiasm and respect for the individual.

Money is all cleared away, and it is lunchtime now at 12.30 p.m. I make sandwiches and tea for lunch. This is what we always have, as anything else becomes too expensive. Then Calvin goes down for his nap. Sometimes we all have a rest depending how mother is coping. The painkiller is wearing off, and I need to take another one and lie down. We all get on our beds with books for half an hour, and I read my book *By Right of Conquest*, by G.A. Henty. It is about Mexico being conquered by the Spanish in the seventeenth century—excellent historical fiction.

When I get up and release the children, they run outside to the playground to swing and climb, play in the sand pit, and in their small, wooden playhouse. Calvin will sleep for about an hour and a half to two hours. The girls love to learn new tricks and moves on the ropes and bars, and sometimes they do a "circus" performance for us. We plan to add parallel bars and some rings that we will make ourselves. These all hang from the big tree in our garden.

It is now 2.00 p.m. I get laundry out of the tumble-dryer and then get ready to go shopping and put petrol in the car. I appreciate my mother being so near when I need to dash out quickly, because taking all the children with me is no small mission. This is usually my project time, and everything screams to be done at once—sewing, mending, baking, music practice, music for church, planning and beginning supper, sorting stuff, and catching up on mail and paper filing. I don't like to have to go out because there is usually so much to do at home, and shopping in Zimbabwe these days is not a thrilling experience. However, it must be done.

I say goodbye to the girls and tell my mom I am going out for a while. I fill the car and then go to the supermarket. Parking is easy, but getting out of the car is not! I am immediately surrounded by street vendors who all sell the same produce at the same price (I have never understood that!), and homeless street children who insist they want to "guard the car" to earn a little bit of money. I brace myself to get out, hold tightly on to my bag (purse) and politely refuse all solicitors (they can be so persistent), escaping into the supermarket. It is a new shop—clean, spacious, and bright. I locate a trolley that has all four wheels present and moving in the same direction. It's such a new shop, and so many of the trolleys are ruined already! I see some people I know, and others I recognize from around Mutare. This is a very small town. We are all experiencing the same feelings of wanting to get this ordeal over with. At least half of my purchases have gone up in price since I was here a week ago. Dental floss has gone up five hundred percent since I last bought some! Sigh. We trust that God will continue to supply our needs as He so faithfully has all through the past. On my way back to the car I haggle with one of the vendors for some tomatoes and cucumbers, then head home. Finding and purchasing anything besides groceries can be a very frustrating experience. The other day I tried to find eight-millimeter nuts and bolts for one of our woodwork toys that my dad made. I went to four different shops, only to be told that they are either out of stock, no longer will be getting them in, or don't know where I can find any. This is a most common experience.

It will be good to get back home. I am always troubled by the great needs there are all around us, and though I do not want to be an escapist, it is impossible to address even a fraction of the immediate needs. We are doing what we can through the church, and we are fully committed to long-term change. It is the reason we came here as missionaries to do the writing and printing work.

For my children, the desire to read has naturally tended toward a desire to write. I make a point of doing my writing of letters, making cards, writing recipes, songs for church, my diary etc., amongst their activities. We started writing as early as the children showed an interest, beginning with tracing over

---

dots. This mostly happened when the children had their thank you letters to write. They progressed to wanting to copy the thank you letter, rather than trace it. Now they are launching out into writing sentences on their own. I work with them when they want help. The only compulsory writing they do is thank you letters, and they understand the reason for this (that it is the culturally correct thing to do). Other writing they do is inspired by themselves and usually for a reason—such as birthday cards, love letters to Derek and me, phone messages, birthday "wish-lists," labeling pictures, and writing about pictures they have painted or drawn. This approach also goes against the entire teacher training that I had, and from time to time, I have a "wobbly" over it and need an emergency "support group" meeting with Derek. He usually reassures me that I am in line with our long-term goals and that forcing them to do things for which they don't see the purpose creates an unnecessary negative reaction to a wonderful tool that will serve them all their lives. They know how to form all the letters correctly (Taralyn is still getting there), and they spell phonetically. Sometimes, in a relaxed way, I will show them how a rule works on a word they have written, and they understand that there is only one correct way to write each word. (Some American exceptions, of course, are color/colour, program/programme, catalog/catalogue, gray/grey, and many, many more.) Mostly, I give them an enthusiastic response for their efforts, because writing is hard work. Tasha is beginning now to ask for correct spellings, so I have made her a "dictionary." An exercise book with a thumb index alphabet that she brings to me to write new words that she wants to use. From there, I guess I will teach her how to use a beginner's dictionary. Our dictionaries have a special, easily accessible place in the den, and we make it a practice to use them whenever there is need. This is the spelling habit I would like to instill.

Back home, I find the children all outside in the playground. I decide to get supper into the oven. I joint two chickens that farmers in our church gave us, and decide to do lemon and herb. There isn't time to marinate it first. Oh, well, we can't do everything, can we? I put it in the oven and scrub some potatoes. I cook double quantities whenever I use the oven (as it is a large expense) and freeze half for one of those days—you know, "those days" when you don't know why you aren't running away! I let the children know that they have ten minutes until pack-up time. I clean up my mess in the kitchen and call them in. We usually pack up at 4.00 p.m., unless we have afternoon visitors, at which time the routine goes out the window. But that is fine as long as it is not too often. We love visitors. The children must now switch to a different "mode," so I remind them that playing is finished and that they must do their tidying up quickly. The quicker we get through all the tidying, the more time they will later have to play before bedtime. I line them up and pretend to "switch off" their play button and "switch on" their work button. I give them their assigned area and leave them to it. Tasha is tidying the den and Taralyn the bedroom and lounge. Calvin needs to be given a specific little pile of stuff to put away. We try to pack up and clean up as we go, but I also try to keep a relaxed approach during the day, knowing that we will pack up and tidy up at the end. I am a tidy person so relaxing toward the mess during the day is a discipline for me!

The children are doing fine. I cannot manage to establish a "relaxed, fast pace," so I have settled for starting earlier and establishing just a "relaxed pace." I run the bath for Calvin and get him in. Then I check on the chicken, make a salad, and take washing out of the drier. We have to bring everything in from outside that could be stolen during the night and lock the doors and the security gate. All is tidy and ready for tomorrow's new projects and play. Usually, the girls or I help Calvin wash and get into his pajamas, but tonight the supper is taking care of itself, so I do it. Tasha has finished tidying the den, has fed her rabbit, and she gets into the bath. Once they are in, it is often difficult to get them out!

Dad's home! This is a highlight of our day, and I like to have everything ready before he arrives. Most of the time I don't, so he pitches in and helps me finish off. He usually arrives between 5.30 and 6.00 p.m. When the children are all bathed and ready, we sit down to eat and chat. Now that the children are getting bigger, conversations are more interesting and go beyond lessons in table manners. We discuss our day and anything and everything else (the guinea pigs, agreed by all, shall be sold!). We have children who love to talk (don't we all?), so we have to teach them to listen to each other and be considerate (this is hard for Calvin!). Derek and I take opportunities between their stories to catch up.

After our meal, Derek and I (and usually the children) do the dishes together and chat some more. The girls then do their teeth, Derek does any necessary doctoring, and hands out vitamins (when we have them). I make Derek's sandwiches for lunch the next day. When all is ready (phew!) this is where my wonderful husband gives me "timeout." He takes over reading to the children, praying with them, and putting them to bed. Calvin goes to bed at 7.00 p.m. and the girls at 8.00 p.m. I take a bath. I don't just take a bath. I relax, I unwind, and I have blissful, uninterrupted time to think. It is wonderful. Often, I bath in bubbles or essential oils by candlelight that Derek often prepares for me and, on special occasions, an accompanying glass of wine (what a guy!). By the time he comes to bath, I have left the day behind and can focus on him.

My tooth hurts tonight. After I bath, I take some more painkillers and antiseptic mouthwash, brush my teeth, and head for bed with my book. I am more than ready to sleep. Because of my tooth, I go to bed at 8.30 tonight, though our normal bedtime is 10-11.00 p.m. It has been a tiring but good day, which characterizes most of them. I would not give up any aspect of this full-time calling of motherhood for anything in the world. Derek is a wonderful support and encouragement, and I have to say that I couldn't do it without him. I often phone him, any time of the day, for advice or help, or just to chat because I miss him. He is always ready to listen and help. I really appreciate the hands-on help he gives when he gets home, so that I can step out of the picture for a little while. My husband and my three precious children are the dearest treasures I have. I count it a privilege to serve them each day that God gives us together to do what He has called us to do for Him in this wonderfully fulfilling life on earth.

Derek, Elise
Tasha, Calvin, Taralyn

Michael, age 42
Geri, age 32
Lex, age 13
Chena, age 2
Penelope, age 1

Interview with Geri, a year ago in the Kenai Peninsula town of Nikiski, Alaska

BRAIN-COMPATIBLE LEARNING

Long, long ago, when I was only four, my mom made a rather unusual decision. She was very involved in politics and had lots of inside information on our school district's curriculum, policies, and teachers, and she just wasn't very enthusiastic about sending my brother or me to school. Additionally, some of her best friends homeschooled their children, and she saw it as very conducive to Alaskan living. Weather was harsher then, and it was tough to get kids to school everyday.

So Mom decided to homeschool my older brother (who is fifteen months older than me) for kindergarten. Although I was only four, I learned all of my brother's schoolwork, too! After that, I did first grade in three months! Mom wasn't sure what to do with me then, so she put me in private school from second grade until the school shut down during my sophomore year of high school. I was homeschooled the rest of that year, then enrolled in an academy for my junior and senior years of high school.

What I remember about homeschooling is that I had a teacher somewhere in California who would check my work and send me glowing letters of praise with stickers on them. I sure wanted to please her! Mom, too, of course. We had music everyday, and Mom had a whole set of instruments we could bang on. I really loved that. I remember reading my first sentences about Dick and Jane and Sally and Spot and Puff. I even remember reading a story about Sally that made me cry. I was so young, but I remember it so clearly.

Also, when I was a little girl, my best friend had a brother who was Deaf. He was about five years younger than me. I spent a lot of time with her family, and a continuing issue that they talked about was his education and the problems he was having. I am not sure why, but I was very drawn to these conversations. It upset me that he was doing so poorly in school because the only thing he couldn't do was hear! The family used American Sign Language, and I picked it up quickly. It was like a language of the heart to me—so real and unaffected. I wanted to know everything about ASL. I took lessons from his mother. At the age of ten or eleven, I knew exactly what I wanted to do with my life—teach Deaf children. And from that point on, I never wavered. I graduated from high school, went to college for my elementary education degree, then on to graduate school for my Masters in Deaf Education. It was so exciting to reach my goal. I completely love my field and I hope to return to it someday. When people ask me if I teach sign language, I tell them no, that I teach *using* sign language. It is like teaching Hispanic children—you aren't teaching them Spanish, you are using it to teach them! Teaching Deaf children is incredibly exciting to me. When I sign, I use my whole body, facial expressions, everything. The best communicators in sign are very animated. When I taught, I fairly danced through my day! I miss it so much.

It was while I was teaching the Deaf in Fairbanks that I met Michael. He was in Anchorage raising his son Lex on his own. Mike and I married when Lex was eight years old. I taught school for another year in Anchorage, then we moved to Kenai where we decided to homeschool Lex. When people ask me why I would homeschool a stepchild (and lots of people have asked), it may sound strange, but I honestly never think of Lex as my stepson. To me, he is my son in every sense. Even though his mother is active in his life, it just doesn't sink in that he isn't really mine.

We took Lex out of school when we moved because we wanted to unite as a family before we added our coming baby to the blend. He was very glad to be taken out of school to be homeschooled. He loved having a flexible schedule and was thrilled to be staying home with us.

Our home in Nikiski, Alaska is located on the Kenai Peninsula, south of Anchorage and considered to be South Central Alaska. It lies on the coast, surrounded partially by the Cook Inlet. It is an absolutely stunning place to live. Popular recreation in the winter is hunting, snowmachining, skiing, skating, and ice fishing. Our family loves to skijour.

We live on Parsons Lake, which is just the right size for small float planes. We have small planes, so we fly a lot. Our large cedar home sits square in the middle of the private airstrip and the lake. We can have planes on wheels, skis, or floats. When we lived in Anchorage, the planes were tied down at various airports around town. We always had to run around checking on them. So it's especially nice now to just taxi up the driveway next to the house, unload the kids, and park the plane.

From our house on the lake we can see my favorite mountain, Mt. Redoubt across the lake and also Mt. Spur. We have a huge yard with a lawn the size of the Kingdome and Michael takes a sadistic pride in not purchasing a riding mower! Luckily, I am spoiled and never have to mow myself, unless he is out at the lodge. We have a few neighbors who live on the strip, but our home is surrounded by woods for the most part. We can ski right out of our door and go for miles without seeing anyone. We have to watch for moose and bear though. The moose get ornery during the deep snow times, because they can't find enough to eat, and they tend to want roads and paths to themselves. Bear? We had a close friend mauled by a Kodiak brown bear. That is enough to make one careful about going in the woods alone! Honestly, everyone says I am not careful enough.

We own our own guide service, a big game guide business. We also do flight seeing, fly-in fishing, and custom guided Iditerod tours. Anyway, for the past fifteen years Michael has owned the business, but we recently built a new lodge and expanded our clientele. I, of course, just married into the whole thing! Rather ironic, considering I absolutely hate hunting. I was raised around it and I do believe in hunting for meat. As a child, I never even tasted beef except at a restaurant—we always ate moose or caribou. But I just love animals, and I hate hunting. I will squish bugs though! Detest spiders.

Basically, what we do is take clients from the states (and many from overseas) on a one-on-one guided hunt that includes everything except their personal gear and gun. We provide meals, lodging, transportation during the hunt, meat care, and coaching. Michael doesn't guide anymore, he just oversees the operation and does most of the flying. During the hunts, he flies about three-four hours a day, checking on clients and bringing out more ketchup or salt or whatever they need. They start at the lodge, but the next day he flies them out to a remote camp where their guide is waiting for them to begin the hunt. They stay out there until they get the animal they came for or until their hunt is over. We usually have about six guys at a time out there, so Mike is constantly flying to check on their progress and see if they need to be moved to another camp, need more blankets, need meat or antlers flown to the meat prep building, etc.

It's pretty involved, but those are the basics. We also do bear hunting on the Alaska Peninsula. For that we use a fifty-two-foot (boat) floating hunting lodge. Clients, guides, Mike, and the skipper/cook sleep and eat there and go ashore during the day to hunt. Mike doesn't take the planes out there, since the bears are coastal, and the boat can easily be radioed at any time to pick up cold and cranky clients.

During Michael's off-season, he spends most of his time talking to clients, taking in deposits for future hunts, answering questions, making airline reserva-

---

tions for both our employees and our clients, keeping records, researching hunting regulation changes, paying countless business insurance bills, maintaining airplanes, writing letters on the computer to clients, sending out brochures, and other business details. When the snow falls heavy, he is on call with both Kenai and Anchorage Fish and Game Departments. He uses the planes to track radio-collared wolves, caribou, and moose. Oh, and spruce grouse. He also does arial surveys, counting game while the biologists sit in the back of the plane and enter data on their laptops. This job is really only once or twice a week, and only when the weather is perfect. It doesn't happen very often, but the plane and the equipment have to always be ready.

I like to start my homeschooling day with a letter to Lex. Before I go to bed I write a quick note. It is like *DOL* since I include various "mistakes" for him to find and fix. *DOL* is *Daily Oral Language* and is used in most elementary classrooms for a quick grammar review in the mornings. It is popular with children because it allows them to point out the teacher's "mistakes" in a written sentence. The teacher writes on the board and purposely makes errors using the concepts of punctuation, sentence structure, capitalization, or whatever is currently being studied. It is a quick way to see if the students can apply their knowledge in a practical situation. I always enjoyed using it to praise individual students for efforts in their work, manners, compassion to others, etc. Thus, the letter is a nice way to praise Lex for the bright spots of the day and encourage his efforts. I leave the note on the table for him to find.

In the morning, he finds the letter, and it is his first task of the day to amend it and then write me a letter back. He answers any questions I may have posed, then asks me a few or maybe just chats. He can write about anything on his mind. This morning, he tells me he liked the tortilla chip casserole I made last night.

At this stage in my early pregnancy, it is very handy to have him be independent in the first thirty minutes of the morning. (Gives me time to throw up.) When the letter is complete he does a *Brain Storm* card. These are visual brain teasers that challenge him greatly. I like to get him thinking very early. When I come in to the classroom he is stuck on the problem, and I help him refocus by pointing to the poster on the wall listing problem solving strategies. Eleven-year-olds frequently need refocusing! The visual problem is a familiar format, and he knows he can use the combined strategies of making a chart and using the process of elimination.

While he starts over, I glance over at our frog tank. We are raising frogs from tadpoles from a kit we ordered. I look a little more closely, then I walk over to the door where we loosely sketch out our day on our wipe-off board. I cross out "read chapter book" and scribble in "frog funeral." We have three tadpoles left, and I wonder if we will ever see one become an adult. Briefly, I consider purchasing a grown frog from our local pet store and slipping it into the tank, then dismiss the idea. Not teaching him to face reality would be wrong.

I interrupt Lex for a minute to ask him if he has set his daily goals. This is where he chooses an afternoon project and gathers all materials for the project. I find that getting him to think ahead to the afternoon is a great way to avoid wasting time after lunch with the usual excuses. We deal with lost glue, empty tape dispensers, etc., before it's time to actually do the project.

I hear screaming from Michael's office down the hall, and go in to get the baby. Michael's office is one of the bedrooms. He has a huge L-shaped desk, fax machine, copy machine, etc. It appears to be a regular office except for the box of toys and the baby swing! Oh, and *Sesame Street* is usually playing on his little television. Chena is ten months old and already very verbal. She is in a language-rich environment in either the "classroom" or her Dad's office, where everyday he is always on the phone with clients. Her vocabulary reflects this immersion. I pick her up and the screaming stops. She grins and says "Ech" to indicate that she wants to go see her brother. His name was the first word she ever said. As for Chena's name, when Michael and I met for the first time, I took him canoeing with a group of friends. We canoed the Chena River in Fairbanks. He tells me that as we went down the river that day he fell in love with me. So when we married, we decided the name was so special that we would give it to our first child, boy or girl. We are always quick to insist that she was *not* conceived there! (She was born about two years after we were married.)

Back in the classroom, I place Chena in a bouncer in the doorway where she swings back and forth kicking the door. The "classroom" in our house is actually a bedroom. When I started homeschooling Lex, we used the dining room table, but it soon became very ineffective. He was just too distracted. So we cleaned out a spare bedroom, added a desk, shelves, a table, and made our classroom. Michael hung cork board for one wall and white board for another. The whole wall! It's great because I use drawings a lot to illustrate a point. I love to draw. One whole wall of the classroom became a nursery—shelves lined with plants. We hooked up a grow light on a timer so the more fragile plants would be pampered. Ant farms and tadpole tanks completed the scene.

Lex starts to laugh with Chena and tease her a little. I ask him how the *Brainstorm* is going. "Oh yeah, that," he replies. We finish most of it and bag it for another day. I am anxious to get outside before another bout of morning sickness hits me. Our theme for the year is "Science is Magic." The scientific process has always intimidated me, so this year I decided to dive right in. Lex loves science, especially growing things. One thing I adore about teaching at home is being able to capture his spirit through the lessons we choose. That means I must really know the child and help him to reach his potential within that realm. I know Lex flourishes when he is caring for something or tending something, so I use growing things as a way to teach him mathematics, reading, organizational skills, art, comprehension, problem solving, and even cooking! When he brought home my Grandfather's Christmas cactus last year, Grandma told him it would probably never bloom. But Lex was challenged by the idea, and a few days after Christmas, he beamed as he showed me the one perfect blossom. Considering that Grandpa has been dead for ten years and Lex had never even met him, I nearly cried at the connection they made through that plant. Lex's interest in plants is what motivates him the most and I use it unabashedly! Most classrooms spend so much time trying to create situations that imitate real life. At home, we can do real life anytime! So we are learning about mushrooms and how they grow.

I take little Chena back to the office and tell Michael that we are heading outside. "Feed the dogs," he says and gives me a kiss. Lex grabs his coat, and I stop in the kitchen to get some plastic bags "Do you have your note cards, Hon?" He holds them up and we go out in the yard.

Since we live on a lake, we are surrounded by plenty of mushroom gathering opportunities. My plan is to gather several different varieties. We find lots! Lex makes notes about the growing conditions of each, whether we found it near a dead tree, in direct sunlight, in the shade, etc. We put the mushrooms in the bags and he draws the mushroom and a quick sketch of where he found it. Our dalmatian and yellow Lab bounce along beside us and the Lab puppy eats a few mushrooms before we can label them. But we have enough, so we go back in to the house.

After months of me struggling to make lunch while Lex was sitting at the kitchen counter doing his work, Michael and I finally hit upon a solution. He makes lunch for the teacher and the student! I pointed out to him that most men are gone during the day, but since he works at home during our off-season, he expects a sit down lunch daily. He said he would take on the job daily, unless he wouldn't be home that day at all. So now Lex and I come in to a hot cup of soup and a nicely stacked sandwich. I love it! It is like going to a restaurant everyday and it sure frees me up to keep the lessons running.

After lunch we have the whole afternoon to do our "Inquiries." These are hands-on projects that reflect the learning currently going on. I got the idea of using inquiries when I taught Deaf children in Fairbanks, where the model was that of complete immersion. I taught hearing and Deaf kids using sign exclusively. If a hearing child didn't understand the signing, then I was certainly allowed to speak and explain. But for the most part, I signed or acted out everything. By Thanksgiving, most of the hearing kids were fluent in ASL. The situation called for team teaching, since we had grades one through six in one room. Here is how we handled it: Each year there was a year-long theme, and that theme was turned into month-long units. Each month was then separated into twelve "key points" or hour-long lessons, one for each day with review on Friday. All the kids received these key points together as a class, then we broke into two groups to demonstrate learning using "Inquiries." This way of teaching is called the *ITI* model; *Integrated Thematic Instruction*. It worked wonderfully for Deaf students because it encourages thinking iconically, or in pictures. The lessons were always taught using an overhead projector so that the format was like that of story mapping. For example; a year's theme might be "Down in the Dirt," with the unit being "Discoveries" and a key point being King Tut's tomb. Make sense? What I have discovered about teaching in this way is that it is hard to remember how I ever used to teach before that! This is just so natural and it works! Kids get so jazzed about the projects and learning everything through one topic. This is brain-compatible learning at its best.

So each week on Monday, I hand out Lex's Inquiry sheet. These are always thematic, based on the current unit but can use any subject to challenge him. For instance, I can work on graphing skills in math by telling him to graph the mushrooms we found, the food given the frogs daily etc. Or I can have him do a writing project, art, music, reading, story mapping, or any number of activities. When I was teaching in a public school I used this method, and the kids flourished with it. It encourages creativity, flexibility, and (in the school situation) group work.

Some inquiries we have done recently are telephone interviews with relatives, cooking projects, creating crossword puzzles, acting out a scene from a play, developing a board game, depicting the history of our town in twelve art pencil drawings, training our puppy, writing a poem (about a giant squid—it was terrific!), and making a memory game.

Lex is especially fond of computers, so he has already chosen "Inquiry 4" for today—find web sites that tell about growing mushrooms and find one company that sells mushroom kits. This is what he chooses at goal-setting time this morning.

But first he has to finish up an inquiry from yesterday. School ended early when company came over. Normally we don't leave the classroom until 3:00 p.m., but these were special friends. It would be a shame to ignore the flexibility that homeschooling allows, so sometimes we take advantage of such. I love our 10 a.m.-3:00 p.m. schedule since I am not a morning person and neither is the rest of the family. Ending at 3:00 p.m. is perfect too, as that is when the neighborhood kids come home from school. Lex is free to play with them, and he is not finished so early that he is bored and discontent with his schooling situation. We also observe the exact same holidays and in-service days as the schools. That way Lex can visit his mother, have friends stay over, or go places with his cousins. On in-service days, I go shopping for school supplies, work on computer skills, or plan lessons. Sometimes I get together with other homeschool moms to swap materials and ideas. But all my buddies know that on school days we simply can't be interrupted. I tell them that if I were working out of the home they wouldn't call to chat and that educating my son is my utmost priority. I answer the phone with our homeschool name so it immediately lets the caller know that I am otherwise engaged, without me having to make excuses. Seems to work well.

Anyway, Lex needs to finish yesterday's inquiry. He is creating a cartoon, starring common parasites that eat mushrooms. It is a way for him to research the pests but not in a way that bores him. Discovering and identifying each of them is only a secondary priority for him. It is simply something that must be done before he can write his cartoon—my way of catering to what drives him, but still getting to my learning objectives. Funny, but my objectives have a way of getting revised daily! It just depends on what sparks our interest and sends us careening away into further inquiry.

When he finishes, it is a funny cartoon, and I give him full credit. But I can't help thinking it may have been better yesterday when he was fresh on the idea. Guess the company could have been cut short or waited for another day. Oh well, we need time to flush the frog anyway.

His computer inquiry doesn't take too long. I know he has finished the criteria, but he is too far into the "surfing" to stop now. I write down the phone number for the fungi company he found and go into the office to call. Michael is on the phone, as usual, so I use the fax line. Turns out, there are so many mushroom-growing kits to choose from! I settle for shittake and give my credit card. The shittake yields a big harvest and is relatively affordable. I can't wait for it to get here. Lex and I are going to Washington soon, and I plan to take him to a mushroom farm near Bellingham, so he can see how they are cultivated commercially.

Chena needs a change, so I run downstairs for a diaper and head back into the classroom. While I change the diaper, Lex makes irritated faces at me about my choice of locations. I try to distract him by asking if he has seen the poor tadpole. "Yeah, is it my fault?" he asks. "Maybe," I reply, "What have you been feeding them?" We look at his notes. I am so proud to see that he has kept track of the feeding times and amounts, when he changed the water, and other important things in his notebook. Even the temperature has to be perfect. "Looks good," I note, "They probably just don't like Alaska!"

I sign my initials on his inquiry sheet as he excitedly tells me about the web sites he found. Michael comes into the classroom and Lex tells him all about the mushrooms. I tell Lex about the kit I ordered and he wants to know if he has to eat them once they are grown. Both Michael and I love mushrooms, but we assure him he doesn't have to learn to like them. We are greedy about sharing. (Turns out, the mushroom unit made our die-hard fungi hater have a complete change of heart. Now he can't get enough of them!)

I consult Michael about disposing of our little amphibian and he agrees that we can just flush it. So we all troop into the bathroom and quickly do the deed. No twenty one-gun salutes, but he will be missed, nevertheless. By now, Lex just wants school over so he can go meet his buddies at the bus stop. He runs outside and I walk back into the classroom. I straighten the mess and wish I would have stopped Lex and taught him some responsibility for his learning environment. Chena is trying to bang on the computer keyboard, so I scoop her up and tell her it is her time with Mommy now. Last, I pick up the diaper and head downstairs to throw up again.

This day occurred over a year ago, during our second year of homeschooling. Chena is now two, and Penelope (who was in utero) has just turned one. The girls are nineteen months apart. Lex is now thirteen and he enjoys them very much.

My pregnancy with Penelope was *very* hard on me, and twice I thought I was losing her. Because of this difficult pregnancy, we made the decision to put Lex back in school last year, which was a very hard decision to make. Maybe some mothers don't know how hard it is to let go after they have homeschooled, or to see the rapid deterioration of their hard work. He was happy when we took him *out* of school and happy when we put him back *in*, because he was ready for social interaction and hockey season. I still feel somewhat guilty, and it just kills me to see him lose his spark. But he definitely has. What he cares about now is a passing grade and "getting it done."

During our two years of homeschooling, I worked at getting him to see learning as the goal, not the paperwork! In fact, we went for weeks without doing any paperwork just so he could see that life is learning, not a worksheet. One week in junior high, and he was back to the old ways. It has been very discouraging to see—almost like a plant withering away in front of me. I would do anything to put him in private school, since I feel I can't homeschool him with two toddlers underfoot. Some days I barely keep my head above water here in toddler land—I am so busy just trying to stay ahead of their demands. I can't even imagine trying to school Lex at home right now. Not with the quality I insist upon or the effort I put into it. I don't take the responsibility lightly. When you become your child's teacher, you are all they have! They sink or swim according to your input. So, I know that I can't take that on now. I do feel guilty though, complaining about his current situation, yet unwilling to bring him home. I know he would be miserable at home too. He certainly does *not* want to be homeschooled during this social time of life. It would damage our relationship. I am sure.

Most days, with my little handfuls, there is no time to think— just move, move, move! Yet, already, I am planning for Chena and Penelope's homeschool-

---

ing. I plan to homeschool the girls up to the fifth or sixth grade and then put them in the private school where I attended. I think that homeschool is the best situation when the kids are young (prior to fifth or sixth grade), or when the family has multiple siblings so that they can learn together and teach each other. I want the girls to go to the school I went to when they are older because I think it is extremely important to establish their peer group before junior high. The academy teaches about Christianity and emphasizes morality and character building. We also teach that here at home, so the school would be a parent-support.

For now, though, Chena loves Daddy's office. She has her own phone corner where she does her "paperwork" and "business calls." Mike really enjoys her company, and since he sets his own hours, he is usually not too engrossed to interact with her.

Both girls have been taught sign language since birth. Chena uses about a hundred and fifty signs and Penelope about six. I wanted them to know it because it is such a part of me and also it allowed them to communicate before they could articulate words. It is so natural for them now. Even the baby will make up her own sign for something if I haven't taught it to her yet. When Chena

Geri, Michael
Pennelope, Lex, Chena

was learning to talk and we couldn't understand a word, we would say "Sign it!" and she would. Then we could figure it out easily, and it helped us reinforce those early attempts at language without the usual frustrations that toddlers face.

Anyway, I will definitely make signing a part of their homeschooling. I also want them to learn about the Bible, classic literature, poetry, art (especially the masters), and other things that are dear to my heart. That is what is so wonderful about homeschooling—it isn't a bunch of "curriculum committees" sitting around a table deciding what my child should learn. It is *me* who knows them inside and out, who not only chooses carefully, but has the ability to follow it through to the conclusion and the reality. Then I can see it manifest itself in significant ways in my child's life.

I have been homeschooled myself, I have taught in public schools, I have gone to private schools, and I have homeschooled. I feel like I have the full spectrum of educational situations in my experience. And through it all, homeschool shines like a beacon suddenly visible in the fog. For the family who goes into it realistically, wholeheartedly, skillfully, and creatively, it is the best possible learning environment for the young and willing student.

Lex (13), Chena (2), Penelope (1)

Steve, age 39
Megan, age 37
Katie, age 12
Peter, age 11
Emma, age 9
Molly, age 7
Nate, age 5
Baleigh Grace, age 4
Stephen Jr., age 16 months

Interview with Megan in the one-stop-light town of Cherryville, Pennsylvania

COUCH TIME COMES FIRST

One of the most important tools of study I ever learned was to ask the who, what, where, when, why, and how of any topic, whether it be the Bible, history, or literature. Concerning our family and our homeschooling lifestyle, answering these questions will hopefully show clearly what our story is about.

Who are we? We are a family of nine: Steve, Megan, Katie, Peter, Emma, Molly, Nate, Baleigh, and Stephen Jr. My husband Steve is an airline pilot, Commander in the Naval Reserves, and an almost-finished seminary student. His job has many pluses (free travel, for example) but also requires a good bit of time away from our home. I am a stay-at-home mom with a degree in communications. Little did I know I would be using that degree to communicate as a teacher, director, boss, encourager, and sometimes referee of seven children. The children range in age from Katie (who is twelve) to Stephen Jr. (who is sixteen months). They are all about eighteen months apart with the exception of Katie and Peter who are only eleven months apart. We are very family oriented and the children have found their closest friendships with each other.

What are we about? Both my husband and I have felt a strong calling to encourage men to be leaders in their families and to encourage and help women realize what a high calling it is to be mothers and homemakers. To this end, we teach inductive Bible studies (this is a method of Bible study that teaches us to dig out truths for ourselves before turning to commentary), parenting classes, lead discipleship groups, and do much counseling with young moms and dads. All of this, within the boundaries of keeping our own priorities in order. Sometimes, it's not such an easy task and we have had times that we had to wipe the slate clean of all outside activities simply to regroup as a family. Our oldest children are serious-minded about spiritual issues and it has been a great blessing to us to see them making morally correct decisions—not because we told them to, but because they know how to choose right from wrong. The hard work of the early years is paying off in their lives as they model such an excellent standard for their younger brothers and sisters.

We work hard to function as a team, so to that end, we have "buddied up" each older children with a younger child. Our buddy pairs are pretty much set in cement. Katie has Stephen, Peter has Nate, and Emma has Baleigh. (Molly, in the middle, is responsible for herself!) Peter wanted Stephen and we tried it for awhile, but he was just too crazy with him. Stephen will love that someday, but he is still a baby and much more content with his *quiet* big sister. He plays with Peter and roughhouses, but when it's dressing or bathing time, I was concerned that their silliness might not be safe! Each older buddy is responsible to help the younger child with getting dressed and overseeing that the younger children do all of their chores. This is such a help. When we are rushing out the door, I can simply ask the buddies to check that their buddy has everything they need. Unfortunately, this sometimes works better in theory than in practice! We work purposefully to build a family identity and have many family sayings and even a family song.

Our first year we went strictly with *Bob Jones University.* I'm glad we did, because it gave me a great deal of confidence. One of my strong areas has always been research, so I read and research and then share what I have found with Steve. After a good start with *BJU*, I was very comfortable putting together curriculum from a variety of sources. Even among the children, I will use different things with different children as I observe their learning styles and special interests. This year, for the first time, we went to our state curriculum fair and I was able to look more closely at some things I had been considering, but wasn't sure about. Steve trusts my judgment in the specific curriculum choices, although I would say he sets the vision for our homeschool. He is the one who pushes me to reach long term goals with the kids, and I choose the vehicle by which we will get there. Occasionally, as he looks at some of their work, he has expressed doubts about whether a certain curriculum is meeting our goals. It is very helpful to brainstorm with each other.

We have been involved in many extra-curricular activities, but most of these

---

have included all of us. We have opted out of individual team sports for a variety of reasons, not the least being the running around that all of us would do for one child. We have been involved in *AWANA Bible Club*, gym classes, music lessons, summer and winter camps, science camps, Sunday school, plays, musicals, swimming lessons, etc. We try to be careful not to schedule too much. I have never regretted saying no to an activity, but there are times that I have said yes and then wished we were not involved.

We want our children to understand serving others, so we try to involve them in service opportunities. We live in a neighborhood filled with elderly people, so the children have had great opportunities to bake cookies and go visit the neighbors. We, as a family, go and clean the cabins and bathrooms of the camp my kids attend. The children help set up for and clean up after *AWANA* and in doing so, consider it to be their ministry as well as ours. Besides serving, our oldest children have set up a couple of for profit businesses. Katie makes and sells whole wheat bread and chocolate chip cookies, while Peter has a garbage business. Both children have learned to tithe and save out of the money they have earned. Katie is beginning to be in demand as a baby-sitter. As the oldest of seven, she is quite competent. I was nowhere near as capable as she is at the point I had my first baby!!

Where do we live? Our village in Pennsylvania is called Cherryville, although for years Peter called it Cheeryville. We are about an hour and a half from Philadelphia, so we have family passes to most of the fun places there. Cherryville has one stop light and a convenience store. There are only about ten homes that are actually Cherryville—the rest are attached to the next town over. For years, my husband and I daydreamed aloud about the old farmhouse we would buy and fix up. Seven years ago we bought our "dream" house and now we realize that we like *new* houses, only made to look old and quaint. Live and learn, I guess. We love our old house, but the work is continual. Our hundred-year-old farmhouse has thirteen rooms. It is the type of house where every time you turn a corner, you hit another room. Great for hide and seek! At one time, we had a designated school room with desks, white board, and posters on the wall. That only lasted for a year. The schoolroom was too far from the kitchen where I spend most of my time!! Now the children work many different places. We have desks upstairs for quiet work, the dining room table for group work, and the kitchen island for work that I must supervise. My husband turned one room into a library with built-in shelves around the walls. This room is, by far, my favorite and, as with most homeschooling families, there will never be enough shelves. I love books and have gotten many from library sales, my mom's old collection, and used book stores. We have a wide selection from textbooks to board books, animal stories, collections, art books, biographies, my husbands seminary texts, classics, cookbooks (an especial love of mine). We

Katie (12), Peter (11), Emma (9), Molly (7), Nate (5), Baleigh (4), Stephen Jr. (16 mo.)

have two computers, but only one with Internet access. The little children use the older computer for games and early learning activities, while the older children love researching on the Internet.

All of our children share bedrooms and it is especially fun to hear the boys laughing together in the morning. My middle girls do not share the same room, but often request to have sleepovers with one another. Our house is big enough to really spread out in, but somehow we all generally end up in the same room. I still haven't figured that one out yet!

We have three acres of property with plenty of beautiful old walnut and maple trees, a tree house, garden, and generally lots of room to run. Our backyard feels like the country, whereas a busy road leading to the local ski area is just out front. In our tree-line grow wild raspberries and plenty of poison ivy. We have squirrels, chipmunks, and, occasionally, deer. After the hurricane this fall, we actually had a four-hundred-pound bear in our back yard. We often see red-tailed hawks and Katie and an elderly neighbor made bird feeders that attract everything from finches to our gorgeous red cardinal.

When did we begin to homeschool? Ever since Katie was young, my husband and I talked about the idea of homeschooling. We planned and researched, then the big moment came and . . . we flinched. We had just moved here and convinced ourselves that private school would be good for Katie, so she could meet some other children. It wasn't long before we regretted our decision, as our family-centered little girl began to care more for her friends than her siblings and we pulled her home to begin first grade. At first, we committed year by year, but now the idea of not homeschooling seems very foreign to us. The local school bus parking lot is in view of our kitchen window and my children comment on how glad they are not to be getting on one of those busses! At first, we homeschooled only during the school year. Now, homeschooling is simply a part of our lives. We homeschool year round and the whole family, oldest to youngest, is involved.

Why do we homeschool? At first, the family identity was our primary reason for homeschooling. We didn't want to lose our children to other people's ideas and ideologies. As we've homeschooled, however, the why has become the most important part for us. At first, we worried about socialization. We have seen, so clearly now, that socialization in the family is the best preparation for real life that our children can receive. These are kids that can talk to anyone, old or young, from seminary professors to elderly neighbors to kids in *AWANA*. The strong security of our family bond has made our children unafraid in new situations and initiators of new ideas. As we have seen areas show up in their character that are not pleasing to the Lord, we have been right there to address the area and help them find the right thing to do. Because of that early help, the children now know how to make wise decisions on their own, often coming to us for

---

Katie (12), Peter (11), Emma (9), Molly (7), Nate (5), Baleigh (4), Stephen Jr. (16 mo.)

counsel, but not being told what to do. My husband feels very strongly that the one-age classroom is a terrible hindrance to both academic learning and character growth. In the one room schoolhouse, everyone had someone older as an example, but in today's classroom that is missing. Instead of striving to be older and wiser, it is often the class clown or troublemaker who becomes the largest influence. We have our own one-room schoolhouse right here in our home. We try to take advantage of that dynamic, allowing older children to teach younger children and, thereby, cementing the subject they are teaching in their own minds.

Probably, the most important *why* would be our strong conviction that we are best able to teach our children that which the Lord would deem important. We are able to take subjects back to scripture to see how they measure up against God's Word. This has been great training not only for our children, but for us as well.

How do we go through a day? Today I was up at 5:00 a.m., followed by Katie at 6:15 a.m. She spends time reading her Bible, then generally curls up in our armchair to read whatever animal book she is buried in at the moment. Katie is not a morning talker and neither am I. I love my bed and getting up has always been a struggle, so for years we have started the day behind because of my slow mornings. I've been trying to get up at 5:00 a.m. and it has made quite a difference to all of us. Katie comes down quietly and gets herself hot chocolate, kisses me, and goes about her day. At 6:30 a.m. Peter joins us for his hot chocolate and Bible study, followed by Emma at 6:45 a.m. Peter and Emma cannot resist talking to me, so the day has officially begun!

The other children sleep in or simply stay in their rooms until 7:30 a.m. This gives me time to get breakfast going and to assign chores. We have tried chore cards, chore charts, chore baskets, you name it—we've tried it. This year, the easiest thing for me has been to see what needs to be done, divide it among the kids and write it on sticky notes. I then stick the notes on the kids and they've been "stickied" for the morning. We do all chores before breakfast and they are varied by day. Some chores are daily, (make bed, brush teeth, wash face, all things I would have assumed people just did). Now that I have children, I know the truth—kids need reminders not to be smelly and uncombed!! Other chores such as vacuuming, wiping down bathrooms, and the laundry are assigned daily. Each buddy is responsible to make sure his/her buddy completes all of their chores (especially the hygienic ones!). All of my kids (from Nate up) know how to do any job, but, generally, the girls do the food related chores with me. With Steve gone so much, Peter ends up doing many heavy jobs for me that the girls couldn't do. He, Katie, and I rotate months doing the laundry and, occasionally, he will help cook something for fun. I use this time to get a shower and pull our bedroom together for the day.

Katie (12), Peter (11), Emma (9), Molly (7), Nate (5), Baleigh (4), Stephen Jr. (16 mo.)

Molly and Nate need me to constantly remind them that cleaning up doesn't just mean moving piles to another room. They share a desk to store their materials, so we constantly clean it out. Generally, I set a timer for them, and then when they say they are done, I send them back to double check. Often they have moved their stuff close to the desk, but didn't actually lift the lid to put it in. For Molly, losing the privilege of our family night movie is a great motivator. We don't watch television and really limit videos, so this is important to her. Nate is very laid back and will lose privileges for the sake of slacking off. We continually work on reminding him that every member of this house must work together!

I would characterize our house as tidy, but never as clean as I would like it. With nine people busy in it all day, there are many times it looks out of control to me. We try to "commit a clean" before meals and this helps to keep me from feeling totally overwhelmed. I have observed that both my husband and the children can be more focused and do better work in a tidy environment so I work hard to keep it straightened.

After chores, we head down to breakfast. My kids have always eaten a huge breakfast, fair sized lunch, and smallish dinner. Since this is actually a healthy way to eat, I haven't tried to change them. This does mean that breakfast is a big meal for us. I often make breakfast casseroles and fruit, or baked oatmeal (tastes like a giant oatmeal cookie) with applesauce. We rarely eat cereal because of the cost and the enormous amount of cereal we would go through in one meal. Sometimes, Dad makes his famous pancakes and on weekends we will have waffles. Before eating, we all join hands to sing the hymn of the month, then pray and eat. After breakfast, we read the proverb of the day and discuss what we've read.

We each clear our own place, but I do the breakfast dishes. Having the kids clean up after breakfast drove me nuts because it took so long. Now, that is the one meal I will clean up. I work quickly and the kids have just a few minutes of play time.

We regroup in the library to say the pledge and sing together. This part of school is the favorite time for my littlest children, who pick the same songs every day. We work on catechisms from *BJU* and I am always surprised at how much our four-year-old can remember. *My* brain certainly doesn't work that well! We pass out missionary prayer cards and pictures of friends and family and then spend time praying for them. Often, we will get down the globe to find where some of the missionaries are living. Not today, though.

After our group time, Katie takes Baleigh to do an hour of preschool with her. Baleigh loves this time and Katie takes pride in planning out "school" activities for her. They do puzzles, practice letters, read stories, and sometimes bake together. Peter and Emma begin their *Saxon Math* and I begin working one-on-one with Molly and Nate. The baby still takes an hour nap in the morning, so he

---

Katie (12), Peter (11), Emma (9), Molly (7), Nate (5), Baleigh (4), Stephen Jr. (16 mo.)

is sleeping and quiet. Molly is a strong first grader, so we work on phonics review, math, handwriting, and following instructions.

I wish I had known about learning readiness when we began. Since Katie was an easy reader to teach, I just assumed Peter would be also. He wasn't! I was so task oriented that I couldn't back off and often brought him to tears. About half way through first grade with him, Steve called us to a halt. We basically stopped and waited until the next fall. By then, Peter was much more ready. I don't think my early pushing did permanent damage, but he does struggle with comparing himself to Katie. I spend a fair amount of time reassuring him that he is doing well. He placed third in the history competition at the homeschool excellence day in Harrisburg and won last year's local homeschool support group math bee—things like this are slowly building his confidence.

Nate is a beginning kindergartner, so we work on reading using *Teach Your Child to Read in 100 Easy Lessons.* I have promised myself not to repeat the mistakes I made with Peter on Nate. When Nate is in the mood, reading goes easily. Today, he keeps tapping his head and saying his brain won't let him remember. so we review yesterday's lesson instead and he suddenly remembers that he does know the letters after all. When he is done he will fiddle with *Cuisinaire Rods*, do the computer, or draw dinosaurs (his love).

Molly is a willing, although not eager student. She does very well, but would rather be playing dress-up. She needs me right there to encourage her to keep going and remind her that the end is in sight. She does get excited about memorizing her *AWANA* verses so today we work through several pages together.

By now, Katie's hour with Baleigh is over and Baleigh goes to her room for an hour of what she calls "roomy time." She has a kitchen and dollhouse in her room and spends her hour happily talking with her dolls. After the concentrated time with Katie, an hour alone is restful for her. Little Stephen is up from his nap and after a change, Peter will spend the next hour simply playing with him. Katie begins her *Saxon 76* math (least favorite subject first) and I finish up with Molly. Now, it is time to work with Emma. Sometimes I feel a bit like a yo-yo bouncing back and forth between children, but I always remind myself that the more time I give to the early readers, the less they will need me as they get older.

Emma is an early learner and is a fourth grader although her birthday would make her only in third grade in the public school. She has poor eyesight and it is a continual struggle to remind myself that her handwriting is never going to be great because of her vision. When Peter was eight, after two years of struggling with his reading, a routine eye exam showed that he had such severe amblyopia that one eye had virtually shut down, while the other eye was not focusing properly. Boy, did I feel guilty after all of the reading pressure I had put on him. Consequently, we took all of the children to be examined.

Emma and I read her *Pathway* reader lesson aloud, then do science reading

---

from the *Christian Liberty Press Nature Readers*. I correct Emma's math (*Saxon 54*) then send her back to make corrections. Molly and Nate clean up their schoolwork and I begin lunch preparations. We generally eat sandwiches or soup for lunch. Sometimes, when I begin early in the day, we have hot bread with peanut butter. The middle girls clean the kitchen after lunch while I read to Baleigh and snuggle with little Stephen. They both lay down for long afternoon naps and we begin our afternoon routine.

I like to have us all sit and write something after lunch. It can be a letter, or copying, or making a list. I have a list of suggestions, but the big thing is for us all to write. Including me. I think it is important for the kids to see me in the habit of writing to reinforce the importance for them. Having said that, today we don't get to it!! Instead, Peter practices his piano and Katie and I do her *Runkle* geography. We are learning the countries of the world together. As in the Bible memory work, she is having a much easier time than me. Emma finishes her handwriting and *Daily Grams* and will either do *Winston Grammar* or *Wordly Wise*. Now, her schoolwork is completed, except for working on her *AWANA* verses and practicing her piano.

After piano practice, Peter finishes his *Wordly Wise, Daily Grams,* handwriting, *Editor in Chief*, and a half hour of reading. He loves true stories and biographies, although I have caught him laughing hysterically over *Hank the Cow Dog* books. Peter is an auditory learner and especially enjoys unabridged books on tape. He listens to our *Your Story Hour* tapes over and over and has often looked for biographies to learn more about the people in those tapes. He loves his *BBC* version of the *Lord of the Rings* and discusses the characters and their choices with me. Katie plugs away at her schoolwork, mostly just needing me as a resource now. Her big project this year is writing a health curriculum for Emma to use. She is writing short books, making puzzles, crosswords, and games surrounding nutrition, bones and muscles, and the eyes. This is great for both she and Emma. Peter plans to do the same thing next year with a science theme for Molly. Katie tries to stretch her reading time by disappearing from my view. Katie is an avid reader, especially loving animal books. She longs for a pet, but her dad and I are not pet people. Our one disobedient dog caused me more stress than all of the children combined! I console Katie by reminding her that someday she can have her own home and fill it with all of the four legged creatures she desires! She has forgotten piano and I am anxious to have her finish it. Sometimes having four beginning piano students is a bit noisy. Peter and I sit down to do his science reading, then after correcting math mistakes, he is done for the day. Peter uses *A Beka Science for Christian Schools* for 6th grade and also an old *Silver Burdett* book picked up at a used book shop. The experiments in the *Silver Burdett* are much more enjoyable than the *A Beka*. Peter uses our computer science CDs quite a bit also.

We generally do history together in the afternoon, using *Beautiful Feet History* guides. This curriculum uses biographies and historical fiction. We have loved using it. I began all of my children in American History. We have many friends who study world history in order, but I feel strongly that American History is a much simpler history for our children to begin with and doesn't contain so many morally contaminating subjects. As they mature, we will delve into ancient history with a moral foundation to base it on. On another note, we are a proudly patriotic family and I want my children to have pride in the history of their country. We alternate days between history and science, so science is the subject for today.

The kids have finished academics for the day and drift off to favorite activities. Both computers are in use, Katie is reading, and Molly is wandering around in my wedding dress. She loves to play dress up and is more often than not out of her clothes and into some dress-up outfit. Nate is building with his *Brio* begging his big brother to help.

I go lay down for about a half hour to forty-five minutes. Getting up early wipes me out by mid-afternoon. I used to feel guilty about laying down, but without that little bit of rest, I really struggle through the arsenic hour (you know, 4:00 to 5:30 a.m., when everyone is hungry, tired and grouchy).

When I get up, we begin dinner preparations. I want my girls to see the creativity that being a homemaker can involve, so we try to cook seven new recipes a week. I know there are many other areas to be creative in, but even I can't get excited about ten new ways to scrub the toilet! Katie and often Emma and Molly help me in the kitchen. Katie is a very able cook and has prepared several meals completely on her own. We experiment with bread and roll recipes and both the girls and I find great satisfaction when the rest of the family praises a meal.

We commit our final clean of the day in anticipation of Steve's arrival. He has been gone since early morning, first in class at seminary and then flying for the Navy. The days he is home are much less structured because the children just want to be with him.

When Steve arrives home, he kisses everyone, then he and I head to the couch for "couch time." This is the most important part of our day. We sit and talk for about fifteen minutes with *no* children in the room. They play elsewhere or take the baby outside for a walk. We have found that this time is as important for them as for us. Seeing Mom and Dad together communicating has really served to make the children feel secure. When Steve is gone on a trip, we will have couch time (announced to the children) over the phone. They need to see how important our marriage is to both of us. I certainly enjoy the uninterrupted time with Steve as well.

After couch time, I finish up dinner while the girls set the table. All of the children throng around Steve and want to show him something from their day. We join hands and pray before dinner. After dinner, Katie and Peter clean the kitchen, complete with mopping the floor and wiping the counters with wintergreen oil. They love to make the kitchen smell clean! We supervise the younger children in bedtime routines and tuck everyone but Katie and Peter in by 7:00 p.m. Emma reads in her bed until 7:30 p.m., then turns her light out.

Tonight is a relatively calm night. One night a week Steve has seminary, the next night I teach an inductive Bible study, Wednesday our family has *AWANA*, and Sunday night is church. With only three free nights (and Steve often gone then on airline trips), a quiet night at home is a treat. Steve sits and studies, Katie reads, and Peter and I play *Mancala*. He always wins much to the dismay of his very competitive mother! Peter heads up for a shower and bed by 8:30 p.m., with Katie following at 9:00 p.m. Steve and I sit and talk. We have always been best friends and discuss everything. We are looking forward to a move this summer to Maine, where Steve will pastor a new church. Although we are excited, there are also so many details to be discussed. Tonight, I check back over our records for the day. If I am not careful, it is easy for me to fall behind on the record keeping, then I am wracking my brain trying to remember what we did.

Later than I had planned, we head off to bed. Steve stands reserve (on call) for the airline because it gives us a more flexible schedule, but the "hurry up and go" phone calls are a killer. He is hubbed out of New York and must cover all three airports. This means I must always have his uniform ready to go, and if I am behind on the ironing and the phone rings, I run to iron him a shirt. The children often peek in on us in the morning to see if Dad has gotten called out in the middle of the night. Since Steve is on call for tonight, we both sleep with one ear open to hear that dreaded phone! (No call tonight, though.) I do a final check on the kids.

Although our days are busy, busy, generally they run quite smoothly. We have worked hard to teach our children to obey us, and I believe that has made our homeschooling so much easier. We do run into days where the children are not eager, but quite honestly, they don't fight me on doing the work I assign. We have always stressed doing things "right away, all the way, the happy way," so if I say RAH to a child they know to check their attitude. When I hear homeschooling friends talk about the battles they encounter with their children, I realize how thankful I am that we dealt with discipline and respect issues before we ever began homeschooling.

Have we reached our goals? In many ways, our goals have increased each year. I had no idea the closeness we would see in our family until we were actually into the process of homeschooling. We have seen how much our children appreciate us holding them to a high standard and have also seen that we must hold ourselves to such a standard as well. I have learned at least as much, if not more, than the children about organization and self-discipline. Learning to say no to things that would be fun in favor of keeping our priorities in order has taught all of us patience. Our children have truly been our testimony, as anyone with doubts about homeschooling who meets them has seen the fruit of our labors.

As I look back over seven years of homeschooling, I can see how we have gone from teaching at home to being a homeschool family. What a difference that makes in how we approach everything. This change has helped us to relax and enjoy learning together as a family and has given us the freedom to change direction when we sensed it was necessary. Regarding college and the future, we are encouraging the children in that direction. Yet this is not the main focus of our daily routine. Teaching the kids to teach themselves is the focus. As with all our other decisions, this decision will be made on a child-by-child basis. Both my husband and I are thankful for the opportunity we have to help our children grow and learn, step by step, and are very excited to see the young people they are growing up to be.

The joy we find as a family in homeschooling has come from our change in attitude toward what homeschooling actually is. Homeschooling isn't something we *do*, so much as who we *are*. People comment on how they wouldn't want to

Steve, Stephen Jr., Katie, Emma, Peter, Megan
Baleigh, Molly, Nate

be with their kids all day (especially seven of them) and I feel sorry for them. I enjoy my kids. Yes, we have our share of testing days, not because we're home-schoolers, but because we are nine people living and growing together. We don't deal with bottled up resentment, because we are together to work through problems as they arise. We don't tend to look for places to hand our kids off, but enjoy being together in all situations, whether it is at outings or in church. We worship with our kids rather than sending them to Jr. Church—not because we have a problem with the Jr. Church program, but because we want to model worship for our kids. We see many other families looking for these same opportunities. We have seen strangers in the past seven years go from "You homeschool?" to "I bet you are a homeschooling family." Our children talk about how they will homeschool their children (they also talk about the forty-nine grandchildren Steve and I will have), which tells me they believe in their hearts that we are doing the right thing.

Weekly Planning & Learning Log for Kaitlyn

Week # 5

DAYS COMPLETED: 4 TOTAL DAYS TO DATE: 16

ART / MUSIC
- Art Appreciation: M T W Th F Sa Su
- Class Time: M T W Th F Sa Su
- Composition Study: M T W Th F Sa Su
- Daily Practice: M T W Th F Sa Su
- Group Singing: M T W Th F Sa Su
- Independent Projects: M T W Th F Sa Su
- Music Appreciation: M T W Th F Sa Su → preschool prep.

BIBLE
- Bible Study: M T W Th F Sa Su
- Daily Devotion: M T W Th F Sa Su
- Help Siblings Memorize: M T W Th F Sa Su
- Inductive Study: M T W Th F Sa Su
- Memory Work: M T W Th F Sa Su

HISTORY / GEOGRAPHY
- Beautiful Feet History Lesson: M T W Th F Sa Su
- Geography Reading: M T W Th F Sa Su
- Historical Reading: M T W Th F Sa Su — American Girls, Samantha
- History Game: M T W Th F Sa Su
- History/Geography Software: M T W Th F Sa Su
- History Tape: M T W Th F Sa Su — D. L. Moody
- Map Skills: M T W Th F Sa Su
- Runkle Geography: M T W Th F Sa Su
- Timeline Work: M T W Th F Sa Su

LANGUAGE ARTS
- Building Thinking Skills: M T W Th F Sa Su
- Creative Writing: M T W Th F Sa Su
- Daily Grams: M T W Th F Sa Su
- E-Mail/Pen Pal: M T W Th F Sa Su
- English From the Roots Up: M T W Th F Sa Su (Editor in chief)
- Foreign Language: M T W Th F Sa Su
- LLATL: M T W Th F Sa Su
- Spelling, Dictionary Use: M T W Th F Sa Su
- Spelling Games: M T W Th F Sa Su
- Winston Grammar: M T W Th F Sa Su
- Wordly Wise: M T W Th F Sa Su

MATH
- Computer Math: M T W Th F Sa Su
- Math Game: M T W Th F Sa Su
- Saxon Math: M T W Th F Sa Su

PHYSICAL EDUCATION
- Active Play: M T W Th F Sa Su
- Jogging, Walking, Stretching: M T W Th F Sa Su
- Supervised Class: M T W Th F Sa Su

READING
- Assigned Reading: Mariel of Redwall
- Computer Reading Game: M T W Th F Sa Su
- Independent Reading: ____
- Read Aloud Comprehension: M T W Th F Sa Su
- SRA Reading Comprehension: M T W Th F Sa Su

SCIENCE / HEALTH / SAFETY
- Abeka Science Video: M T W Th F Sa Su
- Articles or Pamphlets: M T W Th F Sa Su
- Experiment or Project: M T W Th F Sa Su
- Health Game: M T W Th F Sa Su
- Health Project: bones — M T W Th F Sa Su
- Health Reading: M T W Th F Sa Su — Christian Liberty Reader
- Home Skills: M T W Th F Sa Su
- Nature Study: M T W Th F Sa Su
- Nutrition, Cooking, Baking: M T W Th F Sa Su
- Science Game: M T W Th F Sa Su
- Science Reading: M T W Th F Sa Su
- Science Research: M T W Th F Sa Su
- Video or Computer: M T W Th F Sa Su

SOCIAL STUDIES
- AOL News: M T W Th F Sa Su
- Cultural Study: M T W Th F Sa Su
- God's World: M T W Th F Sa Su
- Magazine, Newspaper: M T W Th F Sa Su

SPECIAL ACTIVITY / FIELD TRIP
- ____: M T W Th F Sa Su

ACTIVITIES / PROJECT LIST

Sun/Wed Church
piano
art class
Awana
cleaning for Mrs. Jones

Katie (12), Peter (11), Emma (9), Molly (7), Nate (5), Baleigh (4), Stephen Jr. (16 mo.)

David, age 45
Aileen, age 34
Lara, age 13

Interview with Lara in November from her home in Hertfordshire, near London

THE TWELVE-MONTH DIFFERENCE

It's been nearly twelve months since I left school behind. I'd spent eight long years as a pupil at the same private girls' school, so homeschooling brought with it an extreme lifestyle change. It also gave me much time to think and reflect, and to rediscover myself outside of an institution.

One thing I'm sure of is that if there ever was an "average" homeschooling family, we're not it. I am an only child, which in itself puts me in a minority group amongst homeschoolers. I live with my parents and our cocker spaniel Oscar in a Hertfordshire town northwest of London. Our home is a four-bedroomed, detached property, located on a quiet residential cul-de-sac and set into a hill. Though the upstairs windows give views of sloping hills, we're within walking distance of the centre of our town—home to a collection of high street shops, a railway station, and a range of schools and churches. Our town is essentially a commuter zone that blends both rural and urban life. In one direction, you can find green hills and countryside walks; in the other, forty-five minutes in the car will bring you to London.

One thing that distinguishes us from the fictitious "average" homeschool family is that homeschooling wasn't my parents' idea—it was mine. I was attending a "good" school and getting "good" grades, but I just wasn't happy. I'd never liked school, but it seemed to me to be a necessary evil—I didn't know there were real alternatives.

For several years I'd battled fatigue and ongoing viruses. I'd become the target for every passing cough or cold, and regular illness meant that I missed a lot of school; sometimes weeks at a time. I had colds and flu every winter, tonsillitis each spring, and a constant feeling of exhaustion. Surprisingly, my teachers didn't seem to mind. Time and time again, they told my parents that I was capable of keeping up with the class no matter how many weeks I missed. I think this sowed the first seeds of doubt in our minds. Why was I struggling to get to school every day, when it was deemed to be somewhat unimportant? I had kept up with my studies at home, quickly and painlessly. What was school offering that I didn't already have?

It was the Internet that first alerted me to the possibilities of homeschooling. To begin with, I was dubious. Like most people, I imagined a full-time tutor, strict timetables, and total adherence to the National Curriculum. Even these circumstances sounded better than what I was enduring at school, though—so I kept looking. During that summer I researched the topic endlessly, with hours spent on the Internet and pouring over books. Homeschooling was sounding better every day.

Slowly, an idea was forming in my mind. The concept of homeschooling had gone from being an off-the-wall, slightly unreal fantasy to a strong possibility. It was the chance to give myself the kind of intellectual freedom I'd only ever dreamed of. But, what on earth would my parents think?

I am lucky in that both my mum and dad are very open-minded people. They've always tried to listen to my views, and, somewhat reluctantly, they started to look into homeschooling. I know they had visions of a stereotypical school-at-home environment and were surprised by what they discovered. The more we searched; the clearer the picture became. I got in touch with homeschoolers online and questioned them about the practicalities, the realities, the ins and outs, and the ups and downs. And I still couldn't find fault with homeschooling.

I think my parents turned into homeschooling advocates during those summer months. That August, they gave me permission to homeschool—with their full support. The final decision was left up to me. Leaving school did seem pretty daunting after eight long years, but my mind was made up.

I attended school for the winter term, before saying goodbye at Christmas. My friends arranged a surprise leaving party during English class on my last day of school. It was an extremely well-kept secret that involved everyone from our house master to my English teacher! My classmates had smuggled cakes and balloons into school that morning, and they'd done an incredible job at keeping things under wraps. They put so much effort into giving me a nice send-off that I know it's something I'll never forget.

And so, since the start of this year, I have been learning from home. My life has changed unrecognisably during that time. And, for the record, I'd like to point out that I haven't been ill at all since I started homeschooling.

Presently, my daily routine is dominated by studying for *GCSE* exams.

GCSE stands for *General Certificate of Secondary Education*, and, although compulsory for school students when they reach the end of Year 11 (age sixteen), *GCSEs* are completely optional for teenagers who are educated at home. I chose to take them as a way of keeping my options open for the future, and I'm looking forward to having these qualifications under my belt. At the moment, I work by correspondence course. This means I have the support of a tutor through the post and by phone, as well as the opportunity to attend occasional tutorials at my correspondence college. I was lucky to meet another homeschooled teenager at the last tutorial I went to, and we've kept in touch ever since.

There are definite perks to taking *GCSEs* as a homeschooler. The one word that springs to mind when I try to sum them up is *freedom.* Instead of cramming nine or ten exams into one summer as students in school would, I am spreading about fourteen *GCSEs* over three summers. There are no "compulsory" subjects, no scheduling conflicts, and no significant restrictions. I am spending nine months on courses that schools spread out over two years!

My first *GCSE* exams, which I will sit in the spring and summer, will be in Information Technology and Geography. Because of this, I am focusing most of my attention on those two subjects over the next few months. Topics that I worked on intensively earlier in the year—such as maths, French, and German—are taking a backseat until the need arises again, be it for an exam or for personal interest. I enjoy having the *GCSEs* as a goal. Whilst my self-motivation has shot up since I began homeschooling, extrinsic encouragement such as this is still a bonus.

Doing *GCSEs* at home has taught me a lot about motivation and dedication. When I don't understand something, I can't grab a teacher for the answer. If I have an essay to write, I don't spend forty minutes discussing it in class before being landed with writing it for homework. I need to decide how to approach it, how much time to give it, what research to do, and when I should finish it. This is much more like the real world. I take responsibility for my choices and accept the consequences of my actions, and if I can't do something, then I have to sort it out.

These days, I am very much a self-directed learner. I take control of what I do each day, and as an autodidact, I'm my own "teacher." My schooled peers, some of whom are very into the institutionalised way of thinking, find this hard to fathom—being "taught" is all they've ever known. But for me, it works perfectly.

We put together study plans on a termly basis. First, my dad and I will consider which *GCSEs* will be coming up the following summer and what each syllabus requires. We narrow this down to a list of subjects I want to work on over a term. Instead of skimming over many subjects every day, I like to work in-depth on just two or three, and my term plan reflects this.

My dad takes control of drawing up a loose schedule for me. This lists the assignments I need to complete, along with recommended reading, details of modules to cover, some videos to watch, and research to do. Even this, however, is very flexible. If I want to add, remove, or alter something, I just discuss it with my dad. Our priorities are almost always in line, and we come to a quick agreement.

On a day-to-day basis, the work I do is under my control, and I often refer to my schedule to check that I'm in line with our overall plan. At the end of the term we review my work thoroughly, discuss the subjects and material for the following term, and the process starts all over again!

Our record-keeping is simply an extended form of my schedule. At the end of a term, my dad goes over what I've done and compiles a list of the material covered. This could include anything from lectures attended to videos watched. The records are filed and divided by subject, and it is very satisfying to look back on what I've accomplished in the last year. We don't need to keep extensive records—as I was privately schooled prior to home educating, we haven't been required to inform the LEA (Local Education Authority) of our position. This gives us a little bit more space to breathe, and the records we keep are more for personal use than anything else.

The rhythm of our day is perhaps the most changeable factor of all. Flexibility is the beautiful thing about homeschooling. I know where I'm going and what I'm doing, and I can tailor my studies around my life, rather than vice versa. Routines change to accommodate the ebb and flow of energy and interest. Flexibility is a skill we've had to learn over the last year.

My day usually comes to a close at any time between 10.00 p.m. and 1.00 a.m. I am a night owl, so it isn't unusual to find me burning the midnight oil and pouring over a novel or perhaps browsing the Internet. My dad works as a director within a large national cancer charity. He rises at 6.00 a.m. to commute to London, which means he is usually in bed a bit earlier than I am. My mum, who is at home with me during the day, turns in a little later. At long last, the house is asleep—until my alarm clock shrills (usually about 7.30 a.m.) or I am nudged awake by my mum. The start of another day!

Much of my "school" time is spent in my study. This is a long, narrow room at the back of the house, and it's home to my books, desk, files, papers, and, more often than not, my laptop computer. I really appreciate having a quiet room where I can focus on my work. The bookshelves that line the walls make it clear than I am a complete bookworm. You can find books by everyone from Maya Angelou and Harper Lee to Shakespeare and Elizabeth Berg.

My days are usually very computer-oriented. I love technology and gadgets, so whenever possible, I like to work on my laptop. We have also turned our second spare bedroom into a "computer room." This houses our two desktop PCs, along with our printer, my scanner, and my PC camera.

Free time is something that I have a lot more of now that I'm a homeschooler. I spend much of it with my friends. I may have an unusual lifestyle, but I am an ordinary teenager, and I enjoy spending time with my friends whenever I can. When I have no outside commitments or want some time to myself, you're likely to find me reading, writing fiction or poetry, or working on my web site.

If you're going to frown over the subject of that healthy byproduct of schooling called socialisation, please think again. Since I left school, my only problem with socialisation is that I get too much of it! I see my schooled peers every weekend without fail, and we regularly meet up on school evenings—after they've done their homework, naturally. My friends have been great about including me in parties, shopping trips, and sleepovers; and they've all been extremely supportive toward homeschooling. I really appreciate the fact that they're always there for me. Instead of having to sit in a classroom together five days a week, we make a real effort to spend time with each other out of school hours. As a result of this, my close friendships have deepened, and I get a lot more enjoyment out of seeing my friends. I am able to get my academic work out of the way in a shorter, concentrated period of time—and then go and have fun! My "socialisation" has also widened to include a more diverse group of friends, instead of a few people who happen to have been born in the same year as me. I mix with people of any age, race, or background, from adults at my yoga class to teenagers at my correspondence college. And, looking at it from a different angle, I don't consider school socialisation to be very healthy. The age-segregation is unnatural, as it seems clear to me that age and intelligence don't go hand in hand. I don't consider sitting at a desk and being told to be quiet to be a good social life, either! School has one thing you need for socialisation—people. Other than that, it's hostile ground for making friends.

I don't know for sure whether I will homeschool through the rest of my school career. There is always the chance that our circumstances will change, and I don't want to define my future before I need to. I do plan on completing my *GCSEs* at home, but will make decisions about my A-levels (advanced exams taken at the age of eighteen) when the need arises. I don't know whether I'll go to university. Perhaps I'll take a gap year and see a bit of the world, or perhaps I'll go early. Maybe I'll find my way into a career that doesn't require a degree. Either way, I feel that I will be fully prepared for the future. School lulls you into a false sense of security and then dumps you into the real world when you finally graduate. Homeschooling is about never leaving the real world in the first place.

As for a career? Well, I'll wait and see. Presently, I have plenty of ideas—I'd love to be an author, a web designer, an aromatherapist, a journalist, or a magazine editor. However, I have no real plans, and I don't want to slap chains on myself by "deciding" already.

Homeschooling has changed me. I've become more relaxed and more energetic. I enjoy life more as I have more of a say in my world—I'm not pushed blindly from one "lesson" to the next, and I've lost that sensation of swimming against the tide. I've explored old hobbies, taken up new ones, and discovered things about myself that I never knew. For example, I've always had a passion for writing, but this has really taken off since I've been at home. I've fueled my interest in aromatherapy and alternative medicine by taking the time to read and research these things. I've taken up yoga. At long last, time is on my side. I feel more energised, adventurous, and excited about taking on new things. I know I've found the lifestyle that makes my world seem right. Homeschooling has been everything I hoped for, and much, much more. I don't know how the future will turn out, but I'm certain that right now, homeschooling is what I need.

My family has changed, too. We have more time for each other, unaffected by the stresses and strains of school life. The time we spend together has increased from a few snatched minutes in the evenings, to hours working, talking, or relaxing in each other's company. My parents have gone from being total skeptics to homeschooling enthusiasts, and both are certain that I've become a different person over the last year. They've commented on the fact that I'm healthier and happier than ever before. Homeschooling has been an education in many ways, and my parents have observed that my relaxed approach to working proves to be more productive. There is less tension in the house, deeper family relationships free from displaced stress, and a more relaxed atmosphere. Besides, it's a lot of fun to be able to ditch everything and go shopping with my mum once in a while! I think I can sum all this up in a few words that have become my mum's catchphrase—homeschooling is the best decision that we've ever made.

Lara

Lara (13)

George (55)
Jill (51)
Sarah, age 14
Laura, age 12
Michael, age 9
Abbie, age 6
Hannah, age 5
Robbie, died 7 years ago at age 2

Interview with Jill at the end of September in warm and sunny Fresno, California

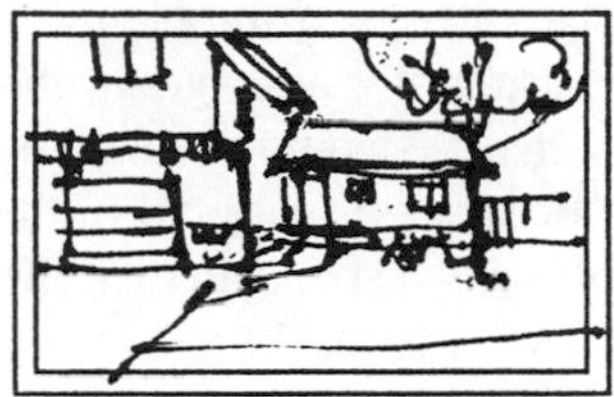

ROUNDING OUT OUR FAMILY

Though stereotypically known as farmland, the larger Fresno area in California's San Joaquin Valley consists of almost a half million people. We live in the northeast area of the city, near California State University, Fresno. I am Jill and my husband is George. We are a blended family with "his," "mine," "ours," and "more of ours"—our adopted children.

The oldest four children are grown and on their own now, and the youngest five children consist of Sarah (age fourteen), Laura (age twelve), Michael (age nine, who came to us at three), Abbie (age six, who came to us as a newborn), and Hannah (age five, who also came to us as a baby). Our first adopted son was Robert (Robbie), who died after surgery when he was two (and now would have been nine). We homeschool all of our "at home" children except for Michael, whom we hope to eventually homeschool, too. He had been in a coma for over a month prior to coming to us six and a half years ago. His needs are especially numerous, as are those of Hannah. The two older girls are creative and bright, even though they have struggles with reading and writing. Homeschool teaching is wonderful for us and is a challenge with the various special needs involved.

After our biological family was complete, we thought about giving a good home to a child who needed one. At first we thought that might be accomplished via adoption, but then we decided that it wasn't fair to all of the many people who were unable to have children and wanted so desperately to adopt. Secondly, we already had, via the process of "his," "mine," and "ours," a large family. George and I only had one sibling each, so our family that already consisted of six children was already far larger than anything we had anticipated. Meanwhile, we heard that our county was in desperate need of foster parents. We decided that foster care would allow us to give a great "temporary" home to a child (or children, as we ended up with forty foster children over time). When we attended classes of about thirty couples, two of us were approached to consider accepting medically fragile, high risk, newborn, drug and/or alcohol exposed babies. We hadn't really ever thought of that aspect of foster care, but we said that we would be open to it, provided that we would be given training to meet the children's needs, especially in the medical area. From the onset, we were given infants with an enormous range of medical problems. It was a very rewarding area, but little did we know, especially after going through so many life-and-death crises with these babies, that we would so deeply bond. The children were like our own birth children. Because virtually all of the birth parents were still involved with their own problems, we soon saw that the placements for most of the children were anything but short term. When a child comes into your family as a newborn with all kinds of serious problems, therapies, etc., and the court system takes forever to free these little ones, it becomes impossible to just send all of them on their way. We were the only parents that most of our foster children ever knew, prior to their leaving our home. There were four of these children that we knew, without a shadow of a doubt, were meant to be ours.

Rounding out our immediate family is my elderly father whom we help care for, and my mother who also lives in Fresno.

George has an office in our home, although much of his work is "on the road" or in two other offices here in town. He is the controller for a local, fairly large construction company. He sometimes does some sales work for them, too. He also works with a partner doing invoice financing. Although I appreciate his hard work, his busy work schedule leaves far too little time for family. We are hoping to work on this issue.

Our home is a four bedroom, thirty-plus-year-old tri-level. We don't have a specific area for "school" but, instead, have various areas around the house where we do different things. Three of our four bedrooms have one full wall, floor to ceiling, of bookshelves. Additionally, our living room and family-room-turned-office have the same large areas of bookshelves. A visitor could quickly spot my "weakness." Much of our "formal" studying, as well as most of our artwork, is done at our kitchen table. In the kitchen, which is bright and sunny, we have an area for evolving/revolving artwork. The kitchen wall changes according to what our current needs happen to be, like the exhibits in an art museum. There are usually two maps there—world and United States. Other than that, it could be a poster of the multiplication tables for one month, the sign language alphabet at another time, etc. Seasonal drawings and artwork usually are displayed in the largest of the kitchen windows. The childrens' "flat" artwork usually is on the refrigerator or decorating bedroom walls. Things such as sculpture are usually displayed on a large old sideboard in our living room. We have a sizable kitchen table which is ideal for all that we do.

Reading is often done in the living room on the couch or on the master bedroom bed, curled up together. On the living room shelves and in our sideboard are various school items like arts and crafts supplies, math manipulatives, games, science equipment, etc. We frequently display our projects and nature "finds" on the sideboard. The children also have areas in their rooms where they sometimes choose to do projects, read, or write. Outside we have a garden, a pool, a sandbox, and some play equipment, including a trampoline. We also have various pets.

When I was expecting (now-fourteen-year-old) Sarah, I began hearing more and more about homeschooling. The more my husband and I heard, the more we were convinced that homeschooling was a natural "fit" for our family; spiritually, emotionally, intellectually, academically, socially. I read everything I could get my hands on and, thankfully, we are now beginning our ninth year of homeschooling.

During these nine years, we have run the gambit from practically replicating the public school classroom, using "canned" curriculum, to being what some would call "unschoolers." Needs and circumstances change and it is important to be flexible. What is ideal for one child one year, might not be what is needed the following year. Life has a way of changing, and it is an important lesson for parents and children alike to be able to roll with the punches, so to speak.

Another area that is important for our family, is the practice of being of service to others. Starting with my young children, doing things like helping our elderly neighbor or baking for shut-ins is important. As the children become older and can step out a bit more into the community, they do things like volunteering at the local no-kill animal shelter or volunteering twice per week at a convalescent hospital. Not only do we feel that it is important to help others, but there are wonderful lessons to be learned from doing so. If my children know all about the three R's, yet cannot go out into the world to make it a better place, what have I accomplished as a parent?

Before I detail a particular day in our homeschooling lives, I'd like to mention a few areas with which we've struggled. I do so, not to be negative, but to share with the reader that all homeschoolers, no matter how "together" they might seem, have difficult days as well as good ones, and doubts as well as convictions. Personally, when I read about the so-and-so homeschooling family whose son just won the national science foundation award, whose daughter is first chair in the junior philharmonic, whose . . . . (you get the picture), on one hand I am thrilled for them, and on the other, it makes me begin to doubt myself as a homeschooling teacher and parent. If my children aren't winning all of those awards (or any of them) what am *I* doing wrong? Of course, that's an over-simplification, but it does point out the danger of comparison. In reality, there will always be those families who do more and those who do less than one's own family. There are so many factors involved in homeschooling and in teaching our children as individuals, that it is seldom beneficial to compare ourselves with others.

Other problems over the years have been: over scheduling of extracurricular events, the telephone or similar interruptions, squabbling over chores, the inability to say "no" to others (many people feel that if you are "only at home," your schedule is wide open for volunteering, baby-sitting, etc.), and far too much switching from one curriculum or style to another.

Our neighborhood currently has no children anywhere near the ages of ours and no other stay-at-home mothers, leading to the (sometimes) problem of lack of friends and support for the children and for me.

The good news is that once we truly "see" a problem, there are usually all kinds of ways to make the necessary changes or adjustments. A good example is the adjustment we made to address this need for making friends. We joined a local homeschooling support group, joined a couple of classes (*Tae Kwon Do* and gymnastics), and volunteered at a convalescent hospital. This way, we are all able to get out and be with other people. One of the major areas of support and helpful ideas has been being a member of several homeschooling e-mail lists. Through them I have made wonderful friends. Their friendship and encouragement has been invaluable. All of these things have helped the children and me to solve the "loneliness" problem and have served to enrich our lives.

We've made other positive adjustments when we've decided (all too often!) that a particular curriculum or way of learning was not working out for a specific child. Although I feel badly about the waste of money involved in abandoning a particular course or book, it is better to do that than to plod along miserably with something that obviously doesn't work for us. Besides, if it doesn't work for one child, there is a good chance that it will work for another later.

A last example involves the area of responsibility. Life has thrown us an unusual amount of curves over the last six or so years. As a result, sometimes I feel like we are getting nothing done other than meeting the challenges of the particular time. In order to hopefully make myself a bit more accountable for some structure, we've joined *Clonlara* this year and are now accountable to a master teacher who will also do some of our record keeping.

In all, our family has usually been fairly good about communicating individual needs, concerns, or problems. It seems like I am usually the one who first sees a problem, but the children have also been known to recognize areas that need to change, as does George. We try to work together to implement the change. I try to be the one responsible for orchestrating or being responsible to see that changes are implemented, but when I meet resistance or am at a loss as to what to do, George is always willing to listen, come up with ideas, or support me.

The important thing to remind ourselves is that we've made the right decision, and in spite of what temporary obstacles we face, we are still doing what is best for our family and for our children.

This Monday in September is as good as any to chronicle a homeschooling day. We'll see what happens. It is warm and sunny outside.

At 6:50 a.m. I get up so that I can wake up Michael, our only child who is publicly schooled. His school bus arrives at 7:45 a.m. and he needs every minute of that time to get ready. Even with medication, the consequences of his previous head injury make it extremely difficult for him to concentrate and stay "on task." I find myself wishing that it were possible to homeschool him along with the other children. Between the needs of the other four children and my ill father, I have not yet found a way to add Mike to our homeschooling bunch. I feel guilty, yet knowing my limits, I feel that he is currently better off in his small, special education classroom with his patient and kind teacher. He genuinely enjoys his friends that he sees only at school, since there is only one little boy in our neighborhood who sometimes plays when he visits his grandmother. Mike loves sports, so he loves physical education at school, especially when it comes to playing soccer. Sometimes he wishes he were homeschooled like the others, but for the most part, he is glad to be at school, accepts it as routine, and truly enjoys himself there. His needs at this time are so extraordinary that our other children seem to recognize that it's best for him to go to school. In fact, one of the issues with which we wrestle is how to meet the needs of the older girls and the younger children. The younger girls can become fairly loud, making it difficult for the older two to concentrate on their school work.

Michael has left for school by 8:00 a.m. Abbie, the only other child who is awake, is outside with her dad, talking with him as he brushes down the swimming pool. Dad is once again explaining to Abbie why the dogs cannot be allowed into the pool; they bring in dirt that causes mustard algae, making pool maintenance a time-consuming nightmare. As Abbie and George talk, I decide to finish reading a book about unschooling. For the most part, I like the idea of child-led learning, yet it is difficult for me to let go of the "what ifs." (What if my child doesn't learn her multiplication tables? What if the children *never* learn to be good spellers? What if they never see the need for . . . . ?) I was trained as a teacher of the Deaf and old habits sometimes die hard.

I've finished the book by 9:00 a.m. I do a bit of research on the Internet. Abbie has taken a shower and is talking about various songs she likes. Hannah has now awakened. She and Abbie begin discussing Abbie's two loose teeth as they play with our pet rat, Elmo.

It's 9:15 a.m. now, and I am thinking about incorporating more Spanish and American Sign Language into our day since the children like both. Aside from our natural love of languages, there are other reasons for our interest in these two languages. Our adopted children are Hispanic and I would like to give them exposure to things related to the culture of their birth families. Also, the Hispanic population is huge where we live. Being bilingual here is quite an asset, both socially and in the work force. All of the children also enjoy sign language. Hannah was born very prematurely with a birth weight of less than two pounds. As a result, she has some lingering challenges—the most apparent one being speech. It is beneficial to her to be able to express her feelings and have others understand. We feel that if she learns sign language while she continues her speech therapy, she will have an additional avenue of expression, as well as a usable skill.

About 9:30 a.m. I call my father to make sure that he is okay. His failing health is a cause of major concern. We will go over to his apartment a bit later. It's also time to roust the two oldest girls out of bed. The younger girls are watching *The Prince of Egypt* on video tape.

By 9:50 a.m., just as I'm getting frustrated about the oldest two childrens' inability to get up, Laura comes downstairs. She shows me a recycling project she took upon herself last night. She found a thrown-away broken picture frame, repaired it, and glued potpourri pieces around the outside of it. It's quite pretty and shows a lot of creativity. I had been planning to discuss ecology and recycling this week so Laura has given me an excellent "opening." Her mood is cheerful and bubbly. She throws an affectionate arm around my shoulders as she greets me. I consider myself very fortunate to have such great kids! Sarah is finally up. She is on my bed talking to me about something nice the kids and the leader of her youth group did.

In spite of the fact that we're getting off to a slow start, I feel warm and good about my children. George has taken part of the day "off" so that he can replace the shock absorbers on my car, thankfully.

Between 10-10:30 a.m. Sarah and Laura eat breakfast. Except for Sundays, breakfasts tend to be in shifts. George is often up at four or five in the morning, so he grabs his own. At seven, Michael needs to be awakened in order to catch the bus. He is usually the only child awake so early, although sometimes Abbie is also. I make a simple breakfast for him (or them). It is usually at this time that I grab a cup of coffee and either a bowl of cereal, a piece of toast, or yogurt for myself. Sarah and Laura are the last ones to get up, and at twelve and fourteen years of age, they are very capable of getting their own breakfast. On Sundays, we usually all eat at the same time. Sometimes George makes our Sunday breakfast.

During breakfast, we look out our kitchen window and notice that the persimmons are just beginning to change color. Soon their sweetness will attract a variety of birds. We are informal bird watchers, although we are trying to get better about bird identification. We've read about the Charlotte Mason school of thought and have thoroughly enjoyed the incorporation of more nature into our "curriculum." Looking out the front window at our persimmon and camphor trees has provided much pleasure for all of us. The persimmon tree, in particular, is our "marker" of the seasons.

Abbie and Hannah have already eaten and are now upstairs making a tent out of sheets and a posture board from our old bunk bed set. They laugh continuously and brighten my day. I had entered both Abbie and Hannah in public school this fall but it lasted less than two weeks. I did so thinking that with all of my other responsibilities, they would be best served with a structured "reliable" environment. Not so!! The changes in them were very negative.

I tried Abbie in public school last year at what would have been midyear kindergarten when my brother died suddenly and without warning. I was overwhelmed with grief and several new responsibilities. I felt that, especially with Abbie being such an eager learner, I would not be able to meet her needs adequately. Academically and behaviorally, she did fine in school. At five, she was already reading, was obviously very bright and eager to learn, won a "citizen of the month, award" etc. In other ways, she showed signs of stress and strain.

By the time school was ready to begin this year, my father who is in poor health, moved to be near us. As my responsibilities again began to mount, I considered putting Abbie back into school. On one hand, she wanted to stay at home, but on another, she was anxious to go back and see her friends. She is very outgoing and made many friends there. Hannah was willing to go to school if Abbie was, even though they wouldn't be in the same grade. I didn't feel very good about Abbie going and felt even worse about Hannah. She just didn't seem ready as a very young five-year-old. I told the office staff and her teacher that her enrollment was very much on a trial basis. Although she was chronologically old enough to be in school, my gut feeling was that she wasn't ready, especially with her speech being difficult to understand.

Once school began, Abbie was bored to tears with her classroom situation. She had even fallen asleep, sitting, waiting to do *something*. There were many serious discipline problems in the classroom already. As for Hannah, she just wasn't ready—a sentiment confirmed by her teacher. After less than two weeks in school, Abbie wanted to come home, and Hannah was happy to come back too. I knew that my heart and intellect had been "right" all along. The place for my children is at home with me. My responsibilities have not changed, only increased, but I feel that I am supposed to have my children at home with me and that God will give me the strength and ability to do what has to be done.

As I look at them now and listen to their laughter, I know that I have done the right thing by bringing them back home. They are, once again, my happy little girls. (Later in the day, Abbie asks me if I want to hear a song she made up. It's about how happy she is to be home with her mommy!) I must remember that after nine years of homeschooling, even though life will throw us challenges, homeschooling is still best for our family. It is only when I have been exhausted and overwhelmed that I have I questioned whether homeschooling is for us.

It's now 11:45 a.m. and for the last hour Sarah, Laura, and I have been discussing emergency preparedness—it's validity, possible effects, etc. We brainstorm ways that disasters might impact our lives and then make an extensive list of ways we might counteract the problems. Our list is extensive: extra food (dried, canned, non-perishable), a lot of bottled water, first aid kits, cash money on hand, lots of batteries, a transistor radio, backpacks for each individual, filled with necessary items (clothing, toiletries) should we need to temporarily leave home, extra medications, other books, paper and writing utensils to be used for "entertainment," flashlights, Coleman stove, lantern, possibly a chemical portable potty, a gas can full of unleaded gasoline, extra pet food, extra blankets, extra firewood for our wood burning stove . . . these are some of the things that come to mind. Even if none of these problems ever come about, it is still a good thing to be prepared for emergencies.

We end up calling the *American Red Cross*, asking them to send us their brochure on the subject. The girls also call the University of California Extension Agency to request a pamphlet on what, when, and where to plant here in the Central Valley of California. We have always had summer and spring gardens but never have tried fall or winter gardens. We are told that we need to come in to pick up the brochure or else send a stamped, self-addressed envelope to them so that it can be mailed to us. We opt for the second choice. Laura writes the letter and Sarah prepares the two envelopes. We then discuss the need for complete first aid kits. We already have several but realize that they've been somewhat depleted.

Somehow this topic also leads to a "life's goals" discussion. We talk a bit about their current interests and possible career choices. We list some of the things they will need to know in order to accomplish their goals. I talk primarily with Sarah and Laura about life goals. Laura wants to "be remembered in the world" (for doing something special, humanitarian, entertaining, etc.) and wants to work with animals in some way. Sarah is far less clear at this point. She wants to take dance as a short-term goal, but has not decided upon any longer-term goals. She says that she wants to be nice and serve people, but she added,

---

"I'm already doing that."

Noon—Time to break for lunch. Sarah wants to create a scrapbook page or two.

It is now 2:00 p.m. Since lunch, we have been spending some time on our scrapbook project, and Laura decided on her own to write a paper about life goals. The little girls are having fun playing together. They often work together on "shows" to be given for their parents and other interested parties. Or they swim in the pool, jump on the trampoline, and do all kinds of stunts on the rope swing. They skateboard, rollerblade, play dress-up, and do "makeovers." Since Sarah takes dance, Abbie gymnastics, and Laura *Tae Kwon Do*, they sometimes practice these endeavors and make up various routines. Other times they will play sports. They might also get together and work out different songs and duets on the piano and vocally. Their friends also like to congregate here.

As requested, I help George with the car repair. I'm having my usual problem with getting the kids to clean up the kitchen. Laura saw our elderly neighbor outside and decided to share her two craft projects with her. This neighbor has remarkable talent and skill when it comes to crafts and asks Laura to come over because she has a bunch of things to give to her so that she can make more projects. She thoroughly enjoys talking and interacting with the children, and teaching them new crafts now and then. She tells virtually anyone who will listen how wonderful homeschooling is and how brilliant, kind, and well behaved her neighbor's children are.

Laura is creatively making "people" out of potpourri pieces at 2:15 p.m. and they're really darling. She is going to give two of them and a little decorated box that she made to a friend of hers at *Tae Kwon Do* later this afternoon. Her friend was ill on Saturday and this is a "get well" gift for her.

The school bus brings Mike home at 2:30 p.m. He wants a "break" before starting homework. I agree that a break would be good. He, Abbie, and Hannah play soccer out front.

At 3:30 p.m. it's time to take Laura to *Tae Kwon Do*. She takes a three hour block of *TKD* classes on Mondays. She prefers to skip class today, but she is on the exhibition team and they have two performances on Saturday. She realizes that she needs to practice. While I am gone, the other children work on the scrapbook.

We're back home again at 4:00 p.m. George is having a tough time trying to get the car back together. Mike is being a diligent helper and feels quite proud that he can help Dad. Abbie and I do some reading together. Abbie *loves* to read and to learn to read. Someone gave us their *Bob Books* series of primary readers. We read through them all at a rapid pace. We also read Dr. Seuss' *Go Dog, Go!* Abbie did all of the reading. We have hundreds of children's fiction books, as well as hundreds of non-fiction. We also visit the library on a regular basis. She has taken to reading and writing like a duck to water.

At this point in the afternoon, I decide to go visit my father. Sadly, he isn't doing well at all. As his health deteriorates, I feel frustrated at my inability (as well as anyone else's) to help him. I silently say a prayer that he will have had a good day today, so far. When I get there to visit, I find that this was not to have been so. I offer to bring Dad some dinner but he declines. The children and I go to visit him daily, and I usually return again alone, so that we can watch *Jeopardy* together and I can take a meal to him. We try to cheer him and just be there for him—all of us work together to clean his apartment and do his shopping. George or I take him to his doctor appointments. I cook dinner for him, usually, and am ready and willing to take him on outings, although he often doesn't feel well enough to do so. I do his laundry and go on errands for him. Death and illness have been an unusually large part of our lives for the last seven years. As difficult as these things have been to experience and endure, they are a natural part of life and have helped us to grow and learn compassion.

At 5:45 p.m. I go back home to make dinner before Laura needs to be picked up. I used to be fairly organized and would plan and list the meals, make out a grocery list for one or two weeks ahead, and would shop for everything so that I'd only have to return to the store for fresh milk and produce. As our lives have become more complicated, I seem to make much shorter-term menu plans, if any, and find myself going to the store too often. Part of this is because my dad oftentimes remembers something that he needs. He's not at all demanding, but considering that he is losing a tremendous amount of weight that he can't afford to lose, if something finally sounds good to him, I try to be accommodating. Especially when George is gone on sales calls so many nights per week, it is all too tempting to either throw a dinner together at the last minute for the kids, my dad, and me, or pick up convenience food—something that we can't really afford. I am the one who cooks dinners about 99 % of the time. Every now and then, George will barbecue something or one of the older girls will cook a meal. I usually makes lunches, too, although Sarah and Laura often lend a hand. Tonight I make salad and put eggplant parmesan in the oven. George has gone on some errands.

At 6:40 p.m. dinner is cooked, but it's time to go pick up Laura from *Tae Kwon Do*. Sarah and her friend have walked to a nearby store. I load the younger three children into the car. We will eat when we return.

We are on our way home with Laura at 7:00 p.m. The instructor's daughter, Laura's friend, is still ill. The instructor was very touched with Laura's homemade gifts for her. We eat dinner and Michael begins his homework. Other than the rote copying of spelling words, the rest of his work is utterly ridiculous, way beyond the ability of this special education student.

Our family goes on it's nightly walk between 7:30-8:30 p.m. This walk has become rather a family tradition. We are surprised at how well our new puppy Molly heels. Her mother, apparently, was a little wire-haired terrier, much like Toto in *The Wizard of Oz*. To look at her, though, she looks like a cross between a Chihuahua and a miniature dachshund. Our other two dogs are much bigger, and both are golden retriever mixes. Then there are, of course, the rat, the cats, the fish . . . .

At 8:45 p.m. Laura is reminded to feed all of our animals. Sarah is reminded that she needs to finish cleaning the kitchen. As with the kitchen, housework is still a work-in-progress. We've tried all kinds of charts, methods, etc., but still haven't found what truly works well for us. Sarah and I do the laundry loads. Theoretically, each person is responsible for getting his or her own things out of the clean clothes pile and putting the items away. Sometimes this works, and other times I find myself sorting late at night. At least the piles are usually clean, but I'd like to find a way to better tame the laundry monster. Sarah and Laura are responsible for animal care and the kitchen. Whoever does animal care on a given day also does the middle upstairs bathroom. They alternate days, and whoever isn't doing one thing is doing the other. Each person is responsible for his or her room. Of course, since they are sharing rooms, there is the customary blaming of the roommate. The three youngest children are supposed to keep the living room clean, although this requires almost constant supervision and reminding by me. George is responsible for the upkeep of the cars, the swimming pool, the yard, and general maintenance, although with his current schedule, it seems like he is always running way behind.

I try to assign chores according to the childrens' capabilities. I also try to pay attention to things they each like to do. The main problem is that no one likes to clean up the kitchen, so it seems there is invariably an argument over whose turn it is, who didn't finish it properly the last time, etc. We've tried incentives and written chore lists, but still have yet to come to a true resolution of this problem. I used to be far more strict about their rooms than I am at the moment. I do, however, want the downstairs (kitchen, living room, bathroom) to be presentable as often as possible. I am trying to choose my battles, so to speak. I fought with my (now) twenty-five-year-old for years to clean, especially her horribly messy bedroom, but now that she is married and has a child of her own, she is an immaculate housekeeper (not to mention that she's a wonderful mother).

When it comes to chores, the children seem to have very selective hearing. Our major hassle is the kitchen where everyone seems to take a hand in messing it up. George and I constantly find ourselves explaining that, if everyone cleans up his or her own mess, it will make the job far easier, but for whatever reason, the lesson isn't being learned quickly enough. Another problem area, though not as bad, involves cleaning the cat litter and feeding all of our animals. I wish we could find the answers to these problems. I resent being a slave to housekeeping.

It seems that one of my lifetime mottoes should be something along the lines of, "She's *always* trying to reorganize and de-clutter." With a family of seven at home, plus all of our activities, somehow we are missing the mark with the area of "chores." We do "okay" but I'd like to do a truly good job of it, with far less hassles than we have.

Every now and then I will leave a Post-it Note about a job, but for the most part, I verbally tell them to do their chores or to refer to the weekly chore chart. Sometimes I feel like throwing away or giving away most of what we have so that the problem will be severely improved, if only via process of elimination. With George, I've tried, off and on, to make a "honey do" list.

Although some areas get more frequent "checking" than others. I have a real "thing" about the need to put food away and to not have dirty dishes on the counters or in the sink. It is very depressing to me to come upon a kitchen that has been "trashed." I tend, therefore, to be much stricter about this area than some of the others.

Sometimes we've ended up taking away allowance because the jobs were not done, were done poorly, or with repeated requests. Some say that allowance shouldn't be contingent upon work done or not done. For a time I felt that way, but ultimately, I believe that, especially with older children, they need to see that they will not be financially compensated or even keep a job if they are unfaithful in carrying out their responsibilities. Losing their allowance now is a less painful but sometimes effective way of showing them that, as part of a family and as individuals, we all have our responsibilities and that if we don't do them, we will not get rewarded.

As the chores are being done, Mike is finishing his homework later than usual and needs to shower and get to bed. George and I are vegging out for a short time in front of the television, watching a show on *The Learning Channel*, about a tornado. The amount of destruction is too much for the human mind to even comprehend. My heart breaks for the victims and I find myself wiping tears away.

At 9:15 p.m. George and Abbie, our two earliest risers, are both asleep on our bed. Mike is in bed, too. Hannah is next to Abbie on our bed. She asks me to lie down next to her, which I do. She is quickly asleep, with her arm around me and her head resting upon my shoulder. Sarah, Laura, and I will, as usual, be the night owls. Tomorrow morning, the two oldest girls will volunteer at the nursing home, as they do every Tuesday and Thursday from 9-11:00 a.m. The girls have been given a number of responsibilities, depending upon the need of the day. Sometimes they help with the two-hour "community" time, when the residents are able and willing to socialize. The girls might read the paper to those who want to hear it, help them with the crossword puzzles, or help them play the game of the day, like *Bingo* or *Hangman*. Sometimes they help with the facility

---

mascots, a huge cat named "Fluffy" or the ten doves that are in a flight cage outside. Oftentimes, they go visiting from room to room. They have already become favorites there. The residents are, for the most part, very elderly and have a lifetime of memories to share. Other residents are unable to communicate or to remember, so sometimes the girls just hold a hand and smile or talk to them. Once Sarah actually hosed down and cleaned the large outside patio, it's chairs, etc. Sometimes the girls help serve coffee or food. They most enjoy sitting, talking, and listening to the individual residents.

During that time, I will work exclusively with the two youngest girls. We will read some children's fiction and probably take a short nature walk, with attendant sketching.

Sarah and Laura come into our room at 10:20 p.m. after I have taken the sleeping little ones off the bed and have turned on *Nick At Night*. I think tomorrow we will also have a discussion about whether to keep the television or not. We watch very little television but I think that with the addition of cable, it is sneaking back into our lives, way too much. We went without it for three years once, and those three years were full of blessings.

Laura showers and goes to bed at 10:30 p.m. Sarah is told that it's getting late and she agrees to shower and go to bed, too. I want to do a bit of stretching and practice *Tae Kwon Do*, which I've just begun. It's late, though, so I will try to do "extra" tomorrow. A hug and good night wishes are exchanged between Sarah and me after her shower.

It's 11:30 p.m. now. This school day has been one that leans toward the unschooling or child-led end of the spectrum. Some days we get more "formal" schooling in. We are ever seeking balance. All in all, it was a productive and happy day. Our household is finally quieting down. I find myself still thinking about where we need to be regarding structure or lack of it.

I don't always have the energy to handle these very busy days. I know that I should be getting more sleep than I do. I keep saying that I will work on maintaining better hours, but it hasn't happened yet. Perhaps prayer for wisdom would help. I hope I do maintain a stable environment, though. On days when things get on "overload," I usually give up on the more formal aspects of our school day and let the kids either play or do some kind of project that will not require my immediate input. An example of this happened recently. The girls had mentioned that they wanted to redo a large, triangular part of our backyard that has always been our vegetable garden. I sent them out to the spot to measure, diagram, and draw up plans for what they would like to see there. After I de-stressed a little bit inside, I went outside and joined them in their project. We ended up tearing out the overgrown garden and replacing it with a park bench, bird bath, goldfish pond and lots of flowers.

It is our goal to raise Godly, happy, well-adjusted, responsible children who love each other and who will be contributing members to our society. I want them to have a strong sense of self-esteem and to be able to be as self-sufficient as possible, realizing that there are other areas in life that are clearly communal, where individuals help one another and work for the collective good. In this respect, I think that we are right on target. Academically, I fear that we are falling behind in some ways. I think that the children have enormous vocabularies and tremendous imaginations, and yet I worry about things like spelling, writing, math, etc. I often find myself second-guessing, wondering if I haven't pushed hard enough. I especially worry that I might not be requiring enough of Sarah and Laura, since they are the oldest of our at-home bunch and will be grown and on their own before we know it.

George and I discuss our children, their needs, and our homeschooling either late at night, very early in the morning, or sandwiched between his appointments during the day. As far as homeschooling goes, George looks upon himself as the principal of our school. He gives me support, helps when there is a lack of cooperation and has, upon occasion, offered to teach a particular subject. I do appreciate the emotional support and encouragement tremendously, although I'd be very happy to have a bit more help with teaching, even if it is infrequent.

Unfortunately, George's work schedule doesn't allow us many evenings together, except Sundays and sometimes Saturdays. He just now walked in and it's already late. All too often there are calls waiting for him or he feels that he

Laura, Jill, George, Sarah
Michael, Hannah, Abbie

Sarah (14), Laura (12), Michael (9), Abbie (6), Hannah (5)

must enter things into the computer. On the few evenings that we do have together, we go for a walk with the children and might watch a rented video or television program of mutual interest. It's rare that George and I have private time together. This is another area that needs work. Even an hour browsing at a bookstore does wonders for me. George asked me out to dinner last week. We went out for a nice meal and actual conversation while Sarah babysat. I'm afraid that we set a rather unhealthy precedent when we had the medically fragile, high risk foster children. Most of them could not, initially, be left with anyone other than a registered nurse. As a result, we got into the habit of either staying at home or else taking the whole family with us. In retrospect, it would have been better to make the time for each other and for ourselves. We are trying to work on that issue now—better late than never. As you can tell, I feel that our current situation needs reworking. Nothing further will be accomplished today, though.

It's time to go to bed. We are blessed and I feel very fortunate.

Stephen, age 43
Kathleen, age 41
Edward, age 13
Amelia, age 11

Interview with Kathleen in rural Maple Ridge, British Columbia, Canada.

AUTONOMY WITH STRUCTURE

We have lived in Maple Ridge, British Columbia, for ten years. Prior to that we lived in Muswell Hill, North London, England. Stephen is a Brit. He was born in Hong Kong and his father was English; his Mum was born and raised in China and is Chinese. I am Canadian-born and spent my first eleven years in Canada, the next nine in the United States, then returned to Canada when I was nineteen. Twenty-one years ago, I went to visit the UK, where my maternal grandfather was from, and I stayed for ten years. Both Edward and Amelia were born in London, and we came to Canada ten years ago, when they were both babies; Edward was two and a half years old and Amelia was five months old. Edward has vague memories of our flat in London, but Amelia only remembers Maple Ridge.

We came to Canada because my cousin offered Stephen a job, and he was very happy to live in Canada near his Mum and siblings. I feel that we are living where we should be for this time in our lives. Stephen's Mum, brother, and sister live nearby. My parents and my brothers live in Washington State. It is much nicer to be able to drive for an hour and a bit to visit them than to have to face a ten-hour flight once every ten years or so to get together. I would still love to live in the UK again one day, preferably in Scotland, which I adore.

Maple Ridge is a 125-year-old rural community of 52,000 people. Its main industries are blueberry, cranberry, and dairy farming; there are also four lumber mills in and around the town. Maple Ridge is set between the Golden Ears and Garibaldi peaks of the Pacific Coastal Mountain range to the north and the Fraser

River to the south. We are thirty-five kilometres east of Vancouver, B.C., in the part of British Columbia called the Lower Mainland or Lower Fraser Valley. Many people who live here, including Stephen, commute daily into Vancouver, for which Maple Ridge has become a bedroom community. We are within a half hour's drive of three provincial parks and six lakes. Being near the mountains and the North Pacific rain forest, Maple Ridge gets a lot of rain. When the sun shines, it is stupendous! We are only an hour's drive from Vancouver and its beaches if we want to go to the seashore.

We live in a four-bedroomed house in a cul-de-sac of two storey, split-level houses. We have a small front garden and a large shady back garden with four huge cedar trees in it. Last summer I planted a very small garden in the back, just to see whether we could get enough light to warrant it. I am proud to announce that we had a harvest of twenty zucchinis, five pounds of tomatoes, two pumpkins, and two pounds of strawberries. I am now eager to put in more beds and maybe even build a little greenhouse that will go where the swing set used to be. When we moved into the house ten years ago, it had only three bedrooms—we have since put in a toilet and shower and a guest bedroom downstairs in the daylight basement. The rest of the basement now has a ceiling, lights, and drywalled walls, but we have yet to finish it. This summer we've been rebuilding our back garden fence between rainy spells—we've got the other two sides to do, but that will have to wait for drier weather.

Stephen is a qualified architect, which he was in England. He also ran the *CAD* (*Computer Aided Design*) bureau for an architectural firm. When we came to Canada, Stephen took a job running the *CAD* computer suite for my cousin's mechanical engineering firm. He also is an engineering draughtsman for this company. They design heavy machinery and those spreaders and cranes one sees loading and unloading containers in the ports of the world. He decided that he wanted to have a job that would allow him to spend evenings and weekends at home with his family, something that being a successful architect can interfere with! He commutes into Vancouver by van pool five days a week, sometimes sharing the driving. He leaves home at 6:30 in the morning and returns home at 6:00 in the evening.

I have been at home with the children since Edward was born. I actually left my job in the travel industry just before Edward was born and have not been employed outside our home since then. I am a full-time home educating Mummy, and I love it that way.

I don't think I was ever happy with the idea of the kids being in school, but put them there so they could make friends. I had read about home education in various publications. I met a family one day at a local park who were passing through with their eight children on a tour of the western provinces. I thought it would be lovely to have the flexibility to show our children the world someday.

We started home educating the children six years ago for two main reasons. The primary reason was that our son was being bullied at school. He was very sociable and always interested in meeting people, but became very frustrated, angry, and shy. This was not our child! We went through turmoil for two-and-a-half school years before we finally pulled the children out of school. It is a decision I dearly wish we had made long before.

Secondly, our daughter was bored silly. She was five and informed us that the only reason she was still attending school was to see her best friend. Amelia went into kindergarten knowing how to read and do basic maths. Her written work was in her own style, but mostly legible. Her major frustration was that her teacher would not let her do the same maths as the Grade 2's in her class. Her class was mixed K, 1, and 2 students—the theory being that children could work to their own ability. Not!

We had talked about home educating when the children would go from the primary up to the elementary school. We had always said we would wait until the kids left the primary school before home educating them. That was a silly thing to do, and I still wonder why we had erected that barrier instead of simply home educating from the very beginning. I find in life that sometimes one is inclined to put decisions off and say I'll do such and such as soon as I've done this, that, or the other first. I try not to do that anymore—rather, I try to deal with things as they come, if possible.

Even when Edward was a little chap and his sister was yet to be born, I was worrying about school. Would he like it? Which would be better, public or state schools? Could we afford a public school on one income? (No—public schools are actually what private schools are called in the UK.) Would he be ready at four years old to go to school?

Since my own feelings about school were always somewhere between intense dislike and boredom, perhaps my own feelings were clouding my judgment about our children? That was what kept our two in school for as long as they were, not wanting to view their schooling with my jaded eye. I know better now.

I never fancied school, though I loved reading and learning. I always dreamt of being educated like Beatrix Potter—at home and mostly by myself. Maybe that's why school was such an anathema to me. I could read when I went to kindergarten and was very happy staying at home near my Mum and two little brothers. I had three routes to walk to school: long, longer, and longest! I always read ahead of the other students and had my work done long before they did—a pattern that continued throughout my schooling. It was not welcomed by any of my teachers, and I was bored silly. Instead of pushing ahead, I languished and didn't do as well as I should have, getting C's when they should have been B's, and B's instead of A's.

When we moved to the U.S. when I was eleven, I was teased and bullied for

---

Edward (13), Amelia (11)

sounding different. I was also being punished for always having the right answer and winning the spelling bees. After a year or so of bullying, I became very shy and never spoke up. This bullying went on through junior high. It left me with a hatred of school and the town we were living in. By high school, I had learned to glare at my oppressors so they left me mostly alone. Also, by this time, most of the students had grown up a tad and were ashamed of their behaviour. I finished high school a semester early and did some college courses. I didn't want to have anything more to do with school, so I took a correspondence course in airline ticketing and reservations and spent a month in Dallas, Texas when I was eighteen. At nineteen I moved to Portland, Oregon, worked for just over a year and then moved back to Canada. I lived and worked in Vancouver and then at almost twenty-one, I traveled to the UK where I ended up staying for ten years.

Stephen's experience of school was vastly different, but I'll let him tell you himself: "I have experienced two types of British education: an almost colonial setup in Hong Kong and a newly formed comprehensive school in a backwater of South West Britain. There were poor teachers in both places, though most teachers were effective. Due to either character, upbringing, school experiences, or all three, I have ended up being very conscious of external standards. Britain sets great store by rigorous national examinations. My concern has always been that we live in a society that has standards and timetables. I feel that to ignore constraints, requirements, and standards is to short-change my children. There has always been an emphasis on set work in our homeschooling. Other pursuits are encouraged beyond that. Trained as an architect, I see it as doing the client's bidding, while designing the dream house on my own time."

Now that our kids are out of school, they are more outgoing than they used to be. We marvel at how comfortable they are in a shop or museum, just going up to someone and asking about whatever it is they are interested in. We certainly weren't like that as kids. They seem to have bags of confidence in any situation.

We started out using the British Columbia curriculum through correspondence for the first three years and then used some parts of it off and on for the next three. One may use the same curriculum one finds in the schools by correspondence (or distance education, as they now call it). It is like having school at home. The texts and supplies are sent by the distance education school. Each subject is done in a module form with daily work and assignments that are done by the children. At the end of each week, the assignments are sent to the distance education school for marking by teachers, and then sent back with grades and comments on them. This is a good way of home educating if the parents want to know just how their child is doing or as a way to ease into home education. Over the past five years, we have used this system in full or have chosen only certain subjects.

By January of this year, we decided that the children were learning more on their own and with more enthusiasm than when they were using the curriculum, so we dropped it altogether. They are still learning about the same subjects, but in a less structured and more autonomous way. Edward is using both CD-ROM and a textbook for algebra, and Amelia is doing the same, using a Grade 8 maths textbook that she is very happy with. If she were in school or using the curriculum through distance education, she would be stuck using a Grade 6 text. As soon as she was able to get into this Grade 8 maths, she stopped telling me that math was boring and that she hated it.

We're still plugging away with French, though both children have started looking at our German CD-ROMS as well. We do the rest of the subjects our own way, on a more autonomous basis and a more interesting way, with more unit studies rather than individual subjects. We prefer to study history, geography, and social sciences as a unit rather than separate subjects. We'll study the whole country, its peoples and history. Most of our studies have a decidedly archaeological/anthropological slant because that is my first love, and the children really enjoy learning this way. For science, we get out the microscope and various science books and do experiments. Last year we gave Edward and Amelia a chemistry set. Since they both are such avid readers and wonderful writers, I don't think they need a language arts course.

A wonderful book called *Sophie's World*, by Jostein Baarder is a great way to introduce children (and adults) to philosophy. I highly recommend it. I read it aloud, and then we have lively discussions about the great questions man has always asked. "Who am I?" "Why am I?" It is exciting to learn from our children as they learn from us.

Stephen has a knack for finding just the books we need during his lunch time forays to the various thrift shops in the East Vancouver neighbourhood near where he works. We have a huge library of books and are always adding to it. My friend always comes to us when her kids are doing a project at school. We also have a computer, a myriad of software (reference and otherwise) and an Internet connection, so we use the computer as a learning tool as well. The children are both very comfortable using the computer and type quite well. They usually choose to use the word processor programmes to write their stories. They are getting quite a fair hand at handwriting as well, thanks to their previous language arts course's insistence upon handwriting. This is good as one must have a legible hand if one wants to communicate on paper. One can't be plugged into a computer continually, after all. Many local bookshops are willing to offer their teacher discount to home educating families, especially if they are already good customers.

We tend to "do school" from 9:00 a.m. to 2:30 p.m. Monday through Friday. Our usual days start at 5:30 a.m. when Stephen gets up, ready for work, and out the door. If I'm not getting up to exercise, I open one eye and say goodbye, then snuggle back under the covers until 6:30 or 7:00 a.m. Not very wifely, I know. If I am exercising, I trundle downstairs at 5:30 a.m. and do forty minutes on the treadmill, then shower and dress, wake the kids at 7:00 a.m., go into the kitchen and put the kettle on for my tea, put *CBC* radio on to catch up with the world, and then go back down the hall to Edward and Amelia's rooms to wake them again. I make the tea, call out to ask whether there is a preferred breakfast for that morning, walk down the hall again to wake the children and *this* time stay there until they're actually out of bed. We discuss what they might want to eat and if they don't come up with any brilliant suggestions, I decide for them.

Then, we all sit down with our books. Yes, we read at the table, but only when Daddy isn't home. When he's home, we discuss things we're doing, have read, heard on the radio, etc. We read out various passages from our books if we think they may be of interest to the others. The kids clear the table according to who set the table in the first place. I am the chief cook and bottle washer. I do the laundry, keep the house tidy, and cook most of the meals. Recently, Edward and Amelia said they would cook one meal a week, but so far it has only happened twice. Edward and Amelia have to feed our dog Oscar on a weekly rotation that is written on the calendar to help their memories (and mine). The person who feeds the dog also has to keep his toilet area clean for that week. Both children set and clear the kitchen table, and load and unload the dishwasher. They now take turns washing up the dishes as our dishwasher has died, and we've had the neither the time nor pennies to get it fixed.

Edward and Amelia are also responsible for keeping their rooms tidy and putting away their clean laundry. Sometimes I enlist them to fold the towels and the socks. If they leave the bathroom particularly messy, then we tidy it together, with me supervising. Edward mows the lawn and Amelia feeds the fish in our pond. Amelia also does the majority of the dog walking as she is doing agility training with Oscar. Amelia is a member of the *4-H Dog Club* with Oscar, is doing obedience and agility training, as well as learning to show and judge dogs. This will also involve public speaking. She can't wait to camp out with her friends and all the dogs.

After breakfast, while one child is doing half an hour of piano practice, the other is doing typing practice on the computer. I have found that this is the best way to ensure that piano is practiced for the required length of time.

One thing that I feel that we are blessed with is that Edward and Amelia get on so well. Sure, they have their spats, but nothing major, and if I feel they're getting too loud and upset with each other, they have to go to their rooms to cool off, and I speak with them individually. Now, before you think this is very civilised, let me assure you that I can get annoyed with the best of them, but I prefer to remain the adult (most of the time), and so try very hard to be the mediator. I assure you; I have my moments. If I've had a hard day bumping noses with Edward, then I tell all to Stephen when he gets home from work, and he helps me put things into perspective and speaks to Edward if need be. Since we've adopted a more relaxed, less structured method of home education, there have been fewer confrontations and less flexing of adolescent muscle.

Sometimes we just have reading or cooking days. We love the flexibility of being at home. I recently set up a home learners' gym time at a local gymnastics centre. Twice a month we join other home educated families at the gym to use the trampolines, mats, parallel bars and climbing ropes. The kids have a wonderful time for two hours, and the Mums have even been known to have a go on the trampolines.

We have tried an unschooling approach a few times, but we seem to be happier with a combination of total autonomy and some structure, with some work days and other days to bake or read, go on field trips, or whatever. I often get more enthusiastic than the kids do about the subjects they've started studying. We think there is room for both structure and autonomy.

We are very conscious of the fact that in four years Edward will be eighteen and university-bound, so we don't want him to miss out on the subjects that matter. In speaking to home educated families with older children, I find that many kids decide to take courses through local community colleges for the first year or two and then simply transfer to the university of their choice after that. It seems a sensible way to go, especially if one doesn't have a transcript of subjects learned and exams passed, which the universities usually insist upon. Having such a transcript is the real reason Stephen prefers Edward and Amelia to do distance education, but he has realized that the children are very capable of covering all or more of the "required subjects" in a shorter time, yet in more depth than they would if they were at school or taking the curriculum by distance.

We do family things on the weekend, so that Stephen can take part since he doesn't get much time with Edward and Amelia during the week while he's away at work. Anytime is learning time, so everything we do has value. Stephen is casually teaching Edward and Amelia the basics of chemistry and physics on weekends. Here is how Stephen describes what he does with Edward and Amelia: "We have various university chemistry and physics textbooks that I read to and with the kids. I have worked on the introductory chapters as they give a good overview to the subjects, outlining philosophies such as testing out hypotheses and developing theories. I do not force them beyond their understanding, but emphasize that it is possible to "calculate this" and "test for that"—it's all in here. I want to nibble away at subjects so that the children are well aware of what the subjects are about, and as their critical faculties improve, the more they will be able to absorb and peruse."

What about socialisation? That is a question that is often asked. Edward and

Amelia are blue belts with a brown stripe in *Aikido*, a Japanese martial art. They have been doing *Aikido* for six years. Edward has archery for one-and-a-half hours. Amelia has *4-H Dog Club* for agility and obedience, and monthly *4-H* business meetings. Amelia has basketball and her Grade 4 ballet class for one-and-a-half hours. We have a basketball net in the front drive and use it when it isn't raining. Our dog Oscar, a lab/border collie cross, gets us out for walks and hikes. Maple Ridge has a wonderful array of places to walk and hike. Since we have an overabundance of rain, there are days when we just stay home. The children both take piano lessons. So, as you see, they are quite active and spend time with other children.

As I've mentioned, Stephen and I plan for the children to attend university. It doesn't matter if they decide afterward to weave for a living, just as long as they have a degree to fall back on should they need to. As it happens, Amelia is (and always has been) determined to become a veterinarian, though lately she's been wondering how to combine a career as a veterinarian with that of a chef, ballet dancer, or famous actress! Amelia has discovered that she likes to cook and bake. She enjoys watching me invent meals and helps me chop veggies for our meals. Having cooked a couple of meals with Edward, she now feels that cooking is something she likes to do and that it might be a neat job to have. She has also tried her hand at baking cookies a number of times.

Edward isn't sure yet. He's narrowed his future interests down to medicine or the law. Since he's only thirteen, he can afford to wait awhile. Edward just knows he wants to help people, and he has a very well-defined sense of justice. It will be interesting to see which path he chooses to take.

A few years ago, a friend and I started our own home education support group. I send prospective home educators information about the legalities of Home Education in B.C. and a list of books they may find helpful. I also invite them along to our meetings. This is the beginning of the fourth year of our little group that has shrunk from its original fifteen families, with three families sending their kids back to school and two more families moving away. There are many groups in the Vancouver/Lower Mainland area—some very active, some not. We arrange field trips or join the field trips that other groups have arranged, so we meet other home educating families that way as well. I have met a number of families who have been teaching their own for ten to twenty years, but they rarely seem to join groups and prefer to do their own thing.

As Edward and Amelia are getting older and we are so busy with lessons and activities, I sometimes find it difficult to take time off for a field trip or a meeting, because we have so few evenings at home. I enjoy getting together with my home educating friends and comparing notes as well as just having a natter, but the times we can do this are getting fewer.

Ten times a year I publish a newsletter for our group. It gets expensive, so I ask my subscribers to give me a book of ten stamps to help offset the cost of paper, postage and ink. In the newsletter I advise of any upcoming field trips, publish articles or jokes submitted by our members or their children, and remind everyone of the time and place of our next meeting. I am thinking of publishing the newsletter on the group web site, but haven't had the time to sit and play with the computer yet. It's on my ever-expanding "to-do" list.

We enjoy being at home with the children and hope that we can continue home educating until it is time for them to enter university. Edward thinks he would like to attend high school. It is something that will have to be considered, but not before Grade 10. Edward's wish to attend high school is strictly social I am afraid. He is a very sociable soul and enjoys the company of others.

Sometimes living on a single income is difficult, especially with so much going out on the kids' activities, but it is well worth the expenditure. I wish that stay-at-home Mums and home educating families could get a tax break, but once the government starts doing us favours, they'll then start legislating how we can and cannot teach our children. This already happens in many provinces, so perhaps keeping a low profile is best.

Whenever I meet someone who is contemplating educating their own children, I am always quick to tell them that it is something we do not regret and enjoy very much. It is so rewarding to see how our children are growing and just how quickly they learn. It's great fun too! We highly recommend home education to anyone who is willing to listen!! I really wish that I had known about unschooling or a less structured approach from the beginning. When one's child is used to sitting in a classroom all day and being told how and what to think, it is very difficult for them to realise that they can be self-motivated and that they are capable of learning in their own way. I thought we had to follow the provincial curriculum, so that is how we started out home educating the kids. I prefer them to be more self-directed but get discouraged if they don't want to do anything at all. I hated being controlled by somebody else's timetable, and the children are finally realising that what Mum has been rattling on about all these years makes sense. They can enjoy learning and writing about their own interests, rather than someone else's choice of subject. They are glad they can tailor their learning to their own interests.

When new home educators or those who are contemplating it contact me, I outline their options and always encourage them to allow the child/ren and themselves some down time to unwind from the school environment and perhaps even unschool for the first little while until they have found their way.

I spend most of my waking hours with the children, other than the odd coffee night out with my friends. Stephen leaves the house early every morning and doesn't get home until evening during the week. Most evenings, except for Monday, we have the children's activities to take them to. Until Edward turned thirteen, we had not really left the children on their own, and now we do so only for two hours at the maximum. They are both quite independent and, happily, quite sensible children.

Stephen and I have a strong marriage, built on our mutual friendship, love, and respect. When the children are at their *Aikido* class, we have an hour to do errands and chat together. To get private time together, we usually go to bed when the kids do and close our bedroom door to read, chat, and have some time to ourselves.

Edward, Kathleen, Amelia, Stephen

Donn (born in 1938 and died in 1995 at age 57)
Jean, age 57
Cathy, age 33
Karen, age 31
Susan, age 29
Derek, age 27

Interview with Jean from rural Glassville, New Brunswick, Canada

ENDURING FAMILY BONDS

After twenty-four years of homeschooling and ten years that the kids have all been leading their own independent lives, this recollection of our homeschooling years will be a retrospective and introspective journey through time.

My husband Donn died five years ago. Because he has written so extensively about our homeschooling experiences in his book, *The Home School Source Book*, I am including many of Donn's quotes from the second edition, which allows *both* of us to contribute to this chapter, as we naturally would have, had Donn been alive. I am now in the process of revising our book for the upcoming third edition.

Homeschooling, when we began in the late 1960s and early 1970s, was almost unheard of. We were unaware of anyone writing about it. We knew no one who was doing it, although we had once met a family who used *Calvert School* correspondence courses. To homeschool at that time meant being able to ignore pressures from friends, neighbors, family, and authorities; to find our own resources, and to develop our own philosophy about learning at home. Like our independent lifestyle before having kids, we learned to look to ourselves and each other for support. Before attempting to say how our lives evolved to center around school at home, it will help if you understand a little about the influences in our lives before we began homeschooling.

Donn grew up in and around a small town in Vermont, strongly influenced by the post-depression era and parents with a very limited income. Donn did well in school. In his sophomore year, his English teacher saw in Donn a mind reaching for new thoughts and gave him a copy of *Walden.* This one book verbalized much of what he already thought. It was a major turning point in Donn's thinking: it was to influence his thoughts and our lifestyle. After high school, Donn traveled extensively throughout the Southwest on a spiritual quest and became a pacifist in 1958, long before it was fashionable.

I, however, grew up in the comfort of a Chicago suburb. School was a nightmare. I can remember not wanting to go to kindergarten. Then, while still in high school, I can remember vowing I would never put my kids through a similar educational process, although I had no idea what the alternatives were. I had friends, but was basically a loner and a rebel. Rebels come in two forms—those rebelling against something and those rebelling to create something better. In high school I was mostly the former, not knowing how to create something better. When I became a pacifist in my last year of high school, I began to see how I could make things better. I took part in an interdenominational freedom ride to Albany, Georgia, in 1962. I worked with *CORE* (*Congress of Racial Equality*). I became a peace activist. During my first semester at Goddard College I met Donn, who had just organized a peace center. He sat down next to me for fifteen minutes on the bus I was taking from Boston back to college. That bus ride changed my life like Thoreau changed Donn's. We married two months later.

Now you have two pacifists who feel that the best way to make the world a better place is to live as simply and as independently of the prevailing socio-economic system as possible. We built our home—a log cabin in the woods, learning the necessary skills as we went. We began growing our own food and raising some animals, again teaching ourselves as we went along. After four years, we decided we were ready to start a family. We wanted to be together for the birth, which we assumed would be in the hospital. In 1966 that was not acceptable hospital policy. We consulted what books we could find, searched, and finally found a doctor who would answer our questions, and we went on to have all four of our children at home. Taking part in all of life together—wanting and needing to share all of our living experiences, including the birth of our babies—has always been of major importance in our lives.

Donn wrote about our earliest experiences with our children in *The Home School Source Book*:

> [Our main reason for having home-birth was that we loved our children (yes, even before they were born), and we wanted them to have the best start in life. We began teaching them at home for the same reason.
>
> In education, as with birth, it was the narrow-mindedness and insensitivity of the "experts" and "trained professionals" which led us to

realize that we could probably do much better without their help.

When Jean and I began our "experiment" in homeschooling, part of our purpose was to determine what things and conditions are most useful, if not essential, in learning. What are the "necessaries" of teaching at home —not just the physical materials, such as books, and pencils, but the methods, the attitudes, and the objectives? What knowledge is really useful or essential in life, and what are the best ways of obtaining or imparting it? Most people who are not homeschooling, whether or not they approve of it, assume that its goals are similar to those of public schooling—to prepare young people for jobs or careers or further education, to make a living, and to be relatively good citizens of the society in which they live. Many homeschoolers agree with those goals, but believe that education at home will provide a better foundation than the public schools can. We . . . want to reach further, to aim higher. Money-earning skills are certainly useful and perhaps even necessary; but there are other skills of far greater importance. This is, and will continue to be a period of rapid and radical change—in society, in government, and in the ecology of our planet. We have the duty, as parents and educators, to help our children prepare to meet those changes creatively and responsibly; to help them develop skills and attitudes with which they can make positive contributions to the world. The ability to evaluate, to make responsible judgments, to resolve conflicts peacefully, and to give helpful counsel to others will be of much more worth to our children and to the world than business management, welding, or engineering. Of equal importance, we want our children to be happy now, as children. Childhood is important in itself; it shouldn't be spent only in preparation for adulthood.]

When the children were all young, they nursed when they were hungry, slept when they were tired, and it always seemed natural to center our adult lives around our children's needs. Because Donn frequently was able to work at home, at least part-time, we were lucky enough to share most days together. Raising our kids was something we shared equally. We never had much money, but we were extremely rich in our living and in spirit.

Our first two children, Cathy (now thirty-three) and Karen (now thirty-one) were born in northern Vermont. Susan (twenty-nine) and Derek (twenty-seven) were born in British Columbia, Canada, where we moved in 1969. Looking back, I can see the seeds of our homeschooling practices and philosophy developed from all these early influences. Donn and I have always been voracious readers—for information and entertainment. As soon as the kids were old enough to enjoy books we spent time looking at the picture books and reading

---

stories to them. Sometimes Donn made up stories and sometimes illustrated them for the kids. Sometimes the kids made up stories, we would write them down (when it was requested), and the kids would draw pictures to go with them.

When Cathy was about four, she started learning the alphabet and a few words. We remembered the *Calvert School* and purchased their kindergarten course. We used it in a manner consistent with an unschooling approach, although we'd never heard of it at that time. Whenever Cathy was interested, we used the *Calvert* materials, otherwise we ignored it. Cathy frequently requested the spelling of words so she could write, and she began reading on her own before reaching school age. Karen, two years younger, became interested in the process of reading and writing because Cathy was. We bought her a six-inch by eight-inch spiral notebook that she filled with writing—it wasn't anything we could read—but she could read it back to us. We never told her the marks she was making on the paper weren't letters. Sometimes she would ask for the spelling of a word and we would write it out for her, but for the most part, she completely filled that notebook and several others, and somewhere during that time incorporated more traditional letters, spelling, and taught herself to read.

For all our nonconformity, when Cathy reached school age, we sent her off to school without much thought. It wasn't long before we *did* begin thinking about it. Cathy became progressively unpleasant upon returning home from school, which none of us liked. She stopped reading on her own and stopped looking at even her favorite books at home. We talked with Cathy. Was anything bothering her? Did she like the bus ride? Did she like the kids in her class? What about the kids in the school? Did she like her teacher? She liked it all. We talked with her teacher. Her teacher could see no trouble spots. We were all baffled. By Christmas vacation, it was an almost unbearable situation for all of us at home. During vacation, Cathy's behavior modified, and the house became harmonious again. After two days back in school after Christmas vacation, it was intolerable again, and we decided that we would take her out of school, even if we couldn't pinpoint the problem. We never did figure it out. It took about six months for Cathy to begin to read to herself again.

A year later we moved to New Brunswick, Canada. Cathy entered the second grade of a two-room school with grades one through six. She had no problems "catching up" with the other kids and no problems with getting along with us at home. It was a very quiet year.

A year after that, we returned to British Columbia, and Cathy entered the third grade and Karen the first grade. Karen's teacher was all one could ever want in a teacher. Karen flourished that year and the year after. Cathy's teacher was a screaming bully, and although Cathy wasn't the object of this behavior, she wasn't learning either. We took her out and began our real homeschooling journey. Donn was confident that I could do "anything." I wasn't, so we compromised by using the *Calvert School* third grade course. That one year with the Calvert School, which we enjoyed very much, was just enough of a confidence-booster for me so that we never bought another packaged curriculum or study unit again.

For the next couple of years we had all the kids home. Susan began to acquire number skills and began to read. Derek benefited from all the fairly structured school time I spent with the girls. I say fairly structured because we discovered that if we waited until everyone was "ready," we just didn't get around to some of the things all of us wanted to learn. We chose 9:00 a.m. as the time to meet at the kitchen table with various learning materials. Sometimes the kids brought what they wanted, and I always had something for each to do if they hadn't chosen anything. We always included lots of individual reading time for everyone, and I always had a book to read aloud.

Are you wondering how I juggled four kids with an age spread of about eight years—some able to work on their own, and others not? Some days felt like a circus with everyone needing attention at the same time. I'd get frazzled and call a "time out" and let everyone go outside to play, go to another room to play or read—anything, but ask me another question! Most days actually went pretty smoothly. I helped anyone in need, and Cathy could always help Karen, who could help Susan. Derek came and went as he pleased. Although I made an effort to have everyone spend some time with math, writing skills, history, and such, I always allowed any special interest to be followed. For instance, Cathy studied dinosaurs until she knew more that we did. Mythology was another favorite subject and many days I would read while everyone drew pictures to go with the story, or just listened. We found that about three to four hours of semi-structured learning exploration was enough to satisfy all of us, and the afternoons were spent in play (inside and out), craft projects, reading, helping with the cooking, music, or visiting. We did a lot of singing together because I played folk guitar, and the kids loved to sing along.

This was a very good period for us. We had money for books and craft supplies. All the kids were learning steadily at their own pace. I wasn't worried about meeting standards, and best of all, the school authorities didn't seem to care what we were doing. No letters or threats. This was also one of the few times we lived within a community. All the kids had friends and spent time with them at our house or at the neighbor's. Learning to play together within and outside of the family happened without effort. There were overnight slumber parties, birthday parties, and picnics.

We moved again about the time that Cathy went into seventh grade, and she decided she wanted to go to school so she could make new friends. This caused a lot of discussion between Donn and me, and between the two of us and Cathy. We finally decided that she could go if that was what she desired. Our only condition was that she had to be committed to completing the year, unless there was a compelling reason not to do so. Although it never came up. I know we would have welcomed her home if she had changed her mind. As it was, she had a fantastic teacher, and she had a very productive year.

The following year, Cathy had the same teacher and Karen decided she wanted to go to school in town too. It became an epidemic! Donn and I were not pleased with this, but felt the kids were entitled to make this decision. Susan wanted to go too. Derek was too young, and I was glad of that. I think I would have found it hard to be childless for so much of the day. I really enjoyed just being with the kids.

For the next couple of years the girls went in and out of the public school system. Derek tried it for two days and quit. He said the teacher was nice, but the kids wouldn't be quiet so he could hear her, and he said that some of the kids were nice one minute and weren't the next. He'd apparently satisfied his curiosity and that was enough.

It was just as well he felt that way because his learning went at a completely different pace than that of the girls. All the girls could all read to some degree before they entered school. Derek couldn't. It wasn't that he didn't want to, but he just couldn't "get it." Over the next three years, we struggled with learning to read. It wasn't a struggle in that we were trying to "make" him read when he didn't want to. He *wanted* to read. He really, *really* wanted very much to read. He loved books and would always stop whatever he was doing if anyone would read to him. Although he couldn't read them, books fascinated him. He'd make up stories and ask me to write them down for him. We made books out of his stories. He loved this. He'd memorize his easy readers that I read to him, and then he'd pretend to read them, but he couldn't recognize the same words out of the context of the book. We tried every trick in the book we could think of to help him. We knew he wasn't stupid. We checked to make sure he didn't need glasses. It was just taking longer for that magic "whatever it is in brain development" that makes this complicated decoding of the written word to develop in him. My biggest challenge during this period was keeping him from getting discouraged.

I haven't mentioned any of the books now available about cognitive development and learning. We didn't have any. The closest books we had for support at that time were John Holt's books *How Children Learn* and *How Children Fail.*

I shudder to think what would have happened to Derek if he'd been in public school during this time. He wouldn't have been able to do the work. He'd have felt like a failure, and it would have marked this otherwise bright happy child for the rest of his life. The magic happened to Derek at about what would have been the end of third grade if he'd been in public school. Decoding the written word suddenly made sense. He could read! So he read, and he read—everything he could get his hands on. Within a couple of years, he became a natural speed-reader with very high comprehension (something I really envy) and was reading on a high school level.

Susan's stint in public school didn't last very long. She developed a lisp when she lost her front teeth, and it remained for a while when her new teeth came in. Her teacher made her so self-conscious by constantly correcting her, by asking her to repeat a word properly, by making fun of her in front of the class, that she almost stopped speaking, even at home where we never corrected her. If asked a question, she'd cover her mouth and mumble. It didn't take very long at home before her confidence and speech came back. Unfortunately, the phonetic spelling she had learned in school took a lot longer to overcome!

Although the older girls spent a couple of junior high school years in public school, we felt they could have been learning a lot more at home, with much more time to devote to artistic activities and music. The girls felt the work to be easy, but time-consuming, picky, and sometimes petty busy work. They liked having friends but disliked the social pressures. It was all fodder for a lot of talk and discussion. They learned some lessons never intended by the schools.

At this point, we uprooted the family again and moved back to New Brunswick to 100 acres and a homesteading lifestyle. All the kids had school at home now, and it included gardening, preserving food, preparing meals, hauling wood, house building, and barn chores. Everyone helped with whatever needed to be done. During the four years it took us to build our "big house (two stories—24' x 42'), we lived in a 16'x16' foot cabin with a small addition just big enough for Donn and I to have a double bed. That's a very small space for six people, a couple of dogs, and a collection of cats. There was no real privacy for anyone, and we all learned valuable, if sometimes very difficult, lessons about conflict resolution. Our kids had disagreements just like all other kids do. There is so much strife, conflict, and war in the world that we wanted the kids to learn how to settle differences. We knew we couldn't solve the world's problems, but we felt that helping the kids learn how to resolve differences would be a good place to start. Instead of dictating solutions, we would sit and talk about a problem. Our aim was to help the kids learn to separate unpleasant or inappropriate behavior from the person doing it. Put simply—not to throw the baby out with the bath water. We felt that learning to compromise, to see another's point of view, and to look for ways to avoid future conflict was more important to us than assigning blame or fault. This was even more important than algebra or any of the standard school courses. Some days, this type of discussion took up a lot of time, and I think the kids weren't sure then whether Donn was a teacher or a preacher!

Eight years ago Donn wrote:

[Having concluded before we started teaching at home that the loosely-structured approach is definitely best, we were sometimes dismayed to find that it wasn't working, and it's hard to find an instruction manual for something that isn't supposed to have instructions. Until the kids were about six or seven, they were certainly eager to learn anything and everything around them. After that, sometimes they were eager to learn, and sometimes they'd go out to lunch for two or three weeks. We watched and waited, and told each other that they'd soon get tired of old Donald Duck comics or television and would return to doing something productive. Maybe they just needed a break. Usually, they did tire of their early retirement, and began reading, thinking, drawing, and making things, and asking us twenty questions a minute about anything at all, but occasionally it looked as if they'd settled down for a long winter's nap.

"Hey, look, kids," we'd say, "we're having school at home. That means you're supposed to be learning something."

"Okay, Dad. What do you want us to learn?"

"What causes gravity? What makes the Aurora Borealis light up? Why was Mona Lisa smiling? What does x represent if five times x to the fourth power equals eighteen? How do you drive a nail without mashing your thumb? How can you collect a dozen eggs in the barn and deliver twelve eggs to the house? How high is up? Things like that."

"Dad, have you read this story about when Donald Duck and his nephews went to Yellowstone park and . . . ."

"Okay, then, where is Yellowstone Park?"

"You mean there really is a Yellowstone Park?"

"That's all, folks. Back to the drawing board. Notebooks, pens, pencils, eager minds, and smiling faces. Nine o'clock tomorrow morning. All drinks of water, toilet trips, and forgotten books to be remembered before then."

"Really? Okay, Dad! We were wondering if you were going to help us learn any more, or if you were too busy."

And so our unschool would become a home school again, and we'd have fairly regular hours, and lots of discussions, and real Assignments For Tomorrow, and after a while we'd try the unschooling again.

The unschooling approach, when it worked, was an incredible experience for all of us. Cathy really studied dinosaurs far beyond her grade level all because of her own interest. Karen did a lot of creative drawing. She researched art history and techniques on her own. She learned far more than we could have taught her. Susan had some of her poetry published. Derek studied sharks with such a passion that we had to go beyond the local library and the provincial library to the *National Library of Canada,* as well as enlist the help for friends and family to satisfy his curiosity—and he learned about a lot more than sharks. His study of sharks incorporated geography, marine biology, underwater photography, history, and the shark's relationship to all the other creatures in the oceans. Derek could identify a shark by seeing the shape of its teeth. We never could, or would have, put together a study unit of this depth.]

At heart, Donn and I wanted to leave the style of learning up to the kids—what is now called "unschooling." Maybe we just didn't have enough patience to let the kids develop more self-sufficient learning patterns. Maybe the time the girls spent in the public schools was too strong an influence. Whatever we may have wanted, it didn't seem to work for our kids all the time. This disparity between what we wanted and what sometimes did and didn't work plagued us all through our homeschooling years. Donn wrote, " . . . If you leave kids alone, and let them study when they want to, they'll educate themselves. It worked for Mowgli and Tarzan, and sometimes it has worked for us. Other times we've wondered why so few of the great educators have children of their own . . . . Sometimes all four (of the kids) scurried through the day, learning and creating and discussing ideas, sometimes one or two would sort of fade out and need a little jiggle, and sometimes all of them would just run down."

We spent a lot of time trying to understand just what John Holt meant by "invited learning." Donn wrote:

[Does "invited learning" mean we shouldn't occasionally try to lead them into areas of which they aren't yet aware, and therefore can't invite us to help them in? Does "invited learning" mean the same kind of choppy, incomplete, fragmented learning that's going on in the public schools?

We never really figured out exactly what "invited learning" did mean, but we decided we couldn't always wait to be invited. Sometimes we just crashed the party and amazed ourselves with the structure and organization we could devise. "Let's hope John Holt never sees this," we'd say to each other. "He'll stop selling our books." But the kids became so interested in Alexander the Great or the Renaissance or Martin Luther and the papal bulls that they forgot all about Donald Duck. They learned psychology and economics and world history and geography and where Yellowstone National Park is. They even began inviting us to introduce more subjects, or help them with the ones they were on, and then we began feeling safe again. We always felt a little like renegades when we taught something without having been invited to do so.

When we were having unschool, the kids mostly set their own schedules. When we were having home-school, it often went, more or less, something like this day, recorded long ago:

6:45 a.m.—Jean and Donn get up with the alarm, feed fires, dress, etc. Feed dog, then let her out. Two cats in, growling at each other. Jean wakes Derek. Donn cleans and sharpens chain saw on ping-pong table.

7:30 a.m.—Jean wakes Cathy or Karen or Susan, who take turns daily setting the table, getting breakfast, and tending fires. Jean and Derek go to the barn, feed and water the pig, cow, calf, and twenty-five hens; clean the gutter; milk the cow; collect eggs. Donn puts fuel in chain saw, then goes out to cut firewood. The one on breakfast duty calls the others, who are usually already awake and reading in bed.

8:15 a.m.—Breakfast: Hot cereal, whole wheat toast from home-made bread, home-made butter and apple jelly, honey, fresh milk, fresh eggs, peanut butter. Coffee for Donn and Jean.

9:00 a.m.—Jean and two girls clear the table, do dishes, and put away. One girl sweeps house, straightens odds and ends. Girls rotate these chores daily. Every fourth day, Derek sweeps, Donn goes out to split firewood.

9:30 a.m.—Derek and Susan or Cathy and Karen bring water, one dipping buckets into the brook (six feet from the corner of the house) and passing them in, the other carrying them to the kitchen and filling the fifty-gallon can, stove reservoir, and large kettle on the stove. In warm weather, the pipes aren't frozen and this chore is eliminated by a gravity water system.

9:45 a.m.—Official school time, morning session, at the kitchen table. Donn leading (or being led). (Jean listens, comments, sews, mends, plans meals, does laundry, plans her afternoon school work, tends fires, bakes bread, etc.) Discussion of daily offering of *Word-A-Day* calendar ("saprogenic") and *Quote-A-Day* calendar ("A sharp tongue is the only edged tool that grows keener with constant use,"—Washington Irving.) We pull the legs and wings off the words, examining roots, derivations, associations, usages, sometimes using the dictionary. We discuss the quotation and its author: Do you agree? Why or why not? What is his most-famous story? Does anyone know when he lived?

10:00 a.m.—(this and other times given in Official School Time are approximate; we have no schedule) — Word play, dictionary and encyclopedia assignments. Cathy: Tass Tacit, taciturn, apocrypha, and anachronism. Karen: cosmos, cosmic, wax, wane, flat, flatulent.

Susan: awesome, awful, offal, neapolitan, obese, obeisance. Derek: auk, gross, grosbeak, eject, elect. Words for tomorrow: faker, fakir, guild, gild, microcosm, macrocosm, zenith, nadir, anathema, spike, bolt, sally, dally. Each student gives definitions, uses the words in sentences; others take notes, discuss uses and usefulness, often making puns and other bad jokes.

10:30 a.m.—Yesterday's Detective Assignment, for encyclopedia and general bookshelf research. True or false? Support your answers. Cathy: The Lutheran Church was founded by Martin Luther King, Jr. Karen: George Fox was an American Indian. Susan: Betsy Ross was a famous opera singer. Derek: "Doctor Livingstone, I presume?" was said by Sherlock Holmes. Students discuss and take notes on each other's research.

10:45 a.m.—Research assignment, to be worked on individually or together, your choice. Problem: A man lost in the woods can find no food except rabbits, which are plentiful and easy to snare. He has all he wants of rabbit meat, yet a few weeks later is found dead of starvation. Why? (Students had to consult several cooking and nutrition books before finding even a hint, and then had to brainstorm their findings to arrive at the answer.)

10:50 a.m.—Poetry: Read aloud the selection you found and practiced yesterday. Cathy: Ogden Nash. Karen: Carl Sandburg. Susan: Edna St. Vincent Millay. Derek: Robert Louis Stevenson. Tomorrow bring one of your own choosing; practice reading aloud beforehand.

11:15 a.m.—Writing assignment: Discussion of more articles for our family newsletter, who will write what. To be done on your own time and submitted for discussion and refinement tomorrow.

11:20 a.m.—Self-image: Design and draw a button or T-shirt that would express The Real You.

11:40 a.m.—Discussion of ethics. How can we know what is "right"? Do values change as society wants them to, or is there a constant right-and-wrong for all people and all times? How can we know? What is "conscience"?

12:00 noon—Donn reads excerpts from biographies, to be discussed.

12:30 p.m.—Research assignment for tomorrow: Find and read the story of the Prodigal Son. What does "prodigal" mean? What does "gospel" mean? Which are the "synoptic" gospels, and why?

12:35 p.m.—Discussion: Where do we get the common expression, "I wash my hands of it"? What does it mean? From last night's readings, what are some of the similarities in Christianity and Buddhism?

Cathy (33), Karen (31), Susan (29), Derek (27)

12:50 p.m.—History simulation. Karen, you are a prosecuting attorney at the Nuremberg Trials; your position is that anyone who contributed in any way to the persecution and murder of Jews should be punished very severely. Cathy, you are Franz Gruber; you were seventeen years old, a railroad guard sixty miles from Auschwitz; you knew that Jews were in the train cars, but you had your orders; besides, you had been taught that Jews were a threat to your country. Susan and Derek, you are judges; you listen to each side as the defendant and the prosecutor argue their cases, then decide if Franz Gruber is guilty of "crimes against humanity," and, if so, what the sentence should be. Explain your decisions. (The students ad lib, with no attempt at drama or entertainment.)

1:30 p.m.—Lunch: sandwiches, milk, carrot sticks, etc. Free reading, ping-pong, walks outside.

2:15 p.m.—Official School Time, afternoon session, Jean leading. (Donn works on business orders and correspondence, or writing.) First aid, instruction and practice. Music, theory and practice; guitar, flute, clarinet, recorder; impromptu drums, and singing. Nutrition and health. Work on individual electives, and help when wanted or needed. Cathy: Spanish, typing, history, literature, counseling, and geography. Karen: French, typing, psychology. Susan: math history, spelling civics, French. Derek: math, handwriting, history, typing, art, Spanish, spelling.

3:30 p.m.—Official Time is over. The kids often continue working by themselves on their own electives or on morning assignments. Some go skiing or hiking. All four bring in firewood. The two that didn't haul water in the morning do so now. Reading, ping-pong. Visiting friends. Begin supper, sharing and rotating jobs.

6:00 p.m.—Donn goes to the barn for evening chores: milk cow, feed animals, etc.

6:30 p.m.—Supper. Many evenings with a dramatized history or story tape to listen to and then discuss.

7:15 p.m.—Supper clean-up shared and rotated. Baking cookies, cakes, pies, sometimes television. Reading books and magazines. The girls sew, knit, tat, and crochet. Derek builds models of planes and spaceships. The girls have each made several articles of clothing. Letter writing, churning butter, square dancing (in town), skating, *4-H* meetings, and board games. Popcorn; maybe ice cream. Donn works in his office. Jean reads or plays guitar.

10:30 p.m.—bedtime. Cats out. Fires fed and shut down. All lights out. Good night!]

As the kids reached high school age, we wanted them to have more experiences out in the community. We wanted them to experience working for and with other people. We felt that these experiences would help them form their own ideas about the kind of work they did and did not enjoy. Because all the jobs they were capable of doing at that time were relatively menial we felt it would inspire them to work toward higher goals if they found bagging groceries etc. wasn't the way they wanted to spend the rest of their lives. Among the various jobs they held were convenience store clerk, helper in a second-hand bookstore, helper in a sporting goods store, helper in the library, stable hand. Some of the kids also traveled in the summer and took jobs as camp counselors. Cathy liked working in the library and was hired as a part-time helper after a few months. A few years later, when she was ready to leave home to live on her own in town, she was able to use her library experience to get a full-time job at the library and support herself. She used this experience later in her life in other places, too. Derek started in the sporting goods store and was soon bored. He had wanted a horse since the time he was two years old and discovered there was a riding stable just down the road. Donn got him a job cleaning stalls and helping with other chores for two dollars. He was then able to trade his wages for lessons. This was the beginning of what he now does for a living—but I'm getting ahead of myself.

To follow us up to this point in time, it will be easier to track one child at a time.

Cathy wanted to graduate from high school with all the normal credits. She decided she would like to try correspondence classes along with what we did at home. The courses turned out to be easy and not involved enough to satisfy her. She used the correspondence courses for a few months to complete the courses she had wanted and was glad to get back to our way of learning. The courses had been easy and not involved enough to satisfy her. When the time came for Cathy's graduation, we created a ceremony and invited the community to join us for it, with a pot luck supper afterwards. The newspaper sent a reporter, and they ran a very nice story with a picture. After graduation, Cathy moved into town (about fifteen miles away) and supported herself working full-time at the library. During her high school years she had spent the summers in Vermont as a camp counselor. On her days off, she stayed with Donn's mother in a nearby town. She liked it there, and after working for a while in the library near home, she applied for a job at the library in Vermont. She was hired and moved into her own apartment. After a couple of years she wanted to see more of the country, she applied for and was accepted by a company in Virginia that raised money for volunteer fire departments and emergency services. She was there for a couple of years and then decided she would like to see the West Coast. We suggested she visit friends of ours. Little did any of us know this would result into something major! Cathy and our friends got along well and Cathy decided to stay in the area and find a job. She drove a school bus and worked in the school offices. On weekends she tended bar and waited on tables in a small local café. It was there she met Michael, who quickly became the light of her life. She moved down to Sacramento to be with him and took temp jobs in various offices. Cathy and Michael were married in Scotland a couple of years ago. Michael works in the computer industry. Their first baby, Jacob, was born last March. Will they homeschool? I couldn't say for certain, but I think it's a possibility.

Karen was in a hurry to leave home. She wanted to attend the local high school but we didn't think it was a good idea for several reasons. We felt we could give her a better education at home—one more fitting for a very ambitious learner. We didn't like the all-too-common tales of drinking in the school. This particular area didn't, and still doesn't, have many activities for high school kids, and too many of them drink as the only social activity outside the pool hall. Karen's greatest ambition was to go to New York City and study art. We told her she needed to finish high school before we would help her. Along with working with us during the normal school days, she proceeded to work her way through *High School Subjects Self Taught*. She did every course in the book — all twenty-eight courses—within two years, even though there were many we didn't feel she needed to do. We arranged for her to stay with relatives and attend art school. This worked for a short time, then Karen came home. A few months later my mother and her husband (my step-father), both professors, invited Karen to stay with them and attend the University of Florida at Tallahassee, providing she got descent SAT scores. We were somewhat concerned about the SAT, but Karen wasn't. She took the SAT, scored in the 90th percentile (without cracking a book for over a year), and moved to Florida. She attended classes (making the Dean's list) for a year, then moved to Vermont. She went to work first, for a newspaper working in the public relations department, got bored, and found a job with a high tech optical company. They started her as receptionist, and when she wasn't busy, she explored the computers which fascinated her and expanded her skills. She then moved to the outskirts of Boston and ran the accounting department for a small company and met her future husband, Gary. After getting married, she attended the University of Boston for advanced computer training and then took a job teaching software design for Clark University on a part time basis. She is now an independent software designer and has worked with several large firms. She and Gary have two wonderful daughters. Will they homeschool? No. Karen loves her work and is able to work at home a couple days a week, and so for her, she has the best of two worlds.

Susan attended a boarding school for her last two years of high school that looked very good at first, but wasn't. Donn and I were not satisfied with the academics at the school, but Susan felt she had made some good friends, learned valuable social skills, and learned enough to earn her diploma. When Susan graduated, she applied for, and was accepted into college in Arizona. She was interested in pursuing a career in outdoor education. She had been on two *Outward Bound* trips, one in Maine and the other in Texas while in high school, and she loved the experience. The college disappointed her. She found it next to impossible to get the courses she wanted. She dropped out and worked a variety of jobs. She began to study *Intrinsic Breathwork* as a means of learning about herself and went on to qualify to lead workshops and do individual counseling. She took a job at a nearby rehabilitation center for abused and delinquent youth. A few years later she moved east and worked for another residential rehabilitation center outside New York City and became interested in psychology and decided to go back to college before going back to Arizona. She now works part-time at the rehabilitation center, does individual *Intrinsic Brathwork* counseling, and is part of the adult degree program at a nearby college, and is on the honors list with a 4.0 average.

Derek loved his job at the stable in town and was lucky enough to work under a very talented trainer who recognized that Derek had a gift for working with horses. He encouraged and taught Derek many invaluable lessons about riding, stable management, veterinary medicine, and much more. Derek soaked it all up like a thirsty sponge and received far more than his two dollars an hour wage. Derek started riding Western and winning ribbons in local classes. Then he decided that riding over fences looked like a lot of fun, so he began riding English. His time at the stable increased, and sometimes he was left in charge of everything over weekends and sometimes longer. Then this stable closed due to personal problems, and Derek's friend, mentor, and coach moved to Alberta. Derek found another stable to work in and was soon teaching beginning riders and training some of the horses.

At this point, all our girls moved to the States, and we decided to move to Vermont to be closer to them. I took a job in town, while Derek and Donn built a small house for us. In the fall, we encouraged Derek, at sixteen, to take at least a semester at the local high school so he could make some friends. He declined and continued to work with Donn on his school work and took a part-time job in town. Since that time, he has worked in stables in Vermont, Québec, North Carolina, Florida, and Nebraska—each time learning what he could and expanding his knowledge and talents. In North Carolina, he finally met someone who understood and shared his passion for horses and could live with his self-imposed working schedule—usually from about 6:00 a.m. to about 9:00 p.m. in the barn. Derek and Stephie now work as a team. When not training, Derek competes over fences that are higher than I stand. He works hard and loves living his long-time dream.

Was our homeschooling all we wanted it to be? It wasn't all easy. Looking

---

Cathy (33), Karen (31), Susan (29), Derek (27)

back, there are things we would handle differently. Homeschooling didn't entirely keep the kids safe from alcohol or drugs, or some difficult life situations, but it did give the kids a strong basis for dealing with these problems. More than that, it created amazingly strong family bonds that will endure. When Donn died four years ago, I couldn't have survived without the love and support from the kids. In all, I can see that Donn and I learned at least as much from the kids as they did from us. I can see in the closeness of our kid's relationships with their partners, that they came away from home with the ability to love and be loved—to create their own strong families. They are people I'd be proud to know even if they weren't my children. Each of them is contributing to society in their own way. Each of them has been able to create a life that satisfies them.

Donn, Jean
Kathy, Karen, Susan, Derek

Andy, age 36
Jane, age 36
Amri, age 5

Interview with Jane at the end of summer on Vashon Island, Washington

LEARNING FITS OUR RHYTHMS

Amri turned five a month ago. She has an angel face, longish strawberry-blond hair, and very fair skin. Her name dates back to Andy's and my college years, when we played a role-playing game. While trying to pick out a name for a new character of mine, Andy and I opened a book and randomly poked at letters: A-M-R-I. Over the years, Andy named a computer system "Amri" and I chose it for the name of a character in a story I never got around to writing. Finally, it became the name of our daughter.

Amri is an only child, extremely verbal, and a girl who does things on her own time schedule. She started talking at one year, but finally crawled after she learned to walk at eighteen months (she scooted in the meantime). She'll only do something when she's ready and when it will be somewhat easy for her. Our job, we've come to realize, is to present her with opportunities, but also to give her the space to pursue new skills when she is ready and willing. We only make her miserable when we push.

Andy is a computer software engineer with a big company in San Jose, California. As a telecommuter, he travels to the San Francisco Bay Area for meetings, usually once every four to six weeks. Occasionally, he flies elsewhere in the country on business. When we lived in the Bay Area, Andy often had to commute an hour each way in traffic to his job. Although he feels much less connected with the day-to-day interactions of his coworkers (despite e-mail and frequent phone conferences), he is thoroughly enjoying telecommuting full-time.

I'm a part-time musician who performs and records as a Celtic harp duo, and I also own a small mail-order business. Basically, it's a business that takes as much or as little time as I can offer, and so is well-suited to the ebb and flow of activity in our lives. My duo partner and I practice together once a week and have performed a few local gigs. We are gradually working up material for an album we'll record with another harper next spring. Mostly though, I'm a full-time mom.

Six months ago, Andy, Amri, and I moved from the metropolitan San Francisco Bay Area to Vashon, a small rural island near Seattle, Washington. For years, Andy and I dreamed of living on a Pacific Northwest island. We longed to abandon the crowds, traffic congestion, noise, stressful pace, and consumerism that is so prevalent in our society. But both of our families live in the San Francisco Bay Area, and it was almost impossible for me to conceive of leaving them—especially since it is important to me that Amri be close to her grandparents, cousins, aunts, and uncles.

A conviction grew that I didn't want Amri to grow up in a place where she couldn't climb trees or play in creeks. I didn't like the fact that our "community" was not in our neighborhood, nor even in our city. We regularly drove from twenty to ninety minutes to visit friends and family. Though we worked to live at a more relaxed pace (homeschooling helped us here) and in a way that was somewhat gentle on the earth, it seemed that the entire thrust of our environment was bent on discouraging these goals. When we visited Vashon early this year, I looked at our dreams and realized that I was too young to stop taking chances. My sister and brother-in-law live in Seattle, so I was able to ease some of the anguish of moving away with the knowledge that now they could become more a part of Amri's life.

Andy was ready to move for years and already knew that he could telecommute full-time. The move provided everything we've dreamed: beautiful surroundings, a sense of peace, and the end to the frantic rushing around we experienced so frequently in the Bay Area. We especially enjoy the warmth and closeness of this community and the feeling of connectedness. It's also been a revelation living in a place where you can't take your resources for granted or operate under the assumption that waste disposal will take care of itself.

Our house is a two-story beige-colored farmhouse with a red roof. It is bordered to the south and west by fields and orchards and by five or so acres of forest extending to the north and east—all part of the property. The living room has big wood beams across the ceiling, a brick-and-slate fireplace, and tall windows. A bunch of Amri's toys push against the front wall below the tall windows. Livening the walls around other parts of the house are Amri's artwork and a few of my own experiments in painting and poetry writing, inspired by the spontaneous creativity that is characterized by young children. There is a wonderful wood-floored addition to the house. This room has a wood burning stove, floor-to-ceiling built-in bookshelves (completely filled with our books),

French doors, and a window-wrapped nook that I use as my music room. A crate of toys and art supplies resides in a corner.

The front of the house faces a lawn, an apple tree, a playhouse, the detached garage off to the side, a ramshackle barn, and our forest. The back of the house, where the addition is, looks out on our old orchard and down a hill, with a glimpse of Puget Sound. We love being able to view the changing tides.

We have a huge basement (lots of great storage) that has the small room that serves as Andy's office. This space works well to keep Andy free from distraction, though he's good at focusing on his work anyway. And, because Andy has telecommuted on and off since Amri was a baby, we're used to leaving him alone while he works.

Andy and Amri have a fun relationship, lots of teasing and rough-housing, and Andy certainly contributes to her homeschooling. *Legos, K'Nex*, the wooden train set, and the *Chaos* construction set are toys and projects that they tend to work on together. Andy also takes time to show Amri and explain things he does around the house or things that come up—like repairing toilets, wiring, building fires, playing on the computer. Andy and I agree on how to raise Amri, including discipline (usually quiet time when Amri gets out of control—a fairly rare occurrence). Amri does turn to me first for most things, and when she was younger, this meant that I didn't have a whole lot of energy left for others after being a mom. Andy was very supportive during those exhausting younger years.

Amri is old enough now that she no longer comes first for everything. If Andy and I are having a conversation, and she wants to tell us something, she needs to wait until a breaking point. Likewise, we try to accord this kind of respect to her. Our parent-child interactions still dominate the day, but more and more Andy and I are returning to the partner relationship we had before Amri was born.

Because I had relied on family for babysitting and my friends for advice, sympathetic ears, and playdates for Amri; when we moved to the island, we left the convenience of all that behind. Suddenly, I had no breaks, no afternoons for myself, and because of the disruption the move caused, I *needed* time for myself. Even more, I needed *not* to be Amri's primary and virtually (except when Andy wasn't working) only playmate. We visited the library story time every week, went to the park, and I offered a music playgroup at our house to encourage meeting friends. We met a homeschooler Amri's age. Still, making friends was slow going. Desperate for friends for Amri and time for me, I finally enrolled Amri in preschool.

Only three other children attended this home-based preschool. The small size of the class and the interest shown in encouraging the kids to work together, work out their differences, and treat each other respectfully, seemed a good thing for Amri. As an only child, she can't quite get this type of interaction at home!

The kids go on weekly walks to the beach, visit a local senior care center, go on field trips to meet people and visit places on the island, and the children help tend the school's garden. These activities, I felt, offered Amri the opportunity to begin connecting to our new community and the island.

We enrolled her at this preschool last spring, but with so many changes in her life, Amri was slow to warm up to this new environment. She was clearly thriving by the time summer arrived and was interacting with the kids much the same way she had with her cousins—something that did much to ease my fear that I had taken her away from a special dynamic that she could never get anywhere else!

This year, Amri will attend afternoon sessions, which will suit our routine better. She'll know three of the four children who will be in her class. I think the school will offer Amri some needed continuity as we continue to establish our new lives here.

Andy was the first to bring up homeschooling, back when Amri was eighteen months old, and we were realizing how much we disliked the idea of eventually sending her to school. At the time, I was only aware of the school-at-home stereotype of homeschooling and thought I'd have to give up my own life and interests to prepare lesson plans that we would grind through each day. But I truly enjoyed being with Amri, watching her discover the world, and helping her to explore it. The idea of being able to remain a primary part of her learning process excited me enough to seriously explore homeschooling.

I soon discovered that there were any number of ways to pursue homeschooling, and that the "unschooling" philosophy—that of allowing your child's interests to lead the learning process—resonated deeply within me. I knew from my own experiences that any subject tends to blossom forth and incorporate knowledge from numerous disciplines. This had been common experience for me since my own childhood. What a marvelous idea: to focus on what is meaningful and interesting to the child herself and allow those things to be the spring board to discovery and acquiring new skills. It is something we allow babies, very young children, and adults to do: why not the very age group our society is so bent on "educating"? To be able to witness not only Amri's process in learning to talk and walk, but also to read, work equations, and any number of skills academically, socially, and in the realm of her passions was something I realized I didn't have to miss and didn't want to. Amri may well be our only child so these opportunities to remain so intimately a part of our child's learning may never come again for us.

I feel that *whatever* type of learning activities we pursue must in the long run fit our rhythms, schedule, and ideals—rather than the other way around. This particular preschool works for us because I can sign Amri up for as many or as few afternoons as makes sense to us (right now three works well for both Amri and me, but eventually it may be just two). Also, the convictions of the preschool are consistent with my own: that the best way to pass on ideas or knowledge is when a child is interested and engaged; and that if children are in the midst of something exciting, they should be allowed to run with the activity and see where it leads, instead of being enslaved to an agenda. Each child is nurtured individually and encouraged, but not forced to try new things.

It's 6:30 a.m. I awake to Amri's voice down the hall in the master bedroom. I'm actually lying in her bed, the bottom bunk of a maple bunk bed. And she is on our bed, having padded in during the night and crawled in between Andy and me, sharing the middle with our cat Spook. It can be cozy, all of us (plus cat!) snuggling in bed together, but that actually works better when Amri comes in upon waking up in the morning. At night she tends to be a bit of a bed hog and threatens to squeeze me off the edge. I could (and probably should) take her by the hand and lead her back to her own bed, but I've been a bit under the weather this past week and had trouble sleeping, so last night it seemed like too much effort. Instead, as I resumed my own too-familiar night prowl, I decided fair was fair—she was sleeping in *my* bed, I'd try out *hers.*

It's a surprisingly cozy room. Built to be a playroom, it has no closet space, and is fairly cluttered with toys and books (and yes, a few clothes) spilling off the short upright bookshelves and dresser. But the hardwood floor is a warm color, with yellow and red bands, and the old window with its watery glass presents a lovely view of the tops of the fir forest. The light in the sky is pale peach and pearl. Sunrise! We'd talked about trying to wake up in time for sunrise someday and we'd actually done so today. It looks like it will be another clear late-summer day.

We're pretty casual about getting up most days. Amri will trot in at anytime from 7-9:00 a.m. (usually depending on how late she went to bed the night before). Since Andy telecommutes, he and I can take our time getting up. One or the other of us will make coffee, and we might chat or read for a bit, or get up and check our e-mail. Right now I hear Andy and Amri talking together. Then Amri pads in, grabs the book *Stinky Bugs* from her shelf and looks at it while we talk. We head back to my room. Andy is there, so silliness and teasing follow.

As Amri tucks some of her stuffed animals into our bed and sings to them, I lay out some possibilities for today: maybe we could check out a little wooded nook that I found on one corner of our property—a "secret garden." Since today is Wednesday, we'll go to the organic farm on the island where we are "subscribers" and pick up this week's bag of produce. But mostly we have an open-ended day before us. Amri doesn't have very many playmate friends yet on the island and the ones we have are away or busy today. It will be another two weeks before Amri's school resumes, adding more shape to our week.

Andy returns with some coffee for me and a snack for Amri (a cereal bar, glass of milk, some raisins, and an apple) on a breakfast tray. I'm thinking that this morning Amri will want to stay close to me. I'd spent the past week busy with rehearsals and two performances with a summer choir. Andy had been away on business, so I'd had to drag Amri to all of these things, and she'd had to endure my fretting and trips to the doctor when I feared I was getting sick. The best way to help her along is for me to be relaxed and nurturing, but not overly-concerned. Easier said than done, but occasionally I'm able to do this!

I resolve to be less distracted today and to "give the day to Amri." She can put up with a fair amount of me being focused on other activities and having little energy to spend much meaningful time with her, but eventually I need to put everything else aside and give her the time and attention she needs. This is one of those days. Things like filling out forms for reestablishing my mail-order business can wait.

As Amri eats her breakfast, I read aloud Roald Dahl's *James & The Giant Peach*. As we read, she asks questions and we discuss details of the story: Do grasshoppers really have ears on their sides? What does "rambunctious" mean? When I accidentally read the word "desert" as "dessert," I spell the words for her and we talk about why I misread it. Amri has me skip a section she finds scary, and we finish the book.

After that, we play with a cardboard farm we constructed from a kit. There are all kinds of farm animals and buildings. If I put my whole self into the make-believe play, it really works best. But, often Amri's attention span for this kind of play is much, much longer than mie. Today I resolve to stay attentive to the game. If I work to keep it interesting to me, then unexpected fun often results.

This farm game provides us with the opportunity to play with some of the concepts we've learned lately. Andy and I are planning to start an organic garden, so we've been doing a lot of reading and discussing. An exciting thing about our planning is that it is a passion that Andy and I share. We hope that Amri will want to be involved in the garden, and think she will, but first and foremost it is something Andy and I are working on together. Amri and I use plastic star beads as crops. We put the chickens out to eat insects. We discuss the roadside farm stand we may someday build in real life. And as we play, we discuss other things. I go horse riding once a week, and Amri likes to hear about what the horses do. I mention that one of them had been showing off, posing in a glamorous way. We then discuss the meaning of "glamorous." "Am I glamorous?" Amri asks. I laugh and say no, then search for a way I can explain this concept to her. I think of movie stars, but Amri doesn't watch much television or videos—certainly nothing where any of the characters are "glamorous." I do my best to explain, and maybe she understands.

We go back to playing. "That night there was magic . . . ." Amri says and sounds the bar chimes that perch near the window. She plucks my African harp and dramatically narrates how the pigs wandered to the mountain (a chair) and are out here on a windy night. I find myself mentally categorizing her play into academic subjects: drama, music, storytelling. Even though it will be several years before we'll need to keep a portfolio on our homeschooling, I find myself mentally evaluating things that we do. For instance, our discussion of grasshoppers and where and how they breathe would count as biology. When we discuss the horses' behavior, that usually could be considered psychology as well as animal sciences.

In Washington, you do not have to formally declare your intention to homeschool until your child is eight years old. Then you must either submit her to periodic testing or have her signed off by a teacher. Since I dislike standardized tests and question their value, we will probably pursue the latter route. A portfolio, in any case, would be useful in chronicling Amri's learning—as a yearbook for ourselves, if for no other reason. I'm sporadic about keeping records now, but occasionally I jot down the things we do in a day. I also keep samples of her artwork and take pictures of projects we do. In the future, I may save checkout tickets from the library to help keep a record of some of the books we read, and become more systematic about taking photos of events, projects, and outings as a means of charting her learning and activity.

Imaginative play is valuable for so many reasons. As we turn back to the farm we find ourselves discussing ideas, points-of-view, values. My pigs want to run free in the mountain. Amri's pig only wants to be in the farmyard and is anxious to bring the other pigs back to the farm. We explore compromise: if Amri's pig will go on an adventure with my pigs, my pigs will come back to the farm afterward. After a while, I give Amri a warning: five minutes more, then I'm going to take a bath and check my e-mail. This is a good time to get a couple of everyday things done. I get some laundry going, help Amri get dressed and ready for the day, take my bath. Amri plays on her own all this time, but now that I'm back, she wants me to immediately return to playing with her. I try talking for the pigs while I comb my hair, but Amri wants me to be on the floor with her, moving the pieces around—*really* playing. We're both frustrated. I'm resentful (again) that I'm her only playmate. This is no good now. I try to be honest with Amri in all things, which means being honest in my play with her. If I'm too tired or just can't get into the mood to play, I'll tell her so. She's usually pretty good about shifting gears when I'm up front with her about what I'm not willing or able to do. But I can't just play with Amri out of a sense of duty. And, of course, during moments like this, when I feel frustrated and a little desperate, I wonder about the future of our homeschooling. I cannot homeschool against a backdrop of duty and self-sacrifice on my part. It can only work if we can both be eager and fulfilled by our time together. I have to find our time as interesting and new as she does.

Amri (5)

A difficult part about Amri being an only child has been a clash of needs between herself and me. I'm happiest when I have chunks of time to myself—when I can work on music or writing. When I wake up or before I go to bed, I like having time to myself to read. Having these spaces to myself gives me energy and spirit. With Amri, it seems that the reverse is true. To truly be happy, she needs to interact with someone. Playing by herself or doing projects on her own seems to come much more easily to her after she's spent a good chunk of time with someone else—usually with me.

Mostly, I combat these clashes by trying to be realistic. I know that in order to minimize my frustrations, I need to write or work on music on a predictable basis. I actually don't need much time to accomplish a lot—when I recorded my solo album last spring, I spent an hour after dinner each day working on the piece or two that I was planning to record the following week, sup-plemented by fifteen minutes here and there during the day. This was enough time to get done what I needed and to feel good about life. Reaching for small blocks of time, rather than large ones, means that I'm more likely to accomplish what I set out to do and that Amri is more likely and more able to allow me to do it.

My other strategy is to give her the time she needs first. Then, I take time for myself a little later. When I'm frantic to get something done, I try and give her a good hour (sometimes it's as little as twenty minutes) before I move to my project. I might divide my project into chunks, devoting my full attention to her between the chunks and being sure to tell her that I'll be playing with her this long, then I'll work on such-and-such. When that task is done I'll play some more. Whenever possible, I try to include her in whatever needs to be done. If I'm frantically cleaning the house for guests, I'll have Amri help me scrub the bathrooms (something she enjoys). When I practice for a concert, she'll often turn the room into a concert hall: dimming the lights for the performance and tooting on a pennywhistle or singing while I play. I love it when she joins in with me and find that I can focus on what I need to accomplish, despite her participation. In fact, I often feel energized by it.

Actually, this is my philosophy regarding chores, too. I've discovered that I enjoy doing even my most loathsome chores (such as cleaning bathrooms or washing floors) when someone is working cheerfully alongside me. Amri may not always directly contribute a great deal to completing the task, but if she's scrubbing walls and cabinets and making up stories about what she's washing, then I'll happily scrub the toilets and bathtubs, and anything else I can think of. Amri doesn't have any particular chores and responsibilities yet, except to help take care of Silly, her hamster, which she usually does cheerfully enough. Often enough she asks to help with various tasks that Andy and I do, so that I don't feel a tremendous urgency to give her chores. I want her to keep feeling that helping is fun or satisfying. Sometimes, though, we do ask her to do something (usually to help clean up her toys) and she'll absolutely refuse. Even when I point out that we'll be helping—and that any job we do is so much more fun when she helps—she'll still refuse. Telling her that toys she doesn't pick up will be removed for three days doesn't seem to help much either. This is pretty frustrating, but I have to admire Amri for her strength of will!

The best thing I can do in these cases is to remind myself of Amri's successes. Occasionally, she does clean things up on her own. I also know that she helps clean up at the preschool. Sometimes, letting something go for the moment is a lot better than making a big deal about it, which just causes Amri to feel even more stubborn and defiant.

Turning the situation around so that both Amri and I can feel satisfied and interested is usually the best thing I can do in any number of circumstances. And as I sit here being frustrated about our farm-playing, that is what I resolve to do.

After a little thought, I decide to bring out the penguin set I bought at a book store close-out a month ago. Sure enough, this works for both of us. The kit comes with a book about polar life. We recognize penguins, orcas, leopard seals, and skua birds from a favorite book of poetry of Amri's, *Antarctic Antics*. We've met the Arctic fox before in one of our fox books, and we know the musk ox and polar bear from our trips to the *Tacoma Zoo*. In one of the pictures we see a hamster-like creature. We examine the picture key and see that it is a lemming.

We discuss lemmings and hamsters. Are they closely related? Lemmings have short tails like hamsters. Do lemmings gather food into cheek pouches as hamsters do? Where are hamsters found in the wild? We decide to check out a book about hamsters to find out, as Amri says, "if a hamster is a kind of lemming."

We look through some coloring books from Alaska and find more information about wolverines and musk ox. Amri notes that in one of the pictures one musk ox is wanting to charge the wolverine: its horns are curving downward, threatening. Somehow, we end up discussing why animals fight for mates and whether or not humans do. I ask Amri if she'd be interested in going to the zoo today. "Read on!" she says. We decide that we might go tomorrow. In the meantime, we continue reading the polar life book.

At 11:15 a.m. it's time for an early lunch. We decide to have a picnic on the bedroom floor. In the kitchen I heat up a frozen chimichanga, pour out salad greens from our subscription farm, and apples and blackberries from our field. Andy wanders up, wearing his phone headset and continues upstairs to say hi to Amri.

After lunch, Amri wants me to read *James and the Giant Peach* again, from where the peach starts rolling away. Andy emerges from his basement office for lunch. As he eats, he reads about food preservation. I go down to the basement to turn on the computer modem and remember to put the clothes in the dryer.

The dryer is already filled with dry clothes from a couple of days ago. Well, better a bunch of dry clothes lying around in the dryer than wet clothes in the washer!

Having Andy at home all day is marvelous. Basically, Amri and I treat Andy's presence as if he were away at work. We leave him alone when he's in the basement or on the phone. We don't often eat lunch together, but we do check in with each other when Andy comes up to make himself coffee or to see what we're up to. If Amri and I are having a bad time together, Andy coming up for a break will diffuse that tension, offer a sympathetic ear, or tease one or the other of us out of our bad mood. Back in California, when Andy went off to work, that was it—Amri and I were on our own until he came back at 6:30 p.m. or sometimes an hour later. Now, at least, even if he's "working late" and on an evening call, we've probably chatted with him sometime recently. We're all a part of each other's day.

The only disadvantage is that we have only one phone line, which is also used for our e-mail. I feel pretty constricted about making calls, much less calling friends and chatting with them. Because Andy is a full-time telecommuter, I want be sure that his colleagues can reach him when they need to.

Upstairs in my office, I check my e-mail. I don't have a good desk or a decent set of shelves, so this room is pretty cluttered with papers piled on top of the scanner, folders haphazardly organized in wooden crates, and my computer monitor and keyboard sitting atop a tablecloth-covered card table. Silly's hamster cage perches next to the printer, and Amri's plastic picnic table shares the space. The room also has a large walk-in closet (complete with a big window and a nice view of trees and the Sound) that has drawers full of toys for Amri and office supplies for me. While I take care of e-mail Amri plays at her table. Using beads in her little *Polly Pocket Village* she says, "This is a story about a cat food boat and a cat food river. It's an old river . . . . " Amri almost always narrates aloud as she plays.

I make arrangements for Amri's friend to come over tomorrow. That's settled! These days, when friends come over, it's like a gift. Amri and her friend will play for hours, cooperatively, creatively—only seeking me out when they're hungry. Even with listening for trouble or just keeping track of them, I can get all manner of work done while they play, and it certainly takes the burden of being Amri's only playmate away. I suspect that Amri has begun to discover that her friends are more satisfying for some kinds of extended make-believe play than I am.

In the *Polly Pocket Village*, marbles are now in the house, serving as "pigs." A metal bell puts the pigs to bed. Amri moves to the closet room, where some old jewelry of mine that I've given her lies scattered on the floor. We take out the white board and write a new menu for our "Seafoam Cafe"—sugar rose crumble cake and violet-mint pancakes. From the closet window, we watch crows soaring from all over to land in some bushes and a tall tree. "Listen to them chant," Amri says. "Maybe they're having a meeting." "Like a parliament of owls?" I ask, and try to remember what a group of crows is called. (I remember now: it's a "murder of crows").

Now, all the crows up and fly to the trees down the hill and across the road. As they fly back and forth, we wonder whether this happens very often. "They must be getting their exercise," Amri says.

Amri digs up her *Vikings Treasure Chest*. We look at a chart of Viking runes. Amri says what each rune is, looking at the Roman letter or letters underneath. One rune is for the "ng" sound. I say and spell some words that have this sound: king, ring, sing. "Like in 'single.'" Amri says.

Now Amri comes up with some letters and asks what they spell. "What's M-A-R? What's M-A-R-Z?" I sound out the words for her. Then I write some words in runes on the white board: king, sing, etc. So, just like that, we explored some phonics, spelling, and history, all in the natural course of our play.

Amri starts constructing a monster with some odds-and-ends we've given her. A telephone connector is the monster, some telephone wire is its teeth. Amri makes up a poem as she winds the 'teeth':

I use my teeth all tangled up,
I do not brush my teeth myself
oh, oh
I do love myself this way

All my teeth
all my teeth
all my teeth
come from my body

This creature is quite something. It has three "teeth" dangling from its head and a long tail that is a chain attached to the end of a telephone wire, with paper clips and a key ring at the very tip. The monster dangles and prances. And this inspires us to set up the jewelry box as the seats of a performance hall. The Viking pieces are arrayed on the box to watch the monster dance to the rhythm of *Jingle Bells*. At this point, I'm now in the role of an approving watcher rather than a participant, so I give myself permission to divide my time and hang up the clothes that are piled on the shelves here.

Eventually, though, I'm lured back to being a Viking. We look at a map from the kit and note that the black arrows designate trade routes. I (as Viking King) speak of trading in Byzantium and Baghdad, places where there are such things as camels, spices, and bazaars. "I haven't seen any camels," says Amri's monster. "Go to Arabia then," my Viking King answers. Amri dresses the monster and has it perform another piece. Andy appears. "My, that's a well-dressed connector!" he says of the monster.

It is mid-afternoon now and we have not yet been out of the house! I tell Amri we'll be heading out in a half hour. One of our stops will be at the farm. I mention that the farm's llama is a relative of the camel. Amri pulls out her butterfly puzzle, a rather difficult one that she was given when she was two. We haven't worked on this puzzle for at least half a year and it is fascinating to watch her work it. She systematically lays out the pieces that show the stages of caterpillar growth.

"What are you doing?" Amri asks.

"I'm thinking about how you first did this puzzle."

We talk then about her change of approach over the years of working puzzles, how I used to lay two pieces next to each other so that she could easily see where they connected, and how she didn't really think to look at the patterns on the pieces for a long time when choosing ones to piece together. I realized again that it is perfectly okay to leave things (projects, work on various topics, or skills) aside and go back to them later. Amazing leaps take place during the between times.

Our discussion of changing approaches to doing puzzles leads to a discussion of what Amri was like as a toddler. "Did I help you make food?" Amri asks. I start to say no, then remember when she helped me make pancakes in the kitchen. When she tossed flour onto the floor, we moved our preparations outside. Toss away!

Amri wants me to help her with the puzzle. Part of me disapproves and feels that she should do as much as possible on her own. I'm not sure why, although I suspect this is a holdout from my school experiences, where I was expected to work on my own, with only a few hints and explanations from a guiding adult if I was stuck. I have to remind myself of something I've realized over the past few years—that there is great value in working side-by-side on a project. We can learn from each other and we can share the experience.

This is definitely one of our " go-with-the-flow" days. I've come to recognize that these can be some of the most fulfilling days we have. It's hard for me to shed agendas, "must-dos" and "we shoulds," but when I'm able to, I find our time full of surprises, interesting conversations, and learning in the most unusual of guises. They end up being times I could never have planned out in a lesson book. We finish the puzzle get ready to go to the farm.

As we drive there, I note that although it is the beginning of September, autumn has already snuck in. Maple trees have begun to turn colors and the slant of the light has changed, becoming more golden, less up front and in our face. At the farm, we go to see the llama in the front orchard. "Flash" walks toward us then turns his back to us. "Cluck, cluck, cluck," he says. We run alongside the fence and he joins the run on the other side, easily passing us.

On our way to the farm stand, we notice that the corn is now quite high. We pull out our produce bag from the cooler. Amri runs out into the sunshine and I choose two tomatoes (a half pound's worth) and leave money in the money box. Then, downtown, I buy this week's edition of the island newspaper.

"Why do you always buy it?" Amri asks.

"To find out what's going on, what people are doing and thinking around here."

We talk about why that is important to me.

At home, Amri has a snack of trail mix and milk, while I put the farm vegetables away and unload the dishwasher. With the bag of produce is a sheet describing what's happened at the farm during the past week. I read the sheet to Amri, who doesn't respond. But that's okay. She may be absorbing these details or ignoring them. Someday, it may be something we talk about. Amri checks out the huge garlic clove from the farm, then goes off to play in the living room. I glance through the newspaper and then start cooking lasagna. The recipe on the farm sheet is for rhubarb-blackberry cobbler. Amri and I will make that this week, I decide.

Amri, meanwhile, returns to the kitchen and has a snack of grated cheese, which she rolls into a ball and calls "kneading dough." Andy has finished his workday. We chat, then he and Amri roughhouse. Andy settles into reading more of *Growing Fruits and Vegetables Organically*, and Amri follows me upstairs. While I catch up on e-mail, she settles into looking at a *Busytown* book. Soon the lasagna is ready. Amri is still busy with her book and says she isn't hungry. Although we almost always have dinner together, I let her off the hook for joining us tonight, but she soon comes down on her own.

After dinner, Andy and I go to put out the garbage. Garbage night is no longer the trivial affair it was when we were living in the suburbs. This chore now involves hauling our garbage can and recycling bins in a wheelbarrow up our winding driveway to the road, sometimes in pitch dark since there are no street lights. I enjoy these walks though. When I take the garbage out on my own I don't use a flashlight and just make my way up the drive by the feel of the gravel and by memory.

We return and I help Amri get ready for bed. Somehow we get into a discussion about her needing to sleep in her own bed. It's fine for her to sleep with us sometimes, but not always. She's upset by that—she wants to be with me. I go downstairs, weary. I should have just started leading her back to bed if she came in and not have made an issue about it. Well, what's done is done.

Downstairs, Andy is starting a fire in the wood burning stove, as it's rather chilly tonight. We talk about Amri and Andy suggests we take turns leading her back to bed.

Amri (5)

Amri comes down with a motion clock she got for her birthday. We all sit by the fire and watch the last bit of light leave the sky. We talk about telling time and counting by fives. As Amri takes the clock apart and puts it back together, we both recover our spirits. Andy is now reading his bible of organic farming, *The New Organic Grower*, by Eliot Coleman.

Amri asks what time it is. 8:50 p.m. "Then it's late," she says, "probably time for me to go to bed."

First, we visit Silly and put him in his hamster ball so he can run around the upstairs. We decide to move his cage back into Amri's room. Amri asks again, "Why should I sleep here? I should cuddle with you and Daddy."

"We're going back to how it was: you sleep in your own bed and I'll stay with you for a bit." (Andy and I need to have space for ourselves!)

Then we read *Diffendoofer Day*. We also read *A House Is A House For Me*. "A cage is a house for Silly," Amri says, joining into the spirit of the book. "A shell is a house for a seed."

Andy calls out that he's just organized my web site bookmarks. I find him looking at a web site for an organic farm supply business. I return to Amri, lie down with her, and she is soon asleep. I talk with Andy, then read and think about going to bed early. I think, too, about the things I'll do tomorrow while Amri's friend is here: clean the house for an upcoming visit, do paperwork, and send e-mail to some family and friends. But then I discover that our cat has thrown up big time in our bedroom. With loud groans, Andy and I clean up the mess. I'm on a roll now and proceed to clean the kitchen and vacuum our room. Finally, I settle down to read and to sleep.

For an unscheduled week day, this one was quite typical. My ideal week is one where we have at least one of these go-with-the-flow days, and where most mornings unfold on their own. I do find that we are all much happier when we have a few things scheduled during the week: a class or our part-time school, friends that Amri can play with, a trip to the museum, beach, or the zoo. The trick is to find a balance between our time exploring or just being together, time with friends, time in activities. For me, I've come to realize that I need not be afraid that, as an only child, Amri will be devoid of contact with other children if she homeschools. There will likely be plenty of opportunities for rich relationships and activity. Also, it is fairly easy to include her in whatever activities come our way. I often bring Amri to my music practices, and Andy and I have taken her with us to scientific talks, concerts, dinners, gallery openings, and other events that are typically considered grown-up activities. I like it that she can see adults working hard at something they love to do, and that she can meet so many people in a variety of contexts. When homeschoolers talk about how homeschooling allows their children to be part of the world, part of the community, I agree—and think how especially easy this is with one child.

Homeschooling an only child can definitely be difficult, especially when our needs and personalities conflict. The trick is to face the challenges and have the courage to work through them, using these times as opportunity for growth for all of us. When homeschooling, it's crucial to keep in mind the bigger picture—that life is a process, and that we are always learning and growing. Over the years, I've learned that when I'm tense about some aspect of Amri's behavior, I only intensify it. If I'm more relaxed, Amri is less stressed as well, and there is less of an issue. Usually when I'm tense, my reactions are focused more on a "what will other people think?" mentality, complicated by my own need to have a little space. When Amri is doing well, I don't think much about how she and other children her age compare, but I do compare her with others (and I know I shouldn't!).

But I don't find I compare myself with other moms. I guess I must be pretty confident that we're homeschooling in the way that's best for us. When we have times of frustration, I sometimes wonder whether we should be more authoritarian, or whether we really should consider sending Amri to school. But those thoughts are immediately jarring—they don't feel right for us. Then, I'm able to move ahead and think about the positive aspects of our situation—how what we're doing is benefiting all three of us and how rich our lives are because of the approaches we're taking.

Homeschooling gives us the opportunity to allow Amri to achieve skills at her own pace. We can look at her journey and realize that she is progressing quite nicely, and we can be awed by the process. I find enormous satisfaction and excitement in being able to witness her growth and in being such an important part of it. Being part of Amri's journey stretches my creativity and my own perceptions of life, challenging me to live more mindfully, joyously, and flexibly, and to act with conviction, care, and spirit.

Amri, Andy, Jane

Eric, 34
Leslie, 33
Jessica, 8
Landon, 6
Adrienne, 3
Marissa, 8 months

Interview with Leslie after a hot, dry summer in Hershey, Pennsylvania

THOSE HAPHAZARD DAYS

The smell of chocolate floats through the air in the surroundings of Hershey, Pennsylvania, where our family lives right on the edge of town. People here are middle-aged and have very busy lives. Everyone is usually quite friendly, but no one goes out of his way to get to know anyone else. It's a good location because we have a cornfield behind our home, and the library is only a fifteen minute walk away.

My husband Eric has owned a lawn care/landscaping business for almost thirteen years, and he coaches soccer, which helps us to get to know the people in our community better.

My name is Leslie (or Mom) and I homeschool, run the bookkeeping end of Eric's business, and try to keep my household organized. A friend and I are starting a Mom's support group that meets once a month. There were twenty-four ladies at the first meeting. Homeschooling seems to be something that more and more parents are doing, and I find that I don't get many strange looks anymore about homeschooling.

We have four children. Our oldest is Jessica. She's eight (soon to be nine) and is very interested in art and writing, and very *not* interested in being outside or anything that takes a lot of physical energy. She's tried several team sports over the past few years. This fall she's decided not to play a sport, but she will get involved in our local *4-H* instead. That suits me just fine, as team sports really make for a crazy evening schedule. She's also very responsible and helpful, especially with taking care of the younger children.

Landon is six and doing first grade work. He's a typical boy who loves trucks, sports, playing outside, getting really dirty, and making a lot of noise! We're really focusing on reading right now and it can be frustrating. I don't want to push him, yet I do want to keep working at it because he's doing pretty well. He likes math, and he loves for me to read to him from *Ranger Rick* nature magazine. He will try anything for a few minutes, but grows bored quickly. This fall he will play soccer with the local recreation league, which Eric coaches, so this is a nice family activity for us all.

Adrienne is three (she'll be four in only two weeks). She and Landon are good friends and spend hours outside in the sandbox or playing with trucks. She loves to do "school," so I ordered the *Brighter Vision Learning Adventures* series for her. It includes a nice hardback book, a workbook, a craft, a poster, and a game or puzzle centered around a specific theme. She really enjoys it. That is our whole preschool "curriculum," although we also have quite a few games, puzzles, and manipulatives that she frequently gets out during school time.

Marissa is our eight-month-old baby, and she has added a whole new dimension to homeschooling. We love her dearly and thank the Lord for her. She's a bright and happy little girl. The older children absolutely adore her and she adores them, too. Although she causes some disruption to our schedule, she's well worth it!

When I first mentioned homeschooling, Eric was very hesitant, but he allowed me to try it for Jessica's first year of kindergarten. We chose to homeschool primarily due to the immoral and godless teachings of the public school system and the many disrespectful and unkind classmates. I just didn't want to see my little girl go off into the cruel world of school (Christian or public) where children are teased unmercifully if they are different, and where they find out about sex and drugs long before it's necessary. I enjoyed Jessica's company and wanted to be with her, and since I am fairly creative and organized, it actually sounded like lots of fun to me!

As we have moved along in our homeschooling, I have come to realize many of its benefits. I truly enjoy the amount of time I get to spend with my children. I also appreciate that they can stay up late enough to enjoy precious time with their dad when he gets home late. Since we are not tied to the school's schedule, we recently bought a camper and can go on short trips when we have the chance. It is important that the wonder of learning be present for our children. As I look into my past, I realize that my enjoyment of learning was squashed by uncaring teachers and rote assignments. I hope this won't happen to my children.

I've found some disadvantages to homeschooling, though. I do sometimes feel very overwhelmed by having *no* time without children talking, asking,

---

Jessica (8), Landon (6), Adrienne (3), Marissa (8 mo.)

cajoling, shouting, hopping up and down, arguing—well, you get the picture. This is especially difficult since Eric usually arrives home in the late evening during his busy season. This means very long days for me. Since homeschooling and "The Business" are my main two priorities, there just isn't a whole lot of time left in my life to do things I'd like. I do try to stay involved at church, but even that has had to suffer. However, I really believe I am where God wants me to be, and ministering in the way He wants at this time of my life. If I didn't believe that, I would be discouraged much more often than I am.

Last winter I was feeling overwhelmed with homeschooling, the business, the new baby, and was about ready to give up. Eric expressed his disappointment and his wish that I keep going with homeschooling. He had become as much a proponent for homeschooling as I was. He was there just when I needed him. I am fortunate to have a very supportive, very *pro* homeschooling best friend who also provides me with much encouragement. I think most homeschooling parents feel overwhelmed on a regular basis and that God has many ways of lifting us up.

Eric (the ultimate handyman) has made our home into a real haven. It is a nice three bedroom rancher. The front door opens into the school room. It's really meant to be a living room, which we would love to have, but I just couldn't stand to have a room with no true purpose when we needed a school room. So, we moved our old table there, along with some shelves and cabinets. They are right beside our "good" furniture and our piano. When we got a second computer (for family use), it went into that room, which has become our all-purpose room. I actually love having a sofa in the school room because it's so much fun to all sit together to read books and magazines.

The kitchen is behind the living/school room and the bedrooms branch off to the right. We have a family room that we added on that's behind the kitchen. In the family room, my husband built a huge closet, so along with lots of toys and games, I store my school things there that I'm not currently using. I have the books broken down by subject—science, history, crafts, etc. I also have two stackable drawers full of craft items—pipe cleaners, felt, watercolor paints, etc. We have another box full of craft items in the school room. I used to be very picky about when the kids used these items. It would have to be for some special project I was overseeing. Last year I realized that they would get used much more often if the kids could use them when they wanted to. So, although there are times when there are things on the floor and no order to my box and drawers, I still do not regret that decision.

I also keep the children's portfolios in the family room closet. I keep a portfolio of their work even when they're in preschool. It's a nice "memory" book for them. I also have a cabinet in the family room full of fiction books. I'm very picky about what my kids read, and I want them to be books with good moral characters that are not disrespectful or unkind to their family members.

My sister-in-law used to be an elementary school teacher and had developed quite a large library of children's books, so she gave us a big tub of them to borrow until her eighteen-month-old will need them. The big tub also sits in our school room, along with the playpen. We are definitely out of room in the school room.

We start our school year in July, which helps me to take a break in March when I need to be getting the business up and running for the new season. We usually take off a week or two in March. It also gives us some extra days off to use for sick days and for holidays, without worrying that we won't get our 180 days in. We like taking a break in May and June when the weather's nicer. The kids really don't mind starting in July. In fact, they're usually ready to get back to it, especially when we have some new books and items to use.

I started out five years ago as a very structured "school" at home kind of person. However, the longer we homeschool, the more I relax. We still stick to "curriculums" for language arts and math, but I'm much more flexible with science and social studies. This year, we will all read *A Beka's* fourth grade science together. Next year, I don't think we'll buy any science curriculum. We are trying *Beautiful Feet* this year for social studies. It's a unit on American history, and the kids are really enjoying it so far. It uses "real" books, rather than dry textbooks. Plus, it's something they can all use together. I also purchase the *God's World* newspaper for the children, so that they can follow current events. Jessica is also using *A Beka Language, Spectrum Spelling*, which I really like, and *Saxon Math.* Landon (first grade) is using *Sing, Spell, Read, and Write* (sort of), *Explode the Code, Teach Your Child to Read in 100 Easy Lessons, Italic Handwriting,* and various easy readers *(Bob Books, Christian Liberty Press* reader, etc.) and *Horizon Math* (which I really love).

I have a ton of stuff around (probably too much) for homeschooling. Lots of reference books, field guides, kids books on lots of topics, kids' cookbooks, craft books, *Cuisenaire Rods*, pattern blocks, flash cards, various *Discovery Toys* and *Lauri* toys, lots of puzzles and learning games, maps and charts, CD-ROMS, etc.

I've purchased a piece of glass for our good dining room table, under which I've put a map of the world and a map of the United States. It has been a wonderful way to familiarize our children with geography. We've used it to follow current events, show where a missionary family resides, and to chart Grandpa and Grandma's trip out west.

So, here we are with another year started. Eric does not do a lot of the hands-on work with the kids, although there have been times when he has pitched in with a math lesson when I just couldn't get a concept across to a child. We have the benefit of having Daddy around a lot in the winter. He does need to work in his shop doing equipment and truck repairs. He also does snow removal, but his schedule is much more flexible. He has even taken over school if I have some pressing matter to attend to, and he goes on some of our winter field trips with us. Not only is Eric my best friend, he is my best support. We normally spend an hour or two talking after the kids are in bed at night.

I have several good friends who homeschool, and I can relate to them when the kids are irritable or I've had an especially hectic day. I have someone come in every other week to clean the house. I used to feel incredibly guilty about this. Now I realize that homeschooling and running our business are really a full-time job for me. On the weeks that the house doesn't get cleaned, we all work together on Thursday to clean. The kids are learning to do the actual deep cleaning. It works out great because whatever they "miss" on the week they clean, I know will be caught by our cleaning lady the next week.

We need to schedule my "office" time. Last year, I worked on Wednesday mornings, while Grandma watched the children. (Both my parents and Eric's parents live nearby. They are quite involved in our children's lives, and we have a lot of support from them.) By the time I'd finish my office work, I didn't have the energy for school. So this year, we're going to try something different and have Grandma come in the afternoon. Soon, Jessica will be old enough to babysit when I need a few uninterrupted hours in the office. To keep on top of things in the business, I really need about four uninterrupted hours on Wednesday afternoon (when Grandma can help) and three or four hours on Saturday morning (or some afternoon, whenever I can fit it in). Since Eric works almost every Saturday, Jessica gets a lot of practice babysitting.

Last year, we were involved in a field trip group, a co-op group (which did a study of our state), Jessica took piano lessons, and both Jessica and Landon were involved in fall and spring sports. The co-op meets twice a month on Thursday mornings. It starts at 9:30 a.m. and goes until "whenever"—usually, somewhere between noon and 12:30 p.m. The original group has been meeting since Jessica started kindergarten, so it's been five years now. The members have changed over the years, although three of the five families are still "originals." We keep it to only four or five families and have found that to work very well.

This year, I decided to cut way back. Landon will play fall soccer, Jessica will continue with piano lessons, and we will continue with our co-op. We have dropped out of the field trip group. It's just too much. This year in our co-op we are doing music, arts and crafts, art and music appreciation, physical education, and cooking. We're all excited about it because these are the things it's so hard to make time for at home.

August 23

It's 7:20 a.m. and I've pushed the snooze button three times and realize it's now time to get up if I want to get a decent start to my day. Eric kissed me goodbye a little after 7:00 a.m. but I just couldn't get myself up. We had an especially busy weekend, and I think, "just a few more minutes." I usually try to get up by 7:00 a.m., but more often than not, it goes a bit (or a lot) past that. Anyway, I hop into the shower and then get dressed. I then take a few minutes to start out my day with the Lord. I'm currently reading through the Bible and I'm at *Judges.* I also spend a few minutes praying about my day and for my family. I love when I can start out my day like this, although there are (many) days that my prayer time is in the shower. As I'm finishing my chapter in *Judges*, Landon wakes up and comes over to my bed, asking me what we're doing today. Landon always wants to know what's on the agenda. I tell him to wait until I'm finished with my devotions. Normally, the kids will sleep until 8:00 a.m. or so, when I go wake them up with whatever made-up song that comes into my head that morning.

Landon gets tired of laying on the bed waiting for me, so he goes and wakes his sisters. Right now, Landon and Adrienne share a room, and Jessica is supposed to be sharing a room with Marissa. Marissa has been waking so often through the night, that Jessica has been sleeping in the bottom bunk with Adrienne for the past month or so. Marissa started sleeping through the night by six weeks, but in the last two months, she's been up every night two or three times—sometimes until the early morning hours. It's very frustrating. She was up twice again last night, so it's good Jessica didn't sleep in her room. The bedrooms are fairly small and we only have three of them. If we had to do it over, we would have had the three older children share, at least until Marissa is older.

By now Adrienne is awake, and she and Landon wonder what we'll do for the day. Eric has mentioned going to *Hersheypark* (it's a very nice amusement park located in "Chocolatetown, USA") this evening, as we have free tickets and can get in for a few hours the evening before going for the full day. So we talk about that a few minutes.

I tell the kids to get dressed, while I throw a load of laundry in the washer. By this time, the baby's awake, so I change her and get her dressed. The kids are dressed by now, so we all head to the kitchen to eat left-over pancakes from yesterday. One of our favorite family traditions is our Sunday chocolate chip pancake breakfast that Eric makes with one of the kids each week. They take turns. They love it and so do I!

After I'm done eating, I feed the baby. After she's done, I grab a handful of cold cereal and put it on her high chair tray to keep her busy for a few minutes. I then go over the kids' chores for the day. I have a chart I made up that lists each child's name with a place I can tack on different chores for the day. These chores are in addition to the "regular" chores of making beds, brushing teeth, cleaning up their own rooms, etc. Jessica has jobs such as cleaning the bathroom counter, folding laundry, and cleaning up the living/school room. Landon has jobs such as cleaning out the car, emptying the trash, and sweeping the kitchen floor. Adrienne is supposed to "help" Landon. This morning he complains a little about Adrienne helping him, because she can be somewhat of a hindrance. He asks if she can help Jessica instead, but for this morning, I keep Adrienne with him, promising him that later on this week we'll switch it around. Sometimes it takes them a long time to finish their chores, and, yes, they fuss and resist—so much depends on my attitude and motivation for that day. It feels like if I'm not constantly on top of them, chores don't get done properly. Sometimes I'm just too tired, and I let them get away with things I shouldn't. Usually, chores take them about fifteen minutes to a half hour for the younger kids, and a half hour to forty-five minutes for Jessica. I've tried lots of nifty things (charts and incentives) over the years, but what it usually comes down to is that they do them because they're part of this family and that's just how it is. I try to teach each chore to the child, go over with them how it needs to be done, and I usually give more responsibility to the oldest and respectively on down the line. I go over their jobs each morning before we get started.

Before the kids start on their chores, though, we head to our school room and sit down on the sofa for our Bible time. I put Marissa in the playpen to play for a while. Sometimes she's quiet and plays with her toys. More often than not, though, we need to take her out because she's crying and frustrated that she can't be roaming. I don't like to give in to her, but we can't get much done with a screaming baby in the same room. So, she will often wander. I put a gate up so that she can't get out of our school/living room. I've tried to really child-proof the living room so that she can wander around and not get into too much trouble. We take the time to go over many of the Bible verses (we use the *Memlok* system) we have been learning. I'm very pleased at how well they remember their verses. We are also doing Gregg Harris' *21 Rules of This House* right now, so we also go over Rule #5 "We speak quietly and respectfully with one another. Each of the kids comes up with a short story to demonstrate the rule in either a positive or negative way. Adrienne's story sounds quite a bit like her brother's, so I wink at him, while he sighs and huffs and puffs that she's taking all his ideas!

The kids then color a page with today's rule on it. My kids love to color and this is a highlight for them. As they color, I get out a chapter book (*Scout*) that we started weeks ago. I have a very difficult time reading to the kids regularly. I love it and so do they, but it just seems there's always something else to do, especially in the summer. Anyway, we do a quick review about what happened the last time we read, and then they color as I proceed to read another chapter.

Today the kids are anxious to know about *Hersheypark*, so I call Eric to find out what he thinks about going tonight. He says that we can go if it works out. Jessica normally has piano lessons on Monday nights, so we will need to cancel it if we do go.

Then, I set Landon up with his *Sing, Spell, Read and Write* book and tell him to write a list of about twenty words. I can't give him much more than that or he gets frustrated. Sometimes I handle his frustration well, and sometimes I don't handle it well at all. I find that if I don't show my frustration, though, it goes much better. If he's trying to figure out a word and I know that he should know it, I find it goes much better if I just sit back and say something like, "I'm not in any hurry, so we'll just sit here until you figure it out," (in a kind tone) than if I get frustrated and yell at him, "You should know this!" A lot of this hinges on whether I'm in a hurry or not. It's amazing how fast he gets it when he knows he's going to have to sit there until he gets it right!

I then head back downstairs to check on the laundry. I hang this load out on the line. (I'm not real faithful about this, but if it's beautiful out, I just can't resist). Then, we go into our normal schedule about an hour later than normal. What we just started this summer is that while I teach Landon, Jessica does her chores. Then, when I work with Jessica, Landon does his chores. Adrienne does puzzles and various games and activities that I have saved just for school time, but I can sometimes work with her in a workbook while Jessica is doing her work.

Before we go any further, I put Marissa down for a nap. We are now ready to start Landon's reading lesson. We are using *Teach Your Child to Read in 100 Easy Lessons*. I love this book! This is what we used to teach Jessica when she got stuck in the process of first learning to read. I went through about half of it with her but I'm going to finish it with Landon. He starts out with slumped shoulders , but also starts off reading the words with a bang, which is always a relief, since he gets frustrated very easily. I breathe easy until we get to the story and he struggles and struggles. I think a lot of it is carelessness and attitude, but we make it through and he's proud of himself once he's finished.

Once we're done with the reading lesson, I set him up with his handwriting (the *Italic Handwriting* series) and then phone information and find out that we can get in *Hersheypark* at 7:30 p.m. with their "twilight preview" deal. I call Eric to let him know, and he says, yes, we'll go for a few hours. I call Jessica's piano teacher and ask her if it's any problem for her if we cancel at the last minute, and she says no. I ask her about twenty times (not really) to make sure. She doesn't seem to mind, so I tell her we'll see her next week.

I then go on the Internet to check out *Nick Jr.* for the kids. I've been meaning to do this for months, and I don't know what drives me to do it today, except that Adrienne was looking for something new to do. I print out a couple of coloring pages for her (and for Landon and Jessica as well). Adrienne starts coloring. Jessica says she's done with her chores, so she starts coloring. I then realize that she might as well get started on school work if she's done with her chores, so I get her started on her *Spectrum Spelling*. I really like this series and she does, too. Somewhere in there, I also do another load of laundry.

Landon and I sing "The Clusters" song from *Sing, Spell, Read, and Write*, and he colors the corresponding pages in his workbook. As we sing, Adrienne comes to join us. She likes the catchy tunes.

About this time, Eric stops in for his lunch. I try to make it for him in the morning, so that he has it when he leaves, but today he tells me it will be convenient for him to pick it up before lunch. He stops in and says "Hi." We chat for a few moments, and then he's off to work again.

After Eric leaves, I do a simplified version of Landon's math lesson. We're using *Horizon Math*, but it's just too easy for Landon at this point and I hope it gets more challenging for him soon. Anyway, as soon as he's done with that, he heads off to do his chores, with Adrienne trailing behind him.

Jessica and I discuss her spelling a bit, and then she goes onto her *A Beka Language*. When I look at the clock, I see that it is almost 11:30 a.m. already. I usually like to have her do her math in the morning, and we normally do science or social studies in the afternoon. I can see today that it's just not going to happen. I need to go grocery shopping, so we decide to eat an early lunch and let Jessica do her math when we get back from shopping.

The kids eat lunch in front of *BusyTown*. I used to feel guilty about letting my kids watch television while they ate, but I realized that this is one of the few breaks I get in the day, so I do it anyway! Marissa wakes up from her morning nap. I give her some formula and then put her in her highchair for her lunch. Jessica feeds her baby food, while I clean up the kitchen sink and stack dishes in the dishwasher. My good friend calls while I am doing dishes and we chat for a few moments. As I hang up the phone, I think what good timing grocery shopping will be, since Marissa just woke from a nap. Normally, she is horrible in the grocery store, but I have high hopes for today! While I finish doing dishes and hanging out another load of laundry, Jessica finishes feeding Marissa and then gives her some more cereal. I wash her bottles and wipe off the table and counters. I take Marissa out of her highchair and let her crawl a bit. I tell the kids to get ready for grocery shopping. They put their shoes on, and I brush Adrienne's hair, put a barrette in Jessica's hair, and change the baby's diaper. Sometimes I forget to brush someone's hair or wash a face, which is why I keep a brush in my purse and wet wipes in my car *and* my purse at *all* times!

We finally get out the door and I'm tired. I never seem to remember how hard it is to get four kids out the door, just for a simple shopping trip. But we did it, and now we're on our way. Landon sees a local limestone quarry and we talk about it. I don't know much about it so I mention that it would be a good thing to look into. Whether I will or not is another story! As we pull into the parking lot of the store, the kids see a fast food restaurant, and Landon asks if we can eat

---

supper there. Since it is only 1:45 p.m., I tell him that we can't.

We get Marissa in the shopping cart and walk into the store. The first aisle is uneventful but by the second aisle, Marissa has started to fuss. I try to be patient and loving, but I'm a little edgy as I have a *really* long list today. By aisle three, she is screaming at the top of her lungs so I give her a plastic ketchup bottle to play with. This keeps her happy for a few minutes then she's back to screaming. By the last aisle, I am almost in frustrated tears, but I am hanging in there, snapping at the kids occasionally. The children do listen, for the most part, so it takes only one or two reminders. I must admit they behave very well today. Usually, I try to leave Marissa home with Eric in the evenings. It will be much easier this winter when it gets dark earlier and Eric's home earlier.

I am so thankful when we get out of there. I had such high hopes of getting home and doing some more schooling together, but I decide that what we all need is a very long quiet time.

I turn on the radio to something soothing, which happens to be a classical station. I don't listen to classical radio that often, although we will often have classical CDs on while we do school work. At any rate, we have a really fun time trying to pick out the different instruments in the orchestra and using our imaginations about the music. What does it make us think of? What culture? Or people? I'm almost drawn out of my grumpy mood (but not quite!)

Once we arrive home, we all work together to bring in the groceries. Jessica first takes Marissa back to her bed for her nap. As I put the groceries away, the kids each have a snack and some juice. Next, I get Jessica started on making the chicken for supper. She's my "Cook's Helper" this week and so starts mixing the ingredients for the marinade. We have a "Cook's Helper" every week, with the children taking turns. Jessica finishes the marinade and the kids head to quiet time. Jessica takes her math along with her. She's using *Saxon 54* and can do most of these beginning lessons by herself. In fact, there's so much review that we skip some of the lessons, or I have her do just half the homework problems. Landon reads a few easy books to Adrienne. I love when he does this because it's such good practice for him. Adrienne loves it, too. After about fifteen minutes, Landon heads up to his bed and they both fall asleep for awhile. I normally don't let them sleep, but since we're going out this evening, I make an exception. I grab a snack and a nice large glass of tea and sit down to read for a while.

After an unusual couple of hours to myself, I realize that I'd better start supper and get the laundry in. Usually, we have a mandatory half hour to an hour quiet time. I find that it is necessary for me and my sanity. This is the time I take to read. I love to read a variety of fiction, non-fiction, and magazines. I'm hoping this will eventually rub off on my kids, although my eight-year-old still isn't real thrilled about reading, and I have to "strongly suggest" that she read for awhile.

Anyway, I put the chicken on the grill and then start taking down the laundry. Meanwhile, Jessica takes the whites from the dryer, wakes Landon and Adrienne, and then they all start folding the laundry. While I'm in the middle of the laundry and the chicken, Marissa wakes and wants her bottle. I take a few minutes to feed it to her while the chicken gets a bit burned on one side! While I'm feeding her, I hear the children arguing while doing the laundry. They're excited about going to *Hersheypark*, so I'm a little bit more lenient than I normally would be. I call Jessica out to hold Marissa's bottle while I check the chicken.

Now the children are laughing and being silly and basically being how children are when they are excited to go somewhere! The next thing I know, the kids have gone down to the basement to play. I don't think much about it until I think about the laundry and wonder if it's done. I go to my room and see laundry scattered all over my bed—nowhere near to being complete! I am very frustrated by this and promptly call the kids to tell them we will not go out before the laundry is finished.

Eric is home by this time, and we all wash our hands and sit down to a nice family supper, although it is a bit more hurried than usual. After I'm through eating, I feed the baby. Meanwhile, the kids empty the dishwasher and then go finish folding the laundry. I need to check into something on the computer for one of our employees, while Eric showers.

Finally, at 7:15 p.m. we head to *Hersheypark*. We have a nice time there and arrive back home at 10:45 p.m. Jessica insists on a shower, and while Eric oversees the kids and bedtime, I finish feeding Marissa her bottle and tuck her in for the night. By now, it is after 11:00 p.m. and I am tired. We watch the evening news at least until the weather's over. It's quite necessary to watch the weather if you live with a landscaper. After a few minutes into the news, Landon comes out and says he can't sleep. I thought this might be a problem, since he had such a long nap, but I thought our busy evening would more than make up for it. I guess I was wrong. He joins us for a few minutes, and then I ask Landon if he wants to lay down with me in our bed, while Daddy unwinds in the family room. He grabs a few library books, and we head back to my bedroom to read for a few minutes. It happens occasionally that one of the kids can't sleep, and I really treasure this time. It's one-on-one time where I get to read and talk with that particular child. It doesn't happen very often, maybe a few times each month, and it's not always the same child. It can be any one of them. At any rate, it's a very special time for us.

When Eric comes to bed, I send Landon to bed. Usually, the children are in bed by 9:00 p.m., and Eric and I will talk for a couple of hours, until we go to bed at about 11:00 p.m. Sometimes we'll talk most of that time, and sometimes we'll do our own things. It really depends on what has happened that day. I find myself often wanting to be alone at this time, so it is a bit of a struggle to make time for us. We usually want to share our days with each other, so we'll talk at least for a half hour.

At first, I would have thought that the kids would go to school in ninth grade, but both Eric and I are gradually opening up our hearts and minds to homeschool through high school, though we do take a year at a time—you just never know what life will throw at you. Happily, we have lots of support from friends and family, but I do have several friends who think I'm crazy (they don't say it, I can just tell), and it does mean that we have less in common than I do with my homeschooling friends, but it hasn't ruined the friendships at all.

I went to public school for twelve years; Eric went to a combination of public and Christian schools, and we both graduated from a Christian college. I am really a firm believer that any form of schooling can work if parents are doing what needs to be done at home (providing a secure and stable home life, being involved in their children's education and providing clear boundaries).

I had a good friend that started homeschooling her children the year before I did, and she really helped me get my feet off the ground. It's amazing how much kids learn on their own and how naturally a lot of it comes. I wish I had known not to pressure myself so much at the beginning.

I think homeschooling can be hard on a marriage, if you're not careful. Mom is so wiped out from giving all of her time to the kids that it takes real effort to make sure Dad gets his fair share of attention. (I'm speaking from experience here!) But, that's something to be careful about no matter what Mom puts her efforts towards. I think being at home together is absolutely *wonderful* for family life. I can already see positive differences in my children and in my relationship with them.

When we're in a restaurant and an older couple comments on how well-behaved our kids are, or I have a good friend who tells me that she loves to have my children over because they are such good children, I feel very positive that we're doing something right. When one of the kids lies, has a bad attitude that lasts for awhile, or is constantly bickering, then I question what I need to be doing differently, such as being able to handle things without getting so irritable and grumpy at times. I would like to learn to speak more kindly *all* of the time and not just when I *feel* like it. I would like to develop more discipline in planning the school days, rather than throwing them haphazardly together (not always, but often). I try to pray for my children most days and give them to the Lord. When it comes right down to it—they are gifts from the Lord to Eric and me and they each have their own wills. Our job as parents is to do the best with what God has given us and trust Him to make up for our weaknesses. That's all we can do.

Eric's and my biggest goal in life is to raise kids who love the Lord with their

---

Jessica (8), Landon (6), Adrienne (3), Marissa (8 mo.)

whole hearts, souls and minds. We want them to serve Him in whatever capacity He desires of them. Most of all, we want to stay in the Lord's Will for our lives.

Adreinne, Jessica, Marissa, Landon

Jessica (8), Landon (6), Adrienne (3), Marissa (8 mo.)

David, age 48
Mary, age 40
Dan, age 19
Elizabeth, age 17
Michael, age 13
Rachel, age 11
Matthew, age 6
Emily, age 3
(and now baby Katherine)

Interview with Mary on a warm fall day out in the country in Iowa

NO NEED TO PUSH

It's going to be another beautiful sunny September day with temperatures over 70° F. Emily comes to our bed at 6:00 a.m., and I pull her in between David and me, where she quickly falls back asleep. Matthew comes to our room at 6:30 a.m., raring to go! I reluctantly get up, and we go downstairs. Normally, David will get up with Matthew while I stay in bed another half hour or so, but today I have a lot to do, and I know how much more I can get done if I start early. Matthew is our early riser, and he wakes up very energetic, unlike me! I have to force myself to greet him enthusiastically, when I'd much rather be grumbling and complaining.

First thing, I put the teakettle on and mix up a large batch of bran muffin dough that can be refrigerated and used throughout the week. Then I head down to the basement to start a load of laundry. Meanwhile, Matthew has turned on the television to watch his favorite show *Arthur*. I am not happy with the amount of television Matthew watches, but it is mostly educational television, and I do remember that each of our other children went through a phase around the same age, when they wanted to watch two to three hours of television during the day.

By 7:15 a.m., David is up and enjoying the tea and homemade muffins. We are lucky to have fifteen minutes to talk before Matthew's show is over, and he wants to be read to. David heads to the couch with a stack of library books and starts reading. Soon he is joined by Emily who comes downstairs. Sometimes she wakes up needing a good cuddle for fifteen minutes, usually from Mommy, which makes it hard for everyone if I've left the house early for my biweekly breakfast and writing session. Every two weeks or so I'll head to a local restaurant for breakfast and lots of coffee, and I'll write for almost two hours straight. I really look forward to these sessions and find myself writing frantically as soon as I am seated, trying to catch up with all the thoughts that have been bouncing around in my brain for the past two weeks. For the past two years, David has encouraged these solo outings of mine, but I know they are a luxury I won't always have, because after our seventh child arrives, I will be busy mothering a newborn again! I have been writing and selling articles on parenting, saving money, and homeschooling for over ten years, and I met my goal of having a book published before the age of forty. While I started researching and writing a book of support for very busy mothers like myself, I haven't gotten very far with it. Writing shorter articles for magazines and newsletters doesn't take as much time or effort.

When David tires of reading books, Emily and Matthew get out the farm set and begin playing. David heads upstairs to get ready for his maintenance job at the nursing home twenty-eight miles away. He will leave by 9:30 a.m. to get there on time, earlier if I have errands for him to run. It was only a year ago that we lived in town only a few minutes from David's work, but we all agree the thirty-minute commute is well worth the opportunity to live in the country. Other than our public-schooled oldest son Daniel, we were all miserable in town. Neighborhood children were a negative peer influence we had hoped to avoid by homeschooling. Because of the two years we spent in town, our children were exposed to swear words, cigarettes, and off-color jokes. Since negative peer influence was our main reason for homeschooling in the first place, we couldn't avoid it in town, unless we kept our children in the house whenever school was out.

David and I were both raised in a country atmosphere and yearned for the same thing for our six children. Other than Dan, none of our children seemed to need peer group interaction over and above the time they spent with cousins. Even Dan admitted the peer-group environment was not one he thrived in. He decided for himself to homeschool the last two years of high school, but by then he was so peer-dependent that as soon as school was out for the day, he would meet up with his schooled friends and spend time with them until late at night. Rather than move to the country with us, Dan (who had graduated by then) decided to get full-time work and remain in town as an apartment complex manager. It wasn't difficult for him to find work, as he had been doing part-time work ever since his paper route at age ten. Finishing school as a homeschooler didn't seem to be detrimental to his job possibilities, since he ended up having to choose between three job offers!

It was difficult for us to locate a country home, but we eventually found a beautiful five bedroom brick house with lots of room for the children to roam and a landlord who encourages pets, enjoys children, and is very friendly and helpful. We all sleep upstairs, and the downstairs bedroom is home to the thousands of books we sell in our home business.

Today I need David to check the mailbox in town for book orders so he leaves at 9:00 a.m., just as Michael and Rachel are getting up. They were both up late last night. David checks the mailbox at least three times a week for orders, payments, or books that customers send, in exchange for cash or credit toward other books on our list. We have been selling used books through the mail for almost five years, mostly to homeschoolers. Locating the books has become a family venture and we attend book sales all over Iowa, within a fifty-mile radius. Next week we will travel fifty miles in our trusty old station wagon to a huge sale. David took the day off as a vacation day, so we've decided to spend the entire day book-hunting at thrift shops and book stores in the area.

Michael immediately starts work in his *Spectrum Math* workbook, even before he gets dressed. Each child has their own bin of schoolwork in the office/school/playroom where two tall white shelves hold all our school materials. Rachel eats breakfast, reading a book propped up behind her cereal bowl. Matthew decides he wants to do math, so I get out his *First Grade Spectrum Math* workbook and show him how to do the next few pages, which he does with prompting from his brother and me. "What is 6+2? What is 6-4?" he asks. We've made charts up to the fours and posted them, but Matthew doesn't know them yet. If he were in school, he'd be in kindergarten, but most kindergarten curriculum is too easy for him, so he insisted on having the same purple workbook as Michael does for math. I ask Matthew if he'd like to do some reading from his reading lesson book, but he doesn't want to today. For a while, Matthew was really gung-ho on learning to read, but lately he hasn't been interested in pursuing it and would rather be read to. Since he isn't even six yet, I don't see any reason for pushing it. Michael and Rachel were closer to age seven when they learned from the same book, *Teach Your Child to Read in 100 Easy Lessons.*

By this time Emily has found her own workbook and wants to know how much "2 + 8" is. No, she doesn't know her math; she's just mimicking her older siblings. Rachel reluctantly starts on her own math. She is stuck on long division, and no matter how many times her Dad or I explain it, she just doesn't seem to get it. We think she understands it, she does a few problems correctly, and then the next thing we know, she'll be lost again. We tried using *Saxon Math*

---

for awhile, but Rachel preferred the *Spectrum* workbooks. Sometimes it helps if Elizabeth or Michael will try explaining a math concept. We know she will master it eventually, but this phase is frustrating to her and to us. Rachel would love to spend the entire day reading and some days she does, but our mutual goal this year is to also work on math, geography, and spelling.

At the beginning of each school year, I write out my goals for each of the children and then add the childrens' goals for themselves. We use these goals as a very loose framework from which to plan and order materials that will be helpful in meeting those goals. Michael wants to work on spelling and handwriting this year, mostly because Rachel writes so much and so often that her writing and spelling surpassed his last year.

The mail here arrives around the same time that Beth gets up at 10:00 a.m. Beth is a night owl, staying up past midnight to work on the computer. Initially, I was upset with these odd hours until Beth explained that this was the only time she could enjoy quiet, without siblings around. Beth has e-mail penpals and works on the newsletter she edits. When we got Internet access, Beth started a group where she introduces topics and is a moderator for the replies—topics such as abortion, euthanasia, homeschooling, and teen-age drinking often send her to the library for more research. It takes me over a half hour to sort through all the mail.

Lunchtime arrives when the children start complaining of being hungry. I stopped planning lunches when I became pregnant and didn't feel like eating anything except chicken livers, peaches, and sausage and egg muffins! The older children take turns planning and fixing a light lunch, usually sandwiches or soup. This is when I head for the computer to check my e-mail. Today I have several messages to answer, so I let the children watch an educational program while they eat. Today it is *Reading Rainbow*.

Michael and Beth feed their animals after they finish their own meal. For someone who doesn't really like animals, I am surrounded by them since our move to the country. Michael inherited a Lab puppy from the landlord, Beth has a stray white puppy who wandered here from a cornfield, Rachel has a gray cat, and there are three bunnies in cages behind the house.

Emily and Matthew gravitate to the office/playroom and play with the toy box toys as I work at the computer. There really isn't much room on the floor to play so I insist on a ten-minute clean-up before play. This means I must leave my computer work while I help. We have bins on shelves for toys, so it doesn't take too long to get them organized. While Matthew, Emily, and I clean, Michael heads outside to play with his puppy, and Rachel goes out to play with her cat. Beth disappears upstairs to work on math or answer letters.

Since the children are all occupied peacefully, I decide to spend some time packing book orders in the book room that adjoins the playroom. I have to step over our oldest son's bed on the floor, and get around his pile of dirty laundry. I miss my nice, organized book room, but Dan's stay with us is just temporary until he can find another apartment. He started a new job with a cleaning crew thirty miles away, and if he would stop buying cheap automobiles to fix up and re-sell, he could move out much quicker! Since he had been on his own almost a year and is now relegated to a very small space in our book room, he wants his stay to be a short one.

I get a couple of boxes packed before Emily decides to join me and "help." I give her a box, a roll of tape, and a black marker, and get two more boxes packed while she works on hers, doing surprisingly well at taping the box shut. By now, Matthew has joined Michael outside, and I can see that they are riding their bikes up and down the driveway. Matthew has been riding a two-wheeler without training wheels ever since he was two and a half years old. He is my child with no fear—a quality I admire, but one that scares me as his mother.

By 3:00 p.m., we are all ready to "veg out" a little, so Emily and I go up to my bed where she sits and plays with her box of markers, stickers, and paper, while I try and rest a little. Rachel is writing letters on the old computer in her room. She saves the letter on a disk and prints it out downstairs on our printer. Michael is working on his geography, another *Spectrum* workbook we thought we'd try, and Matthew is watching *Old Yeller*, a video he has seen a dozen times. Elizabeth is still in her room, listening to country music and writing. She has basically completed her high school requirements except for a year of math, which she does off and on, changing books and materials as she goes. She has started the *Key to Geometry* and *Key to Algebra* series, but now is working on practical math with a Holt, Rinehart textbook we picked up at a school auction. Since her future plans don't include college, this "real math" is the most appropriate for her anyway.

Matthew joins us upstairs, bored with the video, so I read a couple of books to Emily and him. When Matthew heads to his room to play with Lego, I convince Emily to stay in my room with me while we sort through our fall clothing. Matthew does not like to share his Lego with Emily, and I am trying to avoid the conflict between them. I check the clock and see I need to start supper before I finish dealing with the clothes.

With a pot of chili simmering on the stove, I enlist Matthew's and Michael's help in getting the clothes that need to be washed down to the basement. Then I see that they have emptied their out-of-season clothing boxes on their floors while I was busy! It is evident from Michael's small pile, that we will need to be doing some shopping for clothes for him.

Dan arrives home around 6:00 p.m., and David by 6:30 p.m., shortly after the children and I have finished eating our chili and rolls. Matthew and Emily are clamoring for David's attention, when I head to the computer for a few uninterrupted minutes to check my favorite couponing site and the e-mail once again. Then I head upstairs for a much-needed soak in the tub. Sometimes I am lucky and can spend half an hour alone, soaking and reading.

By 8:00 p.m., both Emily and I are in our pajamas and relaxing on my big bed. Matthew comes up with an armload of books, and I only read a couple of them before Emily falls asleep on my arm. David, Michael, and Rachel are downstairs watching television. This is David's "down time," after the two youngest are getting ready to sleep. He's usually too tired to do much more than watch television, but will occasionally play chess with Michael or read a book.

Beth goes on the computer as soon as her dishes are finished. The kids take turns with the dishes and several times a week we post a morning "chore chart" if there are particular things that need to be done around the house. Through trial and error, we have settled on a written chore chart each morning, so the children know what they are responsible for that day. Everyone chips in when major house-cleaning needs to be done.

By 9:00 p.m., my youngest two are asleep and carried to their respective beds. They won't necessarily stay there the entire night, as one or the other often comes to our bedroom during the night. We have a mattress on the floor next to our bed for them. I go downstairs and talk to David for a few minutes before I decide I am too tired to stay up. I wish I could share this time with David, but since hitting the last trimester of this pregnancy, I'm more apt to fall asleep. Rachel is reading a book in the too-dim light of the television. She usually heads upstairs by 10:00 p.m., but Michael stays up for the news every night. I go to bed at 9:30 p.m. and am asleep within a few minutes. David comes to bed at 11:00 p.m., and Beth is in her bed when I make my first bathroom trip of the night at midnight. It is the end of another busy day at our house.

Elizabeth, Michael, Mary holding Katherine, David
Matthew, Rachel, Emily (Dan is not shown)

Dan (19), Elizabeth (17), Michael (13), Rachel (11), Matthew (6), Emily (3)

Cheryl
Phil, age 10

Interview with Cheryl on a cold, rainy day in an urban city in Ontario, Canada

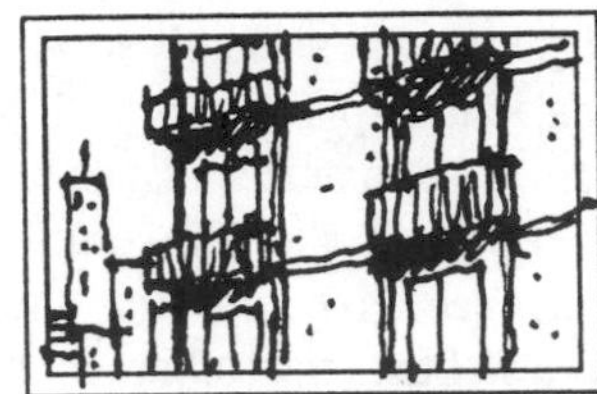

LIFE UP TO THIS MOMENT

It's early November, rainin' an' cold outside but not dismal in appearance. The colourful leaves on the ground and the character of the neighbourhood make it look rather pretty. Even enticing. However, we're goin' t'avoid goin' out before this evenin.' I don't like wet or cold weather, eh.

We live in a poverty-stricken urban area in Canada. Even the main streets here are run down, and many buildings are boarded up. Most of them are dilapidated. Our street's a row of medium-sized apartment buildings and rooming houses. It's also the exit off a highway, so the traffic's often noisy. Area's not well-kept either. Streets need a face-lift (sidewalk repavement, etc.).

But as my son Phil would point out as we walk up the street, there're many trees around. They're pink an' purple an' white during the summer. They provide shade as my son plays in the ugly, run-down tiny playground by the high school 'cross the street. When we go t'the park just south of us, huge trees shade me while Phil romps in the pretty wading pool an' about the barely-equipped play area. The closest parks almost always have children in 'em during the daytime, eh. In summer, it's a beautiful sight t'behold. The beach parks are the most beautiful. As the breeze caresses my skin, I watch Phil play against a backdrop of enchanting blue or grey water, dependin' on the time o' day, eh.

Everything's close to our home. Three major transit routes are within walking distance. The grocery store's about two minutes away. A better grocery store's about a fifteen-minute walk away. The three community recreation centres in the area're all within five minutes' walking distance, eh. One of 'em has a lovely public pool that has a heated tot pool attached to it.

We're in a one-bedroom, medium-sized apartment with a nice layout. Phil "works" in the bedroom or the livin' room and sometimes at the local library as well, eh. Our home is more messy than tidy, that's for sure. Well, when he goes 'way for a while, it's tidy. I'm not a good housekeeper when he's around, eh. Our garden's on the window sill. Phil usually tends to it. I'm going t'ave t'get my own, though, 'cause it's awfully tempting t'do his.

Anyway, I'm Cheryl an' my son's Phil. I grew up in an upper-middle class area of Canada. My family was workin' class while I was growing up. My parents were raised in Jamaica and immigrated to Canada before I was born. My parents were both creative, dexterous people who worked very, very hard to give us the life we had. I didn't grow up having to stretch food, live on a budget, shop carefully, or spend cautiously. As an adult, it took me a long, long time to learn how to live in poverty.

I started kindergarten with the same children I went to school with until grade six. There were only about five or six Black children in my school at one time, but not in the same grades. I never liked school—racism prevented me from enjoying it. My everyday struggle to battle its effects were overwhelming. It took up nearly every cell of my being. For one thing, I grew up having to always watch the eyes and body language of everyone else (in my world, mostly everyone else was Caucasian) to know how much racism I should expect. Sometimes I'd walk down the street and people'd yell racial slurs from their cars. Peers would stare at me, even though we practically grew up together. Teachers seemed to have a difficult time having to adapt to having a Black child in their classes. I was socialised to despise myself and my people. That conditioning was successful enough to keep me ashamed of my people and myself—especially around Caucasians.

First World foreign countries were greatly landed in my parents' homeland, so they were not expecting the racism I experienced. Because of my difficulties at school, my mother was very concerned about me, and so decided to send me to Jamaica when I was eleven t'go t'school for a year and take the common entrance exam.

I stayed with my aunts' families. I was between their homes until I earned a scholarship to one of the best schools in the country. I boarded there for two academic years. Hated it. It was very North Americanised, and I'd gained a lot of weight by the time I reached that school. That weight gain devastated me. It destroyed almost everything I might've had left of self-value.

Beside the culture shock of being in Jamaica, I was totally unprepared to learn that the children were terribly classist—I didn't have an acceptable wardrobe or parents who drove up to the dorms in upscale convertibles. What's worse, I didn't fit their image of whom a foreigner should be. I hadn't before seen classism exist so intensely, and they were even less forgiving of what they perceived of as my inferiorities than the children back home.

The incidences of racism and classism I experienced in Canada and Jamaica probably nourished the roots of my thoughts to some day homeschool if I were to have children of my own. I certainly thought that a mentally safe environment would be a better experience than the one I had!

But, I did learn in the classroom in Jamaica. For the first time in my life, I understood math in a classroom setting. I retained the knowledge passed on to me in the other classes as well. However, I was so withdrawn that I often missed classes. But when I was there, I learned. It was joyous. It was wonderful to look into a teacher's eyes and not see dislike of my skin or hair or lips or nose. It was great to know that I was graded based on merit alone. It's really too bad that I was finding it so difficult to adjust that I couldn't perform well. I was just too homesick and out-of-place in Jamaica.

Later, in Canada, I gave birth to Phil. I didn't know how to live with very limited money, and I didn't know how to motivate myself when I had to do something that wasn't challenging. I was unprepared at the university because I was wracked with guilt about having to put Phil in day care while I went to classes. I also had no direction, really, so I always found myself dropping all or most of my courses when it was too late to salvage the year. I jumped between programmes frequently. For the longest time, I'd go back and forth between history, English, and philosophy. When I finally discovered a programme that I greatly enjoyed, I had to drop out because I couldn't afford to stay. I do hope to return to the university, though, when my son is grown, and when I can afford it.

I don't work outside of my home anymore. When I have to, I do a temp job for someone else. I'm an artisan who paints in acrylics and oils. I also do some photo imagin' an' sketchin.' I bring my pieces t'fairs an' festivals (crafts or arts ones are the best). My work is moderately priced, Black-oriented, and my market segment is mostly Black. My works mostly have images of people, but also shapes, animals, or symbols. I also haven't had th'money t'build up my supplies, so I've missed out on some good opportunities.

My workspace ain't great, but at least I'm able t'do th'work. My living/dining area is L-shaped, and my studio-office is in what would have been the "dining" area. My three desks serve as a partition between the studio an' living room. Who am I kidding? It ain't a livin' room—it's a play room! One wall of my studio-office has tables against it, and on those tables I store materials. I can't wait to get some proper shelving along that wall. I'll be able t'store more items, and I'll be able to access 'em better. My three desks are in an L-shape as well. The third desk, the one closest t'the kitchen, is where my paints, jars, and brushes are. A couple of craft kits are there as well.

We do not organize schoolwork. I've learned not to. I dropped out of university partly because of my difficulty with time-management, and this has continued to be an impediment in homeschooling as well, eh. After much frustration, I decided to try unschooling. I had to stop myself from demanding that tasks be completed within certain time periods. I had to stop myself from being angry with my son for not wanting to do something, even though I felt he needed it. I believe I've reached a happy medium with a bit of consistent structure in an unschooling type of environment. On this he thrives.

Actually, I only need to see that he's gotten at least some academic tasks done—usually English and math—and I'm okay. That is, I'm not frantic an' freakin' out. Oh, he also has t'practice reading aloud to me. The most important thing for me to remember is that my son must not be turned off from learning. I had to keep this in mind as I trained myself to let go and adapt to being this new and looser kind of mother. I do require that Phil finish his task work (workbooks, a spelling text book, etc.) within the morning hours. Believe me, that's an improvement over specifying times for each subject. Yes, he even had to complete his task work in a particular order!

Our curricula is self-devised, eclectic, and focused on my goals for him to be self-sufficient and well educated in an Afrocentric manner. That is, I use materials from different sources and create lesson plans myself. The only textbooks Philip uses are *Nelson's Spelling in Language Arts 3* and *Nelson's New West Indian Readers 2*. His spelling text is a reading-readiness curriculum—vocabulary, spelling, and sentence composition. I used to be a workbook fanatic, but found that they don't work well for Phil. He got pretty much everything right, but didn't always retain the information well. For some reason, the *Nelson* texts work very well for him. Phil's typing CD is *Mavis Beacon*.

Afrocentric learning is important for Philip because he needs to be raised with self-knowledge. He needs to know that he has a good Black heritage and a strong history of achievements by Blacks. I believe that this conditioning will enable him to become a self-confident, loving man. When his spirit is assaulted with negative images and opinions of Blacks, he will have a defense for himself. That is, he'll be able to say to *himself*, with *certainty*, "That is not true." Too many Black children cannot do that. I certainly could not, right into my adulthood. Philip needs to *know*—not just believe or think, but actually *know*—that there is nothing wrong with being Black and that being Black is normal and good.

Hence, I look for Afrocentric materials in alternative (non-mainstream) bookstores, on the Internet, and in educational catalogues. I've found that *Wintergreen* (Lakeshore in the U.S.) and *Peoples Publishing* (in the U.S.) catalogues are good to have on hand. On the Internet, I've found that *Nelson* and *MacMillan* are other good companies to receive catalgoues from because they publish material for Caribbean and African schools. These materials display mostly images of Blacks. When I'm in a mainstream bookstore, I seek the "Black Studies" or similarly named section.

The books we use are numerous, so I'll only name some: Almost all Fred Crump Jr.'s books (Afrocentric fairy tales—*Mgambo and the Tigers, Sleeping Beauty*, etc.); almost all Bill Cosby's *Little Bill* books (*The Best Way to Play*, etc.); *Rabbit Ears Books* with tapes (*Koi and the Kola Nuts*—told by Whoopi Goldberg; *Anansi*—told by Denzel Washington); *Towards Freedom: The African-Canadian Experience, Nelson's New West Indian Readers, Ladybird Caribbean* readers; almost all Sandra Boynton books (*Moo, Baa, La La La!*, etc.), *Book of Black Heroes From A - Z* (Vol. 1 and 2); *Women in the Struggle; Black Inventions*, etc. Phil also loves *Brain Quest's Black Heritage: African American History in 850 Questions & Answers*.

Other materials we have are craft kits from *Creativity for Kids*. We also have lotsa craft materials in a box. Craft kits and catalogues are also great for ideas on how to stock your craft bin. I've seen things in 'em I haven't thought of and haven't seen in juvenile craft books. Also, we use science kits. The only one we have left is *Magic Rocks*.

Beside basic texts and workbooks, we like t'use board games. I think creating board games is a great way to learn new things and to use and the skills one has, so we've started t'do that We haven't finished the first one yet. The board games I've bought so far are *Alpha-Bug Soup, Alpha Animals, Mad Math, Canadian Trivia Jr.*, and *Caves & Claws*. We also have chess, although I'm going to have to get a new one because too many pieces are missing.

I choose learning materials based on Phil's levels of capability as well as what I want him to learn. In the long run, I want my son to be very knowledgeable about his people's history. Having a good and strong history means having pride in oneself and one's people. Also, teaching him from African and Jamaican perspectives (without denying his Black Canadian heritage, of course) makes education relevant to him. If he can identify with his education, he's more likely to succeed. I also want him to know Afrocentric facts inside and out. I want him to be a well-mannered, self-sufficient, and Afrocentric adult who loves Black images as a part of himself. I want my son to see Black art, Black literature, Black playwrights, Black everything, as good and necessary in his life. I want my son to be pro-Black, to believe in the progression of Blacks and the elimination of the concept of Caucasian supremacism. This doesn't mean that he should dislike Caucasians. Not at all, for I believe that dislike of others is self-destructive and only retards progress.

One of the other things I intend to make sure of is that he knows the public learning centres (science centre, museums, etc.) as well as he'd know his own neighborhood. I also want him to know other countries. But, above all, he must know Jamaica as I did. I think it's paramount for his self-esteem to see it through childhood eyes. My having done so made Jamaica a part of my psyche. It gave me roots I didn't know I could have. I visited and lived there only briefly, but it had an incredible impact on me. I drew strength from knowing what it was like to live in a Black and racism-free society. Being in a place as a child makes such a different impression than discovering it as an adult.

Everything Phil does while I am occupied in my work is self-initiated, unless he hasn't completed his task work. He plays with educational games—some of the "Blaster" CDs (*Reading Blaster, Reading Blaster Vocabulary, and Math Blaster*), a *Thinking Things* CD set, *Blinky, Nikolai's Trains* and *Pharaohs, Arthur*, etc. He also plays with toys (*Lego*, cars), works on the computer, creates art, practices karate, and likes to watch television shows for children—mostly about science, nature, and machinery. Television's back in the living room again and it's a bit of a drag, but it was given t'me for free, so what th'heck, right? I've been able t'make sure that he gets stuff done without much fuss. For a while, I had locked the television away. After the initial shock, and after realising that there was no way I was gonna take it back out, Phil got more done and entertained himself in more creative ways. If he keeps up this positive behavoiur, the television'll stay. If not, it's going into th'closet until I can get a VCR. Then, it'll only come out about twice a week. However, I did learn, much to my dismay, that much of his general knowledge comes from educational television.

Shoot, my boy told me stuff I didn't even know. I was asking some things from a juvenile fact book about a particular spider. He was telling me all about it before I could even get to my questions! He told me he'd learned about if from one of those educational television shows. I then started noticing that he knows a lot of stuff—all of it from the television! I am so glad I restricted his television to educational programmes only, since Phil is an audiovisual learner and retains knowledge that way. My mind was so closed that I hadn't seen this before because I do not retain much from television. I can't even describe what I've seen—certainly not even close to the level of detail Phil can.

I do task work one-on-one with Phil when he asks for help, and I try to do what works best for him in setting up his assignments. I write Phil's assignments in his assignment book. I also made a pouch out of paper. It's quite shallow, because the cards to place in it aren't big. (They're small cutouts from the backs of calendars—each picture is a small copy of the twelve large photos inside the calendar, eh. The cards have a nice picture on one side and the name of the card on the other side. (The pictures are relevant to us, as they are of African women from the continent.) I place the corresponding cards in the pouch (the math card, spelling/grammar card, karate card, etc.) the night before. In the morning, he picks up the cards, then looks at the assignment details in the book. When he completes the assignment, he puts the corresponding card back into the pouch. This enables him to go about his businesses smoothly. I'm making a bonus pouch chart this weekend. The bonus chart (also cut from the back of a calendar) will work in a few ways. If he does the bonus work I assign; he gets one ticket. If he does bonus work on his own, without any prompting from me, he gets two. Then, he can apply the tickets toward some benefit.

For meals, I always ask what he wants out of what we've got. But, I'm the one who chooses the groceries, *I'm* really the one who decides what he eats. Chicken, rice, pasta, ackee an' sal'fish, frozen fruit juices, sliced bread, pita bread, veggies, porridge, potatoes, tomatoes, pancakes, and sometimes pizza. These are usually the items my son gets to choose from—he just *thinks* he has some choice. Forgot t'mention dat Phil cooks chicken. He's begun his laundry duties, too, eh. I don't want him t'grow up t'be one o' those men who need someone else t'do stuff for 'im! I should've begun earlier, but c'est la vie, eh?

As far as clean-ups go, sometimes I remember to remind my son to make his bed. Sometimes he does the dishes, sweeps, and mops. He almost always takes out the garbage. He has t'clean up after himself as much as he can, 'cause I just don't have th'energy or patience t'do so. My child's cleaning duties are at least weekly and I usually remind him t'complete his chores.

Some days I need to have a nap. I try to do that if I got to bed really late the previous night, because then I can't function properly later, eh, when I have to take him to the community centre. If I get too tired, the day's just a goner. I can't even focus on keeping Phil in tune with his task work. Bedtime's routine, though. He brushes his teeth, gets stories read in bed if he wants—if I'm up to it and don't have to tend to biz. Then, I read to *myself* before I go t'bed.

Read-alouds and other interests are just a part of our lifestyle. We play when we feel like it, read aloud when we feel like it, and listen to music when we feel like it. Phil is a beginning guitar player, but I haven't been able to afford more lessons for a long time now. He's probably forgotten everything. Maybe he's even grown out of his guitar—it's a small one.

Phil loves his community centre activities. Karate's five times a week for two-and-a-half to four hours each time and swimming is weekly. I have him signed up for other sports, but we haven't been able to make it to those programmes. He didn't want to do any of them in the beginning. But, knowing my son, I signed him up anyway.

We also take local trips to Afrocentric events. I don't drive, but if there's a Black artists' display or Black festival or other event, we try to make it. The library and community centres're all within a short walking distance, so not much money or time're spent on commuting. I'd like local trips by public transit t'be weekly, but I can't afford that. We have to settle for a monthly (or less) trip to the zoo, to a movie, etc. Such places of interest are about thirty minutes to an hour away. The big zoo's almost two hours away. Phil is consulted about trips and activities, but I decide in the end. That is, I'll give him choices, but I'm the one who makes up the choices. I also use a solo parent organization for family socialisaton, and I try to get to the Thursday homeschoolers' hangout for my son. It's a huge open gym with lotsa homeschoolin' kids.

His friends are from karate and swimming. He sees and interacts well with other children, but he doesn't have a *real* buddy. Oh, he does have a friend who lives beside my parents, but he doesn't see him often.

Finances have been the biggest struggle in this lifestyle. I also don't tolerate stress that is due to resistance to schoolwork or chores. Time-outs (bathtub play when he was little) or distractions are used to diffuse tension. Homeschooling's also helped Phil respect my decisions. He doesn't argue much with me anymore. At the most, he'll say "not fair" or he'll try to bargain with me to get what he wants. Mess is another thing that gives me stress. In addition, there're external problems such as a troublesome landlord or not having bus fare. Financial, health, and housing problems are causes of ongoing stress.

My values often seem vastly different from everyone else's, even on the Black-oriented homeschooling lists. For instance, I strongly believe in Afrocentric education for Black children in North America. I believe in egalitarianism as opposed to equality—equal pay for equal work, but not *everyone* has to be *able* to do the work. I approve of the freedom to choose midwifery and at-home births. I am strongly anti-racist, and I abhor the persecution of the poor. I also very, very strongly believe that children's welfare should come first. I believe that the fulfillment of this is inevitable when one has a strong family. While I think that two good parents (and/or extended family) are best for children, I have worked hard to ensure that solo parenthood doesn't need to be seen as inferior. I am also not materialistic, but I feel it's okay to desire material things. Essentially, I believe in freedom of choice.

I am one who mostly does not allow her life to be dictated by societal opinion. I do like nice things, of course, but I don't base my self-value on the amount of typically-admired possessions. That is, I'd rather spend thousands of dollars on books instead of a car. I'd rather use money for music lessons than for clothing. I'd rather live in poverty and provide the best chance at life for my son than work for someone else during the day for a good salary.

Homeschooling's been a very rough journey, but well worth it. Phil was previously in and out of public school because of our financial hardships. I also had a very narrow mind regarding homeschooling and felt that structure was paramount and that paper records were necessary. I believed I had to see the evidence of learning in workbooks. I had to let go of all that. I also had to work out our personality conflicts. I had to compromise and see our differences as acceptable.

Plus, I was still wrestling with my own childhood demons, eh. Homeschooling's easier now because Phil respects me more and because I'm not as pigheaded as I used t'be. Plus, his karate's helped a lot. It took me a terribly long time to get everything "right," but things're sweet now.

As I mentioned, I wanted to homeschool long before I gave birth to Phil. I hadn't heard about it from anyone, but probably my own negative experiences at school helped to trigger the idea. My mother taught us during our early childhood, so I believe that I actually got the idea from her. The black and white movies I'd watched about shipwrecked families and whatnot prob'ly helped me keep my fantasy alive. Who knows? I must've been about six or seven. At that age I just wanted to grow up and have a huge family and live on a farm. We would tend to the farm, and I would teach my children. I really wanted to do it! It was a spiritually compulsive thing. So, like my art, the desire to homeschool was there from the beginning of my life.

Perhaps I committed to it in the back of my mind when school in an institution seemed to be so much worse than school at home. I *enjoyed* my mother's blackboard and the pictures with words all around the basement walls. I *loved* it when she held chalk, when she taught me from phonics workbooks, used self-made flash cards and picture guides. I loved the closeness. It was unbelievable. I still get a little thrill, remembering how she looked and how it felt to be taught by her. Her face was so peaceful, and her eyes shined. I just loved everything about it. I thrived under her loving gaze. Schools used similar materials, but what worked for me was that *she* was the one teaching. My father used a regular clock to teach me to tell time, and he showed me how to tie my laces. What worked was that *he* was the one who taught me. My parents were very conformist, mainstream people, but they sure knew how to reach kids.

However, I hated school elsewhere from the very start. So I am doing with Phil exactly what I saw work in my childhood—frequent puppet shows, children's theatre outings, regular library trips, and visits to the cinema; coupled with our home, backyard, community skating rink, and swimming pool. These were the things my parents provided to create such a rich environment for us, and most of these things I now provide for my son. I can't stress enough that both of my parents instilled the love of books in me, as well as the love of fantasy and drama. My mother always took us to the library, which was my most enjoyable local trip as a child. My father read Bible stories to us and took us to movies. He also made sure that I learned how to ride a bike. When I was in Jamaican schools from age twelve to fourteen, I'd cherish my return home to them during summer holidays.

Though I would have liked to have been homeschooled, I recognise that if I hadn't lived my life up to this moment as I have, I wouldn't be who I am—wouldn't have this child, etc. I do wish I'd known that keeping Phil out of school was the most important thing—even more important than my going to university. If I had homeschooled Philip from the beginning, we'd both be much better off right now. He'd be where I want him to be academically, and I would not have had such a hard time trying to go to school while being a parent in poverty. He'd also be surer of himself and my love for him.

Phil (10)

In healing myself from the injuries I picked up at school, I had to analyse my experiences. Books helped me to do this. *Ain't I a Woman*, by bell hooks, expressed what I knew but in clearer language. I learned from Black authors and also became aware of how visual and print media are effectively used to cause Blacks to have low self-esteem. Indeed, beauty is defined by audiovisual and printed media. Imagine a Black child watching the representations of beauty as only being Caucasian or Caucasian-like. Imagine Black girls reading books where beautiful women are always being described as "pale." Posters, billboards, photo ads in magazines—they all portray people of worth as being *only* Caucasian or Caucasian-like—particularly slim Caucasians with a lot of (or long, in the case of females) hair. Black children need something representing themselves in a positive way, just as other children of varying backgrounds do.

Imagine little boys growing up reading books, watching television, and looking at posters that only had females in them and only referred to females. Imagine having only feminine dolls available—never "boy" toys. They'd never read "he" or "him." They'd never see a male figure in any type of media during their whole childhood, even into their adulthood. Well, perhaps they would occasionally, but he'd always be referred to in a negative way. This is not what I want for my son.

Our homeschooling has not yet reached my ideals, but it's satisfactory. My early goal for Phil was to be an intense reader by this age. When I was his age, I was reading very thick novels. I was supposed to've had him know museums and galleries inside out. He was supposed to've physically been familiar with each province by now. He was also supposed to've been well-versed in the rules of etiquette. Ain't nuthin' doin', though. Ain't happenin.' None of those goals have been met. What I really need to have now is a real connection with other Black homeschooling families. I'd like us to have swap meets, and I'd love others' children to go on trips with us, have slumber parties with us, etc.

Meanwhile, we just roll with the punches. Change has been very much a part of our life. We work our plans around what we've got no control over, such as when the karate and swimming lessons are scheduled by the municipality. That is, we get done what we need to outside of those times. I had no choice about starting a home biz. I had to find a way to bring in some income, and I've always wanted to work for myself anyway.

Homeschooling is our life. It's enhanced the quality of our family life significantly. I am wary of the racism Phil would face from other children and teachers if he were at school. I am hoping that his enjoyment of homeschooling will grow so that he won't want to go to school. Phil's childhood memories probably won't be as good as I'd have liked them to be, but he'll have many good ones.

In my experience, mainstream schooling has long-term damaging effects on children. They are conditioned to disrespect others and themselves, to undervalue the opinions of those who're less fortunate, and to view females as inferior to males. They are also socialised to think that varying ethnicities should be valued differently. I think that even alternative public schooling (perhaps unwittingly) conditions children to subscribe to racism and classism (among other "isms").

My main reason for homeschooling is that I can't afford to risk having my son's talents and brain power thwarted by this society. But even if he were to become financially and academically successful, I abhor the idea of him having a low self-esteem. I believe that mainstream schooling ensures this in most children, regardless of ethnicity, but that Black and poor children are most at risk. My son is both, eh.

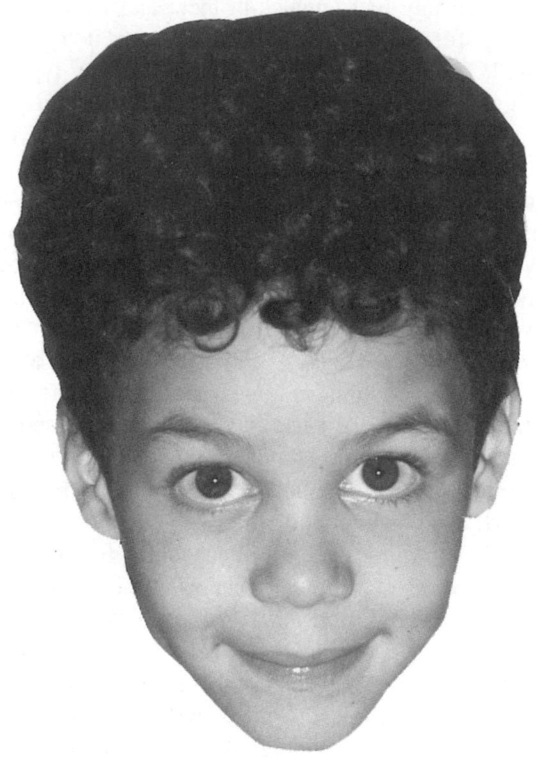

Phil

Phil (10)

Michael, age 40
Caryn, age 36
Katie 10 1/2
Maggie 7
Johnny 4

Interview with Caryn on Labor Day in Chico, California

AT THE OFFICE

Seven years ago I was teaching at a public high school. I loved my job, and I loved teaching, but I did not love the stress and rushing around. I would get up in the morning and drop Katie (who was three and a half) off at a *Montessori Preschool* here in Chico, then Maggie (who was only a few months old) and I would drive thirty minutes to the little town where I was teaching. Maggie was in a wonderful family day care that was only a few blocks from the high school. I would go over to nurse her during my prep period and again at the end of my teaching day before we headed home. I was teaching a short schedule (five of seven class periods). Meanwhile, Michael would pick up Katie at the end of his workday as a dentist, at about 1:00 p.m. Then in the evenings, I would go into Michael's office and do the insurance billing and other financial paperwork. I would do my lesson plans and grading between everything else. I felt like I was always rushing everywhere. At the end of that year, Michael and I decided that I would take a leave of absence from teaching and see how I did at home full-time. By that point, Katie (four and a half) was reading and Michael and I decided that I would try homeschooling her. I had always thought homeschooling would be interesting, but until we decided to try it, Michael and I hadn't ever discussed it. We figured that we'd try homeschooling, and the plan was "to continue as long as it works for our family." That was five-and-a-half years ago, and we are still going strong. When I first started homeschooling, we made lots of trips to the library, did lots of reading on the couch, and took walks in the park (for exercise and plant and animal observations). Whenever the receptionist in the office would call in sick or need to be gone for the day, I would scramble to find a last minute babysitter, and when I couldn't find one, I would pack up the kids, a few books, and go to the office for the day. (Michael has a two-person office—he does all of the dentistry and the receptionist does all of the scheduling and phone calls). At that time, I continued to go into the office in the evenings to do the insurance billing and financial work.

When Johnny was born we continued as before, but slower. Less trips out and more activities at home. We made paper, we made butter, we baked bread, and read books.

Then, our receptionist had another baby and decided that she wanted to stay home with her kids. Michael and I discussed hiring someone new and the training involved to teach everything and decided that it would be easier for me to become the receptionist/office manager. So I started bringing Johnny to the office (he was still pretty young), and the girls would stay home in the mornings with various college students we hired—each would do a couple of days per week. Michael is a morning person (so am I), so he has always said that it is best for him to work when he is at his best. That takes care of mornings. As for which days, how many days, and so on, that has been based upon when patients like to come in. At that time we switched work to weekends "on" with a couple days off midweek. It was easier to get sitters on the weekends, and most importantly, when we had offered an occasional Saturday for patients, they were very popular!

As we talked about the possibility of buying a lot and building our own office, we started to get excited about the possibility of designing it so that there would be ideal space for our kids to be there with us. We've designed our office with the hallway next to my desk connecting straight into the "staff rooms." Our "staff" has a break room (for resting and playing), a lunch area (with a sink/microwave/counter), and four different computer/workstation areas (one computer area and the others have various activities and bookshelves). We are installing counters and bookshelves right now, and then we will do the landscaping. After the landscaping is complete, we will be able to move into the new office, and we'll all have enough space!

We live in a suburban medium-sized city with a mild climate, located about one hour north of Sacramento, California. Our city has a network of creeks that run through it. Our large city park runs along several miles of this creek, which also runs through the middle of the city. There are trails and paved paths that run the length of the park and cross it as well. We live two blocks from this park. Our cul-de-sac is fairly new. Our house is only four years old and was the first house on the street—there are still only four houses. (When finished, the cul-de-sac will have nine houses). The end of our cul-de-sac meets another area of city park land. Since we live at the end of the cul-de-sac, our house backs up to the park land. We can walk out our back gate and be on a path that connects to the park land.

Our house is a two story Victorian-style house. It is a cheerful yellow house surrounded by trees, shrubs, and flowers, mostly planted by Michael. We had it built so that the "front" of the house faces the park land and the "back porch" faces the street. So the side of the house with all of the windows faces our backyard and the channel, with an enormous sycamore, black walnut, and cottonwood trees. It makes for beautiful and restful views!

Living next to the park lands and channels gave rise to our growing political involvement. Although it is wild and beautiful, the creek has salmon and other fish, herons, egrets, ducks, red-tailed hawks, quail, deer and so on; some residents of Chico just think of it as a "flood control ditch." So began my first political involvement beyond voting. We did some research, attended council meetings, and have learned much about the political process.

We have also learned much about the media—especially how things are reported in the newspapers. We've had favorable coverage and unfavorable coverage, but the most important thing that we've learned is that even the best coverage cannot tell everything about an issue. There is always more to the story than what can be reported in the newspaper, and the television coverage is often only two or three sentences—if there is any coverage at all!

Since I've told you about where we live, how we got involved in our neighborhood politics, and how we mix our homeschooling with our dental practice, now it's time to invite you to spend a day with us.

I know it's early, but if you want to really see my day this is where I start. I look at the clock and it is 4:30 a.m., so I get up and go downstairs. My husband Michael goes in to shower and get ready for work. I put some water on to boil—I'm having brown rice for breakfast, and I'll have some herbal tea, too. (Hmm, that makes me sound rather earthy, doesn't it? Well, don't make any assumptions until you get a bit further into the day, okay?) I'd better pick up the living room a little. Three of Johnny's puzzles are spread out—the number puzzle, the ambulance one, and the garbage truck puzzle. Oh . . . there are also several books left out—Katie's *Little House* craft book and *Inside the Body.* I wonder who had that one out? Probably Johnny, as he especially likes to lift the flaps to see what is underneath.

I put in the rice, then I go to sign onto AOL. I answer an e-mail from my stepdad. He, my mom, and youngest sister are living in Japan. They sent birthday greetings for Johnny and me (our birthdays were on Saturday). I also read an e-mail relating to local politics and then go to write in my journal. Whoops, I haven't finished Katie's school schedule for the week yet, so I'd better do that first. (I wrote Maggie's up on Saturday.) Katie already finished the book she was reading, so I'd better make another trip to the library on Tuesday or Wednesday.

Michael comes downstairs to have breakfast—he eats his breakfast while mine finishes cooking, and he reads the local editorial page on-line. There is a letter criticizing one of our favorite council members. Michael frequently writes letters to the editor, so we usually read the local news and editorials on-line in the early morning and discuss them. At 5:30 a.m. Michael leaves for the office, where he will sterilize instruments and set up trays for his dental practice. Johnny and I will join him there later in the morning. I eat while writing in my journal.

5:50 a.m.—Time to wake up Katie, my eldest. She is ten and a half and has the job of fixing the kids' breakfast each morning so that I have time to have a quick bicycle ride before work. Last night Johnny picked pancakes for today's breakfast, so I direct her in how to cook them—this is the first time she's done pancakes, but she does a great job. She makes fabulous scrambled eggs and knows how to do grilled cheese sandwiches (another very popular breakfast here), and she also does cream of wheat, cold cereal, and toast. I run upstairs to wake Maggie (almost seven years old) and Johnny—I carry Johnny downstairs because he really likes to be carried down, but that is getting harder and harder to do—he turned four on Saturday and is quite a big kid!

I call out good-bye to the kids as I take off on a bike ride through the park. My ride will be a loop through my favorite park, and I will be back in almost exactly half an hour. I try to ride in the park everyday. It is beautiful and peaceful. I love large deciduous trees, and the park is filled with them. The trees form a canopy over the trails and paths. I suppose that I ride for my health—mental as well as physical. It renews me to be out under the trees! It is cool but not cold, and I'm comfortable in my shorts and short sleeved shirt. It is still half-dark, but the sun will start to come up as I do my bike ride. No owls today (I saw one last week but haven't since), but I hear a pair of sharp-shinned hawks calling overhead as I ride the loop. It is a beautiful time of day, and because of the holiday, there aren't the usual singles and pairs of people walking and riding through the park. I have it almost all to myself—it is lovely!

As I pedal toward home, I think ahead to what I need to do before we leave for the office. When I roll the bike up onto the porch I notice the rats' cage is open. Then, as I come in the door, I see Katie and Maggie in a big recliner in the living room. They are giggling and conversing with "Burps" and "Gneiss," their rats. The rats used to reside inside the house but are temporarily kept on the back porch until the girls can establish a better cage cleaning schedule. The cage got pretty yucky and Mom threw a tantrum. It was not very pleasant!

Maggie tells me Johnny had just started his bath. I go upstairs and curl my hair while I chat with Johnny. I don't wear makeup and my new haircut is still taking some getting used to, so it seems like I have to fiddle with it for awhile.

Johnny hops out and goes to "blow dry his hair." He likes to do that because that is what Daddy does! He gets dressed, and I make my bed. We have a few more minutes before 7:00 a.m., so when I go downstairs I ask the girls if they want to hear some of Maggie's book. We are reading *These Happy Golden Years* a chapter or so at a time. *These Happy Golden Years* is the next to the last Laura Ingalls Wilder book. It is about Laura's late childhood leading into her marriage to Almanzo Wilder. Lately we have been reading about Laura's "first teaching job" and the first time that she was away from home. It was very difficult for her to be away from home, but Almanzo came every Friday to take her home for the weekend. The descriptions of Laura's emotions and the cold weather are quite vivid. The children are delighted with this book, so we traipse over to the couch and read a chapter. Then we have a quick prayer for a good day for everyone, especially for Johnny who will have his first dental checkup today, and for Daddy because he fixes lots of people's teeth.

Johnny and I kiss the girls goodbye and head for the car. The babysitters don't do schoolwork with the girls. Katie prefers to work alone and usually doesn't need any assistance, and Maggie prefers to work with me individually and to do "fun stuff" with the babysitters. The best babysitters have done activity-oriented things with the kids: built a cardboard clubhouse, played a multitude of games, gone to the park, gone to the library, and many, many art projects. We've had good luck with college students who want to teach or work with children, because they like doing activities with the kids.

Our current office is quite close—about eight minutes away and we drive along a peaceful road. Today we see several yellow-billed magpies. I think they are so wonderful to look at with the long tail and the shine of iridescence on the feathers. When we arrive at the office, the parking lot is empty except for Michael's car. I take out the trash and pick up the reception area before our first patients arrive. I read the front page of the local paper and also the Sacramento paper most days, but today there is not enough time. I pull some patient charts, then Johnny goes back for his checkup. Michael explains everything to Johnny as he works. Michael sees a lot of children and his style is to tell the kids everything he is going to do. He is honest and soft-spoken, and this makes him a great dentist for working with kids.

When Johnny's checkup is finished, he returns up front with me. Between my conversations with patients in the office and on the phone, Johnny keeps me busy. He works on workbooks that deal with letters and sequencing pictures. I read to him. Today, one of the stories is *Island Boy* by Barbara Cooney—a wonderful gentle story. Throughout the day, Johnny acts as my "copy assistant." He loves to turn on the copier, make the copy, then remove the insurance card to hand back to the patient. Some days Johnny "uses my calculator" but not today.

Several patients converse with Johnny about his checkup and about his recent birthday. Later in the morning, the wife of one of our patients talks to Johnny for a long time about accents. She is from the Philippines, and she tells him about the different accents for herself and her husband who is from England. She tells him about "the lollipop ladies" (crossing guards in England) and we discuss the "chemist" vs. the "pharmacist." When the children are in the office, they have the opportunity to interact with adults and children from Mexico, Spain, China, India, Laos, Eritrea (in Africa,) and of course the United States. Johnny likes to sort the brochures and coloring books at the office. He pulls out the ones that have been colored on and tells me "we need more of the ones in 'Panish.'"

Throughout the morning, I have plenty of chances to help Johnny with his "schoolwork." He insists that he needs to do some, because his sisters do! Today, the only phone calls are from the girls calling to tell me how they are doing and to check in. Katie has started on her schoolwork, Maggie hasn't yet. This is pretty typical since I don't insist on completion of their schoolwork while I am gone. Since Katie has more experience with trying to rush through it later, she usually does all or almost all while I am at the office. Maggie likes to check and make sure she is doing everything right. Having a babysitter or Katie tell her how to do it hasn't usually been satisfactory for her, since she doesn't like to have other people see her struggle with something new. Often, I will work with Maggie later in the afternoon or in the evening. We usually work upstairs, sitting on the floor of the master bedroom, leaning back against the bed. Working this way, Maggie and I probably spend about one hour a day on her "written work." She does short segments from *Daily Language Review* by Evan Moore. This has four to five items to do each day—correct one sentence, pick the word that is spelled correctly, etc. She also copies short paragraphs from a *Dale Seymour* workbook that has a picture at the top of the page and then four or five sentences about the picture. She doesn't like "having to figure out what to say" so I'm trying to relieve the pressure and just give her some practice with writing words, sentences, etc., to strengthen her finger muscles. Maggie also just recently started writing letters to her friends. I don't assign, correct, or at all get involved in those. I would if she asked, but on those I think she usually asks Katie for help when she needs/wants it.

After we finish with our morning patients, Johnny acts as Michael's "lunch assistant," bringing him the different parts of his lunch while I vacuum the office. Today we have an emergency patient so we stay after lunch to see one more patient. When we don't have emergencies, we leave right after lunch. Our usual work schedule is from 7:30 a.m. until 12:00 noon on Monday, Thursday, Friday, Saturday and Sunday. Two Sundays a month we take off so we can go to church and those weeks we add in Tuesday. The weeks that we work on Sundays, I take the kids over to church so that they can still go to Sunday

School every week. Our schedule developed because we see so many children who do not want to miss school, and we have many working parents that work six days a week. As I mentioned, our weekend appointments are the most popular!

Johnny and Daddy drive home together, sometimes driving by "the new office" to check on the progress. I often stop to do a quick errand on the way home. I debate about it today and decide that I'd rather not fight the Labor Day crowds. Living in a college town, the end of August and beginning of September and on through to Christmas tend to be very busy in the stores. I'll wait and do my errands on one of our days off.

There are so many advantages for us in being able to set our own schedule. It is more convenient for our patients and it enables us to take our time off in the middle of the week so that when we want to go places, we don't fight crowds. It has also prove to be very useful for when we attend Monday night Park Commission meetings or Tuesday night City Council meetings. The next day we can sleep in a bit and not have to worry about getting someone ready for school, grumpy and tired.

The kids attend political meetings with us, and enjoy watching them on the local public access television channel. Johnny likes to "discuss politics." That means he tells which are the "good council members" and which are the "bad council members," but more than anything else political, Johnny enjoys going down to the council chambers before the meetings or in the afternoon so that he can sit in the chairs and pretend to be a council member, a park commissioner, the park director, or the city manager! His sisters like this too, but they are quite particular about which "characters" they play.

The girls generally have Saturday and Sunday without assigned written schoolwork because their public schooled friends tend to have more time available on the weekends during the school year. We generally school year-round, but are not at all formal about insisting on everything being done at a particular time or in a particular place.

Johnny does much of his "schoolwork" in the office—but he is really learning all of the time and everywhere. One of his birthday presents was a large puzzle of the United States and another one was a *Miquon Mathematics Orange* workbook. He was very excited about that one because he knew Maggie had one before. His favorite presents were the silver and gold pencils and his own hand pencil sharpener!

We all are home and coordinating schedules at about 1:15 p.m. Maggie already did her schoolwork. She and Katie are hoping they'll be able to play with their friends when they return home, so they've finished up their work early to have more time available later.

1:15-1:45 p.m.—I sit at the kitchen table and check over a few day's worth of

Katie's schoolwork. This is longer than it usually takes because, due to errands and birthday preparations over the weekend, I got behind. We had a family celebration, which is typical for us since we don't do "big parties" for Johnny's and my birthdays. We made "chocolate cake with gummy bears on top" that Johnny requested and wrapped Johnny's birthday presents. Truly nothing fancy, but enough extra work that I was out of my regular routine for a day or two. Hmmm, as I think about this, it is more typical than not for me to be checking several days of Katie's work at a time . . . there is always something that seems to come up!

2:15 p.m.—I am still at the kitchen table. Katie is making corrections on her Spanish lessons from last week. Maggie and Johnny are on the floor in the kitchen with the pieces of a small battery powered train engine. They have all the gears spread out and are listening to Dad exclaim "I don't think I can get all those gears back in!" I try to assist when the frustration level gets too high. I succeed in getting all of the gears in, but the engine still doesn't work. Maggie takes some out and rearranges them. The engine now has its sound-effects back, but still won't run. Johnny decides to just throw it away since it is his train, and I agree that is okay. About six months ago, we had a discussion and experience with throwing away and how "once the garbage men pick it up, we can't get it back." So I am confident when I ask, "Are you sure?" that he knows what he wants to do. Into the trash it goes.

2:20 p.m.—I ask Johnny to take his puzzles upstairs. I get bugged by too much clutter, so periodically I'll pick up my stuff and ask the kids to put some of their stuff in their rooms. I had asked the girls to put away some of their things earlier (before I went to the office) so theirs was done. I help clean their rooms and weed out old, broken, and unused stuff about once a month, so "putting it away" just means moving the visual clutter out of the living room or off of the kitchen table so we can eat! He isn't thrilled but does it.

Maggie asks to work out of a new spelling workbook *A Homework Booklet* from Instructional Fair, Inc. that I bought for her this weekend. I did buy it in the hopes that it would not be intimidating, but fun. She seems to be delighted with it . . . hurrah! I also bought some *Magnetic Poetry Words* for her birthday later this month, and I hope she will like those, too.

Johnny is hungry and goes to heat a leftover banana muffin in the microwave. "How many tens, Mom?" I reply, "Two tens." Snacks throughout the day for Johnny are fairly common, and the evenings are common for the whole family. Katie takes the comics into her room to read and has some "quiet time."

I start dinner at 3:20 p.m. We usually eat dinner at 4:00 p.m. everyday. Sometimes I cook, sometimes Katie cooks, and sometimes Maggie or Johnny helps me cook. Today I fix pizza—instant pizza crust and sauce from a jar, topped with shredded cheese. I make a quick lettuce and cucumber salad and open a can of peaches. Our dinners are usually fairly simple. Tonight would probably be considered a fairly typical meal for us. We also eat fast food out quite often. That's not something I think is healthy, but it seems to be a tradeoff—the more we are involved in work and projects outside of the house, the more we "eat on the run." I put drinks out on the table. I hear Johnny "reading" *The Very Hungry Caterpillar* from memory.

Since we're in the kitchen, I might as well tell you that I don't like clutter, but my kitchen counter collects it, and I feel like I need to bulldoze through it at least once a week to keep it from becoming completely unmanageable. Since the clutter bothers me the most, I generally try to pick up things as I go through the day, but sometimes the background general house cleaning waits for longer than I'd like. The kitchen floor won't have toys and paint bottles lying all over it for longer than an hour or so, but it might go as much as two weeks before it is swept and mopped.

Talking about cleaning, the kids have to do a set "value" of work each week, based upon their age. I wrote up 3" x 5" cards with jobs and how much each job pays. The kids pick what jobs to do and when to do them, just so long as they've earned their total by the end of the week. If they don't earn their set amount for the week, they can't play with friends outside of the family for the following week. However, this method does require a fair amount of "bookkeeping."

Our theory is that each family member needs to contribute to the upkeep of the household, and if they aren't, they need some extra time at home to give them more time to help out the next week. The money the kids earn goes into an account that we keep track of for them. They decide how to spend their money. Some purchases the kids have made are: toys, candy, science experiment kits, books, pets (so far lizards, rats, fish, and a bird), as well as all the "pet gear" and food. Additionally, the kids have started paying for their offerings at church from their earnings. They are not currently required to save a particular amount, although I plan to encourage that as time goes by. The chore-earning method works pretty well for our family. The kids have money they earn, we get chores done without complaint and without reminders because the kids pick what they do and when they do it. In the past, before we put in our "chore system," they almost always griped. Sometimes at the end of the week there was a frantic rush to try to finish enough of their chores. There was some whining, but that was due to not feeling that they had enough time to get it all done. That does not happen so often now since they've gotten used to the system. Johnny isn't on the system yet—assigned values for chores start at age five and then increase yearly. He can do work and earn money, but he doesn't have to earn a set amount each week. A few times Maggie or Katie have "slacked off" and then just decided to "forget it" until the following week. That has been their decision and they would start fresh with the new week. I don't really do reminders with this system. Throughout the week, before I do housecleaning, cooking, or whatever, I first ask if anyone else wants to do them. The most popular jobs are cooking dinner and doing laundry. Since doing laundry is a popular job and "pays" well, there is usually not much laundry laying around.

Dishes collect between meals until I can get to them. We don't have a dishwasher because we don't like how noisy they are. The kids don't usually wash the dishes since it doesn't "pay" as much. How much the job "pays" is roughly determined by the amount of time it takes to do a job.

During dinner tonight, the kids plan a trip for frozen yogurt and a bike ride after dinner. Johnny discusses the "silly table manners" of his imaginary friend "Caffeine." "She never says please and she gulps all the time."

As I finish dinner, I discuss the food pyramid with the kids. We have discussed it often before, but whenever I think about it, we review it. Usually, this also serves to make the kids more aware of eating more fruits and vegetables when they are hungry for a snack. Leftover pizza goes into the fridge. Often, Johnny will eat some as an "evening snack," again checking for "how many tens?" and watching the countdown on the microwave. Maggie and I like leftovers for breakfast, and we all like leftovers for lunch.

I clear the table and get some dishes started. The kids are checking bikes and fiddling with air pressure in tires and so on. They put the bikes in the car and we are off. We drive over to a short looping trail on the other side of town that is about a quarter mile loop. Michael and I walk and talk. The kids ride the loop—Johnny one time, Maggie two times, Katie three times (their idea).

We get home at about 6:00 p.m., and I ask if anyone is willing to help with window washing. Since this job "pays" well, I get three quick volunteers. Johnny vacuums window tracks, with Maggie loosening crud and wiping the sills, Katie sweeps cobwebs and junk out of the screens and I wash the windows.

It's 7:10 p.m. Hurray!! We finish. I take out the trash

We typically have "evening class" at 7:30 p.m. five nights a week, alternating who teaches each night. The evening class was Michael's idea. He wanted to do something with homeschooling, but wasn't interested in doing reading, writing or mathematics. Since he really enjoys the natural sciences it seemed to be an extension of our hiking trips to learn about the plants and animals that we see. When it is each of the kid's turn, they decide what to teach and where class will be. Typically, class is upstairs on the floor of the master bedroom. Usually, the subject is something from the natural sciences—lizards, birds, butterflies, and so on.

At 7:30 p.m. Johnny "teaches class" on butterflies, rocks, and snakes. Johnny's classes often contain an "exercise break." He runs around, jumps, or something else, and we are all supposed to imitate his actions.

Class is over at 8:00 p.m., and I take my shower.

Katie (10 1/2), Maggie (7), Johnny (4)

We do have a television. We often watch City Council meetings when we can't be at them or when we need a break. We also watch a lot of "nature-based" shows. *The Crocodile Hunter* is a favorite at our house. Michael and I watch a lot more television than the kids. We have more of a tendency to sit down and turn it on and then watch for hours without really thinking about it. The kids usually watch more when there is something "good" on. They also watch some videotapes. Michael and I don't watch (or allow the kids to watch) any standard network sitcoms or other stuff like that for several reasons, but the biggest one is that the "canned laughter" really annoys Michael (another is that the kids seem to fight more—and that annoys me). We do watch *CNN* (Michael and me, mostly), *CSPAN* (mostly me, with Michael sometimes), *The Outdoor Network* (all of us), *The Animal Channel* (all of us), and sometimes *PBS* (Michael and I, mostly for political shows and sometimes news). When the kids were younger, they watched more of the kid shows. No television tonight.

Around 8:15 p.m. I gradually mosey kids through tooth brushing, etc., and everyone goes to bed at 8:30 p.m.

Because Michael and I get up early, we set the early bedtime before the kids were even born, and we have maintained the habit. Katie sometimes stays up later reading, but there aren't any noisy activities after 8:30 p.m. Each child at some point wanted to "stay up late," and we allowed them to, but we weren't up. There wasn't a lot to do, so it wasn't usually very interesting and no one has wanted to make a habit of it. Everybody gets up early and Michael and I are both definitely morning people, so an early bedtime makes sense for us.

This day was a pretty good one—pretty typical, although I spent less time with Maggie than usual, and we spent less time on politics than on some recent days. We spent more time on housework, and the kids spent less time in just playing without any particular goal in mind. Also, most days they spend some time playing with their friends from the neighborhood. The kids usually play a lot throughout the day and fit their schoolwork in around the other things they enjoy doing. They have a large measure of control over when the schoolwork gets done, where, and how.

We try to live in a practical and common sense way. We don't orchestrate every minute of our childrens' day. Our goal is to raise children who are self-sufficient, organized, hard working, and who give back to their community in some way. Goal-wise, they are often pretty self-sufficient but not yet with their learning. Maggie and Johnny are usually enthusiastic. Katie is more reserved, so it isn't always possible to tell. She tends more toward bursts of enthusiasm when something sparks her interest.

I was a good student who pretty much followed all the rules in going through my years in public school. I find that as a result, that I am good at taking on jobs that are assigned by someone else, but sometimes have a much harder time getting started on self-selected projects. I believe that is one of the things that I most want to pass onto my children—a strong sense of their strengths and what they want to do (without worrying about "what others think") and the ability to develop a project and dive into it with enthusiasm and effort until they accomplish it.

I think that my life might have been quite different if I had homeschooled. I think I would have been more independent and perhaps less externally motivated. Michael went to an alternative school where he says, "The teachers didn't teach at all." But he did not consider this "homeschooling." Michael is very independent and quite internally motivated as it is, so I don't know that his life would have been different if he had homeschooled. When I was in school I didn't know that homeschooling existed, but looking back, I think it would have been great!

On Sundays I usually record the assignments for Katie and Maggie for the next week. Currently, I select materials and items to study that I think will work well for each child, but I plan eventually to have the kids take on some of the direction for what they want to study. I save the "assignment sheets" after the week is over and about once every month or two, I take the sheets and transfer the notes about what was studied into the computer. At the same time, I take out samples of the kids' work and put it into their "portfolios." The "portfolio" is just a large (about 10" x 14" x 3") expandable black pouch for storing the work I save for each child.

To find the materials I want to use, I subscribed to *Home Education Magazine* for several years and also got *Homeschooling Today* for about one year. I always order new homeschool catalogs whenever I hear about them. Then, I browse the catalogs and read about resources. Through trial and error, I figure out what is best for each child. Homeschooling catalogs can be addictively wonderful to read. You can find out what other families use and recommend, and often it is like just sitting down with another homeschooling mom and chatting. *Timberdoodle* is one of the ones that is excellent that way. We use many resources for our "schooling." I would describe my resource selection as "eclectic."

These are some of the specific resources that we use:

The History of US books—Katie adores these! Katie usually reads them and rereads them and rereads them. She devours them! I don't assign her questions or any other assignments out of them at this stage, but she absorbs much on her own.

What Your 1st Grader (etc.) *Needs to Know*—Sometimes I read these aloud, Katie enjoys reading them solo sometimes too.

Miquon Mathematics—Katie completed these and loved them, and

Maggie and Johnny are now beginning them. As a former high school mathematics teacher—I think these are marvelous! You can see what you are doing.

Key to Mathematics workbooks—Katie has worked through all of these and is now starting the final set of *Key To Algebra.* She has always loved these except for a few pages in *Key to Decimals.* Again, I think they are wonderful.

Backyard Scientist books—Some great experiments

TOPS science materials—We have used *Corn and Beans*—a great unit on monocots vs. dicots; *Pendulums*; and *Electricity.* These are units designed to be used in public schools, but they are wonderful for homeschool use. They use very cheap materials that are easy to find and use to do real science, with observations and testing hypotheses, etc. The materials we used for *Corn and Beans* included popcorn, pinto beans, paper towels, and a milk carton—used for growing and observing differences in plants. We also used a straight pin, clothes pin, masking tape, and a can to make a small balance (for weighing seeds and sprouts)! *Pendulums* used string and paper clips—wonderful!! I plan to get more of these units very soon

Elementary Language Lessons and *Intermediate Language Lessons* are used, so far, by Katie. An "old-fashioned" set of writing exercises.

"Mom assigned" writing—Sometimes based on literature being read, sometimes the topic will relate to City Council issues or events we have attended

Library books—many and often, and still more!! We usually have piles of them around.

Pathway Readers—We have three sets. Maggie is the one who primarily uses these. They are straightforward stories of family and farm life that are used by the Amish. Conflicts in the stories revolve around common household events . . . small disagreements.

Art Postcards—from *Dover Catalog*—I bought seven or eight different sets of artists. The kids take them out, play with them, sort them, etc.

In years past, when I was home full-time, we sometimes went to "story time" at the library and "homeschool skate day" at the roller-skating rink. Currently, we do not have time to do those things. It can be tricky to coordinate schedules for outings with other families when our schedule is different from the norm, and ours sure is. However, our flexible schedule works well for our family and that more than outweighs the drawbacks. So, homeschooling for our family means that we miss out on school friendships, organized homeschooling activities, and a perfectly cleaned house. On the other hand, our children still get to play with their schooled friends after school and on weekends; they have friendships that develop at church and Sunday school activities; they have much more time to play together with each other without it taking away from their time with other friends; our children have met many of their council members and know all of them by name; they have seen and understand well how the political process works and understand its strengths and weaknesses; and they can attend meetings of the *Native Plant Society* with us in the evenings. They also go to special presentations given by the *League of Women Voters*; we, as a family, can go on hiking and backpacking trips midweek when the roads are less crowded; and we can teach and learn from each other. I think that homeschooling makes our family stronger and better. We have the time to work together, talk together, play together, disagree and compromise together.

We plan to continue to homeschool for as long as it works well. We want the kids to go to college and would like to see them continue homeschooling until they start taking college classes. We try to plan for that goal in the materials we use and in the expectations that we set for them. I hope that someday my grandchildren will be homeschooled.

When I was teaching school, Michael and the kids and I spent the major portion of the day away from each other. Now we don't. I think it has greatly improved our lives and I wouldn't ever want to go back to "the usual way." This way works much better for us.

I know homeschooling has also strengthened our marriage. Michael and I share much more of our days now, and we are therefore building from more "shared experiences." I know what his day has been like in the dental practice. We spend more time together during our time off, now that we have all become involved in our local politics. We are closer to being "on the same wavelength"

Johnny, Maggie, Katie

Katie (10 1/2), Maggie (7), Johnny (4)

now, whereas before we were often hurrying around in two separate directions—actually three or more with Katie's preschool added into the mix!

The children, too, feel good about their homeschooling. Maggie says, "I love it!! It is fun because I like it." Johnny says, "I love it. It's fun." (Yes, he did listen to Maggie's answer!) Katie says, "I like homeschooling because I can decide when I do my work and I can get it done early if I want. That means that I can have more time to play if I choose. It also means that I can get help on something that I need quicker than if I were in a room with thirty other kids. It is also quieter, usually (grinning), unless Johnny or Maggie has a cold. Can I go play now?"

When first beginning, I would have wanted to know that it is okay to "do homeschooling" differently from how anyone else is doing it, and so I've learned to relax, enjoy our kids, and to listen—they'll let us know what they need and what they like and don't like. We don't expect any two kids to be the same, even if they are our kids! We take our time and work at finding what is best for *our* kids in *our* family.

Katie (10 1/2), Maggie (7), Johnny (4)

William, age 40
Marie, age 35
Joyce, age 10
Jake, age 5
Trace age 2 1/2

Interview with Marie from Davie, Florida

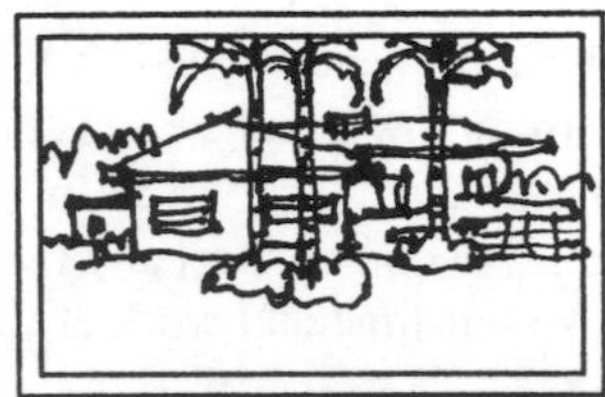

EMPLOYEE ONLY DOORS

One of my strongest desires early in my adulthood was that I would be able to stay at home with my children. I have wonderful memories of my mother experiencing life with me and my siblings, and I have wanted to have the same for my children. I respected the way my mother balanced being with us and finding her own place in the world as we got older. She was a wonderful teacher. She took us everywhere and gave us rich experiences—from hosting underprivileged kids to attending major theatre productions. Sadly, I lost my most precious mentor when I was twelve. But I remember so much of those early years, and Mom was my first and best teacher. She taught through child-centered learning. I was talking to my Dad today, who is very supportive of homeschooling, and I said, "I bet Mom would have homeschooled us if she knew it was a possibility." He answered, "Absolutely . . . no doubt."

And I wish I *could* have been homeschooled. I played the school game well. I read early and didn't have to suffer the drill and practice of the reading curricula. I suffered in another way though. I felt that many hours of my life were wasted in boring classes on boring subjects. I was rarely challenged and when I was, it was not according to my own interests. I feel I was never allowed the time and resources to just think for myself. I had to put up with the school bells signaling the end of each period, which meant I had to arbitrarily switch my mind from one subject to another.

Looking back, that seems a ridiculous way to learn. I was a gifted student in gifted classes. These classes were probably the highlight of my school years and reconfirm more than anything that homeschooling is a better way of learning. There were about ten students per teacher in the gifted classes. They were set up for "child-centered" learning. Although we were not given complete free reign on what we wanted to study, we were given a lot of choices. Our classes were also mixed grades. We were allowed a lot of time to brainstorm and socialize with each other. I remember there was such a mix of students; one girl's mom and dad owned an auto paint shop, and she came to school in a black leather jacket. Another girl was miss "prim and proper" and very sweet. Yet another was a son of a state representative. We all got along—I can't remember anyone having bad feelings about another. It was very different when the bell rang and we had to go back to our "regular" classes. The sad thing is that I believe we all are gifted in different ways and every child should be able to have the opportunity to lead their own learning. Homeschool is the ultimate "gifted class" to me. I feel that I could have learned or accomplished so much more if I had been home educated. There is no substitute for the unschooling environment—no testing, no grades, just pure learning because the human spirit craves knowledge and experiences. I have this rooted belief that learning is a natural instinct and that life is filled with so many interesting things to explore. It baffles me that someone should decide for someone else what is worth studying and what is not.

I find that an involved parent or mentor is the key to children's success. A homeschooling parent takes this involvement to the extreme. I take such joy in being there for my children's first "anything." It isn't as though I pat myself on my back for their accomplishments, but that I sit back in awe and appreciate each step they take. That step may have been getting a small pea on a spoon and then getting it all the way into the mouth, getting a key in a keyhole, or discovering how a spider makes a web. As they get older, the awe changes. Now, I am in awe at the way they develop new theories, teach themselves how to read, and work through complex social problems. Since I feel that the mentor or parent's job is to encourage and foster the natural learning instincts in the child and not to thwart them, I don't want to give the teaching of my own children to anyone else. I love this job.

Sometimes, my husband William says, "Well, we did the school thing and we came out okay" when, in fact, he believes that many people didn't come out okay. My husband and I don't believe that the government should be regulating education. I guess you would say we are free-thinkers and want our children to be also. I truly believe that, in the next few decades, we will look back on the ways and means of mainstream education today and wonder why we, as a society, let this primitive form of education take place.

One book that was an early influence on our decision to homeschool was *What Do You Really Want for Your Children?—How to Raise Happy Kids* by

Dr. Wayne Dyer. I have read it over again many times. It has an unschooling slant and really made me think about our own values, goals, and morals, so I could look at what we *really* wanted for our children. Another great influence was *Dumbing Us Down* by John Taylor Gatto. Over the years, I went to a state conference, read all of John Holt's books, and decided the child-centered or unschooling approach is what I felt would work best for us. I am glad that I found out about homeschooling before my children went to school.

William has always been supportive of homeschooling and the unschooling philosophy. However, he has said that he didn't think he could stay home with our children everyday! Yes, sometimes it can get crazy, and we have the normal ups and downs, but I think that having so much time together to work things out, the ebb and flow of life is smoother. Dad does a lot of "teaching," mostly by example and by sharing things. We spend many "family" hours together. We like each other and like doing things together.

I take most of the responsibility for the family's spiritual guidelines as well as handling the daily stresses. This is a learning process for me and the children. As I ask them not to yell, I must remember not to yell myself. It seems that my mood can set the whole family's mood. If I react positively and calmly to a stressful situation, then usually everyone else does too, including my husband. If I am stressed, the kids don't handle things as well. I try not to take responsibility for their happiness, because that is up to them, but I realize that my emotions as "Mom" affect the mood of the family. We have not been without our share of hardships and pain. Looking for positives and dealing with hard things is taught by example.

A few years ago we were moving while I was pregnant. Trace almost died at birth. William's dad was dying of cancer. At six weeks old, Trace was in an intensive care unit, and again was on the edge of death with pneumonia. William's dad died a month later. Needless to say, it was a tough time. However, life is a journey, and we never stop learning throughout this journey.

Most of our outer family is supportive of homeschooling. It takes strength and trust not to worry about "conforming" to other's expectations. Most who question the "unschooling" approach worry about basic skills. Once they get over that, they can see the benefits of child-centered learning.

Creatures of habit we are not. We don't have "typical" days. Our unschooling learning-all-the-time philosophy makes each day unique. I wondered which day I should pick and decided to use today. We have had many more exciting days, but this is what happens today.

Dad is off to work at the nursery, before any of us gets up—sometimes one of the kids will go to work with him.

We start stirring anytime between 7:30 a.m and 10:00 a.m. Sometimes Jake (five) will sleep later because he stays up later.

Joyce (10), Jake (5), Trace (2 1/2)

Trace (two and a half) was up around 8:00 a.m. wanting to nurse. I make a small wish that he'll fall back to sleep. No luck. He is up and wants "boy" pants on. He's potty training himself and wants the diaper off. The other two wake up soon after.

Joyce (ten) is pretty self-sufficient and likes to cook. She bakes from scratch. She will usually make breakfast for herself and whoever is up at the time. Today, it is just cereal and some cantaloupe. We tend to eat "healthy," and the kids enjoy a variety of foods. I think growing an organic garden makes kids more aware of what they are eating and where it comes from. We have a 30'x100' garden in our yard. Our garden season is October through May. There is not much out there now, as it is August. There are a few small eggplants that haven't given up. I don't eat or cook red meat. I gave it up years ago when I started having pigs and goats for pets. Sometimes, the other members of the family eat meat when we eat at a restaurant or at someone else's house. We all love fish.

I don't have a set routine for the day, but we do keep track of field trips, classes, obligations, appointments, and such. We do a significant amount of learning outside the home. We discuss places we like to visit, schedule field trips there for our homeschool group, or just go as a family. The kids are interested in the "employee only door" and want to know what goes on behind those doors at different establishments. We visit the library and the bookstore about every other week. I pick up a lot of "classics" at garage sales and our large playroom is filled with bookshelves.

Since I don't like to be late, I make a point to be on time to things we have scheduled. Today, we don't have any appointments or field trips. I make a mental note of what I need to accomplish today and some spiritual notes on how I want to handle my day. I pray and ask for spiritual guidance. Sometimes, I share a quote with the kids.

In reference to structure, I am getting a bit more organized as the littlest guy gets bigger and my older ones can help out more. My dishes are almost always done everyday, the laundry is semi-caught up, and a closet may get cleaned out once in a while. I focus on the children first and the house second. Someday, I hope to have a happy balance, as it is nicer to have a clean, organized house rather than a messy one. I just wish I had someone else to do the cleaning!

This morning, Joyce spends some time working with a map of our county. She is planning her birthday party and it involves mapping the guest's addresses, so we can pick them up. I found this big county map at a garage sale. My "sale-ing" Saturday mornings have brought many of hours of fun and learning to our family and at a cheap price too!

Jake is really into the *Thinking Things,* by Edmark and *3-D Body Adventure* computer games, by Knowledge Adventure. Jake has been thinking a lot about numbers. I hear him whispering himself to sleep saying things like, "500+100 = 600." He explained to me the other day that 2, 4, 6, and 8 are even numbers because if he had 4 of something and gave me 2, we would both have an "even" amount. He said you couldn't do that with 1, 3, 5, etc. It may sound simple, but to me it was amazing to see him developing his own math theories. We had never labeled the numbers "even" or "odd." When I mentioned that some people call the 1, 3, 5, 7 "odd" numbers, he gave me a funny look. He also loves to do mazes now, which has helped him in writing and drawing. A few months ago he seemed to be struggling to get things on paper, but now it is getting easier. And all three kids are left-handed. Sometimes I forget this and buy the binders with rings and it is hard for them to use them.

He and Joyce play *Thinking Things* and *3-D Body Adventure* for a bit. Trace wants to play too, so they let him. Trace's job in life now is to follow his brother around and make him feel important. Jake is a great big brother and is patient with him . . . well, most of the time.

We do a lot of reading aloud. Joyce reads to her younger siblings. I taught Joyce phonics in our early homeschooling years and she could read early readers when she was about five years old, but she didn't feel really comfortable reading until just this past year. I feel the most important thing is to develop a love for reading. Reading gives us basically two things—pleasure and knowledge. I am glad we found the unschooling philosophy and didn't force skills on her or stifle her love of reading. She is now reading chapter books that she picks out at bookstores, in magazines, and on web sites.

Our children are very athletic and love the outdoors. Joyce excels in gymnastics and horsemanship. She doesn't want to compete in either, although she has been asked. She has also been performing in theatre groups since she was five years old. Joyce is looking into volunteering at a local zoological and botanical garden. She has raised a couple of ducks and would like to work with their injured/unreleasable birds. As the kids get older, we will look for any opportunity for them to learn from real people, and do real things in the areas they are interested in.

Jake is joining soccer this fall and is very excited, though I have mixed feelings. It is our first "organized" sporting event for the kids, and although there are no official games at his age, I hope the cooperative spirit is regarded more than the competitive. I may need to change my outlook on the "competitive sports" as it seems to be a passion for my youngest. He thinks he's on the soccer team.

All of our "curriculum" is on the computer. The kids choose what to play. I make suggestions occasionally. We have many manipulatives available and even workbooks if they feel like doing them. With three kids and one computer, we have to set a timer for how long each person can be on the computer. This gets

---

to be annoying when someone is into a game/educational program. So we purchased another computer as part of our homeschooling budget this year. The only other expenses are our memberships to a few local museums and occasional books. We have a yearly membership to our science museum, our art museum for kids, and a garden/wildlife park, where Joyce wants to voluntee. We will check with them when the worst heat of the summer is over.

Later on, while Trace takes a nap, Joyce and Jake play "magic tricks" with a laser pen we picked up. I check some e-mail. A friend calls and says there is a special on *C-Span* about homeschooling so I turn it on and Joyce watches a bit of it with me.

One of the kids turns on *The Weather Channel.* They check *The Weather Channel* for storm updates. The kids are always interested in the weather, and hurricane season makes it even more interesting. There are a few storms to keep our eye on.

All three kids model for ads or local fashion shows. Joyce had been asking me about it for a few years, so last year I thought we were ready. (She was ready before then, but I wasn't, since Trace was an infant.) We have fun. It's not the high-fashion, high-stress stuff you hear about with adult models. The kids get to meet all kinds of people. I'm hoping they can make enough money to have a nice savings account to use when they are older. They can go to college, take a trip around the world, start a business, etc.

We tell the kids that they don't have to wait until they "grow up" to do real work. They know they can start a business if they want to. We tell them that they don't have to wait to be a photographer, a baker, an animal sitter, whatever. We also talk about doing something they love that will also serve others and not to think of work as only a means of making money.

I believe the constant example and explanations we give the children help them form proper values and make good choices. Being with my kids everyday, I am the trusted source whom they come to share their feelings. They express their opinions on other's behaviors and things they see in movies or on television. Although the oldest is just turning ten, we have had many discussions (many during our "car" learning) about social problems such as racism, war, sexual abuse, violence, and murder. We also discuss different types of religions, beliefs and talk about the soul. We discuss world politics, sex, love, and how our bodies work. I believe this constant dialogue will serve them now and in the future with many of life's choices. Communication is a big key to solving many of life's problems and making the world a better place. I hope this open communication that I have with my children will carry over to their teens and beyond.

Dad comes home at 5:00 p.m., but has to go back to the twenty-five acre nursery to fix something on the tilapia (freshwater fish) tanks. I have a homeschool support group meeting, so William takes Trace with him. William is very supportive of me and he is always willing to help. He enjoys his time with the children, but he also looks forward to the long talks and "alone" time we share as husband and wife. The close relationship we have really helps us with our homeschooling and the flow of our daily life. Giving to each other is just as important as what we give to the kids. We work a lot on our marital relationship, continually aiming to improve it. It helps our children understand the complexity of relationships as they see us work on ours. The children also are coming to understand that we need time alone for ourselves, which we have counted on since before they were born!

Joyce usually comes to the support group meetings to sell sodas, socialize, or sometimes listen to the topics. Jake comes with me this me time because it is an "orientation" meeting, and we have booths set up but no speakers. I don't think he'd like sitting for the hour while someone talks. I oversee the "unschooling" table by answering questions from the people who have gathered around my table. Some are in awe, some are curious, some are frustrated with the "school-at-home" approach to homeschooling. I also volunteer at the "computer" table since I am considered the "expert" on computer issues in our group. I answer

Joyce, Marie, Jake, William, Trace

questions concerning our e-mail list, recommend good learning software, etc. I had Joyce's portfolio there for people to see how we document learning and meet our state's requirement. It's mostly a book of pictures of events and field trips, some samples of her work, a list of the dozens of computer programs she uses, and a reading log. Everyone said it was great. Looking back through her portfolio, I was impressed at the amount of things she had experienced. The truth is, even with the impressive portfolio, it still did not show all the learning she had accomplished. There is no way to know or document all the learning that runs through her head everyday.

We get home around 9:00 p.m. Everyone is still up at 10:30 p.m., reading or on the computer. Joyce checks her e-mail and returns a letter to her grandmother. She asks me how to spell some words.

Then, they start to drop off. Trace, Dad and Joyce go first. Jake is a night owl, so he and I sorted through, then read some "easy" first readers that someone gave us.

Jake and I head to bed together. Sometimes I will stay up late when it's quiet and work on the computer. I do the web site for our homeschool support group, our business, and a few other businesses. But tonight I'm tired, and I go to bed.

John, age 34
Rachel, age 34
Daniel, age 10
Michelle, age 8

Interview with Rachel in Canberra, Australia on a lovely spring day in August

CREATIVELY RESTRUCTURING

It's a lovely sunny and warm day—the last day of winter, with a hint of spring at last. We're near the middle of Term 3. The Australian school year starts in late January, with four ten-week terms. We finish for the year in mid December when our summer and Christmas holidays begin.

Canberra is the capital city of Australia. It's unusual since it's not yet 100 years old and is a planned city (a bit like Washington, D.C.). It's a city of public servants, politicians, embassies, two universities, and many national institutions. A lot of people have tertiary qualifications, and there's not much heavy industry in the area. The population is only 310,000, so it's a nice mix between a city (with the benefits of theatre, concerts, art galleries, libraries, and other cultural and sporting facilities) and a small town where people know each other well. We enjoy living here very much. My husband and both our children were born in Canberra, and we've lived here on and off for most of our lives.

We live in a suburb on the west of Canberra, near Mt. Stromlo Observatory, where my husband John works as a research fellow. He is a theoretical astrophysicist and studies the interstellar medium (the gases and stuff between the stars) and shock waves from when stars explode. He really loves his job, but it's demanding, and he works long hours. He also studied chemistry, so he's a valuable homeschooling asset! As an academic, he has some flexibility and can sometimes stay home with the children if I have an early morning meeting.

I was born in Melbourne, and have lived in Canberra for most of my life, punctuated by years in America (with my father and husband's work commitments). I spent much of my childhood in Connecticut and Arizona, and three years recently in Boulder, Colorado. When I finished high school in Canberra, I studied and worked in the biological sciences (genetics, biochemistry and botany) for several years, but then shifted to graphic design. Science and art always featured highly in my schooling, and this change gave me more flexibility to have a career *and* children (something which is notoriously difficult for women scientists). While the children were young I didn't do much paid work, but for the past two years I've been able to start my own small home-based business doing graphic design, web site design, and fine art. I usually try to work three to four hours a day in my business. Sometimes this is less when not much work is on, and sometimes it's much more when a deadline is approaching.

I must admit that I find it very hard to balance work, homeschooling, housework, and the rest of my life. The only way I can cope is to not have very high expectations of what will happen each day. Too bad if the house is messy, I don't get all my record-keeping done straight away, or the kids don't write anything. I've found that having wishful and unrealistic goals has made my life extremely difficult, and I've had to seriously drop my standards and expectations so that I can continue to be with the children, earn a small income, and stay sane.

August

8.30 a.m.—I get up later than usual (7:00 a.m. is more usual)—we've all been battling the winter flu for weeks now, hence the need for more sleep. Daniel also wakes up, but doesn't get out of bed just yet. My husband John is home sick in bed today, so I have the luxury of not having to drag the kids around with me on my errands. I have an appointment with my podiatrist, to check my orthotics (shoe inserts). I have a shower and quickly check my e-mail.

9.00 a.m.—I drive down to the podiatrist. On the way home I drop past one of the several libraries we go to and get some science fiction novels for Daniel and "easy to read" books for Michelle. Daniel has read all our SciFi and fantasy novels that he's interested in, hence the search for something he'll like. He loves Terry Pratchett and Harry Harrison, and he prefers funny books, although he also loves Sherlock Holmes, too. He can't stand it if he has nothing to read in bed each night! I also pick up some groceries at our local shops—just milk and bread for now.

While I'm out Daniel has had a quick shower, dressed and grabbed the computer while he can. He's logged onto the Internet, found the web site for an *FA-18 Hornet* flight simulator game he loves and has downloaded a keyboard overlay for our extended keyboard. He prints it out, and John staggers out of bed to help him cut it out and put it onto the keyboard. Daniel plays his flight simulator game for about an hour.

Daniel tends to get caught up into things. He'll be totally into a particular game, author, activity or interest for a day or weeks and not want to do anything much else. He feels interrupted if we ask him to do anything else. I find this quite frustrating at times, but realise that this is the way he does things.

10.10 a.m.—Michelle wakes up at last. She goes out to the living room and watches Daniel play his plane game for a little while. Then she gets out their mice, Coco and Caramel, who are sweet and tolerant and put up with endless handling! Our Chihuahua Lily is also a favourite with Michelle, who wants to be a vet when she's older.

10.40 a.m.—I get home, and make a few business phone calls—one to a client, and one to a printer. The kids know they need to be quiet when I make business calls. I have to work in the living room, as we live in a small house and there is no "spare room" to be an office. This makes life very difficult at times. Daniel has got tired of his game for a while and has gone to visit dad in bed, while John checks his e-mail and tries to get a bit of work done on his laptop computer. He's updating the Observatory's public information web page, one of his many duties for work. We have a fax/modem line in the bedroom and living room, so we're pretty well connected!

11.00 a.m.—Michelle grabs the computer and plays the games *TombRaider, Super Maze Wars,* and then *Spin Doctor* for half an hour. She goes down to our bedroom to visit John, and we all end up sitting on the bed for a while. She and I muck around with "Baby Bear" (a small soft toy bear)—I play the bear, and she talks with him. We're talking about numbers and stuff — "What's a number?" I ask in a squeaky voice, wiggling Baby Bear's head. "It's a thing you count with," she explains to her toy. John eventually gets fed up with the noise and company and turns us all out of the bedroom.

11.40 a.m.—I help Michelle make a banana milkshake, the first thing she's eaten today. Daniel rarely has breakfast. Michelle's still in her pajamas and now plays with Lily the dog for a while.

12.10 p.m.—I helped Michelle count her money (she has $10 in coins). We talk about how 100¢ make $1 (in the past she has become confused about cents and dollars being the same thing), and she calculates 50¢ + 20¢ = 70¢ in her head (Daniel especially is good at mental arithmetic, largely because he doesn't like writing.) She also calculated that three $2 coins make $6. So the 2x tables work is sticking! She swapped all her coins with me for a $10 bill from my purse, which is now very heavy!

12.15 p.m.—I finally get the kids to sit down with me, and I read three chapters of our current novel, *The December Rose* by Leon Garfield. We hadn't read any chapters for a few days, so I did a quick recap of the story up to now. The novel follows Barnacle ("on account of me amazin' powers of 'oldin' on"), a young orphan chimney sweep in Victorian England, who accidentally gets

---

involved in political intrigue and corruption by falling down a chimney at the wrong time. The story is exciting, scary at times, and historically accurate. We often "study" history by reading novels set in various time periods and places.

After a few chapters, I also check with the kids that they understand what is going on in the story—Daniel is fine, but Michelle is struggling a bit (the story is aimed at older readers), so I summarise what is going on for her, and make sure she gets it. We also discuss various difficult words (truncheon, barge, etc.) as we go. That's something I like about reading aloud to Daniel and Michelle—we can stop when they don't understand a word, or the plot, or they want to find out more. There's always time for asides.

While I am reading out loud, Daniel is playing on the flight simulator. Michelle rolls out pieces of aluminum foil to make them very smooth, and then makes a little girl paper doll from a wad of newspaper covered with masking tape, a drawn on face and body, and strips of tissues paper for hair. She says "I'm really proud of that girl."

12.50 p.m.—Michelle finally gets dressed. She comes outside with me to help me hang the washing on the clothes line behind our garage (this is one of her daily chores, and I have to coax her into doing it, as usual). She then plays in the sandpit, building a sand house, for about fifteen minutes. She comes in and does some piano practice for about ten minutes. I do some more business work (phone calls and filing), things I can do while my computer is being used by the kids. Since most of my design work relies on the computer, the conflict of the kids wanting to use it is difficult.

Daniel is still using the computer, but then proclaims himself to be officially "bored." He goes to his room and sets up a bed for Lily. He wants to hang up one of his model airplanes and experiments with different ways of hanging it up. He tries an arrangement with rubber bands at first, and then John suggests using black thread. This works and Daniel then makes a sliding and adjustable holder for the plane on its thread using *Lego* blocks. While Daniel is doing this, Michelle is outside again, making tunnels and houses in the sandpit, using bits of wood and leaves for structural strength.

2.00 p.m.—I put a load of clothes on to wash and do some more work for my business—working on the design of a web site for a client. Both Daniel and Michelle are now outside flooding the sandpit ("the end of the world" apparently!), watching their tunnels and houses being washed away. A good demonstration of erosion I suppose?

2.30 p.m.—I wash a few dishes, clean off the kitchen bench, visit John to see how he's feeling, and hang out the clothes on the line. The kids watch the video of *The Borrowers*—we've read a few of *The Borrower* books, and the kids always enjoy seeing the difference between the original novel and the film adaptation. While they're watching the film, I get to use my computer again for a bit, working on my client's web site.

3.40 p.m.—Michelle's friend comes over to play—she is a year younger, and they have a great big/little sister relationship. The girls play make-believe games outside. *Animorphs* is a favourite, along with other animal games.

4.40 p.m.—Daniel is back on my computer playing the flight simulator. He was goaded into doing some of his daily chores. It is always a struggle to get the kids doing these, and entails a lot of supervision from me. They have a weekly list of what is required each day—usually five or six small chores. I generally have to encourage them to get going and do their chores. They will do a few things unasked, like feeding the pets and some chores they do with me (laundry, cooking).

Every day includes a kitchen chore, another chore of their choice, feeding pets, and then one or two other chores such as helping cook dinner, tidying their room, vacuuming, taking out rubbish bins, and helping with laundry. Their allowance is 50¢ per year of age per week, so Daniel gets $5, and Michelle gets $4—if they've done all their chores. If they've not done a chore during the week, they lose 20¢ for each missed chore (they're paying me to do it for them). Some weeks they only earn half of their allowance, but usually they do better than that. We've been running this system for about five months now, and it's been the most successful chore/allowance system we've tried yet. It does require the parents to be on the ball, though (as does any chore system, I suspect), so when we're busy or unwell, it lapses.

6.00 p.m.—Michelle's friend goes home, and Michelle hops into a bath to wash away the sand and mud (after leaving sandy footprints all down the hallway, sigh). I do some tidying up in the living room. I'm sorting through some of the huge piles of papers and stuff that build up. Because so much of our life happens in one small area (the kitchen/dining/living area of the house), it's extremely hard to keep it tidy. I don't have a separate room for my business desk, which sits in the living room a few cluttered feet from the piano, television and stereo system. There is only the coffee table and dining table to use for craft, art, writing, and other projects. I feel that homeschoolers need a large house to stay sane. Most other families are out of their homes most of the time, with kids at school and parents at work, so they can live happily in a small suburban home. We're only renting, so one day we'll find ourselves a larger place. For now, we try to put up with the cramped lifestyle with good grace, although sometimes the frustration gets to all of us.

6.15 p.m.—Michelle's out of the bath. Dripping and wrapped only in a towel, she does another ten minutes piano practice. We put the note names onto two octaves of keys, using masking tape and a pen. I write and cut, and she sticks them on. She plays two pieces. I play the teacher's part for one of them as a duet with her, which we both enjoy. She loves playing and has a great ear, but isn't so keen on anything structured and formal, so we'll try to help her maintain her enjoyment of music. Daniel decides that he wants to earn extra money from chores so he can buy a model airplane kit. He suddenly becomes very willing to work! He looks down the chore list, and chooses to wash the bathroom floor and bath (sandy from Michelle's efforts).

6.30 p.m.—I take ten minutes out to play the piano myself, and Daniel is back on the computer playing you-know-what. Michelle talks to me about *CPR*, and the movements you need to make, which she is learning at *St. John Ambulance Junior Cadets* (it's a bit like *Scouts*, only the children learn first aid techniques and human biology and can eventually can go on duty to provide first aid care at sporting events, festival, and other public events).

7.00 p.m.—I'm doing housework again, cleaning the kitchen and getting ready for dinner. John is working on his computer in the bedroom and doesn't want to be interrupted. Michelle starts watching *The Borrowers* again. Daniel helps me cook dinner. The kids help on alternate nights. He makes a white sauce and slices vegetables for the casserole—a pasta bake (noodles mixed with a vegetarian sauce, topped with a cheesy white sauce, and baked). He's a good cook and we encouraged him to start cooking as early as possible, when he was three. He can now make cakes and dinners unassisted.

While we're working he comments, "It would be weird if pepper dissolved, wouldn't it?" We talk a bit about the origins of different spices and herbs. Michelle got hungry while we were cooking, and cut up heaps of oranges for us all to share. She ate five!

7.45 p.m. —John gets out of bed for a while, and we all watch the end of *The Borrowers* video while we have dinner together in the living room. The dining table is covered with the papers I was sorting out, so we can't sit there. After dinner I read out silly poems from a library book to the kids while they clear the dishes. Daniel's back on the computer, playing that flight simulator yet again. His interests drive me crazy at times, but they usually only last for a day or two. I guess I would be happy if he were focused on maths or writing, so maybe I'm just being biased here?

8.30 p.m.—We're washing dishes, and doing our evening chores (the kids are rushing to do some of the chores they were supposed to have done during the day that have been left until the last minute). I help Michelle tidy her room, for fifteen minutes. John returns to bed.

9.30 p.m.—It's officially Michelle's bedtime, but I do half an hour of "puppet maths" with her, which she loves. By using hand puppets, she is much more enthusiastic about doing things like maths and spelling. We have an ancient wolf puppet (Hans) and a frog with an outrageous French accent. Hans is an especially helpful character, as he is pretty dumb and silly, and I make sure that Michelle always knows more than he does! As the youngest in the family, this is a situation she enjoys. We work on her 2x tables, using *Cuisinaire Rods* and a ruler (she lines the blocks along the ruler, and reads the answers off the ruler—the blocks are in 1 cm units). She also investigates the 8x tables (Michelle's age, which is why she chose this number). I asked her to ask Hans questions to solve. She explains multiplication to him by saying it's "adding up lots of the same thing." French Frog asks her to count by 2s, which she does up to fifty (the frog was only expecting her to go to twenty-four!). She knows most of her 2x tables from memory now. She started guessing for 2 x 6, so Frog asks her to figure it out from 2 x 5, which she knows. When I first hit up on this idea for teaching my theatrical daughter maths, she was so taken with it that we didn't stop for three hours! My hands suffered from constant puppet use and my voice started to give out, so now we limit it to an hour at a time.

10.00 p.m.—Michelle reluctantly finishes "Puppet Maths" with some over-tired grumbling (she'd happily keep going with the role playing for hours) and gets ready for bed. Daniel comes in reading aloud from his kids' gardening book. He read about how to dry herbs and decides to try drying some of our fresh marjoram tomorrow. Because he's interested in cooking, he's also interested in growing herbs and food in general. He also likes gardening in itself, especially growing flowers.

10.15 p.m.—Michelle is lounging around, avoiding bed (as usual). She pretends that there're tiny people inside John's portable radio and uses the earphones as a microphone, pretending to talk with the inhabitants: Parliament is being broadcast and she advises the "trapped" politicians to "get out while you still can!"

Daniel *finally* "retires from the Air Force" as a Lieutenant Commander with four medals. He's completed all the missions in the flight simulator—thank goodness! Daniel discusses the finer details of his accomplishment with John. I don't really want to hear any more about flight simulators and jet planes today!

10.30 p.m.—I read Michelle a bedtime story, eight pages from *Asterix in Britain*—her most treasured daily routine. (We have all the *Asterix* books, and both kids learnt to read with them; first looking at the pictures as they're read aloud, then reading more and more by themselves. We've replaced many books in our collection several times over the years as the books are literally read to pieces!)

Daniel tidies up his room a bit at last—one of his daily chores. Talk about leaving it until the last minute. He goes to bed, listening to Bach's *Well-Tempered Clavier* (his favourite composer) and reading the Terry Pratchett novel, *Guards, Guards!* He says he can only read when it's very quiet, so bedtimes are it. I often don't know how late he's reading—later than I would like, I suspect!

10.40 p.m.—Michelle's upset that she can't have Lily on her bed. I just want her to go to sleep! I'm in bed now but sit up reading and writing until 11.30 p.m. By then, everyone is asleep. Wait, I think I hear a giggle, which means Daniel is still reading!

December

Since our day in August, we have gone through some major restructuring in our family. I got to the point of collapsing and burning out. Trying to run my business, home educate the kids, and manage the family was becoming totally overwhelming. We have been home educating for nearly eight years. For most of this time, I have been the only parent homeschooling and knowing what the kids were up to. John is supportive but not as involved. A more recent problem was that the kids were always wanting to use my computer that I depend on in my business. I practically never had time alone, and the lack of any routine in the days made me feel that I didn't know what was going on or if the kids were learning anything at all some days.

I went through some severe depression and desperation as to how I could continue to do all these things that are so important to me. We called a "home school holiday" for a few weeks—the kids continued to do their own thing, but I didn't feel as if I had to be achieving anything with them. It took the pressure right off. John and I talked a lot. We reviewed all our reasons for home educating—the state of school in general, our social and moral standards, the children's enjoyment of home education, and what we could offer them. Did we still want to home educate? Yes! However, we had to change things to make it bearable and even enjoyable again.

What was clear was that I desperately needed more time alone, more help with the homeschooling and household tasks, lower standards, a lighter workload with my business, and we all needed more structure.

The first step was to buy a second-hand computer for the children's use. This has made things a lot easier and was a worthwhile expense. The children don't compete with me now for the use of my work machine. The new problem now, of course, is that Daniel won't get off the computer all day if I don't prise him away and encourage him to go outside for some fresh air! Still, it's made things a great deal more relaxed in the family.

I now try to take a few hours once or twice a week to go off by myself—not to run errands, but to wander in the Botanic Gardens, draw, visit galleries, have morning tea at a café—just relax alone. This doesn't happen every week, but I'm doing my best to make this sacred time for me happen. John also tries to do more activities with the children—reading stories and doing science experiments on the weekends. He joins in discussions about their activities when he's home. He's doing his best, within his busy life at work, to be more aware of what we're doing at home. However, he hasn't been able to do a great deal more.

We've started Family Meetings on Sunday nights, where we discuss what is coming up, what things we've achieved, celebrate our triumphs, resolve any problems, and plan the family and homeschooling week ahead.

The major attitude shift for John and myself is one of becoming a bit stricter. Before, if I asked them to do, say, a multiplication table work sheet, most of the time they'd say "No!" and be difficult. I would back off and not insist —but then we'd get to the end of the day without anything much being covered. I would feel frustrated and the kids would get the negative fallout from that. Now, I tell them that they're expected to do this and that by the end of the day, and when they say "Do we have to?" I say YES! I only do this with two or three activities a day, but it helps us all to feel like we're making more progress and covering the basics like spelling and maths in a slightly structured way.

We've also decided to have a cleaning lady come in once a week (I wish it were every day!) to help out with the heavier cleaning chores like washing floors and whatever is overwhelming at the time.

We have always been unschoolers, with not a lot planned and no structure. John Holt was our main source of inspiration (and he still is!). However, as the children get older, we feel that they can take on more responsibilities and more set activities. They both want to go to university (Michelle for veterinary science, Daniel for computing or zoology). They still have a very free lifestyle, but now I make the time to sit down with them and do some planned things every day. It's early days yet, but I realise now that if we don't have *some* structure, we're not going to be able to continue to home educate and achieve our goals.

Some things I still find difficult are their reluctance to write (John and I do a lot of writing, both by hand and on computer, so it's not as if they don't have role models here—they just get very stubborn about it and refuse) and their lack of interest in suggested projects or activities I've put before them. I guess in these cases I just have to leave them to their own devices, as I'm not about to force them to do something they're not keen on. Still, I also know that if I do insist gently, they often end up being drawn into the activity and become absorbed by it. It's always a precarious balancing act!

Michelle and Daniel have other out-of-home activities they go to regularly. Michelle goes to drama classes once a week and *St John Ambulance Cadets* one night a week. Daniel belongs to the local *Herpetological Society* (they study reptiles and frogs), has occasional golf lessons and comes along to the evening meetings of the local *Wildlife and Botanical Artists Group* that he and I belong to. He's the only child member, and the other members (mostly older women) make a great fuss over him and encourage his drawing and painting efforts. He is happy with mainly adult company, while Michelle is the social butterfly, who needs hours of play time with kids every day. She makes friends quickly and easily, while Daniel is shy and happiest at home.

Daniel (10), Michelle (8)

We decided to home educate when Daniel was only two, and Michelle was not yet born. My mother brought over an article on home education from an Australian newspaper. As we read it together, I thought, "Good grief, what would you want to do *that* for?!" Then I read it a second time and got very excited. Something just clicked in my head. I read any book I could find and started thinking seriously about what the modern education system would mean for Daniel. I didn't like it.

My next step was to convince John that this would be a good idea. He was cautious about it at first, but over the years he has become a more vocal supporter and is now reluctant for the kids to go to school. Our goal is to help the children grow up in a supportive and interesting environment, with their creativity and curiosity in tact. They do constantly amaze and delight us, with their insights and interests, so I do feel we are on track. We enjoy the laid-back lifestyle of homeschooling. Even though I do yearn for more time alone, we would all be loath to give up our companionable evenings, sleepy mornings with no rushes out the door, no school uniforms to iron, no lunches to make, or projects to finish to deadlines

I suppose that homeschooling is a big part of how I see myself as a parent. I want to do the best I can for my children to give them a great childhood.

Michelle is the one who has shown interest in trying school. She imagines that there is endless playing and fun. We have always said that they needed to be at least eight years old before they went to school—the age that Dorothy and Raymond Moore speak of as being one where they have a strong sense of self well established. Since she is now eight and we're nearing the end of the school year, we have given her the option of attending the local school next year. She's thinking about it, but isn't terribly keen at the moment. She would like to try a few hours a week, but not every day! The local schools are not this flexible yet, but this may come one day.

Daniel shows no interest in trying school at the moment. We would like them both to be attending for Year 11 and 12, which will give them an easy entry point into higher education if that's what they want to do. If they choose not to attend university, that's fine with us, too. We mainly want them to follow their interests and dreams.

Many of my friends "admire me for homeschooling" but "couldn't do it themselves." They feel they don't have the intelligence, knowledge, or patience. I sometimes sense that they feel threatened by our choices—that they're bad parents because they don't want to do homeschooling. Others will talk up the great benefits of school and how their children are having a great time there and that I'm depriving my kids, but this response is rare.

When we're out and about at shops and on excursions, we get a lot of interest from the community about why the kids aren't in school. Most Australians have

---

Daniel (10), Michelle (8)

now heard of homeschooling, and many people will say either they wished they'd been able to homeschool their children, wished they'd been home-schooled themselves, know someone who homeschools, and that it's great. We almost always get a positive response.

Whenever I have trouble with feeling overloaded, I get a fair bit of advice from friends and family about putting the kids back in school, as if that's the main source of trouble and the obvious and first thing to be jettisoned. It is our *last* choice of what to stop. Maybe I'm being terribly stubborn, but that's the way I feel about it. I can always postpone some of my goals, and live in a messier house on a lower income for a few years, but Daniel and Michelle won't be growing up again. These years are the time it's most important to be committed to them.

Since my parents homeschooled my younger brothers years ago, they are supportive of what we're doing, although they do worry about the pressure and workload I'm under. Some of our other relatives aren't so convinced, but they can't deny that our children are wonderful, lively, intelligent people!

When I look back, I am surprised that I have ignored the system, the established ways of doing things so much, and achieved as much as I have. I was always the "good girl" at school, petrified by the system—a conscientious high achiever, "Straight A" student who never handed anything in late, mucked up, or talked back. I think that my experience of school as an oppressive and overbearing master has helped me to take my children's education into my own hands.

Michelle, Rachel, Daniel

Daniel (10), Michelle (8)

John didn't have such a difficult experience of school, so he doesn't have such a strong insistence about homeschooling as I do. I wish I had been homeschooled. I spent much of my time in school being mysteriously sick and frequently anxious. I still have nightmares about having to go back to high school. I found any way I could of being at home. I hated having to do sports (I had a great deal of surgery on my legs as a child and was never good at sports activities). I spent holidays doing the things I *really* wanted to do like studying ancient Egypt, drawing, learning music theory, reading, and making things. My free time throughout the year was spent playing music (I have played the violin since I was seven), which was a great joy. I had the personal drive, interest, and self discipline to be totally self-taught. I would have loved it. Perhaps home educating my children is a way that I can create the childhood I wish I'd had. Both Daniel and Michelle say they would like to homeschool their children, so hopefully our efforts now will have lasting and positive effects throughout their lives.

Home School Diary

for the week 20 Sept - 26 Sept '99 Daniel

Day	Time	Activity	Science/Technology	Maths/Problem Solving	English/Language	Social Studies/History	Computing	Arts/Music etc	Physical Activities	Life Skills	Social Skills	Spiritual/Religious
Monday 20/9	½ hr	Walk to shop, posted letter							✓	✓		
	15 min	Practised 6x, 7x, 8x tables		✓								
	45 min	Listened to 3 chapters 'Dec Rose'			✓	✓						
	1 hr	Designed boat model, drew plan		✓				✓				
	1 hr	'3-in-3' game, spelling			✓		✓					
Tuesday 21/9	½ hr	Bought wood for model, started boat						✓		✓		
	2 hrs	Played 'SimCity 2000'				✓	✓					
	1 hr	Sewed sail for boat (on machine)						✓		✓		
	2 hrs	Herpetological Society meeting	✓								✓	
Wednesday 22/9	3 hrs	Completed his model boat - floats!	✓	✓				✓				
	1 hr	Helped out during business lunch here								✓	✓	
	40 min	Listened to 3 chapters 'December Rose'			✓	✓						
	1 hr	Reading library books to himself	✓		✓							
	15 min	Reading [illegible]			✓							
Thursday 23/9	1 hr	Listened to 4 chapters 'Dec Rose'			✓	✓						
	2 hrs	Swim at Erindale Pool							✓			
	15 min	Reading aloud 'Never Kiss an Alligator'	✓		✓							
	½ hr	Multiplication tables		✓								
	15 min	Helped cook dinner								✓		
Friday 24/9 End of Term 3	1½ hrs	Listened to last 4 chap. 'Dec Rose'			✓	✓						
	1 hr	Played game 'Scrabble'			✓							
	½ hr	Atlas work - finding Bali etc				✓						
	1 hr	Origami - making boxes		✓				✓				
	½ hr	Walk to shops							✓			
Saturday 25/9	2 hrs	Helped with grocery shopping								✓	✓	
	2 hrs	Sailing model boat on lake	✓						✓			
		Stayed overnight at Aunty J's								✓	✓	
Sunday 26/9	2 hrs	Golf lesson							✓			
	½ hr	Watched Dinosaur show on TV	✓									
	1 hr	Worked on aircraft model		✓				✓				
	2 hrs	SimCity 2000				✓	✓					

Books read: "Eric" by Terry Pratchett; Sherlock [illegible] adventure [illegible] the Dancing Man' 'The Three [illegible] - The [illegible]'

Other things: (adaptation by Murray Shaw)

Daniel (10), Michelle (8)

Jerry, age 41
Susan, age 40
Zach, age 21
Jessica, age 19
Nathan, age 17
Hannah, age 11
Rachel, age 7
Ben, age 4

Interview with Susan on a cool, crisp Autumn morning in Northwest Louisiana

---

WE DIG AND BUILD

I am waking up to a kitchen I wish I had taken time to finish last night. By the time I got my last batch of soap in the mold and the gumbo put away, the dishes didn't seem to be calling loudly enough!

We have a cottage business making and selling handcrafted soap and other handcrafted toiletries, dried herbs, and handrolled candles. We have a catalog and have just added gift baskets containing our products. That is keeping me very busy during this pre-holiday season. I am very excited to be doing a home business that can include the children . . . and they are *big* helps to me.

My husband Jerry's job takes him away from home for two weeks, and then he is home two weeks. When he is away, he is a driller on an offshore oil rig in the Gulf of Mexico, and when he works at home, he is a carpenter. Because Jerry works two jobs, which he does with a glad heart, it is possible for me to stay home and take care of the things that are most important to us . . . our children and home life. We have been married for twenty-two years, we certainly appreciate our time together, and we try to make the most of the precious little time it is.

We have six children and have homeschooled them for the past twelve years. The eldest three have finished their formal studies, the next two are my current scholars, and my youngest is not yet a scholar. Zach is twenty-one and an aspiring author who wrote his first novel by the time he was seventeen. He works in produce for a local grocer to pay his way while he writes. He is an accomplished guitarist and loves music almost as much as writing. Jessica is nineteen and in tech college studying business, and she is the first of our children to be in a serious relationship. Nathan is seventeen and has worked full-time since he finished his formal schooling in May. He will start college next fall studying electronics, and then he hopes to transfer to the university to study electrical engineering. Nate is an avid outdoorsman and loves hunting and fishing. Hannah is eleven and loves to read, read, READ!!! She recently found the *Harry Potter* series, fell in love with the characters, and anxiously awaits the next in the series. Hannah loves herbs and is quite learned in the medicinal properties of many common herbs. Rachel is seven and our little artist and author. She spends many, many hours drawing, painting, sculpting, and writing. Her command of the English language is astounding for her age, probably because she's been exposed to so much reading since she learned to read at age three. And, there is little Ben who is three and a half . . . a joy to all of us. He wants to grow up and be Nathan! He dearly loves his siblings, but Nathan is special to him for some reason. They look alike, and I see many of the same character traits in the two of them.

When Zach, Jessica, and Nate reached high school level, we pretty much gave each scholar all the responsibility and the freedom of finding their own path. I had a little problem with "letting go," but Jerry and I felt that by high school, they were old enough to begin to decide what they loved, what interested them, and what they wanted to pursue for their life's work. We allowed them to take the reins, and our only requirement was that they do *something*.

I have equated our style of learning with the way Plato or Socrates taught—lecture, discussion, one-on-one interaction, and small groups. For us, this is the ideal situation for sharing thoughts and information. Sometimes our discussions are done in conjunction with other duties such as washing dishes or making soap.

I tend to be more and more like "Charlotte Mason meets John Holt" as time goes on: Charlotte Mason because of her emphasis on art and literature, and John Holt for his unschooling approach. I have become more and more relaxed about "subjects" such as math and grammar.

Our reading consists of what is more or less unit studies. We pick a particular time in history, a famous person (artist, scientist, musician. . .) or a literary work and study until we have satisfied our curiosity about the particular subject. The year before last, we went through three of the *American Girl* studies. This year, we have read and studied *Little Women, Anne of Green Gables*, Mozart, and Van Gogh. The subjects took us into history, geography, home economics, as well as reading. They were also the source of our vocabulary and many arts and crafts projects. We do time lines, dioramas (the girls love these), sewing, cooking, charts and graphs, book reports, as well as daily narration. If we are studying an artist or musician, then we study their works as in-depth as is appropriate for the ages of the children. We are just beginning a study of *Carl Linnaeus, Naturalist*, whom we discovered while reading *Linnea in Monet's Garden*, the children's book. This will cover science, history, and geography, as well as the basics. We have found that presenting material in this way, with an outline/subject, then building on that and adding materials as needed, has been the most satisfactory for us. We don't believe in feeding a child information with the sole purpose of asking them to test their comprehension later via a written test.

The way we approach science is by introducing them to the greats. Leonardo was a natural choice because of our love of art. By studying his life and work, we were led into other great minds of his time, which naturally led into how all of what was learned and discovered in the early days is so much a part of our scientific world today. But, we have never had a science text book or work book or test. We just read and read and read and talked about it all—kind of what we did for every subject and still do.

We do have a schedule, but we do not strictly stick to it. We just use it as a guide. Though we do use texbooks for math and grammar, everything else is from living books. We use *Hearthstone Math*, a consumable, practical math program that uses real life in the problem solving, with lots of word problems. And it is a great primer to *Saxon Math*, which we change over to at the fifth grade level and use through high school. Then, for grammar, we use *Primary Language Lessons* and *Intermediate Language Lessons*, both by Emma Serl. These books are hardback, non-consumable grammar books reprinted from the early 1900's. They teach the traditional principles of grammar and spelling in short lessons. There is quite a bit of copy work and memorization of poetry and narrative passages. For vocabulary, we pull words from whatever books we are using for other subjects and have a spelling/dictionary contest. First, we take turns spelling out loud, then giving the definition we believe is correct, then looking it up as fast as we can. No prizes, just the satisfaction of a job well done.

We are very flexible and do make concessions for "more important" things that come up. We are not above taking an impromptu field trip, nature walk, picnic, or trip to library if we get on a subject and need a book. We do try to complete the majority of our "book work" before we take a lunch break, leaving the afternoon free for fine arts and fun. All our work is done in the kitchen at our seven foot dining table, so I can work on my many projects (soaps and such) and still be very available to the girls, should they need assistance. They seldom do. They even check each other's work and do many things together. They like to read the same books back-to-back and discuss them. I encourage this camaraderie between them. Indeed, they are best friends.

When we decided to homeschool, we took full responsibility for our children's lives. How good or how bad things turn out is up to us. So in a sense, we are "on trial" more than other parents. We have stepped out and up to the plate. Many days, my personal batting average is not so great! Many times I have to defend our choices. And at the same time, we put others on the defensive —teachers and other parents who have not made our same choices. I asked a teacher what the big deal was about our homeschooling, and she very honestly said it appeared to her and many others that the message they got from us taking our kids out of their school was that it was not good enough for our family. Well, I couldn't argue with her—that was actually how I felt—only I prefer to say it in a way that does not immediately put an educator on the hot seat. Sometimes I say we found a better way. Sometimes I am more bold and admit we hated all the wasted time they spent doing brainless tasks for endless hours.

Our main goal for our scholars is to be able to think independently, to respectfully question authority, to do what is right because it is right, to take very little at face value, to have a working knowledge of numbers and their purpose, and to be able to write out their thoughts without hesitation so that they will be

Zach, Jessica, Jerry, Susan, Ben, Nathan
Rachel, Hannah

Zach (21), Jessica (19), Nathan, (17), Hannah (11), Rachel (7), Ben (4)

understood and their opinions respected. We want them to appreciate art, literature, and music. We want them to be able to communicate not only in person, but in other mediums as well.

I cannot imagine my children in a classroom situation . . . how dreadful, how sad, how *confining!* My children are such thinkers, and they are so profound in their observations. I am very thankful we saw a better way for them to learn before it was too late. Their curiosity has never been stifled, their questions never go unanswered, and they keep digging and researching, which leads to more questions and more reading and more observing. Is that not what learning is supposed to be?

Zach (21), Jessica (19), Nathan, (17), Hannah (11), Rachel (7), Ben (4)

Tony, age 44
Linda, age 46
Benjamin, age 13

Interview with Linda on a cold September day in rural Baltic, South Dakota

SHIFTING ROUTINES

The Setting

Hi! We're Tony, Linda, and Benjamin. Benjamin just turned thirteen years old and is in the eighth grade. We've always homeschooled. We planned to homeschool since the time he was a baby. I found a book by Raymond and Dorothy Moore, *Home Style Teaching*, and I devoured it and knew for sure that homeschooling was for us. I had always wanted to teach, but I also knew that I wanted to stay home once we had children. In the area in which we were living at the time, public school was not an option, and there were no Christian schools nearby. Believing that God expected us, as parents, to teach and train any children he gave us, this book was the encouragement and motivation I needed. It was full of practical suggestions for everything from getting started to teaching methods, to dealing with state issues. I believe my finding this book when I did was the Lord's timing.

When we first began homeschooling, we were living in Virginia. We now live in South Dakota (I still haven't adjusted to the winters). We live in a rural area, a few miles outside a small town called Baltic. Sioux Falls, the largest city in South Dakota, is approximately fifteen miles away. That's where Tony works as a boiler plant operator at a medical center and where we attend church, buy groceries, etc.

Two years ago we found this house—the perfect place to homeschool and to compliment our lifestyle. We live in an old farmhouse (emphasis on the old!) on about fifteen acres, complete with huge red barn, pasture, shelter belt, and various outbuildings. It boasts large, spacious rooms and storage space for all of our books and homeschooling supplies. The gardens, animals, and outbuildings provide opportunities for training in many areas, including science, work skills, physical education, etc. When we first moved in, we replaced some upstairs windows and found the walls were insulated with newspapers dating back to the 1880s! There is a long lane leading up to the house. When I walk down to get the mail, I often joke I should pack a lunch to take along!

One would think that, because we live in a rural setting that has no children Benjamin's age, it would be a problem to homeschool an only child. However, we do not really consider this to be a problem, because Benjamin has friends from church. He is also invited to participate in our church school's activities (chapel, field trips, etc.) as our schedule allows. He attends summer camp with children from the church school each summer. We enjoy entertaining families with children of all ages. Recently, some friends came over to do some target practice, and next week friends are coming to butcher chickens. What pleases us is that Benjamin gets along well with children of all ages and converses easily with adults. I don't believe that a lack of daily contact with other children is going to be harmful to his development. We believe that our child most needs his parents, his pastor, and other adults for examples to model his life after. We are, after all, striving to rear a child to become a God-fearing, mature, well-balanced adult. Why should it be necessary to pattern his life after a group of children whose attitudes, behaviors, language, etc., will not aid, but may possibly harm his growth? Is it necessary to experience "peer pressure" in order to some day become a well-adjusted adult? I don't think so. As he grows and develops interests, there will be other outside activities (possibly karate, volunteer work, etc.). We do not feel a need to overload his schedule with outside activities in order to "compensate" for his being an only child. Our nearest neighbors are within eyesight, but not within throwing distance.

We have a black angus-simmental mixed cow named Bovina, who recently had her first calf, named Calfene! Bovina and Calfene are meant to be used for breeders. We hope to raise cows to sell for beef. (No, we won't be eating anything that has a name.) There are chickens for butchering and for laying eggs, various barn cats, three dogs, and two rabbits. (You're probably getting the idea of what some of Benjamin's chores include.)

Planning the Year

We do our "formal school work" from late August to early May. On our farm there are two seasons—winter and getting-ready-for-winter! Early spring we plan our gardens, and on the first day of spring we were hauling next winter's firewood. Our summers are full—gardening, canning and freezing, hauling and splitting firewood, mending fences, animal care, building projects, etc.

At the end of the summer, I write a brief summary of Benjamin's activities. For instance, this past summer, he and Tony built a fort, repaired the chicken house, and put up a tent in the back yard. He attended camp with our church, went to the fair, etc. We go to the library two or three times a week during the summer, and he reads more books than I can keep up with—about five books a week. By the time school starts, it's past time to pull out all those winter coats, boots, mittens, etc., and see what fits—usually, not much!

In past years, I always did most of the "setting up for a new school year." This year we spent the first week of school working on that task together. We moved Benjamin's desk and shelves into the dining room. He uses a comfortable student chair (a smaller version of an office chair). The computers are right next door in our office, which makes it quite handy. Benjamin picks up any new computer function quickly. (He and his dad put me to shame in this area!) He sets up files, folders, makes changes in programs, installs new programs, etc. Last year he learned the basics of typing and is gaining skill this year as he practices with assignments. He recently put together and printed ads for free puppies to display in area businesses. What really impresses me is how comfortable he is on the computer. He's always changing things around and experimenting. ("Benjamin, what have you done to my computer now?") Of course, he also enjoys computer games.

We decided to use the dining room for our main schoolroom. Until now it has only contained a woodstove and my sewing machine. (We are not dining room people!) Our new school room is in the central location on the first floor, convenient to the computers. We are surrounded by the living room (where we often read or watch videos), the office, laundry room, and kitchen (the latter two being convenient for me!).

We have a small bulletin board on one wall with a decorated border and a calendar where we can change each month. On another wall, there is a bulletin board for keeping our Bible reading calendar, a current list of library books and their due dates (this has really helped to cut down on the problem of overdue books!), a library schedule, etc.

Some other things that grace our new school room are an 1828 *Webster's Dictionary*, a U.S. map surrounded by pictures of the presidents, the poster for *The American Adventure Book Club*, etc. There is a square work table that we use to work at together when needed, and it also comes in handy for projects, puzzles, games, etc. Shelves containing *The World Book Encyclopedia* and other reference books are almost within reach of Benjamin's desk. Just inside the office door is a storage cabinet containing art supplies, paper, learning games, etc. My old sewing machine table now serves as a display table for projects, the globe, hole punch, a file with extra assignment sheets, calendars, worksheets, etc.

Scheduling and Getting Ready

Since Tony's rotating shift work schedule includes clusters of day shifts, night shifts, relief shifts, and afternoon shifts—each followed by two or three days off before starting all over again—this can make homeschooling even one child a complicated task.

We have developed some sort of routine for each of the different shifts, and I've learned to be very flexible during the relief shift week. During this week, Tony will work the day shift, unless he is replacing someone who is on annual or sick leave.

Benjamin and I try as much as we can to keep to a regular schedule during the school year, but we work his physical education and other activities he does with his dad around Tony's schedule. Sometimes our weekends fall in the middle of the week, and other times they are on a regular weekend with an extra day. This is an advantage for running errands, going on field trips, etc. But it can be a disadvantage for keeping a regular schedule, though we do try. We always have at least one meal together each day, no matter what shift Tony is working, so some days our "big" meal may be in the middle of the day. This forces me to plan ahead!

I shop once every two weeks and try to plan menus for those two weeks. I don't try to assign certain meals for specific days. I have them handy to choose from according to our schedule and activities. (The hardest part for me has always been deciding what to cook.) Planning ahead relieves the stress.

I love reading books on homeschooling, organizing, clutter control, cooking systems, time management, etc. Tony just grins when he sees me reading another book and wonders what part of the house will be affected next. For me, it is an endless challenge, and I never give up.

I'm constantly looking for ways to make our days go smoother and easier, with less work and more productivity. Benjamin and I decided that our mornings would go smoother if we plan ahead the night before. Also, if he makes sure all his school work is in one place, clothes are chosen, animal feed ready for chores, etc., we are done much quicker and ready for school on time. (Less nagging is an added bonus!) The thing that probably helps our day to go smoother is having the meals planned ahead of time. (I can waste a lot of time trying to decide what to prepare!)

Also, I keep a "to do" list. It's nothing fancy, just jotted down on notebook paper usually. I don't always accomplish everything on my list, but it is encouraging to see how much I do actually accomplish. I don't trust my memory anymore, so I just add everything to my list! Calendars are also helpful for everything from appointments to paying the bills.

I begin planning for the next school year in the spring. I have the subjects we will study decided upon, so when the spring catalogs come out, I can begin

---

placing orders. (I have learned to order early to reduce the number of backorders and to give me the summer to prepare.) We started out years ago using *Bob Jones University* materials. Then, as Benjamin got older, I began putting together a lot of my own curriculum, choosing materials from different sources. We still use *BJU* for math, and this year we are using them for earth science. I enjoy putting together many of the other subjects according to what we want to accomplish for the year. I spend a day or two at the library doing research to compile reading lists for several subjects. Of course, we may not read all the books on the list, and we will read many more books that are not included on the list. Even though I have always taken Benjamin's interests into consideration, this is the first year that he helped to set things up for the school year. As he gets older he will help to choose electives. I do most of the curriculum planning alone, but I do go over everything with Tony, and I welcome his support and advice. (His faith and trust in me are a little scary.)

I compile a master check-list (which is adjusted each year) to make sure I remember everything that must be set up: catalog orders, grade books, attendance records, teacher log, etc. I also set up a file for each subject and eventually write a "Subject Summary" for each subject we study. (This is not required by the state of South Dakota, but I need it to keep myself straight!)

I used to be (notice, "used to be") the type of person who liked to make plans once, and did not feel the need to ever change them again. Homeschooling sure cured that! It took a while for me to realize it was okay if some method, or even a particular book we were using, was not working for us. It was okay to make changes—even during the school year! For instance, when Benjamin was in kindergarten, the curriculum called for him to begin printing. He was clearly not ready for this, and I had to decide that the roof would not cave in if we delayed handwriting until he was older. When he was in second grade, I tried a curriculum that turned out to be too advanced and very boring. After two months, I scrapped the whole thing, and we started over. (We were both happier!) Also, it didn't take long for me to realize that what worked in lower grades (large visuals, coloring books, etc.) would not work for junior high! So, I grow with him and realize now that nothing is set in stone. I realize that it's normal to make changes and I look forward to the variety of each different school year.

After the first year of homeschooling, I realized that every year would be different. Each year I would wonder what I could possibly do differently next year. Hadn't I thought of it all by now? But as Benjamin grows, I am growing with him. We change methods, materials, schedules, and incentives as he grows and matures.

Years ago, we chose a theme song for our homeschool (*Onward Christian Soldiers*) and a verse (Colossians 3:23, "And whatsoever ye do, do it heartily, as to the Lord, and not unto men"). Bible reading, scripture memory and Bible lessons are a part of our work each day. In fact, we try to include the Bible in some way in all of our subjects. This is quite easy in some subjects such as science, where we learn about creation and talk about why we do not believe in evolution. In *Heritage Studies* (we have been studying American history for two years now), we study about the Christian foundation our country was based upon and read about the men who were led by God, as they were instrumental in giving our country its beginning.

We are most interested that Benjamin study subjects and receive training that he can actually use in life. Now that he is getting older, it's becoming easier to apply math lessons to real life situations and to help him understand why he needed to learn those boring basics! This year Benjamin and his dad have been spending time together every week on various building and repairing projects. He has found that the ability to measure correctly comes in very handy! They are nearing completion of a two story fort, which they began this summer. Measuring lumber, then deciding the amount needed, and figuring the cost has been good practice. Also, they just recently measured and cut new shelves for a pantry closet. Benjamin also measured portions of old storm windows in order to replace the broken glass. When he opened a savings account, depositing (adding), withdrawing (subtracting), and figuring earned interest became more real.

Benjamin and I read some books with each other, usually taking turns to read aloud. At the moment we're reading a book about Lewis and Clark, and another book, *Pilgrim's Progress* in this manner. We discuss these books as we go along. Other books, he reads silently on his own, and I read the same book on my own. Then, we discuss these books. (I never get around to reading some of the books, but I do make a real effort to keep up!) Benjamin reads most of his biographies and other books on his own and I am desperately trying to keep up with him.

As it gets closer to the first week of school, I like to set up lesson plans to give us a jumping-off point. We like to ease back into a regular routine after a long busy summer. This year we are trying to spend at least a certain amount of time on each subject, but not limit it to that time. I've learned not to put a time limit on accomplishing a certain amount in some subjects, such as *Heritage Studies*, but to just keep moving along.

Now that we've made our changes for this year, have set up our schedule, and have had a chance to settle in, we'd like to share a day with you from the middle of September.

Tuesday, September 14

6:00 a.m.—The alarm goes off, and nobody moves. Tony's on day shift and he likes to set it a little earlier than he plans to rise, so we have the pleasure of sleeping a few more minutes after the alarm sounds. Tony gets up and checks his e-mail, while I roll over for a few more minutes. When I come downstairs at 6:40 a.m., I see Tony's flashlight out in the pasture. He discovers a leak in the stock watering tank, so he fills a barrel in the barn for our cow and her calf. This will suffice until the tank can be repaired or replaced. He also checks our seven one-week-old puppies in the barn. We were concerned because the temperature was in the 30's. Mother and babies are just fine.

I pack Tony's lunch, while he eats breakfast and showers. After he leaves for work, I fold mounds of laundry, while watching the latest news about the coming hurricane. (Being originally from Virginia, I always follow the news of hurricanes closely.)

Benjamin's alarm goes off at 7:30 a.m. and a few minutes later, he comes downstairs. This is a recent development that has helped me a great deal. Not having to keep after him to get up in the morning saves me lots of time and energy, and the start to our day is much more pleasant!

Benjamin heads out to feed and water dogs, cats, rabbits, and chickens. The morning's quite chilly and he informs me it will be time to get out the winter coats soon. After breakfast (cereal this morning), Benjamin gets our two min-pins (yes, they are dogs—miniature pinschers) Molly and Boomer up and lets them outside. It's cold for them and at first they don't want to go out!

I like to begin our Bible reading by 8:30 a.m., but this morning I want to get the dishwasher going and the bed made first. (Hearing appliances running makes me feel so productive first thing in the morning!) We finally settle down after we're both dressed, teeth brushed, and read our Bible. We're doing a chapter each morning using the *Alexander Scourby* tapes. Right now we are in *Leviticus*. We also read on our own some time during the day. Benjamin is reading the *Book of John*. Also, on Monday, Wednesday, and Friday, he's doing Bible lessons from the New Testament.

After Bible reading, we talk about the Sioux Indians, which we are studying in South Dakota history right now. We're using *South Dakota, a Journey Through Time*. We watch two segments of a set of tapes called *South Dakota Adventures*, on loan to us from the public television station. Today's segments are "The Sioux People" and "Tiyospaye." We learn how the Sioux Indians live together in groups and depend on each other for survival, rearing children, etc.

In math, we are working on sets. After a short break, we sit down at our writing board, armed with markers and an old sock (our eraser!), and practice recognizing unions and intersection of sets. (Benjamin took a break during math to eat a peanut butter sandwich.) Then it's time to practice some skills by subtracting and multiplying fractions. This refresher is needed, as we ease back into the school year.

This year we're trying to take a small break between each subject, and it seems to be working well for both of us. Benjamin may run upstairs to play for a few minutes, read, or do a chore. I'm usually getting ready for the next subject, doing laundry, or getting the mail.

Benjamin takes his first vocabulary test for this year and does well, missing only one word. Then we go over some notes I put together this summer on study skills. I typed these up before receiving my new glasses, without a spell checker on the computer, so I decided to have Benjamin proof them as he reads them. Tomorrow, during computer time, he'll make the corrections on the computer for me. (Last year's typing practice has come in handy for him!)

While Benjamin is working on his new vocabulary lesson, I'm fixing leftover chicken and grilled cheese sandwiches for lunch. While we eat, he tells me about *Swiss Family Robinson*, the first book he's reading for literature this year. He compares the differences between the book and the video.

After lunch, I notice that the mail carrier has left the mail on the hood of my car since there is a package, which means no walk down the lane for me today! As I let the dogs out, I notice once again, the baskets of tomatoes, apples, potatoes and onions waiting for me in the entryway. As we gather the last of this year's harvest, there's still plenty for me to do this week! The baskets represent apples to be made into apple butter and canned for apple desserts. Also, there are many apples to be dried for snacks this winter. Some of the onions will be frozen and others will be stored in the attic, where they will keep all winter. I will can tomatoes for soups, stews, and casseroles.

Earth science is next. Benjamin had previously read the first chapter (*BJU*) titled *Science and Origins*. We discuss some questions at the end of the chapter and he is very enthusiastic (as he always is) about discussing creation vs. evolution. This discussion lasts about an hour! One thing I enjoy about homeschooling is that we can take the time to discuss various subjects and interests, not just read about them. When he listed some of the things that scientists cannot control, it led to a discussion about the coming hurricane. This led to my telling him about some of the hurricanes I remember from my childhood in Virginia.

At about 1:15 p.m., we begin the last subject for the day: American history. We are continuing our study from where we left off in seventh grade (another thing I like about homeschooling!). We've been reading about the American Revolution, Boston Tea Party, July 4, 1776, etc. We use a variety of books for this study, including *American Adventures* by Morrie Greenberg, *Exploring American History* by Christian Liberty Press, a book about Presidents, and many library books. The library is my best friend when it comes to this course. Benjamin loves to read and I take advantage of that.

Today, after reviewing a time line of events we've studied up to this point, we read a story about Mexicans moving into California. We tried a little debate as to whether it was worth it to suffer for a chance at a better life. Benjamin warmed up to the debate-style of "creative thinking" and did well. He's working on a four-day diary, imagining that he is a settler telling about his trip from Mexico to California. (This is an exciting development for me, as he has not been very fond of writing prior to this year.)

By the time we are through, it is just about time to start supper. We go out to the barn to check on the puppies, and Benjamin plays in his half-built fort for a while before hauling a dead hen out of the barn. Then he reads a book from the *American Adventure Club* series. He receives two historical fiction books about every six weeks. There are forty-eight books in all, and he devours them as soon as they arrive. He's reading *Marching with Sousa* now. This club has been a lot of fun for him. He received a membership card and a poster to put on the wall with places to put stickers for the books as he reads them. Also, he receives a newsletter with each mailing with activities and previews of the next books he will receive.

Tonight I decide to try a new recipe "Hearty Ham Casserole" from my *Quick Cooking* magazine (I love the *Taste of Home* and *Quick Cooking* magazines). While preparing supper, I hear on the radio that the Minnesota schools are now requiring students to read twenty-five books during the school year—not a problem for us!

Benjamin helps me unload the dishwasher and set the table. When Tony comes home from work around 4:30 p.m., we all agree that the casserole is a keeper. After clearing the table, we watch the news, and then I pick the last of the tiny pumpkins from the garden.

While Tony and I haul a load of wood and stack it, Benjamin reads about Daniel Boone, works a few math problems, writes his vocabulary words, studies some verses, and reads a chapter in the *Book of John*. Then he picks some apples before dark. (Someone should remind me not to give him assignments during wood hauling season. Next time, it's his turn to help haul wood.)

By now, it's 8:30 p.m. and I'm winding down. Hauling wood really finished me off! Benjamin's asking me to make a batch of hot chocolate mix, and since we accomplished so much today, I think that's a good idea. After he takes a shower, we all sit at the kitchen table drinking hot chocolate.

Finally, I sit down to plan tomorrow's lessons (mostly just making sure everything is ready) and do a little reading. I'll fill in my teacher log in the morning. I'm just too tired now. Benjamin heads to bed at 10:00 p.m.

Looking back over our day, I realize this is a rather calm day—no trips to the library, no significant interruptions, no visitors, no stray cows wandering onto our property, etc.! The phone was even quiet except for once when Tony called to give me some price quotes on a new water stock tank.

When I think back on how far we have come, I am amazed (and perhaps a little proud) at what's been accomplished so far. I hasten to add that we are ever-mindful of our dependence upon the Lord and are thankful for His guidance. There are days when things do not go well. For instance, if one or both of us wake up tired and cranky, all we may want to do is hurry up and get through the day—Benjamin may not be interested in doing his best handwriting, and I may not be interested in explaining the same math concept over again. I may question what we're doing, but it doesn't take long for me to realize everyone has bad days and that's no reason to quit. Some things we may do to relieve frustration or stress is to take a break, get some exercise, or just do something completely different for a while.

My mom and dad were always so proud of our choice to homeschool that, even though they are both gone now, it continues to encourage me when I think of them as if they are watching over our shoulders. Actually, I can't imagine our family life without homeschooling. It has always been such a huge part of us!

Lights out! Is it too much to hope for two calm days in a row?

Linda, Benjamin, Tony

Sept. 14 - Studied Sioux Indians.
Math - union & intersection of sets.
Subtracting and multiplying fractions.
Voc. Test. - Did well. Missed one word.
Finished reading notes on study skills.
Began American Adventure book. Read
about Mexicans settling in California
in 1781. Checked Timeline to see where
we're at. (1700's) Debated the pros and
cons of settling a new land. This was
fun! Also reading a book on Daniel Boone.
Sci. - Finished discussing chapt. 1. Benjamin
enjoys discussing creation vs. evolution.
Test on chapt. 1 on Thursday.

Benjamin (13)

Date	Subject: Bible	Subject: Math	Subject: Study Sk.	Subject: H.S.
9/13	pp. 32-39 Quiz #2 mem. Jn. 1:1, 14, 29 (Due Fri.)	45 Union & Intersection of Sets pp. 12-15 [Skills 21-25]	Read notes on Testing. Find typos.	Video (Where America Began - Jamestown, Wmsbg. Yorktown) Bk. - Daniel Boone
	Subject: S.D.	**Subject: Math**	**Subject: Voc.**	**Subject: H.S.**
9/14	Discuss chpt. 3 Act. p. 11 Tape Seg. 4, 5, 6 Bks. The Sioux - Legends of the Mighty Sioux	↓ H.W. [Skills 26-30]	Test 42 Suffixes pp. 56-57 St. Sk. Finish notes (write voc. wds.)	Am. Adv. ✓ pp. 6-11 Timeline - Story - Activities Bk. - Dan. Boone
	Subject: Bible	**Subject: Math**	**Subject: Gram.**	**Subject: H.S.**
9/15	pp. 46-53 Quiz #3 pp. 54-59	46 Wd. Problems pp. 16-17 H.W. [Skills 1-5]	chpt. 2 - Pronouns pp. 17-19 Personal Pronouns	Dan. Boone - chpt. 7-9 H.W. [10-15]
	Subject: S.D.	**Subject: Math**	**Subject: Gram.**	**Subject: H.S.**
9/16	Bks. - Buffalo Woman Return of the Buffalo Pray. 6 [Assign chpt. 4]	Skills 5-12 Wd. Prob. 31-35	pp. 20-22 Indefinite Pronouns Demonstrative " Interrogative "	Complete D.B. chpt. 16-18 Add to booklist - Assign John P. Jones Bk.
	Subject: Bible	**Subject: Math**	**Subject: Lit.**	**Subject: H.S.**
9/17	pp. 60-65 66-71 Quiz #4 vs. Lk. 2:14, 52 (Due next Fri.)	47 Natural Nos. Whole Nos. Integers [Skills 13-17] [17-23]	Swiss Family Robinson Bk. due Watch Video	Work on Diar.

Subject: Art	Subject: S.D. Hist.
Begin next week	Mt. Rushmore Video
Subject: Sci.	**Subject:**
Chpt. 1 - 6-13 Terms Review	
Subject: Comp.	**Subject:**
Correct study skill notes	
Subject: Sci.	**Subject:**
Test - chpt. 1	
Subject: Comp.	**Subject:**
Magazines - List of games	

Notes:

"Old Indian Legend" [Cckr]
If You Lived With the Sioux Indians" (
Return Videos Mon. [ML]
Science Test - chpt. 1
Type Math Wd. prob. pp. 26; 31-35
Type " " " p. 27: 32-35

Demetrius, age 46
Shellie, age 49
Caela, age 13
Seth, age 13

Interview with Shellie from Washington, D. C. and Pennsylvania

LESSONS WITHOUT BOOKS OR TESTS

10:30 p.m. at last. As I sit with my last cup of tea for the evening and my kids' lesson plan books in front of me, I think back over the events of the day and realize that it's such a blessing to be able to homeschool my two children—both aged thirteen, but as different as any two siblings could be. Until recently, my husband was in the Air Force and we had moved every two to three years. Ah, but I must digress a little.

Demetrius and I met while we were both working for the U.S. Military in Germany. De was an Air Force officer, and I was working with the U.S. Army as a counselor. We met the first Sunday after my arrival in Germany, while I was still experiencing jet-lag. Although I was a civilian working for the Army, I knew that I would spend the next three years experiencing German culture, language, food, and fast driving on the Autobahn.

When we decided to marry, only four months after we met, the one thing De asked me was, "Please, don't do Santa Claus or Halloween." This was fine with me, although I had grown up with both of these holiday concepts—and enjoyed them. I knew that De was very religiously devout, and I just assumed that was the basis for his request. When Caela (pronounced Kayla) and Seth came along, they seemed to accept it as the natural thing.

Although both De and I had received our education through the public school system, we discussed homeschooling our children. I had done some research on homeschooling while we were stationed at Osan, Korea, and I was pretty convinced this was the best route to take for the education of our two kiddlings.

I've been a certified teacher in five states, and was pretty confident that I could do the job, but De wasn't so sure. So when we returned from our two year assignment in Korea, I just naturally thought that homeschooling was what I would do with the kids. De, however, had other plans. He wanted them to go to the best school available for kindergarten. They were enrolled that September (nine years ago) and all went smoothly until his two precious little children came home the first day of October singing about ghosts and goblins and witches, oh my! Well, let's just say he was dumped off that proverbial fence and realized that perhaps homeschooling might not be such a bad alternative.

While in Korea, I had over two years to research homeschooling curriculum and decided to use a "canned" curriculum. I used this method for the first two years of homeschooling and then decided to branch out, rather than burnout, on the canned curriculum route. During grade three, I used some canned curriculum and began to integrate a couple of unit studies in social studies and science. I realized that this was much more fun and reaped longer retention/recall rewards for my children.

We started with *KONOS* and *Greenleaf* unit studies, based around historical time frames. From grades three through six, we took two years to do American History (while we were stationed in Washington D. C.—what better place to be for American History) and two years to do World History through the Renaissance Era (yet another move, this time to Pennsylvania). After the first year of *KONOS* and *Greenleaf* unit studies, I branched out and developed my own. I was having a ball!

It was two years ago, during our last year in Washington, D.C., that our world changed drastically. If we hadn't been homeschooling, times could have been even more traumatic. It all started in June. First, my oldest son Jason (a twenty-three-year-old college student in Forensic Investigation) died unexpectedly. That July my husband decided to retire from the Air Force and proceeded to move us to Pennsylvania—where we knew no one and where he had a new, civilian job with the state. In August, my mom was diagnosed with inoperable cancer, and she died two months later in October. Finally, in January I had to have major surgery.

Because of the flexibility of homeschooling, my children and I were able to face all of these traumas, partly by making a "unit study" out of death. They do say that a homeschooling mom can find something educational in any situation! Previously we had done unit studies on how horses were important to the colonization of America, how various people discovered scientific advancements; and even comparing/contrasting the importance of Egypt to the Hebrews. Why not a unit study on death? The Lord knew we had first hand experience dealing with death each day during the last half of that year.

Thus, for seven months we experienced death in various forms. We didn't

---

Caela (13), Seth (13)

read about it, and we didn't take tests on the course material. We just observed and experienced.

DEATH OF LOVED ONES—And now, I present to you some of the topics we covered in our unforeseen unit study on death:

- •cancers and the various treatments available
- •the hospice program, nursing, and funeral director careers
- •the stages the body goes through in "shutting down" and preparing for death
- •cremation vs. embalming
- •funerals vs. memorial services and the planning of these
- •wills and what to do with the personal property and effects of your loved one
- •estates
- •death certificates
- •notifying businesses and colleges regarding the death of a relative
- •vehicle registration, retirement, and bank accounts of the deceased
- •medical insurance and doctor/hospital bills
- •coroner and police reports
- •filing documents in court

We discussed the different stages individuals and families go through in dealing with death: denial, anger, and (eventually) acceptance. We encouraged each other verbally and in writing to deal with our emotions and our concerns about death. I answered questions my kids had about the whys and what ifs (what if Mom or Dad got cancer, what would happen to *us*?), could this happen to me, and what kind of pain was associated with cancer and with dying? We spent time together in prayer, realizing that life is so precious but can be ended in a blink of an eye.

DEATH OF FRIENDSHIPS LOST THROUGH OUR MOVE—coincidentally, during this same time, my husband retired from the Air Force and accepted a job with the Commonwealth of Pennsylvania. Once again, my children had to deal with the loss of leaving their friends behind in Washington D. C. They now realize, though, that if we hadn't moved, their friends eventually would have, as that's the nature of the military. To counter this loss, we tried to encourage Seth and Caela to keep contact with their friends through e-mail and periodic visits back to Washington, D.C. I realized they would be angry for a short while, leaving their friends and being in a new place where they knew no one. Since we had moved to the country, there weren't even any neighborhood children for them to get to know.

I found out there was a homeschool co-op meeting at the church we started to attend. My kids and I truly wanted some new friends. We wanted a new support

---

Caela (13), Seth (13)

system. But, the Lord knew we *needed* to rest and that I *needed* to get my kids back on track in their schooling. Through *Scouts*, church, musical activities, and eventually the homeschool co-op, we have more than enough socialization now. We do still have contact with our friends in Washington D.C., but we have all met new friends in our new community as we always have. The other change was adjusting to homeschooling in yet a fourth state. That meant another set of laws and adjusting to having to keep records.

POTENTIAL DEATH ASSOCIATED WITH SURGERY AND HOSPITAL STAYS—when I was told I would need to have major surgery, we were (once again) faced with possibilities, questions, and concerns about death: What will they do in surgery? What is surgery like? How long will you be in the hospital? How long before you will be out of bed? How long before we will start school again? What will we do while you are in the hospital? How long will you be in bed recovering? Will you be in the hospital or at home recovering? When will you come back home? What happens to us if you die during surgery? Who will take care of us? How will Dad handle everything? Who will homeschool us or will we have to go to government school? What school would we go to if not a government school?

We had to deal with the all the possibilities and "what-if" questions my children had. We took one question at a time and we dealt with one concern at a time. And because we discussed every concern that my kids had, we all went confidently into the hospital the morning of my surgery, knowing that God had a plan

Caela, Demetrius, Shellie, Seth

and purpose for everything. Luckily, we didn't have to face many of these concerns, because everything turned out fine.

Yes, homeschooling has proven to be the best decision De and I made. As I take my last swig of now-cold tea, I realize that homeschooling has provided the flexibility we needed in curriculum choices, scheduling, and teaching techniques; the new friends we have met through each military move, church and homeschool coops; and the academic growth of our children in traditional and non-traditional learning experiences. We have experienced, what some people call "Death—The Last Frontier." And despite the tragedy associated with death, we have carried on and grown—spiritually, emotionally, psychologically, and academically. God has promised us He will not give us anymore than what He knows we can handle. But Lord, I'm really ready not to not have to handle quite so much at one time.

Caela (13), Seth (13)

Harry, age 34
Sandra, age 34
Rachel, age 10
Callum, age 9
Joshua, age 6
Sarah, age 5
Hannah, age 3
Samuel, age 1

Interview with Sandra on a cold and windy November day in Ontario, Canada

SHEEP AND SHEPHERDS

We live on a sheep farm in Ontario. In mid-August we moved here to a great house with barns and a hundred acres from a six-acre property about an hour south of us. We had up to fifty sheep there and now have 220 with another fifty arriving sometime next week. Eventually, we'd like 1,000 sheep, so we plan to keep the females from next year's crop of lambs and expand fairly quickly. My husband Harry works full time for a feed company as a sales manager, dealing with pig farmers. He loves his job but finds it fairly demanding, and he generally works a ten-hour day.

I am Sandra, married to Harry for eleven years, and we have six wonderful children. Rachael is ten, Callum nine, Joshua six, Sarah five, Hannah three, and Samuel will be one on Christmas Day. Harry and I are both from Scotland and immigrated to Canada eight years ago with Rachael and Callum. Harry was working for his father's feed company, selling animal feed in the southwest of Scotland. He became a Christian and from then on felt the need to relocate and grow in his Christian life.

We started to look for other options including relocating within Scotland, changing area of employment, and moving abroad. We considered France because we both had been there a lot and liked it; Australia because it sounded all right; and Canada because we'd heard good things about it. We ruled out France since we thought the language barrier might be hard to overcome; Australia because it was too far away; so that left Canada! Through an agency, I got a job as a physiotherapist, and we left in October with the plan that Harry would look after the two children for the year that I was signed up to work.

I became a Christian shortly after emigrating, and it was at the Baptist church we attended that I was first introduced to homeschooling. I thought it was an interesting idea, but not one that I would follow.

Anyway, Harry found a job after a few months, and I started working part-time so I could be at home with the children more. The company I was with was very accommodating. After a year, Harry started a new job, one that required us to move house. He had been working for a large feed company and moved to a smaller one that was closer in nature to the one he'd been working at in Scotland.

Now, eight years later, we live on a farm, have six children, and are home-schooling—not the lifestyle I'd expected when we moved, but I wouldn't change it for anything.

In our last house we had a schoolroom with loads of shelf space and wall space for everything. When we moved, I had the choice of using the basement, the kitchen, or different areas. I didn't want to use the basement, as I like to see daylight and our house has superb views of the surrounding countryside. We can't even see any of the neighbors, and we look out over the sheep pastures, with some trees on the rolling hills in the distance. We move around the house a fair bit when doing schoolwork, so we use different areas to learn and try not to be distracted by the view! There is an area for the math supplies in the room Harry uses for an office. It is actually a sunroom but was the only place for his rather large desk to fit. I put a couple of old school desks there with the math supplies so the kids can have peace to get on with math. We do any taped studies (French, geography, music) in the kitchen where the tape recorder is. Rachael also keeps all her singing materials here since she accompanies a tape during her practice. She has started singing lessons this year and loves it. No one was interested in learning to play music, and we didn't have space for our piano when we moved, so we left it for the new owners.

For read-alouds, we choose the living room since that is where the books are kept and also there are puzzles on the lower shelves for the younger girls to do when I want quiet. We have a large kitchen with a sitting area, which has another couch and my small desk in it. I often do number and letter practice here with the younger children while Rachael and Callum read in the living room. I also do our Bible study with all of us on the couch. We keep our Bibles and study books at one end of the kitchen counter, so it works well for devotions after supper and study during the day. I still need to find a spot I like for the arts and crafts supplies. At the moment there are some in the basement and some on the living

---

room shelves, so it means bringing them to the kitchen from various places. Consequently, we don't do as much art as I would like, so I do need to change that. When it is easy to locate supplies and to put them away afterward, the subject is easier to do.

The basement houses the *Duplo*, dress-up clothes, and various other toys. One recent addition is a table tennis set. We are having a lot of fun with this and I think it will prove to be the winter equivalent of the trampoline we use outside in the summer. I truly am blessed with the choices of living areas in this house, so not having a schoolroom is working out fine, despite my initial concerns. The laundry room is centrally located, so it is easy to chuck a load from one machine to the other whilst passing.

Years ago, when I registered Rachael to start junior kindergarten, I watched our friends who homeschooled with growing interest. Harry and I saw in their children the attitudes that we desired in ours. We decided to homeschool for a year to see how it went. After all, how hard could kindergarten be? I read everything I could find about homeschooling, borrowing books and teaching manuals from anyone who would lend them! Advice was to use a complete program from one publisher until I had the feel of what I was doing. But, the way the teacher's manuals told every word to say and exactly what to do did not appeal to me at all. So I scrubbed that idea and decided to choose just one program that I thought I could use to teach Rachael to read. Other subjects didn't really cross my mind since I figured reading was the main thing to learn that year. We bought the *Play'n'Talk* program, our first major purchase since buying a mini van. I thoroughly enjoyed watching our clever daughter glide through the alphabet and short vowel sounds. We came to the long vowels with the "magic e" and her comprehension abruptly stopped. *My* panic abruptly started and was not helped by some friends' children who progressed quickly to fluent reading! Was it me? Was it Rachael? Was it the program we were using?

For six weeks no progress was made, and I felt like a failure. This was my first challenge in teaching, but as a mother, I didn't want to put undue pressure on Rachael. So we reviewed the things we'd done already, played games and read stories together. What seemed like ages later, we tried the long vowels again and it clicked. I was thrilled and Rachael was excited to be able to read many more words. On looking back, I think my expectations in the first year were high. Rachael was only four when we started, so she was actually doing really well, but when you don't have a clue what you're doing, the first stumble can be a major blow to your confidence. When I started to teach Callum I waited until he was five. He took longer then Rachael to learn the letters and sounds so I expected at least a six-week break when we came to the "magic e" thing. I was stunned when he understood it on the first lesson. This was my first realization that children actually learn differently and at different ages. Why it came as such

---

a surprise I do not know, since they hadn't walked at the same age or started to talk at the same age. I'm now teaching Joshua and Sarah using the same program, but going at the speed they individually need and waiting as long as necessary before moving on to the next lesson. I now know to tailor whatever program to need rather than doing exactly what is suggested. Children are able to learn very quickly when they are mature enough to grasp a new concept.

Harry is away for a two-day conference at a university in Iowa for vets to learn more about disease in pigs . Because he's gone, it's not a typical day, but it's the one I've chosen to keep track of. Normally, he is away to work between 6.30 and 7.30 a.m. He doesn't usually bother with breakfast, so just showers and is away twenty minutes after getting out of bed. This morning, I am up around 7.00 a.m. Rachael takes Sam downstairs while I have my shower. Hannah is chattering away to me, oblivious of the fact that I can't hear anything she says when my head is under running water! Sarah is in and out of the bathroom a few times; the boys are awake and playing with *Lego* in their bedroom. I dress Hannah and myself and head downstairs for some breakfast. Usually, we are all eating breakfast at the same time, but this morning the boys are engrossed in building a new design for a *Lego* competition and don't appear until 8.00 a.m. By then, I've eaten my cereal with Sam and the girls and have started the first load of laundry. I like to get this going as soon as I am up, so it can all be dried and put away by the end of the day, but often there are various piles of clothes seemingly glued to the top of the drier. The children are responsible for putting their clothes away; the older ones helping the younger ones find the right place.

I dress Sam and Sarah starts the breakfast dishes. Each child is assigned chores according to age and ability. They are expected to make their beds and tidy their room after dressing in the morning, and each has a chore at breakfast, lunch, and supper time. They generally do them without complaints, but when a new chore is introduced, it can be met with some resistance. I like to keep them at the same thing for about four months so they can learn how to do it well. Then I'll rotate or move them up to a harder job. I have used stickers as incentives, but I am not consistent with it so it only lasts a short time! I have also used a chart for when I see them exhibiting certain positive character qualities, but it needs my follow through to work, so it fails!

Its nearly 8.30 a.m., and Rachael is reading again. On their way back upstairs, the boys comment that Sarah's plates aren't really clean. Surprisingly, this doesn't upset her and a few minutes later she carries a dripping plate upstairs to show them how well she can do the job. Hannah is following me around contentedly and Rachael has decided she would like to have a shower before getting dressed., I try to speed her along a bit, and the boys appear downstairs, having made beds and done their morning chores. (Callum has to wipe the bathroom mirrors and counters, and Joshua brings dirty laundry downstairs.)

I put Sam back to bed and clue myself in to what we are learning today. Joshua has started math, Sarah has done some pre-writing zigzags, and Rachael and Callum are reading. We do a lot of reading in our house. There is a wall devoted to shelves in our living room, and I think that could be the reason we bought this place! I think that once kids have the ability to read on their own, my job as teacher becomes a lot easier. I encourage them to read in their free time. I have started reading *Treasure Island* aloud to them, so I continue with a few chapters from that to start the school day. Sarah and Hannah are doing some puzzles on the floor, and Rachael is cutting things from a magazine for a scrapbook. Callum gives his full attention to the story, and Joshua listens from a variety of positions (including upside down on the couch).

I talk on the phone to Harry, and Rachael and Callum have begun math—their least favorite subject. It could be a reflection of my enthusiasm for it. There have been times when they had math to do, and it would take an hour to get it done. Some of their behavior frustrated me immensely, and I found it very draining, so we changed our ways. I now limit math to twenty minutes and demand full attention during this time—no whining or delaying tactics accepted! They often cruise through it and get more accomplished than in an hour of dragging it out with a bad attitude. Today Callum has a problem with an addition fact he keeps getting wrong, but Rachael needs no assistance.

I sit with Joshua to practice letter sounds, while Sarah and Hannah are colouring. Rachael and Callum have moved on to their handwriting, and Sam sleeps on. Its 10.00 a.m. During the next half hour, Rachael and Callum read and then narrate to me what they've read. They then have a twenty minute break during which Callum races outside to check out some birds he's seen, and Rachael joins the others upstairs, playing, before bringing them all down to have a snack—today it's oranges and apples. I process some laundry, and Sam wakes up, no doubt from the noisy playing upstairs!

We have started French this year. Rachael was desperately keen to learn . . . who could say no?! I chose *The Learnables*, based on reviews I'd read. Joshua has been doing the French listening exercises with the older two but it's now progressing to reading, so he's excused if he wants to leave. Sometimes he'll stay to listen, but not today. Sarah and Hannah have now gone down to the basement to play with *Duplo* and Sam is finishing someone else's apple core!

It's around 11.00 a.m., and I prepare for the science lesson. We have been using *Critical Thinking Through Science* and this is a major hit with all of us; easy for me to prepare, and fun for the kids to do. We are doing a section about the properties of water, so preparation doesn't take long. When science is finished, I do grammar with Rachael, and the rest disappear downstairs to play table tennis or *Duplo*.

Sadly, the boys argue too much and are banned from table tennis for the next

---

hour. They slump off to their room for more *Lego* creation time, and I read to Sarah and Hannah, while Sam crawls around his toys in the kitchen. Usually, the children get along very well. Rachael loves to read to the little girls, the boys are each other's best friends, and everyone loves Sam. Rachael continues reading to Sarah and Hannah, while I start making lunch—nothing too complicated here; bread, cheese, tuna mix, jam, fruit, and chopped vegies; so everyone can make what they want. After lunch, each child has a chore to do (and also one after supper). Rachael has to clear and wipe the table, Joshua does the dishes, Sarah and Callum get the mail (soon it will be just Sarah, and I'll give Callum something else to do.)

I am thinking of having a snooze. I try to get in two naps each week. I tend to get snappy with everyone by supper time if I'm tired, so I try to make sure that I get some time without noise during the day. This works well since the kids are used to quiet time now and it's just part of the days' routine. Some days I'll jump into bed and snooze. Other days I'll sit and read in the kitchen where it's the quietest. Actually, I usually lie on the couch there! During quiet time, lately, I've been reading *Season's of a Mother's Heart,* by Sally Clarkson, and find I can relate to a lot of her experiences. It's a very encouraging book for a homeschooling mum.

The younger children have quiet time in their beds each day, and the older ones can stay downstairs but still have to be quiet. First I mix some salt dough for a map the older two need to make for their study of Greece. We use the *Greenleaf* guides for history and have really enjoyed them. I leave them to work on it themselves and send Joshua upstairs for quiet time. I jump into bed for about forty-five minutes and around 2.45 p.m. I make my way downstairs for a cup of tea. The maps are finished and don't look too bad, but the mess looks bad! By 3.00 p.m. everyone is up again, the girls have a snack, and I nurse Sam. For the next half-hour everyone has some free time and then we head out to the barn to do chores.

The sheep aren't too hard to look after, but finding an extra hour in the day to feed them is hard. We've had the sheep for three weeks and are still adjusting to doing the chores on the days when Harry is unable to. To encourage them, I mention that we can all treat ourselves to hot chocolate when the sheep are fed and watered, and the children can play. The faster the chores are done, the sooner they can play. Sometimes it works, other times not, and often its not necessary. Generally, they are fairly helpful, but when they are tired, the attitudes can be hard to tolerate.

At 5.00 p.m. we are all back in the house and I process more laundry. Everyone has a general cleanup, and Rachael helps me with supper. Hannah and Sarah are playing with the remains of the salt dough, and Sam is again crawling around on the floor. While we are eating supper, Harry phones to say he is on his

---

way home. It's good to speak to him and have some moral support, for now I'm getting pretty tired. He's looking forward to his drive home and plans on listening to a series of tapes to keep him awake. He expects to be home around 6.00 a.m.

After supper, Rachael does Callum's dishes for two packs of gum! Sarah and Joshua are clearing the table, and I quickly vacuum the living room and hallway carpets.

I put Sam into his pajamas, nurse him, and he is in bed by 7.00 p.m. The girls are putting away another puzzle and since the boys are fighting, I send them upstairs to get ready for bed. I am really not in the mood for any more arguments, and need some quiet time of my own, but they're not all ready for bed yet.

I read another two chapters of *Treasure Island,* and during that time, Sarah and Hannah find a game of *Mastermind* to play. The others then want to know how to play it. Will I ever get some peace? I quickly show them, then scoot them off to bed. Usually, I'll pray with them all, but tonight I just pray with Hannah and tell the rest to pray by themselves. It's 8.00 p.m.

This has been quite a *good* day as far as accomplishing things. We had a very slow start to the year with moving house, having parents visit from Scotland, and going to visit my in-laws when they stayed in Boston from Scotland for a week. I found it very frustrating to try starting schoolwork one week, then having some interruptions stop us again. I definitely work best with a schedule in place; even a loose one is better than none at all.

Mondays always start off badly. I think it's because we've been up late on Sunday night with the evening service at church. Sometimes Harry will go alone with the oldest three, and I'll get the younger ones to bed, which seems to work better.

A typical *bad day* would include a lot of interruptions in the morning, such as phone calls, someone arguing with someone else, sales representatives calling at 11.45 a.m., or someone finding something they really want to know more about and needing help to find the information. If I get distracted, I forget what I was doing. The children tend to need to be kept on task, so if I make a phone call for example, by the time I'm finished, they have all disappeared outside or upstairs to play. Then I have to call them back and figure out what they still have to do. It is very frustrating, but doesn't happen too often. Most of my friends are homeschooling their children, so they don't have time to interrupt me in the morning. I try to keep any phone calls I need to make until the afternoon, so we can keep the morning clear for the majority of school work to be completed.

Keeping a good attitude during bad days can be very hard. When nothing seems to be going right, we'll sit on the couch and read. I figure that at least the children will calm down and will probably learn something, even if it's not what was planned. I might grab a book and go sit in the bathroom for ten minutes! Its a good place to pray, and if I can humble myself to pray, things work out well. I am learning that I need to keep seeking the Lord in everything. I have been getting better at handling the interruptions, and perhaps I've had more opportunity to practice recently.

Before we moved, I had a babysitter for the children every Wednesday afternoon, so I could go out for groceries/haircut, etc., without everyone else tagging along. I haven't started this since we've moved, and I am really noticing a difference. I generally go out on Saturday morning now. Harry takes the kids to spend their pocket money, then to the dump with the garbage, and to the barn. Sometimes I'll take one or two with me, but I find I really need some time away with just me!

I have been implementing some of Charlotte Mason's ideas this year, and see this as the way I would like to progress with our schooling. I love the idea of short lessons and frequent changes of topic. The children are responding to it well. I also like the narration idea, where the children talk to me about what they've read, and I'm gradually working more of it into our work. I meet once a month with some other homeschoolers from our support group to discuss the methods of Charlotte Mason, and it is always an encouraging evening. Our homeschool group consists of about thirty families, and we meet each Friday morning to have a field trip or some group activities. I have decided not to go to any outings in November because our schedule has been so slow in getting established. This gives me a whole extra morning each week, which feels really good.

Our week generally looks like this:

Daily—Bible study, read aloud, math, language arts, French

Twice a week—History, geography, science, critical thinking skills

One time a week—Art, music appreciation, nature journal.

We use *Math-U-See* as our basic math programme, but I find it doesn't have enough drill, so we also use *Calculadder* daily. This has really helped them get their math facts secured in their heads. We did use *Saxon Math* with Rachael at the beginning of this year, but she preferred *Math-U-See* because she was so familiar with it already. I use *English for the Thoughtful Child* and *Simply Grammar* for grammar. I bought a used *Winston Grammar*, but I still haven't had time to explore it yet. I like to spend the summer reviewing any new material we'll be using, but this year was too busy. The children use the *Italic Writing* handwriting series and I'm going to start Rachael doing copy work after Christmas. I have *Wordsmith Apprentice* for Rachael that we use on an infrequent basis. I find she does a lot of writing to friends or relatives, both on paper and by e-mail, and I'd rather she did that than some textbook work.

We are using the *Greenleaf Guide to Ancient Greece* and have already done their *Old Testament History* and *Egypt*. I also bought *Spelling Power* this year, but haven't really used it yet. We read lots of books individually and as read-alouds, some from the library, and some I buy. I love used book-stores, library sales, and homeschool catalogues. I have also bought some used books from some Internet sites and have used that way to sell some things, too.

In addition, the children have a kids' club they go to at church on Tuesday nights, and Rachael has singing lessons on Wednesdays. We usually trade off watching each other's kids with other families at church for Sunday afternoon, except when we've had a busy week and we need some rest time. I am generally happy with the way things are right now, although I do need some slowdown from too many hectic days; the last six months have been too busy. I go through periods when I don't think we're getting enough schoolwork done. I think this is a common problem with homeschoolers. But when I look at all the times the children are reading or investigating something independently, learning how to get along with each other, or helping someone else, then it allays my fears. I constantly have to remind myself that I can't do this without the Lord, and when I'm having a bad day, it usually reflects the amount of time I've spent with Him. I also need to keep remembering that I want the children to have good attitudes and values more than I want them to have academic results. I think academics are important since we need to be able to express ourselves clearly and reason with others, but it shouldn't be the only goal. I am excited about what the future holds for them and envisage them being home for their schooling years right through high school. I know there will be challenges at every stage.

I wish I had known from the start that children will learn something in a short time when they are excited about it. Actually, someone probably told me that, but learning from experience is the best! I also would like to have known that they don't need to know everything and that pushing information into them just so I'll think we've "done" that subject doesn't work. Also, I allow lots of extra time to complete things and expect to stroke something off our schedule for the year! Last year, for example, we did one month of science and then rescheduled without it. There wasn't time for everything, so I removed some pressure by deleting science completely. That way I didn't feel guilty at the end of the week if we'd done no science! We're having a great year with science this year, but have dropped Canadian history to make space for it. Next year we'll do more history, and maybe manage science too! I wish I would have known earlier to trust the Lord more to direct our paths, but I think that also is learned through experience.

I have learned so many things over these years. Children will learn in spite of our imperfections. They learn without forcing them when they are mature enough to grasp a concept, or when they are interested in a subject. And on the bad days, we don't have to give up in despair, for the good days far outweigh the bad ones. There's the immense joy of seeing our children grow in all aspects of

---

Rachael (10), Callum (9), Joshua (6), Sarah (5), Hannah (3), Samuel (1)

life. The materials our family selects will be different from what another family would choose, so we try not to compare our family with someone else's. The freedom to teach our own way is, after all, one of the reasons for homeschooling. And, when things are going badly, we humble ourselves before the Lord and try not to keep battling away on only our own strength.

Sandra, Hannah, Harry, Samuel
Callum, Sarah, Rachel, Joshua

Rick
Suzanne
Kevin, age 9
Tracy, age 7

Interview with Suzanne on a cloudy and humid fall day in San Diego, California

NON-STICK SCHEDULES

I'm Suzanne. Rick and I have two never-schooled children, Kevin (age nine, grade four) and Tracy (age seven, grade two). I was introduced to homeschooling when my sister loaned me *The Teenage Liberation Handbook*, by Grace Llewellen. Kevin and Tracy were both years away from school-age. I mentally argued with the author through the entire book, and I returned it to my sister saying that those ideas would never work for me. It planted a seed, though, and over the next few years, Rick and I talked about our public school experiences and how people really learn. I didn't think I had the patience to homeschool, though.

Kevin was always a quick learner, but he was a late talker, so we kept him out of kindergarten the first year he was eligible. By the next year, when we were required to enroll him, he was academically ready for first grade, but we were hesitant to toss him in over his head socially. We had also come to the conclusion that children should be given time to learn what they are interested in and not be forced to learn what they are not interested in. I enrolled Kevin in kindergarten, but we didn't like the idea. We noticed posters on the walls and a note on the chalkboard about things that didn't mix well with our religious beliefs. There was a room full of computers that was so noisy I couldn't wait to escape, and I did not want to put my child into such conditions. Since I didn't know where to find out about homeschooling, I wrote to the school district and learned they had a homeschooling program. I thought I might use their program for a year, while I learned more about homeschooling.

However, thanks to a cousin, a friend, and lots of library books, I learned how to homeschool outside of the public school system. All of this happened in about four months, before the school year even began. I enrolled Kevin in a private *Independent Study Program* (*ISP*) the first year, which is a private school that allows students to be taught at home by their parents. Different ISPs provide various services, such as curriculum help, support groups, and field trips. This one just did the record-keeping. The next year, I decided to file to be a private school and to keep my own records (which are minimal).

In California children must be enrolled with either a public or private school, or taught by a certified tutor. Most parents don't have a credential for the subjects being taught and don't want to hire tutors, so they either enroll their child with a private school that offers an independent study program or they form a private school themselves. There are private schools that are exclusively for homeschoolers. It is also very simple to establish your own private school by filing a form and offering the specified subjects. What you want to teach in those subjects is up to you, and no testing is required. I love this freedom, because to me, grade levels are arbitrary and unrealistic. We accept the fact that children learn to walk and talk at different rates, so why can't they learn academics at different rates?

I sometimes wonder if we ever would have started homeschooling if Tracy had been born first. She was an early talker and reader, and she probably would have loved a classroom. I know she will benefit from homeschooling, though, and she likes having plenty of time for her own interests, such as reading and art.

Four years ago, Rick got fed up with unsatisfying management jobs and jumped at an opportunity to drive a truck with a friend. The newfound freedom allowed him to be open-minded about homeschooling. In fact, I recall him mentioning it first and me resisting, but he remembers it the other way around! He and his partner would be on the road for up to three weeks at a time, then home for a week or so. One awful time they were away for about three weeks, came home for a Friday morning, and were called away again that afternoon. I thought, "If Kevin had been in school, he would have missed seeing his dad!" Kevin learned a lot of U.S. geography during those years by highlighting the cities where Rick was delivering. Now Rick owns the truck and drives alone, so he's home more often—almost every weekend and usually a few days during the week. Often he's either home all week or gone all week.

Due to Rick's twenty-four-hour on-call job, we have a very flexible lifestyle, which meshes beautifully with our unschooling philosophy. For example, last week Rick took Friday off and we went to *Disneyland*. We like to play miniature golf and have played courses up to an hour or more away.

We enjoy getting together with the grandparents and chatting. Our parents have always been our best friends. We see them twice a week at church, and we often get together for dinner or to watch baseball games on television. Both of our moms are available to babysit, too! The kids have only had a non-grandmother babysitter about four times in nine years. Our parents are all very supportive of our decision to homeschool. My mom has actually gotten involved in the statewide organization to which I belong, and is answering the 800 telephone number. The grandparents all enjoy spending time with Kevin and Tracy, answering questions and sharing knowledge. We've gone on vacations together, and my parents drove the kids to Colorado and New Mexico to visit cousins and a friend.

Homeschooling also allows us to cat-sit for our parents when they go on vacations. We've only been doing this for a couple of years. We just moved back home yesterday from two weeks at Rick's mom's house, and soon we'll go to my parents' house for about two months. My parents live about fifteen minutes away, and Rick's mom is only about one mile away, so it's easy to go home every day or two to pick up the mail and get anything we may need. Our yard gets ignored, but fortunately the grass grows slowly.

I don't like clutter; a place for everything and everything in it's place. However, the ledge around the den often collects a few piles of things to do, and sometimes the kids leave out *Lego, Monopoly*, or other large projects. I get frustrated trying to find places for their possessions in the room they share, even though they don't have much stuff.

Our house is even less cluttered than usual because it is for sale. We plan to move to South Lake Tahoe with Rick's mom. It's actually nice to be house-sitting elsewhere, because it helps to keep our house immaculate. The kids are looking forward to living with Grammie, although they will miss our house. There will probably be several changes during the next year, but homeschooling allows us to be closer, so the changes aren't as upsetting.

Last night, Rick got home at midnight after a run to Las Vegas.

7:30 a.m.—Rick gets up and showers. I had intended to get up, but bed was just too comfy! We only set alarms when absolutely necessary, and it's unusual for Rick to get up so early. We still resent all those years of getting up for work at 4:30 a.m.

8:20 a.m.—Rick leaves to do errands and I get in the shower.

8:45 a.m.—Kevin comes into my room and gets in my bed. Sometimes I make the bed as soon as I get up, and he's disappointed because he likes to snuggle in our big bed. He started asking questions right away this morning. ("Where's Dad? Did you think the pedals on the Autopia were easier this time?" I pushed the pedal at *Disneyland* and had already told him that it seemed easier.) Some days Kevin talks a lot, and I have to tell him that I'm maxed out on questions and need a break. He immediately stops talking—he doesn't even say "okay"—and then I feel strange in the silence. I try not to tell him very often to be quiet because I want him to have someone who is interested in him, but I console myself by telling myself that I am teaching him to be considerate of others. When he talks, I want him to know that I am listening. I don't want to ignore him. To do that, I have to let him know when I just can't listen. He doesn't seem to mind. Tracy is quieter, but not shy.

9:00 a.m.—Tracy comes wandering out. She's usually up a bit earlier than this, but she didn't turn off her bed lamp until 11:00 p.m. last night because she wanted to finish reading the entire *Lego* catalog that arrived yesterday. She's usually asleep by 10:00 p.m., as Kevin was last night.

The kids want to start filling out their "Memories" books right away, because they see them sitting on the den ledge. These are spiral-bound books with a pocket for each grade and questions written on each pocket. Kevin's is purchased (a gift) and has very schoolish questions (favorite subjects, what I would do if I were the teacher), but I made a book for Tracy with more appropriate questions for a homeschooler. It's the beginning of a new school year, so I got the books out to start new pockets. Kevin needs to write his weight, height, and clothes size, so he grabs my hand and skips down the hall. He likes physical contact like holding hands.

9:35 a.m.—Makeup's on and the bed's made. Tracy got dressed quickly, because she wanted to go through the pockets of her Memories book, and I said she had to be dressed first. We don't have a rule about when to be dressed, but I knew she would dress faster if she were looking forward to doing something, so I took advantage of the situation. She usually plays around for twenty minutes instead of dressing.

Rick just came home, turned on the radio ('60s and '70s music), and is doing church work and going through a stack of mail.

Breakfast: ooops! We left the butter at Grammie's house. The kids want plain, cold bread. Blah! Kevin will eat fruit spread if I insist, but I don't this morning. Chocolate milk as usual. While eating, Kevin uses his calculator to figure out what *Lego* he can buy with his cat-sitting money. I usually have toast with 100% fruit spread and a glass of orange juice, but this morning I just have a breakfast drink.

The kids look at their bank statements that came in the mail and see that Tracy, who has more money, earned more interest. Tracy and I then look at a Spanish story, while Kevin brushes his teeth. I have some videos, cassettes, and books with Spanish stories and songs. Tracy likes them, but Kevin just endures them. Rick and I like to toss around Spanish words (we're not anywhere near fluent), and I'd like the kids to at least start developing a vocabulary, so it will be easier later on if they decide to study a language. Besides, it's nice to know a little Spanish in Southern California.

10:10 a.m.—To the grocery store. I make up a week's menu at a time, then a shopping list from that, so we only go to the store on Thursdays. On the way out of the house I notice the kids' unmade beds, so I "Beautify" them, since a prospective buyer could tour the house at any time. (I made up a morning list that I call the "Beginning B's": Bathroom, Bedeck Body, Beautify Bed, Breakfast, Brush teeth, Books are read. The "books" refers to the Bible or anything else religious, but this usually doesn't get done. I just try to mention things during the day about how my beliefs are helping me in a specific situation.) I used to make the kids beautify their beds, but bunk beds are difficult even for me and they need to look nice with the house for sale. Kevin reads *Calvin and Hobbes* aloud in the car. Tracy reads *Highlights* and *Ladybug* magazines to herself.

11:30 a.m.—Back home, but Rick is gone. There isn't a note, so I guess he just had more errands and not a run (a trucking job). I put away groceries. Tracy lies on the couch and continues reading her magazines. They aren't new issues, but she enjoys them like a favorite book. Kevin plays with a plastic light saber. On the way to the store, we stopped by our new church that is being built. There's now tar paper on the roof and windows in the walls.

Kevin is at his desk designing a theme park ride. The kids usually "work" at the dining room table (it's an informal dining room, part of the main living area), but sometimes they clear off a spot on their desk and work there. When I check again, he's playing with a *Lego* car. Then I hear the piano. He's been composing a simple tune for his haunted house ride.

The piano is a good example of how we do things. Rick plays the piano well, and I can read a simple melody and play the guitar chords. I've played some *Keyboard Capers* games with the kids, but never forced them to learn to read music. Kevin decided he wanted to play a specific song, so I showed him the fingering and he memorized it. He's learned several songs that way. Then he wanted to make up a song and write it down, so he had to learn how to read music. He probably doesn't remember how to read music now, but he was able to write a song. He also played a song and told me which notes to write. Tracy then got interested and memorized the fingering for a song. She finally did what I had planned for Kevin: she learned a song on a toy color-coded piano and transferred it to the big piano. Their interest in the piano comes and goes, as does mine. We don't want to give them lessons like we had, though, and make them hate it. They have been able to ask questions and absorb information at their own pace.

I make chicken salad, wash grapes, cut up watermelon, and make lunch for the kids. I'm not sure whether we'll have the salad or enchiladas for dinner. It depends on whether Rick's home. I'm learning to be flexible about which meals I have when. I'm used to planning meals, but the kids rarely like what I would fix for Rick and myself, so the plans go out the window when Rick leaves town.

I've probably done them a disservice by not serving them whatever I've fixed for Rick and myself. After formula and baby food, I just continued to make separate meals for them when they didn't like what the grown-ups were having. Lately I've been insisting they try more things, and I usually don't fix anything separate for them. They can have their favorite foods for breakfast and lunch, but must have whatever we're having for dinner.

Lunch—Both read while eating (*Calvin and Hobbes* for Kevin, *Ladybug* for Tracy). They love boxed macaroni and cheese, as I did when I was a kid. I finally eat some watermelon and macaroni and cheese, although I don't like it as much as I used to. Breakfast and lunch aren't very interesting to me. I never know what to fix.

I hear the red-shouldered hawk on the golf course. Sometimes it sits on our fence. I've learned a lot about birds in the past few years, because we live on a golf course and see a variety of birds. Kevin shows me his theme park rides; one on paper, one acted out with *Lego*.

1:00 p.m.—More "Mom Time." I'm trying to plan one or two things to do with the kids each day, to introduce them to new things or sooth my conscience that I'm actually "teaching" them things. I find unschooling to be very natural, but once in a while I panic and wonder if Kevin and Tracy are learning enough, since I don't force them to study. I haven't bought many schoolish things and the ones I have bought usually sit on the shelf because they don't fit naturally into our life. They are usually books of science experiments and math ideas, since I don't know much about science, and most people think math needs to be learned from books. We seem to cover plenty of math and science in everyday life, though.

Basically, I don't use anything "schoolish." Math is learned through money, cooking, games, and real life situations. Science is answering Kevin's questions about how the world works. Language arts is reading books, magazines, writing thank you notes, and sometimes keeping a journal (when I insist). Fine arts could be building with *Lego* (they both love following directions from *Lego* kits, as well as building on their own), arts and crafts, playing the piano, listening to classical CDs, or making a movie on videotape (making up the plot, acting, filming, editing). Physical education is swimming, walking, playing tennis, riding a bicycle, or riding the kettcar (a pedal-powered four-wheel low vehicle).

I can't seem to stick to a schedule. Sometimes I feel guilty about not having a schedule. Am I lazy? Or am I being flexible and open-minded? Even a housework schedule, like dusting on Tuesdays, doesn't work for me. Tuesday will arrive and I'll think, "Nothing looks like it needs dusting. Besides, the kids want to . . . ." I'm trying to jot down a daily schedule the evening before, if we have specific things to do, just to be sure they get done and in an efficient order. If the day seems busy, the kids will know what to expect and when they will have free time. Housework gets done when the dirt bothers me enough, laundry when we're out of underwear. The kids don't have assigned chores, but they like to help me.

There are certain things that Kevin asks to be allowed to do. He likes to operate things. He used to always want to do the laundry with me (open the water valves, put in the soap and fabric softener, turn the knobs). He puts gas in the car, uses my credit card to pay for gas and groceries, and helps Rick mow the lawn and wash the car. His greatest wish is to be allowed to stay home alone instead of having to go on errands with me. Just recently, I gave the kids their own grocery list and let them have their own cart. We met when we were finished. They had a great time, and Kevin said he always wants his own list now.

I help Tracy write a few names on her family tree. We're tracing our roots back to those who emigrated to California, as part of studying California history. This was my idea, just because Kevin is in fourth grade and someone mentioned that's when they study California history in public schools. At the same time that I was thinking of this project, we received family tree charts and stickers in the mail from *Highlights*, and three other people gave us the ones they had received. Tracy loves stickers so that was the thing that really made me start this project. I thought it would be interesting, but the kids haven't caught my interest, probably because it's just doing what Mom tells them to do.

We listen to *The Three Bears* in Spanish and follow along in the book. Tracy wants to listen to a second story. I suggest she listen to it on her headphones in the car on the way to Grandma and Grampa's house and she agrees. She was able to look at a previous story to find the word for "pig" and she asked what a few words in *The Three Bears* meant. (I had read it in English first, translating.) She loves words—listening to cassettes and reading books. Kevin prefers videos, which I limit to thirty to sixty minutes per child, per day. We don't watch television at home.

1:45 p.m.—To my parents' house. From the little bit of Tracy's tape that I can hear, she is turning the pages at the proper time in the story. I'm surprised, because we haven't worked on reading Spanish or how to pronounce the letters, and I don't think she's even heard this story before. Kevin reads *Calvin and Hobbes* aloud to me. I don't really like being read to and cartoons are even worse because the picture must be described, but I am pleased that Kevin wants to read. Tracy taught herself to read when she was three years old, and she has natural phonics. Kevin patiently endured several months of my own made-up phonics games, but they didn't do any good. He just wants to be told what the word is and get on with the story.

At my parents' house, Tracy watches thirty minutes of cartoons, while Kevin plays with *Lego*. Then they watch *The Disneyland Story* video together. I got tired of having to arbitrarily decide if the kids could watch a video, so I made construction paper tickets (each for thirty minutes of video time, five tickets per child) to use Monday through Friday. Weekends are free; we may watch movies together, get busy playing miniature golf, or be with family and never watch anything. They could combine tickets to watch more one day and nothing another day. That worked for a long time. They would watch short kids' videos or spread out a movie over four days. Recently, though, they've been wanting to watch an entire movie at one sitting. They are more mature and aren't watching the short kids' videos very often. I decided they could each get about an hour per day, and they often either pool their time and agree on one movie, or watch Kevin's two hours one day and Tracy's two hours the next day. Kevin would watch videos all day if permitted. I like to think that if he were given complete freedom, he would eventually want to do other things, but the effect and attraction of television is just too subtle and insidious to take that risk. Besides, our house just has one main living area, so I couldn't get away from the sound of the television.

I only have a few e-mails, which is a pleasant surprise, but the kids want to watch their video, so I look up California history on the Internet. It's so time-consuming, overwhelming, frustrating, and exhausting. Rick and I do not want the Internet in our home, although I may need to get e-mail, eventually, for my work on the Board of Trustees of our state-wide homeschooling organization. I don't like having to come over to my parents' house three times a week to spend an hour or two in front of the computer. I don't want to spend a lot of time in front of my computer at home, either. Our old computer is just good for word processing, which is all I care about. To e-mail or not to e-mail, that is the question. Thanks to the Internet, I stay longer than planned and hit traffic on the way home.

4:45 p.m.—Kevin reads to me in the car again. There are many big words for him to sound out this time. Tracy heads straight for the couch and her stack of magazines when we get home.

Kevin and Tracy decide to play *Monopoly* on the board they made a few years ago. We had some old money and markers, but the board disappeared when we moved into the house. We borrowed Grampie's board to look at, drew our own board using some stickers, then had it laminated.

Kevin and Tracy usually set the table, but since dinner is in the oven (enchiladas), I go ahead and do it. Dinner is usually on the stove, with me juggling three different dishes and trying to get them finished at the same time. Rick helps Kevin figure change for a *Monopoly* transaction.

Rick and I love the new enchilada recipe, but the kids hate it, as I expected. They like the green salad and watermelon, though, so they won't starve. I wash dishes, Kevin and Tracy play *Monopoly*, and Rick selects hymns and the benediction for Sunday.

Kevin (9), Tracy (7)

7:00 p.m.—We four go for a walk. We live in a typical suburban neighborhood, except that the houses are attached by two's, we have common ground in front, and a community pool. We didn't use the pool much until Kevin was about four years old. I subjected him to a few weeks of swimming lessons, which he hated and were therefore useless, but years of going to our pool made him feel comfortable in the water. When he was tall enough to stand in the shallow end, he took off the floating ring and taught himself to go underwater and to swim. Now Tracy is tall enough to stand in the shallow end and has taught herself to dog-paddle, although she doesn't want to go underwater. I told them I don't care if they never put their faces in the water, I just want to be sure they can get to the edge if they ever fall into a pool. On our walk tonight, Tracy rides the kettcar. Kevin would have ridden his bike, but we left it at Grammie's house. I like an after-dinner walk, but we don't do it very often. I struggle with the feeling that I should exercise, but lack the desire to make time for it. I enjoyed swimming laps this summer when I could read afterward, while the kids continued to swim. During winter, I sometimes do an aerobic workout or ride the exercise bike.

After our walk, we all play *Monopoly*. Rick and I both like to play games, but we don't always take the time to do it. Whenever we do play a game, I think, "We should do this more often." At 8:30 p.m. the game is over.

Kevin and Tracy eat crackers for dessert. I try not to have desserts, because I would eat more than anyone else, but the kids are usually hungry right before bedtime. I haven't figured out how to handle this situation. I would prefer they eat healthy snacks and desserts, but that's not what they like.

Rick works on the church treasurer's report and I start to put out the trash, then look around at the other houses and remember that trash day is one day later this week because of Labor Day. Holidays don't make an impression on me since they aren't days off from work or school. Rick usually puts out the trash when he is home.

Kevin is still hungry and pouting because I want him to go to bed. Rick and I experimented with no bedtimes. We each like to stay up as late as possible, and we figure it's because we are still rebelling against bedtimes. We thought it would be nice to give the kids a chance to listen to their bodies and learn to go to bed when they were tired. The freedom would supposedly take away the feeling that staying up late is a reward. I knew it would take some time for them to actually choose to go to bed before us, so I told them they were not allowed to fall asleep on the couch. I couldn't handle not having a break from the kids, though

8:45 p.m.—While the kids are getting ready for bed, I jot down a few notes in my records. I've already written about *Monopoly* under math and family tree under social studies, so I just mention listening to the Spanish story and how Tracy could follow along well in the book. I write "walk" under physical education. They also talked about bank interest for math.

By law, I only need a course of study and attendance record for each child. A course of study is difficult for unschoolers, but I write a page of things like "improve reading skills." My attendance form is just a grid, twelve down and thirty-one across. I cross out non-days (Feb. 29-31, for example), write "W" for weekends, and "H" for holidays. I pencil in some vacation weeks around Christmas. Every week or two, I try to remember to write "P" for present in the squares up to that day. I try to make a 185 day school year. It's just for show, though. Some weekdays seem like vacation days, while Sunday lunch at a restaurant usually turns into a math lesson.

I make one page per subject (language arts, math, science, social studies, fine art, physical education) in each child's spiral-bound notebook. I make a fresh set of pages each quarter. I don't list every book they've read, just if it's something unusual. I only write things once, even if we do it every day. I try to note change and progress, but I also write the basics (like "watched *Bill Nye The Science Guy*").

At the end of each quarter, I summarize each subject, adding onto the previous quarter's summary, so at the end of the year I have an evaluation. I give copies to the grandparents and put one in each child's file.

9:15 p.m.—Kevin and Tracy usually pick out their own bedtime stories, but since we're later than usual, I just want to read one book. I know they'll never agree on the same book, so I choose *The Cookie Tree*, which I haven't read aloud yet. When the kids choose their own books, they often like to have Rick read *Calvin and Hobbes*—they like his tiger voice. Sometimes we read chapter books. I usually read, but sometimes the kids want to take turns reading chapters. We cuddle on the couch, and I read the story, then Rick gives Kevin a piggyback ride to bed. Tracy asks Kevin if she can sleep on the bottom bunk tonight, and he says okay, so she tosses his stuffed animal-of-the-month up to him. He chooses the *Disneyland* map and Tracy picks out a few books. Rick and I say prayers with them and kiss them good night. Kevin comes running out a few minutes later to use the bathroom, before turning off his bed lamp. He says he heard the radio and thought we were going to bed. When Rick's home, we sometimes put the radio on a sleep timer.

9:40 p.m.—I prepare for reading practice tomorrow, which means I read selected passages aloud from the Bible and research any unclear passages. Rick will be reading with me. He has jazz on the radio; not my favorite music, but I can tune it out.

10:10 p.m.—I'm finished reading the Bible. This week has fairly easy passages. Although religion was one reason we chose to homeschool, we don't force the kids to read the Bible. Sometimes they are very interested and will read on their own, but they usually don't think about it much. We insist they attend

Sunday School, and we discuss our beliefs when occasions present themselves.

I heard the kids talking for a minute, but their lights are off.

Rick and I have some intimate time, then he plays the piano for a few minutes. We go to bed with the radio tuned to his favorite trivia show. I don't fall asleep easily with the radio on so Rick usually sets the timer for thirty minutes. We like to talk in bed. Lights out at 11:45 p.m., which is a normal time for us.

Was this a "typical" day? I suppose so. The kids go through times of being very interested in and focused on certain things, like *Lego* or theme parks. Kevin doesn't usually read as much as he did today, and even Tracy read more than usual. Some days we never leave the house, and I play more with them. We rarely have visitors or go to a home other than the grandparents. School holidays are nice, because Kevin and Tracy can get together with their best friends who attend public school.

I enrolled the kids in a drawing class last fall, mostly for Tracy. They liked it so much that we did it for three months. Tracy would have continued forever! I hated the long drive each way and the wait. That's the only formal lesson they've taken.

Rick and I want our children to grow at their own pace, maintain their love of learning, learn basic life skills, and pursue their interests. So far, we feel we are achieving this goal. Unschooling is challenging because I have to trust that they will learn what they need, when they are ready to learn it. Whenever I need to boost my confidence, I look back at my records or journal and see how much Kevin and Tracy have already learned.

Though I have the list of categories for what I'm supposed to be teaching and an idea of what's being taught in public school, I'm not forcing my children to learn those things. I get asked if the kids would be up to "grade level" if they were to enter a public school and it makes me wonder, even though I know all school kids aren't at the same level and that standards vary among schools. It takes a lot of trust to let children learn not only at their own pace, but according to their own interests.

When Rick is home, he enjoys spending time with Kevin and Tracy. Rick is the one who answers most of Kevin's questions when I don't know the answer. He shares his knowledge of airplanes, trains, geology, meteorology, movies, music, and miscellaneous. He teaches specific things like how to ride a bike, tie shoelaces, count money, and cut up food. He reads stories, dances with the kids, lets Kevin help mow the lawn and wash the car, and writes math problems on the backs of paper place mats. (I have to keep two pens in my purse. The minute we sit down at a restaurant, the kids ask for the pens and beg Dad for a word problem or an addition problem with lots of carrying.)

I hope Kevin and Tracy never want to go to school. They are good friends, and Rick and I feel close to them. Homeschooling is a natural way of life for us. It blends well with our personal and religious beliefs. Nothing changed for us just because our children reached age six. This is just life, and we love it.

Tracy, Suzanne, Rick, Kevin

Loren, age 41,
Mary age 41
Delnora, age 18
Patty, age 12
Shannon, age 12
Margaret, age 10
Nancy, age 7
Ralph, age 4

Interview with Mary during spring in suburban Columbia, Maryland

VICTORY OF THE THREE-HOLE PUNCH

Background

Columbia, Maryland, grew out of rural cow pastures in the 1960s and is now a typical suburban planned community. There are nine "villages," each with its own community shopping center, winding streets, neighborhood play-grounds, and specified percentages of single family homes, townhouses, and apartments. Residents are not allowed to have permanent clotheslines, boats parked in the driveways, or chickens, according to the covenantal agreements.

Despite Columbia's close resemblance to Stepford, we have enjoyed our six years here. We have a single family home on a small lot, but since our house backs up to the power lines, there is a large field behind us where the kids can run and play. There is a creek nearby where they find tadpoles, salamanders, and lots of poison ivy in the summer.

Columbia serves as a bedroom community for many commuters who work in either Baltimore or Washington, D.C., including my husband. Loren is a Lieutenant Colonel in the U.S. Army—a preventive medicine physician. He either commutes, travels out of state to various conferences and meetings, or has an occasional trip overseas. This is our third stay in Maryland and the longest we've ever been in one place.

Loren and I met in science classes at the University of Washington in Seattle and were married after our junior year. Our first daughter was born a year later so my full-time career has been caring for my family. However, when Delnora was a toddler, I did go back to college part-time, and I completed my BS degree. Meanwhile, Loren had begun medical school in Maryland.

Our first daughter Delnora is now eighteen, and a plebe (freshman) at the United States Military Academy at West Point. We were somewhat bemused when she made this choice of colleges, but she is thriving there and enjoying the challenges. She completed her first semester with all A's.

Delnora started out in public school and stayed through the fourth grade. That year in North Carolina we were dismayed by both the low academic standards in the school and by the growing lack of respect that Delnora displayed toward her family. There were several families in our Baptist church who were homeschooling with, what seemed to us, excellent results. We thought that we probably couldn't ruin her in the fifth grade, so we decided to give homeschooling a one-year trial run.

The positive changes in her character and attitude were readily apparent by the end of that school year, and we knew that she was thriving academically as well. We have been a homeschooling family ever since.

Delnora returned to public school as a sophomore in high school. When we began her high school years I turned away from our project-oriented unit study approach and went with a more structured, prepackaged textbook type of curriculum in preparation for college. I had to spend hours and hours making up the required tests, grading papers, and trying to motivate an increasingly reluctant learner. It became a struggle to get her out of bed each morning, but it was not difficult to see why—her course work was so unappealing.

Meanwhile, a brand new high school was being built only three blocks from our home. There would be a plethora of interesting activities available to her there, and in a high school of 1600 students, plenty of rigorous academic classes. We enrolled her as a sophomore. Delnora loved her three years there. She was selected for the varsity cheerleading team even while she was still a homeschooler in the spring! She was elected a class officer within her first three weeks of attendance. Her calculus teacher asked me what math curriculum I had used since she was so well-prepared (*Saxon Advanced Math*, of course). She helped begin a weekly Bible study group that met at 6:45 a.m. every Wednesday. She set her own alarm clock and rarely was late to classes.

Being in a new school made this transition a lot easier. Delnora was a wonderful representative for homeschooling: her principal told me he had never met anyone like Delnora in all his years, who could succeed in everything she tried. They easily recognized her maturity and strength of character. She is a gifted leader—West Point recognized that, too!

Delnora (18), Patty (12), Shannon (12), Margaret (10), Nancy (7), Ralph (4)

We will soon be facing the high school dilemma again, since our next two daughters, Shannon and Patty (twelve-year-old fraternal twins) are in seventh grade. From the first books I ever read when I knew I was expecting twins, the main advice was—don't treat them like twins! I use the word twins far more in this interview than I ever do in real life. We don't refer to them as twins at home and we don't think of them like twins. They have very disparate appearances and personalities, are just like two siblings who happen to be the same age, and are very good friends. They are pleased to finally have their own rooms, now that Delnora is off to college. Shannon, especially, expresses a desire to attend the same high school as Delnora, being attracted to the whirlwind of social and extra-curricular activities offered there. We will be giving it careful consideration over the next two years. I am more aware now of better curriculum choices, weekly homeschool group classes, and other opportunities that would be available to Shannon and Patty if they remain homeschoolers. I have always used the same academic materials for them, primarily out of convenience to me. They still have time to pursue some of their own academic choices. Patty is a serious fiction reader and has tackled such books as *Jane Eyre* and *Pride and Prejudice* this year. She has joined a church basketball league. Shannon enjoys non-fiction books about subjects she is interested in, especially pets. She spends many hours cleaning cages and caring for the guinea pigs, the mouse, and the aquatic frogs.

Margaret, age ten, just recently decided that gymnastics three times a week was cutting into her free time too much and keeping her from exploring other interests, so she resigned from her Level 5 team. We located a violin teacher, and she'll be joining a jump rope club. It's hard to give up something familiar, and we are proud of her decision. We're also very glad to have her back with the family for dinner on those three evenings.

Now seven, Nancy spent one year in the public school system when she was four years old. She had speech delays that entitled her to a spot in the special education preschool. Her sisters were all jealous that she got to ride the little yellow bus that picked her up right at our house.

Although I had initial misgivings about sending her to this program, we could all see the incredible leaps of progress that she made. She was back at home for kindergarten and began to learn to read without a hitch. Nancy doesn't like to try new things without having some time to get her mind around them, but when that process is completed, she will then give everything she does a 200% effort.

Ralph is four, a sweet and compliant little boy. He loves every activity we do, and he plays fairly quietly around the house while we work on academics. Nancy has the most free time to play with him when she's not doing her book work. They are roommates, too, and get along wonderfully.

Anyone who has been in my home knows that not only do I have a fairly relaxed approach to academics, but to housecleaning as well! So, join us while we share a day at our house last year, when Delnora was a still a senior in high school.

March 8

I am awakened by Ralph (age three then) in the hallway at 4:30 a.m., sounding distressed. Apparently he woke up feeling sick, went to the bathroom to get a towel, and now wants me to hold him while he thinks about throwing up. After a few minutes of empty gurgles he slumps against me, and I put him in my bed for the rest of the night (Loren is on a business trip to Thailand). Where did Ralph learn about going to get a towel? None of the other kids would have thought of such a thing . . . .

At 6:45 a.m. I hear Delnora (then age seventeen) getting herself ready for public school. She is a senior in high school. Usually, a few of her friends gather in our hall and dining room and catch a ride with her to school. I keep my pajama-clad self upstairs until they've cleared out. I also hear a familiar truck out on the street and realize that I have forgotten to put the newspapers and soda cans on the curb for recycling.

At 7:15 a.m. my early risers, Nancy (age six) and Margaret (age nine) are up and ready to watch their two morning cartoons before school. I spend a few minutes checking the e-mail.

Patty (age eleven) is now up without any fussing, which is unusual; she is almost always the last and hardest to get going each morning. But I made the twins go to bed earlier than normal to recover from a "sleep-over" on Friday night—you know, they should be called "*no-sleep*-overs"! At 8:15 a.m. I go tell Shannon (age eleven) to get up.

The children all get their own breakfast: oatmeal, cereal, toast, frozen waffles. A big sister usually helps Ralph. As the girls finish their breakfast, I tidy our schoolroom (the dining room) and write today's list of assignments on our dry erase board. Normally, I have the whole week laid out on a computer-generated assignment sheet, but I spent Sunday night watching a video with Delnora instead of doing my usual lesson planning.

This week I'm transitioning from what we've been doing to what I want to do. It dawned on me that I don't have to wait until September to change course if things aren't going as I want them to! We've been following a curriculum called *Prepare and Pray*, based on the book *Swiss Family Robinson*. I like the book and the activities, but it is all too scattered for my tastes—one day we're learning about poisonous snakes, another day we're doing caves, another day slavery in the colonies. I'd rather live with material for a week or more. So we're going to finish reading *Swiss Family Robinson* during this week, and then we'll spend the rest of the year on mini-units of my choosing.

I often use a textbook as a "springboard" for a unit study. *BJU* (*Bob Jones*

University) texts work fine. I'll choose a grade level that has topics that interest me, or ones that we haven't studied for a long time. We've been working more or less chronologically through history, and the *BJU* seventh grade world history text begins with the Renaissance, which is where we left off before doing *Prepare and Pray*. I'll read a short section aloud to everyone from the textbook, then we'll expand on it. For example, when the text mentioned Bach, we spent a day listening to his music in the background while we did our usual work, I read a biography aloud, and we listened to *Mr. Bach Comes to Call*, a cassette from the library that interspersed biographical information with excerpts from many of his compositions. We added Bach to the time line books called *Book of the Centuries*. Each girl has her own copy.

A chapter on the Mongols might only take us two days, but when we cover African culture, I plan to spend several weeks doing a lot of art projects, cooking, and visiting the local *African Art Museum* in Columbia. It all depends on the availability of extra resources and my own bias as to how much time a subject should receive.

After a few weeks of history we'll begin *BJU*'s fourth grade science. I use the accompanying work text pages and the recommended projects and experiments, but I'll add in additional library books for the twins to read that address some concepts in more depth. We'll take about two weeks to cover the plant classification unit. In addition to *BJU's* materials, I'll do some library read-alouds, assign the twins extra books to read, make some slides of mold to look at under the microscope, and they'll be putting together an overview booklet of plant classification as a review at the end of the unit. If it warms up a few degrees, we'll take a field trip to the *National Arboretum*. It's about an hour away in Washington, D.C., but probably worth the effort (and free).

My problem is usually *too many* ideas for a unit study, not too few. Spending a couple of weeks on a topic and then moving on to a different topic helps keep me fresh and excited all year. This is my ninth year of homeschooling, and I rarely experience educational burnout using this approach. I choose the books that go along with our unit studies. For "literature" I generally choose the books, too, although if Patty is reading something like *Pride and Prejudice* on her own, I won't assign her something extra. I browse through homeschool catalogs for suggestions and try to expose them to different types of literature or topics. Sometimes I'll just say to choose a book this week to read, and they can pick their own. Nancy is working through some readers, but she can read aloud from books of her own choice, too. Margaret has been doing some of the *Childhood of Famous Americans* series and historical fiction like *A Cabin Faced West*. Off and on, I do a literature read-aloud, usually outside "regular" school hours. We read *The Count of Monte Cristo* last year, and we are in the third book of the *Lord of the Rings*—a three year project. I try to remember the little guys, and

I've read several of Beverly Cleary's books this year to them. Otherwise, they are all certainly free to read whatever they wish, and they do. I bring home a lot of library books, keep them in a box, and they scrounge through there for lunch-time reading when they're not in the middle of their own books.

But back to today. On the dry erase board I write: Math, Writing, Bible, Read Something, *Swiss Family Robinson*, Spelling, Music. I leave places for Margaret, Shannon, and Patty to check off each subject as it is finished. Patty starts in on her writing assignment from *Wordsmith Apprentice*. We had completed half of this book last year, but I was using a more traditional grammar and writing textbook for sixth grade this year. By now, we are totally convinced we all hate it.

Shannon joins Patty at the table, and they are both eager to try something different. They begin working on an ad for our church, using descriptive adjectives. After they're done, they compare their work with each other, and I show them real ads for churches in both the *Columbia Flyer* and the *Columbia Yellow Pages*.

I spend a few minutes folding some of the laundry. We run about ten loads on the weekend when the electricity is cheapest, and my folding area is the living room carpet. I call it "Mount Laundry." I had polished up the living room to perfection yesterday, but like moths to a flame, the littler kids had gravitated to the one lovely clean room in the house while I was watching the movie last night, and several creative projects have now taken over.

There are four chore charts taped onto the back of one of the kitchen doors. Each of the four charts lists one week's chores, roughly organized by the main room of responsibility. An example for the living room is Monday: Tidy and vacuum living room; clean mirror in upstairs bathroom. Tuesday: Tidy living room; dust living room. Wednesday: Tidy living room; vacuum stairs and hall. And so forth. Between these four charts, most of the regular tidying and cleaning gets done. I have a photograph of each girl by each chart, and on Monday I rotate the photos, so that they get a different list of responsibilities each week. That way if they despise collecting the garbage from wastebaskets, at least they know they only have to do it once every four weeks. I take care of most of the kitchen responsibilities myself, and I do the laundry, although the girls are all capable of helping out when they are asked to do so. Capable, if not always eager.

I generally ignore the state of their bedrooms. They get fifty cents a day for a clean bedroom; otherwise, they receive no allowances. They freely receive food, clothing, and recreation in abundance. They have to earn money for anything else. There are always extra chores available for extra pay. I love it when they are trying to save up money for something! That's when my kitchen floor gets scrubbed, the basement tidied, or a closet straightened. There are also extra chores available for squabbling sisters, or for those who are reluctant to do their schoolwork in a timely manner. The twins get paid for babysitting for me on occasion and, at thirteen, they will be old enough to babysit other people's children for pay.

Ralph is in charge of emptying the dishwasher, putting away his toys, and being helpful to someone during chore time (carrying clean clothes to rooms, picking up stuff, fetching paper towels, etc.). Needless to say, some of the girls tend to do their jobs more thoroughly than others, but since I rotate the photos, no one room stays overly-neglected for more than a week or two before a more industrious cleaner comes along. Occasionally, I have to retrain or help move furniture to finally get them to vacuum in places that they tend to skip. I've used this system for two years now, and it has worked longer than any other I've tried. It is perfectly "fair" since they know the jobs rotate around. It adds some variety over the course of the four week rotation, so they are not always stuck with one particular room.

Most days, I just have to remind them that their chores must be finished by a certain time of day (usually 4:00 p.m.) or before they go out to play. If they are not done and this comes to the attention of Dad, then they have learned that there will be all sorts of chores to do, some that they never even knew existed. And Dad does not pay attention to assigned chores on the chore chart, either.

After I fold the laundry, I grab Nancy, who is in first grade, and have her read to me on the sofa in the living room, which is cluttered with cardboard box houses, scattered dress-ups, and Ralph's *Brio* train set. She reads one easy reader book from the library or our own bookshelves and then four short stories from the *Horizon K* reader. She cheerfully does a couple of accompanying workbook pages that reinforce her phonics, and she does about a fourth of the handwriting page, which is enough for her at this time. She is then free to play for a while.

Mid morning, it occurs to me that Ralph is still up in my bed. He is running a low grade fever but not complaining. He follows me to the kitchen where he eats his waffles from the toaster and demands yellow juice, which puzzles me until I realize that the rest of us call it "orange" juice.

I discover that Margaret loaded the dishwasher last night as requested, but did not actually run it, so I shuffle dishes and squeeze a few more in from breakfast, then I start it. I add some more toys to the pile at the bottom of the stairs that the girls are going to sort through and put away later. I find both parts of the tape dispenser. I have lost the Battle of Misplaced Office Supplies. We have resorted to having three staplers, three tape dispensers, twelve pairs of scissors, forty pens, and forty pencils in the glorious hope of actually being able to locate one of these items when needed. I have, however, managed to get through nineteen years of married life with the original three-hole punch. A small victory.

At 10:00 a.m. Shannon is lying on the sofa reading, trying to catch up on some 100 pages that she didn't do last week in *Young Fu of the Upper Yangtze*. Margaret read some poems from Roald Dahl's *Revolting Rhymes* and is now playing hangman on the dry erase board with Ralph. He is getting very frustrated, of course, since he can only think of a few letters and doesn't read at all. The answer is "Funny Mom." Patty read from her most recent Redwall book, *The Bellmaker* and has finished all her school work that she can do by herself. She jumps rope in the hall. Nancy is dancing around and around the kitchen table and talking to herself.

Time for math with Margaret. I like *Saxon Math*, but the grade three lessons can take a looooong time, and it gets frustrating for both of us to get through it. I usually skip a lot of the drills when I feel she has "gotten it," but I will be so happy when Margaret finishes this book and goes into *Saxon 54*, which she will do pretty much on her own. I'm learning to encourage her more when she does well in math, since she puts in the time and is very accurate once she finally "gets it." I praise the Lord that she is such a forgiving girl, to forgive me for the times I get impatient. Margaret is also very affectionate, so I try to remember to give her more hugs and pats, on which she thrives.

Shannon is practicing her guitar chords, and Ralph is playing in the cardboard houses. Patty starts the *Amazon Trail* computer game, which attracts Nancy, Ralph, and Shannon. However, I see Shannon still needs to do her *Saxon 76* math test and her spelling, so I shoo her away from the computer and back to the dining room, where Margaret is working through her math test. Shannon arrives to do spelling with a shawl over her head, pretending to be a gypsy, although she reminds me more of Yoda from *Star Wars*. We use *Spelling Power*. The girls spell words from a list until they miss one or two, then they study only that word. We do this twice a week. They still misspell words like "their" or "you're" over and over during their writing assignments.

While Margaret is working on her math, I go to the upstairs computer and call up the library to print out a list of books that are due tomorrow. Shannon is feeding Cookie, her guinea pig, and I spend some minutes on the phone trying to sign the girls up for an owl program nearby. It turns out to be full, with a long waiting list.

Margaret finishes the math test, and we shelve the rest of her math lesson for later in the day. I call the older girls to the living room sofa and read aloud three chapters of *Swiss Family Robinson*. The girls notice that Jack in the story uses a yoke to carry two heavy ostrich eggs, just like the girls did to carry maple syrup buckets on our field trip last Friday. Nancy has the liberty to listen or not to this particular book, and today she interrupts us once to ask where the craft books are—two shelves up from the Bibles.

It is after noon, so we break for lunch. Sometimes someone cooks macaroni and cheese for lunch (several of us know how) or Japanese noodles, but often we just have sandwiches or heat up leftovers. My husband almost always takes left-over dinners with him for lunch the next day at work. He saves us a bundle of money by not eating out every day and says he likes my cooking the best. I prepare all the dinners. The girls can help, but I usually prefer being by myself for a few minutes in the kitchen and not turning it into another learning opportunity. We eat pretty simple meals. I have a floating list of menus in my head, but I seldom write down a week's menus, unless we have overnight guests. I usually plan dinner the evening before, in case I need to thaw out something from the freezer or start something right away in a crock pot. Occasionally, we have homemade bread or cookies. Anytime the girls are eager to bake something I give them full reign of the kitchen.

We have poor table manners, and we generally read at the dinner table and at the lunch table and, of course, at the breakfast table (the comics and the rest of the newspaper). But Loren and I do look up on occasion and talk to the children, who generally finish meals in about seven minutes and are then excused.

Ralph puts together more train tracks in the living room and Margaret and Nancy play together congenially. I take my lunch upstairs and read the rest of the newspaper while listening to Rush Limbaugh on the radio. Shannon enters my sanctuary to get permission to bake a cake. No problem. Then she comes to say there are only two eggs and the box calls for three. I assure her it will be just fine. Another visit to find out if our corn oil counts as "vegetable oil." Yes, corn is a vegetable. One last trip to find out which shelf in the oven the pans should go on.

After our leisurely lunch break, I have Shannon and Patty go over their mistakes on the math test. Margaret goes back into the school room to do her subtraction problems. It is her choice to do them timed or not, and she decides to be timed. I call out the five minutes one by one until she finishes up the rest of the drill sheet.

Shannon, Patty, and Margaret work with me on our Bible study, using *Bible Study Guide for All Ages.* Actually, I find this program works best with stronger readers, so Nancy hasn't joined us yet. I work with her separately with *BJU* materials. She memorizes her verse very quickly, and she likes to sing and do the little projects. The older girls have questions and drills, some memory verses to recite, and some review of previous lessons. Today, it is Patty's turn to draw the little stick-figure picture of the story, while the other three of us read through the chapter. We are in *2 Samuel*, and Absalom is about to rue that glorious head of hair. I provide some commentary as we read to make sure they are comprehending the text. They usually have some good questions, too. After the study, we will read a recent missionary letter, or if I don't have anything new, we read from *Voice of the Martyrs.* We take turns praying for these needs or for family concerns. We finish with a hymn at the piano.

After we finish Bible study, Shannon goes to frost the cake, and most of it disappears rapidly as an afternoon snack, including a piece to their public school friend who stops by our house nearly every day at 3:00 p.m. I notice that both Shannon and Margaret are still in their pajamas and I wish I could say this was highly unusual. Their friend's arrival generally prompts a rush for more formal attire.

Margaret still has one more worksheet to do in math, and I get Nancy to do her last schoolwork for the day. She does a page or two in a social studies work text, which is pure "twaddle," but serves the purpose of assuaging my conscience about educational neglect of a first grader.

Then she tackles her *Saxon Math 1* with little difficulty. The new concept is counting tally marks and nickels by fives. She says she had been wondering how much a nickel was! She does most of her "subtract two" worksheet using her fingers as a convenient math manipulative.

Patty and Shannon each do their chores, and Ralph picks out a math game that he wants me to get down off the shelf so he can scatter it around the dining room. I comply. Shannon works on making a kite out of a black garbage bag, cut and taped to some very heavy dowels. The kids go outside briefly to try it out, with minor success, as there is no wind to speak of. Patty brings in the mail, which includes three boxes of *Scholastic* books. Shannon helps me sort out the orders for several families and then sits down with our new book about a migrating wood thrush. She is tickled that it is set here in Maryland, but later she says it was a sad story. I also bought a book about Betsy Ross since we visited the *Betsy Ross House* in Philadelphia last week. Nancy enjoys her two new "maze" books, while Ralph looks on in admiration. Margaret has gone next door with her three-quarter size violin to ask her third grade neighbor to teach her to play.

Delnora gets home from after-school activities, so I escape for a half hour to run some errands. I return our videos and take Delnora's cheerleading outfits to the dry cleaners. I suddenly realize that I am standing in front of the supermarket with no children. I go in to get more eggs, and, of course, $50 worth of groceries fall into the cart as well.

At home, the kids help carry in and put away groceries, looking hopefully for new cereal and good treats. Yay for the root beer! Yay for the grapes!

At 5:00 p.m. Margaret arrives back home with her violin and her new tutor. I get a kitchen concert of *Hot Cross Buns* and *Mary Had a Little Lamb*, which is two more songs than I was able to teach her. She wants to know when I will go to the music store to get the special violin sponge for her chin, and I recommend a dish towel.

Delnora is going through the house collecting props for her upcoming spring musical, *Bye Bye Birdie*, and I have a very good laugh when she asks if I possi-

---

bly have an unfinished cross stitch project somewhere. Ha ha ha—That's a real funny question, Delnora. Ralph is playing in the box world in the living room, and Shannon is making a yoke from a dowel so that Nancy can carry two loads of dolls. Can I now write this down for science?

I turn on the oldies station, clean the kitchen, and put fish sticks and tater tots from the freezer in the oven for dinner. When Dad is out of town (or nation, in this case), there is always some question about whether Mom will actually provide a meal or not, but they get lucky tonight.

Patty is back on the *Amazon Trail.* I field a phone call about getting some meals to a friend who is on bed rest with twins and another one about the special education preschool program at the school Nancy attended two years ago. I start in on my third diet cola. I have miles to go before I sleep.

I eat tator tots and read *U.S. News and World Report*, while a large theatrical production begins to develop in the living room. It is *Cinderella*, complete with an ingathering of many props, many costumes, and (for a change) not too much bickering. They get out the video camera, and I retreat upstairs for a few moments. Something is blocking my bedroom door; it is Ralph, who has fallen asleep on the carpet right inside my door. I have to kind of shove him with the door until I can get an arm in to roll him out of the way, so I can get in the room and carry him to bed. He is obviously not quite himself today, and I think it will be best not to take him out tonight to Bible study. I call the small group leader to let him know I won't be coming.

The theatrical troupe heads next door to show off their latest video release to the neighbor's family, but when I come downstairs, I find Nancy back at the dinner table with the last fish stick on her fork. I offer to reheat it for her, and she thinks that might be an improvement. Just call me Betty Crocker.

At 8:00 p.m. the girls are back home, and I check out what they are watching on television. It is *Seventh Heaven*, which is on our acceptable list, although during the five minutes that I watch with them, I notice that one of the plot lines includes the horrors of too much caffeine. Humph!

Nancy is at the school table, a little frustrated with the craft books that she has found. But then she spots a beginner's book on drawing that captures her interest; I'm glad I invested the twenty-five cents it cost when I found it on the library's used book shelf.

Apparently, I have forty-five minutes of free time, hurrah. I have an e-mail from my mom in Washington, and I spend some time on the homeschool "Swap" board online, seeing what the ladies are posting recently. This will have to count for adult conversation for me this week, while Loren's away.

At 9:00 p.m. Delnora is back from *Bye Bye Birdie* practice with a friend in tow and they spend the next hour reading through a play that is assigned for English. The girls brush their teeth and head for bed after I brief them about tomorrow afternoon's busy schedule: guitar lesson for Shannon, the last *Math Olympiad* problem solving contest, library, flute lesson for Patty, and gymnastics for Margaret.

We belong to a Christian homeschool support group with fifty families. We have a monthly Mom's Support Night and a myriad of voluntary activities such as field trips, small clubs, classes, and parties. I have led the *Math Olympiad* team for the last three years. We have about five or six students each year that are interested in challenging themselves with these difficult math problems, but we have fun, and I treat them to pizza after the last contest in March. We could be quickly overwhelmed by all the activities that this group offers, so I carefully pick and choose ones that supplement what we are learning, that fill in gaps in our curriculum (especially physical education), or are just too unique and excellent to be missed, such as a field trip on a skipjack in the Chesapeake Bay.

I start the dishwasher. I ignore the unfolded laundry. I step carefully around the pile of toys that is still at the bottom of the stairs. Shannon is reading in the hall outside her bedroom door, since Patty wanted lights out for sleeping. How did ten o'clock arrive so quickly?

Commentary

As we've gone along during our years of homeschooling, I have learned to be more realistic about what I can get done in a day. I know how to cut back on assignments when we have other activities scheduled. I don't cringe if we don't finish everything I had planned for the week. If it was truly important, then it goes on the next week's schedule. If it was just for fun, or for filler, then it gets set aside.

I don't feel any pressure to cover every single topic. It can't be done, anyway. I do want to give my children tools for lifelong learning, so that they can continue on as adults, pursuing their interests in a thoughtful way.

When we first began to homeschool, my North Carolina friends were very helpful, and they gave me no unreasonable expectations of how it really looked day to day. They brought me along on several of their field trips before we began homeschooling, they invited me to watch them one afternoon, and they brought me with them to North Carolina's most excellent state conference. I was immediately attracted to the unit study approach, so we have never really tried to duplicate public school at home (except for Delnora's freshman year, I suppose).

Usually, I am able to find small bits of time for myself. I take a few mini-breaks during the day to check e-mail, although I am still available to the kids. I usually like being alone in the kitchen to cook dinner. Once every two weeks or so, I get to run some errands by myself or browse in the library alone. It is terribly hard to get out the door without a child or two begging to go with me. They appreciate the rare one-on-one time, too, so it's easy to feel guilty about going

---

out solo. Every so often, I stay up very late at night, so I can just have some time all alone without interruptions. I like all sorts of movies when I'm too tired to read. I am thoroughly enjoying my French horn lessons and weekly band rehearsals, where I am not a mommy or the teacher, but just a musician, albeit a much older one than the average band member. I look forward every month to our Mom's support meeting, where we conduct minimal business, are encouraged by a devotional and teaching tips, and meet in small groups for sharing and prayer. And then there's time to schmooze and talk shop.

Loren and I have some time to visit each evening, but as he often gets up at 5:30 a.m. for work, he cannot afford to be much of a night owl. We rarely go out. Occasionally, we will rent a movie, make microwave popcorn, and shoo all the kids upstairs, so we can pretend we're out on a date. I have a morbid fear of calling a babysitter on the phone—it has to be something desperately important to attend. Soon, the twins will be teenagers and this will cease to be a problem.

Loren's role in our homeschool is to support my efforts, provide a listening ear, and to provide correction and motivation for good behavior in the children. He is not interested in the finer points of which curriculum to use—he just wants to know that the children are being properly educated. He gives me free reign to spend what I think necessary. His salary allows us a lot of breathing room to afford things like a quality microscope and music lessons, and the occasional take-out pizza to relieve stress on Mom. I try to make good decisions and resell used or unused curriculum, but I don't have to continue using something that is not working for us, just because it is already paid for.

Loren doesn't mind a flexible schedule, but he does like most of the schoolwork and chores to be finished before he comes home at about 6:00 p.m., primarily because I get pretty stressed out if it isn't done by that time! He encourages us to take advantage of the unique opportunities that homeschooling provides: no book work during visits from Grandma (but lots of extra field trips), hiking on a beautiful mid-week fall day, or attending a special event like an Army promotion ceremony.

When people ask for advice on how to begin homeschooling, I advise them to start very simply, with the minimum of basics. Then start adding what interests your family most. If you are teaching more than one grade, consider the unit study approach, so that you are all studying the same topics, even if at different levels of comprehension. I think a fourth grade level science book has almost all the content you need, unless you major in that subject in college. Read, read, read. Snuggle together on the sofa, and read your children great books. Give all the characters different accents and voices. Certainly, consider having some kind of schedule or master plan, but maintain the flexibility to capitalize on what is happening in the world around you.

Of course, you will make mistakes. Apologize and move on. How easily children forgive! They have big hearts. Ask them to pray for you.

Relax. Enjoy your children. They are with you for an incredibly brief time. It will take your breath away how fast the time will go. You can still remember what your baby's neck smelled like when you nuzzled her after a bath, and there she goes out the door to college or away to be married. Too soon, too soon.

You have been given the incredible gift of having them at home for a season. Cherish the gift.

Margaret, Shannon, Delnora, Patty, Nancy
Mary, Ralph, Loren

Delnora (18), Patty (12), Shannon (12), Margaret (10), Nancy (7), Ralph (4)

Rick (43)
Naomi (41)
Elisha (11)
Karissa (8)
Leah (almost 3)

Interview with Naomi in November from her rural home in Washington

EXPOSURE AND ACCESS

We live in a rural, unincorporated town in northwest part of Washington, approximately sixty miles from the base where my husband is stationed. It is the first time in eleven years that we are not living on base, and we elected to do so in order for our family to have five acres of land and animals. It was my husband's decision to commute 120 miles each day to offer the children a rural lifestyle, and he does not regret it. We purchased five acres of pasture land and put a new double-wide manufactured home on the property, with three bedrooms, a family room and two baths. My husband did the fencing himself and also built a barn, primarily to store feed for the horses and to have a tack room. He also made a heated and insulated play-room for the children in the barn, so they have a place to play on rainy days when I need some quiet in the house. It even has a window, so I can see them from our kitchen. The horses are out on pasture, and the only critters living in the barn are the barn cats, the dog, two rabbits, and a guinea pig. The chicken coop is alongside the barn, and my husband built that also.

Rick, my husband, is a United States Navy Chaplain, currently assigned to a carrier air wing. He is presently at sea. As a Naval Chaplain, he is a Pastor to the military (preaches, leads Bible studies, counsels, performs weddings and memorial services, conducts seminars such as stress management, delivers *American Red Cross* messages to military members, conducts the prayers at official functions such as change of commands and retirements, and he participates in military training along with the troops). The "needs of the Navy" is what determines where we live, and sometimes we have a say as to where we'd like to be if an opening exists.

We have enjoyed moving approximately every three years, experiencing the unique positive and negative aspects of each duty station. For instance, Okinawa was a blast because of experiencing a foreign culture; yet we lived too far away to be with family during a crisis and had no access to little things such as toll-free phone calling, which was often frustrating. Hawaii had beautiful weather and scenery, yet the centipedes, scorpions, roaches, and geckos could cause quite a stir. Bridgeport, California, (southeast of Lake Tahoe) offered seclusion and beautiful scenery, but my husband's job there created much stress on our family. Washington state, where we are now, is lovely and green, but to get that green grass, we endure much rain. Now that our children are getting older, however, the moves are getting more difficult, so we're hoping to stay in Washington for another assignment.

Prior to having children eleven years ago, I was a graduate teaching assistant at Montana State University (teaching shorthand, keyboarding, office adPministration/procedures, and business machines to freshman and sophomores), while earning my Master of Science degree in Business Education. I have been out of the work force since I was pregnant with our first-born son, and we were sent to Japan. My name is Naomi, and I am now a stay-at-home, homeschooling mom.

My husband and I went to Catholic schools in our elementary years and to public schools from fifth through twelfth grades. We had never discussed schooling choices for our children prior to having them. Our firstborn was just an infant when we were stationed in Okinawa, Japan, and we attended an *Officer's Christian Fellowship* (*OCF*) Bibles Study on base. A few couples who attended were homeschooling their children, and that was the very first we had ever heard of such a thing. We liked what we saw in their children . . . they were well-mannered, siblings had a genuine concern for the well-being of one another, and they could carry on an intelligible conversation with adults. We then read several books on homeschooling which left, in our minds, no other option for educating our children. It was a decision and commitment that we made from the start for their entire education, not a year-to-year try-it-and-see-if-I-like-it-deal but rather for the long haul. My desire and excitement were so strong at the time that I started reading any and all books I could find on the subject. By the time my son was three, I was already researching various curricula options, and I had another child. The decision to homeschool was a mutual decision, and although I make the curriculum decisions, I often consult with my husband first. He is extremely supportive of my decisions, he encourages me, and he provides for us.

We started homeschooling Elisha in Hawaii at age four, using a *Bob Jones University Press* kindergarten for four-year-olds. Since he was not compulsory

---

Elisha (11), Karissa (8), Leah (almost 3)

school age, I kept no records. We set up a "schoolroom" on our back lanai (closed-in porch), complete with number and alphabet charts on the walls, an American flag, a blackboard (okay, it was actually green), and school desks from *Salvation Army* for our son, as well as our almost two-year old, so she could "do school" too. We "did school" every weekday morning for two hours. I was not only organized back then, but also structured! You could say we had "school at home" rather than "homeschooling."

Our second year of homeschooling brought us to kindergarten for five-year-olds. My son really wanted to read, although I was hoping to put off reading until he was six or seven. (My "research" had indicated that boys didn't learn to read as early as girls and that later was better than early for structured education.) Yet, my son's desire to read was too strong to delay any further. I signed up with a full service curriculum, *Covenant Home Curriculum*, so that I would have someone to whom I would be accountable, someone to answer my questions if I ran into difficulties, as well as having the entire program laid out for me. All I had to do was follow their instructions! It worked so well for me and made me realize that I could not only teach my own children how to read, but I could also select our own curricula and make my own lesson plans for our third year of homeschooling: first grade.

We moved to California prior to beginning our third year and were treated there as a private school, which meant keeping more records, now that my son was compulsory age (attendance, grades, publishers/books used, and I even typed up qualifications for myself as teacher and my husband as teacher/ principal). We did continue to homeschool in the mornings and early afternoons covering *A Beka* first grade math, language, phonics, and penmanship in the family room, which we again made into a "schoolroom," but I was starting to feel that the entire setup was too sterile. These were my children I was teaching, why couldn't I do it more informally, as when I was reading books aloud to them on the couch? Why was I doing the *academic* subjects (math and phonics) in the schoolroom and other more *fun* things on the couch? That's when we got rid of the school desks, purchased bedroom desks to match their furniture, and moved our "academic" subjects to the couch or kitchen table, while maintaining a schedule where schoolwork was completed by the early afternoon hours.

For our seventh and current eighth year of homeschooling, we're in a smaller home in rural Washington state. My desk is piled with papers in the study, along with my daughter's desk (another baby came along, and the girls' bedroom isn't large enough for the beds, dresser, and a desk), my son's desk is in his room, my homeschooling resource bookcase is in the kitchen, as is our homeschooling "you-name-it" shelf (craft items, puzzles, felts, etc.), and penmanship is the only subject required to be done at a desk or the kitchen table. We don't have the wall space for all of the posters I like to have up. Most days, we don't begin academic

---

Elisha (11), Karissa (8), Leah (almost 3)

subjects until 10:00 a.m. or later, and we're still completing them in the evenings. On sunny days, since they are few and far between in the fall, winter, and even spring, we tend to slack off on the academics and enjoy the outdoors—even if it's just playing outside all day. Since we go into town one day a week for shopping, appointments, lessons, to visit friends, and a library run, we now homeschool four days a week from September through July, having two weeks off at Christmas and one week for a spring break.

My minimum daily goal is to cover our Bible lesson, and anything beyond that, I feel, is a productive day. Our textbooks include *Saxon Math* (beginning with fourth grade and *Horizon's Math* for grades one through three), *A Beka* English (phonics, spelling, readers, and language), and *Bob Jones University Press* Bible for the earlier years. Science and history are explored through real books we either purchase or borrow from the library; and since our children are avid readers (we don't have television reception or cable) and they explore art on their own, we don't formally cover these subjects. For literature, we use real books and purchase study guides. For instance, my son and husband have gone through *Johnny Tremain* together, with my son e-mailing the study guide answers to my husband on ship and my husband responding via e-mail. They will also be studying Latin together when my husband returns from sea duty in a month.

We utilize the public library weekly and join the summer reading clubs annually. Our field trips are done primarily as a family, and occasionally we'll go with one or two other homeschooling families to the zoo, a museum, or the pool. Elisha has had swim lessons and plays baseball every spring, and Karissa has had gymnastics lessons and now takes weekly piano lessons, presently in her fourth month. (She'll have her first piano recital next month, the day after Dad gets home from his six months at sea.) When weather is nice, we'll go on a family bike ride, or I'll jog with my toddler in the jogging stroller while the older two children ride bikes with us.

Daily chores for the children include taking care of our animals and helping me inside the house. Each has a room they are responsible for picking up daily, in addition to their own bedrooms. Elisha usually handles the dusting and vacuuming twice weekly, while Karissa handles the kitchen (sweeps and mops the floor, sets and clears the table, gets beverages ready, empties the dishwasher, puts away leftovers) daily. Occasionally, they swap duties so that my son will know how to function in the kitchen. Both of them enjoy cooking, they fold and distribute laundry, and clean out the vehicles. Chores and all schoolwork need to be done in order to earn time on the computer. They receive an allowance only if their rooms are kept neat (nothing on the floor or beds, things where they belong) and *all* chores for the day have been completed. Karissa and Elisha have not had allowance now for two months because their rooms have not been kept tidy,

---

which means my house is not as tidy as I like. They still are required to do what I've told them needs to be done, such as sweep, vacuum, or fold laundry; but they earn no money. Now, they are realizing how much they miss that allowance, and they are starting to get things in their rooms put away. There are many days, however, when keeping the animals fed is all we accomplish in addition to schooling, and this is my greatest weakness; I will often let them go out and play rather than finish what needs to be done in the house. I justify it by saying that they are "just kids," and they need to expend playful energy. Also, I need the quiet. My solution is to make daily chore sheets that I can reproduce on the computer, but I have continued to put off doing it. When they were a couple years younger, we used the *Choreganizer* system (with the picture cards and "mom money" and "dad dollars"), which worked well for us then.

It is November 9, and as I slowly awaken, I glance at the clock and think that I could not have possibly slept in till 8:30 a.m. We are all sluggish today, since we had a day of errands yesterday in a town ninety miles away. Also, last night Elisha Karissa (eight) had their *AWANA* Bible Club at a church thirty miles from home. Elisha and Karissa have just awakened by themselves; and Leah, not yet three years old, continues to sleep soundly, snuggled up against me where she's been since the middle of the night.

8:30-9:30 a.m.—As the older children get their breakfasts (blueberry-chocolate chip pancakes or waffles that I make in large quantities and freeze, cold cereal, or hot cereal), I check e-mail to see if there are any messages from my husband who has been on an aircraft carrier in the Persian Gulf for the last five months. I don't e-mail him in return until the end of the day, since he is going to bed as we're getting up. Plus, at that time, I'm able to fill him in on our daily happenings.

While I have breakfast, I go through some paperwork, writing out some bills that must be in the mail today. Elisha does his morning chores, consisting of feeding our seven horses, two rabbits, one duck, and one guinea pig. Karissa joins him in the barn, feeding our four chickens, one rooster, two barn cats, and a chocolate lab. When they return indoors, they fold and put away laundry from the night before.

9:30-10:00 a.m.—Elisha watches a drawing instructional video we borrowed from the library while Karissa practices her piano in the study. We are all amazed that Leah is still sleeping, but she is so tired out from our long day in town yesterday.

10:00-11:00 a.m.—Elisha works on writing his fiction book at the computer. He started this on his own, using his friends from church and *AWANA* for "characters," combining attributes of three time periods into a story entitled "Rickland" (named after Dad). While he does this, I instruct Karissa in *A Beka* second grade *Letters & Sounds* (she was a late reader), *A Beka Language 3* (sentence types and punctuation), and *A Beka* second grade cursive penmanship. As the children work independently for part of this hour, I clean up the kitchen. We have had a very productive morning, since Leah has been sleeping.

11:00-11:30 a.m.—Leah finally wakes up, and I snuggle with her on the couch to give her time to get functional. She asks whether "Mr. Golden Sun" is out today, to which I must reply "No, Mr. Rain is once again visiting," although on these fall days in Washington, his visits often resemble a permanent residence. I get her breakfast together and she watches a short video while Elisha and Karissa read history books that cover a time period they've chosen (using real books from the library).

11:30-12:00 noon—Elisha and Karissa pick up their rooms, while Leah plays with her toys in the study.

12:30-1:00 p.m.—Lunch time. I usually give the children a choice of two items for lunch (any leftovers, a sandwich, or macaroni and cheese), and usually Karissa makes it, with Leah's help. Elisha helps to make sure the kitchen table is cleared and he gets the drinks.

1:00-2:00 p.m.—Leah asks for a bath, so Elisha and Karissa alternate watching her in the tub (usually they read a book and play with her) and have a little "free" time. This is my time on the Internet, searching a web site for used homeschooling books or classics for literature, searching for Christmas presents (great for cheap *American Girl* outfits!), and getting on some homeschooling web sites for my "professional" reading.

2:00-3:00 p.m.—Playtime for all the children, while I do my aerobics tape and take a very quick shower. Sometimes they do aerobics behind me; other times they play together; and still other times they play separately. Today they are playing together. Karissa and Elisha get along extremely well, but on occasion we have to deal with their selfishness and have them consider the other person before themselves. We have always tried to be within earshot of them to teach them Biblical methods for conflict resolution. The biggest hassles these days consist of Leah desiring her independence and not wanting any other person near her or helping her—other than Mom. This takes much more of my time now to correct, but in the end it should pay off.

3:00-3:30 p.m.—Outside chores for Elisha and Karissa—they're feeding the animals earlier now, since it's getting darker earlier. Leah continues to play inside, but often when it's warmer, she'll go out in the barn with Elisha and Karissa. I've elected not to give Leah a nap today, since she slept in until 11:00 a.m. Otherwise, she'll be up until midnight with me tonight.

3:30-4:00 p.m.—Elisha goes to his room to work on his *A Beka* sixth grade English text, which he usually does independently. I go through his book at the beginning of the week and write the weekday and date on the pages I expect him to complete. Leah asks for Karissa to play house with her, so they make "blanket houses" with the living room furniture. The living room remains a mess for the remainder of the day.

4:00-4:30 p.m.—Leah is now off playing by herself again, so I cover *Horizon's* second grade math with Karissa (we're moving her into third grade math later this month). Elisha does his *Saxon Math 76* independently, doing a lesson per day and a test after every fifth lesson. Leah interrupts me to change her doll's clothes, and I continue explaining math to Karissa as I maneuver the doll.

4:30-6:30 p.m.—The children have free time to play or read, while I reorganize closets and make dinner. I normally choose what we have for dinner (meat or poultry, steamed vegie, rice or potato), although with my husband being out at sea, often I'll give the children a choice of two things (hot dogs or chicken nuggets, a vegie, and a starch). Leah chooses to watch a video tape, although by the time it's half-over, she's playing in the study with the *Barbie* dolls. Elisha plays a civil war computer game, and Karissa occupies herself with arts-and-crafts, writing a letter to a friend, and practicing her piano.

6:30-7:30 p.m.—It's dinner time, and tonight we eat together at the table as a family, even in Dad's absence, since it provides a great time for family communication. Sometimes, however, when my husband is at sea, I will get on the Internet while the kids eat dinner at the kitchen table, just to have a little bit more quiet to myself.

7:30-8:00 p.m.—Everyone helps to pick up the living room, study, and family room (where the computer is), which means putting toys, clothes, books, and any remaining folded laundry (needs to be refolded after spending a day on the couch!) where it really belongs. After dinner is "quiet hours," so there's no rough-housing permitted . . . it's the time of day I need quiet.

8:00-9:00 p.m.—I now realize we haven't had our Bible lesson today, which I normally like to get done first thing in the morning. We sing one or two hymns, I read a Bible account using *Bob Jones University Press* third grade Bible as a guide, then I read the same account in a children's Bible storybook, and we close in prayer. Often, the children ask me to read more from the Bible storybook, so I usually will do so, or I'll select a short missionary book to read to them. As we read, Leah will play near us for a bit and then come on my lap for a while, too. Then, Karissa and Elisha work on their memory verses for their *AWANA* Bible Club. Sometimes I will read aloud a chapter or two from a fiction book during this time, too.

9:00 -10:00 p.m.—I allow Leah to watch one more video, which is a good night type of video and then get her ready for bed. Leah and I listen to classical piano music as she lies her head on my lap and goes to sleep on the couch. Karissa and Elisha also get ready for bed, and they must have their lights out at

9:30 p.m. and 10 p.m. respectively. However, since my husband is away, many nights Elisha comes back out to talk with me in the living room, while I get Leah to sleep. This has been a precious time for both of us, and sometimes he's up till 11:00 p.m. with me.

10:00 - 11:00 p.m.—I've held Leah all this time, while reading a book. This is the time I need for myself and for quiet. Even when my husband is home, I have my last two cups of tea for the day and usually work on a Bible study or read a book relating to motherhood and/or homeschooling (as encouragement to press on in our lifestyle). When he's at sea, I borrow fiction books from the library and occasionally rent a video. These help me to escape the loneliness I feel when he's deployed.

11:00 p.m.-midnight—I correct language and math sheets for Elisha and Karissa. Then I e-mail my husband about our day's events and end up playing *Mah Jongg* on the computer until just about midnight. I put Leah in her bed before retiring myself. On the days when Leah naps, I usually nap with her (Elisha and Karissa play together, catch up on school, or use the computer), so I can make it until midnight. On days when I don't nap, I'm usually pretty tired by 10:00 p.m., but I still need "my time" at the end of the day. Some days, the kids will play at a neighbor's house from about 3-5:00 p.m. when I feel I need time alone (although, when my husband is home, he'll take the kids out somewhere and let me have my time at home to sew or work on lesson plans, etc.).

When my husband is home, things usually run about the same, although we do get up earlier, and thus retire a bit earlier at night. He leaves for work between 5:30-6:00 a.m. and arrives home about 5:00 p.m. The biggest difference is that he is a great help with the kids, and he takes care of things outdoors (that's my added stress when he's at sea), while I focus only on things in the home. He also leads us in a Bible devotional after dinner.

We remain committed to homeschooling the children through high school graduation. While we've met many of our original goals from the earlier days, such as teaching them to read and basic math foundations, many of our goals will be in the process of being achieved throughout all the years of homeschooling. For instance, training the children to treat each other with respect, as they would want to be treated; working toward correcting their selfishness and thinking of others before themselves; further developing a family cohesiveness; continuing to instill Biblical morals and values into their thought processes to aid in decision making; and developing the children's problem solving skills.

I am more comfortable now with our less structured methods of homeschooling, even though we still use textbooks. While, in my mind, I believe the ideal would be to have a set schedule, it has not worked well for us in the last two years. I admit that this does cause me more frustration on the days we don't accomplish what I think we should have accomplished—namely in keeping the house picked up and clean—but I'm learning to go with the flow of things and enjoy the children more than a picked-up-house.

I have learned to say "no" to things that take me out of the home and away from the family. We are very family oriented and enjoy our time together. We're trying to teach the children that saying "yes" to something says "no" to something else. So, during this phase in my life, I am not active in church meetings or ministries that take me away from the kids. They are my priority; my job is to raise them in a manner pleasing to the Lord, so that they may grow to serve Him with their whole heart, soul, mind, and strength.

I have found that some homeschoolers get much more accomplished than I do, such as science experiments, history projects, etc. I often feel inadequate, since I can't seem to work these into my daily life. So I have had to lower my expectations and be careful not to compare myself with others. And I've heard it said that even the worst of homeschooling situations produces a better result than the government schools. I do see that as my children pursue their interests (such as Elisha's desire to draw and Karissa's creativity in arts and crafts), they are learning just by having the exposure and access to other facets of learning. The only thing I would like to change about our present homeschooling lifestyle is that I would like to incorporate unit studies, along with our math and language texts. I have purchased *Prairie Primer* and hope to be organized enough to begin using it soon.

I used to doubt and worry that maybe I don't cover enough in history or science with the children, since we allow them to chose library books in areas of interest within these subjects. However, their annual test scores (since we've moved to Washington, where annual testing is required by law) as well as their general conversations in these areas, indicate to me that there isn't anything to worry about. Plus, I consider that topics in these subjects are repeated at least twice through the elementary/junior high years, and I don't know how much I really remember from those years of repeated information. I'm counting on the high school years to concentrate on these other subjects, while I concentrate on getting the basic information into their heads and teach them to think, based on the knowledge they've already gained.

Our children appreciate being homeschooled, mainly because they see how much more time they have to play and pursue their interests. Karissa is our social butterfly, and she had wanted to go to school the first couple of years we homeschooled. At times, it was difficult to remind her that this was not an option for us, because we believe it is what God has called us to do. Now, she is content and wouldn't want to go to school. Our first-born has always appreciated the security of Mom and Dad and never did want to go to school, so it's been easier with him. Our toddler knows no other lifestyle; she scribbles in her tablets while I work with the other children. Their curiosities with regard to school come in

---

Elisha (11), Karissa (8), Leah (almost 3)

the form of what physical education class would be like, how neat it would be to have a locker, and having lunch with their friends every day—obviously not major issues.

Homeschooling is a reflection of our love and commitment to our Lord Jesus Christ and our Biblical instruction to teach our children. Character development is a major part of our instruction as we live out our lives daily. We try to deal with frustrations and stress from a Biblical standpoint in being content in our circumstances; not by allowing our circumstances to regulate our reactions, but rather to have a dependence and trust in the sovereignty of God.

Rick, Elisha, Naomi
Karissa, Leah

Elisha (11), Karissa (8), Leah (almost 3)

Greg, age 39
Jeanne, age 39
Macia, age 13
Megan, age 11
Marla, age 8

Interview with Jeanne from a suburb of Grand Rapids, Michigan

GOD DOES MY LESSON PLANS

While my home would never be featured in a magazine (unless maybe a homeschooling magazine!) it is comfortable for our family. We have four bedrooms, allowing each of the girls their own space, and two bathrooms that are almost a necessity now that our girls are reaching their teen years! Our family room, dining-school area, and hallway are wallpapered with posters, time liness, and maps relating to our current studies. The dining-school area is open to the kitchen, making it very convenient for me to work on lunch or dinner while going over spelling words or quizzing multiplication tables. There is a built-in desk where I keep my books and supplies. The majority of our school supplies are stored in the three bookshelves (usually overflowing) in the family room, which is also where our big white (marker) board and computer are located. Only the living room does not look like a school room, except when Macia takes over the couch with her books! While the girls all have tables or desks in their rooms, and they will occasionally go to them to study, the majority of our education time is spent in the living and family rooms (especially when cuddling on the couch to read, one of our favorite pastimes!), and in the dining-school room at the table.

We are always planning to replace some of the carpeting and remodel the kitchen and downstairs bathroom of our home, but we are very slow about getting it done. Camping, traveling with our kids, sports, and other activities regularly take priority over home improvement projects. I think that we will probably visit friends in Panama next year, moving the remodeling project back again. I think the experience of traveling will be of more lasting value to the girls.

Our yard has seven big maple trees in it, which makes it one of Megan's favorite places. She is positive that God created trees for climbing! Our backyard is divided into two different sections—the fenced part where the dog plays and we have a wooden play set with swings and slide, and the hill and creek. The hill runs down to the creek, which runs along the back of our property and provides the girls with a wonderful setting for summer adventures. They spend many hours playing on the neighbor's wooden bridge over the creek and walking in the water down the creek a half mile or so to the neighborhood park. This is where we spend our days.

I am not a morning person. My husband, Greg, is. Quite often, he is awake and out of bed before his alarm goes off at 5:30 a.m. Greg is a computer software engineer for an aerospace company. He develops web software and supports *CAE* (*Computer Aided Engineering*) systems. On Mondays, Wednesdays, and Fridays, Greg leaves home about 5:45 a.m. and goes to the gym to work out. He showers there and then gets to work about 8:30 a.m. He leaves work at about 4:30 p.m. on those days, and gets home at about 5:00 p.m. On Tuesdays and Thursdays, Greg works 6:30 a.m. to 3:30 p.m. and is home early. I like the days when he gets home early!

I, on the other hand, have worn out the snooze button on my alarm. And that is how my "real" day begins. "Beep, beep, beep, beep!" I hit the snooze button repeatedly, hoping to find the spot that will make the beeping stop, but it is no use. The alarm goes off and the television news goes on. My goal in setting the alarm for 7:15 a.m .is that I will get out of bed by 7:30 a.m. It didn't work this morning.

It's 8:00 a.m. on this first Wednesday in November and my daughter Macia (thirteen) has risen just before me. She rubs the kinks in my shoulder as I pour my first cup of coffee and settle down with my Bible. Megan (eleven) and Marla (eight) straggle into the kitchen as I read from *The Inspirational Study Bible* and spend some quiet time in prayer. Macia and Megan are eating grapefruit for breakfast. Marla spends breakfast time looking at slides under the microscope that was left out after last night's biology lab. "Macia, what is this?" "That's an amoeba. See those long things sticking out that look like legs? Those are called pseudopods. The amoeba uses them to move around like legs, but it also uses them to eat. When it finds some food, it just wraps them around it and swallows up the food." "Cool!"

I've gotten into the habit of discussing whatever I read during my personal devotions time with Macia as her Bible lesson. This morning, the verse is *2 Timothy 2:22* "Flee also youthful lusts; but pursue righteousness, faith, love and peace with those who call on the Lord out of a pure heart." God knows exactly which verses Macia and I need to read and discuss. I love it when God does my lesson plans! Our discussion of these verses is particularly meaningful today because they address issues that have come up in our homeschool teen group. Today we talk about what is appropriate behavior between Christian girls and boys in relationship to the Bible verse. In many families this kind of discussion would be uncomfortable to say the least. Macia, while not always in agreement with our feelings on this kind of issue, listens, accepts our guidance, and honestly shares her opinions. The wonderful sharing relationships that we have developed with our girls top the list of things that Greg and I cherish most about homeschooling.

By the time our Bible discussion ends, it is 9:30 a.m. Megan is reading an American Girl magazine and Marla is reading one of the *American Girl Felicity* books. Last Friday, we had our first *American Girl* history class. I am using the *American Girl* stories and the *America at School* history curriculum to teach the class to Marla and five homeschooled friends. I taught the class with Macia, Megan, and several of their friends during our second year of homeschooling, and this year it's Marla's turn. Over the course of the school year, we will read through the books, do projects from the curriculum and the *American Girl* craft books, try food from the recipe books, and end the year by presenting an *American Girl* play at the Celebration of Lessons—our support group's end-of-the-year program. As a part of the reading incentive program, when each girl finishes the entire set of books, she gets to choose an *American Girl* poster. Marla hopes to be the first one done, so she can get the Molly poster.

Macia and I spend a few minutes going over what work she needs to do today. It is important for Macia to keep on schedule in biology as we are doing the high school biology labs together with another family. Using the *Exploring Creation Through Biology* textbook (published by Apologia), we try to do two labs each Tuesday. Last night's lab was at our house, which is why the microscope was still on the table at breakfast this morning. Macia settles in on the couch to get started with her day's work.

I usually try to start the laundry and take something out of the freezer for dinner before we get started in the morning. Since all the girls are reading quietly, I take a few minutes to do this now. The chore chart shows that Megan will fold the laundry later today. The ground beef is thawing. I will decide what to make for dinner later.

"It's almost 10:00, Megan and Marla, we need to get going or we'll still be doing school at dinner time tonight." "I'm hungry," Marla replies. "Can I eat something before we start?" It irritates me that she is not ready to start, but I agree to a quick sandwich. My typical breakfast is three or four cups of coffee until midmorning when I grab a quick sandwich or bagel. I can't blame the girls for taking on eating habits similar to my own. As Marla makes a quick sandwich, I work on the log for last night's biology lab.

During our first year of homeschooling five years ago, I tried several methods of record keeping. In my frustration over trying to match our homeschooling style with record books that had too many little boxes, I designed a log book that worked for our family. I print the forms on our computer and have them copied and spiral bound with a vinyl cover at a local copy shop. Each one-hundred-page log covers one semester and gives me a few extra pages to jot down educational activities we do on our breaks.

By 10:15 a.m., Megan and Marla are working on their math. All three girls are in *Saxon Math* this year; Macia does *Saxon Algebra*, Megan's in *Saxon 76* and Marla is in *Saxon 54*. Marla is technically in the third grade, but each year she has finished her kindergarten, first grade, and second grade *Modern Curriculum Press* math books by January. So last year during the second semester, I used the third grade *MCP* teachers manual to cover multiplication, fractions and the other subject matter she had not mastered yet. This fall we moved her into the *Saxon Math* at the fourth grade level. So far she is doing wonderfully! Today her lesson is on metric measurement. She and I use masking tape and a centimeter ruler (I really ought to get a meter stick) to mark off a meter on the living room carpet. How much farther is it than our yard stick? Can Marla step that far? She can, but it's a stretch!

As Marla works her problems, I check Meg's practice problems on converting fractions. She has them all right and moves on to do a second lesson. The way our homeschool schedule is working so far this year, Megan and Marla only do math on Monday, Wednesday and Friday. So that we don't get too far behind in the book, and in order to get through all the review at the beginning of the book, I have them do two lessons a day. They read and do the practice problems of both lessons and then work every other problem of the second lesson. When they reach a point in the book where the concepts take more time and repetition to master, we will slow the pace to one lesson a day.

Occasionally I do the math lessons orally with Megan or Marla. We began this last year when Meg was frustrated with math. Even though she was doing one lesson a day, she was getting several wrong and it was taking a long time. So I now read the lesson with her, and then she does as many of the problems as she can in her head. Any that can't be done in her head still have to be written out. One time last year, after we had been doing most of the lessons orally, Megan's math book fell open to the back as I picked it up. Written in the back cover was "I Love Math!" "Megan, this is your handwriting. Do you really love math?" "I really do, Mom. When we do it out loud, it's like exercise for my brain. It stretches it and even hurts sometimes. But it's fun and it feels great when we're done!"

I write down these oral math lessons as "Mental Math" in my log book and try to do them once a week or so with each girl. Today I have prep work to do for the rest of the day, so the girls will do written math work as I put away the microscope and put up a human body poster on the pantry door in preparation for our science lesson later today.

About 11:20 a.m. Macia has finished today's assignment in *The Witch On Blackbird Pond*, and gives it to me to check. For high school language arts we are using *Total Language Plus* (*TLP*) for literature and *Blended Structure and Style* (*BSS*), published by *The Institute for Excellence in Writing* for composition. I had originally planned that Macia would do *TLP* this year and *BSS* next. But there is a lot of writing in the *TLP* curriculum, and I felt that she needed the *BSS* to strengthen her writing skills. Why don't we use *BSS* this year and *TLP* next? Because the stories that we have chosen in *TLP* go so well with the American history that she is taking this year. We will probably do both curriculums for two years. There are so many good books available in the *TLP* curriculum, I might have Macia use it for all four years of high school.

As Macia collects her *Saxon Algebra* book from the school book cabinet and settles back into the corner of the couch, Marla finishes her math and brings it to be checked. She has twenty-one out of twenty-two correct. We redo the missed problem together and then discuss her "Neatness Counts!" grade.

One of my goals for both Megan and Marla this year is to teach them that neatness counts. We are working on it in their school work and hopefully it will carry over into other areas of their lives as well! In order to accomplish this, I am giving them a "Neatness Counts!" grade on all of their written work. The grading scale goes from A to F: A—Alright!, B—Could Be a little Bit Better, C—Come on!, D—I Don't think so!, and F—You Flunk! Today all of her answers are circled and the numbers are legible but the problems are all scrunched together on the notebook page, so she gets a C. I am trying to use a bit of humor to make the "Neatness Counts!" point, and hoping that with enough repetition the point will get through. Since she received a D yesterday, Marla is happy with today's C.

I need to help Meg again with her math, so Marla grabs her *American Girl* book and disappears. Yes, Megan is still doing math after an hour and a half. She is distracted. Today would have been a good day to do mental math. We will do it that way tomorrow.

Because it was easy for Megan to become distracted, we began to look into homeschooling. There were several families in our church who homeschooled. I had done some reading on it and even attended the state homeschool convention. Not convinced that I could homeschool, when Macia reached school age we enrolled her at the local Christian school. I was an active parent, volunteering as room-mom, helping with fund raisers, and serving wherever I was needed.

Macia was reading quite well before she started school. By the end of her first grade year, Macia was beginning to be bored with school. "Mom, I know how to do this, you know that I know how to do this, and the teacher knows that I know how to do this. How come I have to do this?" Macia skipped the second grade, going ahead to third, and we enrolled Megan in kindergarten. About eight weeks into the school year, it became apparent that school wasn't working for Megan. Though she had been excited about starting school and making new friends, now she was discouraged. Megan didn't go back to school after Christmas break. She finished kindergarten at home. Macia finished third grade at the Christian school and began fourth grade at home. Would either of the girls wish to return to a regular school? They both answer that question with a resounding "No!"

As Meg perseveres with her math, I give Marla her spelling quiz. She spells ten out of thirteen words correctly today, but that is not good enough for her. Tears begin to flow as she rewrites the missed words. When she doesn't respond to my "Let's look at how many words you got right!" speech, I get frustrated and send her down the hall to take a break. I'm about ready for one too!

Meg is now done with her math and agrees to get her spelling quiz out of the way before lunch. Spelling used to be Megan's worst subject, and today she has a perfect score!

When we began homeschooling, Megan picked up reading so quickly that after a while I just abandoned the phonics lessons. Why spend time going over "sh as in ship" when she could read all the "sh" words? It wasn't a problem in first and second grades, but by the third and fourth grades Megan was really having a hard time with spelling. Phonics not only helps a child with sounding out words in reading, but it also prepares them for spelling those words. Now that Megan needed them, she didn't know the phonics rules. Oops! We spent her fourth grade year rebuilding the phonics foundation for spelling using *Explode the Code* and Gayle Grahams's *Tricks of the Trade*. I didn't make the same mistake with Marla. Even when she thought that the phonics was boring and babyish, I stuck with it.

I am using the *Spelling Power* curriculum for both girls now. At the beginning of the school year, I tested them to find out where to place them in the curriculum. Meg was still not very confident about her spelling, and the test made her pretty nervous. But the results made her happy. She placed in the first month of the seventh grade level and she was only beginning the sixth grade. On her placement test, Marla scored in the eighth month of fourth grade. I take the opportunity today to remind her that she is in the third grade but spelling words from the end of the fourth grade, so she shouldn't be so hard on herself. That reminder, packaged with a few hugs, kisses, and tickles has Marla smiling again

---

and ready to work on her *Spelling Discovery Activity.*

The girls have mixed feelings about our switch to the *Spelling Power* curriculum. They are not wild about having a spelling test every day, but they like only having to study the words they miss (and they especially like it when they don't miss any!). Marla really enjoys doing the game-like spelling discovery activities. Today we are trying to find smaller words in her spelling words. In "chocolate" we find late and cola. In "office" she sees off and ice. "Just like Macia's off ice training for ice skating," Marla comments. "I won't miss that one again!" In the word "problem" she finds rob and pro. Megan comments from the kitchen that "pro" is not really a word and we talk for just a minute about prefixes. Next we try to make other words from the letters in the spelling words. This activity is a lot like *Boggle*, one of Megan's and Marla's favorite games, and everyone joins in the activity. Between us, we found fifty-nine words:

"Chocolate": ate, cat, coal, coat, cocoa, cola, cool, cot, eat, halt, hat, hate, he, heal, heat, hoe, hole, hoot, hot, latch, late, locate, loot, lot, oath, tale, teach, the, tool. "Office": fife, foe, ice, of, off. "Problem": bop, bore, lob, lobe, lop, lope, lore, mob, mole, mop, mope, more, poem, pole, pore, pro, probe, rob, robe, role, romp, rope.

We all sit around the table talking together while eating. The girls are laughing over the similarity of the signs for pregnant and football in sign language. Several of Macia's and Megan's friends are taking an American Sign Language class as their foreign language through one of the local homeschool co-ops. The signing and laughing escalates as the girls use their limited knowledge of sign language to try and make sentences.

I am using today's lunch break to correct papers and update our lesson logbook. Meg has three math problems wrong today. If the errors had indicated that she didn't understand the math concept we would have gone over them together. But, because the errors are what we call no-brainers (like 5 x 5 = 20), she can redo them after lunch for half credit. Any problems she misses twice, we will go over together. Macia has a perfect score on her algebra lesson. She seems to be understanding it much better since Dad took over the teaching.

Megan and Marla have gone outside to play.

"Mom, the telephone is for you." Another homeschool mom calls to commiserate with me about our busy schedules, a problem very common among homeschool families. In our area, we are blessed to have many active support groups that offer field trips, kid's clubs, extra-curricular activities, and cooperative classes. We even have a homeschool concert band and the only homeschool marching band in the country! When you add all these wonderful activities to family commitments, church commitments, and the task of getting school work done, they can become a problem.

"You can't do it all," I remind her. A wise homeschool mom once told me that every time you say "yes" to something outside your family, you are saying "no" to your family. Keeping outside activities from taking over can be a difficult but important task—one I struggle with regularly.

At 1:00 p.m. I finish my phone call and call the girls back to work. Megan and Marla read out loud to each other from *By The Great Horn Spoon*, an historical fiction book about the California gold rush. Macia practices her guitar.

God has given Macia a wonderful gift with music. She sings occasionally with our church's praise and worship band, plays the piano and the flute, and is now teaching herself the guitar. I loved marching band when I was in high school and hoped that Macia would decide to play her flute in the homeschool marching band. But, as I said, you can't do everything, and Macia chose competitive figure skating over band. Even so, she practices her musical instruments regularly. I am pleased that she is learning to play the guitar, and I allow her time today while I correct her Spanish quiz.

Macia moves on to biology after I review Spanish with her. Megan and Marla have finished their reading. After we discuss the reading questions, Megan redoes her missed math problems, and Marla practices penmanship. The house is completely quiet for a few minutes—a rare occasion. I use the time to whip up a meatloaf and put it in the fridge for supper. Normally, I try to do this at lunch time, but the meat wasn't thawed at lunch time today because of my late start this morning. I tend to think of homeschooling as an educational lifestyle, rather than just "doing school" at home. In addition to the regular academics, I am mentoring my girls in the skills they will need as wives and mothers. So, it isn't unusual for me to include cooking, laundry, cleaning, bill paying, and more, along with our regular book work.

The clock says 2:00 p.m. already! My prediction about doing school at dinner time might not be too far off if we don't get going! Grammar is next for Megan and Marla, and this elicits a few moans and groans. While they don't enjoy the grammar songs tape that I am using to introduce verbs, it seems to be effective. The girls remember the songs from one lesson to the next. After listening to the verb song twice, we discuss the different kinds of verbs. Megan has had all this before and is able to recite the "being" verbs: "am, are, is, was, were, be, being, been" from memory. While Marla understands about action verbs, linking and helping verbs are new and confusing. We will spend time this week and next focussing on each of them. Our lesson finished, the girls complete a noun or verb worksheet, and I use the five minutes or so to correct their work and catch up on my log before we move on to science.

Science is one of the girls' favorite subjects. I attribute this to our use of the unit study method that is fairly unstructured. My lesson plans generally begin with reading about the subject, progress to experimenting and designing arts, crafts and projects to show what we are learning about, and usually include some kind of writing activity. We are currently studying the human body, system by system. Today we are starting the skeletal system. I read aloud from our "texts" for this unit that include *World Book Young Scientist Volume #7*, *Considering God's Creation*, and *Blood & Guts*. After we have finished reading, we look at the poster in the kitchen, read the names of each of the bones, and try to feel them in our bodies.

Megan wonders aloud if our dog Galaxy has the same bones that we do; she wants to be a veterinarian someday. The question takes her to the encyclopedias for a little bit of research. This wasn't part of my lesson plans, but nurturing natural curiosity and a love for learning are two more of our educational goals, and I encourage her. After just a few minutes of reading about dog's skeletal systems, her question is answered: Yes, many of the bones are the same. We are ready to move on to writing, our final subject for the day.

Today Megan and Marla will begin a writing project related to our American history unit. Typical of my teaching style, the assignment is unstructured: Write something about Oregon. Some of the choices I list for them are: write a report about the book we finished reading yesterday (*Moccasin Trail*) or any of the other books we have read about Oregon, write a description of Crater Lake National Park or one of the other places we visited in Oregon last summer, or write a fictional story about traveling on the Oregon Trail.

One of my goals as a home educator is to make history, science, and the other subjects as real and meaningful to my children as possible. When we first began homeschooling, one of the things we said was, "Instead of just reading about all these places, we are going to take the girls to them." So this past summer, when family reunions and commitments called us to Arizona at both the end of June and the end of July, we took our homeschool on the road for seven weeks, traveling a loop around the western United States between the two Arizona reunions.

We traveled for fifty-one days, putting over 10,400 miles on our mini-van. We visited the beginnings and the ends of the Oregon Trail, the Mormon Trail, and Louis and Clark's route. We spent time in fourteen national parks and numerous state parks in the twenty-two states we traveled through. We crossed the continental divide ten times (five times in one day at Yellowstone National Park), listened to twenty books on tape (mostly from the *Sonlight* American history curriculums), and renewed acquaintances with my college roommate and many, many relatives that we hadn't seen in years.

While the girls remember all too well the long hours in the car (they never want to take a trip that long again!), they also remember camping in a Conestoga wagon on the banks of the Columbia river in Oregon and trying to light our campfire with a steel and flint. As we study the pioneers who settled our great country, the girls understand how far it really is from the mighty Mississippi to the Pacific Ocean. When we talk about how God shows Himself to us through

---

His creation, they have a sense of His awesomeness, revealed to us as we saw and climbed on giant redwoods, rafted the rapids through Glacier National Park, and observed the beauty of the Badlands as He sprinkled them with rain, to which Marla said, "Mom, I think this is how God does art!" As we continue our study of history and science during this school year, we draw on our experiences and memories from our cross-country adventure, our journal entries, and our photo album (still in progress six months later) for our writing assignments and projects.

Today for writing, Megan writes a first-person story about traveling on the Oregon Trail. "Megan, I hate stories that end with the main character waking up from a dream." "But Mom, it took a really long time to get to Oregon and this is supposed to be a short story!" "Use your imagination to let your character solve the problem." Meg took out the dream part and turned the story into a journal entry—a good solution. "But, did they have BB guns back then?" The story is a bit rough, but it's a first draft. We'll work on it.

Marla writes a report about our visit last summer to Fort Clatsop, a recreation of the fort built by the Louis and Clark expedition during the winter of 1806. She brings her souvenir candle out of her room and sits at the table smelling it. "What are you doing?" I ask. "I'm smelling the candle to find the right describing words to say what it smelled like when they made candles out of animal fat. But I can't think of any words that smell as bad as my candle."

It's now 3:30 p.m. and the book work of our school day is done. Well, almost. Macia hasn't done any history yet. She complains that she has brain overload from her biology and promises to do history tomorrow between classes. I agree.

Thursdays are a catch-up day at our house. With Macia figure skating from 8:30-10:00 a.m., Megan and Marla in drama class 11:30-12:45 p.m., Macia in drama class 12:45-2:00 p.m. and Megan and Marla in art class 2:00-3:30 p.m., our day is full without trying to fit "real" school work in. We car-pool with three other homeschool families to or from the various lessons, leaving me some free time in the afternoon to catch up on housework and book work.

Once the school work is done, I allow the girls to take a break before the housework begins. Marla plays on the computer. Normally she would play an educational game, but our CD-ROM drive isn't working, so today she plays solitaire. Megan fixes cheese and crackers for a snack, and Macia jumps in the shower to get ready for church youth group this evening. I finish the day's log book and put the meatloaf and some potatoes into the oven to bake.

Our after school and evening hours vary from day to day. We always have housework to do and dinner to get ready. Sometimes there are errands to run. Quite often, one or more of the girls will have a field trip, service project, or social activity scheduled with other homeschoolers from our support group.

Today's plan has me getting some grocery shopping done and Macia at church youth group this evening.

At 4:30 p.m. the girls begin their chores, household jobs that rotate from day to day. I realized soon after we began homeschooling, that I wouldn't be able to do it all by myself. God didn't put us down here on earth all by ourselves, with every man for himself. He put us down here in families, to work together like a team. Greg is our team captain and my strongest support system, helping me as we set goals for our girls, teaching biology lab and algebra in the evenings, and providing the spiritual and emotional support I need to keep going.

In order to manage the household chores, we've devised a pocket chart that hangs on the side of our refrigerator. I used colored index cards to make the chore cards, a different color for each day of the week. They are sorted and redistributed in the pockets weekly. With this system each of the girls knows what her chores are without my having to tell them. (I do still have to remind them regularly!) When a chore has been completed its card is flipped over in the pocket so Greg and I can see at a glance what's been done and what remains. If a job hasn't been done sufficiently when Greg or I checks it (inspections take place sporadically), it has to be redone. In order to distribute the chores fairly, each of the girls has the same number of pockets on the chore chart as she is years in age. Each year, as their birthdays are celebrated, our daughters receive a new pocket on the chore chart, along with their birthday presents. The idea behind this is that the older the child is, the more responsibility she has.

Periodically, I will take a day or two to do some serious scrubbing and cleaning, but for the most part, the house cleaning is maintained by the girls. When we started this system, I had to teach each of the jobs to the girls, and I still occasionally have to remind them what my expectations are for each job. We have been using our chore card system for about three years, and as time goes by, I notice that the girls are becoming more proficient at cleaning. They are also becoming more responsible about getting the jobs done, with "becoming" being the key words here!

Today's chores include dusting, vacuuming, sorting the recyclables, and folding the laundry. We also have a kitchen helper and dishes person each evening. Since Macia has dishes today, she empties the dishwasher during chore time. This could have waited until after dinner, except that she has church youth group this evening, and she wants to be finished quickly.

After her chores are done, Macia uses the grocery advertisements from the newspaper to help me make the shopping list. We're still working at it when Dad gets home at 5:00 p.m., and he helps us finish up. Megan is the kitchen helper, so she feeds the dog and sets the table. She'll also help Macia with dishes after dinner.

Dinner today is meat loaf, baked potatoes, green beans, and family conversa-

---

tion. The news media regularly reports that fewer and fewer families are sitting and eating at the dinner table together on a daily basis. In our family, this time together is a priority. Our general rule is: "If outside interests (friends, sports, television, etc.) are more important than family time, then you are spending too much time on the outside interest." We are a busy family and, while exceptions are made occasionally, we sit around the dinner table, eat together, and discuss our day, every day.

After dinner, our busy family goes in three different directions. Greg drives Macia to her church youth group meeting. I leave to do the grocery shopping and will pick Macia up later. Even though I spend my evening in a busy grocery store, I enjoy the time by myself, a rarity for most homeschool moms that I know. I am not the only homeschool mom in the grocery store! I visit a few minutes with my friend, arrange tomorrow's skating car pool and discuss what groceries are on sale. I pick Macia up at 9:00 p.m. Eleven-year-old Megan is left in charge during the fifteen or twenty minutes while Greg and I are both gone. Greg, Megan and Marla spend the rest of the evening at home. The girls play computer games, watch a little bit of television, and shower before bed at 9:00 p.m. They are allowed to read in bed until 10:00 p.m. The girls consider this an unreasonably early hour, but they have agreed to it since they aren't given a choice. Macia won't have time to read tonight, as it is after 10:00 p.m. before we get home and get the groceries carried in and put away.

Our day has been a long one, and I am tired. The last thing I do is set up the coffee pot so that the coffee will be ready when I get up in the morning. Greg is already almost asleep as I kiss him good night. He'll be up again at 5:30 in the morning. I turn down the sound on the television after the news and set my alarm. Tomorrow morning will be here before I'm ready for it. I wish I were a morning person.

In years to come, I know I will think back and know that there were times when homeschooling went extremely well, and times when I wondered if my kids were learning anything. I think this is typical of most jobs, occupations, and careers. In the beginning when I was doing kindergarten with Megan, Marla sort of tagged along. As we progressed through that first semester, and I saw how much they were learning, I gained the confidence to teach Macia, too. Our first year with all of the girls at home was the most difficult one.

Each year since then has gotten easier, yet more difficult at the same time. It is easier because we are used to homeschooling, and the girls are good about doing the work. It is also easier because I have a better idea of what I am doing. The years are getting more difficult though, because now we're into the high school subjects. High school algebra and biology take more time and attention than the elementary subjects. For the first several years that we homeschooled, I taught the girls together, using the unit study approach. I don't feel like I can do this anymore. Macia needs to study high school subject matter, and I need to do elementary school with Megan and Marla. This has been an adjustment for me, but it is going well. I still plan, supervise, and go over the subject matter with Macia, but it is also hard not being as involved with her as I used to be. I think this is the beginning of letting go. It won't be very long before she is driving, then going to college, and beyond. I'm glad we've had these years with her.

We have goals each year that relate to the curriculum and goals to improve weaknesses, such as our "neatness counts" goal. Beyond that, we also have several long-term goals. It is our goal that each of the girls will be strong in her faith and able to draw on that faith when making life decisions. To accomplish this goal, we include Bible in our curriculum, attend church, and participate in church activities as a family. Our main educational goal is to prepare the girls for college. We are doing this by working on the basics: reading, writing, and arithmetic, but also by guiding them in the development of their thinking skills through study of geography, social studies, and science. We are striving to nurture their natural curiosity and creativity, encouraging them to look carefully at how things work, and to ask questions about what they are learning. We challenge them to come up with ideas and to act on them in order to improve the world we live in. I hope that each of our girls will attend college and study about something that interests and excites her. We hope that each will marry for life and enjoy raising a family. But most of all, we pray that our girls will know God and follow His plan for their lives.

My homeschool friends and support group help with "me time." When I first joined this group seven years ago, there were about seven families involved. Homeschooling is a growing movement in West Michigan. There are over twenty-five support groups in our area and more starting all the time. Our support group membership has now grown to nearly seventy families. The moms meet once a month in both large and small groups. A few years ago, when fellowship was becoming difficult due to the size of the group, we started going out for coffee and dessert at a local restaurant after our meetings. I now plan the day after the support group meeting to start a little later than usual, as our coffee, dessert, and fellowship time sometimes lasts until after midnight!

I have become close friends with several of the moms in my group who have children close to my children's ages, and we have become a support system for each other. Recently, when I was feeling over-worked and under-relaxed, I called them on the spur of the moment, and we all went out for Saturday breakfast together. After I had surgery in October, friends cleaned our house and cooked meals for us for more than a week. Another time, after our big trip, two of the families took our girls camping with them so that Greg and I could have time alone. We will be returning the favor next week.

Macia (13), Megan (11), Marla (8)

I don't spend much time doing hobbies by myself (except reading in the summer) but that is okay. I have ten more years with my kids and then the rest of my life after that for hobbies! (Thirty years or more, I hope!)

Time alone with Greg has always been a priority. From the time that Macia was a baby, Greg and I had a regular weekly "date night." We actually went through four regular babysitters before Macia was old enough to sit for us. What we did on our date nights varied, depending on budget and interest. Sometimes we would eat dinner with the kids and then go out, other times we would eat out. We became regular customers at the discount movie theatre, did our Christmas and birthday shopping together, took walks on the beach at Lake Michigan, or sat and talked over coffee and dessert.

Homeschooling has been very good for our marriage. While I am the one at home, guiding the education of our girls and doing the majority of the teaching, Greg and I are working together in this venture. We discuss our goals, large and small, and together come up with ways to reach them. I think that working together as homeschooling parents and the communication that this requires has strengthened our marriage.

Homeschooling has been the best decision that our family ever made. We have wonderful relationships with our children that I don't think would have been possible if they were not at home. I think of homeschooling as a lifestyle. Whenever a learning opportunity presents itself, whether on a trip or sitting at the dinner table, we are able to spend the time learning. I love it when God does the lesson plans!

Here is a list of some of the many things God has taught me during our seven years of homeschooling:

RELAX!
Enjoy your children!
Involve your husband however you can.
Don't get over committed with outside activities.
Trust yourself.
Read all that you can about homeschooling.
Don't compare yourself with other families.
Figure out what you want to do and do it. It doesn't matter if it is unconventional—if it works for your family that is all that matters.
Set realistic goals—if you are not a morning person, don't set your goal to be out of bed at 6:00 a.m.
Find a curriculum that works for you—don't be a slave to your curriculum, it's just a tool.
If the curriculum doesn't work, get rid of it and try something new. (I don't know a single family that hasn't goofed on curriculum purchases!)

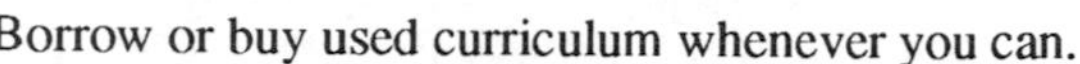

Borrow or buy used curriculum whenever you can.
Get to know your librarians.
Do a unit study at least once, just for the experience.
Simplify your life.
Don't worry about socialization.
Don't worry about what others will say or think.
Ask your child what s/he wants to learn—desire-directed study is successful study.
You are the parent, take control.
Read out loud as a family.
Take fun trips and talk about what you learned.
Cook.
Do crafts.
Paint.
Camp.
Go to museums and count them as school time.
Say yes to your children as often as you can, then it won't be so painful when you have to say no.
Don't forget to study art, music, and drama.
Have fun!
Remember that your relationship with your children is more important than any school subject.
Pray a lot.
God will provide exactly what you need.

Marla, Megan, Macia, Jeanne, Greg

Unit Human Body - Oregon Trail Date Wed. 11-3-99

MACIA	MEGAN	MARLA
Bible- discussed 2Tim 2:22-26 w/Mom in relation to Teen group	Math- Converting Improper Fractions to Whole Numbers or Mixed Numbers + Converting Mixed Numbers	Reading - working on AG questions. Math - Metric Units of Length + Naming Fractions
TLP- reading + bookwork	Spelling -	Spelling -
Algebra - 14 More complicated evaluations	History - reading from "Great Horn Spoon"	← History Penmanship (cursive) a, e, l, i + h
Spanish - bookwork and quiz	Redid missed Math problems	Grammar - Verb Song talked about action, being, helping + linking verbs.
Biology - reading and bookwork	Grammar →	N + V Sheets
	Science - Human Body Unit	← Science
	Writing - began creative writing project on "Oregon" related to books or trip →	← Writing - putting in the capitals + punctuation

Date 11-3

UNIT- Human Body

Read about Skeletal System - how bones support your body and give it shape. Bones are alive and grow. The outside covering is the Periosteum. Next layer inside is called compact bone - long hollow bones have bone marrow in the center - produces red blood cells. We have about 300 soft bones as a baby - they harden + fuse as we grow until at 18-25 your last bone (collarbone) hardens. Adults have 206-209 bones.

Looked at Skeletal System poster naming bones and finding them in our bodies. Meg looked up the dog's skeletal system in the encyclopedia to compare which bones we have in common.

BOOKS READ

World Book Young Scientist - Vol. 7 - World Book
Considering God's Creation - Mortimer + Smith
Blood + Guts - Linda Allison

Macia (13), Megan (11), Marla (8)

Matthew, age 30
Kathleen, age 29
Chantel, age 8
Talen, age 6

Interview with Kathleen in November from the mountains of Prescott, Arizona

FOLLOWING OUR DREAMS

Homeschooling is something that Matt and I planned to do since before we were married. We both felt that the public school system squelches children's natural love of learning. When Chantel was about four, we talked to some people who were homeschooling and read some books on it. But at the time, I hadn't heard of the more alternative styles of homeschooling. The only thing I could imagine was school-at-home that could somehow be made more interesting to the child. I also didn't know of any legal way of homeschooling in California that didn't involve a public school's "homeschool program." So we signed up with the public school in our town's program.

The teacher we met with once a week was great! She was, without a doubt, the best thing about that program. She had homeschooled her daughter for several years so she knew what we were going through. She spent a lot of time that first year telling me to relax! Chantel was doing fine and was far ahead of what they expect for kindergarten. I tried sporadically to do structured, "school-at-home" stuff for a few months, but it didn't work well for us. I found that if I pushed things, even things she liked, she would balk. Even if I forced her to finish it, she wouldn't remember it. Plus, she wouldn't want to touch anything remotely like it for weeks. If, however, I backed off and just gave her ideas sometimes, answered her questions, and went where she wanted to go (learning-wise), she loved it and could remember incredible details for the longest time. So, we got more and more eclectic, with me only pushing certain things when I got nervous.

As time went on, I read more and more about different homeschooling styles—John Holt, Mary Griffith, Montessori, Waldorf, etc. I also actually saw my daughter learning (reading, writing, math, science, history, etc.) even when I wasn't "teaching" her in the traditional way or assigning work. I relaxed more. Finally, we decided four months into our second year to try unschooling. We figured that if it didn't work, we could always go back to more structure. Needless to say, it did work. We have found that our children have a wide variety of interests and they love learning. We believe this is due, in great part, to unschooling.

If someone had told me at the beginning that there were a lot of ways to homeschool out there, I wouldn't have tried to pattern myself after the public school system! I think if someone had pointed me in the direction of some of the books I read later on, our first year might have gone a little more smoothly. Or, at least, I wouldn't have been freaking out quite so much that I wasn't following the public school pattern well enough! In the beginning, it's so helpful to see what is out there and what is going to fit best with our family. We thought about and talked about what our goals and reasons for homeschooling were, then decided which homeschool style would fit best with those goals. Homeschooling should fit our family, not the other way around.

My husband is Matthew, I am Kathleen, and our children are Chantel and Talen. Matthew works outside the home. He is the office manager at a psychiatrist's office. I worked at several different jobs from the time we got married until I was about seven months pregnant with Chantel (answering service, kennel, and temp work). Then, I became a stay-at-home mom and have been since my daughter was born. Chantel is now eight and our son Talen is six. Our children have never been to school and this is our fourth year of homeschooling.

We live in Prescott, Arizona, in a three-bedroom house with Matthew's mother. We moved in a year and a half ago when my father-in-law was terminally ill in order to help care for him. He passed away six weeks after we moved here, but we have all chosen to continue this arrangement for the time being. We are up in the mountains and there is a wooded area in the back yard and big granite boulders in the front that the kids love to play on and in. It is a large yard and the kids spend a lot of time outside playing and learning. Chantel has been keeping a nature journal for a couple of months and she loves to collect leaves, bugs, and flowers out of the yard. They also love to watch the many birds and squirrels that live in or near our yard. Both children like to pack a picnic, books to read, paper to write or draw on, and go outside for the day. I feel this is a very healthy way for children to live and learn. Chantel has strong artistic, linguistic, and musical talents. Those are the ways she learns best, so she is constantly drawing, writing, and singing. Talen is very physical. He is a kinesthetic learner. He is constantly moving, climbing, and hanging on things, which is one reason why he is so talented in gym!

They each have a desk in their room but they don't work at them. They use them to store things! Okay—pile things. Chantel has a computer in her room (it is not hooked up to the Internet), but Matt needs to put a CD drive in it so they can use most of their programs on it. They usually use the computer in my room to play games like *Carmen Sandiego* and *Math Blaster*. We usually read together in the living room on the couch, and Chantel reads almost every night in her bed before going to sleep. They like to do other projects at the kitchen counter or on the kitchen table. And, of course, the floor is always a popular spot!

Really, our learning spreads out all over the house and yard, as well as the car! We have musical instruments, art supplies, and books all over the house! We have a piano, a guitar, a flute, two fiddles, Talen's drum set, and two banjos. Matt plays the piano and banjo. Over the years, I have taken piano, flute, and guitar lessons to get started, and then try to go forward on my own.

We keep both of the kids supplied with real art supplies, good paper, watercolors, oil pastels, pencils, pens, crayons, and clay. Chantel has a bag in her room where she squirrels away any potential craft supplies she finds. Talen is into *Lego* right now, so we consequently are constantly stepping on them! We have broken electronics in the garage that they can take apart when they feel like it. Matt has a number of woodworking supplies and he is starting to show the kids how to use them to make things. They are working on a project right now, but I don't know what it is. It is an anniversary present for me that Matt is helping Talen make.

Our Day

It is a Friday morning in early November and the weather is cool (something like 32° F.). I wake up as Matt is getting ready for work . . . about 7:40 a.m. I lay in bed for about ten more minutes, talking to him as he finishes getting ready. After he leaves for work, I get up and check my e-mail . . . I had asked some questions on one of the unschooling mailing lists I am on about homeschooling laws in other states, and I wanted to see if I had received any responses. I send questions out and then people who know the answers post them. The *Unschooling List* (*UL*) is great! I can ask questions about almost anything, and someone (or several someones) will know the answer or can direct me to a place to find the answer. Plus, I can get sympathy when things are going badly, and cheers when things are going well! I receive some responses, so I read them and look up some of the sites I am directed to. I also answer some personal e-mails I receive.

While I am doing that, Chantel wakes up and comes in and gets into my bed. Her grandmother is in California right now so both kids slept in her bed last night. Chantel tells me that she had better sleep in her own bed tonight because

Random (our dog that sleeps with her) tried to sneak in and sleep on Mamaw's bed with her. She says she knows Mamaw wouldn't like that, and that she had better stay in her room so Random can sleep with her. I am almost finished with my e-mail when Talen wakes up. We all discuss what to have for breakfast and decide on pancakes and bacon. I ask the kids to get out the stuff for pancakes while I read my last few messages.

It is about 9:00 a.m. when I get to the kitchen. Chantel has looked up the recipe in the recipe box and has gotten out all of the ingredients she could find. The only things she hadn't gotten out were the oil (because she didn't know which kind) and the flour (because she thought we would use the flour in the canister). I show her the oil I use and explain that the flour in the canister is Mamaw's and we have a different kind of flour that we use. I show them that I make pancakes from one third whole wheat flour and two thirds unbleached white and explain that it makes the pancakes healthier for you. Chantel has recently become very interested in which foods are healthy and why. I also show them how to divide up the cup of flour the recipe calls for into thirds. Chantel reads me the ingredients as we need them. She and Talen take turns measuring everything out. Then Chantel cooks the pancakes. She likes her pancakes just so, so she cooks her own now!

While they are eating and I am finishing up cooking the bacon, we discuss what we will do today. They recently got a number of books from the library and I tell them I will read to them if they want. Talen asks if we can read a whole *Bunnicula* chapter book. That is what we did with the first one . . . read the whole thing in one two-hour marathon! I say sure and tell Chantel that I will read her anything she wants . . . she always has several books going at once. For instance, right now she and her dad are reading *Harry Potter and the Prisoner of Azkaban*, she and I are reading *Knights Castle*, she has some flower identification books she is using, and (on her own) she is reading a *Pony Pals* book and some fairy tales. Plus, she is listening to *Tom Sawyer, Peter Pan* (both original and unabridged), and *Ramona the Pest* on audio tape. I am sure there are others that I don't know about. Right now, she is reading a lot of fiction, but other times she reads a lot of non-fiction. A couple of months ago she was reading everything she could find about dolphins and whales, plus some books about foxes and squirrels. This morning she says she wants *Knights Castle* (about these four kids who get transported back in time to the medieval period) that she got at the library. She feels it is a little too hard for her to read on her own. I say fine, but then while I am eating breakfast, Talen asks if they can watch the television show *Wishbone*. About ten minutes later, I hear him watching *Scooby Doo*. I call him in and ask him if he is finished with *Wishbone*, and he says yeah. I remind him that he can only watch so much television each day so he needs to choose what he really wants to be watching—not just something because it

---

comes on. He decides that he wants to watch the two *Arthurs* (one in the morning and one in the afternoon), *Zaboomafoo* (a *PBS* show about animals), and *Wishbone*. He goes in and turns off the television for half an hour until *Arthur* comes on.

I am not super restrictive about television. I usually let them watch a couple of hours per day. Mostly, they watch *PBS*, although they also have quite a few movies on tape that they like to watch sometimes. I feel that television has it's place and that they can learn from it. For instance, they have learned many things about animals from watching *PBS* and *Discovery* channels. Also, I started reading *Tom Sawyer* and Shakespeare to Chantel because she saw them on *Wishbone* and said that she thought she should read the "real" story. I am trying to help them learn to pick what they want to watch—not just anything or having the television on all the time. They are pretty good about this, although sometimes I have to nudge them, especially Talen. But, once I say something about it, they turn it off and go find something else to do with little or no grumbling.

Talen has gymnastics twice a week and he is on the junior team. He is very good at it! Chantel takes gymnastics once a week and has recently made it to level two. They both really love it! I noticed that they were offering a gymnastics class in town and I asked the kids if they wanted to try it. They both did so we signed them up. Talen's teacher said he was very talented and asked me if he could be on the junior team they were going to form. I asked Talen if he wanted to do it and he did. I thought he might like gymnastics as he has always been a very physical child, but ultimately he made the choice.

It is about 9:40 a.m. by this time and I am drinking a cup of coffee and reading the newspaper, with the dogs lying under my feet. Talen is talking to his sister on the couch, but keeps asking me if it is time yet for *Arthur* (there is no clock in the living room). Finally, I say, "Why don't you go get dressed and make your bed while you are waiting?" So, they wander off to do that, with much discussion about who is the most responsible for the bed being messy. Then they come in to watch *Arthur*.

The kids have two types of chores. The first type is the kind that they have to do because they are part of this family and, as such, they need to help with the smooth running of the household. Examples of this type of chore are cleaning their rooms, putting away the things they get out, cleaning up the messes they make (to the extent of their abilities), folding and putting away their laundry, taking their laundry down to the machines, etc. I also expect them to make their own breakfast and lunch most of the time, although I will help with certain things if they need it. These chores are not negotiable.

The other type of chores are open for discussion if they are unhappy with them, and they get paid three dollars per week for them. The paid chores are taking out the trash (they split up the trash cans in the house), getting the mail and newspaper (they each get one), and feeding the dogs (they each do one). Most of the time, they are pretty good about doing these chores. I do usually have to remind them one or two times that they need to do such and so now. Sometimes, I have to stand on top of them and point out every toy and piece of paper two or three times to get the job done! Fortunately, that doesn't happen too often. It seems to happen in clusters. There will be two or three weeks where I am pulling my hair out because of this and then a month or two of overall co-operation.

I go in to get dressed and check my e-mail again because I sent out some more questions. As I have some responses, I look up the information I've been given. All in all, this takes about an hour. Chantel asks me to cut up an apple for her, so while I call Matt on the phone to tell him what I found on-line, I cut up her apple. While Matt and I talk some more, I cook the rest of the pancake batter—Matt and the kids like to eat them cold with peanut butter. Talen comes in and asks if I will take them swimming today. He says, "There is nothing going on today, please!" Matt reminds me that today is the homeschool swim at the indoor pool. We went all the time last year, but haven't been yet this year, so I say I will take them. Later in this conversation, Talen asks me where his paper airplane that Daddy made him is. I tell him I don't know, but he must have found them because when I get off the phone, he is throwing them down the hallway. He comes into the kitchen and starts explaining to me the differences between the two planes and how one flies better than the other does. I ask him why he thinks one flies better and he starts speculating on what particular features in one plane make it fly better than the other. Then, I tell him if he wants to try to copy the plane Daddy made, he can use some more of my computer paper.

So, Talen is working on a new airplane and Chantel is reading on the couch. I clean up the kitchen from breakfast, make my bed, and fold the clothes that are all over the bed. Cordless phones are great! I can get so much done when I need to answer a call. Chantel takes her backpack (full of workbooks, paper, and her journal) out to the front porch. I find her out there working on her journal. She has also done some cursive practice. She decided that she wanted to learn cursive a couple of months ago, so I bought her a book on it. She works in it sporadically.

I don't give assignments so Chantel works on what she wants to. I bought her a complete third grade workbook (she has had one every year) because she likes them and asks for them. She hauls it out when she feels like doing something in it, as she does on this day. Sometimes she shows me what she was working on and sometimes she doesn't. Either way is fine with me. Talen, on the other hand, doesn't like doing worksheets and will very rarely touch one—that is fine, too. We don't really do structure here (except, of course, for outside classes, music, and gymnastics) other than what is needed for real life, like chores and appointments.

I see that Talen is still working on making the paper airplane. I tell the kids to get their swimming stuff together as it is almost time to go. They inform me they already have done that. They are way ahead of me! About this time, Matt comes home for lunch. I talk to him for a few minutes, then the kids and I leave to go to the swimming pool. Normally, when Matt comes home for lunch, if we are not going out somewhere, the kids are off doing whatever it is they are involved in and I come in and help him put together lunch. Then, I sit and talk with him until he has to go back to work.

When we get home from swimming, I send Chantel to get the mail (at the bottom of our very steep driveway), which is one of her jobs, and Talen takes out the kitchen trash. Since it is 3:30 p.m. when we get home, it will be an hour until the afternoon *Arthur*. I tell the kids that I want them to make a pick-up sweep through the house as the clutter is getting out of control. On this particular day, they are pretty co-operative and they pick up with almost no nudging. They put their stuff away, let the dogs out, and then go on the back patio to write a message and draw a picture on the cement in sidewalk chalk. Normally, the kids play outside a lot and one or both of the dogs plays with them, but today they haven't spent too much time outside.

While they are picking up their stuff, I call a friend of mine to get her recipe for homemade dinner rolls. While we talk for a few minutes, I do my own sweep through the house, picking up things. The kids come in to watch their show and make peanut butter and pancake sandwiches. They hadn't eaten lunch before we left for swimming at 1:00 p.m. They weren't hungry since they had eaten a big breakfast and had an apple later in the morning. After they eat, I tell them that while they watch television, they need to fold the load of their clean clothes in the laundry basket. While they do that, I throw the ingredients in the bread machine on the dough cycle and start the chicken roasting. I had set it out to thaw before we went swimming. I peel an apple from the backyard tree for the kids, as they are still hungry.

After the show, Chantel goes to her room to work on some math worksheets she wanted to do, and it is time to take the dough out of the machine. Talen and I take it out and shape it into balls, which we put in the oven. Then, I peel the potatoes and Talen puts them in the pot to steam for mashed potatoes. Talen stays with me and we talk the whole time about many things. He also helps me baste the chicken and I explain to him why we are doing it.

Chantel comes in and wants me to check the math she did. She is adding numbers in the hundreds and thousands as well as columns, all with regrouping. There are also some subtraction problems mixed in. There is one thing she hasn't quite understood so many of the problems on one page are wrong. After I explain it to her, she easily fixes the rest. This is very typical of her, since I don't insist she correct them. To her, the emphasis is on "am I understanding this?" When she brings something to me and asks if it is right, I will explain to her what is wrong and why (if any are wrong, of course). She is usually very attentive at such times because she wants to know why it is wrong. Then, she is free to redo those particular problems or not, as she chooses. Many times she will because she likes to be right. But either way, she usually remembers what we talked about and doesn't repeat the same mistakes.

Meanwhile, Talen decides that we are going to eat at a "restaurant" tonight so he sets the table like a restaurant would, with the silverware rolled into napkins etc. He also very carefully makes a "credit card/check" to pay for dinner. He asks me how to spell all the words he wants to put on it and writes it out himself. He was about to do a worksheet with Chantel but decided not to because he thinks the directions are stupid. He is to color the moon shapes blue and the stars red. He says, "But that is not what color they are!" So, he makes the credit card instead. Matt comes home from work just as I am taking dinner out of the oven and he carves the chicken. It is right around 6:30 p.m. when we finally sit down to eat.

After dinner, Matt and I clean the kitchen, while the kids feed the dogs and then play a game on the computer about the plants and animals of Alaska. Since Chantel loves writing a nature journal lately, she picked up this game a couple of days ago, after two years of thinking it was boring and refusing to touch it.

After about thirty minutes, they each get into pajamas and have dessert. Then I notice that Talen hasn't finished folding his clothes so I sit with him while he finishes and puts them away. Daddy builds a fire and reads a chapter of the *Harry Potter* book to Chantel. She is really into them, but Talen isn't. Since it is an hour past Talen's bedtime, I send him to get in bed while I finish talking on the phone to my father. Then, I go in and read Talen *Arthur's Family Vacation* and tuck him into bed. A few minutes later, Matt finishes reading to Chantel. She comes in to kiss me good night. She says she doesn't want me to tuck her in tonight because her room is not clean and I say okay, but then she asks me to come help her fix her bed since the covers are very messed up. I help her with her bed and tuck her in. She snuggles down to go to sleep right away, which is unusual, as she normally reads, draws, writes, or something until quite late (11:00 p.m. or midnight). It is only 10:00 p.m., so I guess she is tired. They are allowed to stay in their rooms with the lights on reading, or whatever, as late as they want. but they have to stay in their rooms. This is Matt's and my time to be alone. We can read, watch television, talk, or whatever, but I need this adult time without the kids running around. It makes for a peaceful relaxing evening. It didn't, however, work out that way today!

I now have time to think back on our day. I don't keep records, really, since

Arizona doesn't require any, but I do keep a folder of written work and projects the kids have done. Every few months, I sit down and write out, journal style, what we have been up to. All of that is more for us to look back on in the future, not for the state. If I had to put down what we did today, I could translate it into education-ese like this:

Chantel:
Reading: silent and being read to
Math: fractions, measuring, addition to third place with regrouping, subtraction with regrouping, reading and deciphering recipe measurement
Writing: journal writing, cursive practice
Science/Health: studying the plants and animals of Alaska, nutritional value of wheat vs. white flour, *PBS* show about animals (panthers)
Social Science: discussion about doing things to keep peace among family members, American Indian legends (*Wishbone*), social behaviors (*Arthur*), read fairy tales from another country
P.E.: swimming
Art: drawing (with sidewalk chalk)
Discipline/self-reliance: doing chores, picking up after self, cooking

Talen:
Reading: read-aloud
Math: fractions, measuring, reading recipe measurements
Writing: printing/spelling practice, creative writing (made up story/situation)
Science/Health: studying plants and animals of Alaska, nutritional value of wheat vs. white flour, *PBS* show about animals (panthers), aerodynamics of one shape vs.. another, scientific thinking, making a theory about why something works and then testing it
Social Science: American Indian legends (*Wishbone*), social behaviors (*Arthur*)
P.E.: swimming
Art: drawing, making paper airplanes
Discipline/self-reliance: doing chores, picking up after self, cooking

Unschooling, for us, is allowing the children to choose what and how they will learn. During our first year of homeschooling, we spent some time thinking and talking about our reasons for homeschooling and our goals for our children. What it came down to for us is that we want our children to keep the natural love of learning that all children are born with. We want them to know how to find out whatever it is they want to know. We do this by helping them find the answers to their questions. They are learning how to easily use the resources at the library. We want them to be able to think and reason for themselves and not just blindly follow what someone else tells them. We want them to be self-sufficient adults. Unschooling fits perfectly with all of these goals. Our whole family loves unschooling and being able to watch our children grow and learn every day is proof to me that it works!

Our whole family lives an unschooling lifestyle. For us, unschooling means all of us should follow our dreams and interests, with the support and help of the rest of the family. That, obviously, means that when the kids want to learn about something or pursue something, we help them however we can to follow up on that. For instance, since Chantel read about nature journaling in *Ranger Rick* magazine and wanted to try it, I bought her a composition notebook and a small magnifying glass. She decided she wanted to have *lined* paper rather than *blank* because she wanted to *write* more than *draw*. She puts the notebook, magnifying glass, tape, a pencil, and usually water and a snack in a backpack, and goes outside for the afternoon. I also helped her find plant and bird identification books at the library so she can try to identify what she finds. I told her that I would buy her some binoculars so she could observe birds and squirrels without getting too close and scaring them away.

It was the same way with Talen and dinosaurs. He would check out thirty or forty dinosaur books from the library every time we went, which is about once

Chantel, Kathleen, Matthew, Talen

every couple of weeks. I would read them to him over and over again. This encouragement works the same way with the adults. For example, when I was interested in learning the guitar, Matt said that I should get one, so I asked a friend of ours if he knew anyone who had an extra. It turned out he had an extra that he gave to me. I spent two years playing around with it and reading books about it, and when I realized I wanted to take some lessons to figure out a certain technique, Matt was very supportive of that. And the kids are very happy that I am learning to play the guitar! Chantel told me that it was great that I would know how to play because then I could teach her how to play—she already has Daddy to teach her piano and a fiddle teacher to learn fiddle! We all have many interests and we all try to be helpful and supportive of each other's interests and goals.

Chantel (8), Talen (6)

Bob, age 50
Jackie, age 41
Dawn, age 13
Charles Tyler (C.T.), age 11
Jackson, age almost 8
Sam, age 5

Interview with Jackie in October in the foothills of the Appalachian Mountains

THE POWER TO FLY

This time of year is absolutely breathtaking. Frederick County, Maryland is considered rural. However, where we live is also minutes from interstates that take us to Washington, D.C. and Northern Virginia. We can be in Baltimore, Maryland within an hour. We have an acre of property that is not wooded (unfortunately), that borders a fifty acre horse farm in the back and ten acres of land that can't be developed in the front, and neighbors on either side of us. We have a half-court basketball court, a huge wooden play set with two towers, and an in-ground swimming pool/spa combination all in the back yard. Everyone that visits claims we have our own slice of paradise.

However, it isn't much like a paradise inside! We have a two story traditional-colonial style house with a finished basement. In the past year we've remodeled the kitchen, painted most of the rooms, and replaced some of the carpeting, so it's starting to look civilized. (When the oldest boys were around a lot, the living room was a boxing ring, a knee hockey arena, and it had that sports arena "look" to it. You know—marks on the walls.) Having had babies for so long, I do not have many things displayed, but I have some great framed art on the walls, and I have been told my house has a "homey" feel to it.

We have three older sons who are in their twenties and our four younger children who are still at home are: Dawn (age thirteen), Charles Tyler (or C.T., age eleven), Jackson (almost eight), and Sam (age five).

The only exposure I ever had to homeschooling was through my brother's wife. She has been homeschooling for eleven years now. I thought what she did was really great, but didn't entertain the thought for myself until I had my own day care for two years when I had children come to my home. It was very difficult, but we had a lot of fun. When I saw how influential kids can be on other kids and how they totally absorb the environment that they're in, I thought I needed to homeschool for my own children. I wanted their childhood to be filled with lots and lots of positive input.

I start my day be getting up with my beloved at 4:30 a.m. Bob travels an hour to work where he is the director of operations for an Internet company. (I'm so glad to have someone computer literate in the family!) On a perfect day, I work out for an hour and a half, eat a little breakfast, then sit down and go over the scheduled work for the day. I've found that I do better when I schedule weekly instead of daily. It lets me be a little spontaneous each day! The kids usually start getting up around 7:30 a.m. They eat, take a shower, mess around, and when they have fifteen minutes left, I put on a timer (one of my most used possessions) as a signal to get started. That way, we begin somewhere between 9:00-9:30 a.m. When the timer goes off, everyone is pretty good about getting down to the school room, which is a room I have in the basement (one that has a lot of windows and a walkout so it is not like a dungeon, thank goodness).

I used to do school at our dining room table, but got tired of having all that mess all the time. Now that the little one is five, he isn't exploring all over the place as much. Also, I have a desk with all my stuff, and they have fold up tables (small) where they can spread out with their work. *Many* pencils have to be sharpened before we actually begin. I have an answering machine that takes calls, and we hardly ever turn on the television before 4:00 p.m.

We do our Bible study for a half-hour, and then the kids look over their schedules. Their schedules are made according to their understanding of the material they're working on. Since I make the schedules in three-week intervals, I'll change the amount of time they're given for working on something they might be having a hard time with. They are happy with the scheduling I do, so they don't have input (even though I would allow it). I looked at many software applications for designing school schedules, but my husband set up a spreadsheet for me on the computer, and it works out great. I plan three weeks at a time and print out one week at a time.

Dawn learns very methodically. She understands concepts and likes things to be taught in an orderly fashion. C.T. doesn't, and I'm still learning how to teach him. Jackson *must* have a routine, and when I deviate, he falls apart. However, I occasionally let him fall apart just so he can see that he does get his work done, and that he can handle it. Sam loves to learn and he is really quick. Sam does simple reproducible geography, science, *Saxon Phonics K*, and *Saxon*

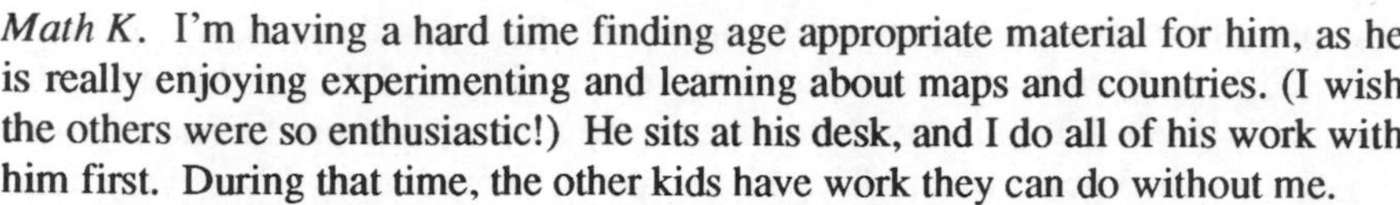

Math K. I'm having a hard time finding age appropriate material for him, as he is really enjoying experimenting and learning about maps and countries. (I wish the others were so enthusiastic!) He sits at his desk, and I do all of his work with him first. During that time, the other kids have work they can do without me.

Next, I work with Jackson. There is a lot of work he does on his own, but I do *Saxon Phonics 2* and *Saxon Math 2* with him. And, yes, I do use all the annoying punch out cards and babyish books. I think he's one of those kids who needs constant reinforcement of what he's learned.

After him, Dawn or C.T. will ask me for help or to go over some of their work. I always do their math with them. (*Saxon Math*, of course!). Most days, we are done by 2:00 p.m. Then I start on some light housework. There's *always* laundry and starting dinner. I'd love to say I've finally found the way to get the kids to do chores on a regular basis, but I haven't. They do help when I ask, and my daughter will automatically pitch in when I start getting really behind. I believe it is very important, so I am going to find a way.

The kids like to play dinosaurs, go out back and play basketball or baseball, or draw. My daughter usually plays her CDs, talks on the phone incessantly, or reads constantly—*Star Wars* books. They have four game systems (*Super Nintendo, Nintendo 64, Sony Playstation*, and *Gameboy*), but are only allowed to play them on the weekends or if mom is perimenopausing. It's not very often, but I will allow myself to kick back and read a book or draw then. But I won't put any stress on myself that day.

Bob gets home around 7:00 p.m., eats dinner with us, and then cleans up the dishes. Ideally, the kids are in bed by 9:00 p.m., but usually it's more like 10:00 p.m. I read and fall asleep.

Since I've been doing this for four years now, the days have become less stressful and more productive. I'm not as hard on myself and I've become more confident. For example, now that Dawn is thirteen, I agonized about *high school*. Can I do high school? How do I do that? After reading about kids who go to college when they're fourteen and recognizing that I can be real creative with their future education, I now know I can do this and even Dawn is excited about our plan. We've planned together for her to start college when she's sixteen or seventeen. I have to check with our junior college for requirements. Nancy, I have you to thank for the idea because I remember reading about your kids taking college classes at a young age. When Dawn and I started talking about her future, she said she really wants to be a dolphin trainer. I told her she might be able to get an early start. It's exciting because in this day and age there are so many options!

Our family culture includes more than our homeschooling. Sometimes we take trips to the museums, do things with other families, or take a day off just because it's finally *spring!* But I am always aware and in tune to the needs,

---

Dawn (13), C.T. (11), Jackson (almost 8), Sam (5)

strengths, and weaknesses of our children. I've tried different methods of homeschooling—structured, unstructured, unschooling, and in the beginning I tried to follow what the public schools were doing. I've read just about every homeschool book and child/family psychology book in my efforts to be informed (and to keep my sanity, sometimes). I believe there is no wrong or right way to homeschool, just your own way for your family. But we are always driven by the intense love we have for our children and our determination to instill in them a value system and a *love* for learning *anything* and to be passionate about *life!* Our children are important and unique because they believe that, not because their peers said so. (Step down off soapbox—breathe 1,2,3!)

I have been fortunate in that I have had a lot of support and few naysayers. My husband was skeptical and cautious at first, but now he tells everyone at work that it is the best thing in the world. In fact, every year we go on these company trips, and one year I met one of the wives who happened to be a teacher. She showed slight interest in my homeschooling. However, the following year when I met up with her, she was so glad I was there because she was considering homeschooling and wanted to know how she should start!!!

As great as homeschooling is, I have also learned that it can't always be fun, and that's okay. I almost lost my mind worrying about what I was doing wrong because I never seemed to keep my children happy! Life is that way. Sometimes you have fun and sometimes you don't! We have fun almost every *day* doing

Jackson, CT, Dawn, Sam

Dawn (13), C.T. (11), Jackson (almost 8), Sam (5)

school, but not every *minute*. I *love* to have fun, and by nature I'm very free-spirited. However, too much of a good thing is not good either.

I love to learn from people and books, and I always have a mind open to life. The more I, as a parent, can be open to knowledge and learning and don't put limits on my abilities, the more I think our kids will pick up on that model.

Because they are so honest, and wear their hearts on their sleeve, our children teach us to be patient, present in the moment, and to recognize the power we have to make them fly. We believe in them because we see they truly trust us and it's just the way we know it should be.

Dawn (13), C.T. (11), Jackson (almost 8), Sam (5)

Gerry, age 41
Leonie, age 39
Luke, age 19
Gregory, age 16
Nicholas, age 15
Jonathon, age 10
Alexander, age 8
Thomas, age 6
Anthony, age 4

Interview with Leonie from Perth, Australia on a November day in spring

FLEX MODE

Our home education itself is nearly always in flex mode. We are very flexible and open to change and spontaneity—what I often call "the serendipity of homeschooling"! Thus, the current daily routines in our home do not reflect the previous ten years of our varied home education routines. Home education, for us, is an ever-changing lifestyle, changing to suit family and individual needs.

We live in the outer northern suburbs of Perth, which is on the west coast of Australia, and are right near the ocean. We currently live in a nice large home near the beach and are building a home just two suburbs and a nine-minute drive away, not too far from the beach, but opposite a golf course, the bush, and a great park for children. The older boys play golf with their friends. We expect to move to our new house soon.

For the previous two years, we lived in a very small rural town, four hours from Perth. It has a population of 450. Gerry was deputy principal at the school down there and so our time in the country was prompted by his career. We opted to return to the city since we felt the isolation was not beneficial for the boys. We did love our country stint, though, and there certainly are advantages to living in the country. We have moved a great deal, especially when Gerry was in the

RAAF (Royal Australian Air Force), and I feel that every place we have lived has had its advantages. Gerry is a native of Western Australia, while I lived a fairly nomadic life as a child! I went to so many different schools, and while I did well academically, I feel that homeschool would have been a great option for me. Gerry attended parochial and private school.

We are a family of nine. My husband is a high school maths teacher, I was trained as an elementary teacher, and we've both tutored students in a variety of subjects. Gerry was also an Education Officer in the RAAF for six years. Together, we have written *Measurement in Maths*, that is a series of activity-based inductive reasoning master sheets for the measurement strand of the maths curriculum. I am a writer, homeschool consultant, leader of a Charlotte Mason homeschool support group, and publisher of a homeschool newsletter that helps Australian homeschoolers inspired by Charlotte Mason to keep in touch. There are seven boys in our family. The eldest is Luke (nineteen), and our next sons are Gregory (sixteen), Nicholas (fifteen), Jonathon (ten), Alexander (eight), Thomas (six), and Anthony (four).

Luke is the first graduate of our home education adventure and is studying externally for a Bachelor of Arts degree, majoring in history and politics. He is enrolled at university; but the lecture notes, tapes, videos, and course work are mailed to him. He returns assignments, speaks to his tutors or to other students when necessary, and sits exams either at the university or with a private invigilator. We initially began external study during our rural stint, but Luke has chosen to continue this option as he feels he is then in charge of his own time and can fit study around his interests and outside work. This is like a continuation of homeschooling for him. Since he has attended classes for university level chemistry and other areas, he has experienced classrooms and their trappings. He studies a full-time load—four courses each semester. Three of his current units are Irish Nationalism in Australia, the Vietnam War, and Economic Dynamism in the Pacific Region.

He also has two part-time jobs. He works at a food hall (an open-plan restaurant area with a wide choice of stalls and food) in the city, serving customers and managing the till. His other job is as a tutor and marker for the *KUMON* learning centres. *KUMON* learning centres are based on a Japanese model of individualized and accelerated learning. Luke works at a centre where he tutors in maths and English. Students are given diagnostic tests and placed at individual levels. They have work to do each day (fifteen to twenty minutes) and the centre is open two afternoons a week so pupils can come to have work corrected, learn new concepts, or get help as needed. Here in Australia, the cost per student is a bit less than the cost of a standard tutor, and all the work materials are provided. Luke marks students' work and explains concepts to them if they come to his desk for help. Additionally, he is active in our homeschool group, does volunteer work (filing and cataloguing for a maritime museum, and volunteer work through our local parish, and in the homeschool group), is passionate about reading and music, and is a help to us all at home.

Today in Perth, it is a sunny 25° Celsius on Monday, 8 November, in late spring. I wake up at 6.00 a.m.—not my usual time. I usually wake at 7.00 a.m. but am finding that the warm and sunny mornings have been encouraging me to wake earlier. My husband Gerry and I discuss the day's plans. He has woken with a terrible bout of hay fever, but plans to teach school anyway.

After showers and tidying upstairs, we wake the boys. They all know to start morning chores and grooming. We have always tried to work on this, but sometimes we are more consistent than other times. We have family meetings every three to six months to determine chores. Everyone keeps the same chores for about six months—this makes it easier for me and makes them really good at each chore, with so much practice! We don't give pocket money or allowances—chores are considered part of family life and any money has to be earned. For example, Nicholas "employs" Thomas, Alexander, and Jonathon to help with his midweek and weekend deliveries of papers and pamphlets. In the morning Greg and Nick tidy their rooms, Greg sorts and puts away laundry, and Nicholas is the "vacuuming person." Jonathon unloads the dishwasher, clears the table, and makes his bed. Alexander tidies the room he and Jonathan share. Thomas tidies his and Anthony's bedroom/activity room. Anny cleans the breakfast table and empties waste paper baskets. Luke empties the kitchen bin, does his room, and is our general helper and errand runner, especially since he now has his own car. Alexander selects clothes for Thomas, and Jonathon for Anthony. To stop distractions and arguments. I help Anthony dress, and supervise chores.

We have always been a family of routines, avoiding time slots but having regular activities to which we peg other things we want to do. This last month we have been implementing more of a schedule, following the guidelines in the very helpful book *Managers of Their Home* by Steve and Teri Maxwell. I read about this book on an e-mail loop and, being a true bibliophile, wanted to buy and read it for myself. Why has it been so helpful? I think because it is not prescriptive, but guides you through thinking about your goals and routines for your individual family. The younger boys have loved this schedule right from the start—they have scheduled time with Mum and with their older brothers, and I find I need to reiterate chores less.

I start the semolina porridge, and Jonathon makes a pot of tea. Everyone helps themselves to breakfast—porridge and fruit, toast, and milk/tea. While I eat, I pack a lunch for Gerry to take to work, check chores, and start laundry. Gerry and I discuss brick paving for the new house. He rings to order some more packs of bricks, and I have an extra chore added to my list—paying for the bricks

---

and purchasing materials needed for painting the house.

At 8.10 a.m. we have Bible and prayer time. We are Catholic and read about the Saint of the day, the relevant Scripture readings from the missal, and say morning prayers. The close of prayers is Anthony's signal to begin his time on the computer, and Alexander remembers that it his turn to help Anny during his computer time. The older boys are finishing chores, and Jonathon and Thomas begin a game using little figures and blocks to create an imaginary world. I drive Gerry to school. We have only one car, but at least I now have older children who can stay at home to watch the younger ones while I am gone. It takes only ten minutes, and most days Gerry walks home from school.

Home again, I check on everyone and clean up the kitchen. Someone forgot to turn the dishwasher on last night after dinner so it is on now, and the breakfast dishes have to be done by hand. Thomas begins his turn on the computer; today he elects to play a simulation game called *The French Revolution*. He asks others for help with making decisions on his troops and moves. Anthony has his time with Alexander, and they swing on the swings outside, laughing, and chatting. I assign Jonathon some extra chores—watering plants and giving the tile floor a quick mop. He discusses the value of free time with me, and I point out the schedule that has this time slot listed with "Free/Assigned Chores for Jonathon." This master schedule solves all disagreements! This schedule is very loose—just brief times listed and some activities alongside. We very rarely refer to it, but it is there if we are looking for more structure or organization, or to solve a disagreement.

The older boys are busy. Luke is reading and Gregory is doing fitness exercises. We all decided to get fitter this year! Gerry is in the RAAF Reserve and has a list of exercises to undertake for fitness and to maintain a certain standard of fitness. These are the exercises we all aim to do each day. Nicholas practices the piano or guitar.

At 9.00 a.m., Luke has his time with the younger children. He takes them outside for a game of cricket on the patio. I have meeting-time with Nick and Greg. We always discuss our school plans during this time, and sometimes we read together any relevant books or articles. We usually have our time together for review after lunch. We go over their work, discuss, share, and correct if needed. Today, Greg will be working—he works part-time two days a week at the same food hall as Luke and studies Grade 11 at home. Nicholas has a weekend delivery job and employs the younger boys to help. We have encouraged our boys to undertake part-time work, home businesses, and volunteer work. For us, learning is not restricted to formal academics, but encompasses all of life, and real-life experiences play an important and enriching role in our homeschool. We see this all as part of the home education curriculum.

We tend toward classical education, using living books and some of the ideas that are popularly associated with Charlotte Mason. Classical education is a term that is used widely now, but I think our definition of it may be a bit looser than those of others. We see classical education as a way of providing the children with the tools for learning, to think for themselves, to be introduced to various writers and culture from our tradition, and to be able to use real or whole books (especially those of traditional or classic writers, rather than using a text book approach). Occasionally, as a result of family circumstances and needs, we have taken a unit study or unschooling approach, but always with a classical bent. For me, classical education provides a child with the tools needed to learn and discern, and to "teach men how to think," to quote from Dorothy Sayers in her essay *The Lost Tools of Learning*. We also hope to integrate our faith and values throughout our homeschooling lifestyle.

Time to hang some laundry on the clothesline before the next time slot. Maths time is at 9.30 a.m. I make a couple of telephone calls, the older boys start *Saxon Math* and the younger ones begin work on different maths texts. We don't have any particular text that we use regularly in the elementary school years. Since we have written math texts ourselves, we use those! We also use a variety of Australian texts and games, and I sometimes take a more activity approach—using ideas as they spring up in every day life or from books such as Ruth Beechick's *3R'S* series or *Family Math*. Today, Jonathon works on *Boomerang Maths*, Alexander on a sheet from a homework series, and Thomas on our *Measurement Activities, Stage 4* book. Luke is at the computer working on a university assignment, and Anthony has play-alone time. He is playing with *Lego* ships and toy cars a bit too loudly!

I usually sit with the younger boys and help with maths. Jonathon generally needs me to read his lesson with him and to illustrate the concept with *Cuisenaire Rods* or something similar. If Thomas or Alexander finish before the half hour is up, they work on handwriting (copy work). Not today, though, especially since Thomas' maths includes hands-on measuring activities from our book and also a bit of drill. Jonathon has music practice (piano or recorder) and copy work later in the morning, but again, not today because of errands. The copy work we do varies and is not too planned. Sometimes, the boys choose a passage from their current novels/reading materials, the Bible, a poetry book, or something related to our unit study. Presently, the boys are copying out definitions from *The Catholic Dictionary Colouring Book*, a book which has text in addition to pictures to colour.

Today, I can correct work straight away and work with Alexander on his mistakes. Often, I leave corrections until later in the day at a more quiet time.

Greg has time with the younger boys and plays various card games at 10.00 a.m. Thomas complains about losing and I give a nice little lecture on having fun and not aiming to win. Anthony would rather listen to his *Madeleine* story tape, and looking and following along in the book, so he does that in the family room. This is the main room where we all congregate, although we do have an activity room for games, toys, and books; and the older boys have desks in their rooms. In addition, we have books *everywhere!* We do have a rule for the younger boys—no playing in bedrooms. Otherwise, the bedroom is a real mess at the end of the day. They have the sitting room for reading and music, and the activity and family rooms for play and work. And the garden and patio!

I begin cooking some meat mixture for tortillas for lunch—a treat as we normally eat either sandwiches or leftovers. I make a couple of cakes for snacks and for our visit tomorrow to a homeschool family, where we will swim in their pool and then do art. Nick and Luke are still working on their own assignments.

At 10.30 a.m. I discuss with the boys the recent referendum held here in Australia. It was over the issue of Republicanism, making Australia a republic rather than part of the Commonwealth, and a proposed change in the constitution. I have cut ads from the newspapers about this issue and read and discuss both viewpoints, trying to explain our points of view to the younger children. Greg and Nick go to their desks to write a report on this referendum, and I give Jonathon a sheet of paper with the heading The Referendum. I ask him to write a description of the referendum. His choice of phrases and obvious understanding of the issue pleasantly surprise me. I use this time to define some relevant terms with Thomas and Alexander—terms such as monarchy, democracy, and so on. Anthony uses this time to play with his farm animals, and then Alexander has a quick game of *Solitaire* on the computer. Thomas reads silently. His reading has really taken off this year, and we often find him curled up with a book.

On Mondays, I ask the boys to tell me the title and author of one book they are currently reading. I don't like to list all their reading as I think there is a privacy issue involved. I feel that listing one book a week is proof of wide reading, and it gives me an idea of where they are in reading. Would you like someone to run around after you, writing down everything you read and/or do? Sometimes, I might direct their reading to a different genre or a change of author if I feel they are getting into a reading rut.

Their books this week are:

Greg: *Napoleon and Hitler* by J. Seward, a historical discussion and comparison. Greg loves history!

Nicholas: *Carry on Jeeves* by Wodehouse—all we older people in the family from Jonathon up, love the Jeeves and Wooster series. Everyone, including the younger boys, loves the *BBC* videos of these stories.

Jonathan: *Jeeves in the Offing*, again by P. G. Wodehouse

Alexander: *Finn McCourt* by Rosemary Sutcliffe

Thomas: *Little House on the Prairie* by Laura Ingalls Wilder

At 11.00 a.m. it is time to leave the house for errands and to take Greg to the train station. Luke also decides to come as he wishes to look at a new music shop near the station. We pack books and drinks and set off. On the way to the station, we listen to *Haydn's 43rd Symphony* with frequent interruptions to answer Anthony's many questions and to discuss words and word roots with Alexander, Jonathon, and Thomas. Alexander asks about the word "chameleon," and we also talk about quad, quadrangle, quadrilateral, and counting in Latin. This conversational style of education—learning through impromptu observing, discussing, and sharing plays a big role in our homeschooling.

On the way home from errands, we buy ice creams for snacks and switch tapes in the car. We now listen to the book tape of *Swallows and Amazons*, by Arthur Ransome. We are great *Swallows and Amazons* fans and love the literary style, the descriptions, the freedom of the children in the stories, and their adventures. The books, written in the 1930s and 1940s in England, are well-crafted novels describing the adventures of two families of children. Much of the activity is set in the Lake District of England.

We arrive home for a late lunch to discover that Dad is home early—his hay fever having taken a turn for the worse during the day. Gerry spends the rest of the afternoon either sleeping off his hay fever, reading, or doing planning and marking for his kids at school. We clean up, Jonathon plays *Civilization* on the computer, Nicholas plays his guitar, Luke gets ready for his afternoon work (marking and tutoring at the *KUMON* maths centre) and the younger boys do drawing and colouring in.

It is time for Nicholas to be with his younger brothers at 3.00 p.m. I use this time to check e-mail and favourite bulletin boards on the Internet. Nicholas sets up a running and chasey game of gangsters outside, so there is much laughter and noise and, yes, some fights and tears.

I round up the younger boys at 4.30 p.m. to help me do a general tidy inside and outside the house. They have quick baths and showers. It has to be quick tonight—time seems to be running away from us! Greg arrives home and chats about his day, and I talk to a homeschool mother on the telephone.

Usually, Thomas, Alexander, or Anthony helps me cook, and sometimes all three. This can be hectic, but I like to know where they are, to keep them busy, and to spend time with them. Moreover, learning to cook is a useful skill! Jonathon sometimes makes one part of the meal by himself, such as muffins. All the older boys are good cooks and can step in and take over when needed. We have done once-a-month, biweekly cooking, and set nights for each older person to cook or for a younger one to cook with Mum and enter a recipe in their cookbook. Each season of family life seems to necessitate a change in the way we approach meal preparation. I like to try different ways of managing the food shopping/cooking as I am a person who craves variety, and I hate being tied down to any one system. Having no system at all seems impractical and expensive with a larger family.

Luke returns from work at 6.30 p.m. Gerry is starting to feel better and has been doing some marking for school. We say the Angelus and Grace (this time in Latin) and sit for dinner. We usually have simple dinners and occasionally dessert. I have a standard summer and winter menu, which I know will change again at some point in the future. We have meals like potatoes baked in their jackets with salad, spaghetti bolognaise and pizza all year round. We have meals like soups in winter and meat and salad in summer. I also have a "real budget" menu for times when we need to be a bit more careful financially! I adapt these meals according to taste, specials, or outings. I grocery shop every two weeks. The boys and I do the shopping and errands together and often visit the library at the same time.

Housework we do on a daily and weekly basis. The boys have regular daily and Saturday chores—things like vacuuming, sorting laundry, and tidying bookshelves, videos, or the toy cupboard and activity room. I have a usual 10.30 a.m. time slot on weekdays (which did not make it on today's schedule!) for either cooking or cleaning. We do extra cleaning or garden chores on Saturday or in school holidays.

We homeschool year round, but our schedule is lighter and different when Dad is home and public school is on holiday. We also do more big chores during this time. Here in Western Australia, the schools are open during four ten-week terms; and there are three one-two week holidays and one five-six week holiday over Christmas (our summer) each year.

Around 7.00 p.m. we continue our dinner discussion of arguments for and against a monarchy and a republic. This is obviously a topical issue for us. Anthony wants to tell Dad all about the *Swallows and Amazon* tape. Mostly, dinner is a good time for discussing and talking, and these topics generally arise naturally. Sometimes, however, we have a time of each child narrating his day or some part of schoolwork to Dad. Sometimes, too, we play games like *Twenty Questions* or "Sixty Second" talks—we all take a turn to stand up and talk for sixty seconds on a topic chosen by another member of the family. Sometimes everyone is too noisy, or there are accidents and disagreements!

While the older four boys do dinner dishes, Gerry works on the computer, and I read another chapter from *The House at Pooh Corner* to Anthony. "Winnie the Pooh" is an all time family favourite and before long, Alexander and Thomas wander over and peer over my shoulder and listen to the story.

I next read a chapter from our current family read-aloud, *The Merchants Mark*, an intriguing historical novel by Cynthia Hartnett. It is set in England in 1492. Thomas and Anthony listen and play with *Lego* and cars on the floor as I read. We are taking a break from *The Lord of the Rings* series by Tolkien to read this novel and have read several other mystery/historical novels by Hartnett that we have enjoyed. At the moment, during what we consider school time, I am reading through some articles on St. Robert Southwell with Greg and Nick for a unit study on English history and poetry. St. Robert Southwell lived in England during the time in history that is commonly called the Reformation, so this has led into a good study of England and other countries during that time period. He was also a metaphysical poet, and the unit covers poetry study as well. I am reading the *Frances* books by Russell Hoban with Thomas and Anthony and using Valerie Bendt's study guide and *The Long Winter*, by Laura Ingalls Wilder with Alexander and Jonathon. Most nights, when the younger four boys are in bed, Gerry reads to them for ten minutes from a book titled Children Of the Court of St. Peter, and Alexander and I take turns reading together for five to ten minutes from an old Catholic history reader. Not tonight, as we decide to watch part of our *Jeeves and Wooster* video. Wodehouse is obviously on everyone's mind today.

At 8.30 p.m., it's time for the Rosary and other prayers.

By now, at 9.00 p.m., it is quite late, so it's cleaning teeth and straight to bed for younger boys. Gerry tucks them in, and I go, reluctantly, upstairs to do my exercises. The boys often read, chat, and play in bed before falling asleep. Sometimes, too, we need to quell the noise or the constant coming out of their room! They can read and play (quietly, we hope!) until they drop asleep or until we think it is getting too late (or noisy) and turn off the light. Luke is using the computer for his university work and Greg and Nick update their homeschool logs. I keep a brief homeschool log, which I like to do, but is not required by the state and would be proof of regular and efficient instruction. This year, we gave Greg and Nick attractive, hardbound diaries in which to record their daily activities and academics. We want the responsibility for learning to rest with the learner and I, for one, would like to encourage time management and organization skills.

I come back downstairs at 9.30 p.m. and make a cup of tea for those who want. Luke and I talk about one of his current university courses; Irish Nationalism in Australia. I really like these discussions and proofreading his assignments because I feel I am learning so much. In addition, these discussions often flow onto the other children. For example, Luke is also studying a unit on the Vietnam War and our family discussions have lead Nicholas to be in interested in the incidents leading up to and during the war. Nicholas and Greg have discussed the ideas at length with Luke, and Nick recently borrowed a book on the subject from the local library. When Luke studied French, Greg watched the videos with him and picked up various phrases.

Children start getting ready for bed at 10.00 p.m. while I tidy up and check my diary, making a list of things to do tomorrow. Gerry is relaxing with the

---

computer game *Civilization*, and I fill in a few items in my general homeschool log for all the children. I keep a log of some of our daily activities, sometimes in subject areas, sometimes in narrative form, sometimes detailed, sometimes not. I do like these logs, however, as family records. The law requires home educating parents to provide regular and efficient instruction. No education department personnel has ever looked at my log during our yearly visits, but I like this idea of proof of education if ever needed and of keeping a family memory book.

We make general school plans at the start of each school year, but look in more detail at the start of each term. I do other plans on a week-to-week basis, following either our scheduling or book work routine, or planning what we want to accomplish each week and how to fit this around appointments and outings.

Our week looks roughly like this:

MONDAY: maths, reading list, homeschool log, music, art, Greg works.

TUESDAY: maths, unit study, sometimes ice-skating or activities with other homeschoolers. Greg sometimes works.

WED: maths, unit study, science or nature study (Greg and Nicholas study chemistry and physics and have both been part of a *Chemistry Olympiad.*) Jonathon and Nicholas have spent three terms doing activities at the *CSIROSEC* (Commonwealth Scientific Information and Research Organization) lab with other homeschoolers while I have taken the younger ones through a hands-on science museum. Science with cousins at our house (older kids act as tutors) or art with cousins at their house (older kids golf with friends). Greg and Nicholas use a variety of approaches toward physics and chemistry—participation in the science labs mentioned above that are run at a local science museum with the cooperation of the *CSIRO*, they work in the *Chemistry Olympiads* for "gifted students" at the University of W.A., use standard textbooks, and the activities in two great library finds—*Teaching Physics with Children's Toys* and *Teaching Chemistry with Childrens' Toys*.

THURSDAY: maths, religion, Latin or Greek (once a fortnight we skip these and shop and then do activities with a couple of other Catholic families based on the *Lives of the Saints).*

FRIDAY: maths, book making—we are making books about the construction of our home, and Greg is writing his autobiography. This fits into the technology and enterprise area of our state curriculum framework. On the first and third Fridays of the month, we have picnics with other homeschoolers. Greg works 12.00-4.00 p.m., and Nicholas organizes for his weekend deliveries with one of the younger boys in turn.

DAILY: there is silent reading, reading aloud, use of the computer for school and personal projects, hobbies such as model making, putting together a little newsletter, practicing and listening to music, discussing the news, games, outside play, and sports.

Some of the older boys are reading and some are in bed, now that it's 10.30 p.m. They choose their own bed times. Gerry and I are reading and talking. Gerry is reading *Hell West and Crooked*, a biography of what is termed "a real life Crocodile Dundee," a book that he thinks will make a great family read-aloud. I usually have several books going at once—*Managers of Their Homes*, by the Maxwell's; *Designing Your Own Classical Curriculum*, by Laura Berquest (these are both re-reads.); *Thrones, Dominations*, by Dorothy Sayers, and *Ring for Jeeves*, by Wodehouse—an eclectic mix!

I am a different and better person through home education. I have been forced to reflect on my role as a mother, as a person, on how I interact with my children, on the true nature of learning, and on organization. I see all these as ways of growing in a positive manner and developing skills that I might have allowed to lie dormant. We have been homeschooling eleven years now. When we began homeschooling, we did so for issues of freedom and family unity. One thing that struck me about schools was the fact that, because of general administrative reasons, children tend to be treated as a group, with little leeway for individual interest or for the child who marches to a different beat. We want our family to be strong and close and to share. We want freedom for our children to develop at their own pace, to follow their own interests, and to be free from peer pressure. We desire our family to be free from outside constraint and to be self-empowered. In addition, we have a glimpse of children with the tools of learning who enjoy learning. All these are lofty goals and there are many times we

Gregory, Nicholas, Luke
Leonie, Anthony, Thomas, Jonathon, Alexander

Luke (19), Greg (16), Nick (15), Jonathon (10), Alexander (8), Thomas (6), Anthony (4)

despair of ever reaching these ideals. When we reflect, however, we can see that many of these goals are on their way to achievement through our numerous daily interactions. Luke, our first "graduate," believes strongly in home education as an educational and lifestyle choice and would like any of his future children to experience homeschooling.

SUBJECTS	Monday 6th November
HEALTH/ LIFE SKILLS	• Weekly meeting
	• Reading List ~ note books in logs
ENGLISH	• MATHS: (G) SAT prep
	(N) ADV MATHS
MATHS	(J) } Choice of texts
	(A)
	(T) Measurement sheet
SOSE/ORAL SKILLS/ ENGLISH	• Discuss w/e REFERENDUM. What do terms mean? Why referendum ~ republic, "monarchy". Look thru newspaper clippings on topic. (J) write brief report, (N)(G) summary + report, discuss + define terms w (A)(T)
LOTE/ENGLISH	• Talk about Latin/Greek words + counting ~ also "chameleon". Related to (A)'s reading
ARTS	• Listen to classical music tape
LITERATURE	• Listen to story tape ~ SWALLOWS AND AMAZONS by Ransome
SCIENCE	Discuss sailing and adventures
PHYSED	• Fitness exercises
ARTS	• Undirected drawing/colouring
ARTS	• Instrument practice
T+E	• Computer games
LITERATURE	• Family read aloud MADELEINE TAKES
SOSE	COMMAND ~ Ethel Bill. Talk about pioneers, Indians, occupying a country, lifestyle, bravery. Greg use ENCARTA CDROM + look up
LOTE	Vercheres. Read French words in Ant's alphabet book + look at scenes from Montreal
HEALTH/ LIFE SKILLS	• (G)(N) update his log
MEDIA/ LITERATURE	• View WODEHOUSE'S JEEVES + WOOSTER video

Luke (19), Greg (16), Nick (15), Jonathon (10), Alexander (8), Thomas (6), Anthony (4)

HOMESCHOOL OPEN HOUSE

Part 2

Gary, age 54
Nancy, age 52
Brian, age 18
Kate, age 16
Neil, age 12
Kevin, age 9

Five-year follow-up interview from the Rocky Mountains of Bozeman, Montana

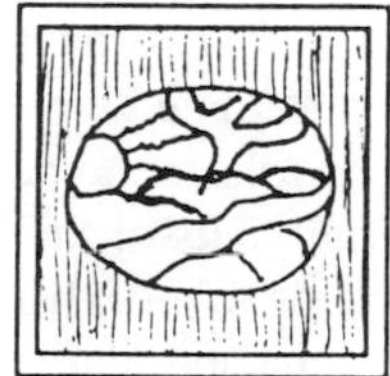

THE GIFT OF TIME

From Kevin (age 9)

I have all the time I want of the day—I can pick out what books I want to read, what subjects to study (except for the ones Mom and Dad say I need to do), when I want to do them, and spend time around home. My favorite subjects are philosophy, science, history, music, and a little math. I like to read. Those are just some of the things I like about homeschooling, except for the fact that I'm not in a social life—but it's still really good.

When you're in a social life you meet people, talk to them, have friends, and hang out. When I'm homeschooling I don't have a whole bunch of kids around our house since we live in the mountains, so the hanging out part doesn't work so well. When I am around a lot of kids, though, I can see how they behave in ways that I sometimes don't like, so I act different than that and try to be a better person. I am friends with the *Scouts,* some of the kids and adults where I live, with my brothers and sister, some of their friends, and I meet new people all the time when we go places. Probably the biggest part of my social life is spending time with my family because I have so much fun with five other people who I do things with so often. I like to be alone just with Dad, Mom, Bri, Kate, or Neil; be with different mixed parts of the family; or be with my whole family together. I did once try out school for half a day. It was fun but I wouldn't want to go all the time. Still, I like homeschooling better than I think I'd like school because I can be more independent and work to get smarter.

Being with my family is one of the best things that ever happened to me, except for being born. My dad is great because he helps me with a lot of things when they get broken or when the computer needs to get fixed. I mostly like having philosophic conversations with my dad, asking him all kinds of questions and learning about post-modernism. Post-modernism, in a simple way, is that there is not only one way to see things. For instance, you can take several families and have different members write down what they think about their lives and how it is and what they do. Then you mix them all together and you could not tell which family everyone belonged to, because their ideas of what it's like being in a family are different from each other. In other words, different people have different experiences and realities—even if it's about the same thing. Dad's a professor at MSU (Montana State University) and I like it when he takes me to his office there and when he asks me to help him find films for his classes. He's so smart that he sees how all kinds of things in life connect to each other, and he can explain almost everything to me when I ask him questions.

I like my mom because she helps me out with my work when I need it, she cooks for me, she's a good person, she does really good art work, and she wrote this book you're reading. She also likes to sew old looking counted cross stitch samplers and make her own kinds of quilts. We have them everywhere in the house and she makes them for her friends, too. (Katie also sews samplers and quilts.) When I want to meet somebody but am too embarrassed, Mom (the embarassing-proof person who can never get embarrassed in her whole life) will walk up to someone and start a conversation. She likes to and ask them lots of questions about themselves or their work, so we get to meet some really interesting people and some of them even get to be friends. Whenever I'm writing letters or papers, she always gives me these questions to think about, so when I'm finished writing, it comes out a big thing.

I like my biggest brother Brian because he has a sense of humor and he's the best. He does and says amazing things, we watch the same movies and shows, and he's truly a great person. I want to be just like him and I already am a lot like him. He's going to Europe and then Morocco for half a year. I know I'll really miss him. His first stop is in Scotland where he's going to stay with Penny, John, Johnny, and Jenny—they're friends Mom made from the PATCHWORK book she did (and you can read about them in "We're Doing It Otherwise"). Some other people he's going to visit in France and Switzerland are people embarrassing-proof Mom went up to and started talking to, and they became good friends. We've known some of them since Brian and Katie were little, and now Brian gets to visit them. Brian and Dad got these cameras that they set on their computers so we can video conference.

I like my one and only sister Kate because she used to take good care of me

---

when I was little and she can drive me places when Brian, Mom, or Dad can't. Sometimes she takes me to town with her and we go out to lunch together. She bakes good cakes and goes swimming and skiing with me. She also buys me some nice things as treats.

My other big brother Neil and I ski, swim, play *Lego*, and play computer games like *The Sims*, *Age of Empires*, *Unreal Tournament*, and *Oracle III Arena*. Dad and Brian look for interesting and complicated strategy games for us that help us think and learn new things. It's fun to do almost everything with Neil, unless we get into a big argument (which I admit isn't too often). We like a lot of the same films, games, books, activities, and things to do. He's the one I do the most with and the most *fun* things. Mom says we're like best friends, but it's different with a brother!

Now we're down to me. I like myself because I'm like my biggest brother, I watch good films, I'm supposedly smart, I'm a nice guy, my mom and dad think I'm funny, and I think up interesting things to do. I like going on the Internet to check out things I want to do, look up movie reviews, or play free on-line games. I also made a pretty neat home page and I like adding on new ideas. I listen to music and I like to write songs. I'm interested the army, so I like writing to generals, receiving letters and brochures back from them, and giving them ideas for improved warfare technology. One of the generals said he'd have to send my ideas to the Pentagon, but that it would take a *long* time to hear back from them because they take so long to make all their decisions! I know all about military clothing, warfare, technology, weapons, bases, etc.

Besides writing letters to lots of people, my mom also taught us all to make phone calls when we were little. I call places to find out information or to see if they have something I need at a store. I do jobs for people in the neighborhood (sometimes with Neil), I make the brochures, the phone calls, and the people call back and ask for me. I do things like take dogs out for a walk, feed them, water plants, rake leaves, shovel walks, check to see that water pipes don't freeze when people are on vacation in the winter, and things like that. I charge a fair price and do a good job. Also, I like to help my parents fix the wood fences around the pastures and even help with the electric wires that keep the cows in. I can't say I like stacking tons of hay though, since it makes me sneeze non-stop. Usually I don't have to do too much of that, especially when it's a hundred degrees out!

I feel more grown up and in charge of myself being able to work, write letters, and talk on the phone to people. Since I'm learning how to play the electric guitar, I make all the calls and set the times for my guitar lessons. I write songs about things I think about. Here are two of my songs—one is about going to the edge of things, and the other is about time:

"Going to the Edge"

I came back home
found my friend on the couch
asking where I've been
and I gently reply
I've been to the edge of the world
fighting dangerous storms
pushing past vice
I've been to the edge of the world
and back!
sailing enormous waves
and back!
I sailed the seven seas
past the Pacific Ocean
down the throat of a beast
into the mouth of fear
fighting past evil
(guard of the edge)
to the end of the world
I've been to the edge
and back!
the end of the world
where east meets west
earth meets the universe
down the cliff of
the edge of the world
I tried to tell the whole story
but they stood there and laughed
Son, you have great imagination
but don't push it to the edge
when I try to tell them the way
they will never listen to me
even if I have a microphone
they just stand there
to watch "the game"
and that is the lonely story
of going to the edge
and back!

"A Matter of Time"

It's just a matter of time
that's in your hand
(200 lbs. = two o'clock)
it's just a matter of time
in your pickup truck out back
it's just a matter of time
(10,000 lbs. = ten o'clock)
it's just a matter of time
that you're holding right now
soon it's going to be so heavy
that it's going to be too late!
time is just something
you truly can't waste
whether you're going to use it
early in the morning to fish
(12:01 a.m. = one ounce)
or use it to go crush
that building in your yard
(11:59 = 1159 lbs.)
it's just a matter of time
that you're pulling
in that wagon of yours
that very strong wagon of yours
time, it's just a matter of time
that's in your hands

Brian (18), Kate (16), Neil (12), Kevin (9)

Our whole family likes to talk about everything in the world, laugh, watch films together, and go places together. We always talk about what is real and important and how to be a good person. You know then that we almost always have a good time together (unless, of course, Mom gets into the mood of cleaning the house).

I love movies when they are uncut and interesting. I mainly like action packed, comedy, science fiction, and post-modern films like *Matrix, Fight Club,* and *eXistenZ.* I like another post-modern film called *Six String Samurai* which is set in a time when the Russians have taken over the world. One of the few cities left was Las Vegas. Since Elvis Presley used to be "The King" of Las Vegas, the only way you could be king was to be a great warrior samurai who could play the guitar very well. It was funny, brilliant, and great. We watch all kinds of foreign films and one of my most favorite ones is *The Power of One* which is about apartheid in South Africa and how people can come together to be powerful as a group. I'll never forget that film.

If I tell you I love television, what I mean is I like the television *set.* We use it to watch tapes, movies from satellite, educational channels, and comedy (including stand-up comedy, comedy movies, sketch comedy, spoofs, and just funny shows). I also like shows that are satires of current events or politics. We almost never watch the shows that most people call "television." I really like to listen to music and so do my brothers and sister. Sometimes we listen together to the same music, and we like a lot of the same songs. We share our CDs but if it's really a favorite one, we don't share it as much. We usually listen to music, when we're doing other things, too. We like classic and alternative rock the best.

From listening to music so much, we were excited to go to the *Pink Floyd* laser show that *The Museum of the Rockies* made. I loved the music and then Brian found *Pink Floyd's* music and movie *The Wall.* It was about how we build up walls around us to feel safe and protected but we also lose out on life. That's when I *really* got interested in playing the electric guitar, and when I asked my neighbor's dad to teach me. I practice for hours everyday and enjoy learning. I like to write my songs about important ideas I think about.

I am in *Cub Scouts* and am a second year *Webelos.* I am working to get the *Arrow of Light* and move on to *Boy Scouts* in the spring. I like *Scouts* because we do a lot of great activities, but mostly I like going camping. I like earning *Scout* activity pins and work on them as part of what I like to do when I'm homeschooling. Our pack sometimes goes on hikes, goes fishing or boating, and to historic places. We live practically right on the Lewis and Clark trail.

Skiing is my favorite activity of all because I love the feeling of it and am getting really good at it. I've been skiing for two years (since we moved to Montana) and will ski the ridge on my third year and join our ski racing team. My favorite terrain is moguls because they make you practice fast reflexes, fast turns, not falling, and they make you practice for jumps and balance. Sometimes when I finish my studies early enough, I can go skiing in the afternoon. Or, if Neil and I do two days of work in one day, we can go skiing all day the next day. Mom drops us off and picks us up if she's working on art or writing. Neil and I take our two-way radios and talk to each other on the mountain and make plans where to ski.

Sometimes I ski with Dad, Brian, or Kate, too. And sometimes we all ski together. I used to ski with Mom until she wrecked her knee and had to use crutches and wear a brace all winter. (I thought is was really fun using her crutches, but she got tired of it!) Skiing gives me good social abilities, because when I go on the ski lift with different people I don't know, I can have conversations with them. I got to know the lift operators and even got invited to the "employee only day" at the end of the season. On the ski mountain we can eat lunch, take a bit of a rest, and have gotten to know some people there.

I like interesting books. One that I really like is called *Sophies' World*, which is a philosophic novel. Since I've always liked knowing about philosophy and especially about Plato, Socrates, and Aristotle—the three best philosophers ever (and Plato is by far my favorite), this book is perfect for me. I also love watching videos called *The Great Ideas of Philosophy* (published by The Teaching Company). My favorite fiction series of all time is definitely *Harry Potter*. Harry is a boy who lives in a very bad family but learns he's a famous wizard. He goes through all sorts of adventures and thrilling activities. I also like *The BFG* by Roald Dahl. I'm in the middle of Isaac Asimov's *Norbie* series—very good futuristic books about robots.

I've liked *Lego* my whole life, so I get a subscription to a *Lego* catalog that has all these new sets, as well as a magazine called *Lego Mania* that has new sets built by kids, winners of contests, and comics about the new sets that are about to come out. I even sent some photos in of my own *Lego* creations but don't know if they're gong to use them. Neil and I have a huge box under our bunk bed that is filled with *Lego* pieces and *Lego* booklets. We like to build a lot of different environments—cities, space stations, military bases, and anything we can imagine. We rummage through the box, which makes all kinds of noise, looking for the particular pieces we need. Sometimes we leave them all over the floor if we're not finished building, and let me just tell you, stepping on *Lego* pieces barefoot can really hurt!

I really like homeschooling. It's a great thing for me because I get to learn about what I'm interested in, work when I want, where I want, and how I want. I work hard and try to do my best. I always have something I'm interested in. When I'm older, I would like to go to college and major in post-modern philosophy and psychology. I've decided that when I'm old enough to have a career, I am just going to find a job that fits me.

Brian (18), Kate (16), Neil (12), Kevin (9)

From Neil (age 12)

For me, homeschooling is way more than just doing "school work" at home. It changes everything. I have choices and a lot of independence. We do all sorts of activities. It's sometimes hard to tell the difference between "homeschool" and just living my life, so it's difficult for me to separate them if people ask me to.

Since I like to learn about science and history, I do it all the time for fun. Besides *History of US* and other books, I love the videos from The Teaching Company. I like their courses *The Great Principles of Science, Europe and Western Civilization in the Modern Age* and *Economics.* I'm always reading, listening to music, and watching films about everything in the world. I don't think I'd do as much math or vocabulary if they weren't things I had to do though. I think homeschooling can be too much like school for some people where you have to do what you're told even when you'd rather be doing something else. Since my learning isn't like that, life is mostly just doing more of what I'm already doing. I can build a fort, and do jobs for people.

In the morning I get started by searching under all the junk on the floor of my room for my books and magazines. Once I do find them, I take what's on my desk, put *that* on the floor, and then I start. My mom has tried to help me keep my room clean, but she has underestimated the power of *ME.* So, I live in a room with my little brother Kevin (who is clean and doesn't have much on the floor) where the mess is all mine! There's a mess almost all the time, except when we have visitors. My room is clean then, except for my closet where I shove it all. Only one person who has ever come over has seen my closet at that stage, and he's regretted it ever since.

My mom and I discuss what I want to learn about each year by talking about what I'm interested in and what I want to know. She and Dad also tell me what they think I should do if it wasn't already on my list. We choose the books or materials together. Brian and Katie also have "opinions" about what Kevin and I should be doing and "participate" in the discussion. Usually I really like what I study, so that makes my day fun because I get to learn new things all the time. I have a small note pad that I bring to my mom each morning (once I find it) and we plan what I am going do that day. I'm the one who decides the order, usually with my favorite subject (science and astronomy) first. Subjects I like include science, history, biology, math, geometry, geography, computer science, economics, and astronomy. I don't necessarily do every subject every day. Obviously, I do my least favorite (vocabulary) last. (But I don't necessarily process information if I'm going on a camping trip the next day, because I keep thinking about what I have to pack instead.) By the end of the day, I usually have everything checked off, except when Brian and Kate are home from the university on their holidays. My brain just figures, "It's a holiday!" However, it turns out that my brain is sometimes wrong and I get caught up doing things and don't finish my list.

The good thing about being home for learning is that I can plan my own time. There are days I like to study all morning, but sometimes I get interested in doing other activities or projects and keep switching what I'm doing. It seems like my days are filled with things I want to do, so I don't get bored very much, especially during ski season!

I do think about going to school though. All my friends tell me it's fun and that I should go because there are lots of kids who are all doing the same things as each other. But that would mean not getting to choose what I want to do. I imagine I'd have more fun and more friends, even though I already have a bunch of friends who all like me. I think it would be fun to do group projects, too. Even though I think I could have fun at school, I wouldn't get to ski as much, since I usually ski several times a week.

What I especially like is that during winter I can try to finish my work early and then ski in the afternoons since we live just a few minutes from the ski area. I have been skiing for two years, but because I homeschool, I get to ski so often that I've been able to learn to be a good skier very quickly and to ski some of the hardest terrain on the mountain (which is one of the most difficult ski mountains in the country). When I first started skiing, I took lessons once a week. After those lessons, Dad started helping us with our form and after that, Kevin and I started skiing the intermediate trails with Brian, Kate, or Dad. Kevin and I started skiing so much (once we figured out to finish our work in the mornings!) that we were able to go on the most difficult trails called black diamonds and double black diamonds. We usually ski as a family on the weekends and once a week we go with Brian and Kate when they have their ski class from the university. Next winter Kevin and I each plan to get our own avalanche shovel, probe, and radio transmitter, which we will need to ski the areas on the ridge where there is avalanche danger. Every morning at home we can hear the ski patrol setting off dynamite blasts to break up the avalanches. But, still, it's a rule that skiers need proper avalanche gear to go up to the ridge.

On ski days, Kevin and I usually pack a lunch for ourselves (if we finish our work early enough, which isn't all that often) or go skiing after lunch. We live to ski. We meet lots of people who ride the ski lifts, who operate the lifts, or who work at the cafés. Sometimes we take a break in the afternoon and order a hot chocolate. I plan to be on a racing or free-style team next winter and so does Kevin.

Also during the winter, the *Boy Scouts* go camping every month. It can get really cold. One time it got thirteen degrees below zero!. I got ninety-eight "frost points" (a point for every degree below thirty-two) last year on overnight camp outs. I needed 100 points to earn the polar badge, though. On winter camp outs we bring our skis and build ski jumps, go sledding, have races, and make snow shelters.

During summer, the *Boy Scouts* still go camping every month, but we also do other activities like going on canoe trips, taking long hikes, going on thirty or forty mile bike rides, and going on fishing trips (you should see me with a fly rod—casting over and over again—with no fish!). Also, our troop went on a special trip to a *Boy Scout* camp in Washington that was a twenty-hour drive, but it was really worth it. Next summer I hope to be a C.I.T. (counselor in training) there. I hope to earn my *Eagle Scout* rank soon.

Katie is in *Venture Scouts*. That's the co-ed part of *Boy Scouts* for older kids and they go on more high adventure types of trips. They've gone caving, canoeing, biking, backpacking, and other kinds of outdoor activities. Sometimes *Venture* and *Scouts* do activities together, so Kate and I go on some of the same trips. Since Brian is an *Eagle Scout*, he comes to some of the *Boy Scout* activities or meetings with me and he might be an *Assistant Scout Master*. He taught me how to pack for backpacking trips, so I do all of my own camping preparations—everything! I even pack for Dad, too. For two years I was the den chief for Kevin's *Cub Scout* pack. We all do things with each other and are often part of each other's activities.

It's neat not to just have my own activities, but to share activities with the rest of my family. When there are movies, concerts, comedy or other events at the university, Brian and Kate usually take us with them if we don't go as a whole family. We get to do a lot of activities on campus and I really like it there (especially skate boarding there in the summer). Sometimes we go to guest lectures on topics we're interested in. It's really fun having an older brother and sister there (and Dad, too). Dad teaches in a few departments—at the business college, in the honors program, and in health and human development. He takes us on campus to do things, and Mom gets her art supplies at the bookstore. We all love the campus bookstore. Brian and Kate go places with us, too.

Each summer Katie, Kevin and I take advanced swimming and diving lessons to improve our form. Our instructor is teaching us what she learned when she was on a swim team. We love to swim and could stay in a pool all day, except that we're not allowed because the sun is so strong here in the high altitude, even though we keep using sunscreen. I also earn money by cleaning neighbor's hot tubs. Dad taught me how to drain them, clean the filters, clean the sides and bottom of the tub, and add chemicals to the fresh water. I like that job and it pays well. I also work sometimes with Kevin on the jobs we get from neighbors.

I especially like if we go on trips to places like *Yellowstone National Park*, *Glacier/Waterton International Part*, or drive around the mountains. I also enjoy when we watch films as a family, which we do all the time, ever since I was born and we used to watch all the *Star Trek* series. I especially like *The Matrix, eXist-*

enZ, *The Thirteenth Floor* and *The Truman Show*—they all show that reality is not what it seems. We also like to use the Internet and play computer games. I love to go on-line and look up things that help me with my work, look at interesting sites, and play games against other people on-line—mostly action, strategy, or racing games. Brian has a group of friends at the university who like to play computer games. They all bring their computers and hook up a *L.A.N.* (*Local Area Network*) and play games together. Kev and I wanted to play computer games, too. At first Dad and Mom didn't think it was a good idea, but Brian convinced them it *was* a good thing. That's when it's really useful to have an older brother or sister!

Speaking of an older sister, I've always also wanted a little sister. Mom takes care of a six-month-old baby all week and it's like having a little sister. We all get to be with her. It's really a lot of fun to watch her learn to sit up, crawl, and now she's starting to stand up by herself by holding onto things. I like to make her laugh and play little games with her. Everyone loves having her here and we even miss her on the weekends!

Being at home also gives me the opportunity to cook, which I love to do. Mom, Brian, Kate and I are all good cooks (*very* good cooks) and I've always liked to watch cooking shows on television and help with cooking. My grandparents and uncle are good cooks too, so it must run in the family. My uncle even owns three restaurants. I cook whole meals on my own including Mexican, Chinese, Italian, American, and the classic hamburger. I'm also a pro on the barbecue. I'm the family omelette maker since I create the number one omelettes in the world. The one thing I *don't* like about cooking is cleaning up. I hate chores and wish I didn't have to do them. (And sometimes I don't.) I especially hate doing the dishes and kitchen chores. Oh, yeah—and cleaning my room.

Outside, now and then I help Katie feed the dogs and cats and throw hay to the cows. When we first got our cows they would sometimes break through the fence and wander around. Luckily, they don't get out and go for walks up the mountain anymore, because getting them back home was almost impossible. All the neighbors would come out in their trucks and try to help us. Once we had to get our neighbor who is a rancher to bring his border collie over to get them back home. Now that Mom has trained them, she just has to bring their food buckets out and they follow her all the way back, while Dad fixes the fence before they can get back out! At the end of summer we get a huge load of hay, which is fun to watch being unloaded, but definitely is *not* fun to stack up since they're heavy and my allergies go crazy. During the winter, the cows love their hay and the oat mix. When they hear Mom's voice, they moo and run (like a gallop) to her and follow her around wherever she goes, like puppies. It's so funny to watch them. They're very gentle even though they have horns.

Last week we saw a young bear out back and a smaller one near the dog kennel. You should have heard the dogs bark when the bears just stayed around them. We have lots (two local herds of about a hundred each) of deer (including one who lives at our house), elk (a *huge* herd just down the road), moose, two foxes, occasional mountain lions, and all sorts of little critters. Don't forget the skunks—we have one of those who lives here also. The moose are the most dangerous, though, because they actually come after people. Once Kev and I met a moose just on our road. If we go out for hikes around our house in the summer, we have to take bear spray and our two-way radio. That way, we can let Mom know where we are and that we're safe. The radios give us the chance to explore around the mountain and still be in touch.

Since I've always homeschooled, I'm used to it and really don't think I know enough about school (just what I imagine) to compare them. But I do know that I enjoy having the freedom to do what I want most of the time, to go at the speed I want, and put more time into the subjects I really like. When school kids ask me about it, I basically say that I have five hours of "homework" everyday!

From Kate (age 16)

From my position today, I don't think that even if I were given the chance to go back in time, I would change much. My academics have far exceeded my expectations, although my social life has been a disappointment. What I can't say, though, is to what extent my success or disappointment is based on homeschooling. So much is embedded in our family style, my personal temperament and choices, and on unexpected opportunities. Over the years, I have experienced many positive and negative aspects of homeschooling, which I will share with you.

Since starting to homeschool when I was eight, I have loved having the freedom to learn what I want and at the pace I like. Though none us had planned it, I started college young, an option that would not have been available had I been in school. At thirteen I really wanted to take a course in biology since Brian had already done so. I knew it could possible because Cabrini College (in Pennsylvania, where we lived then) was open to the idea of giving homeschoolers a chance. Initially, after meeting with the head of admissions (with portfolio and letters of recommendation) and discussing our homeschooling history, they were willing to let Brian start taking courses right away. The following semester I decided that I really wanted to try also. They were willing to also let me try, and I loved the classes and did very well. After my first semester, we began looking at other options and found Saint Joseph's University, a Jesuit university with a strong academic program. We were shocked when they gave us each a scholarship to take two courses each semester. We were each A students and loved our courses. The next year, we moved to Montana and were able to transfer as full-time students. Preparing for this move, Brian and I took the *SATs* and, along with our past university grades, we were accepted into the excellent honors program at Montana State University where I am now a full-time junior. None of this was planned, but we took advantage of opportunities that came along, making choices all along the way. It was not always easy to know if we made the "right" choices, but they seemed like the "best" choices at the time.

My first university courses in Pennsylvania included biology, astronomy, sociology, and two film courses. These courses didn't seem that different from other things I had done before, however I found them to be more exciting than everyday homeschooling. I also took two sessions at one of our local hospitals that certified me to use a transmission electron microscope. I had taken music and karate lessons because I was interested, and these college courses seemed just like more of what I'd always done—learning things I was interested in from others who knew about the subject. It was a continuation of my homeschooling, but with lots of different interests to choose from. It was as if I were at a top restaurant with a menu full of things I wanted to order. And it still is that way for me as I look forward to searching the course catalog for courses each semester.

Homeschooling allowed me to learn quickly at my own pace. My first awareness of what homeschooling meant to me was when I discovered historical fiction during my first year. I truly loved it, spent lots of my time reading about every time period, and found I could really relate to learning history—something I couldn't have done in school and wasn't able to do with most textbooks. I realized that my learning could be based on what I wanted to know from the inside, rather than being told what I had to learn. I dedicated a great deal of time to music, poetry, writing, reading, having fun, and getting my writing published. I discovered the Internet and explored the world, getting involved in interactive projects on the westward expansion, Arctic treks, bicycle tours across Africa, etc.

As one who has always loved comfort, I spent my first homeschool years curled up in one of our living room chairs, doing my work in many odd positions. As I grew older, I wanted more privacy (and quiet!) and discovered that I loved studying while listening to music (a habit that has not faded). My very small room, which had a slanting ceiling and mattress on the floor (a bed would never fit), became my new space of study. I hid away for hours at a time, happily reading, doing some math, reading, then finishing other subjects, then reading some more. I think that having my own personal space for studying and living (and being surrounded by my three brothers) led me to be rather possessive of my belongings and it's still not easy for me to share them.

From the beginning, Brian and I participated in all kinds of homeschool and other group activities. Our homeschool groups included a writing group, an arts and ideas group, and a nature group. Our other activities included years of

---

Brian (18), Kate (16), Neil (12), Kevin (9)

karate, swim lessons, and music lessons. After homeschooling about two years, Brian and I made the decision to drop out of most of these groups. From my perspective, our homeschooling was based on the freedom to follow our natural rhythm of learning, and it felt like these groups interrupted my day. We'd all have to stop what we were involved in and get ready to go out somewhere, when we were happy doing what we were doing in the first place! We were also members of *4-H*. Raising pigs for three years and participating in other programs (veterinary science, gardening, etc.) was a great experience that I wish I had continued. Now that we have cows of our own (beautiful Scottish Highlands), I realize how valuable *4-H* was in getting us started raising animals. We have since bred cats and dogs, and I would love to be able to raise more animals. If we didn't live at such a high altitude with a very short growing season (and plenty of hungry wildlife around), I'd love to have a garden. I finally see and appreciate the skills that *4-H* imparts to children. Again, it was our choice to stop going because we got restless at the meetings and it interrupted what we were in the middle of doing. I think, however, that I'd take a different stance now.

I have always had a competitive nature, taking great pride in my grades and achievements. It seemed like second nature that Brian and I (only two years apart) tended to be somewhat competitive with each other, comparing grades and knowledge. Naturally, Brian (being older) usually won, but it was (and still is) fun and made me stronger and more independent. Brian and I have a very close relationship. We commute to the university together, we take a few classes together, we studied Arabic together, attend activities, and even share some of the same friends. We do have occasional tension about being together, but we come out ahead with advantages like practicing Arabic together. We've learned how to argue and settle our differences. Usually. Though I think I would have had a wonderful experience going to Morocco, I felt I wasn't old enough to be a foreign exchange student at sixteen, and may regret this setback. However, aside from putting my Arabic to use, I would like to possibly study in Ireland for a semester. In the end, it may be better not to use up my chance so soon!

For many families, homeschooling has no noticeable effect on the children's social life. Across the country, there are many tightly-knit homeschool groups and families who do everything together from math and writing to field trips. I went from being very popular in first and second grade to keeping mainly my two best friends over the next few years. As time went by, I seemed to grow more independent and have less and less in common with kids my own age. They didn't seem to share my interest or enthusiasm. I felt a growing gap that I might not have experienced had I remained in school. More and more, I experienced the widening of this gap until it became difficult for me to relate to most people my own age. Without the influence of school peer groups, I was not focused on "cool" things, but *my* things. This is an area I would not want to change, but at the same time I think I did miss out on many social events that I would have enjoyed.

Even now, my peer group at the university is years older than me. The problem of age arose because of my accelerated studies. We didn't plan this to happen and my parents aren't sure it was a wise choice. It seemed more important to me to keep learning than to slow down so I could relate more to my own age group. It seems to be the only choice I could have made, and if I had the chance to go back, I would make the same choice—but might be more prepared for the social discordance.

I never wanted to go back to public school, although I think I may have eventually questioned my position, based on my social desires to have friends and a group to do things with. Once I took my first college course at thirteen, however, I couldn't imagine going anywhere else. High school seemed like it would undo all the choices I had. I love the structure and independence that college gives me and the opportunities that are available—interesting subjects I can learn in depth. I enjoy competition and the wonderful professors I talk to. Not all my professors have been inspiring, but two have especially challenged me and encouraged me. Though professors have office hours available to all students, most students only make appointments when they want to complain about grades. Luckily, from the way I have been brought up, my frustration with other student's lack of striving only makes me compete to study harder. My comfort and experience in dealing with adults has given me a great advantage as a college student. It seems totally natural for me to talk to my professors and make use of their office hours to explore questions further and get feedback on my ideas. This makes college seem more like the kind of mentoring experiences I had while homeschooling. I am at an excellent university with a large and talented faculty and very few graduate students. Therefore, all my courses are taught by senior faculty and their accessibility is wonderful. I feel that I am ending up with an individualized and quality education, much like my homeschooling was.

Most students assume I am the same age as my other classmates, though I am about five years younger than the majority of students. There are many non-traditional students at MSU who have come back to school at the age or thirty, forty, or fifty. Because of this mixture, it is ironic that it is difficult to tell how old *any* student is! Classmates treated me nicely when I was thirteen, but I was, for the most part, ignored by social groups. Now that I'm older and attend the university full-time, it's no longer obvious that I'm a different age. I have less social experience than most students, however, and have a hard time relating to students who date, have children of their own, or go to bars and such.

I began as a media and theater arts major. I also enrolled for a second degree in business accounting, so I do *not* intend to graduate when I am seventeen.

Brian (18), Kate (16), Neil (12), Kevin (9)

There are so many more courses I want to take with specific professors and other areas to explore (such as Native American studies). I don't think it would be a good idea to graduate at the young age of seventeen, and my new major in business assures about three more years of study.

I recently got my drivers license and my life changed dramatically. I've always leaned on my parents for safety and support (even though they have encouraged and trained me to be independent) and on my brothers for their company. I didn't like doing things by myself (outside of my home), and my first few days of running errands by myself was a nerve-wracking experience. I also have a hard time being with people outside my family when I'm by myself. I don't know whether these difficulties are due more to my personality than to homeschooling. I now have the mobility to do things on my own, whether it is shopping, meeting people, attending meetings, going to new places, or going to work. Though the transition is difficult for me, I am moving forward and am pleased to be able to be competent on my own, knowing I have my family's support in the background.

My brothers and I, while very different in personality, are more alike than we would have been had we gone to school. We talk and think, for the most part, in the same way. We are very connected to each other and a big part of each other's lives. Brian is leaving in a few days for Europe and a semester at a university in Morocco. He will be gone about six months, and I easily admit that I will miss him. I will miss talking and being around him, especially since we have done so much together throughout our education. I have always been able to talk and joke with Brian and I will especially miss that. Homeschooling has allowed Brian, Neil, Kevin and me to be more than siblings related only by blood. We are friends who laugh together, learn together, argue, grow together in each other's company, and, *of course*, ski together.

Since moving to Montana, I have happily discovered a new way not only of learning, but of experiencing the world. Our house has a satellite dish (the mountains act as a barrier to receiving television signals). Dad's love of technology and film has greatly influenced us as a family. I know many homeschoolers who are against television and don't own one. While we don't watch network television, we devour films, documentaries, science fiction, comedy, etc. I have found that I cry, laugh, and altogether experience more emotions while watching films (and reading books) than I do in my own life. This has not been for lack of emotion, but the wide variety of films and books offers me many experiences that I could not possibly have experienced in several lifetimes.

I've just recently discovered the fun of setting goals for myself. Through setting goals, I realize that I've started to challenge myself to raise my personal expectations. For example, though I've always been an avid reader, this summer my goal was to try and catch up on my book list. Creating this list has made me want to read books not only for the pleasure of reading them, but for the pleasure of seeing my list grow. So far, I've been reading about five books each week, ranging from *Great Expectations* to books by Barbara Kingsolver, Billie Letts, Anna Quindlen, and Wally Lamb. While I eagerly plunged through some excellent books, I've also plowed through some unfulfilling ones with the purpose of adding them to my list and moving along to the next book. I've also challenged myself to make a bed quilt each summer and I'm really pleased with the results of that!

My main goal in life, the goal that all my other goals point to, is to be a mother, have lots of children, and live in the country. I can imagine nothing more special than staying home with them, nurturing them, and watching them grow. Many people are surprised by this. Expectations of "intelligent" homeschoolers are often to become scientists, mathematicians, etc. Most people, therefore, have a hard time comprehending that I want to help the world, not through the sciences, but by having children and teaching them to be contributing citizens who are kind, loving, and helpful. Naturally, I plan to have the financial resources to live comfortably and, naturally, I see business and accounting as a way to do that.

Beside art and writing, Mom works full-time taking care of our neighbor's baby during the week, and I also babysit her some evenings or weekends, as well as helping Mom on the days I'm home. This is giving me the opportunity to experience having a little sister (which I've always wanted) and having a baby around. It's been amazing watching her grow and develop. I love helping to take care of her and she's helped me appreciate people more. It was such a miracle when she started to use her hands or began to crawl that it gives me a greater respect for the natural life force that creates an actual human being.

I've had businesses of my own since I was ten years old, which is probably why one of my majors is business. I started a pet sitting business when I was ten. When we moved to Montana I continued my pet/house sitting business and now take care of neighbor's horses, chickens, and ducks so they can go away and not worry. I also started babysitting, interned for one of our U.S. Senators for a summer, and I now work two part-time jobs in the College of Business—one as the assistant for the development director and the other as a secretary for faculty services. Homeschooling gave me the opportunity and the incentive to work when I was young, and I always felt it was an important part of my learning. My parents have encouraged my interests in business and work—they see them as valuable for me as any subject area. I am learning responsibility along with business and communication skills, which I could only have learned by relating with people while doing real work.

Moving to Montana has been a dream come true. I have always longed to live in the country or the mountains. As the primary caretaker of our cats and dogs, I love watching them play and spending time with them. Our cats (who think they are dogs) spend time with us around the house and in the pastures with the cows. Our dogs (who think they are part horse and part cow), spend their days grazing and digging. I think our animals love Montana, the freedom (as I do), and the dirt to roll in.

We live in the most wonderful place in the world and I am even now considering saving to buy a little piece of Montana for my own. Homeschooling has given me opportunities I can't imagine living without. Educationally, I would never give up what I have. Socially, I don't know where I would have ended up had I stayed in public school. I do feel a lack of friendships, but don't know how many friends I would have chosen to have even if I were at high school. I am selective enough about everything in my life, that I am just as selective about people and have realized there is an element of randomness in friendships. For me, I think homeschooling was the right decision, even with its various pluses and minuses. I would still recommend homeschooling to anyone who has considered all the tradeoffs and feels it would be worth it in face of what is lost. It is very adaptable to any child's circumstances and needs, whether educationally or socially (for many homeschooled children have very active social lives). I think and hope that, in the end, my own academic and socials needs will happily balance for me.

From Brian (age 18)

Before beginning to homeschool, I was socialized in a public educational institution similar to those across America. I didn't even know there were any alternatives to the familiar cookie-cutter style of education. My assumption that there was only "one way" to school partly speaks to the power that societal institutions and cultural traditions have on framing our everyday reality. A good analogy to delineate this social phenomenon is one of skiing moguls—hilly bumps that form on heavily skied runs. You cannot always just ski straight down a path to the bottom of the slope. New skiers must keep turning to dodge the moguls since they are incredibly difficult to escape, and when you do, it is quite a jolt! Society is much like the moguls on a ski hill, although society's hills are higher and more difficult to escape, since you have no awareness they even exist, what lies over these hills, or that there are other moguls to ski beyond the ones you're in. Advanced skiers have the control to ski right over the tops of moguls, edge their skis into the snow, and choose their own path.

Homeschooling has been my way of learning to ski, to navigate skillfully around and over the tops of moguls, without getting stuck into the grooves created by social institutions. The result of this has been an education that, for me, can be best described as post-modern in character, decentralized of any metanarrative of education, and filled with a skeptical inquiry and deconstruction of the world in which I live. To the extent that my education has been post-modern, there is the sense that it has existed in a type of hyperspace, where space and time have collapsed, no longer behaving in a predictable fashion. I owe this fresh outlook to my parents, since they did not rely on any set curriculum, nor did they make any specific assumptions about the ultimate destination or composition of my education. Thus, homeschooling was always in a state of perpetual flux, never bound to any temporal rules of age or linear progression. I was exposed to a montage of realities: apprenticeships, cyberspace, trends, reading, movies, math, science, etc. I was brought up in an interconnected world of humor, playfulness, and skepticism in order to be aware of my point of view, biases, and cultural assumptions. I see myself as questioning everything—no longer polarized in mind and body, self and others, or nature and nurture. The key to my education, and to my *life* for that matter, is that no medium or method has been privileged over another. Books were not given greater weight than films, nor was mathematics placed above social theory or music. For me, traditional fixed polarities have been replaced. I find no distinction between the real and the simulacrum. Hence, my web site is called simulacrum—a place for humor, irony, stepping beyond "everyday reality," and a beautiful kaleidoscope of truths, stories, beliefs, and emotions.

At the time I began homeschooling at age ten, it did not strike me that my family was doing anything particularly radical or that my five years of homeschooling would be the most formative experience in my development. I was just happy that I could learn at my own pace, delve deeply into my interests, and spend extra hours playing with my *Lego*. My siblings and I have been lucky to have parents who have the ability to think and live outside the box. They have been good guides for us.

In retrospect, the most critical educational skills my parents have imparted to us have come in three major dialectal progressions: critical thinking, clear thinking, and what is frequently referred to as sociological imagination. I was taught critical thinking early on by reading books by Carl Sagan and from my first forays into the biological sciences at the university when I was fourteen. I learned to think clearly and concisely by (endlessly) studying and practicing essay writing. I learned about sociological imagination from my father and from studying sociology and anthropology—the ability to discern patterns in social events, deconstruct social contexts, and view personal experiences in light of these patterns and contexts. This dialectal process results in my ability to critically analyze the world and myself. I try to find the beauty, grace, and control to ski right over the moguls that get in the way and hope I will build enough competence and awareness to find the challenge of moguls wonderful rather than the terrifying experience it is for many. I strive endlessly for the ability to see beyond the moguls of assumptions and illusions of which our world is con-

---

structed. As I build the skills to either ski around the moguls or ski across them, my life, like skiing, increasingly is an experience of joy, enthusiasm, and beauty.

It was because of this method of homeschooling that I feel my education has been superior to the traditional alternative. I believe that the abilities to think and to deconstruct are the keys to uncovering knowledge. Putting that knowledge into practical use leads to success in the world. Homeschooling has given me something else that I never would have gotten from traditional schooling, making risk-taking and adventure part of my educational process. The biggest adventure (and risk) my family ever took (after deciding to homeschool!) was to move from the suburbs of the city of Philadelphia to the rural Rocky Mountains outside the town of Bozeman, Montana. We had no guarantees how the change would work out for us or if we would find social or economic security. We just knew that we needed an escape from suburban culture—a change of scenery and a change of life. It seemed like the next logical step on our journey of homeschooling. As a matter of fact, I have not just metaphorically learned to ski in

Katie, Gary, Brian, Nancy
Kevin, Neil

Montana, but my whole family now successfully skis high moguls of hard-packed snow throughout the winter!

Since I had been taking college courses in Pennsylvania from the time I was fourteen, I was able to transfer to MSU as a sophomore. I am now a senior, majoring in psychology, philosophy, and arts and honors; with emphases in Arabic, statistics (my minor), and social theory. MSU is a world of opportunities, and I plan to stay beyond next year in order to explore as much as I can. The binary opposition of school and homeschool seems like one more arbitrary division in life. For all these years I have been on an incredible journey in learning. The adventure first began by leaving the confines and limitations of public school. The adventure continues because no other limiting structure has since been placed on me—either by homeschooling or by college. Instead, my education has been like skiing on an array of different mountains. My parents provided the support that allowed me to freely open myself to the world of resources and opportunities. I have an independent life, friends, and a great deal of freedom, yet I spend time with my family, do things with Mom, Kate, Neil and Kevin, and I see my dad on and off campus. My life was never in little boxes or categories. I have become a person of questions, not answers.

At the time I am writing this, I am on my next journey—on my way to the African nation of Morocco, where I will continue my studies of Arabic for a semester. This, and my travels through Europe beforehand, will be yet other resources to explore like exciting new ski mountains, grooming me to become ever more able to ski right across those moguls.

Brian (18), Kate (16), Neil (12), Kevin (9)

Joe, age 39
Barb, age 36
Matt, age 13
Nicolas, age 11
Max, age 3
Emily, age 8 months

Five-year follow-up interview with Barb in Derry, Pennsylvania

PAPER RAILROAD

We are now the parents of four children. Matt (thirteen years), Nicolas (eleven years), Max (three years), and Emily (eight months). I am still working ful- time, which I do not recommend to anyone unless they are organized! I have been promoted to supervisor and work the afternoon shift Tuesday through Saturday. I work for the Postal Service and oversee a group of seventy-six employees who type the addresses from the front of each envelope, before a bar code is sprayed on the front of the mail piece. I have many opportunities to answer people's questions about homeschooling while at work. I work with a total of 350 employees and many of them know I homeschool by the bumper sticker in the window of my car! I also hand out past issues of our homeschooling newsletter and encourage them to homeschool.

It is tough working and homeschooling the children. I have a supportive spouse, reliance on God for strength, and the willpower to carry it all out! When the younger children begin to homeschool (at eight years old), then I will most likely quit the work force and stay home with them. Joe works for the state police as a dispatcher. He just started there a little over a year ago. It is less stressful than working as a 911 dispatcher, and he no longer has to work the midnight shift. It was getting hard to keep four children quiet while their dad slept during the day!

Joe's work schedule rotates from daylight to afternoon shift, so about six to seven times a month we employ a wonderful homeschooled teenager to come and stay with the children while we both work the afternoon shift. Other days that I work (I leave for work around 2:00 p.m.), the children are usually at home until their dad arrives home from work at 4:00 p.m. When Matt was eleven, he attended the Red Cross Babysitter's Course. So we've always felt confident that the children are well-taken care of.

Our homeschooling methods have changed, and I laugh as I look back at some of the methods I have tried with children. Our long-term goals have also changed. Previously, I think I had envisioned my children becoming scholars and attending college with high honors. Now, we want our children to graduate with a well-rounded education, being able to relate to both sides of an issue, and base decisions on what they know to be correct in the eyes of the Lord. We want them to be sensitive to the needs of others, and to be able to carry on a coherent and intelligent conversation with their peers and adults. Whatever endeavor they may try to accomplish, we want them to complete it with the love of the Lord in their hearts.

I have changed curricula often, and this year I have focused on a curriculum that gives our children the goals I have previously stated. I debated long and hard (for over a year), and I have decided to try using *Sonlight Curriculum*. The children love to read, and I feel that I am organized enough to try it. Another plus to this program is that all preparations are completely spelled out. I do not have to make up lesson plans or figure out what questions to ask to see whether they are comprehending what they are learning. *Sonlight* has it all written down for me in one binder! I had to give up using complete unit studies as I did not have the time to prepare everything, to drive to all the field trips, or to do all those crafts!! Using just workbooks or texts to school the children resulted in moans and groans because it was boring and filled with busy work. I found that workbooks are okay to use on a limited basis, but the children learn best and retain what they've learned by a cross between unit studies and workbooks—and *Sonlight* doesn't use textbooks. We are very happy with this curriculum and plan to use it with our younger children.

My oldest, Matthew, is in seventh grade and I believe he needs more structure to prepare him for our state homeschooler's diploma. *Sonlight Curriculum* is just what he needs. It is loaded with great books to read, two or three papers each week to write, thoughtful questions, and oral assignments.

Nick will be in fifth grade this year. He will also be sharing his brother's curriculum. Workbooks are scorned by this child since handwriting is a struggle for him. I use *Getty-Dubay Italic* handwriting books for him, although he does use the computer for typing a myriad of assignments.

Both boys use *Saxon Math*, but this year we may try something different with Matthew. I bought the seventh grade *Scott Foresman* math book that has less paper work (they like to do oral work with Joe), uses a scientific calculator, and

---

has real-life applications. *Saxon Math* seems to be great in the early years, but as the boys got older, they wanted something different.

We sometimes attend enrichment classes for homeschoolers for a semester or two. This involves meeting with other students during the week and having parent-run classes for a ten-week stretch. I do not do this very often as it takes away from what free time I do have with the children. Matt is taking chess and biology. Nick is taking gardening, crocheting, and chess. We will not be attending next semester.

Both boys are active in our church *AWANA Bible Club*. I truly love this nationally run program that is provided at local churches. The boys have each won top honors for memorizing hundreds of Bible scripture passages. Additionally, since parents are involved with their children in this program, it helps them to think and learn along with their children. *AWANA* teaches children to witness for God to other people in helping to solve problems. The monthly Bible quizzes are held in front of a large crowd, and the children must speak with a microphone, which prepares them for public speaking. Another plus is that every Wednesday night is counted as physical education since they have organized gym time. The children love to go to church on Wednesdays. Since Max turned three this year, he will get to participate in the *Cubbies* program.

Back to the curriculum choices that I made this year. This first semester of science will be covered under the enrichment classes. After that, I have a science kit that covers human anatomy, and then a three-week study on designing blueprints for a home. I also purchased a *Weather Trackers* science kit, and in the spring we will study weather in-depth. I also have the *Sonlight* sixth grade science course, but I will not be completing the entire unit.

Both boys will be studying Latin and Greek this year using *Grammar from the Roots Up*. This is great! The boys love it and so do I. They are also using some *WordSmith* and *Simply Grammar* products. Matt is using the *Easy Grammar* series for grades six through twelve. This is what homeschooling is all about—flexibility in the education of your children.

Art consists of knitting and crocheting projects throughout the year. As a bonus, these same projects will be entered in the county fair. They each had six entries in the fair this past summer. They will also be learning basic drawing skills—I'll have to use a video for this one!

Both boys take English horse riding lessons each week. They also love to bike, ride and swim. Matt and Nick both take music lessons twice a month, and this will be the start of their third year of music. Nick plays the piano and Matt plays the acoustic guitar. They both play we'll together, and every once in a while, they will play for the church. They also attend the yearly music recital which is a big event.

As you can see, the boys are both active, and I try to tailor curriculum choices to their learning styles. I find that, as a parent, I must limit myself in extracurricular activities. All choices must be able to accommodate all members of the family. For example, is there a place where I can nurse the baby or have the toddler play while the boys take music lessons or riding lessons? I do not let them get involved with *Boy Scouts* or *4-H*, as these would take up even more time that I don't have.

Our church plays an important part in encouraging me when I feel overwhelmed. Most of the members are homeschoolers, so we all share in the trials that await us. We exchande curriculum reviews, triumphs, failures of homeschooling, and AWANAS program events. I have never wavered in my conviction to homeschool. At times it has been trying and other times rewarding. I often wonder if the children are learning enough or if am I pushing them to learn too much. I used to get angry when a child didn't seem to immediately catch on to what I was teaching him. I had thought that it was deliberate disobedience or not wanting to learn. I can look back and see how my misperception and anger affected the child's learning capabilities, so I have relaxed. I used to push them to get ahead at an early age and to get through texts and workbooks, which they disliked and complained about. I wish I had known that the joy of learning to read and making weekly trips to the library teaches them so much of what I had wanted anyway. They also *enjoy* the learning and don't need to be pushed. Now I *know* that the work eventually gets accomplished, and I make sure that the child tries to do his best.

My husband Joe had decided to take over teaching math this year. He knew I was struggling with teaching it and that I don't like the subject. We were afraid that *my* negative attitude would rub off on the children! Also, Joe loves math and patiently works individually with the children. It is his responsibility to teach math in the evening or morning, whatever his schedule allows, and he plans on teaching it all year to make up for days we miss, which helps with their retention. Joe's help frees up time for me to expand on what I am teaching, so I don't have to rush through math in an attempt to get it over with and crossed off my list!

Max and Emily are waiting in the wings to begin their educational process. In Pennsylvania we do not have to send our children to school or teach them at home until the age of eight, so I usually do not formally begin teaching the children until they reach that milestone. But at around four or five years of age, I do teach them to read using *Teach Your Child to Read in 100 Easy Lessons.* After they learn to read, I make sure we visit the library on a regular basis. Once children can read, they can learn for life. No other formal schooling takes place until they reach eight years. Again, I've learned my lesson from the first children that pushing them to learn with workbooks or text books before they're ready creates needless conflicts.

Matt (13), Nicolas (11), Max (3), Emily (8 mo.)

As a family, we do take field trips to local museums, science centers, and community events. These are a nice break from school work and fun, too. Last year, the whole family was able to take a week vacation. Joe had a business trip, and the family was permitted to tag along, as long as we provided our own transportation. I jumped at the chance. So, we packed our school books and had school in the hotel during the morning. We took a field trip every afternoon on each of the five days, and in the evening there was the hotel pool to swim in. If we did not homeschool, that trip would never have happened on such short notice. I still think fondly of that week.

Just one last note. Two years ago we got rid of the television. Let me just say we have never missed having it. What a time waster! The only thing I miss is seeing home videos of the children. This year we may get a VCR because I know that there is some good curriculum out there that requires a VCR. Joe and I are still thinking it over at this point.

A few hints that I learned along our homeschooling journey are: Don't give up easily! Taking the time to teach our children can be rigorous at times, so there may sometimes be no time for myself. Our children will always be with us during the day. Faults, bad habits, and disobedience will have to be dealt with on an hourly basis, or so it may seem at times. But the rewards of hearing our children read with delight and knowing that we've taught them makes it all seem worthwhile. Also, I try not to become discouraged. I pray daily with the children before we begin the lessons for the day. I also try to buy used curriculum to

Matthew
Nicolas, Max
Emily

save hundreds of dollars. I try other means of teaching our children besides plunking a textbook in front of them and telling them to read, then answer the questions at the end of the chapter. Because I was taught in the public school system, I thought this was how all children had to learn. After all, *I* learned this way, why couldn't the boys? I have found that workbooks are filled with too much "busy work" for us and are meant for use by a harassed teacher in a busy classroom. There is so much curriculum published *by* homeschoolers *for* homeschoolers now. I couldn't seem to find that sort of curriculum when I began teaching, but now it's everywhere, and I take advantage of it whenever possible.

In summary, we love our children. I love to teach them new things, and American history has become my favorite subject. I like being around my children on a daily basis. When we are out in the public eye, my older sons will let me hold their hands or hug them and think nothing of it. They carry around the smaller children and tend to their needs when asked. They don't excessively tease each other. We are a strong family unit, weathering all life's triumphs and tribulations together. Homeschooling is the only way we could have accomplished this.

Matt (13), Nicolas (11), Max (3), Emily (8 mo.)

Ed. age 43
Jane, age 38
Anna, age 13
Anthony, age 9

Five-year follow-up interview with Jane in Ryegate, Vermont

THINGS MAKE SENSE

At 6:00 a.m. my alarm sounds and I turn it off, knowing that it's really only 5:50 because I set my clock ten minutes fast. That gives me ten minutes to doze, think about what today holds, and slowly wake up.

We live on a fifty-five acre farm in northeastern Vermont, raising beef and sheep. We also currently have five pigs, eight laying hens, a Jersey dairy cow, four dogs, three cats, a horse, and two ponies. The breeding beef and sheep alone total over a hundred, so it frightens me to think how many animals are actually here at any given time, adding in the young stock and other animals. Ed works full-time as an animal health inspector for the state, dealing with animals from small pets to livestock to emus and elk; and situations from inspecting pet stores to investigating animal welfare complaints to blood-testing herds for import requirements. He's an interesting dinner companion! He also works extremely hard, but loves it. The kids learned at a pretty young age that they had to be able to run to keep up with Dad—we have to be fit enough to run and talk at the same time, if talking is important to us! His hard work is what enables us to have the farm and certainly sets a great work ethic example for the kids. They cherish time with him (as I do), even if it's doing work together.

I am an at-home mom (resource assistant, chauffeur, dog-handler, gardener, cook, sheep midwife, volunteer, veterinarian's assistant, nurse, farm-hand, etc.). Our children have both been homeschooled since age five. This year, Anthony (nine) has chosen to attend the local public school, while Anna (thirteen) is continuing to homeschool.

Ed has been up for at least an hour and is outside in the barn or fields, doing his chores. I know he wanted to leave for work around 6:00 a.m., so I wonder if he has left yet. Just as I sit up in bed, Anthony comes through our bedroom on the way to the bathroom; his alarm has gotten him up. I get out of bed, noticing that it is dark and rainy outside, and Ed's car is still here. I ask Anthony if he wants help picking out his clothes for school. Normally, we do that at bedtime, but last night he had a *4-H* meeting that kept him out later than his usual bedtime, throwing off our routine. He says he'll pick his own clothes, so I dress, make our bed, and go to make sure he has made appropriate choices. I veto yesterday's dirty pants, but he picks clean ones agreeably.

As I go downstairs, I hear Anna call me. I'm surprised because she usually waits until the last minute to get out of bed and get dressed to go outside for chores by her 7:00 a.m. deadline. She wants to know if this would be a good morning for her to make scrambled eggs. I tell her that would be great if she's willing. We're still trying to adjust to mornings dictated by a school bus. Unfortunately, it comes right in the middle of the time we are usually in the barn. For the time being, I go out and do half my chores, come in and eat with Anthony, make his lunch, walk him to the bus, and then return to do the rest of my chores. I know this won't work much longer because cold weather will make me unwilling to dress and undress for the outdoors any more times than absolutely necessary. I also found that the routine was so tight that when I tried to make oatmeal for the kids one morning, the mere fifteen minutes it took to prepare set us back enough to almost make us miss the bus! The next time the kids asked for French toast or oatmeal, I told Anna that if she would get up and start any hot breakfast while I was in the barn, we could all eat it together. I say "all" meaning the three of us. Ed eats fried eggs for breakfast every morning as soon as he gets up, which is usually much earlier than the rest of us.

Downstairs, I shudder at the temperature: mid 30's is too cold for early October. I bundle up and step into the garage, greeting our three border collies. They race around me just as though Ed hadn't already had them out for a run, which I know he has. I find that it isn't really raining, just wet and still dark and cold. Halfway to the "pony barn," I meet Ed in the mist, and he asks me to check on a ewe when it gets light. She looked as though she were aborting last night, but it's too dark for him to find her yet this morning. As he leaves, I check to see what time he thinks he'll be home. He thought yesterday and today would be long days but things went well yesterday, and he was home by four, so he hopes for the same today. His days can start as early as 4:00 a.m. and can go into the evening, but the overtime allows him to take time off to work on the many things that need to be done on our farm, and most days are reasonable. I'm especially glad today won't be bad since he has succumbed to the rotten cold that the kids and I have already had.

In the pony barn, I feed my horse Teddy, who actually belongs to our *Pony*

Club, but is mine for a year to "check out" his abilities and loan to any child in the club who is in need. Horses and riding are what I did with my life before Anna was born. I even rode through my seventh month of pregnancy, but once she was born, I knew I couldn't devote myself to both motherhood and riding with the intensity that I wanted so horses were taken not only off the burner, but entirely out of the kitchen for quite a while. Then, when Anna was old enough to ride, I slowly got involved again—first, as her instructor and groom, then as *Pony Club* volunteer, then as *Pony Club* DC ("district commissioner" or "leader"). Just this past May, Teddy was donated to the club, and I began actually riding again for the first time in thirteen years. It has been absolutely wonderful. This morning I also feed Anna's pony Skippy and give a token handful to her outgrown mount, Sophie. We are currently looking for a new home for her to make room for Anna's next horse! I begin cleaning Teddy's stall while they eat. As soon as they are done, I put them out in the paddock, turn out the lights, and take the dogs back to the house. The sky is starting to lighten, but I have no idea what kind of day is in store because of the fog that will stick in this river valley until up to 11:00 a.m. some days.

When I enter the mud room, Anthony is dancing around happily because Anna is making scrambled eggs. He had dressed, made his bed, and gone to the barn to feed and water his dog while I was out. The dining room table is half covered with paperwork; my end is the worst with a catalog, a horse lease, my to-do list, pieces of paper with important information of various sorts on them, car registration, sheep record books, and more. Ed has piled his similar heap onto a chair and table behind him. Although we have lived here for twelve years, trying to renovate an old house while homeschooling and farming has been slow work. While many rooms are complete, the back room is next on my list of priorities. Right now, it's a junk room, storing craft supplies, rolls of insulation, and cans of paint, the file cabinet for anything that makes it to that stage, and a desk buried under I don't even know what. Some day it will be our office, but for now, the dining room doubles as an office for the farm, *Pony Club*, homeschooling, and household.

I quickly cook the eggs Anna has prepared and we sit down to eat them with toast from bread that Anna made yesterday. I made all our bread until about three years ago when my schedule became such that something had to give. In the beginning, it was kind of nice to have sliced bread that always held together for sandwiches or specialty loaves from the health food store, but the past year has even found Anthony pining for homemade bread. Anna has decided to try to take on bread-making as a weekly chore, in exchange for giving up cleaning the bathroom and weeding the carrots in the garden.

We enjoy our hot breakfast on this cold morning, and as I get up from the table and tell Anthony that he has to get going, Anna casually asks him what he's taking for lunch today. Aughhh. I forgot to make his lunch. There's one yogurt left in the refrigerator so I ask him if that's okay and hustle him into the bathroom to brush his teeth and wash his face while I toss the yogurt, a granola bar, a box of juice, a fruit roll, and the last tiny cinnamon pastry ring into his lunch bag.

When I'm done, it's 6:55 a.m. and time to leave, but he's not ready. I yell that I'm leaving and he'd better run to catch up. If I leave on time, I know I'll get there on time and he just needs to run until he catches up to me to make it. I grab three leashes from the mud room and start down the road, with the dogs galloping ahead. When I am halfway to the corner, I hear Anthony running to catch up and I turn to check that he has his backpack and a coat and hat. On the way, we chat and he identifies bird calls for me and stops to examine things on the side of our dirt road. When we can see the paved road, I stop to put the leashes on the dogs and shortly after, hear Anna running up behind us. Anthony is thrilled that she has come and drops back to walk with her while I keep up the pace I know will get us to the bus stop on time. The bus is late and we are quickly chilled through from standing so Anna convinces Anthony to run to the neighbor's driveway and back with her to warm up. Finally, the bus comes, and we wave as Anthony climbs on, choosing the seat right behind the driver "where you get the most heat."

Anthony is not a child I thought would do well in a school setting. He is independent, easily distractible (unless zeroed in on something of his choosing), a reader of non-fiction on specific topics of his choice, a naturalist who lives to be outdoors, and very, very energetic. But there he goes and he's loving it. Homeschooled up until this summer, he had started saying school would be better whenever I asked him to do anything that resembled school work about a year ago. When pressed, he'd say he'd rather stay home. But he continued complaining. He seemed to think that we were unreasonable in what we asked of him, and we thought school would help him see that the rest of the world also operates on time schedules, responsibilities, honesty, etc. A lot of discussion, worrying, and thought went into our decision to send him to a small private school for just two days a week this year so we could continue to homeschool, yet he'd get a taste of school. Unfortunately, that school did not get enough enrollment, and at the last minute, we found out it would not open. We scrambled and decided to send him to the public school. He goes happily every morning, practically bounces off the bus each afternoon, and looks forward to Monday all weekend. Don't ask me why, but it's working. He does the work they ask, complies with their rules, meets most of their deadlines and enjoys the people and atmosphere. All we can say is, if this is what it takes to teach him these things, then this is the place for him right now. And of utmost importance to us, he's happy.

Anna and I briskly walk the half mile up the hill to warm up. We go straight to the pony barn where I finish my chores, and she does hers. I check on the ewe now that it is fully light and find that she has definitely aborted, although I can find no premature lambs in the field. She acts fairly chipper, so I hope that she doesn't need medical attention until Ed gets home because it's a long way to the barn through many fences to get her there. I say good morning to our livestock guardian dog who lives with the sheep and thank her for her good work.

We put Skippy and Teddy out into a paddock with good grass for the morning and I can now see the mountains on the other side of the valley but no sunshine through the fog. We take the dogs back to the house and feed and water them. It's 8:20 a.m. before we are back inside. I guess the late bus, checking on the ewe, and the fact that Anna stayed in to make breakfast put us behind because we are usually in before 8:00. Anna has hot cider and I have tea to warm up but then I realize that we'll be doing that all day if I don't build a fire because it's cold in the house. In the cellar, I build a fire in our wood furnace and realize how pleasant it has been not to have to do that all summer. Anna begins working on her English lesson while she drinks her cider.

We consider ourselves unschoolers, and when the kids were younger, it was probably pretty obvious to anyone who observed us that the kids were doing what they wanted in terms of learning. Now, however, Anna's schooling might look much more traditional to an observer, but we still consider ourselves unschoolers because she is still doing what she wants educationally. When she was seven years old, studying what she wanted meant having me read to her for hours—as long as it was a good story. It meant playing board games at every possible opportunity, by which she learned basic math concepts and skills from the dice. This year, she is still choosing the what, how, when, and where of her studies. But the why has matured. It's no longer just because she is interested in something. Now, she knows that there are steps to a goal; she has discovered for herself that one needs to learn the basics of a subject before expecting to progress. And she has learned to enjoy learning, so that even if a topic may not interest her at first, her curiosity takes over quickly to keep her going. With high school coming right up and a definite interest in college in the future, this year finds her reading analytically, writing, thinking about intangibles, and studying.

Up until this year, her education has been 95% reading and 5% writing. We knew this was not what would greet her in a traditional setting. We knew practice would improve the writing like nothing else. We knew the thoughts were there but the organization, the cohesiveness, and the continuity of thought would need practice. Anna wondered if a licensed program would look better to colleges and/or prepare her better. So we looked into the *Oak Meadow* curriculum that I had loved when Anna was six, but she had quickly shown me was not going to work because no canned curriculum would. Now, as before, I liked what they offered, and *this* time she agreed with me. We were able to purchase individual subjects and chose civics and English. Civics is certainly a weak point of mine, fascinating to Anna at her age and for her personality, and the curriculum offered the structure and writing demands that we were looking for. English was closely paired with the civics and only required minimal reading but had maximum writing practice, allowing Anna to continue to read a lot of her own choosing. The weekly deadlines would give her a feel for what school would require without my having to come up with essay questions and be the bad guy saying, "Finish this by Friday." I wanted to be an ally.

I know she did some of her English yesterday and only has one piece left: to read about weak verbs, alliteration, onomatopoeia, cliches, dialect, and slang. Then she is to write a one page story using these in different paragraphs. She is already familiar with all of them from previous years and asks if she can just mix them all into one story. I say sure. Since she is busily writing, I go upstairs for my half-hour of solitude.

I started this a year or so ago when I needed some time each morning to clear my head and be able to focus on the day. It seemed like I rolled out of bed and was immediately immersed in chores, responsibilities, and mothering, so that my head was spinning by 8:00 a.m. The hardest part of beginning this practice was shutting my bedroom door on my children and telling them not to bother me unless it involved blood or fire. I had never done this before, and there was definitely an adjustment period before they understood that meant no phone calls, no bickering, and no obnoxious noises outside my door were going to get me out. Now, it is a heavenly retreat each morning that they respect while I write in my journal, read something meditatively, or simply stare out the window and just breathe.

As part of my half hour, I brush my teeth and wash my face. I notice that the bathroom needs to be cleaned—desperately. Today is the first day in a long time that we are just home with no errands, appointments, dates, or meetings to take us away, so I take the opportunity to scrub the toilet, sink, and tub. When I go downstairs, Anna has finished her story and has begun typing it on the computer. This is a surprise because she does not enjoy typing, and her previous assignments have all been hand written. I know she has a lot planned for today, and I hope the typing does not take so long that it wastes this precious day at home. But I also know that learning to type will help immensely and so I bite my tongue. This was her choice. I also know she will need a break so after puttering for a bit, I pop some popcorn and make hot cocoa. When she is half done with her page she stops, and we play a game of backgammon on the living room floor (a game that easily leaves one buttery hand free) while fending off the dogs. Then she returns to her typing, while I clean up the kitchen and wash the breakfast and snack dishes. I can hear her laughing while she types; she's obviously enjoying this assignment. The sun has finally broken through the fog and clouds, so I tell her to meet me outside when she's done, and I take the youngest border collie down for a training session on the calves. Anna comes out just as I finish, so we move the horses to a paddock where there isn't so much grass to stuff themselves on for the rest of the day.

By this time it's noon, but we're both still full from popcorn and hot cocoa so we postpone lunch indefinitely. I read Anna's story. She's done a great job with the dialect and other techniques that were the purpose of the lesson. She has not done the punctuating of dialogue correctly, however. I let her choose the pen I will correct her mistakes with: "Just not red, anything but red." Then, I go back to the computer with her and we correct the whole thing, line by line. She's also a master at run-on sentences, so we correct those and other small errors as well.

After some phone calls, I notice it's 1:30 p.m. and time to ride if we are to be done when Anthony gets home. Because he is at school all day, I try to spend his after-school time with him. There isn't much time between the bus and chores. It has turned into a bright, brisk, and colorful autumn day in New England. We spend a little time working the horses in the field, but the day just beckons for a walk on the dirt road so we finish up with that. We get the horses and equipment put away just before 3:00 p.m., so I think there's time to quickly walk down the hill and meet Anthony's bus, but we find both he and Ed are in the house.

Ed has finished up even earlier than yesterday, and Anthony's driver cut off a long loop because some kids weren't on the bus. I ask him about homework and he does have some math to do. This is the subject he is having the most difficulty with in school. Because we have always used a common sense approach to learning, Anthony knows that if you have seventeen chickens in the pen in the morning and only nine are there at night, eight chickens are missing. The school, however, is following state guidelines of forming a "portfolio" of math work, stressing creative problem solving. One would think that was exactly what he'd be good at. But they expect him to write an explanation for how he solved each problem. This is a challenge for a kid who just does it in his head. Also, he is missing a lot of the math vocabulary at this age. "Write a subtraction story using the numbers 17, 8 and 9" loses him because he doesn't even know what "subtraction" is. He knows how to do it, but I hadn't bothered him with the lingo yet, not expecting him to need it for a bit. I think he'll catch up in time, but math is what he brings home to work on and what he says occasionally keeps him in at recess to finish.

This afternoon, he wants to go with Ed to another farm where we are keeping some of our cattle. Ed says he won't be long and we all value the time Ed can spend with either child, so they go off together in the truck. Anna and I make up for our lost lunch with some cheese and crackers while she gets to work on her civics lesson on citizenship. Since I find myself unexpectedly without someone needing my help, I sit down to design the winter's curriculum for the *Pony Club* members: topics, reading assignments, and special activities. At 4:00 p.m., Ed and Anthony return, and it's time for afternoon chores. Ed checks on the calves and sheep outside and feeds the pigs and sheep in the barn. Together, we bring in the ewe needing medical attention. This time of year, most of the animals are on pasture, relying on grass and large water tanks. There is a lot of fencing to do, but not much feeding or watering. Anthony has to water his dog and feed the cats. Anna and I bring the horses into the barn and feed, water, and put them into their stalls for the night.

I ask Anna to help me in the garden on the way back in, and she lugs all the ripe cantaloupes and watermelons into the garage. It's going to be a cold night. We have been extremely lucky by not having had a frost yet, but I think tonight will be the night. I dig enough potatoes for dinner, glad that they will be safe underground until I get around to digging them all and putting them into the cellar for the winter. Back in the kitchen, I put the roast in the oven—it's time for house-warming cooking again! Anna is back working on her civics and Anthony is now ready for help with his math. *Now*, they need my help, when I'm trying to get dinner ready! Of course. Anna has some questions about family history and is wondering when she can ask my father about his father's immigration into this country. I point out the need to read her assignments at the beginning of the week, even if she can't do them then. She needs to plan the time to interview people, request books from the library, etc., before suddenly arriving at Wednesday night and needing the answers right away.

When she is done, she volunteers to help Anthony with his homework—he's gotten frustrated with my help. She sets the table while I prepare baked apples for dessert. By 6:00 p.m. every night, both kids are expected to have picked up the entire house (their things off the floor, couches, tables, etc.), have hands washed, and be at the table. And I'm expected to have dinner ready. Ed comes in and pours milk for everyone and we sit down to eat. We light candles and it is Anthony's turn to read a blessing from *A Grateful Heart*.

During dinner, we hear about Anthony's day at school and Anna shares some of her day at home. From about 4:00 p.m. on, evenings sort of have a life/schedule of their own. We generally finish dinner between 6:30 and 6:45 p.m., and Anthony is due in the bathtub at 6:45 p.m. Both kids have chore charts that are checked off and their allowances are docked for zeros on the charts. Anthony's consists primarily of daily responsibilities like teeth brushing, taking a bath, and picking up. His biggest challenge is timeliness. If he's late, he still has to do the required task, but gets a zero on the chart. Anna is responsible at all of that (and mostly timely), but she has more family oriented jobs. Anthony only has to take out the trash once or twice a week, whereas Anna has a different job every day: combing our one long-haired dog, cleaning the mud room, sorting

---

the laundry, making bread, in addition to cleaning her room once a week. Of course, she also has the daily chores for her pony. And she's also wonderful about stepping in when I'm in a pinch and starting dinner or whatever needs to be done. Anthony is getting much better about getting into and out of the bathroom on time—and, hopefully, he has remembered to use the soap . . . .

While Anthony is in the tub, we three have tea and Ed and I discuss the plans for the next two days. We frequently need to check in to make sure that our schedules aren't going to conflict. Anthony gets out of the tub with time to spare, giving him an extra five minutes reading time. I read *Harry Potter* to him until 7:30 p.m. and then tuck him into bed. During the summer I read to Anna as well, but when evenings are dark (fall/winter), she prefers to do something that involves Ed, since he stays in the house after supper now. Our current favorite is the card game *Spades*. We play until her bedtime at 8:00 p.m., interrupted by phone calls, as everything seems to be. She can go up and read for a short time before lights out at 8:15 p.m. She has always needed a lot of sleep (and Ed and I always feel like we could use more sleep), so we're pretty demanding about early bedtimes. We all get up early seven days a week for the sake of the animals, so the only way to catch up on sleep is to get in bed early.

After that, I make some more phone calls about finding a new home for the pony while Ed goes back to the barn to milk our cow and finish up any other chores. I wash dishes, glad that the book discussion group planned for tonight at the library was canceled. We enjoy getting together with other families once every six weeks or so, but tonight feels like a good night to get in bed. Ed comes in at 8:45 p.m. and takes his head cold straight to bed. At 9:00 p.m., I go outside with a basket and flashlight to hunt down all the ripe tomatoes and cover the lettuce with a tarp. I can't remember how winter squash fares with frost, but this feels like a hard freeze night, so I take a cardboard box and collect them. I have a weak moment of nostalgia for summer and even grab the last of the zucchinis and summer squash. Then I make my last trip to the horses for late-night check of hay, water, and comfort.

It's 9:45 p.m. when I get in and go upstairs. I admire my clean bathroom (walking into a clean room is always a pleasant surprise in my house). Ed is sound asleep, so I take my "Gratitude Journal" into the bathroom to write. An idea taken from the book *Simple Abundance*, each night I think of and write five things for which I am thankful. This ends the day on a good note, helping me not to be so critical of myself and it counteracts my tendency to lie in bed and think of all the things I screwed up or forgot or neglected. Tonight I write:

- I remembered to bring in the garden vegies, in case of frost!
- Anna made scrambled eggs for breakfast for Anthony and me.
- She enjoyed her English assignment today.
- Anthony had another good day at school.

•Ed's two long days weren't so long after all—good for his cold.

Was this a typical day for us? The unusual aspect was that we were home all day. One day toward the end of September when we were talking about how we'd had yet another busy week, I stopped to realize that we are out of the house three out of five weekdays at a minimum each week. That isn't a lot compared to some homeschooling families I know, but it felt like a lot to us homebodies. That feeling is partially due to the time we spend on chores and farm-related activities that shorten the available time we have when we are at home. Weekends are usually more full than weekdays.

To give an idea what our typical week is, I'll summarize the current one.

Saturday—In the morning, I took Anna to Groton State Forest where she met other homeschooling teens from our group for a two-hour bike ride and picnic. This is a new group we've just started this year to allow the older kids in the group some special social time, other than the "play" time we have each week at the gym. They met this summer and planned monthly outings: bowling, cross country skiing, and a pizza party, in addition to the biking and others. After they biked, we hurried home so I could help Ed with some cattle projects, but he had gotten tied up repairing equipment, so I baked cookies instead. That evening, we all went to some friends' house for dinner.

Sunday—Ed and I started early with the cattle: weighing, vaccinating, worming, and sorting into separate groups for different markets and trucking some to other property. We worked through until 1:00 or 2:00 p.m. The kids were on their own for the morning: reading, playing, and drawing. We did have to leave for a while to truck some cattle. Anthony came with us, but Anna chose to stay home. (We don't ask Anna to be responsible for her brother, even though she does baby-sit other kids.) In the afternoon, one of the girls in *Pony Club* came to ride Teddy to see if she could use him some next year.

Monday—Anthony went back to school. Anna and I went to our weekly homeschooling group—our first weekly commitment (it's still weird to go without Anthony). We meet at a gym with nine other families (about twenty children). The kids have lots of free time and some structured activities of their choosing. This week I had offered to show them how to make little felt people out of wool. I brought lots of wool from our sheep, and since the weather was cold and rainy, I also took tarps and buckets of water so we could work in the gym. All the kids seemed to really enjoy it and I had several take wool home to make more. Next week, the older kids (twelve and up) start a project building toothpick bridges which have to meet weight bearing and other structural standards. They're working in groups of two or three. Other things they do are drama, decorating community Christmas boxes, and field trips to museums or plays. This Monday, we got home late (after 1:00 p.m.) because of the cleanup involved with the felting. We spent the rest of the afternoon going over Anna's schoolwork from the previous week (usually done on the weekend but the past one had been too busy) and planning the coming week. The other subjects not seen on this Monday are math and science. Anna is currently working in *Blueprint for Geometry* for math. It's a book practicing simple drafting techniques and she picked it out of a catalog this summer. I thought we'd use it in mid-winter as a break from *Saxon Math* or *Key To Algebra*, but it looked like so much fun that she wanted to start out with it in September. Since the math, civics and English are all set up as lessons already (very unusual for unschoolers to have that much structure handed to them!), that part of the planning is easy. For science, she is working on the *Biology Coloring Boo*k. It has topics set up as a page to read and a corresponding page to color, which enhances memory of the subject. We aren't going straight through that, but pick things that look fun, interesting, and important. Her English curriculum includes vocabulary words to look up, but I quiz her on them at the beginning of the week and she only looks up the ones she doesn't already know. This week, there was only one. For spelling words, I go through her civics lesson and others to pick out words to quiz her on. I write down only those she can't spell. Sometimes, I give up without finding a full ten. She copies them out each day and then I quiz her again on Friday. Any she misses automatically go on next week's list. After we work out her "assignments" for the week, she looks at the calendar and decides on a plan. She fits everything in around our other commitments, knowing approximately how long each will take, what she can do in the car, what she needs access to in the encyclopedias, etc. She then highlights this on her weekly schedule so she can check each day to see what to do. Like most kids with choice, she tends to do all of one subject at a time, rather than a little of each subject each day. Monday night we ate dinner early because Anna and I had to leave for a *Pony Club* meeting at 6:00 p.m. We got home about 9:00 p.m.

Tuesday—We spent the morning in town running errands, including a trip to the regional library, where I limited myself to only picking out one book for Anthony (he has someone else picking books for him these days). Anna picked out books on dog and horse training and a couple for her civics assignment. In the afternoon, we rode and that evening we ate early again; Ed and Anthony had to leave for *4-H* at 5:30 p.m.

Wednesday—today!

Thursday—Anna's baby-sitting day—our second weekly commitment. She began baby-sitting for two boys, aged two and five this summer. When fall came, we all decided to continue on a trial basis, making sure she could stop if it was too much with schoolwork. So far, it's tight, but she's managing. She loves the job and enjoys the money! She's with them from 9:00 a.m. to 1:00 p.m. With Anthony in school, this means I actually have one morning a week *alone* for the first time in thirteen years. It's still new enough to be a surprise each week. I took the opportunity to can all those last tomatoes and to do some writing.

Friday—Ed stayed home and we spent the morning sorting out the ewes who are due to lamb shortly and separated the others into groups for different rams. Friday is laundry day, so everyone had sorted their baskets into community piles for me to throw into the machine as I had the chance through the day. Anna sorts the clean clothes back into each person's basket (she knows better than I do which clothes she has handed down to Anthony!), and we all fold our own. We also went over Anna's work for the week. At 1:00 p.m., we left to pick Anthony up at school for a doctor's appointment. That was combined with a visit to see my parents, which is our third weekly commitment. My mother suffered a stroke a year and a half ago and has been left with minimal speech abilities and minimal movement. She has (through the hard work and dedication of many, including my father, my siblings and some wonderful care givers) been able to return home to live with my dad. We are fortunate that we are only an hour from them and can go down once a week to visit and share some youthful energy. I won't even try to tell you how important these times have been to all of us. Friday nights are our family meeting nights when we go over chore charts and discuss successes or troubles of the week.

If you were to look at Anna's record-keeping page, you could see how she fit her schoolwork in around our running. Sometimes, I think it would be easier to have "school" each morning, but it just doesn't work that way for us. Anna has a good friend she gets together with every two or three weeks for the day, we have obligations to the farm (you should see what it's like during lambing season!), and we usually spend a full day with my parents. All these things are as important to our homeschooling as the books. Anna is a very social person who is doing a lot of work on her own this year. This needs to be balanced with her interactions with others through *Pony Club*, her baby-sitting, her friends at homeschooling group, and extended family.

It's very different with Anthony in school. The kids are four years apart in age, different genders, and have varying interests, so they've never been the best friends that some homeschooling sibs I know are. But they can have a great time with each other—as well as bug the living daylights out of each other—so to have him gone for the better part of the week is a bit of a hole in her interactions. His absence has allowed me to be more available to help with this transitional stage in her learning approach.

With Anthony in school and Anna doing a lot of independent work, (though the preparation and follow-up at this age is intense), I feel a bit like I'm coming out of a thirteen year fog. I guess I wish I'd been a little less idealistic over the years. This last year would have been a lot easier if I had been less defensive about homeschooling being the only thing to do. I rarely spent time away from my kids until the last couple years. They went with me everywhere and I with them (and I do mean everywhere—I used a sitter about once a year). At the time I was very happy with the arrangement and they certainly do not seem to have suffered for it. But when things were difficult, I was so entrenched in doing things that way, that it wasn't easy for me to see that perhaps we all needed a little breathing room.

We are all very relieved at Anthony's school participation; not just because he is going, but because it's successful. I've been a pretty outspoken anti-school advocate; I really believed sending a child to school was one of the worst things you could do to him/her. Therefore, it was a long and slow decision-making process. Thankfully, Ed has been very, very supportive: first of homeschooling and then of this change. He's always been positive about the kids' accomplishments and capabilities, but when the school issue came up, he was very encouraging of a "let's try it" attitude. This softened my concerns and worries. And really, the original part-time private school option allowed me to hold on to my ideals with only a small compromise. The full-time public school decision was made fairly quickly because we had all come to look forward to the possibility that school was "the answer."

I have a good homeschool friend who has also been a great support. One day this summer, she said something like, "Are you just ready to let Anthony go to school? Because if you are, I'll stop trying to encourage you out of it." And when I replied that I just needed to try it because I'd run out of other ideas, her support never wavered. I knew she knew how hard it was for my ideals to be shattered (that I could and should be anything and everything my kids ever needed) so I could vent to her. It must have been very hard for her not to say "then don't do it!" but she held true and has continued to be supportive. Every homeschooling mother should have a friend like that.

I was definitely looking forward to being Anthony's ally instead of the enemy I felt I had become, even though I really asked very little of him. Last year I began the practice, as I had with Anna at that age, of having him pick two cards from an envelope each morning. The choices on the cards were different subjects: math, history, science, reading, writing and "special". On the backs of the cards were the options; for instance for science he could do an experiment from a book, read any science book, do a dissection or microscope work, play a board game like *SomeBody*, etc. My purpose was to introduce him to some regular work time and have some consistent material to present to the state, while letting him pick from any number of fun things he already like to do.

Even so, he frequently was unhappy and unwilling, getting distracted or anxious to be off. I was tired of trying to coerce him into everything when he is a child who needs to regularly be reminded (I try not to nag!) to brush his teeth, sit still at the table, dress appropriately for the weather, and other life skills. It was exhausting. For both of us. For all of us. The friction had worn on Anna, and of course it was not easy for Ed to come home to the tension and try to take over or patch up or cheer up when he had work and the farm as well.

So now a huge weight has been lifted off my shoulders. When I ask Anthony why he thinks he likes school so much, he says being at home was boring. This I just cannot understand. I offered many things that he refused, because he was too busy doing what he wanted. Our kids have never needed to be entertained—they've never had a television in the house, they have great imaginations and have fifty-five acres to run in, explore, and enjoy. Anthony used it all. In nice weather, he was out the door as soon as possible in the morning, begged to eat lunch on the porch, and never set foot back into the house until required to come in for dinner. He has "conquered" and named every knoll, brook and patch of woods on the farm. Maybe if we had 255 acres, he'd still be home! But instead, he is happy to go into a school building and spend all day working at papers and books. Why? I've come up with several theories. One is—please don't cringe—socialization. Because he was such an independent kid, he did not have the close friendships at this age that Anna had developed in her lifetime. He had lots of opportunities, but just wasn't interested. All of a sudden this past year, he was ready for buddies, and school has supplied him with instant ones. He's had to do a lot of learning about friendships in the past few months and the lessons he is learning have improved relationships at home. My other theory is from watching him succeed at writing and math when the school approach has been one of breaking the lessons down into teeny weeny pieces. I guess I am someone who grasps things better as a whole, and Anna learned this way. It drove me nuts to see people try to teach things in parts that were so broken down that it seemed to completely lose context. But Anthony is thriving on this method.

So in hindsight, could I have done this at home? Probably if I had been able to provide lots of friends constantly and had *known* that what he needed was such-and-such an approach to learning (and had taken a course on how to do it!), it might have worked. But we were stuck and school has provided some answers. I have to give tremendous credit to his teacher who has a great reputation and has definitely earned our grateful respect.

I have to work hard not to see this as a failure on my part. I have to remember that I tried many avenues and that homeschooling is still working for Anna and many other kids. But I had run out of ideas for this particular child. I think it's good that he is seeing other kids having to comply with rules and standards. I think it's good that he has other adults to whom he is responsible. It was a huge relief the first time he got stuck on homework and said, "I can't do this!" because I was able to say, "Okay, tomorrow tell your teacher that you don't understand it" . . . and I walked away. I was so glad not to have to try to push through that wall. In short time, he came asking for help, I could help, and he was grateful. Phew.

At the same time, my heart broke the second week of school when he said, "Are you glad you don't have to homeschool me any more?" I tried to explain that I was glad he was in a place where he was enjoying learning and that we didn't have to argue about it any more.

When we first started homeschooling, it was in reaction to negative reports about the public school. But after a year or two of homeschooling, I said I'd still do it even if we had access to the best school. It fit our ideas of a home/farm based lifestyle. The kids could learn from the farm (and did immensely) and they could help out. Their education would include much more than just the three R's. We wanted the real world right at their fingertips. I think what they have gotten so far has been nothing but beneficial. I think they are wonderful people as a result of their freedom and experiences. They have a wonderful base to build on, however they choose to progress from here. If Anthony stays in school, I'm glad he had nine years of real life to grow into the person he is now. If Anna chooses to homeschool through high school, I'm confident that she has the love of learning necessary to pursue further education without the conventional trappings. Of course, that doesn't mean I've never had my doubts! But I try to focus on the strengths at any time and have faith that we'll overcome the challenges.

Anna
Anthony

Chuck, age 44
Nancy, age 43
Noah, age 19
Jesse, age 17
Joel, age 15
AJ, age 11

Five-year follow-up interview with Nancy in York, Pennsylvania

BUILDING CASTLES

Although my health has not been strong ever since childhood, the past year has been a record low for me health-wise. I shook with chills for months, lived in constant pain, and struggled to walk. With my husband Chuck's constant encouragement, learning to use handicapped aids, high quality nutrition, daily exercise and, most important, the power of God, I am now on the "comeback trail."

I cleared my life of every commitment outside of my family. God provided the strength I needed to travel with my husband for ministry and the stamina to teach my children. I could not do anything else—I did not even take phone calls. I put on my blinders. I stayed under house arrest. I worked with my children when I could and rested when I couldn't. I've had my best two years of teaching my younger children during this illness because my life is much less complicated now than it has ever been.

I lived by Elisabeth Elliot's advice to "do the next thing." Sometimes the next thing is to pass out. Sometimes the next thing is to rest. Sometimes the next thing is to teach the kids. The next thing is never to think about the second-next thing. If I can do the next thing, that is enough.

Since God will glorify Himself whether I am vertical or horizontal, a good day is not defined by whether or not I pass out. There are things that are worth dying for. A clean house is not one of those things. During my illness, I preached that truism to myself.

I cannot possibly overrate the importance of my husband's support. He did everything I could not do from packing for our college trips to proofreading papers. Many nights he tucked me into bed early, then stayed up late to fulfill both my responsibilities and his. He wiped away my tears when the pain seemed too much to bear. He drove me to the doctor's when passing out made my driving too dangerous. He remained cheerful and unafraid as our medical bills mounted. He picked me up (literally) and cheered me on (constantly). Throughout my sickness, Chuck cooked dinners, cleaned bathrooms, bought groceries, and did laundry. Sickness forced me to focus more clearly than ever, taught me never again to complain about what I couldn't accomplish in a day's time, provided endless material for humor, and glorified God's strength in the midst of my utter weakness. And, through all of this, our homeschooling continued.

Noah (now nineteen) ended his homeschool career with his usual flourish and flurry. He was selected as a semi-finalist in the *Westinghouse Science Talent Search*. Being the first homeschooler named to the *USA Today Academic All-Star First Team* ushered in a whirlwind of reporters, photographers, television and radio interviews. Along with nineteen other students, Noah was honored at a luncheon at *USA Today* headquarters, then scrambled back to York for opening night of the play he directed, *Hitchhiker's Guide to the Galaxy*.

Noah is currently in his second year at Harvard. He finds college to be "a lot the same as homeschooling, with the big difference that you lose your days in class and do your work at night." It seems to us that he is using the vast array of resources at Harvard to continue homeschooling himself. Noah also enjoys his roommates, participates in a great church, plays on the ultimate frisbee team, and looks forward to being involved in a play again this year. He recently had his proof of *Mason's Theorem* published in a college text written by Serge Lang (a math professor at Yale University). Professor Lang has encouraged Noah to submit his proof for publication in Germany.

Jesse (now seventeen and in his last year of homeschooling) is focusing on Europe in his studies this year: *Advanced Placement European History*, philosophy, European church history, British literature, and Spanish history (read and written about in Spanish). Jesse is fluent in Spanish and American Sign Language, and hopes to study languages in college. A few years ago, he spent several weeks with a pastor's family in Spain. He also did a construction and evangelism short-term missions trip in Belize.

Jesse is one of the captains of the soccer team at our local high school. He plays with students who come from Mexico, Kosovo, Greece, and several different African nations. Jesse continues to be quite active in our local theater. One of his highlights was playing the role of John Brooke in *Little Women*.

Last year, Joel (who is currently in ninth grade) focused on the theme of business. He conducted some fascinating interviews with local people who had established businesses (raising Hawaiian flowers, importing them, and selling them in York; illustrating/designing books, stuffed animals and movie characters; establishing a center for people to design mugs, platters, vases, etc.); he toured larger industries, did business math, read biographies of business people, wrote business plans, studied the science and history of inventions, etc. Joel's year culminated in establishing his own business. "I cover boxes, frames, pitchers, vases, and more, with beads, china, shells, game pieces, jewelry, and other small things. This shard work makes a beautiful mosaic. To represent memories, you would give me some mementos and I would mix them with my items to cover your box or frame. There are so many little odds and ends you could use for honoring someone: buttons from a wedding dress, pins or medals showing various accomplishments, doll house miniatures showing family memories, souvenirs from family vacations, keys to someone's first car, etc. You could buy memory masterpieces to honor people on birthdays, anniversaries, graduations, bar and bat mitzvahs, and other special occasions."

Eleven year old AJ is as feisty and fun-loving as ever. He pursues his interests with all his characteristic gusto. Although he was first chair in the public school's all-city honors orchestra last year, his musical passion is electric guitar. He also loves playing soccer (both indoor and outdoor) and basketball.

This year, Joel and AJ's work centers around the theme of mysteries. We have developed a fun-filled writing intensive program to strengthen their thinking and writing skills. Each quarterly unit is packed with activities that address every area of the curriculum while focusing on reading, writing, and solving mysteries. I am delighted with the progress they are making this year. They are reading independently every morning and writing a paragraph about their reading. They also write about a wide range of topics in their dialogue journals every day. This fall, they did dozens of interesting labs exploring *The Mystery of Matter*. They wrote paragraphs describing things according to their physical and chemical characteristics. They read mysteries with solutions that hinged on physical characteristics of matter. They reread the mysteries until they figured out the solutions, then wrote explanations of those solutions. They each wrote a mystery that was solved through a physical characteristic. Their reading, thinking, and writing skills blossomed.

While I spend most of my time here at home with the boys, Chuck travels a great deal for his interpreting ministry in American Sign Language, which takes him all over the country and has been richly fruitful. As Deaf churches blossom, there will be an increased need for more interpreters to provide Deaf Christian leaders with access to seminary education. Chuck is now strategizing about how to multiply his efforts and replace himself.

Two years ago, we had a homeschool graduate live with us. She helped with cooking and cleaning, and we taught her American Sign Language (ASL). This year, two homeschool high school students will be living with us. We will sign to them, help them study ASL videos, etc. We are considering moving to an area that has a Deaf school and a Deaf church so we can set up a study center to train interpreters. Several times a year, I travel with Chuck. In fact, we leave York any minute to catch a plane for Atlanta. Later this year, we are scheduled to speak at a missions retreat in France. When we travel, Jesse lovingly cares for his younger brothers and skillfully runs the home. AJ sadly says, "I don't know how I'll even live when Jesse goes away to college." Chuck and I feel exactly the same way. Lord willing, this summer we will travel with the three younger guys on a mission trips to Jamaica where we will do construction at a Deaf village.

Our goal was to raise children who loved the Lord with all their hearts. Chuck and I fail to meet that standard every minute of our lives. Of course, we have been utterly incapable of igniting such love in our children. But the same perfect record that covers our failures, covers our children's failures as well.

AJ, Chuck, Jesse, Noah, Joel

John, age 40
Penny, age 53
Johnny, age 14
Jenny, age 10

Five-year follow-up interview with Penny in Dunblane, Scotland

WE'RE DOING IT OTHERWISE

It's now five years since our chapter was in HOMESCHOOLING: A PATCHWORK OF DAYS. We are Penny, John, Johnny, and Jenny, and we still live in Dunblane, Scotland in our old, whitewashed, terraced cottage but it has been extended with the addition of a small nine foot by nine foot conservatory at the back. Here we have our dining table and chairs, computer desk, and a few large bookcases filled with some of our reference books. We can't think how we managed without it!

Johnny and Jenny now have a bedroom each. Johnny's has his computer, a television and video recorder, a table and chairs, a bed (not surprisingly!), and bookcases filled with books and videos, mostly related to *Star Wars* and *Star Trek*. His walls are painted yellow and are covered in posters relating to the same subjects.

Jen's room, in contrast, is pink and blue, and her walls are covered in ballet and animal posters. She, too, has a computer desk and bed and also a low table, toy cupboard, and *Barbie* houses. Herein lives her thriving *Barbie* community —not fashion dolls, but mummies, daddies, children of both sexes, a Brownie pack, and ballet school.

Our house is (we like to think!) cosily cluttered. We now have a multi-fuel stove to warm the living room and our walls are lined with bookcases. In the few spaces between are quilted wall hangings and cross-stitch samplers (made by me) and favourite pictures. We have old-fashioned furniture and dozens of plants.

Sadly, one of our dogs and our favourite cat died earlier this year, so we're down to one dog (Charlie), and three cats (Boo, Toastie, and Arthur). Also, a late, heavy frost killed the spawn in our garden pond, so there were no baby frogs, toads, or newts this year. We're hoping it'll be back to normal next spring.

"Lessons" take place all over the house. Anything that simply has to be done at a table, like craft work, handwriting practice, or baking, is done in the dining room. Our kitchen's too small to fit a table in, but the dining room opens off it. All our reading together—English literature, history, philosophy, religious studies, science, classical studies, Latin—takes place on the living room couch, with me sitting between Johnny and Jenny, holding the book. Johnny does his maths here, too, with his stockinged feet up on my sewing box (large enough to double as a coffee table), his ring binder perched on his knee, and his text book on the couch beside him. Personal studies and quiet reading are enjoyed all over the house or in the garden during summer.

And, speaking of summer, when the weather's warm and sunny, we take ourselves, Charlie, and our books to the Laighills, where a park bench takes the place of our couch, and Johnny and Jenny can relax and cool off afterward by playing among the trees and paddling in the burn (creek). We're well-known to the other dog-walkers who often stop for a chat and to ask how lessons are going today.

Johnny and Jenny (hereafter referred to as J and J!) have always been home educated, apart from the six weeks leading up to his fifth birthday, when Johnny went to school. Six weeks isn't a long time, but I still remember, with a twist of my heart, the misery he suffered there. If I'd looked into the possibility of home education sooner, he could have been spared it.

He was a fluent reader and had been enjoying maths activities for a few years already. He was bored at school and missed me terribly. Then, after sending for information from *Education Otherwise*, I realised that home education was something we could do. During the autumn holidays, I asked Johnny if he'd prefer to continue learning at home with me instead of going back to school. All the tension left his wee body and his face broke into the happiest smile I'd seen since he started school. "Oh, yes, please!" he said.

So I wrote to the Council and to the head teacher, telling them we'd decided to withdraw Johnny from school and resume responsibility for his education ourselves. We were visited once by an education officer who was delighted with what we were doing, so we had no problems from that source. And that was it! For me, no more walking to school holding the hand of a sobbing child. No more being called to see the head teacher because "Johnny wasn't settling in." For him, no more sitting through lessons on things he'd known for years. Instead, freedom to race ahead at his own pace, to read with me, laugh, discuss and cuddle with me—all the things we'd been missing for the last six weeks. When Jen reached "school age" there was no question of her being enrolled. Home education was our way of life.

How we go about things has evolved over the years. Mostly, J and J work together. We read novels and plays together, watch educational television programmes, study history and listen to music. They learn Latin together (we use the *Oxford Latin Course*) and test each other's vocabulary. One of them reads out a Latin word and the other acts out the translation. There is a lot of hilarity when they practice their Latin vocabulary! We read philosophy together and discuss what we've read. The only subject they tackle separately is maths. Johnny enjoys studying maths but doesn't plan on taking any exams in it. He uses, amongst other resources, *Mathematics—A Human Endeavor* by Harold Jacobs. Jen uses *Ginn Maths*, a scheme used by some schools in the UK.

I have most of the responsibility for J and J's education, although all choices are discussed and decisions shared. I also do most of the housework, with help from J and J and their Daddy; work part-time telecanvassing for a charity; tutor two boys who have trouble with reading/spelling/maths, and am currently studying creative writing and proofreading in the hopes that I can earn enough to give up the telecanvassing, which I hate!

John is head of the department of religious, moral and philosophical education (RMPS) at an academy (high school) near here. He is also in charge of the social and vocational skills (SVS) department, so he is involved with some of the academically brightest kids in the school (the philosophy students) and those at the other end of the scale (the SVS students). We adhere to no religion ourselves and John teaches RMPS purely as an academic subject. Unlike some RMPS teachers, he's not trying to convert his pupils to Christianity! One evening a week, he goes to Glasgow University where he's studying for a master's degree in philosophy (he's already studied it as part of his other degrees). He also tends our allotment and grows delicious veganic vegetables (like organic, but with no animal matter such as blood, bone, or manure).

We are all committed vegans and pacifists. This, along with being home educators, makes us feel just a wee bit different from our neighbours sometimes!

Johnny's voice has broken and he's taller than me and will soon be taller than John. He can't imagine any other life than home education. He is clever, exceptionally funny (not always at appropriate times!), and very kindhearted. Jenny is ten and is small and slim with thick dark hair. She, too, wouldn't dream of going to school and she shares Johnny's positive attributes! J and J adore each other and always have. There are occasional "fireworks," of course, but, like real fireworks, they don't last long! Each is the other's best friend.

Jenny is more sociable than Johnny, who's content with a few friends apart from Jen. They're both members of the local branches of *Young Ornithologists*

---

and *Young Archaeologists* and have recently started tennis lessons. Johnny draws the line there. Jen has "flown up" from *Brownies* to *Guides* (*Girl Scouts*) and goes to ballet class and Scottish country dancing. She wanted to join a drama class, but it clashed with Brownies.

Every Sunday, J and J create and act out an episode of "Galaxy Trek." This is their affectionate parody of *Star Trek*. I asked Johnny if he'd like to join a drama group but he doesn't want to act in anything he hasn't written himself. Do we have, a budding Woody Allen here?

Over the years, we've changed our approach from "school at home" (though always following the children's interests) to a much more natural learning environment. I've asked myself, "What, exactly, is the purpose of J and J's education and what are our goals?" and have come up with this: that they should be literate and numerate (already achieved); that they should be prepared for any exams they may need to pass in order to gain entry to University or similar further education and thus have, we hope, the qualifications needed for whatever career they fancy (working on this!); that they should know how to find out about anything they need—research skills, in other words (already achieved—they use reference books and the Internet regularly); that they'll have an introduction to, and appreciation of, the arts—good books, plays, music, paintings.

Because of this last, a lot of our time is spent reading plays by Shakespeare, Oscar Wilde, Aeschylus and watching films of them. We also go to live performances; read classics which aren't necessarily on any exam syllabus (eg. Oliver Twist, which we've just finished and enjoyed very much); and reading the words, discussing the ideas and humour. and listening to and watching productions of both operas and operettas (like Gilbert and Sullivan).

J and J are also learning to play the piano and the recorder, respectively. Johnny is happy to potter away with a piano tutor book and the minimal help I'm able to give him. He doesn't fancy the idea of formal piano lessons yet, but we're working on him! Jen is learning to play the recorder, under my rusty tuition with, again, the help of a tutor book and tape. She hopes to move on to the clarinet or flute when she's a wee bit older. I hope they'll become competent musicians because of the personal pleasure that can bring. I had to give up my piano lessons in my early teens because of the many hours of homework I had to do, each evening. There just was no time to practise. Now I find that any knowledge I've retained was gained after school (apart, of course, from numeracy and literacy) when I studied things (like Scottish history) that were of interest to me. If I'd continued with my piano lessons, however, I'd now be able to play reasonably well. I know, in theory, that I could take it up again. You just tell me when I could fit it in!

People often ask about the social aspects of homeschooling. I don't think J and J will ever be the types to go around with a large gang of friends. They're used to being considered different and probably a bit weird. Like John and me, they're happy with a few real friends and, in Jen's case, other children to enjoy group activities with. Not being at school, Jen is spared, to a great extent, the on/off "friendships" that girls seem to indulge in. She *has* suffered from it from near neighbours. At least she's not having to cope with it on a daily basis. She has a very loving, trusting, and innocent nature, and it would just devastate her.

Johnny is spared the physical and emotional bullying he would no doubt be tormented with at school. Being clever, an authority on *Star Trek* (full nerd status!), and having no interest whatsoever in football is not a recipe for success among your peers in a Scottish public (state) school!

John, as a teacher, is very pro home education. (By the way, this is the term used in Scotland, as opposed to the American homeschooling.) It began as the solution to the problem of Johnny's misery at school and became our way of life. Just as I was there to hear the children's first words and watch their first steps, and didn't have to be told about them by a childminder, so I've known when they first read independently; I've watched their love of knowledge grow; I've shared their frustrations and joys.

When Johnny was very young, he developed a love of the *Thomas the Tank Engine* books by the Rev. W. Awdry. They became a life-filling obsession. He learned how to recognise numbers from those marked on the sides of the engines. He learned the names of colours from them, too. As he got a bit older, his interest matured into a love of railways in general and when Jen became a toddler, he "brought her up in the faith."

One day we heard from a friend that The Rev. Awdry's son, for whom the stories were first written, was visiting a local library. He had now taken over writing the books, himself. When we arrived, there were a couple of classes from the local school there, too. Many of the children had, of course, no interest at all in *Thomas the Tank Engine*, but were there because it was a school activity. A few were genuine fans, probably, but were keeping quiet about it as they didn't want to appear "uncool"! They sat on the floor with their legs crossed, teachers at strategic points to make sure they behaved well.

Johnny, Jenny, and I sat nearby, also on the floor. I was in the middle with an arm round each of them. Every time the author read a passage we knew well or told us an interesting fact, I squeezed their shoulders and they looked at me with sparkling eyes and delighted wee faces, their bodies tight with excitement. It was a wonderful experience to share with them and I found myself wondering about the schoolchildren there. If their parents remembered to ask how the talk had gone, they would be answered by, "Boring!" "Okay," or "It was great!" but it would all come to them second hand.

After the schoolchildren had left, Johnny spoke to the author and gave him a

---

Johnny (14), Jenny (10)

cuddle. Christopher Awdry told him that he was his "special, number one Scottish fan!" and that he'd very much enjoyed meeting him. Johnny was in raptures! That's the kind of experience you can share when you home educate. Anyway, here's one of our recent days:

I wake up at 7.10 a.m., my brain conditioned to expect the usual sound of the alarm clock. This morning I don't really have to get up at any particular time as John is off sick from his work with some kind of bug that's making him very wobbly-legged and dizzy. I decide to get up at my usual time, however, as today is the day I plan to share what we do, and I want it to be as "normal" as possible.

Usually John and I get up at 7.30 and while he showers and dresses I make his breakfast of tea and toast, and prepare his packed lunch. Today, as I head downstairs, I call to J and J and am greeted affectionately by Charlie and our aging cats. It's a very cold, damp, November morning. I let Charlie out into the enclosed area outside our back door, fill the kettle to make tea and a hot water bottle for John, and switch on the computer to check e-mail. There's a nice letter from Nancy, so I print it out and take it up to John with his hot water bottle.

I can hear Johnny tidying up his bedroom. I expect them to do this every morning and sometimes they do! All is quiet in Jen's room, however. I go in and find her still fast asleep. In true *Sleeping Beauty* tradition, I bend over and kiss her gently. Unlike her predecessor, however, she just grunts and turns over. I shake her (fairly gently!) and tell her it's time to get up and if she's too tired, she shouldn't have read so late in bed last night.

I then phone John's school to tell them he won't be in today. Luckily, I hang up just before the post arrives since Charlie leaps at the door, barking and growling ferociously, as soon as he hears the letters plopping onto the doormat. There's nothing very exciting in the post: some bills and the interesting news that I *could* be the lucky winner of a quarter of a million pounds if I send in my claim form immediately! I pour John some tea, make him toast, and take it up to him with a couple of aspirin. Johnny is now having his shower. I feed the pets. There's still no sign of Jen, however, so I stand at the bottom of the stair and yell. She appears, fully clothed.

As far as meals are concerned, breakfast is pretty much a "get-what-you-want" meal. If J and J are having the same thing, they take it in turns to make it for both of them. If Johnny wants porridge, which he finds very boring to make, he sometimes does a deal with me: I make the porridge and he vacuums the living room. Lunch is usually home made soup (J and J tried the tinned stuff once and thought it disgusting!), pajee (not sure of the spelling here; it's an Indian meal of spicy tomatoes on bread), or bread and crackers plus toppings set out on the table with everyone putting together what he or she wants. Dinner is cooked by me, or if I'm tutoring (and sometimes at weekends), by John. I will tell everyone what I'm planning on making and a general consensus is taken. If I suggest spicy pasta, for example, and someone has a real notion for nut roast, I'll change it. If John and I love a certain dish the kids don't like (cauliflower cheese, for example) I'll keep that for Friday dinner, for just John and me.

Normally dinner is a proper, sit-round-the-table meal, except on Fridays. Then we meet John after school at the supermarket to buy bits and pieces (our big shopping is done in Stirling on Wednesdays, while Jen's at her ballet class) and then visit John's Mum and Dad. After we get home, the kids disappear upstairs to spend the evening together and eat stick bread and hummus. John and I have something on our laps in front of the television. If I'm lucky, I won't have too much phoning to do and we watch gardening programmes and some comedy like *Friends* and *Seinfeld* and just generally relax and enjoy the knowledge that it's the weekend!

This morning as we eat, Jenny reminds me that her *Brownie* uniform needs to be washed before Thursday. She has recently been promoted to Sixer and at the next meeting is going to lead some new *Brownies* up to make their promises. She's very excited about this!

After I've reassured Jen that this will be dealt with, we discuss what to put on today's list. Most mornings, on a sheet of paper divided vertically in three, we note down what we hope to do. The three sections are headed JEN, BOTH, and JOHNNY. J and J are hoping to produce a magazine to distribute among family and friends. The first issue is to be a Christmas one and we want it to be ready by early December, so some of their work will be for the magazine.

Today, under JEN, we list MATHS—Ginn; BOOK REVIEW—*The Best Christmas Pageant Ever*; TYPING LESSON—(we found a CD-ROM of *Mavis Beacon Teaches Typing* on the front of a computer magazine and Jen's enjoying learning to touch type. Johnny has taught himself to type like the wind, often with his feet resting on the computer desk, so we're leaving it at that at the moment!); JOINED-UP WRITING PRACTICE; SILENT READING (*Flour Babies*, by Anne Fine) and PS—*Daily Life in a Victorian House*. PS stands for Personal Study. We have a house full of interesting books, but unless they were being used by J and J to specifically look something up, they sat on the shelves, unread. So I introduced what I called "browsing time"—a part of the day when J and J would choose an interesting book or magazine and just browse in it. This has been a great success. The books are being well used and J and J enjoy it lot. Sometimes I suggest they should choose science or geography, for example, if they haven't done much in that line recently. At other times it's a completely free choice. We've changed the name from "browsing" to "personal study." Well, it sounds better, doesn't it?

In Johnny's section today we have MATHS—write problems for the magazine (of the type in Susan Richman's book *Math by Kids*); ESSAY —Christmas films; KEYBOARD PRACTICE; PS—Confucius; PS—Scottish

History magazine and SILENT READING—(*Brat Farrar* by Josephine Tey).

In the BOTH section we have *OLIVER TWIST*, BIRD VIDEO, and LATIN/ CLASSICAL STUDIES.

Because we moved to a different region of Scotland a few months after withdrawing Johnny from school, we are unknown to the education "powers-that-be." This suits us just fine! Home education is legal and I couldn't be bothered having council officials breathing down my neck, checking up on what we're doing. I know we're doing well! However, I do like to keep records of what we've done, for our own interest.

Our record keeping has changed a lot over the years. This is our current method—different from the one used on the day we've noted. In consultation with J and J, I make up a list each Monday morning of what we hope to do that week. This includes subjects we want to cover, television programmes we plan on watching, etc. (some things like historical novels, come under more than one subject heading: English literature, history, and geography). I print them out and Johnny works from this list, noting how much time he spends on each area. This is purely for his benefit, as he feels bad if he thinks he hasn't worked enough. No amount of my telling him that he does far more work than schoolchildren do has had any effect on him so far . . . . Jenny and I make up a daily list for her from the weekly one. She ticks (checks) each item as it's completed. On the back of the weekly sheets, J and J give more detailed information on some of the things they've done. At the end of each week, the lists are filed in a ring binder.

This binder has divisions for the records I've just described, notes on television and radio programmes we follow (cut out from the television channels' schools programmes catalogues), photos of J and J involved in various activities, like YAC digs, art workshops, our writing group, and programmes from plays, etc. These, apart from the typed records, are in clear plastic folders.

Back to today . . . as we finish writing our list, I notice a bluetit on the peanut (groundnut) dispenser in the garden. I mention it to J and J but they can't see out properly because the window has steamed up. I ask Jen to switch on the dehumidifier and we discuss how we think it works. We're not too sure so we look up various books and a CD-ROM, all to no avail. Then I have a brain wave! I dig out the instruction/guarantee leaflet, and there, complete with diagram, is an explanation of what it does and how! We compare the diagram with what we can see of the dehumidifier and then pull out the reservoir. It's amazing to think of all that water being extracted from the air!

Jen starts her typing lesson, and Johnny and I discuss a maths problem (with a Christmas theme, of course!) for the magazine. He then goes off to the sitting room to work on it. Jen moves on to her joined-up writing practice and very soon Johnny comes back to type up his maths problem on the computer. While they get on with their work, I clean out and light the stove, tidy up the living room, and check on John to see if he's okay or if he needs anything. He's reading and would like some more tea and toast when I've got a moment.

Have you noticed a glaring omission in the saga so far? Yes, I'm still going around in slippers and dressing gown! It's time to do something about this! Johnny has finished typing out the maths problem and because it didn't take long, he wants to do some more maths, so he's now doing some work on *Mathematics—A Human Endeavor*. Jen is still practising her joined-up writing. I interrupt to quickly show her what's involved in the next page of her maths book and then go for my shower. I then clean the bathroom and emerge, eventually, to hear Jen practising the recorder. Johnny has finished his maths and I ask him to make tea and toast for John. He does this and takes them up. I sit with Jen and play duets with her for a few minutes.

When Johnny comes back down, we all have a snack of some fruit. Somehow the conversation gets round to the information, offered by Jenny, that rabbits do not digest their food properly the first time, so eat their faeces to be sure of getting all the nutrition they need. Jen is something of an authority on rabbits. She would love to have a couple to keep as pets and has read every book on the subject that she can get her hands on. However, we don't believe in keeping animals in cages, and with a dog and three cats, the poor wee rabbits wouldn't last very long outside a cage! Jen has accepted this and has built a cardboard box hutch which she keeps in her bedroom with two toy rabbits in it.

Anyway, back to the (rather revolting) eating habits of these animals. I say that it reminds me a bit about cows who swallow their food and then regurgitate it and chew it. Johnny jokes, "Well *that's* something to *ruminate* on—especially as we're just about to eat!" (with an exaggeratedly disgusted face). I laugh and say I'm sorry if I've put them off their snack.

After we've had our fruit, I pop upstairs to chat briefly with John, while J and J have a look at the Latin vocabulary for their next exercise. We've just started translating together when the doorbell rings. It's our neighbour, calling to ask if I know there's a pool of oil under our car? I do! She stays for a moment or two and tells me our neighbour across the street has been taken into hospital. While I'm talking to her, J and J are chatting and laughing together. We then finish our Latin translation and read together about slavery in Ancient Rome. We discuss the slavery that still exists in the world today.

Then we don jackets and shoes to take Charlie for his walk. At first J, J, and Charlie run on ahead, and I walk behind, alone. It's nice to be able to enjoy the quiet and think my own thoughts. Our regular walk takes us through the large area of common ground behind our house called the Laighills. There's a burn running through and some benches here and there. Charlie loves it here. He charges up and down the low hills (that's what laigh hills means) in the fond (but, luckily, unfulfilled) hope that someday he'll catch one of the hundreds of rabbits that have their burrows here.

Sometimes our walks involve looking out for seasonal changes and discussing the plants and wildlife we see. At other times, as now, the kids run on ahead, leaving me in peace and quiet. Today, on the way back, they let me catch up with them and we chat about our video tapes of Christmas films. I know it's only November, but the Christmas season is a big feature of our year, and there just isn't enough time to fit everything into December. We make all our own cards and many of our presents. In past years, as Christmas approached, panic would set in and tempers would become frayed (well, one temper would become frayed, actually—mine!). So now we start earlier and give ourselves more time.

When we get home, we settle down by the stove and while Jen has another snack, I read aloud the next two chapters of *Oliver Twist*. We're interested in Dickens' use of the term "homeopathic" to mean very small and we discuss how homeopathy works and the remedies we, ourselves, use. A character mentions stopping payment on a ten pound note and we discuss how paper money is not *strictly* speaking money, but a promise from the bank to pay you cash in exchange for the note.

It's lunchtime! Yesterday I made vegetable soup and bread. I heat up the soup and take some to John. Then the children and I sit round the dining room table for our meal. I tell them about a radio programme I was listening to about a chimp from Edinburgh Zoo and an orangutan from the USA who paints pictures. After that, I bury myself in my book while they chat together. They're *never* stuck for conversation with each other!

When Johnny and I have finished eating, I wash the soup pot and the milk pan from breakfast, leaving the rest of the dishes to be done by J and J. Jen is still eating. Johnny settles down in the living room with *Brat Farrar*. I take up a fresh hot water bottle and some juice for John. Jen is still eating.

I phone a department store to order an audiotape of *Hogfather*, by Terry Pratchett for us to listen to together at Christmas. At last Jen stops eating! Johnny clears the table and Jen starts washing the dishes. Johnny dries them and puts them away.

Chores are done very much on a "who's available and best able?" basis, with most of them falling on me, with a reasonable amount of help from John and the children. No payment is made to any adult or child who does chores, as we believe we're all working together on our own home. If anyone does a job normally outside his or her sphere, a quick hug and a "Thanks, darling, that was good of you!" is all anyone's going to get, so nothing more is expected. I want J and J to have lots of time to play and read, but I also want them to know how to look after a home, so they regularly wash and dry dishes, load and unload the washing machine and dryer, sort clothes, and vacuum and dust. Less frequently they do some ironing, clean the bathroom, bring in coal (not Jen; she's still too wee), and wash floors. Johnny helps in the garden allotment, too.

There are two jobs they just can't manage, however: feeding the pets and cleaning the cats' litter trays (a job that often seems to fall to John's lot!) Having been vegetarian/vegan since birth (unlike the pets), they gag at the smell of dog/cat food (and its end product!), so these jobs have to be done by either John or me.

To resume . . . for the next hour or so I work at the dining room table at my charity telecanvassing job. J and J finish the dishes and then Jen settles down with *Flour Babies* while Johnny picks up *Brat Farrar* again. After she's read a couple of chapters, Jen starts work at the computer on her book review, while Johnny reads about Confucius in our latest issue of *Calliope*. Jen gets a bit stuck with her review, however, so I tell her I'll write out a few questions about the story to get her going as soon as I get the chance. She shuts down the computer and heads for the living room to read about *Daily Life in a Victorian House*.

Once I've finished my phoning session, I make risotto for dinner. Usually when I have a pupil (twice a week), John makes the evening meal when he gets home from work at 3.40 p.m., unless he's on duty at the "homework club" in which case, as now, I make something that can be reheated later in the day. Jen finishes her reading and comes to ask me if she can do a multiplication square instead of *Ginn Maths*. That's fine with me. Our list isn't carved in stone and changes are often made if something takes longer than expected; if we're unexpectedly interrupted; if something grabs our interest and we go off at a tangent; or, as now, someone finds as the day goes on that he or she prefers to do something different. The list is just a framework for the day. It means that no one has to say, "What should I do now?" We decide together what should go on it and it's then up to J and J to decide when they'll do the work, although we obviously have to come and go a bit on the timing when it's something we're reading together. Also, anything that needs much input from me has to be done when I'm not phoning.

While I'm timing Jen's multiplication square (she tries to beat her previous time) I prepare some work for one of my pupils, who's due to arrive at 4.30 p.m. As soon as Jen's finished, she goes up to her room to play. Johnny is now working on his article about Christmas films for our magazine. Once he's finished, he goes up to his room and continues work on writing a cross-over *Star Wars/Star Trek* script he's doing for Jen, who shares his obsession. Now that Jen's well out of the way, I phone to order some Christmas presents for her. Then I put the finishing touches to the risotto and bring in a bucket of coal.

The sound of ferocious barking followed by welcoming whines tells me that my pupil has arrived and is being ecstatically welcomed by Charlie. For the next hour and a half I tutor him in maths, spelling, and reading. Meanwhile, J and J are keeping each other company in Jen's room. Jen's playing with her *Barbies* and organising a guide handbook for them while Johnny's playing on the computer.

After my pupil is picked up, we all have risotto for dinner. John has his in bed while the children and I sit at the dining room table. Johnny tells us about what's happening on the Internet mailing list he's involved in and we chat and laugh together. Although I often read a book at the table at lunchtime, this is not an option for anyone at dinner time! After dinner, J and J go up to Johnny's room and put on a *Star Trek* video. They watch it with half an eye while Johnny works at his computer on a *Star Trek* book he's writing and Jen makes card dolls. I phone a close friend and tell her we won't be able to have her family over for writing group tomorrow because of John being ill. She wishes him a speedy recovery and we agree to meet next week, all going well. Then I start my evening telecanvassing. Charlie asks out and when I open the back door, I realise that it's now very cold indeed, so I bring in the window box from the front of the house in case the frost kills the geraniums.

J and J help themselves to breakfast cereals for supper, and as soon as I've finished phoning, it's time for our bedtime story. Normally we sit in the living room for this, but since John isn't well enough to get up, we all pile onto the double bed. I sit beside John and J and J prop themselves up against the footboard. We're reading *Redwall* by Brian Jacques and are all enjoying it very much. It's a nice mixture of adventure and cosiness, which suits us just fine! This evening, some of the baddies are described as "hooligans." Johnny breaks in to tell us that the word "hooligan" comes from an Irish thief whose surname it was. He loves reading books about the English language and its origins. When he was tiny and asked me what words meant, I often told him their etymology. For example, if he asked me what "unique" meant, I would say, "Long, long ago, the Ancient Romans had a word 'uno' that meant the same as our word 'one,' so 'unique' means that there's only one of them." He loved this!

It's now time for J and J to go to bed. Jen climbs into my lap for her regular bedtime snuggle and we kiss and cuddle and say how much we love each other. Then she has a quick shower and she and Johnny brush their teeth and go off to bed to read. Johnny can read as long as he likes, but Jen needs more sleep than he does. She asks if she can read for half an hour. It's 9.40 p.m. I tell her she can read till 10 o'clock. "Mummy!" she protests. "I *hate* it when you say a specific time!" "Okay, you can read for twenty minutes..." "Thank you, Mummy!" she beams. Hmm. I can't usually get the better of her so easily! She must be tired!

This is now the time when John and I wash the dinner dishes (if he hasn't done them while I'm phoning) and then sit together, reading and listening to music, watching television or, in my case, sewing. This evening I settle down, alone, with my book (John has fallen asleep), but my eyes start to close. . . . I rouse myself to check e-mail, feed the pets, let Charlie out, and get ready for bed. I go to Jen's room to check she's covered up properly. Her light's out, but she's still awake and wants to tell me about some dolls she'd like for Christmas. I talk to her for a wee while and then kiss her good night.

Johnny's still reading. I kiss him good night and then head for my own bed. John is snoring gently. I hope he'll feel better in the morning. He's slept a lot today so that should help. Then I switch off my light. . . .

Apart from John not being well, this has been a fairly typical day for us, with lots of reading together, discussions, laughter, and hugs! That's not to say that we don't have our ups and downs, however. Some days we're so busy that the dishes pile up in the sink and we have to wash mugs and plates as we need them! Other days (or sometimes the same days!) J and J get up too late to tidy their rooms and they degenerate into what could quite easily pass for bomb sites. That's when I storm in, armed with black bin bags, and threaten that I will *never* buy them another book if I *ever* see any lying, face down, under the furniture, *ever* again! J and J, like most kids their age, can be very irritating and irritable, and John and I sometimes get sucked into their disagreements. Then the walls of our wee house seem to swell outwards with the noise, and folk passing by on the street must think they've strayed into an Italian film! However, there are always lots of kisses and cuddles and apologies and laughter afterwards. At least we always communicate with each other and that is *so* important.

Home educating my children is my life. I can't imagine that the sort of satisfaction I would get from any other job could compare with what I've experienced as a home educator. Most parents send their children off to school and then spend their days either in a job they enjoy very much and would hate to give up, or in a job which they don't enjoy but feel they need to do to earn enough money for essentials or luxuries.

I want my children to have all the resources they need and that's not always cheap. However, the only work I can do and still home educate is home-based and that doesn't pay very well. I feel that my main job is working with the kids and that any other (paid) work has to fit in around it. Apart from that, I don't feel I've given up anything, and I've gained so much: excellent relationships with my children and the pleasure of watching them develop and learn. I don't have to go along to a school on parents' evening to see some of their work on the wall and be told by strangers how my children work and behave.

And, of course, on a purely selfish level, spending a hot, summer's day in the Laighills, reading a book with the kids, the sun shining down on us, the burn rippling past us, really can't be compared with spending the time in an office, a factory, or any other place of work. And in the winter, we can substitute sitting curled up by the living room stove while the rain batters against the windows!

Johnny (14), Jenny (10)

At the end of the day, many parents and children are exhausted. If the parents have been at work and the children at school, this means that they're too tired to communicate with each other. Any questions that are asked often receive a monosyllabic answer. We're exhausted at the end of the day, too, but our exhaustion has arisen out of work that we've done together, things we've discussed together.

So often I've heard women say that their husbands are not supportive of home education and that they, the mothers, have to justify everything they do or don't do. I would find that a terrible strain. When Johnny was so miserable in his few weeks at primary school, John and I read about home education, we discussed it, and we both reached the opinion that he'd be better to continue being educated at home. Johnny was part of the decision as well, but his agreement was a foregone conclusion!

When people ask how we integrate home education into our days, I answer that it's an essential part of our way of life. You could ask how we integrate breathing and eating into our life! Or reading books! Our children are growing and developing all the time. As responsible and loving parents, John and I are interested in helping them to grow and develop into the best people they can be. We're just living as a family. Once we had children, we wanted to spend our time with them, caring for them and helping them to develop until they become adults. Home is where the main focus of our life is.

It seems strange when we hear people saying that they think home educated children must be isolated. I honestly believe that workplaces and schools are the artificial environments. It's at home and in the community that we really live. It

John, Jenny, Johnny, Penny

doesn't mean that it's only the four of us, cocooned in our house. We go out. We have visitors. We meet other people and communicate with other people at different levels and by different means (face to face, on the phone, by post, and on the Internet).

As far as we're concerned, home education is a natural way of life. It's natural for human beings to live in family groups and to interact with people of all ages. School seems, by comparison, very artificial. Pupils are segregated by age, and the influence of the immediate peer group is artificially blown out of proportion. Our children have friends, and they know children of all ages, which means their relationships are much more natural and organic. A lot of the time we're learning together and the most important thing we're learning is relationships and living as a family. When people are growing and developing, although what they learn in terms of content about specific academic subjects is important, much more important is how they learn to be people. I think you learn that much better in a family environment and in friendly relationships with others on an individual level than you do in an institution. And that, in the end, for us, is one of the big differences between home education and schooling.

Johnny (14), Jenny (10)

John, age 51
Pauline, age 50
Andrea, age 22
Jonathan, age 20
Emily, age 17
Susanna, age 10

Five-year follow-up interview with Pauline in rural Fleetwood, Pennsylvania

SEVENTEEN YEARS, ONE AT A TIME

What an interesting experience to reread the chapter about our family in HOMESCHOOLING: A PATCHWORK OF DAYS. It brought back so many memories! When it was first printed, I actually avoided reading the chapter because it sounded almost too idealistic. But reading it five years hence, it seems much more accurate. I think that time truly does have a way of erasing the daily frustrations that can assail us, and we remember with great fondness the joy of those days.

Five years have indeed brought many changes in our family. We are homeschooling only our two youngest daughters now. Emily is a senior this year, and Susanna is in the fifth grade. In many respects the "workload" of teaching has greatly decreased.

Emily is an independent student needing only occasional help with questions, and these are largely answered by John who gives help with the higher math and science subjects. Probably our largest investment of time with Emily this year is in the college search—filling out forms, traveling to visit various campuses, and taking time with her just talking about all the options. Even this is much less intimidating because it is the third time we have gone through this process. We are savoring our days with her because we have learned from experience just how quickly the senior year goes. She will likely be working at a camp next summer and then leaving for college, so her days living at home for any length of time are limited to this school year. As it was with our older two children, it is a great joy to see her becoming focused on what she wants to study and do after high school, but at the same time, we have bittersweet feelings realizing that her remaining days at home are so few.

Even Susanna is becoming independent in her studies. She does math, spelling, language, reading, and writing on her own, and then we sit down together to study and discuss history, science, and health. It is at this level that our children began to learn how to study for and take tests. Having graduated two students and seen their success on the college level, we feel that we have gained a much better perspective on what is required on the homeschooling level. There is not so much the need to acquire a large mass of knowledge, rather the need is to develop a motivated and self-directed student who knows how to study, how to find information on his own, and how to communicate both verbally and in writing.

Our two oldest children have done well in their endeavors since being homeschooled. Andrea graduated from Messiah College in May and is now working as a nurse. She is living near the hospital where she is employed, sharing a house (and the expenses thereof!) with a former college roommate. It brings great joy to know that she is a responsible adult and that many of the values and principles we hoped to teach along the way were indeed transferred and are seen in the choices she is making. Jonathan is a junior art student at Messiah College. However, this semester he is studying in Italy with a consortium of art students

Emily, Jonathan, Andrea, Susanna, Pauline, John

from Christian colleges. He is studying under professors from the participating colleges, as well as traveling extensively to view classical artwork created years ago by the great master artists.

So, we are in the middle of our *seventeenth* year of homeschool and are content with the results. Our plan is to continue home education, even though next year Susanna will be the only student! That will seem quite different, but adjustments are not new to homeschooling. Each year has had its unique situations that, through acceptance, have made the overall picture very colorful. God has been our source of wisdom, peace, and joy, and we fully depend on Him to make these next years equally satisfying. We give God all the praise.

Andrea (22), Jonathan (20), Emily (17), Susanna (10)

Brendan, age 39
Sharon, age 43
Katy, age 16
Colleen, age 11
Ethan, age 9
Eamon, age 5
Erin, age 2

Five-year follow-up interview with Brendan from their California military base

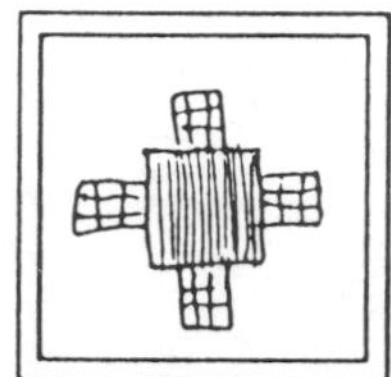

TEACHER DIDN'T SHAVE TODAY

Since you met us five years ago in Nancy's book HOMESCHOOLING: A PATCHWORK OF DAYS, we've gone through many important changes. Most important, we are now a family of *seven* people (Eamon and Erin are our new additions), with two dogs and two cats. We've moved and live on a large military base in California. My wife Sharon now spends her days in *prison*. Actually, Sharon is currently an active duty public health service officer, assigned as a physician assistant to the Federal Correctional Institution approximately fifty miles from our home. Sharon was a navigator for the United States Air Force and the Illinois Air National Guard before going to medical school. In changing careers, Sharon also lost some of the rank she had earned. She is now a Lieutenant, Junior Grade, as opposed to a Major. We also made a not-too-difficult decision to live as far away from Sharon's work as we do because of the cost of living in California. With five children, a three bedroom home is too small and a four bedroom home is way out of the budget for a lowly lieutenant.

What has not changed is that I am still the stay-at-home dad, the homeschooler, and also still an Air Force Reserve officer, although not a traditional reservist. As before, I average one week of duty each month and long stretches of service during the summer. I also commute to my duty assignment that is in Illinois. As you may remember, the time I spend away for the Air

Force is just about my only time to myself. With five children, an over-worked wife, and four pets, I seldom have much time at the end of the day to myself.

When I am only traveling to the Air Force Base in Illinois, my job can be incredibly boring or incredibly hectic. I work at the tanker/airlift control center, which manages all of the missions carrying cargo or personnel and all of the air-refueling missions that make sure that the military cargo or personnel get to their destinations as quickly as possible. My work covers the continental United States east of the Mississippi River; then extends across the Atlantic to include all of Europe and Africa; and also includes Southwest Asia. We do not schedule/create the missions, but manage the missions once they are within twenty-four hours of scheduled departure from home station until the mission has returned to home station.

I travel overseas for the Air Force as well. Since the last book, I spent a few months in Egypt at the beginning of Operation Restore Hope, the military effort to bring food to Somalia. I primarily worked coordinating missions between the United States/Europe and the down range locations where the cargo/personnel were being delivered. On my last trip to Saudi Arabia, I was Chief, Command and Control, for the Air Mobility Command folks at a base in Saudi. Not a lot of interesting work there, just a lot of paperwork being done to run a good command and control facility (command post). My most interesting duty has to have been the time I spent as Chief, Command and Control, Mogadishu International Airport, Somalia. Working with the United States forces there, as well as the twenty-seven other nations providing support to the mission into Somalia was great. Being shot at was an added bonus, although much of the time the attacks on the airport were shoot-and-scoot—harassment firing. Even though we were under harassment fire mostly from people opposed to intervention, I would return to Somalia because of the good we were doing there.

Other more recent overseas assignments have taken me to Saudi Arabia (twice) for several months with brief stops in England, Germany, Italy, and Spain. This type of outside, part-time work is very important to me. Being at home full-time, I am accustomed to dealing with just our children and having little interaction with adults, other than when I go shopping. Being able to get away gives me a sanity check and the time I need to work on lesson planning.

Now, I'll bring you up to date on what we're all doing, how we do it, and why. When I started being the stay-at-home parent eight years ago, there seemed to be very few other stay-at-home fathers. When Sharon convinced me to be a homeschooling father, I was fairly well convinced that I was the only one in the world. I now know that I was wrong. While living in Nebraska, where Sharon attended medical school, we belonged to a large homeschool group that included several fathers who were either the full-time homeschool parent or who equally shared the responsibility for homeschooling. Over the years homeschooling has gained greater acceptance in the community at large. The military, with the frequent need for families to move to new assignments, has been especially accepting of homeschooling, at least from the number of families that do it. This is important for me because I no longer feel isolated as the only homeschooler in the community.

Sharon had already adopted three-year-old Katy from Bogota, Columbia and had her for six months before we married. When I first began homeschooling Katy, she was eight years old and my only student—she was beginning fourth grade. We completed courses through eighth grade and some high school courses at home with Katy, then enrolled her part-time last spring at our community college. Although there are some super high school homeschooling and distance learning curricula available and, although I feel that between us, Sharon and I could teach most of the courses required to graduate, I prefer having Katy at the college. Even teaching just one child at the high school level is extremely difficult, and having three other children also in school would be too much, at least for me. Katy is now a full-time student, doing well in community college, so I see little real need to have her repeat courses that she would be taking at home. Unlike high school, the students tend to be there voluntarily, which I believe leads to more interest in the classes (even the dreaded prerequisites) and a greater interest in success. Katy did well enough that I felt comfortable with the decision to enroll her full-time. She continues to do very well there, taking general courses required of all freshman, along with a steel drum course that she will apply toward her planned-at-least-for-this-week major in music.

Colleen, now eleven years old, was an independent preschooler when I began homeschooling her. Currently, she is doing work at or above grade level in all of her courses except math. Colleen does not like doing any school work; she would prefer to spend each and every day reading books. We have a wide assortment of books crammed into virtually every cubic inch of extra space in our home and some even stored in a storage shed we rented for furniture we have inherited from Sharon's family. Having books available is not the problem; the problem is getting Colleen to read what she is *supposed* to read. Colleen's reading runs the gamut from *The Hardy Boys* and *Sweet Valley Teens* to collections of classics including Shakespeare and Dickens. Sharon and I recently decided that, because we are tired of getting Colleen to read what we believe to be good books, we would get the *Weaver Collection* for her. This course, which we had heard so many positive things about, provides a great introduction to great literature, including non-fiction and biographies. Hopefully, using the *Weaver Collection* will not only improve her reading skills and comprehension, but will also introduce her to more great literature. Lately, I have made her look words up in the dictionary more often than I have in the past.

Colleen did not enjoy dissecting chicken legs to learn about muscles. She kept telling Sharon that the whole thing was "gross" until I pointed out that she needs to practice the skill if she really wants to become a nurse. She is going through the same "I am not going to work on anything" phase that Katy went through at about the same age. Although Colleen and I are frequently at loggerheads, I know that she will eventually outgrow this as did Katy at a similar age. Colleen, as are all of the children, is very smart. Getting to channel that intelligence is a challenge. To keep Colleen interested and working, Sharon suggested that I spend some extra time with her by taking her out monthly to get coffee/hot chocolate and donuts. So we do. I enjoy this extra time with Colleen. It is one of the special times we have to enjoy each other's company and just relax.

Ethan was still in diapers and getting filthy in the garden with me back then. Now that he's nine he loves math. Reading has always been a struggle for him, which has presented a challenge for both of us, so I have pushed him hard to stay on track with his social studies and science.

Eamon and Erin were not even born. Eamon is now a completely train-obsessed five-year-old, whom I have started in kindergarten this year. We are using the *Alpha Omega* books with him, along with a mix of text/workbooks and some computer programs. We are using *Switched on Schoolhouse* for some classes and *LifePacs* from *Alpha Omega Publications* for others. In the past, we have used complete curriculums with advisory teachers and have tried our own curriculum to match each child's strengths and weaknesses. The former was too restrictive and failed to address each child's strengths and weaknesses, while the latter meant too much work for me because I am the headmaster, teacher, bottle washer, chef, diaper changer, chauffeur, head cheerleader, etc. I really like the combination of materials we have been able to pick for Colleen, Ethan, and Eamon. All are highly motivated to work hard on the text books so that they can spend time on the computer.

Aside from the absolutely super courses from *Switched on Schoolhouse*, we have lots of other computer programs, including *Reader Rabbit* and *MathBlaster*, all of which we've had for years and are very popular.

We also have several early childhood programs so Eamon and Erin are included in the fun. (Rumors that I have ever used my computer to play such games as *NCAA Football* and *Andretti Racing* are completely false. So are the rumors that the children do anything non-educational on any of the computers.) Erin seems to get into more trouble than all of the other children combined did. She is into the terrible two's, which explains part of it. My only hope is that she will grow out of this behavior before I go completely gray.

Having Eamon, along with Colleen and Ethan, as full-time students (plus Katy as one of my Spanish students) adds to a lot of work for me. However, I enjoy the challenge (most of the time) and I always know that I will be getting a break when I head out of town for the Air Force. I cannot stress (or repeat redundantly) how important having an outside activity or interest is. Getting away is very important, even if it is only for a few hours or a day. Having a supportive spouse (meaning one who is willing to take the children away or allow you a get-away) is perhaps the most important part of homeschooling.

We also have two dogs, Tom and KC. Tom is Katy's responsibility. He is an almost two-year-old golden retriever, whom we gave to Katy for her fourteenth birthday. KC, which stands for KC-135, the type of aircraft Sharon flew for almost fifteen years, was my first Father's Day present. We re-inherited KC, who was a totally destructive puppy, when Sharon's father died this past August. She is now a delightfully mellow and tame thirteen-year-old with really terrible breath.

As for the final two family members, Rusty and Mystery are completely different cats. Rusty is the dirtiest and stinkiest cat I have ever owned and she is completely antisocial, especially around children. Her antisocial behaviors are understandable when one considers the children she has helped raise. Mystery, a beautiful kitten who adopted our family this past summer while I was gone, has a lovely fluffy tail and understands basic kitty hygiene.

Our decision to live on base has been a true blessing for us, aside from the constant noise associated with huge cargo jets taking off or landing at all hours of the night (they never seem to take off during day time!). Our base is a small town and we seldom have to leave for shopping, church, or other activities. We leave base for no other reason than to change scenery. We are located between Sacramento and San Francisco, so we are not far from a wide variety of activities.

Our home is old and somewhat cluttered, but we do have four bedrooms. We have *lots* of books. We have a dining room table that doubles as one of our school tables and also have the desk and the two filing cabinets which pass for a second desk that we use in the kitchen for some of our homeschooling.

Chores still play an important role in our family. Each child, including Erin, is assigned a chore, rotating weekly. The three older children take turns with either the kitchen, living and dining rooms, or children's bathroom and hallways. Depending on who has the kitchen and/or the dining room, someone is also appointed to clean the grill and/or the smoker, which I use frequently year-round. Eamon pitches in doing lunch dishes, which he actually does well. Erin gets in the way and is responsible for taking the recycling out to the bin. Because of the amount of work inherent with having five children, lessons I learned as a youth living at *Father Flanagan's Boys Town* apply: we all share the chores and we help each other out. I do the laundry and the ironing, but everybody puts their own laundry away. Colleen has to help with Erin's stuff because they share a room. Ethan helps Eamon, especially with clothes that need to be hung in the closet. If the children want things, they must earn them. For example, I have just reminded Ethan that he has to wipe the wall in the hallway where KC rubs herself, or he must hand over all of his trading cards. I have also reminded Colleen that she needs to mow the backyard if she wants to keep the carpenter jeans I bought for her. Both were also reminded that rooms need to be done.

During the week, the children are expected to do the dishes, clean the stove and counters, and sweep and/or vacuum the floor. Additionally, Katy and Colleen, because they are older, are expected to mop at least three or four times during the week. On weekends, the children are expected to spend some extra time cleaning the oven, toaster, spice racks, cabinet doors, dishwasher door, and anything else that needs work. Obviously, this does not always get done, especially when the boys have the chore. Unfortunately, with Katy gone so much to college during the school year, I frequently do her chore for her. I also help whomever has the kitchen by getting the dish drain emptied out, washing any dishes left over from the night before, etc. I also sweep the floor if Eamon is assigned the chore.

As to how the chores are assigned: they are written on the calendar hanging on the side of the refrigerator. I remind each child what chores are assigned every Sunday morning. I have written checklists, which are used about as frequently as Sacramento gets snow. There are no set allowances for chores, but I have set up incentives for the three middle children to earn things for getting chores, bedrooms, and school work done. Colleen, for example, loves clothes, so she earns the "latest" in fashion. Ethan loves trading cards, so those are what he earns. There are no set guidelines for the rewards, but I usually try to make sure that they are able to earn something every couple of weeks, no matter how poorly things have been done. Another way I have been able to get them to do things such as raking or mowing is by buying a much desired item, then offering it for what I want done.

Believe it or not, this system works very well for us. I do not make Eamon wash the pots or Ethan scrub the greasiest of the pans, but I do expect both to do dishes as well as possible. Eamon, who is small for his age, looks rather comic standing on the "time-out" step stool, bending over the kitchen sink, splashing water for thirty minutes or more. I inevitably have to clean up after Eamon cleans up, but he is getting the idea that we all have to pitch in when we are a big family.

You probably notice that Katy is not included in the rewards system. She understands that we are paying for her school books, transportation, etc. She also understands that, because she is not home during the week, I usually do her chore, take care of her dog, and if needed, chauffeur her to whatever happens to be scheduled.

Because we do live so far from Sharon's work, and because she has to be there early, she and I start the day early. Sharon is up at 4:00 a.m., what we in the military refer to as "o'dark hundred." She is gone by 5:15 a.m., after getting the coffee pot ready for me to turn on—perhaps the most important public service a spouse can perform. I usually set my alarm for 5:30 or 5:45 a.m. and drag myself out of bed. I need to get up early because I, like all the children, am a terrible morning person. By getting up early, which is actually an hour and a half after Sharon gets up, but an hour before Katy gets up, I have at least until 7:00 a.m. to load up on caffeine (the only time I have caffeine all day) and become a human being—more or less. I need my early morning quiet to plan my day and get some chores done. If anything interrupts my routine when I am at home, I am a grouch. I have less patience for small mistakes—I am a tougher grader on school and housework. I have less tolerance for extraneous noise from Eamon and Erin. Katy gets up at 6:30, Colleen at 7:00, Ethan at 7:30, Eamon and Erin whenever they wake up. The staggered start helps me a lot, as we are all night owls (except Katy) so our mornings tend to have lots of noise, bickering, and slow-moving grumps and grouches.

Our actual school day starts between 8:00 and 9:00 a.m., depending on how quickly chores and bedrooms are taken care of. The level of chaos is lower than normal today. Colleen has just finished her kitchen chore, Ethan is trying to catch KC so that he can take her for a walk, Eamon is playing in the front yard, Erin has disappeared, Katy is typing an English paper in her room, the two cats are hiding, and Tom is lying on his rug next to Katy.

I write out a daily schedule and a full year's schedule of work for each child, but we need a lot of flexibility. Much of how I spend my morning is largely dictated by Ethan. He is definitely a child who learns by doing, so how much language work is completed depends on whether he is having a good day or whether he is struggling with his reading. On his good days, we spend extra time going over his language and Bible classes. Other days, we spend extra time on math, which he excels in, or science and social studies, which I help him with by reading some of the work to him. I am usually able to figure out if Ethan is going to have a good day or a bad day within just a few minutes of starting his work. I am tough on him and make him work hard, though I do cut some slack on bad reading days. We have been able to keep him at grade level for all of his courses, except for math, where he is above grade level.

Colleen is incredibly patient and helpful with Eamon and Erin. She seems to have an innate grasp of when I am struggling (either academically or temperamentally) with Ethan, and she keeps the others out of the kitchen, where I spend most of my time with Ethan. It does, however, mean that Colleen is not getting as much done as she should.

As you have probably figured out, we do have some structure in our homeschool, but, as Sharon points out, "flexibility is the key to modern homeschooling." Of course, she has a captive audience and does not worry about cooking dinner, since I am the chef. Speaking of dinner, the children get to make requests, which are surprisingly varied. Frequent requests include Jamaican steamed jerk chicken and gungo peas and rice; Thai peanut butter pork chops or chicken; Chinese and Vietnamese noodle salads; Cuban black beans and black bean salad; and Belizean or Lebanese potato salads. Obviously, an eclectic mix. The children also love salads, so we try to have those frequently. And, as final proof that my children are disgustingly influenced by me, and quite possibly irreparably harmed, Ethan loves asparagus!

Our children are very active. Katy swims at the local community college, and Colleen and Ethan have played soccer and baseball for the last two years in youth leagues on base. Eamon wants to start *Little League* next spring, and Erin sticks everything into her mouth that will fit.

When Sharon and I decided to marry, it was commonality of religious beliefs, as much as anything that led to our marriage. That commonality has been strengthened over the years and extended to our children. Aside from the Bible classes that each has taken over the years, the older children have also been very involved in church. Katy had her confirmation two years ago and she has continued to attend Roman Catholic religious education classes on the base since we arrived here, as have Colleen and Ethan. Eamon started this year. Religion and our faith are important aspects of our lives, which is why homeschooling has grown in importance to me. I really enjoy learning and relearning the Scriptures with the children. More than any other topic, I enjoy the growth that comes from the Bible classes.

One of the things that Sharon and I did at the beginning of our marriage (but which we never seemed to have the time nor energy for as our family grew) was nightly prayers. Though we each prayed, it was no longer together nor with the children. We have started praying together again because we believe in teaching by example and because we both realized just how much we missed the prayers and the time it meant we spent with each other as a couple.

I have tried to find some special time with each child. That time is easy to find with Eamon, also known as Yumpy (Lumpy) to my Tickle Monster. We lie down for an hour or so daily. Ethan gets to sleep with me each Wednesday night, after we watch the latest episode of *Star Trek: Voyager*. Colleen and I go out monthly on our "dates." This leaves Katy and Erin. Because Erin is two, I find it hard to figure out when to spend time with her. As for Katy, although I frequently complain about being a bus driver, I do enjoy taking Katy to different activities or to the Base Exchange. These are usually the only times we have to spend alone together, or even talk and relax without the others bothering us, so I look forward to these times.

Katy (16), Colleen (11), Ethan (9), Eamon (5), Erin (2)

Because I homeschool my children, my stress level seems to be very high most of the time. I will usually yell at the miscreant, then send him or her out of the room, but the children know I will usually get over whatever has angered me fairly quickly, except for messy bedrooms, poorly done chores, poorly done school work, arguing, bickering, fighting, too-long showers, or other minor problems that jump up once in a very long while. I am quicker to lose my temper over minor things than Sharon is, but the opposite is true when catastrophes happen. When it comes to school work, I have a lot of patience. I think this is because I enjoy teaching and learning. Though the children know that I will be quick to yell at them to get their house work done, I will spend long periods explaining different subjects to them if they ask.

Our children argue, bicker, and fight. The rooms are frequently messy. The laundry and ironing seem never-ending. The requirements to take one child here and another there means that I spend what seems to be hours driving around. Even so, except for Wednesday nights when Katy has steel drum class and Colleen and Ethan have religious classes, we always have dinner together.

A wise friend told us many years ago, before we married, that sitting down for dinner with the whole family was important. We all learn about Sharon's day and she asks each of us about our day. I wrote about chaos and insanity at the beginning, but there are routines like this that help us all preserve our togetherness as a family.

Brendan, Colleen, Ethan, Sharon, Katy
Eamon, Erin

Katy (16), Colleen (11), Ethan (9), Eamon (5), Erin (2)

Casey, age 45
Nancy, age 42
Ian, age 13
Caleb, age 10

Five-year follow-up interview with Nancy near Bloomington, Indiana

NEVER O'CLOCK

Our little paradise runs well most of the time, but there are a few things that have not worked right, some regrets, and some "hope it turns out okay in the end" moments. Okay, so I'll mention what hasn't gone completely right. I must also tell what has gone well—very, very well—when we knew that the time was right and trusted what we were doing.

Our sons are Ian (now age thirteen) and Caleb (age ten). In our last report, "Never O'Clock," we talked about how our homeschooling consisted of long conversations and nature walks; television and videos; library days and free play with art supplies; curiosity and building onto the house and farm. Most of that still characterizes our learning style.

My husband and I have had some genuine episodes of fear about our sons' futures. We continue to want the children to come to us with what they want to learn, rather than us telling them what they should be learning and when. As someone with a master's degree in psychology, I know the power of motivation. But when Ian didn't read well and was getting to be old by school standards, we started to panic. We questioned what we had done, was there a sensitive or critical period for reading that we missed, what if, what if, what if . . . .?

Then Ian discovered a wonderful card game It was all the rage with the homeschoolers we know from our local support group and Ian wanted in. Now, to play this game, one has to be able to read the instructions on each card. Suddenly, he had to learn some very high-level words in order to play! Virtually overnight (in a period of four to five weeks), he went from very poor reading to the ability to read and understand words like "sacrifice," "regenerate," "enchantment," and "bureaucracy."

I played the game with him, and although some of the imagery was not to my liking at first, the game compares favorably with chess as concerns logic and reasoning ability. Chess is also a battlefield game in which characters "die" and are put in a "graveyard area" and can be "regenerated" (when a pawn is able to reach the far side of the board). There is a store downtown where the cards and other board games are sold. Each night of the week is dedicated to customers coming in to play different games, and Thursday is Ian's night. Ian has been going each week. His opponents are all about ten years older than him—and he's starting to win!

One morning, while watching the *Discovery* channel's *Great Books* series, the Chinese classic *The Art of War* was being discussed. Ian was enthralled. The narrator was talking about how this book is required reading in virtually every military academy worldwide; how, in the movie *Wall Street,* the characters quoted from the book. Ian said, "Can we get a copy of that? It would help me play." So we borrowed the library's copy. We spent a long time talking about the concepts of leadership and what a commander's role is. Now Ian knows he can read and find out anything he wants to know. When the time was right, he learned to read. And Mom and Dad have fewer sleepless nights about it.

Math, in general, is something my kids are behind in compared to schooled students. Way behind. But I take comfort that they know a lot about measurement and angles. It all came together in a time of crisis.

Our house is at the bottom of a hill, and right in front is a ninety degree turn in the road. A previous owner of the property had initiated the placement of limestone blocks (weighing a few tons) between the house and the road. This wall had been smashed into by many cars, but the porch and front room had been left intact. However, a freak accident occurred that collapsed our living room and bedroom wall, destroying a door and a window. We had to rebuild. Instead of hiring a contractor, the boys and their dad did the work. This involved figuring out angles (geometry) and cutting boards and siding to the proper length and angle with a compound mitre saw; calculating square footage of paint, insulation, drywall (measuring, practical math); discovering how much money the family could save by doing it ourselves; and learning valuable, marketable skills such as drywall installation, siding installation, etc. I set up some algebra problems relating to these issues, and the boys understood them. My hope is that as they see the utility of mathematics, they will ask for more. When the time is right, they will learn.

Ian, particularly, is interested in a career in mechanical engineering, architecture, or landscape architecture. For any of these, he will need some advanced mathematics. I'm hoping that the desire to get into a college program will moti-

---

vate him to pick up the math, just the same way that wanting to play the game motivated him to read. Both Ian and Caleb can calculate anything to do with their personal money in a flash and in their heads—so I'm going to trust that motivation will lead to mastery here, too!

Writing. Big issue. I've probably messed up here. Big time. I have not required the boys to put pencil to paper much. Being firmly in the "unschooling" camp as I am, I really haven't required it at all. There just hasn't seemed to be much real world need for that skill yet, although those days are coming. Our local homeschool group had a newspaper club for the children, but that sort of frizzled out. I haven't been able to get either of them interested in pen pals. They have marvelous vocabularies and are very good conversationalists. The boys build whole *Lego* civilizations on what should be a dining room table, but hasn't been used for eating in years, due to all the *Lego* stuff on it. They tell each other stories about their characters, but they have never written them on paper.

I suppose I may have to just push a little bit here—force the situation a bit, although I hate to do that. But the time is coming when they will be required to write down their ideas for essay tests in college; write phone messages; write love letters (girls really like that—hmm, that's a good selling point for writing!); so they will have to develop this skill sometime. I had been hoping that using the Internet to find out information—something they do quite frequently—would inspire them to use their typing tutor program. So far, that hasn't happened. I'm just waiting for the day the motivator shows up. (What's the phone number for hiring a muse?)

We are still doing the tag team parenting thing, although it's more complicated now. Previously, my husband was able to set his own schedule to complement mine. Casey has a new job and my hours are increasing at my primary job so we sometimes have to use outside child care. I work as a clinical and editorial consultant for a company that produces psychological tests and I also teach psychology classes at a community college. My workplace allows the children to accompany me, which is really helpful. The office building is on 200 acres in the country, so they can run around outside, watch videos in an unused office, read books, play board games, or do math homework (that I'm starting to assign). My job is to provide technical support to counselors who use the psychological tests published by the corporation, so I wait by the phone and have a lot of downtime. I also maintain the company web site, but I'm still able to check on homework, talk to them about what they are reading, or what they've just seen on educational videos from the library, or what they are observing outside as the seasons change. They have learned professional office etiquette. They interact well with the staff here, being seen but not heard. However, they have helped out when asked—things like moving furniture, photocopying, etc.

So, the schedule currently is like this: Dad works 7:30 a.m. to 5:30 p.m., five days a week (Sundays and Wednesdays off). On Wednesday he has the kids all day and does things with them. On Sundays, we go to church and have family time. Mom works Mondays, Tuesdays, and Fridays noon to 6:00 p.m. and takes the boys to work; Wednesday, 8:00 a.m. to 6:00 p.m. (while Dad has the kids); and on Thursdays she teaches at a community college. On Thursdays, the children go to the home of another homeschooling friend—one of three different families with whom we have made this arrangement. The other families like having the social time, and it gives my kids a change of scenery, too.

What's gone right with our homeschool? Overall, most things are better than my husband and I had ever dared hope when we started this whole parenting thing. Our children are the absolute center and joy of our lives. We have boys who are kind and gentle to animals, to the rest of the family, to children, or to anyone in need. They care deeply about their pets and about the environment. They have close friends—just a few, but very close. They can work with a group toward a common goal and have demonstrated this ability over and over at home, on sports teams, and at *4-H*. They play baseball on a city league and love the game. They have done volunteer work through our church and their *4-H* club. Caleb has shown a particular skill at taking care of younger children and babies, and he loves to work with me in the church nursery. They both have been in the church choir. They are excellent at conflict resolution, because they have had to live with just each other for companionship so much, that they have had to get along or be lonely. (On one dark day, when they were just getting on each other's nerves too much, I told Ian, "After living with your brother and working out problems with him, just think, being married will be a cinch!" He laughed; I laughed; he figured out a negotiated settlement with his brother; and harmony was restored.)

History and science have been easy. They love learning about how and why things are as they are. We watch movies together and put them into historical perspective. (It's amazing how much history you can teach while watching *Highlander, the Series* or drawing parallels to human history on *Babylon 5*.) For example, we watched the movie *The Tuskegee Airmen* last Veteran's Day. We talked about why it was such a big deal for Eleanor Roosevelt to be photographed as a passenger on a plane flown by a black pilot; why the armed forces were segregated, and why President Truman later changed this policy; how the Tuskegee airmen, having a perfect record of never losing a bomber in their care, earned respect by good performance; why racism is such a bad thing, and how it has hurt people they personally know, like, love, and trust. When they need to know, they ask; when it's important to them, we know the time is right to give the information.

They know how to ask for help and receive it. Ian took a class to become a

Nancy, Calcb, Ian, Casey

certified babysitter. This *American Red Cross* class was for anyone in the community, and he learned some basic first aid, how to price his services, how to keep records for the parents, etc. Each of them knows how to get a librarian to help them search for a book, video, or music recording if they are having trouble finding it through the computerized card catalog. They make their own purchases in stores. They know how to be polite in virtually any community setting.

They have lots of practical skills. Dad's new job is managing a store that rents equipment—chain saws, backhoes, things of that sort. He can bring home these tools for free if no customer is using them, so the boys are learning to run heavy equipment. (I draw the line at chain saws and log splitters, but backhoes are *so cool!*) This is a real world skill that earns significant money—go for it! They can prepare meals and shop for food. They know how to do laundry. They can take care of plants and animals. They use field guides to identify the plants, animals, and insects they find. They do *4-H* projects that require close attention to following instructions, satisfying arbitrary rules, and meeting deadlines.

We are very active with a local inclusive homeschooling support group. This group, which accepts members of any religious background, sponsors many educational events throughout the year. The boys have gone on great field trips with their homeschooling buddies. They have participated in the Science Fair, Biography Fair, and International Fair each year so they know how to do a presentation in front of a group. They have watched their mom set up events and negotiate with museums and other teachers in the community to enable a class or a guided tour happen. They see that there must be something in it for everyone, or the event will not work out well. They are punctual and understand why this shows respect to everyone else.

Yeah, my kids could be farther along in some of the basic academic skills. But they are better behaved and more friendly, cooperative, curious, and just plain alive than most of the people I know—of any age. When they need to come through for us, they always have. My husband and I are seeing the fine young men they are growing into. If it ain't broke, don't fix it. From our point of view, our lifestyle ain't so broke that it can't be lived with. So we will grease it up here, tighten it down there, touch up the paint, and add a few nails—it runs just fine, after all.

Ian (13), Caleb (10)

Clifton, age 42
Edris, age 41
Jason, age 19
Tracy, age 17

Five-year follow-up interview with Edris in Reading, Pennsylvania

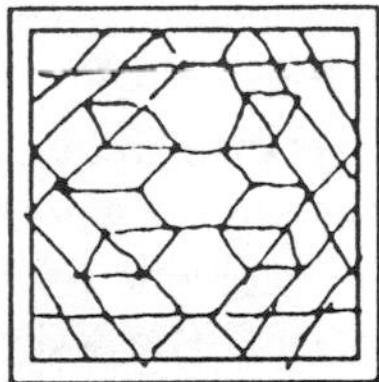

HECTIC BUT ORDERLY

The first fifteen years of my life were spent in Trinidad and Tobago. During a time of drastic change, age fifteen, I moved to the United States. Circumstances allowed me to live with my grandmother and later my uncle and his wife who were all Christians. I learned many life principles at my uncle's home—that is where I decided that if God ever blessed me with children, I would be a stay-at-home-mom. I saw my aunt's contentment in raising her family at home and appreciated the simplicity. And, yes, it was hard work.

Clifton and I decided to homeschool after we realized that our public school offered progressive education—socialized education. We had enrolled Jason in our local public school, and some time after the enrollment, I started to feel uneasy about our decision. The Holy Spirit was definitely doing a work in me. I went to our Pastor to inquire why their children were not in public school. After telling him that we had a single income and that we could not afford Christian school, he referred me to another family in our church who had decided to homeschool. That was the beginning of our thirteen year quest for a Christian education at home.

We live in a neighborhood with different races and desired to raise our children "color-blind." When Jason was in tenth grade, he and I did a presentation at a local college on homeschooling. The instructor was intrigued by what he called our strong desire for success. I attribute that to the fact that both Clifton and I spent the first fifteen years of our lives in another culture. A culture that was not as affluent nor had as many opportunities as the one we now know. I do not ever remember any distinction being made about our family, even when we were the only black family in our homeschool group. We have never made (nor experienced) race or skin color an important issue in our family.

Since our "day" five years ago, the only constant in our lives today is change. This past summer, instead of planning curriculum for the new school year, I was busy working full time. Jason, our first-born, was preparing for college. Tracy was enjoying her first job and preparing to attend a Christian school for the first time. Meanwhile, Clifton was anticipating returning to school at a local technical school. Our townhouse was (and still is) on the market as we anticipate moving—some day.

My return to full time employment outside the home was something we expected. We planned that time to coincide with Jason going off to college because of our increased financial responsibility.

Clifton returned to school—he enjoys working with computers and we felt that the time was right for him to get some formal training. He is studying to become a network Internet technician. His desire is to become certified, so there is a need for some formal schooling before the certification exam. He currently does everything from setting up computers to repairing them. Over the years, he has also "dummy proofed" our computer so I can use it without much frustration. He gained his computer literacy from reading and hands-on training on his own—a simple utilization of the homeschooling concept. He now programs the numerical controlled machines for a small machine shop where he used to work as a machinist. We are not sure if we will want to be involved in our own business or do consulting when he is finished with school.

Homeschooling has been wonderful for our family. Jason is now a freshman at Geneva College in Beaver Falls, Pennsylvania. Jason has had no problems fitting into dorm life. Students still tease him about how normal he is for being homeschooled through high school, jokingly. There are quite a few students at Geneva who were homeschooled. (You may wonder if his campus is mostly white. It is, and I cringe even as I think about that, because it seems so abnormal for me to think that way. Again, we have not made it an issue to have our children in groups that are all black. Actually, our church has had only one Black family for nineteen years—us!)

With a dual major, he will be very busy for the next four years. He chose aviation/business so he could pursue a career as a commercial airline pilot. This love for flying started many years ago. Since he was about four years old, every day at nap time I had to read his Snoopy book about flying. All during his homeschooling he was focused on flying. Two opportunities to take control of an airplane and a glider only cemented his dream. Jason spent many hours playing a flight simulator game on our computer, drawing airplanes, and reading about flying. The two—Jason and flying have become inseparable. Due to the high cost of becoming certified as a commercial airline pilot, Jason has decided to become an air traffic controller, which requires him to get his private pilot's license. Sometime in the future he will continue the necessary qualifications for his commercial license.

Even though it was initially difficult to adjust to Jason leaving home, I am resting in the fact that Clifton and I did the best we could, raising him with a Biblical worldview. The day we dropped him off, it rained heavily on our trip back from Geneva College, so our intense attention to the road meant there wasn't much time to think about the our decreased family size—I was too concerned about those eighteen wheelers alongside us on the Pennsylvania Turnpike. However, after we got home, I felt an emptiness. It was as if someone took away a prized possession. It became almost as wet inside our house as it was outside. Fortunately, I had vacation that week. The following few days were like a grieving period. After about one week, I became used to the idea that our son made his first big step to independence. Now, as a young adult, he must make his own choices and personalize his beliefs. He is only five hours from home, so we see him fairly frequently.

Tracy is adjusting well academically at the Christian academy where she is in eleventh grade, I planned her homeschooling curriculum so that the transition would be easy if she ever had to go to school. I slowly took her from being a non-textbook student to one who used only textbooks. The same subject that she hated at home, she still hates and does poorly in at school. She is on the varsity basketball team and is excited about being able to play for a school, finally.

I am currently working for a local bank in the call center. I started working outside the home over a year ago as a bank teller when Jason was finishing his homeschooling and Tracy was in tenth grade. Even though I only worked part-time, it was very hectic. This past spring, I took a full-time position. I am currently enrolled in an associates degree program in accounting at a local correspondence school. Initially, I was supposed to return to school when the children were finished with homeschooling, but I need to work to help Jason with college. For us, raising our family comes before completing our education.

I started working while both children were being homeschooled because the opportunity was there. We had discussed the possibility of me returning to work, but did not set a specific time. The position of a part-time teller was available close to home, the children were independent learners, so I applied for it. In retrospect, that was a good decision because the teller experience prepared me for what I am doing now at the call center.

I have a good sense of satisfaction to see our children as young adults making decisions and attempting to live for the Lord. He has blessed us tremendously over the years. I would advise black (*all!*) families to focus on educating their children and raising them without a focus on who they are, but on what God can do through them.

Jason (19), Tracy (17)

Those lazy evenings and leisurely suppers together as a family when the children were younger have been traded in for a more hectic lifestyle. Even though I have my moments of longing for the life of a stay-at-home-mom, I am appreciating the changes in our family. We are experiencing many things for the first time: a child in college, one in Christian day school, a working mom, and Clifton and me both in school. I see this as just another season in our lives and accept each day's challenges knowing that God is in control.

Jason, Edris, Clifton, Tracy

Frank, age 52
Sandi, age 52
Brianna, age 21
Christian, age 15
Dmitri, age 13
Svetlana, age 10 1/2

Five-year follow-up interview with Sandi and Brianna in Eagle River, Alaska

UNCOMMONLY FLEXIBLE

BRIANNA: The past five years heralded many changes, tribulations, and much growth in our family since we were in HOMESCHOOLING: A PATCHWORK OF DAYS. We still live on our mountain in Alaska with our bears, moose, wild birds, horses, and house pets. We have pared down to two horses, two dogs, two house cats, two barn cats and a few fish. We are Frank and Sandi (Dad and Mom), Brianna (Breezy, age twenty-one), Christian (age fifteen), Dmitri (age thirteen), and Svetlana (or Svet, age ten and a half).

SANDI: We'll start with an overview of just what some of those trials have entailed and how homeschool is still our favorite choice for educating our family!

BRIANNA: A little over three and a half years ago, Mom developed a very rare heart problem. The main artery to her heart ruptured spontaneously, and the blood flow was 98% blocked. There are only 120 recorded cases of this in American literature and it is usually fatal. Through the miraculous healing power of our awesome Lord, she recovered without surgery after three months. The doctors were astounded. There had been only one case where a woman healed without surgery, and it took over a year! Even after her heart healed, Mom was still very sick from all her medications. Dad said she looked like she'd been in a concentration camp. She is 5' 5" and weighed barely a hundred pounds. I took over being "Mom" for almost two years while Mom was in and out of the hospital and going through menopause at the same time.

SANDI: Between my heart medications and menopause symptoms, I had chronic, intractable nausea, weakness, and severe depression—something I had never before experienced.

BRIANNA: I learned firsthand how much work mothers have to do! Mom is doing much better and right now is learning the virtue of patience in working with our two youngest. Being "Mom" for over a year and a half was a very interesting and valuable experience. The hardest part of that time occurred when Mom came home from the hospital. I kept switching roles. For a while I was the parent. Then a few minutes later I'd be the child again, then back to being a parent. I never knew who was in charge. While she was in the hospital, I took over most of her tasks as a mother. Because Dad's job at the emergency room has extremely erratic hours, and since he was so concerned about Mom, he wasn't around very much. Therefore, most of the family responsibilities fell to me. Here's a partial list of my duties: I planned and cooked the meals, did the laundry and grocery shopping, taught the kids and chauffeured them to their various activities and medical appointments, took care of our menagerie of animals with Christian's help, visited Mom at the hospital, and also finished my own high school work. Parts of it I loved, especially being in charge! It also drew me much closer to my brother, Christian. Prior to that, he and I didn't have a close relationship, but we bonded during this time and are now great friends! Being "Mom" prepared me in many ways to know how to handle my own family when the time comes. It was very beneficial. How many people get to practice being a parent with a ready-made family?! Now, when I start a family of my own, I will have a small idea of what to expect. It might even be easier as I probably won't start out having three children!

In the middle of Mom's illnesses, about two and a half years ago Dad was diagnosed with Multiple Sclerosis. Again, with God's gracious intervention, he is doing well on a special diet, daily exercise, weekly shots, and he is still able to work full-time in the emergency room. He has also been able to fulfill opportunities to teach about creation vs. evolution in various churches around the country, something he thoroughly enjoys.

SANDI: Grandpa and Grandma (Frank's folks) were lifesavers. They flew up from Oregon two or three times over those years to take care of us for a week or two at a time. At one point during the first "summer of siege," we hired an eighth grade student three days a week for a couple of months to come in and help Brianna and me by doing schoolwork with Dmitri and Svetlana. The next summer we had numerous self-sacrificing, loving friends and families from our church take care of them four to six hours a day, five days a week, for five weeks. They also brought in meals during some of the most difficult months. Frank kept everyone updated on our family's struggles through e-mail, and people around the world were praying for us. At times, I was so low I didn't think I could hang on any longer. All I could do was sob and cry out to the Lord for help before I went under. Emotionally, I was a disaster. I clung to God and literally put one foot in front of the other at a snail's pace for nearly two years. He held us all together; there is no other earthly explanation for our survival.

Since Brianna is so much older and more mature, and because we had and have been training the younger ones to respect their older siblings' authority, the transition from Brianna being their sister to being their "Mom" throughout this time was fairly natural. During the weeks that they went from home to home at our close friends', it was much more difficult for Dmitri and Svetlana. It was easier for them to be at home, but the rest of the family required the respite.

BRIANNA: Through all of this, I was still able to graduate from high school at home three years ago in May. I have worked for the past two summers in Missouri at a Bible camp. It is a camp for children who have either one or both parents in jail. I have had the privilege of leading many children to Christ. When I went back this past summer, I was able to see some of the same children that I'd had last year and was able to see the change their belief in Jesus had made. I still take piano and voice lessons and am a leader in our church youth program, *AWANA*, where I work with girls in third and fourth grades.

Last year I worked as a computer teacher for a small Christian school in Anchorage. I taught kids from preschool through eleventh grade. It was a wonderful experience and I learned a tremendous amount. Soon, I will be attending college and plan to pursue a major in history or English and minor in vocal music.

SANDI: The "firstfruits" of our labor of love in homeschooling is a godly, beautiful (both inside and out) young woman with a servant's heart, a joyful spirit, and bubbly personality! Having her away at college will be very hard for us all, especially me. My heart will ache, though I am confident the Lord will help me adjust. God has used her so much in keeping us all glued together that it will be like learning to function minus a major appendage.

BRIANNA: Christian is now in ninth grade and much taller than the rest of the family! He has become an excellent runner, and is in a running club that meets twice a week. He has won many awards for his running skills. He takes piano lessons (along with me), is learning to play the French horn, and keeps busy with all his schoolwork. He uses *BJU* (*Bob Jones Unuiversity*) for English, history, Bible, and science. He is taking Spanish through a wonderful foreign language program called *Power Glide* and in January, hopes to begin *Artes Latinae*. For algebra, he is using *Video Text Interactive*. Last year he started a writing club for some of the homeschoolers in our church. He also writes monthly for our church newsletter.

SANDI: Free-lance writing is something both our older children enjoy and not long ago Christian started working on his first book. In *AWANA*, he is a Leader in Training for his third year. With his older sister and dear friend going away to college soon, Christian will miss Brianna deeply but will, undoubtedly, rise to the occasion and fill in many of the gaps by helping our family in whatever ways God leads him.

BRIANNA: Dmitri (adopted from the former Soviet Republic of Georgia) will soon be thirteen and has been in our family for four years now. Svetlana (adopted from Moscow) is ten and a half, and has been with our family for five years. They both have a lot to catch up on and can challenge our thinking!

SANDI: We are seeing a definite, gradual improvement in Svet's behavior as the years go by. Dmitri is also doing better, but they can both still be trying and frustrating. We pray that by keeping well-defined boundaries, they will function well on their own as they get older. Because of our family health problems and all the difficulties encountered with adopting older children, we believed it was best not to follow through with the adoption of the thirteen year old Russian girl that was mentioned in our previous chapter in HOMESCHOOLING: A PATCHWORK OF DAYS.

BRIANNA: For their schooling, Dmitri and Svetlana used *PACES* (workbooks from School of Tomorrow, *Accelerated Christian Education*) last year.

SANDI: I am now utilizing a more "hands-on" approach and supplementing with Bible reading and discussion, reading *A Beka* science and history to them, letting them read to me, practicing writing with *Learning Language Arts through Literature*, and trying out *Power Glide Children's Spanish*.

BRIANNA: For math, they continue to use *PACES*, plus many hands-on things that Mom creates. They have started taking piano lessons, which they really enjoy, and spend a great deal of time "helping" Dad cut down dead trees, chop and haul wood, and burn brush this time of the year (fall).

Brianna (21), Christian (15), Dmitri (13), Svetlana (10 1/2)

SANDI: Already, they're shoveling snow from the driveway as well. They both love to be helpers in all our household activities, indoors and out. Homeschooling is truly the best option for them. One of the things we struggle with most is not lack of wisdom or knowledge, but putting what we do know into practice—with patience. To be lovingly firm and gentle without getting angry is the area in which I have the greatest battle.

Looking back, we are so thankful that God led us to homeschool our children right from the beginning. It has been, and continues to be, an invaluable learning process for each of us. We are developing an understanding of how to meet each other's needs and truly love one another. None of it has been easy, but it has taught us life's most important lessons: to pray diligently, to read God's word daily, and to spend time getting to really know our Heavenly Father so that we have a hope and a future. Because of Him, we have a hope and a future—eternal life through our Lord Jesus Christ.

Frank, Sandi, Brianna, Christian
Dmitri, Svetlana

Brianna (21), Christian (15), Dmitri (13), Svetlana (10 1/2)

Gregg, age 41
Louise, age 41
Stuart, age 15
Katie, age 13
Martha, age 11
Sarah, age 11
Lydia, age 10
Virginia, age 8
Oliver, age 5

Five-year follow-up interview with Louise in Gardners, Pennsylvania

NOTHING IS EVER CONSTANT

Many things have changed as the children have grown, and so has our homeschooling venture. We now are homeschooling seven children: Stuart is fifteen; Katie is thirteen; Martha and Sarah are eleven; Lydia is ten; Virginia is eight; and Oliver is five.

Some things haven't changed, though. Gregg is still working and pastoring a small church in a local community. He is very involved in our activities. He oversees Stuart's debate team, and he enjoys participating in science lab work. We plan our daily run around his schedule, so that he can run with us every day. Gregg is much faster and usually "runs circles" around the rest of us. We also still live in Gardners, Pennsylvania—the heart of apple country.

Stuart is working pretty much on his own. He is planning on college in his future but is unsure exactly what and where or how. Therefore, he is following a highly rigorous academic program. He is using textbooks for most subject areas. His particular interests include United States history and foreign languages (Spanish and Latin). Stuart is using the *Advanced Placement* (AP) guide by Barrons as an outline to follow for a history course. He is reading through Clarence Carson's volumes on United States history. He has also watched the video lectures from the *SuperStar Teachers* (from The Teaching Company) a video series about geography in United States history. He uses the teacher's guides as jumping off places for reading assignments and essays. He is thinking of taking the Advanced Placement exam in the spring, and if not that, at least the SAT II exam on U. S. history.

Stuart also enjoys foreign language studies. He won an honor award in the first level of the *National Spanish Exam* last year and he intends to take the second level this year. He has used the *Destinos* program for many years and he loves it. He also visited Mexico two years ago and really got first hand experience with the language. This past summer he worked with migrant Mexican workers and was able to practice speaking and translating for the fruit farmers. Stuart first worked along with the migrant workers as a picker, and he was able to speak and learn a lot of vocabulary that way. Then he realized that the grower they were working for knew no Spanish and had a difficult time communicating, so Stuart offered to translate. At the same time, he began visiting labor camps in the evenings with a translator and public health official, informing the Mexicans about services that were available, green cards, etc. He learned a lot about the culture and translating through this experience. He has also excelled in Latin and he hopes to take the *National Latin Exam* this year.

Stuart has been working hard this year with a partner for a debate team. He plans to enter a debate team competition sponsored by the *Homeschool Legal Defense Association.* As a diversion from his academics, Stuart enjoys playing chess. He has a chess tutor and he goes to many tournaments. His rating is improving with each tournament he participates in.

Katie is also doing many activities on her own. She uses some textbooks and participates in all the usual activities including the *National Geography Bee*, the *Scripps Howard Spelling Bee* (that she won last year and went to the regional level), *MathCounts*, and the *National Piano Teacher's Guild Auditions*. Her real strength lies in writing. I am trying to help her develop her style and increase her vocabulary. She would like to work toward taking the AP English composition exam during her high school years. She has had stories written for *Stone Soup* magazine and various other children's magazine. We have a little family newsletter called *The Outlook* that we have been doing for seven years, and Katie is the most prolific and also the most humorous writer of them all. We started it when Stuart was eight. It has book reviews, essays, editorials, poems, real news flashes from our farm, as well as our very famous classifieds and personal columns. We send it to other homeschoolers who exchange newsletters, neighbors, old friends who have moved away, and relatives. We actually have quite a following. People now send us unsolicited subscriptions and stamps.

Katie uses a *Bob Jones University Press* textbook for science. She has been studying world history using *Greenleaf* guides for many years. She is studying the Middle Ages at present. She reads many books on the period. She just finished reading aloud *Macbeth.* She also uses *Jacob's Algebra I.* For all other subjects she uses primary sources. She is a prolific reader and reads many real books.

Katie also enjoys music. She plays the piano, guitar, and recorder. She plays many songs with her sisters, as they all play either the guitar, recorder, piano or lap harp. Katie and all the other girls sing together as an a cappella group. They have sung for many community activities and programs. They sing mostly quartet and trio style.

Katie is not at all sure yet about college. She is likely to try some courses via the Internet, but she doesn't have any definite college plans. I am still keeping her on a college prep program since I know she is capable of the work.

My younger children are my elementary "school." If you remember from HOMESCHOOLING: A PATCHWORK OF DAYS, Martha had incredible difficulties learning to read. She became a "reader" at age nine. She still has difficulties tracking and following, but now she can read and understand without too much trouble. What was the secret to her finally getting it? Time and patience was the answer. I gritted my teeth and listened to her stumble through stories. She read quietly, and I asked questions for comprehension. Now she enjoys reading books if I pick them for her. She is afraid to pick books for herself—fearing she won't be able to finish them if they are too long and too difficult. She is fearful of being misled by a pretty cover or one of her sister's recommendations. She always asks me if I think she will like a book. I know what kind of books she likes: biographies and some adventures—but nothing unbelievable or fantasy. If Martha has free time, she is not going to pick up a book and read. Reading is fine if I require it, but not for free time. During Martha's free time she loves to play "farm" with Oliver or dolls with Virginia and Lydia. She also enjoys singing and playing the guitar. She has an excellent ear and sings second soprano beautifully. She has created potpourri for her grandmother's craft business. She loves making them in her own little "shop" (a corner in our computer room). She bought all the ingredients and she keeps track of the overhead and expenses. She is probably not going to realize any profit this year, but she will have paid back all her original outlay. She is planing to make money next season. She loves to creatively display them at shows. She also makes lye soap using many different oils and textures as well.

Sarah is very good at math and is an avid reader. She is also quite good at writing and I am encouraging her to sending in stories to *Stone Soup* magazine. Sarah is particularly good at running. You would hardly believe it, but our family runs every day, except Sundays. We run about three miles each day. We enter 5K races in our area just to keep us motivated. Sarah is always a winner in her age group and sometimes even a top winner for overall women. Most of my children do not really care about running that much, but I thought it would be excellent physical education that we could consistently do together. (It is also good to keep away the middle age bulge.) They did not always like running with me. We try is make it creative and different. We live near the Appalachian Trail and also two state parks, so we can run through them when we want to. An added inspiration for their running is that the girls enjoy collecting aluminum cans along the way. The younger ones like to see which cans are most popular. The older ones collect the cans, take them to a recycling center, and send the proceeds to an Indian man who has an orphanage for deaf children in India. They never like to travel the same road twice in one week so we are always trying to find new courses close to home. Sarah is particularly good at running and she gains self-confidence, as she is probably the shiest and most quiet of my children.

Lydia, Virginia, and Oliver all enjoy their studies and reading. They also enjoy watching the videos and listening to the tapes from the lessons that their older brother and sisters use. They are ready partners for lab experiments and projects. The younger ones are so anxious to begin. They can't wait to read *Frog and Toad*, color in *Bible Stories to Color*, and read *Your Big Backyard*. The older ones always were looking to finish and go play, while the younger ones want to keep going. The older children were always battling interruptions, baby's feeding time, toddler's potty training, etc. The younger ones rarely have those kinds of interruptions.

My thoughts and focus have changed from less group activities to more individual experiences. As the children got older, their interests and abilities began to show up. For example, although music is essential for any high school education, for Stuart it is only necessary to do the bare essentials. For Katie, it is much more important as enjoyment and stress relief.

I truly love what I do. I am very organized. I have an overall four-year picture that I break down to a yearly picture. From that, I look at a monthly calendar and a weekly planner, and finally I make a daily schedule. I do this for each child except Oliver. Admittedly, Virginia's plan only requires a few hours each day. I am not so rigid that change is impossible. I am also realistic about holidays and certain busy times of gardening.

What about having the energy for seven active children? They do all the work—I just make the plans. My sanity is really based on busy schedules. I enjoy work! My own personal writing, home improvements, baking, cleaning, sewing, gardening (we grow or raise almost everything we eat), schooling, and church activities. I make time for what I want except, possibly, during some very busy times in the summer.

Now that the children are older, they can stay home more on their own. This allows my husband and me to go out for a little while every Saturday night. We also have developed a path around and through our five acres. We can observe

---

the flowers, gardens, fences, buildings, orchards, and animals by taking various paths. This is truly a relaxing time for us to talk and meditate. I also enjoy my daily run as this gives me personal time for reflecting, planning, and just thinking. When I come back after thirty minutes of aloneness on the road, I feel refreshed and revived. I truly enjoy every phase because I have a plan of action.

When I had a four-year-old with cerebral palsy who could not even climb down the stairs, a two year old, and infant twins, my plans were not the same as now. But I still had a plan—play, nurse, change diapers, and help Stuart learn to walk. I also thought about the wash and the dishes. When I felt stressed, I'd think, "Just remember, this too will pass." Don't get overwhelmed! I try to keep moving on, but always with a plan, even if it is a very small one, so that I will never feel overwhelmed. As our children grow, major overhauls aren't necessary, just small changes and variations to "The Plan."

I hope all my children will homeschool. They have never known "school," but they know they have a lot more freedom and opportunities that others don't have.

When the boys across the road get off the school bus, they usually just stare at my children who are climbing trees, lying on hay bales, watching birds, canning tomatoes, riding donkeys, doing math, lying on the sofa reading books, running, playing the piano, singing, baking, hanging wash, or playing in the sand. No matter what the activity, the neighbors are usually watching, while my children are doing. Who do you think is envious?

I have thoroughly enjoyed studying my childrens' personalities and watching as their characters develop. I am trying to guide and help strengthen their weaknesses. I am excited about the future. With Stuart, everything is new since he is the oldest. With the others, I am probably more relaxed. I know that we are on the brink of new experiences with college looming ahead for Stuart and all the girls hitting high school at the same time. It will be very thrilling. When I remember that five years ago I thought we would never get out of elementary school, we sure have come a long way!

Stuart (15), Katie (13), Martha (11), Sarah (11), Lydia (10), Virginia (8), Oliver (5)

Martha, Gregg, Louise
Stuart, Katie, Lydia, Sarah
Oliver, Virginia

Stuart (15), Katie (13), Martha (11), Sarah (11), Lydia (10), Virginia (8), Oliver (5)

Jim, age 34
Ann, age 34
Dana, age 9
Brian, age 6
Peter, age 2
(and now baby Laura)

Five-year follow-up interview with Ann from an academic town in the Midwest

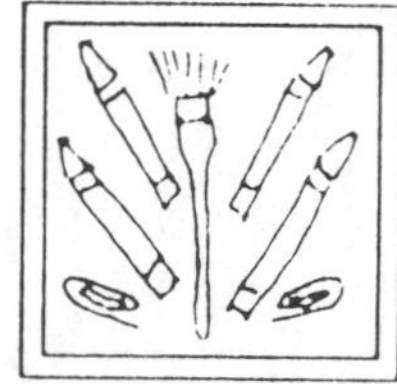

SCRAPPING THE SCHEDULE

So much has changed over the last five years for me and my family. I've had the opportunity to look back and learn from those more trying days when I strove to be a "good homeschool mom." For the first several years, it was very easy to get my role as a home educator confused with my identity as a person. If I did well at teaching my children, then I felt good about myself; and if I did poorly, then I felt lousy about myself. One factor that exacerbated this problem was the feeling that others were possibly disapproving of my choice not to use the public schools and might be observing my children more closely to see if they were "turning out right." Not only would I feel like a terrible person if we did not succeed as home educators, but everyone else would know I was a terrible person because they would see how badly adjusted my children were socially or how poor their handwriting was compared to schooled children. The reverse was also true: if they ended up being socially adept, with fine penmanship, I would feel validated as a person!

Changing this perspective came for me through my relationship with Christ. One day I suddenly realized that I was substituting this "good homeschool mom" image for my true identity—a child of God. As I prayed about this, God reminded me that it was infinitely more important that I be His child than that I be a "homeschooling mom." I needed to rest in my real identity, not to strive for a different one that could only leave me dissatisfied. Since this realization, I have gradually become more comfortable with myself, not just as a home educator, but in all of the roles I fill each day because I am more than my roles—I am a person who is loved by God.

Today, our family is thriving. Dana and Brian are now nine and six, and it is a continual source of joy for me to be able to watch them learn and grow each day. They are both bright, willing, and active children who seem to truly enjoy life. We now also have a two-year-old son and we're expecting a new baby this winter. Peter, our toddler, has been my first strong-willed child, and I am so grateful that God has given me the physical and emotional stamina that I need in order to keep up with the demands he puts on my time and energy!

My husband continues to support and encourage me as I work at home with the children and in the other areas of my life. I teach piano for an hour every day before supper, partly to earn extra money for housekeeping help and other extras, and partly because I enjoy running my own little business doing something that gives me satisfaction. I also meet with some young women from the university every week to help them grow as Christians. It is nice to be involved in helping people outside of our immediate family. I don't do enough relaxing outside of the house, such as going to movies or visiting with friends, but I always know that my husband will stay home with our children if I want to do things like that. Jim also spends time with the children while I teach, which is both a support for me and a benefit for the children since he is a wonderful teacher. Our general agreement about our family priorities and philosophy of education has been a strong factor in our success in teaching our children outside of school.

I've grown to more fully accept the difficulties of raising a child with a physical disability. God has brought me through the stage of depression and fatigue that I was experiencing in response to those difficulties into a new stage of hope and productivity. I was just starting to seek outside help around the time of HOMESCHOOLING: A PATCHWORK OF DAYS and feeling a little guilty about doing so. We now have a housekeeper two mornings a week, which helps me to concentrate more on my children instead of the house. I am not hesitant to get a babysitter when I need a break from the house and the kids, even if I have to call at the last minute. The guilt is gone and my strength is back!

I've also learned to escape some of the isolation that was contributing to the sadness of those old days. I have made friends with a couple of other women in our neighborhood and our outdoor chats on warm days are very strengthening for all of us! I've also tried to care more for my brothers and sisters in the church, and to let them care for me. I've learned that we weren't meant to stand alone, but to lean on others and to let them lean on us.

Five years ago, I was doing away with the schedule that I had imposed on myself because of how difficult it had been to live up to it. Now, I have gone back to a regular schedule, but it is an empowering one rather than a self-defeat-

---

ing one. Empowering schedules are realistic—made up of things we are already able to do, but perhaps do not do as regularly as we should. Self-defeating schedules include some of the same tasks, but also include things we want to be able to do and would be able to do (if we were perfect) but actually are not able to do. They are more like *wishes* than plans. Our old schedule was based on an outside idea of what I thought I *should* be doing as a "homeschool mom."

The new empowering schedule has grown out of a realism that comes from knowing what I want to do each day, knowing what my husband and kids want to do each day, and hopefully knowing more about what God wants us to do each day. We change the schedule when we need to, but we try to stay consistent about mealtimes and waking and sleeping hours for the whole family. The amount of structure in our new schedule seems to give us all a better sense of security and a well-rested feeling each day, without causing me undue stress as I try to keep up with things. It is always better to make plans than to sit around wishing things were different!

Our day in HOMESCHOOLING: A PATCHWORK OF DAYS was a difficult day but our difficult days have become less frequent with time. Our "homeschooling days" are now more productive and more peaceful than they were five years ago. I believe the main reason for the change is that God has been with us all along the journey of home education, on the difficult days and the easier days. He continues to be there, and so I know we can face any kind of day that is to come.

Dana (9), Brian (6), Peter (2)

Keith , age 45
Cindy, age 42
Kendra, age 16
Jonathan, age 14
Tessha, age 12
Aneka, age 8
Anna Mae, age 4
SharaBeth, age 1 1/2

Five-year follow-up interview with Cindy in Mechanicsburg, Pennsylvania

LOTS OF SCHEDULES

In five years, much has changed—such as moving only two miles away from Keith's work to a ten room house.

SCHOOL: We are still using *ATI* (*Advanced Training Institute*) with supplementals. The elder three are totally independent. The eight year old sits in at 6:00 a.m. for *Wisdom Booklet*, but is one-on-one with Mom for math, phonics, grammar, and spelling. The four year old begins kindergarten next month.

KEITH: Having taken a part-time job, his time is limited. Interaction with the children was so important to him, he took the full responsibility of teaching the *ATI* curriculum. Additionally, he also teaches music to Tessha and Aneka. He's encouraged all of us—Kendra, Jonathan, and myself—in starting our own businesses. Without his flexibility, the spoke of the family wheel would be broken.

KENDRA: Twelfth grade, sixteen and a half years old and still rises at 5:00 a.m. She's become a very thorough and diligent young woman—enabling her to graduate high school this June. For the past three years, she has volunteered at a nearby retirement home. They appreciate her willingness to help with whatever is needed. She established her own Suzuki piano studio in our home two years ago. Her students range in ages from three to fourteen, and she presently has seven students. God graciously opened this door to provide funds for numerous

ATI apprenticeship opportunities such as an *International Children's Institute* in Mexico and five weeks in Oklahoma City teaching *Character First*. She looks forward to finishing high school and seeing God's next step for her life.

JONATHAN: Tenth grade, fourteen and three quarters years old and still rises at 5:00 a.m.—fact is, he's our family alarm clock! Jonathan participated in an apprenticeship program for eight weeks two summers ago at Camp WIT (Whatever It Takes). He rose at around 5:00 a.m. and worked from 6:00 a.m. until 8:00 p.m., six days a week, with thirty other boys building our church. We only saw him on Sundays. At the conclusion of the summer, he was six inches taller and ten pounds heavier. He also fulfilled his dream of starting his own lawn care business. As his reputation for being a hard worker spread, so did the facets of his business. Whatever needed to be done, he did it: pet care, plant care, mowing, weeding, raking, shoveling, etc. The Lord used this opportunity to teach Jonathan public speaking and public relations. In addition to purchasing all his own equipment, Jonathan has also provided many gifts of love for his five sisters and mother.

TESSHA: Eighth grade, thirteen years old and rises at 6:00 a.m. She is a blessing to our family. She's a marvelous baker, creative seamstress, and is fabulous with children. For eight months, she's been my assistant in my business when we demonstrate kitchen tools at shows. With this source of income, she constantly blesses others.

ANEKA: Third grade, eight years old. She delights in being recognized as old enough to help with the baby. She's come a long way in learning diligence and truthfulness.

ANNA MAE: Kindergarten, four years old. She is our "high needs" child—quite intelligent and very demanding. I'm hoping the early academic stimulation will level off her "boredom." She's proud to be a big sister and adores the privileges of growing up: making her own bed, emptying the dishwasher, etc.

SHARABETH: One and a half years old and is the sunlight of our day! Quite flexible, lovable, and huggable, she marks each day with a smile

FINAL THOUGHTS: Somehow, with all the activity going on around me, my younger three miss the "mommy moments" the older three had. My guilt has leveled off because I know that with the help of the older three, my younger three are getting three times more attention than I alone could give.

There are times I feel like I am running a marathon in four different directions at once. Yet, when I see the character traits developing— particularly with my older three—I know it's worth the effort. Kendra, Jonathan, and Tessha have learned organization skills (they do all their own logging and scheduling), public speaking, writing skills (Kendra puts together a yearly studio policy and quarterly piano schedule), flexibility (babies seldom "jive" with these organized

---

Kendra (16), Jonathan (14), Tessha, (12), Aneka (8), Anna Mae (4), SharaBeth (1 1/2)

schedules!), and more. Kendra has come to greatly appreciate her family, having been exposed to students from broken homes.

Yes, it's hard to believe I've been homeschooling sixteen years (eleven of those actual "academic" years). Seeing my sixteen year old growing into a young woman—beautiful, bright, and so obedient to God's direction—brings me much joy. Reflecting on the once-tussled hair and noisy lad at my knee, who now stands taller than me, amazes me. Where has the time gone?

Motherhood is but a fleeting moment. It often seems as though time drags forever when we are in the heat of it all. Like a sunset, childhood is beautiful, but swift to pass. As the sunset doesn't wait until we have the time to observe its beauty, neither do children wait to grow and develop until we have the time to invest in the experience. Seeing my children grow into confident and secure adults, obedient to God's call, brings me no regrets. It was worth the loss of that second income, the loss of my time, and I would change *absolutely nothing*. They are a blessing beyond words and worth all the investment I gave.

As our daughter graduates from homeschooling, seventeen years of investment shine bright when we hear our daughter's speech (excerpts):

"It's to my parents that this speech is dedicated and to thousands of other homeschooling parents who have laid down their lives, dreams, goals, and ambitions in order to teach their children to have a heart for the things of God. As I look over the past twelve years, I do not remember so much the phonics lessons, the grammar workbooks, or the algebra exercises. Those things, I assure you, are in there, but they are not what first comes to my mind when I think of my formal years of schooling. The first things that come to my mind are the good times I have had with my family. As a homeschooler, I have gotten to know my family on a level that would not have been possible if my parents had sent me to school. I know that it was a sacrifice for them to homeschool—a sacrifice of time, energy, and money. The amount of this sacrifice can never be fully measured on earth, but neither can the results nor the memories that it created for me.

The greatest gift my parents ever gave me was the gift of their time. Being able to learn together was what drew my family close. I gained a comradeship with my siblings as we shared adventures during everyday life. Because they were my classmates year after year, they became my best friends. Being with my younger siblings on a regular basis also gave me continued experience in teaching various academic subjects that I would not have had if I had been segregated with students of my own age. My interest in becoming a piano teacher was primarily based on the two years of experience I had teaching my sister, before I started my own piano studio.

The learning experiences I have had under my parents' tutelage will always

---

be memorable, because they did not just teach out of a book—they taught from their hearts. Let it suffice to say that *Mom* was the one who created the neat, organized, methodical lesson plans and carried them out day by day. *Dad* added the special spice. Learning with him always meant surprises.

Many of my experiences and memories seem simple, and indeed they are. However, it is this simplicity, hominess, warmth, and security of homeschooling that I have been most privileged to enjoy. A youth who has been homeschooled all her life such as I have, needs only to work a short period of time in the outside world before she realizes all that she has taken for granted, in the face of the hardships that other young people confront.

My desire, as part of the next generation, is to follow in the footsteps of my parents. The homeschooling movement has gained great success only because of parents who were willing to lay down their lives in order to "be there" for their children. These parents have put aside goals, careers, and material gain. The movement that is only just beginning to sweep this country through the lives of homeschool graduates will wither and die if we do not *continue* to use what we have been given in order to carry on the torch to coming generations."—Kendra

Keith, Tesha, Jonathan
Kendra, Cindy, Aneka
Sharabeth, Anna Mae

Kendra (16), Jonathan (14), Tessha, (12), Aneka (8), Anna Mae (4), SharaBeth (1 1/2)

Howard, age 49
Susan, age 48
Jesse, age 22
Jacob, age 19
Molly, age 16
Hannah, age 12

Five-year follow-up interview with Susan from rural Kittanning, Pennsylvania

WE NOTICE THE CONNECTIONS

Some things don't change. We still live in the same old farm house (and it's still pretty tumbled) out in the country in western Pennsylvania. We still work full-time with homeschoolers, since it's part of our family business, and we still do lots of phone counseling, lots of mail order sales of homeschooling books, and lots of organizing of homeschool conferences, graduation ceremonies, and local group activities. But the kids are all older now, with Jesse and Jacob out of the home, and only the two girls here all the time—and even that will be changing soon, as Molly heads off to college next year.

A major technology change is having the Internet at home. I can barely remember time before e-mail, and the constant call around here is, "Are you online? I really need to check my e-mail!" And like many families today, I don't have a teenage daughter who talks on the phone endlessly—I have one who chats with her many friends on *Instant Messenger* on the computer. The Internet has entered fully into our learning too, with all the kids taking part in some sort of Internet-based course, and Howard and I both teaching full on-line *Advanced Placement* courses to groups of homeschool students.

But on to today—it's a balmy, but damp Tuesday in November. We have a day at home planned.

I get myself up fairly early today. I only hit my snooze button about seven times before crawling out in the dark and getting up and about. I let everyone else sleep in a bit, while I shower, fold some laundry (aerobically—my morning exercise), and head to a quiet breakfast on my own. Only Molly and Hannah are at home today with Howard and me. Our home is quite a bit quieter now than five years ago when our two boys were home also! It's one of those days (not terribly common, I'm afraid) when I'm highly organized in the morning— starting a crackpot supper right after breakfast, getting whole wheat bread started in the bread maker (hand kneading has gone the way of the handwritten letter around here . . .), and heading up to do some office work before rousing the girls by 7:15 a.m. It's still not easy to get this family going in the morning. Maybe it's the years of "flexibility" of homeschooling, but we've never been a family to all zip out of bed early—all the kids love to sleep in and do so every chance they get. And as they get older, they do tend to stay up later—I'm often the first one in bed these days.

After groggily getting up sometime after 8:00 a.m., Hannah goes to finish reading *The Master Puppeteer* by Katherine Patterson, while curled up with a blanket over a warm heating duct in our livingroom. In a little while she's eating breakfast, and I join her and give her some oral geography quiz practice questions and also read aloud an article on Sri Lanka from *National Geographic* that I read last night before going to sleep. She just last night took her online chapter quiz for her world geography distance course through the *North Dakota Division of Independent Study* on South Asia, so it's fresh in our minds, and the article is a good review and enrichment— and of course much better than any text. Even though we're doing this textbook distance course, we're not doing "just" the course as is—we are adding a lot, especially extensive outside reading, extra map use, watching videos, and most importantly lots of talking. The value of the course is that it keeps us moving along, and keeps us focused. All on my own, I tend to "scatter shot" and that isn't always a plus.

When Molly gets up, she heads to the living room and is soon reading *A Tour of the Calculus,* a book that talks about calculus from a humanities perspective, cozy on the sofa with a blanket—is she falling asleep?? She says no, that she's just comfortable—very comfortable. The book was given to her by the dean of Honors College at the University of Pittsburgh as a little gift after her interview with him the week before. She's enjoying the book immensely and feels it's a good balance to learning the technicalities of the field. She describes the book as almost being about the spirituality of calculus.

During the early morning I spend some time picking up the house while the girls work independently—I'm getting ready for our junior high *MathCounts* group coming this afternoon. I even vacuum up some cat fur, but decide I can go another few days without mopping the kitchen once I've swept the floor well.

The mail comes—still a highlight and favorite interrupter of our morning. The surprise today is to find out Hannah has gotten a formal letter from our county courthouse stating that she is one of two candidates who tied for the position of township auditor. We're all very confused over this odd mistake—only to find out the facts a short while later when Jesse, now twenty-two and a political science grad student, arrives for a quick visit. Turns out he wrote in Hannah's name on his ballot during the recent local election, just for a joke—never knew our family could have such power in a local election! Hannah decides to write a short piece for our Thursday writing club about this unexpected happening and even wonders if it could be the basis for future short story. Both girls continue to find our writing club a real motivator for their writing, as they know they'll have a real audience for their work. Our group meets monthly, and everyone is expected to complete an open-ended assignment I've given them and to bring a free-choice piece of writing. Jesse and his new wife, Patricia, stay to talk for a while, laughing with us all over the incident—we love having them living nearby right on the farm.

Molly gets only one piece of mail from the University of Pittsburgh today—they have already offered her a four-year full tuition scholarship—and it was special to find out that another homeschooler we know in Pennsylvania has been offered the same. Molly, at sixteen, is a senior, so college mail is a daily inundation.

At around 11:00 a.m. Hannah does a sample exam from the *American Math Competition 8* with me. We do it timed, quiet, with calculators, simulating the real thing, which we'll do this afternoon with our math group. The *AMC 8* is a national junior high math competition for public, private, and homeschool students, with local, state, and national awards. It's a one-time exam that we take locally in our group. It fits in well with our *MathCounts* activities and goals, and will be a good way for the kids to gauge how they are doing compared to other students nationally. It was nice luck that the date we had to give it fell right on our regular *MathCounts* meeting. After finishing up, we then take another half hour at least to discuss most of the problems. "Does this count as a math lesson?" Hannah wonders, as we have an official point system for keeping track of all the math work all the kids on our math team do during the week. It does count. In fact, our favorite way to have math lessons is to find some intriguing problems that are challenging and learn together how to approach them, getting out various texts as needed to help us out. And after working on math with four different kids, I'm getting pretty good at improvising quick lessons on the spot. I'm much better at math than I ever was before homeschooling. We're not too keen on just plowing through a given text, but enjoy the more informal pace of talking and working together. Hannah does much better on this practice exam than she did last year. She's surprised and proud.

Lunch is right at 12:30 p.m. and we all enjoy the warm homemade bread, and I like it that there is nothing to clean up from bread machines. After eating, I wash up the dishes, while Hannah does spelling work in a new *Scholastic* book called *Spelling Works!* by Jim Halverson, that is actually fun and very helpful in learning basic spelling generalizations. Spelling has never been something we've spent enough time on—but with spell checkers and just plain growing up, all the kids have managed to improve anyway.

Then Hannah and I spend about a half hour listening to the next *French in Action* lesson on audio tape together in the dining room. *French in Action* is a full high school or beginning college video course, and we're taking it nice and slow and easy. We love it and have used it for all of the older kids too. For Hannah it's much more palatable to follow along while crocheting a new hat at the same time. French work is easy at this point for Hannah, as she's had a long background of informal learning. She's been to French camp many summers, she's spent time with Molly's French penpal and her younger sister, who've both visited with us here in the summer, she's watched numerous French movies, seen all the videos for *French in Action* when the older kids were doing the series, and more. Doing the program formally now is good for really picking up on grammar and details, and it's fun to be doing this together regularly.

While we're at this, Molly is in the living room reading from her physics text, The *Mechanical Universe*. This college-level text goes along with a video series and is a self-paced (translate: sometimes "slow-paced") course for her this year, with the goal of being ready for the AP exam in May. She realizes it's not crucial to her future plans to really complete this course, but she knows that without the AP exam as a target she might not work as hard as she is. She's finding that physics ties in very well with her *AP Calculus* course she's taking on-line. She's taking her course through a teacher working with us to offer on-line AP courses for homeschool students.

It's soon 3:00 p.m., and the five other kids in our *MathCounts* group arrive, ready for the *AMC 8* exam. Everyone works hard in the quiet room. Only the clicks of calculators and sounds of pencils scribbling out possible solutions are heard for the forty-five minutes of the test. Afterwards the kids burst out in talk as they get snacks and settle in to go over all the problems. Participation is brisk and lively, with oodles of scratch paper consumed as we all try to show one another how we went about our unique solutions to these very tricky twenty-five problems. Molly joins in also, adding her ideas on some of the really hard questions. She does a quick group lesson on exponents right before everyone has to leave—she's getting to be a terrific impromptu teacher. Though I'm loving working with this *MathCounts* team, I still feel a bit of regret that this is our first year in ten years that we haven't also done the *Math Olympiad for Elementary School* program—sad to move beyond these earlier loves, like outgrowing a favorite dress. I highly recommend other homeschoolers check out all these math programs. We've found it really energizing to get together with small groups to work to improve our math in this way, and homeschoolers are welcome to take part in these national programs.

After everyone from the math team heads off, we quickly clean up the dining room. Supper is ready very soon, and I'm grateful that I took the few minutes in the morning to get that crackpot of lentils going. By 6:00 p.m. we're ready for evening cleanup, still a pretty regular family tradition. Molly takes on the task of washing Happy, our little dog, who has been rolling in who-knows-what in the yard again, while Hannah cleans up the dining room and living room, and Howard burns garbage outside and carries some boxes of books upstairs (our hallways are always a bit like a messy warehouse, as we have our small catalog business for homeschool supplies located right in our home). I sometimes wonder what in the world we used our attic for before we needed it for boxes of extra homeschooling stock.

After cleanup, Molly is at her computer again working on her next calculus lesson. She's working with a wonderfully encouraging and helpful teacher (who's also a homeschool father of six kids) and five other homeschool girls via the Internet. She's loving it, even though it takes lots of her time. I'm really grateful that she has this option for learning, as I wouldn't have the time to relearn calculus at this point—nor the interest. My involvement for this course has mostly been just to ask Molly how it's going, if she's gotten her work turned in yet, what topics they're working on now, plus a bit of 'oohing' and 'aaahing' over nifty graphs she comes up with on her graphing calculator. And for Molly this course, with the ready sociability of all the girls working together through any difficulties, is much better than the CD-ROM-based distance course Jacob did several years ago, where no interaction with other students was built into the course design at all. Molly has formed a number of fast friendships with all her many cyber classmates. In fact, this is her third year in online *AP* courses. She completed my *AP US History* course when she was in tenth grade, and last year was in *AP Psychology* and *AP English Literature*. This year she is also doing my husband Howard's *AP Economics* course, so much of our mealtime conversations are centered around discussing everyone's moves in the latest economics simulation game the students are all playing together online. We knew when we first designed these courses that we wanted the students to have ways to discuss and share and interact with one another. We've been surprised to see just how much the students all seem to appreciate this social aspect of the courses.

And what's Hannah doing now? She's been working on resurrecting an old game Jacob created back in early high school called "Catreers," a spoof on the board game *Careers* my kids have always enjoyed. Hannah started on this project last night, making needed cards, writing out full directions, making game tally sheets—and she's is now playing it with Howard in the dining room. Fun to see this old game being used again.

And what's that I hear from Molly? She should be finishing up her calculus, but instead she is beginning to teach herself to play the soprano recorder, using some of the books she found in an old music stash by the piano. This is the first year since Molly was five years old that we haven't been taking weekly piano lessons, and I know Molly has missed the regular focus on learning new music. She is still playing piano on her own, but it's hard to have the drive to really tackle and perfect new pieces without the structure of lessons and upcoming recitals. Her time has been really short this fall anyway. So recorder seems to be taking the place a bit, and she's now practicing every spare minute (and some not-so-spare minutes). Molly and I actually limp our way through some very simple beginning duets together—it reminds me a bit wistfully of my very early days playing recorder with Jacob. We eventually could do all sorts of lovely Elizabethan duets together, but we let recorder playing slide during his high school years. Many things seem to slip by as time is spent on other things. It's nice to come back sometimes and revisit old interests years later in a new way. It helps us feel a sense of continuity. Soon Molly and Hannah are both playing recorder together, sounding quite squeaky but having a fine time. They even try out duets, with Hannah improvising on piano and Molly on recorder.

Molly and I are even talking of learning to play a Shakespearean duet for the next "Sleepover Shakespeare Society" meeting in a few weeks. Molly organized this group this fall. Basically, it's a group of about fourteen homeschooled girls in the region who all meet here monthly to discuss a selected Shakespeare play, followed up by watching a video production, then with more talk, and eventually in the wee hours of the night, by a small bit of sleep. It's been terrific fun, and it's really been exciting to see Molly plan out questions for everyone to talk about—finding ways to lead an effective discussion with the diverse group, and learning to find and use the many Shakespearean resources on the Internet. This month they are all reading *Hamlet*, and last night Molly, Hannah, and I all watched a video lecture from *The Teaching Company* on *Hamlet* given by Peter Saccio. After we first watched a physics video from *The Mechanical Universe*, everyone was too tired to move off the sofa, as both girls were still very sore from Saturday's binge at the statewide co-ed volleyball tournament. We were a good captive audience for a Shakespeare lecture! Hannah is also a part of the Shakespeare group. She and I usually read the plays together, especially tragedies like *Hamlet*, discussing them as we go. We also love first gaining background by reading *Lamb's Tales of Shakespeare*—always good to know the basic storyline and characters when dealing with Shakespeare's difficult language! All the girls in the group plan to take part in the annual *Shakespeare Monologue Competition* this year in Pittsburgh. Molly and Hannah took part last year, and the experience was so worthwhile, even though they didn't come close to winning. The group of girls will also attend a live performance of *Macbeth* in early May, hopefully all wearing their matching "Sleepover Shakespeare

Society" tee-shirts they're designing. Whoever worried that homeschoolers don't have friends or opportunities for group discussion?

After this, Molly works on her web site for "Talk it Out," her math web site for a year-long competition she designed for girls in grades four through seven. The first problem set answers are due this week, and Molly is making sure everything is working correctly for the girls to post their work. In this competition, the kids need to write full explanations of how they think through their solutions; if they just post the answer, they won't get full credit. Molly modeled this program on a similar one for advanced high school students, called the *USA Math Talent Search*, which she's taken part in. She wanted to give younger kids something similar, where they would have to stretch themselves to write out a full solution. Molly first creates three math problems, chooses a fourth problem written by one of the girls in the group, then offers an extra-credit project (such as finding at least five neat math web sites, researching about a famous mathematician, and more). Hannah is part of this group, along with about seven other girls from all around the country.

This whole math activity is Molly's official Leadership Project, planned during the *Pennsylvania Governor's School for Teaching* that she attended last summer on full scholarship. She'll be reporting on her progress with the plan throughout the year, keeping in touch with the *PGST* faculty. So far it's going super—the girls are participating in informal discussion about math on the "talking board" of the site, learning to find good Internet sources for math enrichment, and more. Once they post their solutions on the web site, they'll all have the chance to comment on one another's ideas.

And what am I doing now, as it's approaching 9:30 p.m.? I'm working at my office computer, writing out more responses to essays written by my *AP US History* students and checking our web site for any new discussions or questions raised by the kids. I have a typical busy week ahead, so spend a few moments looking over my schedule that's mapped out in my planning book. Hannah and I have a *Geography Awareness Week* talk we're attending Wednesday evening, our writing club meets here this Thursday, and on Friday Molly, Hannah, and I will be going to see a live production of *Arsenic and Old Lace* in Pittsburgh—a friend of Molly's from *PGST* has a leading role. On Saturday I'll head off to an *AP US History* teachers' workshop to learn more, get recharged, and meet other *AP* teachers. Always interesting to let them know how homeschoolers are taking part in *AP* classes on-line. And also there's that upcoming newsletter I need to start working on, too.

And bedtime routines? They've changed substantially over the years. As I've mentioned, I'm often the first one in bed, as I like to get up the earliest. Howard is currently reading a book to Hannah at night—naturalist Gerald Durrell's fun autobiography *My Family and Other Animals*, telling of his growing up years on a wild Greek island. I stopped being the family bedtime reader quite a few years ago. Howard remembers loving this book when he was younger—Durrell's books were favorites of his mother. But first Hannah and Howard have to talk over moves for Howard's *AP Economics* simulation game—Hannah has been invited to take part, and she's getting quite interested in it all. I have to remind them that it's about 10:30 p.m., and if they actually want to read tonight, it will have to be now.

Molly actually stays up till midnight—when I groggily ask Howard (who's up late reading *Shogun*) to tell Molly to head to bed. She's enjoying knowing that she has the day off of her university class tomorrow and has been continuing to play recorder, working through about a dozen lessons in *The Recorder Guide* all on her own. She's sounding better all the time. She said she's realized how easy it is to teach yourself a second instrument, since you don't need to learn all about reading music, too. It's rather like learning a third language in some ways—it's never as difficult as the second language. And speaking of languages, Molly is planning on really working on her beginning Spanish skills next semester at home, working with the *Destinos* video course and other written materials. It's her third language, and she can do it all on her own, and she may set up weekly Spanish meetings with a nearby homeschool friend who's in the Shakespeare group.

I certainly have developed a changing role with Molly—more of just "How are you coming with this?," "Did I hear you say you have a French essay due this week? What's it on?," "Working on physics? Good." We also listen to audio lectures during long car rides and discuss ideas brought up in the philosophy series of lectures from *The Teaching Company*. The long, extended conversations on all sorts of topics with our older children are a real blessing, something the people who warn you about how awful teenagers can be never mention. But Molly is moving on to a bigger world, and it's a new type of weaning perhaps—she'll be off next year full-time to college. This semester she's actually been enrolled in an upper level French class three days a week at the University of Pittsburgh. After getting a top score on *AP French Language* last year through independent work at home, she felt she really wanted a full class experience for more advanced French work. She gets to ride into the city with Jesse, who heads in to Carnegie Mellon University every day for his grad classes and teaching assistant work in political science. It's helping Hannah and me get used to the idea that Molly won't be here full-time next year.

This change has given me more time to focus on Hannah and her interests—helping her find her niche. We all know the feelings of guilt we have as homeschooling moms over not spending as much one-on-one time with the youngest children—well, it does eventually come full circle, and the youngest gets all our time. And it's always important for us to realize how much our younger ones have gained over the years by being part of their older siblings' activities. It's certainly true even this busy year, as Hannah learns about Shakespeare, philosophy, recorder, and even beginning economics through her time with Molly. I wrote a fun article called "Sister School" years ago about the two of them working together in a play school they'd invented when Hannah was quite young and just starting to learn to read. Really, "Sister School" has just grown up with them, as they still do so much together, and they continue to be very close and special friends.

And it's been a change to have Jacob off at Carnegie Mellon University in Pittsburgh—he's now a sophomore, is living in the dorm, working hard on all his course work in computer programming, staying up late into the night to finish up that paper in philosophy, and tolerating his lab course in physics. Jacob loves physics, but has always hated hands-on experiments. He'd rather just program a simulation than do something with real equipment. He joked the other day that nothing yet in college matched the neat penny pendulum experiments he did with Howard and all the other kids years ago. He did bleach his hair this fall as a lark, but he's letting it grow back in "natural" and says he won't pull that one again. He's in the Computer Science college at CMU—his early interests in computer programming have only grown over the years. Last summer he spent three months working at a programming internship, something that is pretty unusual for a college freshman to do. He's talking now of possibly graduating early. With all of his *AP* credits earned while in high school, he can easily finish up a year early if he chooses to. But he might want to do a senior year honors project in programming, so he's not sure. We like having him nearby for college and love having him come on out to our monthly square dances with homeschooling families. We keep in touch via e-mail and visits to the city in between. He's even cooking for himself this year, with his veritable kitchen of crackpot, microwave, toaster oven, and bread maker in his dorm room. His forte is still homemade-from-scratch whole wheat pizza.

Jesse arrives back to the farm at midnight. As I mentioned, he's living here on our farm again, after being away for four years at college. He graduated from the University of Pittsburgh in the summer, with an honors diploma in political science and a double major in history. But more importantly, he got married last summer to homeschool grad and longtime friend, Patricia. They have worked really hard to fix up one of the little cottages on our farm, with lots of work and love, and it's wonderful to have them nearby. Patricia, who's finishing up her undergraduate degree at Indiana University of PA in teaching children with special needs, is also helping in our office work. She's terrific with phone counseling, getting orders out to people, handling credit card orders from our Internet site, and keeping us all a bit more organized. She even was able to help give achievement tests to homeschoolers with us.

So life has been a real blessing since the first edition of HOMESCHOOLING: A PATCHWORK OF DAYS—the kids are all doing well, working hard, and becoming good people. They are all finding their place in a larger field and making sound choices for their futures. Our sphere broadens as they move out into the world more and also as Howard and I move into new work with homeschoolers all across the country with our on-line courses. Life is good. It's busy and the pace feels probably a lot more hectic these days, but the core of family life is still there, giving us all a strong base to our days.

Susan, Howard, Patricia, Jesse, Jacob
Hannah, Molly

Jesse (22), Jacob (19), Molly (16), Hannah (12)

Blake, age 36
Karla, age 36
Ian, age 11
Rachel, age 9

Five-year follow-up interview with Karla in College Station, Texas

WE LIKE IT THIS WAY

I almost didn't return to homeschooling this year. This summer we kept hearing relatives complain how behind my children are, how their younger cousins are further along in reading, etc. I got discouraged and scared that, in spite of experience, in spite of a teaching degree, in spite of all I know that I've taught them, I somehow was failing my children in their educations. To my husband's credit, he gave me enough support to overcome other's doubts and pointed out how far we've come. He also pointed out the state of the schools, the state of the culture, the lack of depth in the educations of the public schooled children we know, and the many ways that the complaints I received simply were wrong. So, renewed by Blake's support and the sad lack of decent alternatives, I ordered the books for another year.

We began our homeschooling this year in good form. All of the textbooks I selected arrived before we needed them, and I'm extremely pleased with our new curriculum providers. I used to put together my own materials and that worked well. Last year I decided to try a packaged curriculum from a private school that sells its books and teaching guides to homeschoolers. That worked even better for us, yet I still wanted greater depth in some subjects. This year I went with *Seton Home School* and I love the books, the organization, and the depth of coverage of the subjects! What is even better, the children love the books too.

My husband Blake is currently working; I'm homeschooling, editing a newsletter, raising good show dogs, playing with the horses, and hoping to have our new house finished this winter.

Where we live in our part of Texas is very hot and humid. We are in the process of building a home outside of town. We have twenty-one acres, fenced and crossfenced with cedar posts and a tight wire mesh topped with two smooth strands of wire—the top one is "hot." We have a large deep pond that we had dug because the natural drainage for the area had made a ditch across several farms and the water wanted to sit and breed mosquitoes. It filled on the next cloudburst and has remained full ever since. The land is nearly flat with just enough slope to drain well. And in our area there is an almost constant stiff breeze. We built a hay barn and put up run-in sheds for the horses.

The house includes a two-car garage that was converted to an air-conditioned dog-room with a raised tub for grooming and a washer/dryer for dog bedding. There will also be an outdoor kennel area for fresh air and sunshine exercise. The house and garage consist of two large domes. The garage is forty feet in diameter and the house is forty-eight feet in diameter. The house dome has lots of open spaces with the high curved ceilings, three bedrooms, and three and a half baths. We expect to move in sometime in December or next January. This is such an exciting change for us as we have longed to be out of town and have not been able to move before. My children are eagerly looking forward to living where the pony lives. I can hardly wait to have all the horses and us in the same place.

Activities based on their interests have continued to increase. Both Ian and Rachel are in *Pony Club*, piano lessons, and *Tae Kwon Do* this year. Rachel is also in *Brownies* and dance. Occasionally, when the program is going to be especially educational, hubby takes both children to the *Herpetological Society* meetings. When they go, they listen to people who really know reptiles and amphibians. Sometimes it is a person who has visited an area and photographed and studied native species, so there are lectures with the pictures.

This summer was full of firsts. It was Rachel's first week of real camp. She went away to *Girl Scout* camp, and I missed her so much! She loved camp and enjoyed her time with the other girls, the fun of the crafts, the singing, the swimming, the horseback riding, and pretty much everything about camp. She makes friends easily, so as soon as she met the girls in her cabin and her leaders, she was eager for us to leave. When we picked her up, she gave us a quick hug and asked if we'd mind waiting until her leader finished braiding her hair since all the girls were having it done. She began planning next year before we'd even finished the walk back to the truck! And it was Ian's first summer of almost continual martial arts day camp and his first chance to watch his favorite instructor compete in a martial arts tournament. He thinks he wants to compete, and I think we may support that desire sometime in the next year.

The children are at an age now when travel becomes valuable. The end of the summer included visits to the giant arch in St. Louis—the museum in the arch is on the Expansion of the West/Louis and Clark and is very wonderful; *Carnegie*

Children's Museum in Pittsburgh—four stories of hands on exhibits for children—awesome!; all the historical sites in Philadelphia—the places really do look like the pictures in the books; the *Neil Armstrong Space Museum* in Wapakoneta, Ohio—my home town; Lincoln's home and burial place in Springfield, Ill.; and many of the famous sites in New York City as well as the musical *Cats*. Everyone was tired and glad to get back to Texas.

My goals for this year are to see big improvements in spelling, handwriting, and history. I really felt at the end of last year that we hadn't been doing as much in those areas as we ought, partly because I'd not had a spelling curriculum as I do this year, and partly because the children just were not ready for the sort of history reading I wanted them to be doing. Already, my constant adjusting of our program to fit the individual developmental levels of my children has paid off. Ian is jumping ahead in reading and history, now that his reading is finally to a usable level. Rachel is a year ahead in most language arts, so I've put her into some of the same books as her older brother, thus making my teaching tasks much easier.

I purchased the spelling books for first through fourth grades and in the next couple months we will be going through the early books at an accelerated rate in order to pull the basics of spelling into use. I'm finding that at third and fourth grade levels, they are leaping through the first and second grade spelling very quickly. We are using the spelling books put out by *Seton Homeschool*. I really like them. They use both the visual shape of words that is so popular with the whole language concept, combined with solid phonics. This seems to make mastering spelling more effective and easier for the children.

By going early to most activities, the extra time seems to satisfy my children's desire to be with other children. I'm considering giving a standardized test sometime next spring to see where they stand for myself and to give myself proof of progress, though I think I will still encounter doubts. I'm grateful, though, that our church is very supportive of homeschooling.

Our long-term goals have always been the fairly loose desire to educate our children to become solid in all the basics and to give them the foundations for higher education. We include music—piano lessons, music theory, lots of listening, and musical exercises. Our daughter is in dance, both children are in martial arts, horseback riding, and running for fun. We emphasize solid language arts—phonics, grammar, spelling, vocabulary, reading comprehension, and speaking clearly. We have been using the *Saxon Math* curriculum because I still feel it gives the strongest math foundations. I feel that mastery of Latin and the ability to read source materials and classics in Latin is a strong foundation for future learning. Sciences have been a mixed bag of books—usually whatever I felt would best teach each topic. We are also still tinkering with robotics as those machines just seem to be more and more integral to our lives.

Ian (10), Rachel (8)

I don't think our goals have changed over time, but my husband's and my conviction that homeschooling is the best way for us to reach those goals for our children has strengthened. Meeting our goals involves hard work, persistence, and much encouragement for both children. Our daughter finds her schoolwork is easy, so we encourage her to widen her interests and work ahead. Our son doesn't like to read much. Though his reading comprehension is good, reading is still difficult for him, so we point out to him that he needs reading to really take his math ability to whatever goals he sets for himself. At ages eight and ten, both children are a bit more into the short-term vision than the long, but we just keep moving along, and I believe the long term will take care of itself.

I wish I'd realized that homeschooling was such hard work and that it would remain hard work. I kept thinking it would get easier over time, but it hasn't. Also, while I'm more confident, I still second-guess our decision to homeschool. Doubts don't go away, but I do get better at reminding myself *why* we homeschool. Also, unlike some people who finish in less time, our day takes almost the same number of hours as the public schools. I find that refusing to run errands during the "school day" has really taken a lot of tension out of life for me. We get more done when we refuse to allow anything to interfere.

I've come to terms with some of the facts of homeschooling. Most importantly, I try not to let the pressures get to me. Homeschooling *is* hard work. It gets more *comfortable* as we get the hang of it, but it remains hard work. We've learned to step back and look at our children as whole persons. This helps us to see that those inevitable hitches in the learning process are not the whole picture! I find when some subject gets frustrating that just stepping back, looking at my children, and having a conversation shows me that their development in whole is coming along nicely and that, even if the steps forward in the problem subject seem small, they *will* add up.

I also remind myself that I answer to God for how I've raised these children He has entrusted to my care. If God is holding *me* responsible, then I strive to overcome my doubts that I can't do as well as the schools—and to know that I *can* do a good enough job.

So this is our follow-up as we dive into a new year with hope, eagerness, and excitement. It's going to be great.

Ian (10), Rachel (8)

John, age 47
Valerie, age 47
Dorien, age 19
Tyler, age 15

Five-year follow-up interview with Valerie in Johnstown, Pennsylvania

WORKS-IN-PROGRESS

This update tells the story of how our homeschooling family ran blithely, full tilt into more than one brick wall. Though we were happy and comfortable on our side of the walls (which we didn't even realize we were building, trowel in hand), I hope fresh young homeschooling families will be wary of the walls they unintentionally build for their children.

When we last visited with Dorien and Tyler five years ago, they were still eager little, fresh-faced monkeys joyfully answering my reasonable demands. I judiciously determined what was important for them to know in order to have successful future lives, and micro-managed their efforts at learning it. The girls read the newspapers, *Science News, Smithsonian, Discover, Planetary Report,* and *National Geographic* to keep current on happenings in the Global Village and new scientific developments. They wrote three to five page papers and discussed their findings with me. They worked diligently on their respective maths and competently completed courses in biology, ethics, American history, and civics. They gamely produced ten-page research on the topics of their own choosing. Both girls volunteered to spend part of each summer working with special-needs children and adults at several different camps, did odd jobs for the neighbors to earn spending money, and went on vacations with friends and relatives without their parents along to stifle them.

This idyllic portrait does not examine the day to day tussles over: bedtimes and rising times, listening to the radio while working; quantities of work; quality of work; whether truly horrible fantasy novels count on a reading list (not now, not ever); and if we'd ever be able to unplug the television (afraid not). These homeschool clichés are now mostly things of the past; we got over them, and daily homeschooling was pretty much hunky-dory.

Throughout her four years of high school, Dorien worked independently in what I considered to be fairly challenging areas. She intelligently discussed her findings in a physics-made-easy type course, was putting out a steady (if unremarkable) effort in mathematics, and was writing volumes in all subject areas. I especially enjoyed our sometimes fierce political and sociological debates (Dorien is the weepiest of bleeding-heart liberals); and wide-ranging discussions about art literature, and most importantly to her, music (she prefers inarticulate screaming with drums).

Though she'd finally given up on ever mastering the guitar, she continued to spend a great deal of time and money at concerts, and so stayed close to the independent, punk music scene so dear to her heart. Because she also kept up with writing, editing, and producing her own fifty page 'zine, the pieces she had written about both live and recorded music came to the attention of editors of other 'zines as well as editors of mainstream magazines. Her work has been widely published, and she's always being asked to write more. More importantly, she brought up her SAT scores by a hundred points, good enough to earn her acceptance at all the colleges to which she'd applied. Unfortunately, we were unable to afford the women's college that was her first choice, and so she registered at the one closest to home. The thoughtful essays she'd written were specifically noted and were given credit for playing a major role in her acceptance at all the colleges.

Not willing to waste her energy on eccentric class scheduling and archaic courses established merely by years of trial and error and musty old tradition Dorien rewrote her guest appearance as a college freshman. Though she claims in the beginning to have shown up regularly for classes, once there she quickly became bored. I'm going to go way out on a limb here and guess that some of this problem was due to the fact that she bought and read each and every one of her texts before the semester even started.

This bad habit was one she'd learned from me. I had always scoffed at how traditional school texts seem to try to trick students into discovery by withholding necessary information. Theoretically, this would be a good plan if the student were bright enough or had any sort of clue about where the subject would be going. From my own high school experience, I was often in the position of lump-throated, dry-mouthed, faking-it because I was phenomenally clueless in algebra, geometry, biology, German, physics, etc. Since I've never liked this kind of !surprise! education, I let my students in on the secret that courses and books aimed at adults do not stoop to such devious strategies, but inform the learner up front of what they need to know so they can get right down to the business of learning it, rather than "discovering" it. There have never been any "teacher vs. student" games in our house. They knew what I knew, and If I didn't know it, we learned it together.

Dorien was accustomed to reading and digesting all the written information available to her, or at least the interesting parts, and then receiving complementary instruction. That she was so keen to begin her classes was because she was so excited about learning something new, something at which her mother could only hint, something she longed to debate with other eager minds. Instead, she found that she, alone, was familiar with the material, and because of her extensive reading habit into related areas, often ended up holding intense, enthusiastic conversations with the professors, while her classmates sat glumly doodling.

The second semester was more of the same. Because she began to miss classes and did miserably on tests, she was in danger of failing by mid-term. To their credit, the remarkably indulgent college staff recognized her genuine enthusiasm, attributed her boredom to the right reasons, and allowed her to veer off on an independent direction and use her talent for writing. She was given credit for her outspoken class participation and was permitted to write essays in all the subject areas to make up her grades. This resulted in her landing a B average. We should all be so lucky.

Both girls have always been encouraged to find compromises; to work off punishments; to shape the material to suit their own private understanding. They have always chosen material that interests them the most, rather than memorizing the boring facts that can be found on the pages of history or geography books. Therefore, they have never had to develop the patience or discipline to tackle an uninteresting topic nor expect all topics to be malleable.

For instance, if papers were due, they would scout out an angle that engaged their enthusiasm and bend the topic to fit. Dorien wrote a ten-page research paper on Native American traditions in seventh grade and a ten-page research paper on Native American cookery in eighth grade, because Native Americans held her interest for that long, and everyone knows the rest of American history is such a frightful bore. Tyler recited multiplication flash cards aloud while practicing her ballet steps, because the sitting-still kind of memorization is not her bag. Even now I can see in her eyes the longing to spring up and grande jété across the floor to find the product of (8 x 7), or (13 x 2), tondue.

Because I encouraged both daughters to find creative solutions for work that had to be done, I unwittingly built brick wall #1, which didn't prepare Dorien for the realities of "traditional school." My own shortsightedness prevented me from realizing what I was building, brick by brick over ten years, until it was too late. (My husband John is a bricklayer who *deliberately* builds such walls, usually on schools, and gets paid for it.) The only way I knew to facilitate their education was with creativity, interest, and flexibility, because that is how I live and couldn't have done otherwise, even if I'd been able to see the wall and had the conviction to change.

During her freshman year, Dorien worked ten hours a week at the local library as part of the federal work study program. It is a place she has been familiar with since we first started taking her to the Preschool Adventure Library when she was three. She represented the library and won a state-wide poetry contest when she was nine years old, and in consequence of our frequent visits over the years has become friends with most of the librarians. Her duties included a wide variety of tasks, from answering reference questions at the information desk, to assisting genealogy buffs in their research, to shelving books. As challenging and enjoyable as the work was, she felt that she was just being coddled by family friends and wasn't truly working at a real job.

At the end of her freshman year, she went to work at a new electronics/appliance store in the area. From the mandatory drug test, to dealing with many prickly fellow employees and supervisors, to obeying all the assorted employee codes, using a time clock, and working shifts, she feels she has finally entered the real work force. To our pleasant surprise, she has adapted fairly well and is a top salesperson in her division. She plans on keeping her job through college to build up an income to pay for all the concerts, CDs, bus trips, long distance phone calls, and books that are essential to her survival. Dorien also gives her homeschooling experience credit for allowing her to speak easily and competently with a wide variety of people. We've noticed that while most teens are uncomfortable with adults, she and her sister are quite at ease. Since they have spent their lives listening and talking to me, they expect other adults to be as interesting, rational, and witty, and so are courteous and confident. Because her reading, writing, and conversational skills have been nurtured, she is quick to grasp new material and situations, and to deal with them.

Now, at nineteen, Dorien views her homeschooling experience as generally positive. Though she believes she has been misdirected and somewhat retarded by her lack of preparedness for traditional schooling (brick wall), she has also found distinct advantages. The biggest plus that springs instantly to mind, is that she and her sister are best friends. While their shared experiences set them apart from their peers to some extent, it has brought them closer together. I'm afraid they strike other teenagers as being kind of "weird" because of their large vocabularies, arcane knowledge, and creativity they gained on our side of the wall, but both girls say they feel more confident knowing they have a permanent, reliable friend.

Now fifteen-year-old Tyler is a different story. In everything she does, creativity is evident in her drawings to her funny and insightfully written articles. Always a little shy and unsure of herself, she was nonetheless a homeschooler's dream! Up at first light, eager to begin, good-humored, responsive, a hard worker. Therefore, we were not forewarned of brick wall # 2. On our side of the wall, we keep pretty much to ourselves, achieve personal victories, and reel at public attention. But Tyler has mutated into something that causes both her parents and her sister to draw back in horror. She . . . has become . . . a social butterfly.

As she emerged from her chrysalis (I know I'm stepping away from the brick wall metaphor here, but it can't be helped—perhaps the chrysalis was *attached* to the wall), her new-found public persona came about largely in response to the fact that since joining a new ballet school, she performs almost monthly at many different events, before hundreds of people, demonstrates at schools before her peers, and attends the performances and participates in the workshops of several different professional companies. She claims to enjoy this.

In the year that she's been at this new studio, she's become very serious about ballet. The high monthly tuition, workshops, pointe shoes, ballet slippers, leotards, tights, and foot care products were beginning to put further study out of our financial reach, so Tyler began assisting in the teaching of younger grades. This happy exchange was her own idea, and it allows her to reduce our expenses while doubling her class time, because she leads and corrects student exercises, and must demonstrate technique, positions, and routines over and over again.

Standing in the spotlight and being valued solely for her physical attributes and abilities has made her extremely conscious of her appearance. Unfortunately, this awareness has pushed most of her writing, thinking, and conversational skills out the window. (Hmmm . . . a *window* in the brick wall?) Her father and I hope this is only a temporary displacement, and that she will become more balanced with maturity.

Tyler sees our brick walls in a different light. Whereas Dorien can forgive me for putting her through this experiment of homeschooling because she can now often see the advantages, Tyler claims it has been the struggle to overcome her homeschooling experiences that has made her the strong person she has become.

In order not to appear like a freak, inbred, or a member of a cult (all of which we homeschoolers have been called!), she has plunged wholeheartedly into her peer-group identity. She's definitely dumbed down, especially in her writing and conversations (the word "like" thunders constantly against our sensitive ears) to fit in with the boy-makeup-music-clothes-crazy crowd she hangs around with. Nothing, from algebra to biology seems to really "stick" in her mind. We have been enjoying reading and arguing over her ethics book and I believe it is making an impact since she now slightingly refers to her sister as an "egoistic hedonist."

Her transformation on the other side of the wall has been painful for me, even though I understand her drive to be like everyone else and fit in. While I have been single-mindedly, conscientiously, shoving her down the narrow path to unique individuality, she had been gleefully running at top speed in the opposite direction. (This path runs alongside the brick wall.)

To my satisfaction, the changes in her appear to be as superficial as her make-up. Her flamboyant pursuit of fame and popularity are not as important as her genuine kindness and caring for other people. She is well-liked whatever she goes, even though she still cannot spell and has to be forced to read the newspaper. It makes me truly proud when we are out in public to see her warmly greeted by both her peers and the assorted grownups she's met. Sometimes it's hard to move because small children from ballet class run up to hug her legs, or mentally challenged adults overcome their shyness to call out and pat her on the arm. Tyler claims that it is in a counter-reaction to our sheltered, claustrophobic little homeschool, that she has become a social, functioning human being capably dealing with the real world on a personal level.

This is in direct contrast to Dorien. I don't know how long Dorien will be able to get away with chipping and hammering to reshape every round hole to suit her own square peg. It has to be an arduous way of going about life, and one that must take its toll.

There is some good news though. This past year has seen the development of a mathematical phenomena to which I'm sure all experienced homeschoolers will be able to attest. Now that Dorien is nineteen-years-old and a college sophomore and I have only Tyler at home, I've determined logically, statistically, *mathematically*, that I do indeed expend exactly *half* the time and *half* the energy that I did when teaching both girls. Whew! What a relief! All joking aside, I really did expect to have more leisure time for nut-center chocolates and soap operas and it just hasn't happened. Oh well. There is that satisfaction of ethics.

Brick walls # 1 and # 2 were built from my inability to demand self-discipline from my daughters and failure to recognize that it is a wide variety of other people and their expectations that shave down the rough edges to make square pegs a little rounder, a little more suited to fitting into real life. We've provided a protective shelter from and a barrier to life's challenges and hard-knocks. One of my favorite sayings: "What doesn't kill you will make you strong" had been made meaningless because everything's been too easy. In all fairness, my husband John did indeed point out that I had all the tools for the making of brick walls scattered about me.

Being forced to conquer impossible subject matter, face failure, deal with other people's difficult personalities, and overcome your own weaknesses are the things that try your abilities and strengthen your backbone. You can't make too many excuses or bend too many rules when taking a test or keeping a job if Mom isn't there holding your hand and "understanding" you.

Even though Dorien feels handicapped and Tyler feels that homeschooling has backfired, both children have turned out to be unique. Dorien poetically screams her differences to the world at top decibel while Tyler aspires to be the leader of the herd. In both cases, it is their undeniable individuality that makes them interesting to others.

In retrospect, and this will be the brick wall #3, I would not (*could not*) have built my brick wall any differently since I can only be the person that I *am.* My husband, and Dorien and Tyler can only be the people they *are.* We all did our best, to the best of our abilities. It is no good imagining how different things would have been *if* the kids had been put in school or *if* we hadn't moved to a more isolated area which has certainly encouraged our anti-social tendencies (I suppose that could be wall #4, so now we have a house.) However, those alter-dimension, other-timeline children do not and never will exist. To think we could have designed any other kind of wall would be to assume we were other than who we are. I do not believe I could have avoided building these walls even with the best of intentions or the most diligent of efforts. Each family builds walls of their own design, some high and intimidating, others low and fun to sit on, happily swinging legs on either side. Know yourself well enough to recognize your own boundaries and the type of walls you prepare around them. Don't expect to import prebuilt or relocated walls that are not of your own design—it can't be done.

From all that I've learned, I know that my hollow voice can be heard calling over a high brick wall, through time, down an enormous distance, along that one-way street called hindsight: "Don't homeschool if you think you can or should be someone other than *who you are.*"

Dorien (19), Tyler (15)

Keith, age 43
Sandra, age 46
Kirby, age 13
Marty, age 10
Holly, age 8

Five-year follow-up interview with Sandra in Albuquerque, New Mexico

OUT OF PINK CRAYONS

We were the "pink crayons" chapter in the last book, and *still* my kids need pink crayons for all sorts of projects. Kirby's thirteen now, and he's been taking *Shorin-Ryu karate* for nearly three years. He taught his first classes a few weeks ago when the sensei was sick.

Marty is ten and just started writing and spelling lately. He went from nothing to a *lot* in that area, for a few unconventional reasons. First, he saved enough money to buy his own video game. I bought him the manual, and he came to read that and the screen messages and directions. Then he got an e-mail account and started answering *Instant Messages* and e-mail from friends. Now he can write. Not many families are willing to wait until children are nine or ten, but I'm interested in having them develop other ways of taking in information (aural, visual, experiential) before they begin to read, because it seems to me that early reading can somewhat limit one's willingness and ability to take other avenues to knowledge.

Holly is eight and I overheard her brothers bragging to their friends the other day about what a good artist she is. We have a big old light table and the kids have done composite tracings for years and then have moved on to their own designs with the advantages of light tables. Holly can whip out a drawing in no time now, from memory, anywhere. She's also really good at keeping a fire going in the fireplace, at taming cats, and at asking profound philosophical questions with sweet humor.

Our biggest change is that we moved to a bigger house. Now the kids have their own rooms and there is an enclosed porch for their games, art supplies, and commonly-owned toys. They have a view of the back yard which is edged in Arizona cypress and seems a little more like a rural yard than the Albuquerque neighborhood it really is. Our back gate opens to a big vacant lot, and we can walk to the grocery store, copy shop, the credit union, and two video rental places from there. Unschooling families come over on Thursdays in the winter, and in warmer times we meet in a park.

My husband Keith has been working in Minneapolis on a defense contract which just keeps being extended, but he's home about a week per month, and we get to go and visit him there. We've been to Duluth, to the iron mines, and to play in some snow that's very different from New Mexico's snow. In New Mexico, when you sled you get dirty. The snow pulls up grass and weeds and dirt. Snowmen often have dirt or dead grass embedded in them. In Minneapolis I took four days worth of clothes for the kids to sled for four days. They could have used the same clothes every day—there was *no* dirt or dead grass. Our snow melts in a couple of days. We nearly never see week-old snow. In Minneapolis there's four-month-old snow.

We have a housemate who knows biology, chemistry, and physics as well as I know grammar, literature, and music. That helps a whole lot when the kids come upon those learning-rich opportunities without any warning. I'm learning lots of science myself from hearing the explanations. Keith does geography and math easily and with enthusiasm, so as a team we have things pretty well covered, but it never seems like school, just like joyous inquiry.

What I'm proudest of about my kids is that they are sensitive to other people's feelings, they're helpful with younger kids they don't even know, they make friends easily, and they're funny and bright. They have lots of adult friends, too.

Now that the children are older, we've become more active again in *The Society for Creative Anachronism* in which my husband and I have been participating since the late 70s. The *SCA* is a sort of Medieval and Renaissance studies co-op with costumes, sword fighting, and lots of crafts and research. This causes lots of brilliant, artistic people to be in and out of the house, and the kids can't help but benefit from that. My husband's squires and my apprentices and proteges are a wonderful resource for our children. Also, we have traveled to feasts and tournaments in other areas, and the kids gain friends they wouldn't have met otherwise.

Homeschooling gives me a really flexible schedule, and I've made friends in other states from online discussions and from speaking at and attending homeschooling conferences. I have lots of adult friends (and six adult students) in the *SCA* already (plus my husband's two squires), and now I'm more available to do things with them. They sometimes babysit for me in exchange for things I do with and for them. Sometimes they take my kids to movies or to do some-thing interesting. And some of the homeschooling moms have become my close friends.

As far as their higher education is concerned, there are all kinds of classes available in Albuquerque through continuing education, the vocational school, and the university. When the kids are older I'm sure their interests and contacts will lead them to interesting opportunities and situations. I've never been sorry we chose to homeschool.

I'm glad Nancy has given us an opportunity to share our lives with other homeschooling families. If you're just starting to homeschool I have a few words of advice: Breathe. Smile. Your kids will be sharing your stress and fear, so move quickly to get over them. Meet experienced homeschoolers and model your practice on families you like and respect. Deschool yourselves, and the kids will follow easily.

Kirby, Sandra, Holly, Marty

Randy, age 41
Sharon, age 38
Amberle, age 14
Nate, age 12

Five-year follow-up interview with Sharon in rural Ephrata, Pennsylvania

FIFTY CHARACTER TRAITS

Few things have remained exactly the same since our day in Nancy's book five years ago. I had said that spending lots of time together as a family and working on character twenty-four hours a day were two of the reasons I chose to school at home. Both of those things are still very important to me. However, last school year I found that our homeschooling was actually working against those things. My daughter Amber was thirteen years old and, after seven years at home, she was getting tired of being with her brother Nathan and me day in and day out. She didn't want to spend any time with us outside of school. Mostly, I think she was feeling a strong need to pull away and express her individuality and independence. Because our relationship became tense and strained, it was difficult to maintain the loving trust required to work on character together. These are some of the reasons my husband and I chose to send Amberle to a private school this year.

The Lord took us through a transition time over the spring and summer. First, I thought we would enroll Amber in an on-line Christian school. They would provide teacher input and grading that would give her accountability to someone besides me. It was actually a big step for me to consider because I have always needed to feel in control. That is why I rarely used prepackaged curricula; *I* wanted to be the one to choose books and schedules. A friend of mine advised, "You want to meet your child's needs, of course. You have a responsibility to do that. Some children need socialization because of their temperament. Consider whether school would be the best way to meet your daughter's needs." That helped me see it wasn't about meeting my needs or fulfilling my personal desires; but that I must seek the best for my child. This led us to a lifestyle schedule I thought I would never do—one child in school and one at home!

Three years ago we moved our mobile home to a wooded lot and built a house around it. Now, instead of a made-over dark dining room/school room, we have a large sun room that is used primarily for school. We have room for a piano rather than a keyboard for my daughter. It's a good thing too, because she has been very involved in playing for church services and special music. Of course, now that she is in school (ninth grade), she doesn't have even a third of the time to practice. That is definitely one of the disadvantages of being in school. Time for chores, personal interests, and family fun is very hard to find.

Our schedule now looks like this:

6:50 a.m.—Randy, my husband, takes Amberle to a friend's home (where she takes a car pool to school) and will then head into work.

7:30 a.m.—My son Nate and I get up and ready for school.

8:30 a.m.—We start school the same way as before. Nathan and I read over the prayer concerns for the day in our church's prayer calendar. We pray for our church family and our home family.

8:45 a.m—Last year we tried the *Sonlight Curriculum.* They use a large number of "living books" (biographies, historical fiction, attractive fact books) in a sort of unit study approach. It has a missions emphasis and so for sixth grade Nathan and I are studying Asia, Africa, and Oceania. Since I had been doing a huge amount of work choosing, interweaving, and scheduling books for many years previous, my husband asked me to look at a curriculum that was similar and would do the work for me. Ta da—*Sonlight.* They sell all the books they recommend (although I get some from the library), and include complete schedules, teacher's notes, discussion questions, dictation, and more. We have always loved narrative reading, so Nathan and I usually start with one of our fascinating readers (like *Young Fu of the Upper Yangtze* or *Eric Liddell*). My son will always choose the readers for history or science before his own reading or writing projects, so I must carefully intersperse diction, spelling, grammar, and math with our narrative reading.

I believe that concentrating on good books strengthened Nathan's vocabulary and prevented him from hating reading. He must read at least thirty minutes a day with *Sonlight* and has often been so involved as to read ahead or finish a book! This year they have added a wonderful spelling program called *Spelling Power* by Beverly Adams-Gordon. We are making slow, steady progress in spelling.

12:30 p.m.—We take a lunch break and then usually have one or two things to finish.

1:45 p.m.—We are usually done by now, although sometimes we are working up to 2:15 p.m. when I must leave to pick up Amberle. I work at home

---

Amberle (14), Nathan (12)

on our computer, typing about an hour or two a day. Sometimes I can manage to get in forty-five minutes here. Financially and schedule-wise, this has been a big blessing to our family.

2:15 p.m.—I leave for the twenty mile, forty-five minute drive to Amberle's school. While I am gone, Nathan usually has some silent reading or computer work to finish, and then he does his chores.

4:00 p.m.—Amber and I get home. She gets right to her homework, and I must think about supper. Nate runs out to play with the neighborhood children who are just getting home from school.

Our schedule is definitely more hectic, but the Lord gives strength for the work and walks with us along the way. We try to keep extra-curricular activities to a minimum. Most of our energies outside of school go to church service. This sometimes means we must forego a sport or activity that practices or plays on Wednesdays or Sundays, but we feel that setting our affection on things above helps keep eternity's values in view. Basically, teaching character is an around-the-clock, lifetime endeavor. Thank the Lord, He's still working on me!

Amberle (14), Nathan (12)

Bill, age 44
Leslie, age 44
Adrienne, age 16
Jesse, age 13
Brennan, age 10
Zachary, age 6

Five-year follow-up interview with Leslie in Val Morin, Québec, Canada

A COMEDY OF WISHFUL THINKING

Homeschooling has changed quite drastically in our family over the past few years because of two serious illnesses I have faced. Three years ago I had a nervous breakdown that was unexpected and severe. Recovery was long and slow. After two months in the hospital, I returned home, assuming that life would soon return to normal. The reality, however, was that I could do very little besides look after myself, and that I needed large doses of solitude, quiet, and sleep. Bill stayed home for a year and took over the care of the household and the children, which he was happy to do being a homebody at heart. It was a lot like being a single parent, with a greater need for co-operation and sharing of responsibilities amongst the children. It wasn't an easy time. I was in a great deal of inner turmoil and relations between myself and my spouse and children were very strained. There was, however, the opportunity to establish a new family dynamic. The experience helped foster a sense of self-worth in the children, who knew that their contributions were essential and of real value. Bill saw our family healing and thriving under his care.

The following year, everything began to restabilize. I gradually built up to managing the household, although in a scaled-back fashion, and Bill started working outside of the home again, doing small-scale construction and renovation projects on a self-employed basis that provided the flexibility we needed. (If circumstances were different, Bill would be very happy as a stay-at-home father!) Structured homeschooling of any kind was impossible, however. I did not have the inner strength required to motivate and direct our children in educational activities that they would not otherwise have done by themselves. We decided it was our sabbatical year to reframe the experience in positive terms. Then, last year, I discovered that I had leukemia and we have, yet again, lived through enormous upheaval.

The initial period of uncertainty following my diagnosis was very hard on everyone and required lots of explaining and reassuring. The children responded to the news differently, depending on their personality and how they deal with anxiety: one needed to cry and ask "difficult-to-answer" questions; while another wanted to spend lots of time away from home with friends.

There was a need to express anger, sadness, fear, and disappointment in various measures, but we didn't observe any regressive behaviours. This was largely due, I believe, to Bill's sensitivity and availability as a parent and because of the help of supportive friends. When living through really hard times, children tend to respond to the situation in the same manner as the adults around them. If we are able to accept the situation with equanimity and respond with confidence, despite the inevitable doubts, then our children are able to do likewise.

For a while, our lifestyle seemed completely beyond my capacities, but because of the insights I learned from the previous experience of my first illness, it has been easier to find a new equilibrium. Other than the need to rest frequently and reduce the amount of physical work I do, I am now able to live quite normally. I have been doing an immunotherapy treatment to improve the functioning of my immune system for over a year with a gradual, yet steady, improvement in well-being. The greatest challenge for me has been to accept my limitations and to reduce expectations to bare bones. This means constantly reassessing priorities on a daily basis, depending on my energy level, living in the present moment, and following the flow of events rather than trying to impose a schedule.

One of the hardest realisations I've had to come to terms with is that, although I still really believe in the value of homeschooling, I'm no longer interested in being the one making it happen. Our children, however, are still of school age. So how do we do it? Ten years of experience has given us more confidence in waiting for our children to express readiness. Often, what would have taken many hours of sit-down lessons at a young age, is learned independently at an older age. An added benefit of time is that now the older children can help the younger ones with what they want to do. We also have found that around age thirteen, our children have developed a good sense of themselves and what interests them, along with a growing ability to be focused and disciplined without an adult standing over them. They need a little structure and guidance from us, but too much is interpreted as trying to control their lives. It works best for them to focus their homeschooling efforts for short and intense periods during the spring and fall and take two or three months off during the winter and summer months.

For the past two years Adrienne (16) has decided what subject areas she has wanted to explore, generally choosing between math, English, French, history, and science, with no specific requirements from us. She has a limit of four subjects per session (each session is three-four months in duration). We've found her the necessary texts, helped her set up a study plan, and have been available to answer questions. Most of her spare time is spent in artwork and design. When she is ready to get a high school diploma, she will most likely do as other homeschooled adolescents in our community have done and register with an adult education programme to study for and write the required exams.

We've just begun the same system with Jesse (13), but with a much lighter workload. When he was about seven, we made the mistake of trying to teach him to read using a system devised by education experts. The result was quite sobering. He became convinced that reading was a very difficult process that was beyond his abilities and lost a lot of self-confidence. We backed off completely and waited, although anxiously at times. Now, he reads fluently, having taught himself over the last couple of years by trying to decipher the texts on his magic cards. He is also the kind of child that needs constant stimulation and friends, and he works best with company. In a school environment he would probably have been labeled as hyperactive and attention deficient! (Labeling seems to be a convenient way to blame the problem on the child rather than undertaking the more complicated task of identifying and correcting the deficiencies in the educational system or the incompatibility between a child's nature/needs and the programme's structure/context.)

We have no structured programme for Brennan and Zachary (ages 10 and 6), although I do sporadic math and science exercises with them about twice a week on good weeks. They attend a science club at a friend's house once a week and visit with friends frequently. Brennan is being treated by a developmental optometrist for a severe strabismus of both eyes, so he needs to avoid straining his eyes with too much close work. I find the younger children pick up learning effortlessly by observing and interacting with the older ones.

Living in Québec, being able to communicate in French is essential. Our children vary in fluency according to their age, with Adrienne and Jesse being the most comfortable. Adrienne is studying French grammar and babysits for French-speaking friends. Jesse takes his *Tae Kwon Do* course in French. Brennan understands a lot and speaks a little, while Zachary is just beginning. I've observed a similarity in the learning process with each child, where they slowly add to their vocabulary and then try it out with friends and in the community at large. Ideally, I'd like to spend part of every day speaking to the children in French, but so far, despite Adrienne's continual requests, I've been unable to do it very consistently!

Bill continues to read chapters of library books to the three boys most nights. Adrienne prefers to read to herself now—books ranging from mysteries to classics. We have just acquired a computer this fall on which they experiment daily. We were also given a video camera with which the children have created their own *Star Trek* episodes (we're major fans). Other family projects have included landscaping our garden, hauling firewood out of the forest, and building a timberframe woodshed from trees blown down in a large windstorm this past summer. Every fall for the past five years, the children have been involved in a bilingual (English/French) homeschoolers' theatre production, which has

Bill, Leslie
Jesse, Adrienne, Brennan
Zachary

Adrienne (16), Jesse (13), Brennan (10), Zachary (6)

become increasingly elaborate with each year. Recording sessions for music and vocals are done with a father who makes his living as a musician. Adrienne has begun to design and paint the backdrop and sew her own costumes, while we help the boys gather together what they need and help them learn their lines. We also continue to join in monthly activities organized by our local homeschooling group, with regular skiing and skating outings every week during the winter.

Seen from an outside perspective, how we homeschool (loosely based on the free school model) probably hasn't changed much. However, as our motivations and values in life have undergone a thorough reassessment in response to living with our current challenges, so have our attitudes toward homeschooling. Our contribution to HOMESCHOOLING: A PATCHWORK OF DAYS included a tongue-in-cheek look at a typical day in theory versus reality. While humour helped us deal with overzealous plans, the beliefs and expectations underlying them were left unchallenged and continued to undermine our confidence. We tended to evaluate ourselves according to what we thought we should be doing and, of course, always fell short. Our anxieties derived for the most part from our own upbringing and schooling, which was very performance and achievement oriented. Success was largely determined by someone else's approval. Now we understand the enormous benefit of self-assessment. One of my mentors was fond of saying: "Perhaps the greatest challenge is to be able to live on one's own terms without the compulsion to justify oneself." As we have come to see happiness and health as more precious than ideals or accomplishments, we are much less inclined to push ourselves and so are less willing to demand that our children push themselves to fit any preconceived notion of what they ought to be. We are more consistent in being able to see them for who they really are and what they want for themselves. We have become less concerned about academics and how they are doing compared to some norm, and more concerned about creativity, knowledge, and appreciation of oneself and the ability to find situations and conditions that nourish one's whole being.

Adrienne (16), Jesse (13), Brennan (10), Zachary (6)

Vern , age 51
Cathy, age 48
Tim, age 17
Jason, age 16

Five-year follow-up with Cathy in rural Quakertown, Pennsylvania

LOOKING BACK

This is the fifth year that I am not homeschooling. I am relieved and feel that Tim and Jason are doing well learning from others in the public school.

Jason started his sophomore year by earning the distinction of student-of-the-month of September for global perspectives (social studics). I continually shake my head at how well he and his brother do in social studies. I always felt that was one of our weak areas in homeschool due to the fact that I merely read an entire children's encyclopedia of history to them. Jason is taking an *Advanced Placement* computer programming class—a class not usually taken until the junior year. Jason is very skillful on the computer and all family members call on him for help. For a sixteen-year-old, he is very mature, a safe driver, and is starting to go out with his friends. He is gentle, submissive, peaceable, and considerate. Following these Scriptural principles, he is a forceful reason why family life goes so well.

Tim is a senior and was already accepted by Messiah College the August before his senior year. This year, he is taking an *Advanced Placement English* course. Last year, he took two *Advanced Placement* courses and scored a four on the history exam and a five (the top score) on his English exam. This will allow him to skip certain courses in college. In his junior year, Tim was selected to go to the *National Young Leaders Conference*, a program established in 1985 to cultivate and inspire students in their leadership potential. We also enabled him to go to another ten-day "*Law and Advocacy*" session in Washington, D.C., under the same conference. Tim got an almost perfect score on his verbal part of the *PSAT* (and later, the *SAT*) which helped him to become a *National Merit*

Scholar. That would give him a free ride for tuition at Eastern College. In math, he didn't do quite as well and plans to take the *SATs* again. It is exciting to see where Tim will go this year. I am guiding him to a Christian college. First we did homeschooling, then public school, and I think now is the time for Christian higher education.

The Lord led me into substitute teaching, which I have been doing now for about four years. It is a joy to get to teach our teens in the public school classroom!! One of our sons doesn't mind me teaching his classes, however the other expressed his discomfort, and although I would like to teach his classes, I decided to follow the Scriptural principal to consider the interests of others, so I do not accept a job that would be for one of his teachers. Vern is still a heavy equipment operator.

A homeschooling mother once said to me that, instead of studying homeschooled kids, studies should be done on the marriages of homeschooling families. I'm happy to report that my husband and I just celebrated twenty-five years of marriage. I am now working on strengthening our bond and continuing to seek other ways of building our relationship. It will be important since in a year we will begin to experience the "empty nest."

Tim, Jason

Dave, age 39
Ruth, age 41
Elizabeth, age 11
Timothy, age 10
Daniel, age 8
Peter, age 6
Jonathan, age 5
Matthew, age 2
Mary, age 1

Five-year follow-up interview with Ruth from Ellicott City, Maryland

THE BIG HAND'S ON THE SIX

We have moved from the Philadelphia area and now live in Ellicott City, a suburb of Baltimore. The area was developed in the fifties, so the yards are large, and the street is busy. We don't see too much of our neighbors as a result. Though we live near a business district, we are far enough away that we can't hear it. All in all, it's a pretty area, especially in spring when the trees blossom. And we now have seven children—the baby is one year old.

David now works for a small asset management firm, which manages money for two insurance companies. He does several things ranging from asset risk control to investment in structured securities and derivative instruments, to real estate investment, and more. Anywhere that investments and mathematics intersect, David is the one who works on it. He is enjoying the quality and the variety of the investment work. Still, he considers his primary job to be the home front. Earning money is not a priority compared to our marriage and the children.

I think most of what we are all about is the same. Every day has frustrations and rewards. I am still working on setting a good example of patience to my children. And I still wouldn't trade this homeschool lifestyle for anything.

Elizabeth is almost eleven and as tall as I am now. Her life ambition is to marry early and be a mother. Her motivation in her schoolwork is to be able to homeschool her own children well. Timothy is almost ten and can't get enough of books and computers. Daniel is eight, with an easy-going attitude toward life. He learned to read at a young age and especially enjoys science. Peter, at age six, is now in the process of learning to read. He has always been the child with the strongest will, an attribute with advantages I have come to appreciate over the years. Jonathan, who is five, is very musical and loves to be with people. Matthew, our two-year-old, is also musical—he could carry a tune before he could talk. And baby Mary keeps us entertained with her smile that won't quit.

We really wanted a large family, and transracial adoption provided an open door to fulfill our desire. Morning sickness and delivery pain are replaced by the hassles of phone networking, paperwork, and dealing with social workers. It comes out pretty even. In both routes to family—pregnancy and adoption—the end result is the same, a new baby. All our adopted babies were brought home within one month of birth. We didn't pay a fortune, but we did put a lot of time in looking for the right agency/intermediary. In short, it has all worked out very well for us, and we have no regrets. Though we have a transcultural family, we have experienced no racism within the churches we have attended. In the communities we have lived in, we have also had almost no problems. One final note: we view ideas from a Christian perspective, so we want all of our children, adopted and biological, to understand the good and bad points of all cultures.

I finally got my fenced-in yard. How wonderful! On sunny days, the younger children play outside for hours, without supervision. My oldest daughter adores the baby, her only sister. I wouldn't be able to manage without Elizabeth's help. One of my biggest challenges has been finding time to correct the older children's work. Since I'm a "morning person," doing it in the morning before everyone is awake has worked well so far.

I have come to recognize that there is not enough time in the day to do everything we'd like to do. We need to keep our perspective about what is truly important. Of course, we don't want the weeds of this world crowding out our commitment to God. Nor do we want to ever say, "I'm too busy homeschooling you, I don't have time to talk." Academically, I would rank math, after reading, as the one subject not to be neglected. Most other things they can pick up later or on their own. I firmly believe God gives us plenty of time for the truly important things in life.

We've also come to realize that to maintain this lifestyle, we have to do almost everything as a family. It's hard to keep saying no to all the opportunities that would break us up, but chauffeuring the children to different activities puts a stress on the rest of the family. Instead, Dave plays ball with the children after dinner in spring and summer, we rake leaves together in the fall, and we read aloud special books on the Lord's Day. We frequently invite other families over for dinner.

Elizabeth (11), Timothy (10), Daniel (8), Peter (6), Jonathan (5), Matthew (2), Mary (1)

We are confirmed in our belief that homeschooling is the only way for us. We do not want someone else raising our children. There are many times when I am frustrated with such things as sibling bickering or dawdling. But I am amazed at how much my children are devoted to my husband and me despite major failings they see every day. Their hearts seem to be embracing our values. I attribute this in part to the sheer amount of time they spend with us.

By the way, I still can't get through the day without an afternoon quiet time. For the older children, it's reading time. For me, it's still almost always nap time.

Elizabeth holding Mary, Daniel, Timothy, Matthew
Jonathan, Peter

Elizabeth (11), Timothy (10), Daniel (8), Peter (6), Jonathan (5), Matthew (2), Mary (1)

Mark, age 46
Sarah, age 40
Ben, age 16
Nathan, age 14
Aaron, age 12
Rachael, age 11
Ethan, age 9
Reuben, age 8
Isaac, age 6
Maggie, age 3

Five-year follow-up interview with Sarah in the small town of Osgood, Indiana

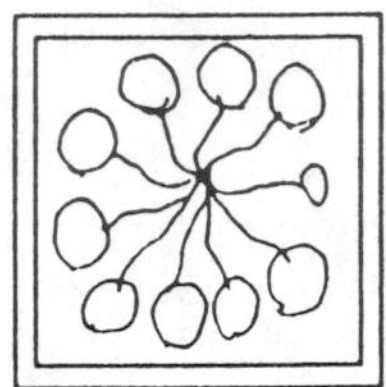

OLDER BOYS HAVE "THEIR BOY"

"Are you crazy?" I'm usually asked this question by wide-eyed, gaping-mouthed strangers when they find out I have eight children, work outside the home, and homeschool. My response? "Maybe." Their next question invariably is, "How do you do it?" To which I reply, "Well, isn't it obvious? I'm superwoman." Not! I'm just an ordinary woman who made unconventional choices.

We have eight children : Ben, Nathan, Aaron, Rachael, Ethan, Reuben, Isaac, and Maggie. And yes, I have had only one husband, Mark. Let's see (big breath), no multiple births, we've homeschooled our children since day one, and I only work part-time. (Whew!) That covers the most common questions people ask us.

We no longer live in a country home in Indiana, close to the Ohio border and civilization. Since then, much has happened, including a move farther west into Indiana and farther from civilization. Has anyone heard of Osgood? Okay, so we did move into a town but, trust me, Osgood is not much of a town. Mark and I were outnumbered in our choice of where to live. The kids wanted some big city; we wanted fifteen acres of wilderness. Do the math. Eight of them, two of us . . . we compromised and chose the smallest town we could find—Osgood. The kids have made friends, which was their goal, and Mark and I got to pick a ten-room Federal style home in which to live—a pretty fair trade-off.

Since our move, much has happened—a new job, the birth of Maggie, and major illness—all of these events have affected our life. Yet, homeschooling has been a constant. Our style of homeschooling hasn't changed too much, though my views about homeschooling have. Let me explain.

Homeschooling was a great blessing because of our ability to have a flexible schedule when a new baby joined our family, something to which we had become accustomed. When a baby arrives, everyone goes on vacation while Mom tries to get some rest, and learning becomes a self-directed affair.

It's a good thing that our homeschooling style vacillates between structure and chaos. My children have learned to learn in any condition, although they prefer structure, and that trait would become very important over the next years. At the end of Maggie's first year, an even bigger and unexpected road block to structured learning occurred.

You may remember that Isaac was born with a complex-congenital heart defect. He had undergone two heart surgeries by the time he was one, one of which was open heart. That December, he was scheduled for the second surgery which would complete his palliation. He was in and out of the hospital in six days . . . amazing, eh? His recovery was fast and problem free (so we thought), and we enjoyed a wonderful Christmas.

With the new year came a major complication, however. On Mark's first day back in school (I'll explain *that* situation in a bit), Isaac woke up from sleep and had a massive stroke. That moment became one of the defining moments of our family. While trying to reach Mark at school to let him know what was going on, I was trying to get our kids dressed and organized, finding places for them to stay, packing for a stay in the hospital, and trying not to panic. Isaac ended up staying in the hospital for three and a half weeks, and my other children (except for Ben and Maggie) stayed with our wonderful friends. Mark, Ben, Maggie, and I stayed near the hospital. My children all stayed with homeschooling families, hence my children did school with them. Their academic progress continued, but what they and I learned through this time was much more important than academics. We learned how precious our time together as a family is and how tenuous our lives are. I am proud of the way my children pulled together and accepted the challenge of having Isaac as a brother.

The first half of that year was terrible for us. Isaac had therapy three days a week, an hour away. During his therapy, the other children either stayed with friends or came to the hospital and did their workbooks while Isaac was busy. During this time, our fun studies came to an end. Math and English? Yes. Workbooks? Bring 'em on. Projects? Are you crazy?

Ben (16), Nathan (14), Aaron (12), Rachael (11), Ethan (9), Reuben, (8), Isaac, (6), Maggie (3)

So often homeschoolers view homeschooling as a better way to get an academic education than traditional schooling. I feel this is true, and I had a certain amount of pride in being able to point this out. But when a family is torn apart for a season, you have to hold on to other reasons for homeschooling when stellar academics become secondary to survival. My paradigm began to shift as I started to see homeschooling as the best way to keep our family intact. We had the time to spend loving our children in the way they needed after such a frightening experience. I still believe, wholeheartedly, that homeschooling is the best way to get an education, but I now know that it is also the best way to keep our family whole.

This aspect of homeschooling was brought home over and over again as the next two years passed. Before we moved, we had the opportunity to be involved in some of the public school district's programs. The very forward-thinking principals in our district offered to let us use their books, facilities, be on their sports teams, and take any classes we wanted. Nathan and Aaron chose to take part in their band. While I was at the school with them, I found that the school offered a preschool for special needs. Isaac was able to get in the class and it was wonderful for him. They had a very low teacher-to-student ratio, and the help he received was immeasurable. Additionally, one of the kindergarten teachers was a family friend, and Reuben ended up going to her class for half of the year. Ben, then fourteen, wanted to try junior high so he could make a decision about whether he might want to try high school. Isaac, Reuben, and Ben ended up in school full or part-time two years ago, and the year became a hectic jumble of trying to keep everyone's school and therapy schedule organized. It was exhausting and depressing.

The next summer another huge change occurred. Mark was accepted into law school, and we decided that in order for us to continue eating, I would have to go back to work as an RN. That summer I got a job at the children's hospital where Isaac received treatment for his heart and embarked on a lengthy orientation process. Seldom does one's life change so drastically overnight. I went from a stay-at-home, lots-of-kids, homeschooling mom to an employed professional in one day. I think I'm still in shock. I am learning to live with ambivalence because of my work. I love my job. I love being a stay-at-home mom. Being able to work part-time has brought a bit of balance, but every time I drive off to work, I think, "What am I doing? Am I crazy?" (I usually nod and keep on driving.)

Mark put off law school for a year to take over running the home and homeschooling. The year went fairly well. It was much harder for Mark to take on homeschooling six children all at once than it was for me to add children one at a time. I think you homeschooling parents will understand that. My working part-time has also helped Mark to find balance.

It was during this last year that we moved. Ben and Aaron pleaded to go to school to make some friends. Mark and I agreed, so we had two in school again. Actually, Ben lasted a week and then decided that school was a colossal waste of time (atta boy!). Aaron finished out the year and did learn some good things, none of which were academic. The major lesson he learned was time management. Having to get his homework done, getting clothes ready for the next day, and getting up to catch the bus on time were good tools for learning this.

They didn't make many friends at school. Most of the kids they know live in our neighborhood. The local homeschooling community has a basketball team that Nathan and Aaron have joined. I think they will end up with more friends from there than they did at school.

So, back to the central question, how has our homeschooling changed? I guess it hasn't. Everyone is home this year and we still plug away. My children have asked for more structure (did I mention they like structure?) in their schooling, and we try to adapt to that while balancing Mark's and my need for spontaneity. We still use workbooks, do few projects, and try to have lots of "real life" experiences available for them.

I have come to love homeschooling more and more. Homeschooling allows us to have our own schedule—our own life. We have the freedom to go to the park at 1:00 in the afternoon and hike. If we want to sit around the kitchen drinking tea and talking till noon, we can. If we want to go to the moon and stay for a

Nathan, Maggie, Ben, Aaron
Rachel, Aanta, Ethan
Reuben, Isaac

Ben (16), Nathan (14), Aaron (12), Rachael (11), Ethan (9), Reuben, (8), Isaac, (6), Maggie (3)

week, we can! And, God forbid, if Isaac should have any more health problems, we could race to the hospital without trying to coordinate a million different factors.

Lastly, Mark and I love the closeness that homeschooling affords. During my nursing orientation, I worked lots of second shifts. In the mornings, before I went to work, we would all drift into the kitchen (the smallest room in the house) and spend hours talking and laughing, catching up on each other's lives and building memories. Mark and I cherish these times and believe that our children do also. How many other parents of teenagers can say that their teens look forward to having tea/coffee with them in the mornings? Our older three children have gotten to be very close. And our younger five play together very well. They are being given time to build close relationships with their siblings, something I wish I had built with my siblings. Perhaps we are more aware of the brevity of our lives because of Isaac. Probably so. All I know is that I wouldn't want to send my children off for hours every day and not have the opportunity to know them.

So, am I crazy? I think not. I think I have been given a gift to have such a wonderful family and the freedom to raise them and to know them—and for that, I am grateful.

Ben (16), Nathan (14), Aaron (12), Rachael (11), Ethan (9), Reuben, (8), Isaac, (6), Maggie (3)

Tim, age 39
Tina, age 39
Jake, age 17
Josh, age 16
Jordan, age 13
Hannah, age 8
David, age 7

Five-year follow-up interview with Tina in very small Temple, Pennsylvania.

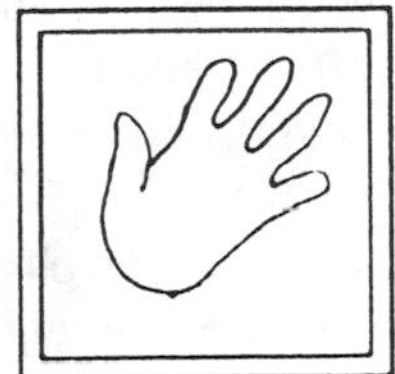

TRIAL AND ERROR

It has been more "Trials and Errors" over the last five years. We still live in Temple, Pennsylvania, but we'll soon be moving down the road. Tim is an electrical engineer. He is a very giving man who volunteers to drive a bus for various ministries in our area, traveling to many places, near and far, often taking the children along. Jake is seventeen, Josh is sixteen, Jordan is thirteen, Hannah is eight, and David is seven.

The last two years Jake and Josh went to a private school. However, they are back home again for the current school year. This is Jake's senior year and Josh is in eleventh grade. Over the two years of not homeschooling, we noticed negative attitudes developing toward family. We needed to find a way to get the "socialization" attitude out of my kids and to instill again the priority that "family comes first."

When it was first decided that they would come home again to homeschool, there was a lot of tension between older and younger siblings. The ones at home liked it when the older ones were away; and the older ones liked to be away, so they could do their own thing. But they were not ready for that kind of freedom. There has been a gradual process of weeding out the poor influences and replacing them with good ones. When I feel uncomfortable about a situation, I pray about it and it seems like God dissolves it.

My husband Tim often reminds me that these are learning experiences, even though we would prefer to not go through the difficult times. He also is very glad for the opportunity to deal with these situations while the children are still at home. Once they are out of the nest, we won't have as much to say on the matters.

So, here we are with more trials and errors behind us. We bought a larger home this summer. We got a great deal on it, but there was also a lot of work to be done. The boys all learned how to do roofing, plumbing, electrical and drywall. With all the repairs the boys have been doing, we have encouraged them to keep track of it in detail, so that they will be able to count it toward school hours.

Jacob is taking two courses at the local liberal arts college—English and math. To help keep him motivated, he is paying for the courses, and we will reimburse him if he earns a B or better. He is also doing a computer programming course and Bible study at home. At this point, he is not sure what he wants to do after graduation.

Josh is doing *Saxon Advanced Math*, physics, Bible, and an *Advanced Placement English* course online. He is doing a fine job with the course and told us the other day that he is glad we got him to do it, because it is so good to have an outlet for his writing.

Jordan is using the *Sonlight* curriculum for the second year in a row. He is in eighth grade but chose to do the sixth level as he has never studied world history. He likes this curriculum because the log is all written out, and he knows what he needs to do each day. He also likes all the reading he needs to do. He often comments about how hard it is to stick to their reading schedule. In January, he will also sign up for a correspondence writing course. He did this last year and really enjoyed the challenges of it. He is also involved with a drama group from our church. He played soccer for the school district this year and learned a lot about living his testimony.

Hannah is in the third grade, using the *Learn At Home* book. She is very much hands-on. She is working on the *Saxon Math* third grade math text for the second year in a row (we are taking it slow) She likes to review flash cards outside where we can play "Mother May I?". I show her a card and, if she answers correctly, she can somersault or hop or move somehow toward the finish line. She is also touring the U. S. this year via computer where there is a wealth of information on each state. After she looks up a state and fills in her fifty states workbook, she makes a little booklet that gives a brief synopsis of each state. We then mark the state and its capitol on a mark-it map. David is using a similar workbook and *Sing, Spell, Read, and Write*. He is working on his reading. Although he is seven, I am not pushing him—we take it slowly.

Just today, we picked up the really cute lop-eared bunnies Hannah and her friend had chosen at a farm. We also bought rabbit food, chicken wire, and a

---

Jake (17), Josh, (16), Jordan (13), Hannah (8), David (7)

water bottle for the rabbits while we were out. The girls wanted to come back home and help the boys, who had agreed to build a cage for them. Josh and Jordan did most of the framing for the cage, I got in the way, and Sarah and Hannah were the giddy cheerleaders. The girls and I stapled on the chicken wire. This took a long time, since I have never worked with chicken wire or a staple gun before. But we got it all done, and it turned out to be a rather nice cage.

While the bunny house was being built, David and his friend ran off into the woods to play in the fort near the pond. This fort has been under construction all summer, and it seems whenever other kids come over, they always add something to it. What started out as a clearing under some brambles has turned into a two story haven for imaginative kids. Hannah and David discovered some old pallets and scrap wood in a dump on our property. They hauled these to their site and made a dock into the pond for the canoe and a ladder to go up to the second story. They were pretty excited the day they had constructed the second floor "We can actually stand on it! Without falling through."

Several things occurred today that convinced me yet again that at this point I do not see how I could send any of my children to a school. First of all, Jacob spent most of the day reading and working. This is the same kid that has not read a book in two years because he went to "school." Josh humbled himself and made this cage for his sister.

I am very thankful for the opportunities that arose today and that we could capitalize on them right away. If the children were not at home, I would not have been able to witness Gods' healing in my children.

Josh, Jake, Hannah
Davaid, Jordan

Jake (17), Josh, (16), Jordan (13), Hannah (8), David (7)

Matt, age 43
Susan, age 40
Sarah, age 16
Caleb, age 14
Ricky, age 9

Five-year follow-up interview with Susan in the wilderness of Chugiak, Alaska

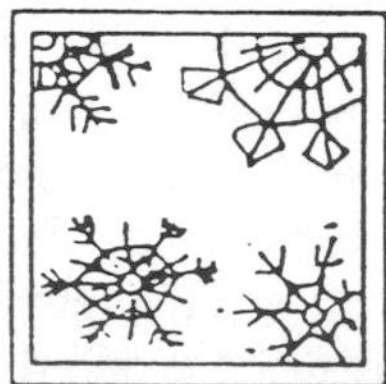

EACH SNOWFLAKE IS DIFFERENT

Homeschooling continues to be a large part of our everyday life. Sarah and Caleb are now in high school, and that has brought new challenges and opportunities. I found that I had to expand and bring in other resources. Whether it meant videos, another homeschooling parent, a college class, or distance learning, it didn't matter—I just needed help providing what they needed. Sarah is way beyond me in English and writing, so we signed her up for English classes at the university. She had to pass an entrance exam but everyone was very helpful. I think that it's important that parents realize they don't have to know all the subject matter (advanced math, etc.), rather, it's just a matter of finding the right help or resource.

All three children are enrolled in a new Alaskan homeschooling distance education program, *I.D.E.A.* (*Interior Distance Education of Alaska*). We do not have to pay for this program that may be used toward any non-religious curriculum, music lessons, college courses, books, or anything that is used for educational purposes. They have never questioned anything I have purchased, and I can still use any "religious" materials to teach—*they* just don't pay for it. Due to the new program, we have been able to expand our educational options to include music lessons and college classes. The program allows us to teach at home and remain in control of our children's education, while providing more opportunities and resources than we would otherwise have. Students that graduate from the *IDEA* program receive a high school diploma, and Sarah is taking Spanish at the local university and high school.

At first, the children were hesitant about our new plans, but both Sarah and Caleb won awards for *ThinkQuest*, where they won contests for their Internet web sites. Sarah also won the local creative writing contest for her age group for the *Anchorage Times*. She did all that her freshman year and I've never heard any complaints since!

As I reflect back on our homeschooling years, what has been most valuable to us is the time we have been able to spend with our children. Our teens know us, and we know them! In a day and age when families go their separate ways everyday, we stay together. My husband Matt still develops software applications as an independent consultant, and I develop web sites. I was doing quite a bit of it over the past few years, but am doing as little as possible since I want to spend more time homeschooling. Since Dad works out of a home office, we have home, school, and work all in one place. The Internet continues to be a large part of our lives and has allowed us more freedom and choices both in education and work. We stay in touch with resources and people right from our desktops.

The day that public school started this past fall, I happened into the local coffee shop in the morning. It was packed with women "celebrating" their kids going back to school. Our homeschooling philosophy is that we rejoice in our children being at home with us. Next year I'll take my kids with me to the coffee shop when public school starts and buy them all a "steamer" to celebrate!

Caleb, Matt, Susan
Sarah, Ricky

Harry, age 46
Jane, age 47
Jen, age 16
Michelle, age 14

Five-year follow-up interview with Jane in East Hanover, Pennsylvania

CRAZY QUILT IN THE MAKING

We still live in East Hanover. Our township was created from several large farms, with many small farms having been saved throughout. There are also many small family-run horse stables. The location is reflected in the street names: Trail Road, Meadow Lane, Pheasant Avenue, and Bunny Lane. It is very nice blend of beautiful Pennsylvania scenery, neighbors, and shopping within a half hour's drive.

What a great time for an update on our homeschooling family. A chance to reflect on what we're doing, where we are, where we've been, and where we're going five years later. This chance to reflect comes as our homeschooling heads in a new direction. After homeschooling throughout her life, Jen is in her senior year of high school and will graduate in June, traveling out of state to college. How did we get to this point? Is homeschooling working? How did we all prepare for Jen's college education? What are her opportunities? Many readers may think that homeschooling may work in the elementary years, but wonder about high school subjects. What about the teenage rebellious years, and what about preparation for college? How could we possibly do that? I'll tell you how the high school years have been as easy, fun, and educational as the first homeschooling years, and about Jen's college experiences and opportunities.

Jen eventually dropped off the gymnastics team but continued with private lessons and began to work as a coaching assistant for beginner girls' classes. By age fifteen, she was a full coach with beginner, advanced beginner, intermediate, and pre-team classes. She worked three evenings a week. Michelle continued on the team, earning many medals, and she qualified to compete in her first national meet—*The State Games of America.* She was taking private dance lessons to improve her beam and floor routines, adding a lot of back tumbling. At this point, she decided she did not want to continue in gymnastics, but wanted to expand in dance.

This past year, Michelle took classes in ballet, lyrical, jazz, hip-hop, tap, and acro (floor gymnastics combined with dance). Handstands and backwalkovers in the living room have become pirouettes and laybacks in the living room and tap in the kitchen. The dance studio attends competitions twice a year, where she also earned several trophies. With the girls' drop in time spent at the gym, I have cut back to working there one evening a week.

Michelle is taking classes at our local homeschool center. In previous years, she has taken general art, composition, literature, earth science, math strategies 1 (including *Math Olympiad* where she was among the top 10% of all students in sixth grade), math strategies 2 (including *MathCounts*), and algebra, where she was one of two honor students. This year in ninth grade, Michelle is taking a literature class and life science. Last year she was a teacher's aid in science, helping with labs, grading papers and helping the teacher as needed. She is assisting the math teacher (that's me) by helping select problems to be given as homework, creating quizzes, grading papers, and helping in Math Club. Michelle has also coached preschool gymnastics and helped with preschool dance class. She thinks she might become a teacher—she would be very good at it. She also thinks she might major in dance, possibly to teach dance or become a back-up dancer for a well-known group. She might end up in musical theater with Jen.

Jen's musical interests were mentioned briefly in our last chapter. At the time, she was taking piano lessons, playing handbells at the church, and performing. Jen has now played handbells for nine years, has played a duet with another teen, and has performed two handbell solos—one at Easter, another at Christmas. Jen is the only person in our church to play a handbell solo. It is really something to watch her since, along with memorizing the music, she needs to choreograph where to put down each bell to make it easy to reach for the next time she needs it, then memorize that the specific bell is in a new position when she reaches for it!

About a year and a half ago, Jen began private voice lessons. She has a strong high soprano voice and a good ear for pitch. Her voice teacher, a mezzo-soprano opera singer has high hopes for Jen. She is learning opera pieces in German and Italian and church pieces in Latin. This summer, Jen performed a mini-concert of musical theatre pieces for the senior group at our church, and she will be singing 1940s swing music for a dinner this fall.

Each spring, the church choir takes a bus trip to New York City where the participants have the whole day to do as they want. Jen and her father have gone the past two years. Each year they see part of the *Metropolitan Museum of Art* that relates to Jen's art or history interest at that time. The first year they also attended a Broadway show, *Phantom of the Opera.* This is when Jen announced she had changed her college major from marine mammalogy specializing in dolphin communication to musical theatre. This past year, in addition to their trip to the *Met*, they went to Broadway and saw *Les Miserables.*

Jen spent five weeks last summer in college theatre classes. At the conclusion of the three-week introduction to theatre class, Jen was voted outstanding theatre student by her fellow students.

After successful auditions, Jen was selected in her senior year to attend college part-time. She is taking acting, theatre voice, theatre movement, and a theatre workshop. These classes are for seniors in high school only. She is one of five students in the classes.

With high SAT scores and a high grade point average, Jen also qualified to take academic classes, so is now taking Spanish. I am pursuing my own bachelors in elementary education, so I am fulfilling my language requirement by also taking Spanish. We are in different classes, with different instructors, but using the same textbook, so Jen is helping me with my homework, especially pronunciation and conjugation.

This was her sixth year performing with a group that is for children from age six to sixteen, and they sing positive, uplifting, patriotic, inspirational, and pop songs. They also learn choreography and *American Sign Language* for many songs. Jen will be seventeen at the time of next year's auditions and will not eligible to perform but may participate as an assistant director.

Jen continued to take dance classes this summer and we researched colleges that offered a Bachelor of Fine Arts in Musical Theatre. We found many colleges that offer a major in one with a minor in the second, but very few offer the B.F.A. in musical theatre. Beside looking for a college with her major, she was also looking for a small college, fairly close to home, and in a rural or suburban setting. I looked for a college that had started as a music conservatory, so she could possibly minor in vocal performance. We have narrowed this to three top choices—The University of Hartford in Connecticut, Ithaca University in New York, and Otterbein College in Ohio.

Both Jen and I feel that Otterbein is her number one choice—music conservatory background, BFA in musical theatre, and a small college in a neighboring state. They also have opera theatre and a variety of choirs, including a chance to tour. Jen applied to Otterbein early in June and received an acceptance letter and an offer of a merit scholarship for her academics. We visited the college in October and enjoyed watching a production of *Death of a Salesman* by the college theatre department. Jen's auditions for the music and theatre departments are scheduled for early next year, so she is postponing her acceptance letter until after her auditions.

Along with college classes, her performing group, voice lessons, dance classes, and occasionally coaching gymnastics, Jen is completing her required high school classes at home. She is studying American government, mathematical problem solving, and English—she is trying to read as many classics as she can, along with the plays she is reading for her theatre classes. She is also contributing to the our state's homeschooler's high school literary magazine, reviews books online, has completed a seventy page novella, and writes poetry.

We see Jen's transition from high school to college as going very smoothly. After all, we never had "school at home." We had an unschooling, real-life approach to education. Jen has volunteered at the therapeutic horseback riding center, coached gymnastics, performed in various music areas, worked on many craft projects, and for most of her high school years has studied areas of interest from college level textbooks. She also has several years experience in proof reading and editing my college term papers. I've discovered that after writing a paper and proofing it several times, it's very easy to miss small errors, since I know what I wrote and I easily "read" what I know I wrote and miss what I've actually typed. A fresh set of eyes to read the paper catches those little typographical errors and minor punctuation errors. This is helpful to me and to Jen, as she has become used to the layout of a research paper, including footnotes and bibliography.

Next year, in Jen's first full year of college, she will be familiar with college level work and the scheduling of homework, term papers, and projects. She will be familiar with many college teachers and the fact that different teachers expect different participation in classes, want different formats on papers, and have different grading practices. Jen is experienced at registration lines and paperwork, scheduling required classes, changing classes, and walking the campus to different buildings. All that will be really new to her will be living in a dorm away from home. She is becoming an expert at e-mail and *Instant Messenger*!

Jen works at her school work seven days a week, twelve months a year. She is a true autodidact, hard worker, and perfectionist. She sets goals of A in every class and works to get them. She schedules her assignments, completes them on time, and keeps her own log book. Homeschooling is a breeze with this type of student. As a parent and homeschool supervisor, I only need to schedule time to drive her to the library and keep alert in reading the newspaper and magazines for activities in which she would be interested.

Since I briefly mentioned my college courses before, here is an update on what I've been doing educationally. When I first went to college, I majored in elementary education and library science. I finished approximately three years before having to take a break for physical health problems. I started working in banking, and the job was actually paying more and had more of a future than teaching at that point in time. I spent ten years as a bank teller, ATM specialist, and branch manager of an all ATM branch. Then, I took time off for full-time mothering and homeschooling. Almost four years ago, I started back to college, taking classes part-time. I try to take one class per semester. It doesn't seem like much, but try to go to class two or three evenings a week, read all your assignments, do projects, and write papers; while homeschooling middle and high schoolers, teaching one day a week, and working part-time. Oh, yes, and getting the children to all of their activities! Then realize that fall finals hit two weeks before Christmas. My family has been extremely supportive.

When the budget allows, I pick up small gifts all summer and tuck them away. All major shopping is handled by Harry, with a joint trip after my finals. Decorating, baking, and all those niceties are cut back, and what is done is done as family projects. Michelle is becoming a great cook and baker. Jen is the expert gift wrapper—she's very creative. I am going for my Pennsylvania teaching certificate in order to do homeschooling evaluations—an opportunity to return to the homeschooling community what help others have given to me.

Harry has also added to his education during our homeschooling years. He studied and took a test for certification as a senior professional in human resources. He has since studied further and received life certification. He also received his Master's Degree.

What has always worked best for us has been flexibility. The best advice I think I've ever received and used was: if the morning starts as "one of those days," don't do planned school work—it would be a waste of time and cause a lot of frustration. I followed Jen's lead on whether it was going to be a focused, planned-activities learning day or a day having fun being together, knowing that learning will occur anyway on another day.

Flexibility was also helpful in realizing that materials I purchased for Jen might not be the ones to use for Michelle in the same subject. They have different learning styles and no one will be happy or learn at their best if the work goes against their style. Since we don't purchase full curriculums and seldom use textbooks, we purchase games, workbooks, and computer software. It doesn't break the budget to get different workbooks for each of them.

I am the coordinator for our local support group, which is very informal. In the early formation of the group we had regular monthly meetings, prepared topics, scheduled field trips, etc. and too much time was put into the group instead of individual families and homeschooling. We now meet informally in the park during nice weather, and try to stay in contact by phone. Field trips are more spontaneous, with several families getting together to do something of interest. When I am contacted by phone by a new or potential homeschooling family, I try to get together with them to give them information such as good books to read about homeschooling, how to get newsletters and magazines on homeschooling, some benefits and drawbacks, and of course, how to get the most accurate information about our state's homeschooling law.

I've realized that parents of four-, five-, and six-year-olds don't need to feel it's necessary to purchase a curriculum and sit down to "school" from 9:00 a.m. to 3:00 p.m., set certain times for certain subjects, or that children must learn to read at six years old, etc. That's what they would be doing if they were at public or private school. I've learned to enjoy being with our children, to share with them, and to learn together. I've enjoyed reading to them and having them read to me. Instead of workbook pages of phonics, spelling, punctuation; we've explored the world together, discovering and investigating. Instead of math workbooks filled with drills, we play math games and are alert for math in every-day life. We give concepts, not rules, and we visit museums and places we enjoy and want to share with our children. We give our children the joy of exploring, discovering, learning, and give them the joy of being together as a family. Love of learning and memories of family and friends are much more important than memorizing facts and formulas at an early age. There are plenty of years to learn the details. It's hard to believe and seems like an old cliché, but they grow up and head off to college long before we realize it.

Michelle, Jen, Ed
Jane

Brad, age 44
Betsy, age 44
Justin, age 16
Sean, age 13

Five-year follow-up interview with Betsy in the capital city of Dakar, Senegal

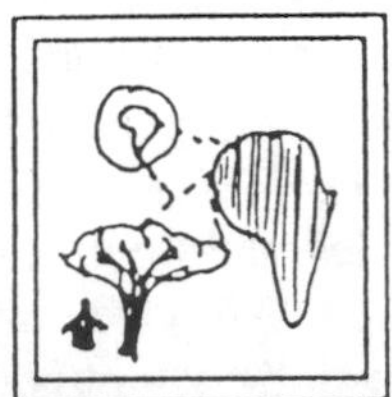

WAITING CONSTRUCTIVELY

About four years ago, we moved from our village to the city. We had been based in our village home for ten years. We had actually lived there during those years for stays of up to four months at a time—with intermittent stays in our mission center in the capital city of Dakar. Our village house was described in the first book—that's where we spent the homeschool day we wrote about.

The capital has over two million people—the whole country only has about eight million in all, so that gives you an idea of the concentration of people in Dakar. This African city is a real mix of the traditional and the modern. Skyscrapers overshadow an amazing array of vehicles in the streets below. Fancy Mercedes Benz vie for road space with horse carts, taxis, crowded buses, and pedestrians. Businessmen in suits and ties stroll along the sidewalks beside women carrying their cook stoves on their heads and their babies on their backs. Stores and outdoor markets carry many imported items along with beautiful local cloth, crafts for tourists, fresh fruits and produce, as well as many other every day items. There is much beauty in the city here—people say the women here are among the most beautiful in Africa! There are public and private gardens with lovely tropical flowers and trees. There are the colonial buildings with their colorful orange clay roof tiles and interesting architecture. But it is also overcrowded, and there is much poverty alongside the wealth—a place of contrasts, to say the least.

We have lived in our present house for almost three years—which is a record for us as a family! This has been the longest stay in one place since Justin was born. We are in a neighborhood outside the downtown area. Our move from the village to this city was a major transition for us. We have traded a consistent village water supply (from a well beside our house) for an inconsistent city water supply. Located on the edge of the dry Sahel region, the country is trying hard to keep up with the enormous demands for water and not quite able to. We have traded our cozy village light supplies (candles, gas lamps, occasional solar power) for unpredictable city electricity. We do still have our gas fridge (brought with us from the village) so our food storage remains dependable! We have traded having our own vehicle for using taxis to get around, or just walking. I could write a whole book of taxi tales!! Those are a few of the more concrete changes we've experienced.

The changes that are somewhat harder to describe, but which affect us at a much deeper level, include adjusting to this urban lifestyle that is noisy, crowded, dirty, and a huge mixture of cultures. Our village life was focused mainly on the people around us. The city is, on the other hand, a combination of the largest ethnic group in the country, memories of the French influence from colonial days, as well as many other ethnic groups. There is also a large international business and diplomatic presence, and a major Lebanese community. As you can imagine, we are faced with many cross-cultural experiences every day as we live and work here.

This rich mix of cultures is, of course, fascinating. And, I must confess, it's overwhelming at times. That is from a middle aged mom's point of view. I must admit . . . it tires me out! I deeply miss and would prefer the village life, but I know that for these years, considering the ages and interests of our kids, the city is where we belong for now.

Our boys are happy here. They don't mind the city as much as I do. They have started to get out a bit on their own. Justin began using the public transport about a year ago, and he travels around now comfortably to some of the mission school activities or to see friends. Sean is wanting now to go out on his own too, but he needs to work on his French more—all the public conversation is either in French or one of the local languages.

Both of the boys have a good group of friends who are mostly American at this point. They found it hard initially to make Senegalese friends here in the city—the difference between living in a small town environment and the city environment was the main reason for that. People here live behind high walls and enclosed courtyards, and the kids are in their schools most of the day, most of the year—their schedules just didn't make for easy interaction. With our own schooling, the boys spend much of their time either at home, with friends during our homeschool co-op activities, or they participate in the mission school activities.

After our move to the city three years ago, Justin decided to go to the mission

Justin (16),

school for ninth grade. (For his eighth grade year, Justin spent half the year in the States during furlough and half the year here.) That spring, it became apparent that the following year there would be no kids his age in our local homeschool group. He had started to get to know some of the kids at the mission school, and he expressed an interest in going there. We discussed all the pros and cons for several weeks, met with the guidance counselor at the school, and prayed about this decision. In the end, we felt the decision should be Justin's and he did decide to try the school for ninth grade. It seemed a good time for the transition, as he was beginning high school. He was very excited. He felt this would probably be the end of his homeschool career.

Mom was less excited about it for several reasons, especially considering the cost. And then, having taught him for almost all his life—I wasn't quite prepared to just stop. Could I trust his education to others? It took much prayer on my part and sorting through my own motives and goals for him. My main concern was the availability of adequate staff at the school, as each year they have to recruit their staff, and some years they just don't have the teachers they need to fill all the positions. Indeed, it looked like they would not have a high school science teacher up to the last week before school started that year.

Despite my fears, Justin did ninth grade at the mission school and, all in all, it was what we would consider to be a successful experience. He liked most of his courses, got a 4.0 grade point average and discovered an interest in drama (which has subsequently grown to be a passion). He was challenged to get along with people, both teachers and students, he would not have chosen to be with had he been on his own. He was also challenged to examine his priorities and develop his own sense of identity among a very different group of people than he had known before.

However, he did have significant adjustment difficulties. Although Justin enjoys being with people and interacting, he had a difficult peer group experience. Many of his peers had an active disdain for academics and this, along with a very relaxed attitude even among some of the teachers, made some classes very frustrating. Justin is an extremely focused student and playing around during class just did not meet with his idea of well spent time.

As you can imagine, this caused friction with his peers to some extent. Handling this became a growing experience for Justin, and he made mistakes, as we all do. It was not all negative, but these challenges led to another consideration of homeschooling for the following year. The combination of the long hours and lack of flexibility, "required" courses that just didn't fit into what Justin wanted to pursue, and our family plans that included a trip to the States the following spring, all led Justin to decide he'd rather return to homeschooling for his tenth grade year.

The original plan was to take the tenth grade year at home and to then return to the mission school for eleventh and twelfth grade. Justin's interest in drama, his desire to be with people outside the home, and his enjoyment of several of the teachers at the school made him want to return to school. In view of this, the school said he should take correspondence courses.

Well, it was a *horrible* year. The correspondence routine was far from my idea of homeschooling. Both my husband and I spent hours sorting through all the required correspondence—I didn't teach or even interact much with Justin. I was too busy filling out grade cards and writing e-mails and faxes trying to keep up with the records! Fortunately, he is able to work independently. If he hadn't been able to basically do the work on his own, it would have been even harder. I felt all year like he was taking courses from a computer—we never even received a name of the teacher for one of the courses. He did virtually no reading except in the texts. He took a tenth grade level history course with *no* outside reading . . . groan. We had one incident where we poorly photo-copied grade cards, which resulted in Justin receiving two failing grades! We also ran into political correctness face to face for the first time when Justin received a lower grade on an essay because his content was politically incorrect, even though it was essentially a grammar exercise.

Well, in the spring of that school year, we looked once again at our options and plans! The previous type of correspondence choice was erased forever from any future considerations. However, we knew there were other possibilities for studying at home. Since Justin had developed an interest in certain authors, especially JRR Tolkien, and since he continued to prefer studying on his own for the most part, Justin decided he would rather finish his high schooling at home by developing courses that suited these particular interests. He had also been invited to participate in the mission school drama program during the year, even though he was not a student. He was invited to join due to the lack of kids interested in being in the play. He was even given the part of the Narrator in the play *Our Town* because none of the students tried out for that part. So, he knew the drama option would probably still be open to him, even if he continued to homeschool.

One of my main concerns at that point was how to get Justin into an accredited program, so he would receive a high school diploma. Although these days, more colleges are looking with interest at homeschool students who do not have a traditional diploma, there are still many who "require" a diploma from an accredited school. Since Justin is not sure where he may want to go to college, or even if he will go, we don't want to narrow his possibilities in either the job or the college market by him not having a diploma. We had been associated with a homeschooling high school diploma program during our furlough years and liked their program, but they do not offer a diploma for overseas students. We looked into several other options, and when we were in the States during this summer (between Justin's tenth and eleventh grade years), we got registered with a private school in the States called *Clonlara School*. *Clonlara* is accredited and will award a diploma. Yet, they are very flexible with how they award credit for work done. One thing we really like about their program is that they allow you to design studies that follow your own interests. They also value having a job as part of the high school experience. We designed a two year program for Justin that fulfills the normal requirements for a college-bound student, but at the same time is tailored to Justin's interests.

So far this school year has been wonderful—a breath of fresh air and many other clichés of that sort. Justin is doing an e-mail course in play writing that is working out really well—not at all like corresponding with a computer. He's also done more drama this fall, including a great part in the mission school play and participating in a student café night in which he did two lip-syncs.

One other great thing about having planned and bought materials for the next two years is that we have all the materials we'll need, so we won't have to do any ordering and buying overseas, which has been one of the most stressful things for me about homeschooling here.

However, I will hasten to add that one problem with planning two years in advance is that our plans may change as time passes! Justin is now rethinking his senior year, and feeling a pull once again toward the mission school. Part of this is social at this point, which is a legitimate consideration in our opinion but should not, of course, be the only factor in deciding. What will he do in the end? Stay tuned!

Speaking of planning, to briefly describe how we work the schooling between Brad and I, I'll start by saying that it is very much a joint effort with the sense that we equally share the responsibility for providing our sons with the best education we can offer them. As far as the hands-on, day-by-day routine we have, I do the planning, curriculum buying, and most of the teaching.

Though Brad works in his job most of the time, he also helps with various aspects of our homeschooling program, especially physical education and the more advanced math courses. He is also our principle encourager and facilitator, helping out with scheduling and pitching in with the household if there is a major homeschool event to be organized.

Our other son, Sean (who is now thirteen), is learning how to be an independent scholar. I decided when he started sixth grade that we would look at the years sixth through eighth grade as a whole—a passage between elementary and high school. These years could be a review in a sense of what he had done so far in his earlier years of homeschooling and also a deepening of his learning in those areas. We could use this three-year period as an integrated time of doing things like a three-year world history study. We've also planned our science as a three-year program.

It has been exciting to see how Sean has grown lately. He is becoming quite the creative writer. He has taken a journalism course via e-mail this fall and is now working on producing a newsletter with a friend about life here in Africa.

Sean is starting Latin this year, which has been really fun and stimulating. Justin really revolted in his seventh grade year against the grammar workbooks that were part of our curriculum at the time. I wanted to avoid a rerun of this with Sean and was interested in a more classic approach to learning how to write well. We had been doing studies of word origins for several years and starting Latin with a list of derivatives for each lesson's vocabulary has worked real well for him.

With Sean, I have been very involved in starting a homeschool co-op here in Dakar. Last year we did things like follow the *Iditarod* dog sled race via the Internet. We also started a desert survival course (as a companion to the arctic focus) to prepare us to follow an annual road rally that runs from Paris to Dakar each year. As part of a three-year syllabus that we are developing, we spent two months learning about prehistory and the early empires here in West Africa. Activities included dance lessons for the kids by a local gal who taught them how the dance steps are all based on daily activities like planting and harvesting, and a field trip to Goree Island, which has quite a long history as a slave port. We also had our own homeschool team in a regional sports event and the kids had a great time despite not winning anything.

Our co-op started out as a monthly get together for about six families who were interested in the kids having some group activities. It was a good mix because several of our participating families were not American, and the exposure for all the kids to the various cultures was great. We did this sort of loose thing for several years in a row. We had an explorers day, an oceanography workshop, a living history day, a Presidents day, stamps day, etc. The kids always were expected to prepare something in advance and present it to the group, and then we planned age specific activities.

Starting just a year ago, three families decided to start meeting each week. This began as a Senegal focus—we committed to a month study of the nation, history, and cultures of Senegal. After that, we moved on to the *Iditarod* dog sled race. One of our families had a relative who was going to Alaska for the race and he sent us an activity book about the race. We spent a month with those activities. It was really fun! We even listened to live radio broadcasts during the race via the Internet.

This weekly idea was working well, so we just began to do various things each week. We usually have some sort of history topic, some sort of science topic, and an art activity. The three moms are the planners and we all share the teaching. We get together most Tuesdays (the kids all take martial arts class then) and do some planning. Then we have the co-op on Wednesdays. We have had a few other families come and go—the core three have stayed involved. We find that some people come and then start to feel like they can't fit the co-op into their schedule—but they don't like to miss what others are doing. This gets to be a drag for those of us who are committed to it, so we try to let people know that they shouldn't feel obligated to come, but if they are going to come, they have to really be involved.

This fall we have been doing a "time travel" through the Ice Age, the Stone Age (we like to call it "the stone and bone age"), the Iron Age, Roman times, and the Dark Ages. We decided that each age group (we usually divide the kids up into three age groups and have age appropriate activities) would invent a Time Traveler whom they would follow through each time period. We have a set of questions about needs and how they are met, which we do for each time period. We'll continue this into the spring and probably even through the fall next year. The kids are doing their own time line, with the various periods appropriately situated. They also each do an illustration each week. These illustrations will be made into a comb-bound booklet when we finish.

We are also having a great time starting a small business with the co-op. We got hooked up with a college student group in the States called *SIFE* (*Students in Free Enterprise*), which is an international group that works with younger students, helping them in business and finance. This has been a very stimulating challenge for us all—including the moms, who are officially the Board of Directors for our business. We are buying up used homeschool curricula from families here and reselling it to others who need the books, hopefully helping to reduce the stress of getting materials for our schooling.

One more homeschool activity we all do together is physical education. We have done the *President's Challenge* as a group for several years now. We had a homeschool team last year that competed in the regional meet. We also have a weekly sports day and the kids are led that day by the dads, which is a special treat.

Another whole area I have been led into is beginning to help coordinate a network of homeschool families in this region of West Africa, including the countries of Senegal, Mali, and The Gambia. We have sixty-five kids being homeschooled in this area this year. The majority of these families are missionaries, although we have known of families associated with the diplomatic communities (they work for various embassies) as well. This year our families are from several home countries including America (the majority), Britain, Australia, Germany, Canada, and New Zealand. For various reasons, there has been little or no cooperative effort in the past. Each family has been doing their own thing, which is okay, but I have discovered that there are lonely moms out there who sometimes end up sending their kids to boarding school simply because they can't do the schooling "alone."

Justin (16), Sean (13)

This year, we are setting up an e-mail network, having a homeschool forum at our first regional ladies retreat, having a homeschool focus day for moms to meet together and share ideas. We have other things we'd like to try such as encouraging the high schoolers with some activities they can participate in through the year, mostly via e-mail (having a *Model United Nations* is one idea—of mostly African nations, mind you!—and possibly setting up a debate club).

As I have entered my middle age years, and look back over almost twelve years now of schooling our boys, I have been doing a lot of thinking and praying about my role as mom, teacher, and mentor to our boys. These various roles are redefined as the kids get older. I am finding a rich relationship with Justin as he matures, yet he still considers his parents his significant others. It's such an awesome privilege and, admittedly, a trial at times. As Sean enters his teen years, he is such a different individual than his brother. I realize in two short years that he, Brad, and I will make up a family of just three when Justin goes to college, and there is much to think about there, too.

There is also the whole area of raising "third culture" kids to think through, since missionary kids aren't really part of either their home culture or the host culture where they grew up. Rather, they make up a unique combination of the two—a "third culture." They have spent enough time on our furlough years in the States to both appreciate parts of their parents' home culture and recognize parts of it that they themselves don't want to incorporate into their lives. For example, they both really like American food and miss the variety and availability of it when we're here. On the other hand, most of their best friends are missionary kids who live here, so they miss them when we're in the States. Since they've spent most of their lives in a foreign host culture, there are parts of this, too, that they also appreciate and parts that they find difficult. They have found the multilingual environment challenging and, as they get older, enriching in some ways and frustrating in other ways. They have also been Americans living overseas which gives them a different perspective, a more international perspective in many ways.

I personally prefer thinking of our kids as "multi-culture" kids. We have passed some milestones recently, like having spent fifteen years here in Senegal, and it's been twenty years since we first came to Africa. I realized that means my kids have basically grown up in Africa. I find that somewhat overwhelming to grasp, since I grew up in northern New Jersey and their father grew up in Pennsylvania!

We often are struck by the fact that compared to most American kids and to our own up-bringing, the variety of experiences our kids have had growing up is really vast. Justin took his first international plane trip when he was seven months old and hasn't stopped traveling since. Airports don't hold a lot of excitement for us—we have made more cross-Atlantic flights than I can count. Justin's first language was English, but the local Senegalese language was also part of his early experience. As a three-year-old, he would speak English to white people and Jola, the language of the people among whom we lived, to black people. He didn't understand when he was that age that the black people we met in the States didn't speak Jola! We lived in a house with no electricity or running water on and off for ten years. We were the only white foreigners living in the whole village except for an occasional *Peace Corps* volunteer who would come to do a project.

Speaking of living accommodations, we also lived in a castle in France for two months when the boys were ten and six years old. And then there was the apartment we had for two years right on the ocean here in Dakar. Each day the kids would go across the street and play on the beach—we watched fishermen pull in their nets and learned names of the local shells and other ocean animals they pulled up.

We have taken trips to a game park that was essentially like our village, except there were still wild animals there because they are protected. We had our own pet parrots, that were caught by friends who climbed the tree and found the nest, and a pet chameleon that was caught near here in a tree . . . different from your local pet store. We had scorpions running around on our village house floors at night—we didn't need to have an encyclopedia picture of them when we studied insects.

When we were studying how people make their living, we didn't read a book—we asked our neighbor to show us how they clear and plow their field with oxen. We interviewed him to learn how the Jola people think of their land and how precious it is to them. We had to learn that trees planted in your yard aren't yours—they belong to the person who planted them. We had to wait to eat the oranges from the tree in our yard until the man who owned the tree came by and harvested them! We learned not to whistle in the village because the people there believe it is dangerous and also how important is to shake everyone's hand when you arrive someplace—always using the right hand except, if you are going on a long trip, then you use the left hand as a sign of the upcoming trip.

Along with the good times, we have had our share of hard times, too—again, things neither Brad nor I had ever come close to in our growing up years. We've experienced civil unrest first hand—seen riots, avoided demonstrations, stayed home because it wasn't safe for us to go out. We've had friends who literally couldn't afford the few dollars to buy medicine for a sick child, and beggars on the street who'd hold their hands out when we pass by

We can't possibly anticipate what all this cross-cultural influence will mean for them in the years ahead. Some missionary kids fit fine into American culture when they return from field, while others really struggle with missing the type of life they lived overseas. Justin has expressed an interest in possibly looking into further education in Europe at some point, instead of the United States—perhaps Oxford. We shall see.

We all realize when we spend time in the States that our world view perspective is so different from our family and friends there. We view issues from a more international grid than most Americans do because we have lived among a different people. When we watch the news in the States, we consider how other countries may feel when America does things that make it more difficult or easier for them. Financial considerations, aid projects, conservation questions, and other issues that may have one side expressed American news—and this viewpoint is all most Americans will ever hear—often look different from over here. Our boys will carry all these experiences and ways of understanding things into their adult years. I think it will help them relate to people with different perspectives they meet along the way. When they go to college and meet an African, they will immediately shake his hand in greeting, and will understand when the African says he misses the food he's used to in his country. This is not to say of course, that all Africans are alike, just like we wouldn't say that all Americans are alike, but there are general cultural trends that you are much more attuned to if you have grown up outside the confines of just one majority culture.

Another multi-culture facet is that I think our sons will be equipped to work in an international context if they so chose. They are used to dealing in several different currencies, speaking several languages on any given day, and being flexible with people who don't consider time as important as relationships and are therefore always late to appointments. I think their perspective may also isolate them from people with more narrow perspectives, unless they have compassionate hearts that can accept people wherever they are and however they think. These are some of the ways I believe a cross-cultural upbringing will affect our sons. Other ways, and I am sure there will be many others, remain to be seen.

As I considered our goals and objectives for this year, I found myself again looking back. I think the basic conviction that we value home education over any other option has remained the same over the years. The privilege, the responsibility, and the freedom we experience when we are in charge of our sons' education are all part of the formula.

One way I think I have changed is to have a much deeper desire to see my sons appreciating their God and His Creation through their education. For a young man preparing to go out into the world on his own, this may mean learning to wrestle before the Lord with the difficult issues he confronts in his studies (like whether euthanasia is right or not, or how to handle hard relationships with peers). For a boy who loves to learn about his natural surroundings, this may mean time to study the birds and reptiles that live around us here, and to recognize the miracles of biological intricacies that God has put in place.

I see myself as becoming progressively more flexible in one way. Schedules are important, and the skill of setting your own time limits on various studies is essential. But, on the other hand, how many times do we get a chance in life to see a comet—so why not take the day before it appears, cancel the scheduled activities and just read all we can get our hands on about comets, and then spend the evening hours marveling at it as it passes overhead?

Another change I have noticed is that the type of time investment required of me as the main "teacher" of a high schooler has evolved. The elementary years are time intensive in the sense that I had to be "on" the young students as they learned their lessons and learned how to study. With a young adult in eleventh grade, I am realizing that my time is also needed and it is no less an intense experience. At times it is no longer necessary to teach, but to interact, to discuss, and to challenge to view things from various points of view. I'm still supervising tests and grading assignments, but I am also acting as a sounding board and as a fellow inquirer in many ways. I certainly don't have all the answers. I seemed to have had more answers when they both were younger and many of the questions were easier! It's really important now, I believe, that if we haven't realized this earlier, to allow my son the opportunity to discover for himself that it's alright not to know. In fact, it's even better not to know all the answers at times! Then faith enters in, needing examining and exploring. All these things are being processed lately.

Have we been "successful"? If we measure success by how our sons think their education was, their opinions will differ from day to day on this point. I am sure they will be different at various points down the road, too. There are times when they are really glad we homeschool. I think our flexibility is a big plus, as they compare their lives to friends who go to regular schools. There are also times when they envy kids in school and wish they could join in activities the school offers that we can not be a part of. As they have gotten older, we have given them the choice whether to continue in homeschool or not. So far, for the most part, Justin has chosen to homeschool, but there's always next year. We take it one year at a time now because we want them to feel that the best option has been carefully chosen. We do think there are circumstances that would lead to school being better for a time.

In my opinion, I feel like things have gone really well, by God's Grace. It hasn't always been easy, by any means. We have each had to decide that, yes, we believe homeschooling is the best way for us at various forks in our road. We

---

Justin (16), Sean (13)

Brad, Sean, Betsy, Justin

Justin (16), Sean (13)

have made mistakes. We regret things we've done. But, we are also learning that we can simply do our best and things will work out as they will. Each of our sons needs to make his own decisions as he grows older. If he has learned to make those decisions in a responsible way, then I feel we have been successful.

Justin (16), Sean (13)

Ron, age 40
Janet, age 37
Christopher, age 13
David, age 12
Emily, age 7

Five-year follow-up interview with Janet outside Pittsburgh, Pennsylvania

HOMEMADE BLUEBERRY PANCAKES

I had forgotten some of the little daily rituals and happenings that were so much a part of our life at the time we were in HOMESCHOOLING: A PATCHWORK OF DAYS. I reread the chapter about our family with the kids and they were as delighted as I was with this trip down memory lane. We shared quite a few giggles and, "Oh I remember when we used to do that!" I felt a tug on my heartstrings thinking what a special phase that was in our family's life.

Five years have passed since THEN. A lot of things have changed. There have been the natural changes that come with the passing of time and the growth of the children. For the last four years, we have not been homeschooling. Of course, our school day is quite different from when the children were at home. However, our beliefs, the values we share, our philosophy on learning, and the importance we place on our family haven't changed. Unfortunately, the kids still grumble about doing chores, and they still argue about who gets to sit by the window. I guess some things never change.

I really enjoyed having the children home with me over vacation this past summer. Of course, kids will be kids, and sometimes they made me yearn for crisp September mornings when the little darlings would be going off to school again, leaving me a few quiet moments to collect my wits. But we had a good time together on my days off. I admit, though, that when they ran down the hill to catch the bus that first day of going off to school, Emily's ponytails swinging, all of them squeaky clean and smiling as they turned around to yell back, "I love you, Mommy," I thought how nice it would be to have them home with me, learning things together again in our own space. But perhaps it's like many things in life, it's not so much the circumstances that we find ourselves in but our reaction and attitude toward them. It seems that the greatest satisfaction comes from "blooming where we're planted" or making the best of whatever situation we find ourselves in.

Making the decision not to homeschool was a difficult one to make. A lot of family discussions, sleepless nights, soul searching, and prayers were behind it. There was no one particular issue responsible for the change. Rather, it was a collection of reasons that, put together, helped us with the decision. These reasons (not mentioned here in any particular order of importance) may or may not seem valid to another family, but they were valid for our family.

For one thing, our family budget required me to go back to work outside the home. Obviously, my children were too young to be left home alone to learn independently. Next, the boys were very close in age and they took up a huge amount of my time and attention, and I felt that the energy I had left for Emily was not enough. I was afraid that I would look back and feel sad that Emily's precious little years had passed by so quickly, and I had been too busy for us to enjoy them together.

Once the boys went to school, I was able to get a schedule at my job so that I could work only in the afternoon. That way I was able to spend each morning with Emily. I neglected some other things like ironing, but I really tried to make that time with Emily count. We read together a lot. In fact, I taught her to read fluently by the time she was a young four. We colored together, made cookies, took walks in the park, and went to the playground. I knew how quickly the boys had flown through those early years, and I didn't want to miss a minute of it with Emily. I sometimes feel a little melancholy that I haven't homeschooled the children these last four years, but I *never* regret that I took the time to bond with Emily and enjoy her in a way that I couldn't have done if I had been divided between her and the boys' homeschool work. Each mom is different, so for another mother the two would have been able to mesh together with more success. But for this mommy and daughter, it was the best decision I could have made.

In addition, although we had some wonderful friends who homeschooled, the majority of the families we knew did not. The boys expressed a desire to go to school like their friends, and in all honesty, I think I wanted to feel like I fit in more, too. It can be a little lonely when the other mothers are talking about things that you can't relate to or sharing ideas and not feeling included in the conversation. It's not that our friends were unsupportive, it's just that our schooling experiences were so different that it was sometimes difficult to find things in common.

Lastly, I reached a point where I just felt burned out. I loved my kids to

---

Christopher (13), David (12), Emily (7)

pieces, and I loved reading to them, playing games with them, and learning alongside them. Realistically, though, homeschooling was not the only thing going in my life. The day-to-day responsibilities, coupled with homeschooling, became a burden and a source of too much stress. Not only did I need to go back to work outside the home, I just felt overwhelmed trying to care for a toddler and focus on the boys' schoolwork at the same time. Also, my dear mother was able to watch Emily for me as I worked, but it was just too much to ask her to watch all three children and to help with their schooling. Lastly, and this is a bit more vague, but I just felt life was so complicated that I didn't want the homeschooling to be yet another source of dreaded stress, and I didn't want to begin resenting the boys' presence. The time came when I didn't feel I was doing justice to either, so I knew we needed make the switch.

With great trepidation we sent them off to the world of public school. It was scary. We had lots of worries. Would a gulf now develop that would pull them away from us? Would they learn all sorts of words and ideas and beliefs that were foreign to our value system? Would they have to fight off drugs and immorality and delinquency at every turn? Would they be behind academically or socially? We heard so many negative things about schools, it's no wonder we were anxious. And it certainly has proven true that things go on at school that we'd rather did not and that many of our worries were realistic.

Just because the children go to school doesn't mean that we aren't intensely interested in what they are learning and how they are doing. We attend parent-teacher conferences, open house, science and art fairs, field trips, etc. I volunteer to help in the classroom when my schedule permits. Last year I went with David's class for a train ride to a new railroad museum and learned a lot of interesting things. This year our whole family was able to go with Christopher's class to an observatory for a nighttime field trip where we saw the moon, Jupiter, and Saturn. We try to stay involved and enthusiastic about our children's schooling, and we don't take the view that someone else is now responsible for their education.

There is a certain amount of freedom we sacrificed as far as curriculum. What the school district thinks is important and what we think is important can differ at times. We've found, though, that when there is something that we just do not want our children to be involved with because of our beliefs, the teachers are extremely supportive and cooperative. On the flip side of the coin, there have been opportunities and advantages the school provides that we wouldn't have been able to provide at home. For instance, recently David won second place at our school district level in a nationwide art contest, and Emily's work went all the way to second place for her age group at the Pennsylvania state level! So we were very excited about that!

The children have done well academically. The boys are both in the gifted program, and although Emily is only in second grade and too young for the gifted classes, she may also be in them later on. She reads very well, so her teacher frequently lets her go down to the kindergarten classroom to read to the younger students. I've had more than one comment from teachers saying that the solid foundation our children received from homeschooling really shows. I was even hired for two years to tutor first and second grade students with special needs, and I was told a big reason I got the job was because of the success I had with my own children. It was a great experience and one I'll always treasure.

Presently, I am working as an administrative assistant for a large investment/brokerage firm. It's a great job, so I feel blessed in that way. My husband Ron is still working as the fleet and buildings manager for a large electrical contracting company, and he has been with them for almost twenty years now. He puts in long days, but he tries to see the kids for at least a couple of minutes in the morning before he goes off to work, and he tries each night to have dinner with the family. We try to discuss a Scripture together for a couple of minutes at dinnertime. It doesn't always work that way, but he tries. He helps look over their homework and encourages them to do their best. He also attends special school events. At least once a week he sits down with our whole family to discuss something that is an issue in the children's lives and then how common sense, discernment, and the Bible can help them make wise decisions. And he plays sports with them as often as he can.

Learning doesn't stop when the children step off the bus either. There is homework to supervise each night. We make sure that we include something interesting and educational when we go on vacation or have family outing days. This past summer, we took a day off from the beach to tour a lighthouse in Corolla, NC, and another day to tour the *Wright Brothers Memorial and Museum* in Kitty Hawk. We still have family reading times when either I read aloud a classic work of literature to them or we take turns reading aloud together. Television and computer games have a place in our home, but it is a very moderate place. The kids know that reading, homework, playing outside, and getting fresh air come first. And when they do play computer games or watch television, we monitor the time spent and the content. We ride bikes together, go swimming, hiking, play board games, softball, football, and card games. They help with the cleaning, cooking, laundry, yard work, etc., to learn responsibility. Both David and Emily are taking piano lessons, and they participate in a yearly recital.

There are times when school can be tough on kids. There are bullies to deal with, bad attitudes to pick up, fears of violence, peer pressure to overcome, academic stress, and the questioning of our family's beliefs and values. It's not always easy. But learning to deal with these things, deciding where we stand on issues, knowing how to fit in without compromising what is right, learning to feel good about yourself even if you're not always like everybody else, getting to know people from different walks of life, cooperating within a group—these are all lessons in life and a part of growing up, whether one goes to school outside the home or in the home.

We have respect for parents who care about their child's education. For some, this means homeschooling their children. For others, this means being involved with their child's public or private education. It would be sad and counterproductive if there were a dividing line between the two: *us* and *them*. Both options can be successful. On the other hand, neither option guarantees success, but I think there's a much better chance when parents are involved. Children need help as they grow toward becoming independent adults and assets to the local and world community. As parents we need to help them set definite goals, and then help them work toward reaching those goals. We have friends who have great homeschooled kids and we have friends who have great kids who go to public school. We've known some young adults who were homeschooled as children and they are now successful and happy adults. We know others who homeschooled and they haven't done as well. But that's certainly true of any adults who were schooled publicly, and of all people in general.

I think our kids are just like most kids, homeschooled or otherwise. Sometimes they enjoy their school projects, and other times they complain. Certain teachers are favorites, and all I hear about is "Miss So and So this" and "Miss So and So that." For a whole year, I know that the teacher is going to be the last word on school work in my child's mind. Other teachers aren't quite so "revered." But I take the grumblings with a grain of salt. I keep in mind the words of one teacher who, at the junior high orientation, spoke, "Here's the deal. I won't believe half the stuff your kids say about you if you won't believe half the stuff your kids say about me." I think the kids sometimes want to homeschool again but they don't say it often. Realistically, I think it's mostly on days when they want to sleep in or not do homework. I'm sure they've conveniently "forgotten" that if they were still homeschooling, they'd have to get up early and do work anyway! Overall, though, I'd say the children enjoy school and have come to accept it as an important part of life—like bathing or flossing their teeth—that they need to do it even if they don't always feel like it.

I was asked to share some advice with other homeschooling families about what helped us while we homeschooled. First, we regularly evaluated our children's progress. We asked ourselves whether the overall feeling of each family member was positive or negative. When something wasn't working, we made the needed changes. Second, we found it very helpful to talk with other families who homeschooled successfully and we tried to learn from them. Because every child and every family situation is different, we listened to their ideas but then adapted them to our family's needs, thereby finding our own comfort zone. We realized that we didn't need to be perfect, but kept a general set of goals before us that we could review periodically, so that we could stay on track. Third, we got together regularly with other families for shared learning time. We often found that having an audience outside our family was just what a child needed to try a little bit harder with a story, poem, or other project. At these get togethers, we also tried to set aside time for the kids to have some unstructured time when they could simply relax and play together. Fourth, we found it more helpful to have a general set of goals before us that we could review periodically to help us stay on track rather than a separate structured time when they could simply relax and play together. Finally, we tried to respect each family member's need to have some quiet, private time. This was a challenge because everyone was home together most of the time, but it really helped to keep tension to a minimum and gave each person a chance to rest, relax, and regroup.

We have not written off homeschooling altogether for our family. We keep the option open. Just as circumstances changed and we knew it was best to send our children to school, if the time ever comes when we feel our children need to be homeschooled again, we will do so. We are always monitoring our family's experience, and we will do what we feel is best for them as time moves along. Although we may look back on our homeschooling days with nostalgia at times, we are confident with the passing of time that we made the right decision.

I want to conclude with a personal anecdote. We went to an apple festival a while back. There were various craftsmen working, and at one stall a woman was working on a loom. We were really fascinated with her work and asked a lot of questions. She stopped for a minute to chat and asked if we were homeschoolers. I told her no, but asked her what made her ask that. She said we just had that way about us, and the children were very polite. She said she didn't homeschool her own children, but it was her experience with others who did that made her think we might, too. I understood what she meant, and I took the comparison as a compliment and felt so pleased. It made me glad to know that even if we don't homeschool right now, it must still show that we love learning!

Christopher (13), David (12), Emily (7)

David, Janet, Emily, Ron, Christopher

Christopher (13), David (12), Emily (7)

Matt, age 43
Leslie, age 42
Jesse, age 16
Benjamin, age 14
Bethany, age 11
Jordan, age 8

Five-year follow-up interview with Leslie in populated Long Island, New York

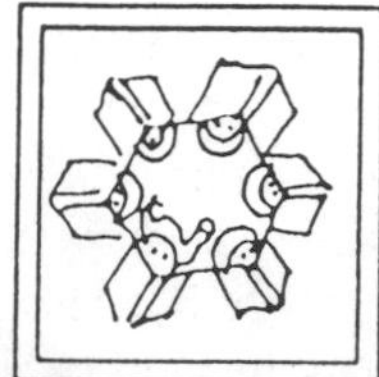

CHARMING CLUTTER

It is a cold November morning, just as it was five years ago in HOMESCHOOLING: A PATCHWORK OF DAYS. As I did then, I arise around 7:00 a.m., shower, say goodbye to Matt as he heads off to work, make coffee, and start a load of laundry. But how things have changed! My husband accepted a change of pastorate here three years ago, so we are no longer in rural western Pennsylvania, but on the densely populated south shore of Long Island, just a few miles from New York City. What an adjustment! We have traded mountains for beaches and coastal plain; and farmland for bridges, expressways, and endless suburbia. Many people have asked why we would want to move here. Quite simply, we felt God's leading. I am reminded of God's admonishment to country-boy Jonah when he protested preaching in Nineveh: "Should I not be concerned about that great city?" And so we are here, striving by God's grace to make a difference in this fascinating mix of cultures, races, and world views.

Looking back over the past eleven years of homeschooling, I have few regrets. Our family has been able to spend extended time together in a way few non-homeschooling families can. One of my favorite parts of homeschooling is our Bible time. After reading a chapter or two from the Bible in the morning, there is usually plenty to discuss and many parallels we can draw from our lives. Bible time is usually unhurried, and each child takes a turn to pray for ourselves, missionary friends, friends who need to know Jesus, and our church. Above all, we thank God for the privilege of the family altar. This is not to say the children don't get distracted at times, but overall this has worked well for us. It is a wonderful feeling to be sitting cozily in the living room together in the morning, reflecting together on God's plans and purposes for us. This alone would have made homeschooling worthwhile.

Homeschooling has been especially helpful to us as a busy pastor's family. Matt's schedule means he must be out most evenings. But he is home for lunch and dinner every day, and we see him then. We also are still up when he gets home from church after his evening meetings. We have been able to tailor many projects to the needs of our church and family. When vacation Bible school time comes around, we paint and act and teach and sing *together*.

Ben (fourteen) and Jesse (sixteen) also help lead our boys ministry program on Friday nights and live for church basketball after. They sing tenor and bass (with Dad) in our church choir and play trumpet and French horn in our little orchestra. Mom directs the music. Bethany (almost twelve) is doing well on piano and has played some in church. She also enjoys singing in church choir. She and Jordan (eight) are looking forward to being an angel and a shepherd in our Christmas musical in a few days. This spring, we enjoyed creating a community outreach we called "Easter Fun Day"—a mammoth egg hunt, games, crafts, plus a retelling of the resurrection story. Our kids worked on it with us for days ahead of time. Crowds of kids and their parents came and listened very attentively to the real meaning of Easter. It was an exciting day for us and great to be working together as a family. Were we not homeschooling, church ministry would have the potential of splintering our family instead of uniting it.

How are the kids doing academically? Jesse took the SAT's this fall and did extremely well in the verbal, and acceptably in the math. (He's a junior so has another year). His scores put me at ease—we've been working toward this for a long time. *He's* looking at private Christian liberal arts colleges and Bible colleges. *We* have sticker shock! He's interested in writing, teaching, pastoring—that kind of thing. He is planning to enroll in the local community college's honors program this spring and will soon start earning college credit. It's a little early to tell about the other kids, but I think they will do fine, too. They have all been able to develop their gifts and abilities with extended art projects, church music involvement, much leisurely reading, and creative writing.

We have had many opportunities to observe homeschooling and non-homeschooling kids together, and we think there *is* a difference. The homeschooled kids generally seem much less peer-dependent, more mature and level-headed, and are often better readers. They rarely present discipline problems. Most of our kids' friends think our kids are lucky to be homeschooled. All our kids do very well with younger children and are well-liked.

A negative for us has been wrestling with state reporting requirements. I was

---

Jesse (16), Benjamin (14), Bethany (11), Jordan (8)

comfortable with Pennsylvania's system and its once-a-year reporting and creation of nice portfolios for each child, which were truly keepsakes. Here, in New York, we must report quarterly, including grades, minutes of instruction in each subject (!), and percentage of material covered. The cost of living here is also very high, precluding our kids' participation in some extra-curricular programs.

Another negative is that being fairly new in the area, it has been harder for our kids to make friends than it would have been if they were in the public school which is, yes, right across the street from us. Sometimes, I feel a little isolated and wonder if we are missing out on something. Homeschooling takes us a bit "out of the loop" with our public school neighbors. This has been hardest with the older kids, so we started a homeschool co-op that provides enrichment classes on alternate Fridays. This has helped our children meet other homeschooled kids and forge some good friendships. For the past couple of years, Jesse's been the gym teacher. He takes the responsibility seriously, and the kids love him. Jesse and Ben play varsity soccer on a Christian school team near here, Bethany takes gymnastics, and Jordan enjoys *Cub Scouts*, baseball, and basketball. All four participate in church activities and clubs for all ages.

I'm at the age now when most moms who are not homeschooling are back in the workplace. I admit, I miss teaching high school and the excitement and self-esteem that went with it. I miss all those students. I still keep up with some of them from my former teaching days. As the college years approach, I also miss the income I would have been making to help with tuition. But, there will probably come a time to do all that again. My husband encourages me that this is where I need to be right now. I definitely have personally grown through homeschooling in many ways. I am always learning new things and there is always a new homeschooling mom to encourage. I enjoy teaching in our homeschool co-op, leading the choir at church, teaching Sunday School, and am challenged at home to put my faith into practice before my kids.

It is difficult for me to turn off the "teacher mode"—I hate to see my kids idle and am always thinking up new projects or chores if they don't look like they are being productive. I would like to be more of the supportive, encouraging mom, and less of the nag that I frequently am. This may come back to haunt me. I am always wondering if we've done enough or if they are getting everything they need to know. Some of those high school subjects are pretty tough, too. We are struggling through chemistry just now and need to rethink our approach to algebra if SAT scores are any indication. Another difficult part has been juggling all four kids' academics. It's hard to get as excited about teaching the same thing for the fourth time with the youngest. I find the new stuff interests me more. Then I realize, "What? We didn't do that with you?"

I think it's natural to have some doubts—after all, we are still pioneers to a degree. But, stepping back and looking at the total picture, I am glad we did it

Jesse (16), Benjamin (14), Bethany (11), Jordan (8)

this way. I am thankful for the relationships we have with our children and with other homeschooling families. I am thankful that we can maybe show others that there is a different path—one they might want to examine for their own lives. And I am thankful for the blessing of having the time to teach our children God's ways.

Jesse, Ben
Matt, Leslie
Bethany, Jordan
